THE OXFORD ENGLISH
LITERARY HISTORY

Volume 12. 1960–2000

THE OXFORD ENGLISH LITERARY HISTORY

General Editor: Jonathan Bate

* already published

This series was conceived and commissioned by Kim Walwyn (1956–2002), to whose memory it is dedicated.

THE OXFORD ENGLISH
LITERARY HISTORY

Volume 12. 1960–2000

The Last of England?

RANDALL STEVENSON

OXFORD
UNIVERSITY PRESS

OXFORD

UNIVERSITY PRESS

Great Clarendon Street, Oxford OX2 6DP

Oxford University Press is a department of the University of Oxford.
It furthers the University's objective of excellence in research, scholarship,
and education by publishing worldwide in

Oxford New York

Auckland Cape Town Dar es Salaam Hong Kong Karachi
Kuala Lumpur Madrid Melbourne Mexico City Nairobi
New Delhi Shanghai Taipei Toronto

With offices in

Argentina Austria Brazil Chile Czech Republic France Greece
Guatemala Hungary Italy Japan Poland Portugal Singapore
South Korea Switzerland Thailand Turkey Ukraine Vietnam

Oxford is a registered trade mark of Oxford University Press
in the UK and in certain other countries

Published in the United States
by Oxford University Press Inc., New York

British Library Cataloguing in Publication Data

Data available

Library of Congress Cataloging in Publication Data

Data available

Typeset by Regent Typesetting, London
Printed in Great Britain
on acid-free paper by
Ashford Colour Press Limited,
Gosport, Hampshire

ISBN 0-19-818423-9 978-0-19-818423-2
ISBN 0-19-928835-6 (Pbk.) 978-0-928835-9 (Pbk.)

10 9 8 7 6 5 4 3 2 1

For Roger Savage

Acknowledgements

My memories of the period 1960–2000 reach back, just about, to early 1960, when I recall asking my father what the word 'decade' meant. For answers to that and many other demands—for introducing me, in every sense, to the late twentieth century—my gratitude extends across and throughout this period to memories of my father, William Stevenson, and to my mother, Helen Stevenson.

It probably wasn't precocious interest in periodization that prompted that question about 'decade', but it did anticipate innumerable enquiries about later years, and much good fortune in finding help and advice in dealing with them, from many individuals and institutions. The Arts and Humanities Research Board funded academic leave in 2002; the British Academy, a grant towards the cost of permissions and illustrations; the University of Edinburgh, further sabbatical leave, teaching assistance, and help with research costs. I'm also grateful to the series editors in Oxford University Press—Sophie Goldsworthy, Frances Whistler, Sarah Hyland, and Elizabeth Prochaska—for their thoughtful, generous, expert support; to Rowena Anketell for her diligent, thoughtful copy-editing; and to the fathomlessly patient staff at the National Library of Scotland.

I'm especially indebted to the General Editor, Jonathan Bate, for much guidance with individual chapters and with the final draft of the whole text—also for the imaginative way the Oxford English Literary History project was conceived, allowing a flow of advice from other contributors, particularly my near-neighbours in twentieth-century volumes. Towards the end of a long career in the University of Edinburgh—distinguished throughout by such generosity, wisdom, and cultural omniscience—Roger Savage read and improved virtually every chapter. Alice Ferrebe proved an equally encouraging, incisive reader, as well as a thoroughly determined researcher: her work contributes to several sections throughout, and forms the basis for the Author Bibliographies at the end—carefully checked in their final stages by Abigail Garrington. Individual chapters were read and improved by Clare Brennan, Ken Millard, and Rick Rylance. For advice with particular sections or problems, I'm also grateful to John Carpenter, Sarah Carpenter, William Christie, John Frow, Heather Johnson, Brian McHale, Drew Milne, Susan Manning, Caroline Root, Anna Stevenson, and Peter Womack. For much direct help, as well as advice, many thanks to Cairns Craig; likewise to others, in the 1990s and beyond, who'll know who you are.

I'm also grateful to Michael Schmidt of Carcanet Press for allowing quotation from work by Donald Davie and other poets. The excerpt from 'Mr Bleaney', from *Collected Poems* by Philip Larkin (copyright © 1988, 1999 by the Estate of Philip Larkin), is reprinted by permission of Faber and Faber Ltd. and Farrar, Straus and Giroux, LLC. The poem at the start of Chapter 8 is reprinted by permission of PFD on behalf of Carol Rumens: © Carol Rumens 1987—as printed in the original volume. Acknowledgements for the use of illustrations appear in the List of Figures on pp. xiii–xiv. For additional advice and help with these illustrations, thanks also to Donald Carroll; Tom Phillips; James Scott; Judith Chernaik and 'Poems on the Underground'; and Jules Mann at the Poetry Society.

R. S.

General Editor's Preface

The Oxford English Literary History is the twenty-first-century successor to the Oxford History of English Literature, which appeared in fifteen volumes between 1945 and 1997. As in the previous series, each volume offers an individual scholar's vision of a discrete period of literary history.[1] Each has a distinctive emphasis and structure, determined by its author's considered view of the principal contours of the period. But all the volumes are written in the belief that literary history is a discipline necessary for the revelation of the power of imaginative writing to serve as a means of human understanding, past, present, and future.

Our primary aim is to explore the diverse purposes of literary activity and the varied mental worlds of writers and readers in the past. Particular attention is given to the institutions in which literary acts take place (educated communities, publishing networks and so forth), the forms in which literary works are presented (traditions, genres, structural conventions), and the relationship between literature and broader historical continuities and transformations. Literary history is distinct from political history, but a historical understanding of literature cannot be divorced from cultural and intellectual revolutions or the effects of social change and the upheaval of war.

We do not seek to offer a comprehensive survey of the works of all 'major', let alone 'minor', writers of the last thousand years. All literary histories are inevitably incomplete—as was seen from the rediscovery in the late twentieth century of many long-forgotten women writers of earlier eras. Every literary history has to select; in so doing, it reconfigures the 'canon'. We cast our nets very widely and make claims for many works not previously regarded as canonical, but we are fully conscious of our partiality. Detailed case studies are preferred to summary listings.

---

[1] Since Volume 1, *to 1350*, covers many centuries, it is co-written by two scholars.

A further aim is to undertake a critical investigation of the very notion of a national literary heritage. The word 'literature' is often taken to refer to poems, plays, and novels, but historically a much wider range of writing may properly be considered as 'literary' or as belonging within the realm of what used to be called 'letters'. The boundaries of the literary in general and of *English* literary history in particular have changed through the centuries. Each volume maps those boundaries in the terms of its own period.

For the sake of consistency and feasibility, however, two broad definitions of 'English Literary History' have been applied. First, save in the polyglot culture of the earliest era, we have confined ourselves to the English language—a body of important work written in Latin between the fourteenth and the seventeenth centuries has been excluded. And secondly, we have concentrated on works that come from, or bear upon, England. Most of the writing of other English-speaking countries, notably the United States of America, is excluded. We are not offering a world history of writing in the English language. Those Americans who lived and worked in England are, however, included.

So too with Scottish, Irish, Welsh writers, and those from countries that were once part of the British Empire: where their work was produced or significantly disseminated in England, they are included. Indeed, such figures are of special importance in many volumes, exactly because their non-English origins often placed them in an ambivalent relationship with England. Throughout the series, particular attention is paid to encounters between English and other traditions. But we have also recognized that Scottish, Welsh, Irish, African, Asian, Australasian, Canadian, and Caribbean literatures all have their own histories, which we have not sought to colonize.

It would be possible to argue endlessly about periodization. The arrangement of the Oxford English Literary History is both traditional and innovative. For instance, the period around the beginning of the nineteenth century has long been thought of as the 'Romantic' one; however we may wish to modify the nomenclature, people will go on reading and studying the Lake Poets and the 'Shelley circle' in relation to each other, so it would have been factitious to introduce a volume division at, say, 1810. On the other hand, it is still too soon for there to be broad agreement on the literary-historical shape of the twentieth century: to propose a single break at, say, 1945 would be to fall in with the false assumption that literature moves strictly in tandem with events. Each volume argues the case for its own period as a period, but at the same time beginning and ending dates are treated flexibly, and in many cases—especially with respect to the twentieth century—there is deliberate and considerable overlap between the temporal boundaries of adjacent volumes.

The voices of the last millennium are so various and vital that English literary history is always in the process of being rewritten. We seek both to chart and to contribute to that rewriting, for the benefit not just of students and scholars but of all serious readers.

Jonathan Bate

Contents

Part III Drama

Part IV Narrative

List of Figures

A Note on References

Brief biographical information on selected authors will be found at the end of the volume, together with bibliographies covering their major works and some recent criticism concerning them. In addition, there are suggestions for more general reading relevant to the history of the period. The bibliographies are intended as starting points for further study, not comprehensive listings. The Author Bibliographies include recommended editions: an asterisk indicates those used in the main body of the text.

Quotations in the text from prose works and plays written in the period are usually followed by a reference in parenthesis. Where possible, these are given in a form that does not depend on access to a particular edition (e.g. chapter or book number, or act or scene number), but for works without convenient subdivision, the citation is of the page number of the edition asterisked in the relevant Author Bibliography, and /or specified in Works Cited. Titles of plays, when first mentioned, are followed by a note of the theatre which originally produced them—in London unless otherwise specified—and the date of this production. Poem titles are generally followed by a date of their first publication in book form, and the editions used are asterisked in the relevant Author Bibliography and /or specified in Works Cited.

All quotations from primary and secondary material are keyed to the list of Works Cited at the end of the book. Anthologies appear in this section under the names of their editors. Footnotes are mostly used to refer readers to other relevant sections of the text, where such connections might not be apparent through judicious use of the index.

Introduction:
Last Things First

'1960–2000: The *Last* of England?' Surely England is more durable than that title suggests? It certainly still seemed so, twenty years before this period began, even at the height of the Second World War. 'Worlds may change and go awry', Ross Parker and Hughie Charles warned in their popular wartime song, only to reaffirm that 'there'll always be an England'. Such confidence is not necessarily contradicted in this volume of the Oxford English Literary History—not entirely, at any rate. 'The Last of England' of its title is in one way less doom-laden than simply descriptive, referring to the last or most recently produced literature in England: the last phase of the millennium-long tradition the History describes. Yet no study of the later twentieth century, doom-laden or not, could overlook how far sureties failed, even in the brief gap between the end of the war and 1960. Historians envisage most periods since the Industrial Revolution as ones of radical transformation: the latter half of the twentieth century saw the pace of change itself accelerate, breaking down a whole range of convictions once considered surely enduring.

England, of course, was by no means the only country to experience change and loss, sometimes encountered much more sharply elsewhere. Even as those wartime voices sang, a wider world *was* going awry. Throughout the West, in the years that followed, the war and the horrors marking its conclusion often seemed to have dimmed or extinguished enlightened ideals—faiths in reason and progress—which had illumined life and thinking for two centuries. Memories of the war cast a long, deep shadow over English life and literature later in the twentieth century, and are examined throughout this study. But in the decade or so immediately after 1945, it was probably French writing which envisaged a blacker, bleaker post-war world most starkly. Uniquely uncompromising vision of this darkened world made Samuel Beckett—though an Irishman, first writing in French, and translated only gradually during the 1950s—a presiding influence on literature in English at the start of the period, in 1960, and for some time thereafter.

Some profound post-war transformations were nevertheless specific to England, or at any rate to Britain generally. 'Red, white and blue; what does it mean to you?' Parker and Charles's song enquired. 'Not all it used to' was the likeliest answer by the 1960s. 'The empire, too, we can depend on you', the song went on, but by 1962, there was virtually no empire left. Most of Britain's colonies around the world had been granted their independence, surprisingly rapidly, during the previous fifteen years. In other ways, too, Britain's world role diminished radically during these years. Even by 1946, the Prime Minister, Clement Attlee, was expressing views very different from those of his wartime predecessor, Winston Churchill, describing his country as no more than an 'easterly extension of a strategic arc the centre of which is the American continent' (Colls, p. 145). Clear confirmation that Britain's world role had been taken over by the United States appeared ten years later, during the Suez crisis, and again in others that followed in the early 1960s. From the late 1940s to the 1960s and beyond, financial crises and devaluations of sterling showed dwindling imperial and military power paralleled by substantial decline in Britain's economic and manufacturing power. As the historian Robert Colls suggested in *Identity of England* (2002), during a period of only about fifteen years following the war, ' "decline", as a peculiarly British characteristic, embedded itself right at the centre' of the nation's politics, and of its thinking about itself generally (p. 143).

While the red, white, and blue of the Union Jack fluttered less boldly, and over far fewer territories, there were also signs that the union it represented might itself be fragmenting. Scotland, Wales, and sections of the community in Northern Ireland contemplated independence increasingly enthusiastically during the 1960s: by the end of the 1990s, measures of autonomy established for each left Britain a rather disunited kingdom. More pressingly than for two centuries, England had to reconsider itself as a distinct unit, politically and culturally. The Oxford English Literary History is symptomatic in concentrating more firmly than its predecessors on writing in England, separately from the traditions of neighbouring nations, or other anglophone ones abroad. A new interest in separateness, and in separate traditions, began to appear in literature itself in the 1990s, in novels such as Peter Ackroyd's *English Music* (1992), or Julian Barnes's *England, England* (1998). It also appeared extensively in critical and historical writing. More than two dozen studies had been published by the end of the century, defining or analysing English life, or, often, worrying about ways its characteristics had blurred or faded.

For several—Roger Scruton's *England: An Elegy* (2000), for example—decline in world role had inevitably been accompanied by slippages and confusions within the country itself. In one way, England did end the period rather as it began, with social stratifications still more clear-cut than almost anywhere else in the world. Yet divisions of class and community had nevertheless altered and weakened, removing many of the frameworks through which social roles and English identities had once been defined. 'Nowadays, almost anyone is more English than the English', Will Self commented in his novel *How the Dead Live* (2000, ch. 4). Jeremy Paxman's *The English: A Portrait of a People* (1998) likewise observed that 'being English used to be so easy . . . [but] the conventions that defined the English are dead' (p. ix). Along with the national character, even the English landscape seemed increasingly imperilled. A mainstay of poetic imagination, nature in England had long been equated with the nature *of* England, and with its supposedly everlasting qualities, yet it seemed more and more menaced by change and decay. 'There'll always be an England | While there's a country lane', Parker and Charles opined in 1939: 'England gone, | The shadows, the meadows, the lanes' was Philip Larkin's more sombre reflection in 1974 ('Going, Going').

For some critics, decline and uncertainty of this kind seemed likely simply to be reproduced in the period's literature. Hugh Kenner's title, *A Sinking Island: The Modern English Writers* (1988) ominously suggested as much, and in discussing 'The Englishness of the English Novel' in 1980, Q. D. Leavis was in little doubt. Along with the disappearance of 'the traditional English life of the countryside', she considered that 'the England that bore the classical English novel has gone forever, and we can't expect a country of high-rise flat-dwellers, office workers and factory robots and unassimilated multi-racial minorities . . . to give rise to a literature comparable with the novel tradition'. Largely as a result, she concluded, 'the decay and approaching death of the English novel' was both inevitable and 'generally recognized' (*Collected Essays*, pp. 320, 325, 303). There were other commentators in the late 1970s, as she suggested, convinced of the novel's imminent demise. Yet their dire expectations were not fulfilled in the years that followed. In Q. D. Leavis's case at least, it is not difficult to see why. Her views interpreted difference far too readily in terms of decline, mistakenly envisaging inevitable change as terminal loss. Much of the same misplaced nostalgia shaped several of the elegiac studies of England mentioned above, Scruton's particularly, also underlying the widespread assumptions of national decline Robert Colls assessed in *Identity of England*.

Neither mid-century renunciation of empire, after all, nor the loosening of class hierarchies and social exclusions in the years that followed, need be understood only—or primarily—in terms of loss. Each marked the last of a certain kind of England, but one which was in many senses a world well lost. As it declined, another England gradually emerged: less enthralled by tradition, freer and more open, as a result, in outlook, lifestyle, and culture. Encouraged by wider affluence and improved education, this new society developed strongly in the 1960s. Many of its influences—described throughout this volume—extended long afterwards. Despite the economic crises of the next decade, and the conservative politics of the 1980s, broadening democratization in society and culture generally continued throughout later years, and came to seem characteristic of the period as a whole. 'You cannot leave England', Peter Porter's poem 'The Last of England' (1970) remarked, 'it turns | . . . majestically in the mind'. Throughout the later twentieth century, England did turn—gradually and mostly affirmatively—towards new mentalities and self-conceptions, in ways often hastened by the obvious obsolescences of the old.

In any case, even if the age *were* somehow defined as one exclusively of historical decline, there would be little reason to suppose its literature doomed to follow the same direction. Literary developments do not always straightforwardly reflect or run in parallel with the wider history of their time, directly reproducing its ups and downs. On the contrary, what history refuses, culture provides: changeful, challenging times demand and direct new vision. Crucially, too, reshaping of the country's social fabric encouraged a range of new voices through which new visions might be expressed. Contrary to Q. D. Leavis's scepticism of factory-workers and flat-dwellers, literature later in the century came to be successfully produced, and read, in ways freer of the social exclusions of earlier decades, and of gendered ones. New diversity in the sources—and subjects—of imagination appeared particularly strongly in the work of women writers: initially in the novel, in the 1960s; eventually in all the genres. Tardier acceptance of women as poets and dramatists incidentally highlighted another characteristic of the period. Sharp asymmetries marked the development of individual genres, and the response of each to the changing life of the times, demanding separate assessment of poetry, drama, and narrative later in this study. By the late 1950s, for example, drama was already finding new excitement in contemporary shifts in social structures and world roles. Poetry, on the other hand—at any rate in the Movement idiom still influential at that time—often followed Philip Larkin in regretting an 'England gone', and in trying to sustain its values and conventions a little longer.

Contrary, too, to Q. D. Leavis's scepticism of 'racial minorities', black or immigrant authors were centrally involved in rescuing the novel from the 'decay or approaching death' she and other critics saw threatening it around 1980. For the Victorians, 'The Last of England' would have recalled Ford Madox Brown's famous 1850s painting of an emigrant ship departing for a new life in the colonies. A century or so later, the empire sailed back, with immigrant writers among those most committed to renewing the imagination of England. In the decade following Q. D. Leavis's judgement, fiction was revitalized in form and vision by Salman Rushdie, Timothy Mo, Kazuo Ishiguro, Caryl Phillips, Fred D'Aguiar, and others. Throughout the latter decades of the century, though on a more modest scale, black writers also contributed significantly to developments in poetry and drama. Their work nevertheless highlighted new uncertainties about 'English' traditions. Through domicile and education, through their subjects and themes, sometimes through outlook and style, the writers mentioned obviously belonged to an English context, though they remained unusually aware of others. In many ways, it was the problematic, partial nature of this belonging which proved so productive imaginatively, rather as it had for modernist authors—also often exiles and outsiders—earlier in the century. A certain distance from domestic life and literary convention encouraged new, transforming imagination of each. Significantly, England was often renamed, as well as reconfigured, by authors involved: as 'Inglan' in Linton Kwesi Johnson's poetry, for example; or in Salman Rushdie's translation of London into the fantasy city 'Ellowen Deeowen' in *The Satanic Verses* (1988).

Along with personal memories of an Indian childhood, influences on Rushdie's writing included the fiction of Günter Grass, the magic realist novels of Gabriel García Márquez, and fantastic cinema produced in Bombay and in Hollywood. Such writing obviously could not be located, uncomplicatedly, at the end of a thousand-year history only of English literature. The era, in other words, in which the Oxford English Literary History chose to concentrate on an English context and tradition was one also marked by new complexities of culture and identity *within* England. Similar complexity more generally affected 'English' writing, attached less and less exclusively, throughout the twentieth century, to the experience of England itself. In 1990, Bernard Bergonzi questioned how, or if, the term 'English literature' could continue to 'relate to a small, ancient nation and a global language' (*Exploding English*, p. 27). The *Norton Anthology of English Literature*—produced in the United States, and used in university courses throughout the world—provided a clear answer in 2000. 'The *national* conception of literary history, the conception by which English Literature meant the literature of England' was no longer tenable, M. H. Abrams and Stephen Greenblatt concluded in their editors' introduction. English literature, they emphasized, had 'ceased to be the product of the identity of a single nation' (p. xxxv). The development of separate traditions among English-speaking nations elsewhere—of many English literatures—made it in some ways more important than ever to distinguish the particular nature of writing in England. Yet it also made it more difficult. In an increasingly globalized culture, 'nation' as a category of literary or even political analysis weakened during the period, and seemed likely to continue to do so. Marking the last of a traditional England, the 1960–2000 period may also have seen the last of English literature as traditionally or nationally conceived, and the beginnings of new, broader categories of analysis. As the General Editor's Preface affirms, the Oxford English Literary History explores in all its volumes the intersection of local, national, and international influences on literature in England. The growing significance of such intersections for the later twentieth century is a particular interest of this one.

This volume also reflects—and reflects on—new questions raised in the period about the survival of literature itself, and not only its Englishness. Some of these are easily answered. From the late 1950s onwards, critics worried that a first age of television might be the last for literature, or for reading generally, especially as video and computer-based forms of entertainment developed in the 1980s and 1990s. Chapter 4 suggests that such worries mostly proved unfounded: reading, and the theatre, generally sustained or even expanded their appeal during the period. Yet the existing influence of cinema, and the new power of television, naturally did affect ways books were written and read. Though a history of literature is limited in the attention it can devote to other media, their influences on the written word, and on stage performance, are assessed throughout. Limitations of space also account for straightforward concentration on poetry, drama, and fiction in later parts—one consistent, in any case, with most contemporary assumptions about literature. Over past centuries, as the General Editor's Preface points out, the range of writing generally considered as literature has expanded and contracted like an accordion. It shrank to one of its narrower points in the first half of this period. By the end of the 1970s, writing in the form of essays, memoirs, and the like had mostly been squeezed out of literary study, and to an extent out of popular appreciation as literature, in favour of more and more exclusive concentration on imaginary or fictive forms. Later chapters mostly sustain this concentration, though Part IV, in particular, considers ways novelistic imagination was shaped by—and influenced—cognate forms of narrative such as travelogue and biography.

Constraints of space and practicality eliminate other organizational possibilities half-implied by critical thinking in some of its

forms after 1980. Academic study of literature expanded enormously in scale throughout the period, and in its concern with critical
theory, especially in the late 1970s and 1980s—often with direct
effects on contemporary authors. Yet this academic study was not
much concerned with tightening or limiting the boundaries of its
subject. On the contrary, conventional conceptions of literature as a
purely imaginative form often gave way to much broader categor-
izations, sceptical of distinctions between factual and imaginary,
and ready to consider history and philosophy, for example, only as
different kinds of fiction. More widely still, culture in all its forms,
written or otherwise, often came to be seen as a kind of text, or a
range of texts or sign systems, all or any of which might be usefully
examined through the practices of literary analysis. Literary history,
in this view, could expand to embrace everything in the bookshop,
and in the streets outside. Yet critical theory also raised the possibility that a literary history might shrink down to a crisply dismissive
introduction, followed only by a few blank pages. While opening out
the literary accordion to include a greater range of texts, academic
criticism also grew more suspicious of the music it had usually
played: of how far, in particular, this might have been music to the
ears only of an elite or class-based minority. Q. D. Leavis was not the
only critic, early in the period, suspicious of factory-workers and
flat-dwellers. Her husband F. R. Leavis, probably still the most
influential of English critics in the 1960s, remained equally committed to a high culture, defined and enjoyed principally by a 'cultured',
well-educated minority. The limitations of such views became
increasingly apparent in later decades. Broadening tolerance, broadening education, and the democratization mentioned earlier affected
criticism as well as culture generally. Several influential critics in the
1980s even considered avoiding any elitism—or just vagueness—
surrounding the term 'literature' by eliminating its use altogether.

Yet this possibility was rarely advanced with complete enthusiasm. In any case, in journalism, reviewing, bookshops, literary
prizes, the media, and public discourse generally—as well as in most
universities—the term 'literature' continued to enjoy as vigorous a
life as ever. Among critics and academics, scepticism about its use
eventually had two main consequences. Critical analysis in the
period extended to cover culture more widely, including areas of

writing—'genre' fiction, for example—hitherto mostly excluded from study. Literary critics also grew warier of treating the object of their study as a given—as a solid, securely established structure, simply awaiting their scrutiny and analysis. Instead, they were readier to examine how, and why, the category of literature was constructed, and what economic, political, or other interests might be involved. In examining not only individual works and writers, but what the General Editor's Preface calls 'the institutions in which literary acts take place'—along with the economies and historical pressures shaping writing—the Oxford English Literary History once again exemplifies the critical thinking of its time. Within this volume, this entails concentration on most of the agencies just named—on media, marketing, education, and the Arts Council, for example—as well as on the shifting patterns of social and historical pressure outlined in Chapter 1.

Concentration on overall patterns and pressures is in any case especially necessary in studying the recent past, its raw immediacies uniquely awkward for literary-historical analysis to digest. Still unsifted by the amnesia of centuries, authors and their works compete for attention in unusual numbers. Little space can be allowed any of them,[1] or for exemplification of their styles, or for more than preliminary assessment of their relative merits. An evaluation is implied, of course, by the extent of discussion allotted each. Readers might also deduce for themselves, within the patterns and developments described, an appropriate place even for a cherished author omitted from discussion altogether, whether for reasons of space, or merely oversight. Readers, too, may be unusually—and productively—disposed to reconfigure these patterns for themselves: it is not only recent authors who remain largely unsifted, but the huge range of recollections of encounters with their work, and of still-vivid memories of the period. What *did* members of Harold Pinter's first audiences make of *The Birthday Party*? What were they talking about after the play, stepping back out into the spring air of 1958? Why did a bookshop browser pick up Ted Hughes's *Birthday Letters* in 1998? What did she or he make of *that*, on a first reading on the bus home? Tantalizingly, answers to such questions are far more

---

[1] Readers interested in individual careers will find a number of them briefly described in the Author Bibliographies.

widely accessible for the recent period than earlier ones, though correspondingly harder to reduce to general patterns and outlines. Essential though these are, they can emerge only tentatively, hazily, from a mass of still-vivid particulars.

Their lasting validity, too, remains inscrutable. Charles Dickens's writing in 1859, for example, or Joseph Conrad's in 1899, can be discussed not only in terms of what these writers followed from, but of what followed from them. Accounts of the later twentieth century, on the other hand, necessarily still look mostly backwards, construing Hughes's writing, or Pinter's, more as consequence than as cause. Constraints of this kind may help to account for the popularity of late twentieth-century analyses and critical movements with 'post-' in their title. The period's unusual haste in defining itself—another symptom of its sense of unusually radical change—probably sharpened its conviction of coming after something, or, especially as the millennium approached, marking the last of an era, or an England, in itself. Before too long, the late twentieth century may well be seen not as 'post-', but as 'inter-', or even 'pre-'. It is tempting to try to outlast the present, look into the seeds of time, and guess how this might occur. Future analyses are probably better served by an account only of what seemed significant during this period itself: of what most moved, shaped, and troubled its imagination; how, and why. That is what this study aims to provide.

Part I

Histories

1

'Gleaming Twilight': Literature, Culture, and Society

'A story has no beginning or end', Graham Greene warns in *The End of the Affair* (1951): 'arbitrarily one chooses that moment of experience from which to look back or from which to look ahead' (bk. 1, ch. 1). Like other stories, histories have no absolute beginnings. Yet some are less arbitrary than others, and 1960 is in many ways an obvious starting point. Factors shaping life and imagination throughout the rest of the century—many patterns in its literature, discussed in later chapters—originated either in that year, or at any rate in the late 1950s and the early part of the new decade. Its opening naturally encouraged reflection about new directions and developments: differing enthusiasm in looking ahead, on different sides of the Atlantic, highlighted some of the pressures shaping Britain's outlook generally at the time. In the United States, presidential-nominee John F. Kennedy talked expansively of 'a New Frontier—the frontier of the 1960s—a frontier of unknown opportunities . . . new invention, innovation, imagination, decision'. The British Prime Minister, Harold Macmillan, more modestly noted only a 'wind of change' blowing across the threshold of the 1960s (Gilbert, pp. 224, 245).

He had reason to be cautious: the new decade seemed likelier to be dominated by Britain's continuing retreat from existing frontiers, rather than by much experience of new ones. Following victory in the Second World War, and the establishment of the Welfare State between 1945 and 1950—and despite slow post-war recovery, rationing, and general austerity—national self-confidence had remained relatively high until the mid-1950s. But it had scarcely recovered from the Suez crisis in 1956—'a climactic year', Doris Lessing considered, looking back in her novel *The Four-Gated City* (1969). Abortive military intervention in Egypt showed that Britain no longer had the authority, or the resources, to impose its will on a wider world, and that its actions abroad were largely subject to the approval of the United States. New uncertainties and shifting attitudes to authority were soon in evidence at home. '1956, or 7, or 8', Lessing added, were 'years that had given birth to this epoch', encouraging 'the idea of change, breaking up, clearing away, movement' (pt. 3, ch. 1; pt. 4, ch. 1).

Vanishing status as a world power was emphasized by the terminal break-up of the British empire. At the start of the twentieth century, Britain had ruled 13 million square miles and 400 million subjects overseas: by the mid-1960s, only a scattering of fragments and islands remained. Much had been ceded shortly after the Second World War, though from a position of apparent strength: the 'wind of change' Macmillan referred to in 1960 rapidly removed the rest, with independence granted to Nigeria, Cyprus, Sierra Leone, Tanganyika, Jamaica, Trinidad, Uganda, Kenya, Zanzibar, Malawi, and Malta, mostly between 1960 and 1962. Other contemporary events further confirmed rapid shrinkage in Britain's influence. Kennedy's insistence that the Soviet Union remove its missile sites from Cuba, though eventually effective, briefly threatened world nuclear war in 1962. The crisis incidentally suggested that Britain, neither directly involved nor much consulted, now figured only as a minor chess piece in Cold War struggles between the new superpowers. For the novelist Peter Vansitartt, it confirmed that 'for the first time in two centuries, Britain had no world role' (p. 1).

Largely dependent on the United States for its nuclear capability, Britain was further humiliated by difficult negotiations for new weapons later in 1962. It hardly fared better with its European neighbours the following year, when application to join the Common Market, the early form of the European Union, was vetoed by a former wartime ally, General de Gaulle—partly on the grounds, ironically, of Britain's supposedly close links with the United States. Membership was deferred for a decade. As the US Secretary of State, Dean Acheson, famously commented in 1962, Britain had 'lost an empire and not yet found a role' (Morgan, p. 216). Anthony Sampson's *Anatomy of Britain*, also published that year, confirmed that 'with those acres of red on the map dwindling, and the mission of the war dissolving', the country inevitably felt 'confused about her purpose'. 'Of all the stages in a great country's history,' he added, 'the aftermath of Empire must be the hardest' (p. 620).

Uncertainties in foreign affairs were compounded by a number of scandals nearer home, including three separate trials of British diplomats and officials, for spying for the Soviet Union, in 1961–2. The following year saw the defection to Moscow of the MI6 officer Kim Philby, and the revelation—accompanied by lurid details of sex, intrigue, and drug abuse—that the war minister, John Profumo, had been involved with a call girl who also had connections with the Soviet embassy. 'Never glad, confident morning again', a Member of Parliament remarked, quoting Robert Browning, during debates on the Profumo affair (Morgan, p. 225). The fabric of loyalty, patriotism, and idealism which had supposedly sustained Britain during and after the war appeared to be unravelling, along with its world role: gaps between high expectation and real capabilities abroad seemed matched by ones opening up between official and actual morality at home.

A measure of disillusion with the government, and with the establishment generally, naturally became more widely apparent at the time, clearly signalled by the growing popularity of satire in the early 1960s. The irreverent theatre review *Beyond the Fringe* transferred from Edinburgh to London in 1960. The satirical journal *Private Eye* first appeared in 1962, and the television satire *That Was the Week That Was* in the following year, employing as its scriptwriters several authors embarking on successful careers at the time—playwrights such as Peter Shaffer, Keith Waterhouse, Dennis Potter, and John Mortimer, as well as the *Observer*'s celebrated theatre critic, Kenneth Tynan. To Mary Whitehouse, whose 'Clean-Up TV Campaign' began in 1963, *That Was the Week That Was* seemed 'anti-authority, anti-religious, anti-patriotism and pro-dirt' (Hewison, p. 29). It was at any rate a startling programme to find on the BBC, still supposed a guardian of public propriety in the early 1960s—as if growing disaffection with the establishment had infected even its own most respected institutions.

Fig. 1. Towards the end of its first year of publication, *Private Eye* sends Christmas greetings to world leaders: Nikita Kruschev, John F. Kennedy, Charles de Gaulle, and Harold Macmillan. The Cuban Missile Crisis occurred a few weeks previously, in late October and November 1962.

Disaffection of this kind led in one way, straightforwardly enough, to a change of government: Labour, under Harold Wilson, replacing in 1964 a Tory party tainted by scandal and national decline. Yet it led in other ways beyond anything even this new government sought to achieve, public life at the time becoming increasingly characterized by the failure of established politics to match popular aspirations. Some of these aspirations had been formulated for the 1960s by a 'New Left' emerging at the end of the previous decade. This centred on the work of critics and commentators such as Richard Hoggart, Raymond Williams, and E. P. Thompson, and around two journals, *Universities and Left Review* and the *New Reasoner*—the latter emphasizing the contemporary implications of a revolutionary tradition identified throughout English history. In January 1960 the two journals merged as *New Left Review*, its first editorial declaring commitment to a 'genuinely popular socialist movement . . . in cultural and social terms, as well as in economic and political' (p. 1). Despite some progressive legislation, Harold Wilson's government never seemed likely to fulfil hopes for a radical reshaping of British society, or for genuinely popular socialism. It seemed reluctant even to meet its supporters' more modest expectation that Welfare State reforms, initiated under Labour between 1945 and 1950, would be continued and completed.

Government adherence to Cold War politics also frustrated the most broadly popular movement to emerge from the late 1950s, the Campaign for Nuclear Disarmament (CND), founded in 1958. Drawing on disgust at Britain's late imperial ambitions at Suez, as well as anxiety at the proliferation and testing of atomic weapons, CND gathered support independently of conventional party allegiances. Its protests and demonstrations involved several public figures, notably the philosopher Bertrand Russell, as well as a wide range of contemporary authors—John Arden, Robert Bolt, John Berger, Shelagh Delaney, Doris Lessing, Iris Murdoch, John Osborne, Alan Sillitoe, and Arnold Wesker, among others. By 1961, annual CND marches to the atomic weapons laboratory at Aldermaston—described in Doris Lessing's *The Four-Gated City*—seemed to Raymond Williams to represent a genuinely popular 'new . . . spirit' at work in British politics (*Long Revolution*, p. 333). Minimal parliamentary response to this spirit fuelled doubts also widely evident in the United States after the assassination of President Kennedy in 1963: doubts about how far anything worthwhile could be achieved within existing forms of government and established political organizations.

These doubts were greatly extended, eventually throughout the Western world, by the United States' military involvement in Vietnam, officially starting in 1964 and lasting until withdrawal in 1973. The first war of the television age, Vietnam was made horrifyingly immediate even by the much-censored footage shown on nightly news bulletins. As the editor of the underground magazine *Oz*, Richard Neville, remarked in 1970, Vietnam proved 'the One Great Youth Unifier', radicalizing a generation and provoking demonstrations on a huge scale—initially in the United States, but also in most European cities by the end of the 1960s (p. 19). In Britain, resistance to the Vietnam war helped to unify both youth and the extra-parliamentary left, rather as CND had earlier: it also made a US novel, Joseph Heller's anti-capitalist, anti-militarist *Catch-22*, among the most popular of the decade. Some of CND's tactics were initially followed by the Vietnam Solidarity Campaign, established in 1966, though demonstrations much less peaceful than the Aldermaston marches soon ensued—in particular, outside the United States' London embassy on several occasions in 1967 and 1968.

Demonstrations against Vietnam, and against the established political system generally, also centred on institutions rapidly growing in influence during the 1960s: the universities. Writing in the *New Review* (Summer 1978), the novelist Angela Carter described the 1944 Education Act, ensuring secondary schooling as far as the age of 15, as the most 'important cultural event in recent British history' (p. 32). 'By the sixties', she also remarked, its effects 'had more or less percolated through the entire system . . . they had to invent all those new universities, and the polytechnics, too, to cope with the pressure' (Maitland (ed.), pp. 210–11). Students numbers had doubled between the late 1940s and the 1960s: following the Robbins report in 1963, recommending the establishment of new institutions and the expansion of existing ones, they quadrupled during the rest of the decade. Fired by the conviction, as Carter suggested, that 'so much seemed at stake in Vietnam, the very nature of our futures, perhaps', and by new opportunity for intellectual enquiry and collective action, this growing student body was drawn further into political activity as the decade went on (Maitland (ed.), p. 212). Almost all universities experienced some unrest, with prolonged occupations in Warwick, Hull, Essex, and, famously, the London School of Economics in 1967. There was even an 'Anti-University' in London for a time during the following year.

Yet student activism in Britain hardly compared with the *événements* which unfolded in France in May and June 1968—much the nearest approach, in reality, to 'the revolution' vaguely but regularly anticipated and discussed during the decade. Student demonstrations around the Sorbonne rapidly grew in scale, extending into riots, nights of violent clashes with police, and the construction of barricades throughout the university quarter of Paris. Matching disruption soon occurred in other French cities. Revolutionary liaisons developed between students and factory workers. A national strike eventually brought the government close to collapse, forcing General de Gaulle to flee temporarily to Germany. Though he returned to curb the strikes and win a general election in July, the world had nevertheless witnessed an unplanned, student- and youth-led revolt coming close to overthrowing a major European state—astonishingly, as if the Paris students' slogan 'imagination is seizing power' had genuinely been put into practice (Roszak, p. 22).

This unexpected near-revolution, and its defeat, naturally influenced profoundly a whole generation of French politicians and intellectuals. Even across the Channel, though there was little direct political reaction, the events in Paris seized the imagination of many authors—comparably, though on a lesser scale, to the effects on English writers which followed the actual French Revolution of 1789. 'Truly, it felt like Year One', Angela Carter remarked of the 'brief period of . . . heightened awareness' which generally ensued at the end of the 1960s (Maitland (ed.), pp. 209, 4). Events in 1968 remained especially haunting for the political dramatists whose work emerged alongside the New Left during the 1960s, and went on to dominate the English stage during the next decade.[1] A sense of huge political opportunity, and its loss, remained unforgettable in their later writing. Howard Brenton, for example, described May

[1] See Ch. 10, below.

1968 as 'crucial . . . a great watershed'; adding that 'it destroyed any remaining affection for the official culture . . . a generation dreaming of a beautiful utopia was kicked—kicked awake' (Trussler (ed.), pp. 96–7).

Other events in the summer of 1968 nevertheless suggested that dreams of 'beautiful utopia' had dimensions beyond the political ones which had been frustrated on the streets of Paris. Fashionable new lifestyles in Swinging London continued to swing, and flower power and dreams of love and peace to flourish in California. By July, flowers and free love were once again on offer on the streets around the Sorbonne, too. As David Caute suggests in *Sixty-Eight: The Year of the Barricades* (1988), 1968 witnessed not only a high tide in revolutionary politics, but also a 'heyday of hedonism, of private pleasure gift-wrapped in permissiveness, of an alternative "revolution" of the spirit and senses' (p. 35). Like the political developments discussed above, origins of this alternative revolution can also be retraced to the end of the 1950s—to new energies eventually emerging from a society wearied by the war but apparently, for much of the decade, still generally content with itself.

Critics at the time often saw some restlessness or rebelliousness focused by the literary figure of the 'Angry Young Man', epitomized by Jimmy Porter in John Osborne's *Look Back in Anger* (Royal Court, 1956). Yet it was only a limited, amorphous, sort of dissent. Jimmy's representative status was best indicated not by his anger but by his complaints that 'there aren't any good, brave causes left'—or even much 'ordinary human enthusiasm'—and that 'if you've no world of your own' there is little alternative to engagement with 'someone else's' (III. i; I). Typically of the mid-1950s, he was a rebel without a cause, unable to find clear, widely shared directions for his disaffection. Other contemporary characters, and their authors, often seemed similarly aimless, or ultimately selfish, in their interests. Popular success for dramatists such as Osborne, or novelists such as Kingsley Amis, usually led them to discard any whiff of radicalism or left-wing politics surrounding their earlier careers. As the critic Gilbert Phelps remarked of a supposedly 'angry' generation, 'they beat against the doors not in order to destroy them, but in the confident hope that if they made enough fuss they would be let in' (Ford (ed.), p. 511). Unable to access worlds of their own, or even to imagine them, they had little choice but to make what accommodation they could, angrily or otherwise, with society as it was currently structured.

By the end of the 1950s, contemporary life had begun to offer new causes, and even a new 'world' in which they might be pursued. Colin MacInnes's aptly named novel *Absolute Beginners* (1959) indicates the nature of the change. Dismissing the Angry Young Men as 'that bunch of cottage journalists', MacInnes's unnamed narrator celebrates instead a still younger generation—a 'whole teenage epic . . . teenage ball' (*Visions of London*, pp. 328, 257–8). Its members are no longer disposed to 'beat on the doors' of established society, but enjoy instead 'real splendour in the days when the kids discovered that, for the first time since centuries of kingdom-come, they'd money . . . we'd loot to spend at last, and our world was to be our world, the one we wanted and not standing on the doorstep of somebody else's' (p. 258). Many factors contributed to 'kids' creating their own world at last. National Service was abolished in 1959—though still explored in 1960s plays such as Arnold Wesker's *Chips with Everything* (Royal Court, 1962) and John McGrath's *Events While Guarding the Bofors Gun* (Hampstead, 1966)—removing the brisk military indoctrination in the establishment ethos previously facing young men on leaving school. Expansions in education opened up a whole new range of opportunities instead, and young people were further empowered later in the decade by the lowering of the age of voting and legal majority from 21 to 18.

Yet from the late 1950s onwards, much the most powerful lever in opening up a new, separate world for the young was financial, as MacInnes's 'Absolute Beginner' suggests. Chilled by winds of change abroad, Harold Macmillan spoke much more warmly of financial affairs at home, famously claiming that the British public had 'never had it so good'. His remark reflected an economic confidence confirmed by the economist J. K. Galbraith's title, *The Affluent Society*, published in 1959. By the end of the 1950s, this new confidence had largely dispelled the atmosphere of austerity, rationing, and bare sufficiency in which the decade began. Wages rose steadily throughout the 1950s and early 1960s, by 34 per cent between 1955 and 1960 alone, and personal disposable income increased by a further 20 per cent between 1961 and the end of the decade. In relation to earnings, the price of many consumer items declined sharply. Along with relaxed credit arrangements, growing spending power became an influence in most areas of society. As Angus Wilson recorded in his novel *Late Call* (1964), 'the washing-up machine, the quick grill, the deep freeze, the cooker, the spin dryer, and all the other white monsters' had become 'everyday things' in many households even by the early 1960s, adding further to a new, more leisured mood at the time (ch. 2).

But the new affluence had more particular—and particularizing—effects on members of a younger generation. Bored by their parents' consumer durables and status symbols, young people preferred to spend their loot, as MacInnes emphasized, on 'luxuries that modify the social pattern': on fashions and accoutrements defining a separate world, identity, and lifestyle of their own (*England*, p. 54). 'You could everywhere see the signs of the un-silent teenage revolution', his narrator records in *Absolute Beginners*, 'the disc shops with those lovely sleeves set in the window . . . hair-style saloons . . . scooters and bubble-cars . . . coffee bars and darkened cellars' (*Visions of London*, p. 311). Even in the mid-1950s, signs of this kind had begun to identify separate forms of youth culture: the Teddy Boys, in particular, setting themselves apart through preferences for skiffle and unusually stylish dress. But the process rapidly gathered pace towards the end of the decade and in the early 1960s. 'Never before . . . has the younger generation been so *different* from its elders', MacInnes suggested of the late 1950s (*England*, p. 59). By 1962, young people were spending £850 million annually on themselves. Anthony Burgess's novel *A Clockwork Orange*, published in that year, nervously satirized teenagers' increasingly distinctive styles of dress and speech, as well as their growing distance from their parents' habits and expectations.

New affluence and a new sense of style naturally encouraged industry and advertising to keep the teenage ball rolling, with more new fashions appearing and more money being spent. By 1967, the 15–19 age group accounted for half the clothing sold annually in Britain. Mods, Rockers, and eventually Hippies and Punks used dress and image—often in competition with each other—to consolidate distinct groupings of shared lifestyle and musical taste. Yet even by the mid-1960s, the teenage ball had begun to roll in directions which neither industry nor advertisers had altogether anticipated. What began only as a separate youth culture grew into a counter-culture: new styles and fashions increasingly signified rejection of conventional society and commitment to alternative values. Teen-agers and young people who might have continued to offer a con-venient, high-profile market fraction began to turn against market and capital altogether, loosely aligning themselves instead with the politics of dissent emerging through CND and the New Left.

Some of this change was visible in, and encouraged by, the evolu-tion of the most 'unsilent' component of the teenage revolution, rock and roll, its growing popularity reflected in the BBC's *Top of the Pops*, first broadcast in 1963. One of the early hits the programme featured was Bob Dylan's 'The Times They Are A-Changin' '. Along with his 'Blowin' in the Wind', and 'A Hard Rain's A-Gonna Fall'—the latter written during the Cuban Missile Crisis—it defined the climate of radical change felt by the younger generation at the time, especially in its warning to parents: 'don't criticise | What you can't understand' (Dylan, p. 132). Partly under Dylan's influence, rock music continued to acquire new seriousness and complexity. It also grew more subversive. Formed in 1960, the Beatles had three number one hits in succession by 1963, but were still considered appropriate performers for the Royal Command Variety show in the autumn of that year, the *Daily Mirror* describing them at the time as 'the nutty, noisy, happy, handsome Beatles' (6 Nov., p. 2). Groups soon rivalling them in popularity—the Rolling Stones and the Who, formed in 1963 and 1964 respectively—would have been harder to describe in such cosy terms. Rock stars, the Beatles eventually included, began to look cool, stoned, and disaffected, rather than happy and handsome, their lyrics becoming rebellious and sexy rather than innocently nutty.

Rock music, Thom Gunn suggested in his poem 'Elvis Presley' (1957), 'turns revolt into a style'. As the 1960s went on, it contributed to conflict not only with convention, but often with the law. Extensively broadcast by 'pirate' radio stations, until legislation closed them in 1967, rock and pop music had always had a faintly unofficial feel, accentuated around this time by its performers' much-publicized drug abuse. Two of the Rolling Stones were detained on drugs charges in 1967: even those nutty, handsome, Beatles were soon implicated, with coded references to LSD on their *Sergeant Pepper* album that year, and John Lennon arrested the next. Among the population generally, prosecutions for cannabis possession alone increased threefold between 1967 and 1970, indicating how far, in ten years or so, the teenage ball had rolled on beyond its absolute beginners' preference for coffee bars. As Jim Morrison's group emphasized in its name, 'The Doors'—borrowed from William Blake, via Aldous Huxley's writing on drugs—a younger generation was no longer standing on anyone's doorstep, but moving on through 'doors of perception' towards new worlds of its own. Increasingly, these lay not only beyond conventional society, but beyond everyday reality altogether.

Other doors were opening, in the early 1960s, more easily than ever before. Philip Larkin famously indicated one of these—another beginning, if hardly an absolute one—when he commented in 'Annus Mirabilis' (1974) that 'Sexual intercourse began | In nineteen sixty-three | . . . | Between the end of the *Chatterley* ban | And the Beatles' first LP'. Sexual intercourse, evidently, pre-dated 1963. But new attitudes towards it did develop soon after contraception became more widely available in 1962, in the form of the Pill. An ensuing 'relaxation of manners . . . changed, well, everything', Angela Carter commented, emphasizing 'sex as a medium of pleasure' (Maitland (ed.), p. 214). As Larkin suggested, new attitudes also followed the lifting of the ban on D. H. Lawrence's *Lady Chatterley's Lover* (1928), always assumed too explicit in its sexual descriptions to be published entire in Britain. Partly as a deliberate test of a new Obscene Publications Act in 1959, Penguin Books planned a paperback edition, duly prosecuted for obscenity in a sensational trial the following year. Penguin's victory had many implications during—and beyond—the decade that followed. Naturally, it seemed at the time to indicate the abolition of censorship, though as it turned out skirmishes between a conservative rearguard and new liberalism in English arts and publishing continued for many years. Even after theatre censorship *had* officially been abolished, with the removal of the Lord Chamberlain's office in 1968, Mary Whitehouse was still able to bring a private prosecution, for alleged public indecency, against the National Theatre's production of Howard Brenton's *The Romans in Britain* in 1980. The

Fig. 2. Huge queues outside a bookshop in Leicester Square, London, waiting to buy the Penguin edition of *Lady Chatterley's Lover*, acquitted of obscenity early in November 1960.

Chatterley trial was nevertheless a decisive move towards new freedoms—ones generally allowing authors later in the century to explore sexuality and the physical more intimately than ever before.

The trial also contributed directly to Lawrence's growing influence on the early 1960s—a symptom as well as a source of new attitudes at the time. A writer whom Graham Hough described in 1960 as the best representative of 'the rebellion, the discontent and the aspiration' of the first half of the century might have appealed in any case to the dissentious 1960s, but it was the publicity surrounding the trial which secured his unique popularity in the years which followed (*Image and Experience*, p. 134). Part of an extended Penguin reissue of Lawrence's work at the time, the new paperback *Lady Chatterley's Lover* sold two million copies in the six weeks between the end of the trial and Christmas, and another one and a half million the following year, making it one of the best-selling novels ever published in Britain. This contributed to a role for Lawrence's writing sometimes less as fiction than almost as the creed, or prophecy, of a newly liberated age. The hero of David Mercer's play *Ride a Cock Horse* (1965), for example, records the healthful effects of 'reading *Women in Love* aloud and eating cornflakes' on Saturday mornings (II. i). Ted Hughes and Sylvia Plath named their first child Frieda, after Lawrence's wife, in 1960, and the biographer Claire Tomalin later recalled that notions 'loosely drawn from D. H. Lawrence via F. R. Leavis, coloured many young marriages' at the time (p. 204).

Some of the testimony in the trial particularly highlighted Lawrence's potential as prophet and precursor of a 'revolution of the spirit and senses'. Penguin called numerous distinguished writers and critics in its defence, including Walter Allen, E. M. Forster, C. Day Lewis, Richard Hoggart, and Raymond Williams, most of them sensibly stressing that Lawrence's sex scenes were contained within an overall artistic purpose, and essential to it. But a number of defence witnesses also sought to justify Lawrence in terms more religious than aesthetic. Among them was John Robinson, Bishop of Woolwich, who described 'the sex relationship as something essentially sacred'—a view of interrelated secular and religious love which he went on to develop in *Honest to God* (1963), greatly disturbing conventional church opinion at the time (Rolph (ed.), p. 70). Such views, Lawrence's general popularity, and an age generally moving away from conventional religion all contributed to a 1960s 'revolution' which left spirit and sensuality in unusual proximity. Love and relationships came to seem not only emotional and sensual experiences, but potentially transcendent ones; sex not only a medium of pleasure, but another of the 'doors' offering escape from conventional life and perception—one which new forms of contraception made it easier than ever to open and pass through.

Views of this kind were encouraged by other 'prophets' and

thinkers popular at the time. Rather like Lawrence in *Lady Chatterley's Lover*, both R. D. Laing and Herbert Marcuse criticized modern society for forms of rationalism, materialism, and systematization which they considered almost insane in their nature and effects. As a practitioner and theorist of psychiatry, Laing expressed reluctance to readjust disturbed patients to a society he thought deranged in itself. For Marcuse, the ostensible liberalism of Western society was merely 'repressive affluence', disguising from its members how far their true natures and psychic energies were suppressed by 'the political machine, the corporate machine, the cultural and educational machine'—by 'the system' in general (pp. xii, xiv, xvii). 'The free play of individual needs and faculties', he added, could be restored by means of 'instinctual liberation . . . from sexuality constrained' (pp. 201–2). Such views allowed 1960s revolutions in spirit, sex, and sensuality to seem not so much an alternative to radical politics as an extension of politics by other means. Private indulgence, sexual permissiveness, and drug use could be construed not only as parts of a heyday of hedonism, but as radical acts in themselves, subverting 'the system', restoring energies suppressed by its machinery, and generally bringing personal and political into mutual alignment. 'Once you have blown your own mind', Richard Neville wryly suggested, summarizing this thinking in 1970, 'the Bastille will blow up itself' (p. 18).

At the time, a whole range of contemporary developments—from mystical cults to alternative theatre; underground newspapers to LSD; new sexuality to the barricades in Paris—*were* construed as somehow sharing an underlying unity of purpose. Later commentators sometimes supported another version of this idea, seeing all the new lifestyles and ideas of the 1960s as diverse manifestations of an 'immense freeing or unbinding of social energies' of the kind Fredric Jameson considered—in his essay 'Periodising the Sixties'—to have been fundamental to the decade (*Ideologies*, p. 208). Its various new energies can also be characterized, and seen collectively, through ideas of the carnivalesque which first reached the West in 1968, translated from the Russian of Mikhail Bakhtin, quickly influencing a generation of critics. For Bakhtin, the popular carnival of the middle ages represented a 'special condition' of social experience still significantly present in later periods and their literatures; one of 'liberation from the prevailing truth and from the established order'. Through emphases on play, parody, pleasure, and the body, carnival offered a 'second life outside officialdom . . . [a] utopian realm of community, freedom, equality and abundance . . . the suspension of all hierarchical rank, privileges, norms, and prohibitions' (*Rabelais*, pp. 6–7, 9, 10). In these terms, the liberating, non-official cultures and politics evident throughout the 1960s can be seen contributing collectively to a carnivalized decade: a period in which energies libidinal, social, and political were all simultaneously unbound.

Yet carnival, Bakhtin explained, offers only a 'temporary liberation from the prevailing truth and from the established order' (*Rabelais*, p. 10). As his critics often warned, it might therefore function as no more than a social safety valve, leaving untouched, even consolidated, the norms and privileges it cheerfully but briefly inverts. John Lennon suggested a comparable view of the decade just completed when he remarked in 1970 that 'the people who are in control and in power and the class system and the whole bullshit bourgeois scene is exactly the same . . . nothing happened except that we all dressed up . . . we are a bit freer and all that, but it's the same game, nothing's really changed' (Wenner, pp. 11–12). As he suggests, the 1960s had scarcely affected 'the people who are in power' or the established order of society, politically or economically, as the re-election of a Conservative government in 1970 helped confirm. According to *The Economist* the following year, 84 per cent of the nation's wealth remained in the hands of 7 per cent of its population—a statistic widely publicized through the naming of the theatre company, 7:84, founded at the time. By the early 1970s, other aspects of the economy had in any case begun to suggest that the carnival aspect and unbound energies of the 1960s *were* largely temporary. Arising from a mood of affluence at the beginning of the decade, they were soon threatened by a sharp economic decline at the start of the next.

Even during the 1960s, affluence was to an extent only another of the decade's beautiful dreams, temporarily obscuring the reality of long-term economic problems. Britain's economy had struggled to recover ever since the war, hindered by military spending which was far in excess of continental competitors', still accounting for 10 per cent of the gross national product even in the 1960s. Production and exports had increased, but less rapidly than in most countries in Europe. Minimal unemployment, rising wages, and a per capita income still the highest in Europe contributed to late 1950s affluence which was genuine enough in a way. But without being matched by a genuine increase in productivity, it created a consumer boom too dependent on imports, causing crises in Britain's balance of trade which eventually required the devaluation of sterling in 1967. Even this measure was somehow construed as a blow to national pride, rather than a warning of fundamental economic problems. By the early 1970s, unchecked expectations of affluence began to exceed what the economy could sustain, at any rate as it was currently structured, leading to industrial unrest on a scale unmatched since the General Strike in 1926, culminating in two prolonged miners' strikes. The second, in the winter of 1973, coincided with a global recession caused by an embargo on supplies of oil, following war between Israel and Egypt, and a fourfold increase in its price. In order to deal with the resulting energy crisis, the Government imposed a three-day week on industry, a nationwide 50 mph speed limit on traffic, and a 10.30 p.m. curfew on broadcasting—encouraging all households go to bed early, even if they had not already been plunged into darkness by cuts in the electricity supply.

Economic difficulties could hardly, any longer, be dreamed away. 'It had all looked so different, four years ago, three years ago', Margaret Drabble recorded in *The Ice Age* (1977)—'so hopeful, so prosperous, so safe, so expansive'. But after the crises of the early 1970s 'the old headline phrases of freeze and squeeze had for the first time become for everyone . . . a living image, a reality: millions who had groaned over them in steadily increasing prosperity were now obliged to think again' (pp. 18, 62). 'Thinking again' generally meant thinking very differently from the 1960s. 'Suddenly there was inflation', Martin Amis recalled. 'That had an incredibly sobering effect on everyone, which we see to this day . . . the wild ideas— political and pharmaceutical—that were going around then had to be dispensed with as leisure-class fripperies' (*Guardian*, 23 Jan 2001, p. 15). Some sober and long-cherished political ideals were also threatened by an inflation rate moving above 25 per cent by the end of 1975, and by growing unemployment. A Labour government had replaced the Tories in 1974: to obtain help from the International

Monetary Fund in 1976, it had to abandon long-standing principles and agree to many cuts in public spending and social welfare. Though these and other measures reduced inflation later in the decade, continuing conflict with the unions and general nervousness about the economy helped the Tories to return to power in 1979. Margaret Thatcher's new government soon indicated that the ideas of the 1960s and early 1970s were not only to be rethought, but as far as possible reversed. In another 'state of the nation' novel, *The Radiant Way* (1987), Margaret Drabble recorded a 'new rhetoric praising the Victorian values of family life' (p. 16) emerging in the early 1980s. Thatcher herself extolled in 1982 'the old virtues of discipline and self restraint' over the 'fashionable theories and permissive claptrap' of the 1960s (Waugh, *Harvest of the Sixties*, p. 18). Renewed 'discipline and restraint' were quickly imposed legislatively, and on the unions in particular. *The Radiant Way* painfully records its heroine watching television images of another miners' strike, in 1983, fiercely controlled and ultimately defeated this time by 'police in their riot gear . . . [and] charging horses' (p. 342). New disciplines and reversals of earlier assumptions were most clearly evident in Tory management of the economy. This was based on monetarist policies intended to control wages and inflation, on re-privatizing nationalized industries and assets, and on reduction of public spending wherever possible. With more than three million unemployed by the early 1980s, these policies had disturbing immediate consequences, contributing to frustrations which regularly erupted into rioting in the weary heart of British cities—in Toxteth, in Liverpool, and in Brixton and Southall, in London, during 1981 alone.

There were also radical longer-term implications for British life in the later twentieth century. Policies based on market forces rather than social welfare—summed up in Thatcher's memorable claim that 'there is no such thing as society, only individual men and women'—reversed much more than the values of the 1960s (Bloom and Day, p. 7). They discarded, or inverted, a commitment more or less supported by both major political parties ever since 1945—the principle, framed around the thinking of John Maynard Keynes, that governments should intervene to manage a capitalist economy and ensure that its benefits were accessible to the population as a whole.

The sense of common cause and shared outlook which had developed during the war evolved through such principles into the Welfare State established in the years afterwards. Much of the expansive mood of the 1960s, described above, resulted from the continuation of a post-war, welfare-capitalist consensus in later years—from a sense of security, improved educational opportunity, full employment, and agreed social priorities which had continued to accumulate since 1945. Some of the 'beautiful utopia' dreamed of in 1968 concerned ways such principles might be extended still further into the future.

As Raymond Williams explained in 1961, the idea of 'a good society naturally unfolding itself' had in some ways a still longer provenance, extending a process of gradual social improvement and democratization whose origins he located in the late eighteenth century. Williams also emphasized that the future of this 'Long Revolution', as he called it, depended on the strength of the economy, and warned that faith in its continuing progress might in the end prove 'exceptionally misleading' (*Long Revolution*, p. 294). After the reversals of the late 1970s and 1980s, it seemed more and more so. Surveying global politics in 1959, C. P. Snow suggested that 'disparity between the rich and the poor . . . won't last for long. Whatever else in the world we know survives to the year 2000, that won't' (*Two Cultures*, p. 40). But it did, globally and locally. Surveys in the 1990s showed gaps between rich and poor in Britain widening more rapidly than in almost any other country in the world, with as much as 25 per cent of the population living in poverty, and corresponding increases in crime, which doubled in England between 1979 and 1992. The economy in the 1990s was more stable than two decades previously, despite continuing overall decline, but its benefits were still less equitably shared, nationally and locally. Between 1980 and 1985, more than a million jobs were lost in the north of England, ten times as many as in the south. Within the cities, a new, relaxed lifestyle of high-street coffee bars and bistros thrived within a stone's throw of rotting, sink estates.

For those educated, employed, and established, life in many areas was more comfortable, affluent, and full of potential than ever. But it was at the expense of a new, growing 'underclass', excluded from full participation in a 'good society' by poverty, low wages, or unemployment. It was also, consequently, at the expense of the relative social cohesion, optimism, and 'never had it so good' feelings with which the period began. Despite worries about declining world influence, Harold Macmillan was ready to claim Britain as 'on the whole . . . the finest country in the world' in the 1950s (Paxman, p. 131). In *British Society since 1945* (1996), Arthur Marwick refers to a poll showing that in 1977 British people still considered themselves among the happiest in the world, even in the middle of Drabble's 'Ice Age'. But by the mid-1990s, another poll suggested that half of the population would emigrate if the chance arose— Marwick concluding that the country had become 'utterly torn apart', a society 'at odds with itself' (pp. 267, 420, 439). The 1980s, in particular, did experience 'the last of England' in one way, in the sense suggested by Derek Jarman's 1987 film of that name. Jarman's *Last of England* showed the failure of all sense of community, radical disparities between the affluent and the underclass, and anarchic, even terminal decline in the life of England's inner cities. Elected ten years later, in 1997, the Labour government's promises to mend divisions and repair the apparatus of the Welfare State remained firmly constrained by market forces. By the end of century, 'New Labour' policies had achieved only a partial return towards the values of post-war consensus which eighteen years of Tory government had so decisively reversed.

*

This reversal, and its timing, invite any history to divide the period from 1960 to 2000 into two sections. It even, conveniently, falls almost into two halves: the first characterized by an affluence in economy, lifestyle, and imagination, growing in the 1960s and fading in the next decade; the second, by a disillusioned, fragmenting society after the late 1970s. Literature in the period did reproduce some of these divisions: forces contributing to them obviously affected writers both directly and indirectly. In the 1970s inflation, and the strategies later adopted to combat it, had a sobering effect not only on the wilder ideas of the previous decade, as Martin Amis remarked, but also directly on the economics of publishing and arts production generally. Inflation and recession in the later 1970s affected the book trade particularly severely, leaving publishers much more reluctant than hitherto to take risks, encourage new authors, promote unfamiliar styles, or to publish poetry at all.[2] Support from the Arts Council was also increasingly restricted in the 1980s, one of several significant changes in its role during the period. These are worth examining further, as they illustrate so clearly, as well as directly affecting, relations between economic and artistic spheres in the later twentieth century. Arts Council Annual Reports offer a kind of barometer of the changing cultural, financial, and social confidence discussed above.

Founded in 1943, originally as the Council for Encouragement of Music and the Arts (CEMA), the Arts Council firmly shared the commitments to a more equable society, and to greater democracy of opportunity, which developed into the Welfare State. John Maynard Keynes explained in a broadcast at the end of the war that CEMA was intended to support both excellence in the arts and the widest possible access to them. Slogans such as 'the best for the most', 'enjoyment of the "high" arts by a wider public', and 'raise and spread', continued to appear in Reports in 1976/7 (pp. 7–8) and 1978/9 (p. 7), confirming that this ambition was broadly sustained over the next three decades. It was probably realized most success-fully in the late 1960s and early 1970s. The chairman at the time, Lord Goodman, had good reason to be confident that the Arts Council would thrive 'so long as the attainment of a more civilized society remains the ultimate objective of all political exertions': suc-cessive governments had steadily increased their support (1969/70, p. 5). CEMA's £235,000 grant in 1945/6 had risen to £1.5 million by 1960, and £4 million by 1965. Under the Labour government, which appointed the first-ever Minister for the Arts, Jennie Lee, it had doubled to more than £8 million by the end of the 1960s. The 1970/1 Report could look back with satisfaction on 'Fifteen Years' Achievement in the Arts'—in particular, to 'remarkable growth . . . a creative outburst' in drama since 1956, including the foundation of a National Theatre, and of the Royal Shakespeare Company, in the early 1960s (pp. 15, 43).

Yet only a few years later, this 'remarkable growth' was im-perilled—like so much else at the time—by the oil embargo and the ensuing recession. With increases in funding falling behind the rate

[2] See pp. 145–6, 186–7, and 430, below.

of inflation, the Arts Council entitled its 1975/6 Report 'The Arts in Hard Times', complaining that it no longer had the resources to encourage new ventures, nor to sustain properly ones already dependent on its support. Under the new Tory government, which reduced arts funding by £1 million immediately, and continued cutting in later years, such complaints soon grew more strident. They also changed significantly in tone. The 1981/2 Report continued to emphasize the role of the arts in 'expansion of consciousness', and to recall that public subsidy had been introduced 'in the darkest days of the Second World War . . . mainly because the arts made an indispensable contribution to the spirit of the nation in fighting the Nazis'. But it immediately added a contemporary note in claiming that the arts could 'contribute even more to the economic struggle' (p. 6). As the 1980s went on, the Arts Council increasingly defined its role in terms of this 'struggle', and of Tory priorities generally, stressing the potential of sponsorship and private-sector funding, and the importance of the arts for the economy generally. The 1985/6 Report, for example, famously suggested that 'the Arts are to tourism in Britain what the sun is to Spain' (p. 10).

Reports in the 1990s continued to highlight contributions to employment, tourism, and the country's image generally—ones formalized by the Arts Council's inclusion within the Department of National Heritage, set up in 1992, before its transfer to a new Department for Culture, Media and Sport at the end of the century. Like many other aspects of national life, in other words, the Arts Council's changing role showed how far consensual, post-war priorities of social and civic improvement, sustained through the 1960s, fell victim to the financial stresses of the next decades. By the 1980s, economic imperatives had largely replaced 'expansion of consciousness' and earlier commitments to 'civilized society' and 'the spirit of the nation'. These changing fortunes obviously affected literature directly, especially in the genres of drama, for which the Arts Council's support was crucial throughout the period, and poetry, to which it often gave significant help.[3]

Expansion and contraction in 'the spirit of the nation' naturally affected literature imaginatively as well as economically. Throughout the 1960s—from Doris Lessing's *The Golden Notebook* (1962)

---

[3] Consequences for each are considered in Chs. 8 and 14, below.

to John Fowles's *The French Lieutenant's Woman* (1969)—fiction often matched contemporary experiments in lifestyle with innovation in literary style. Partly under the influence of rock music, poetry at the time enjoyed a popular revival, poetic imagination also seeming an ideal vehicle for the decade's dreams and utopias. For its growing political commitments, the theatre offered an obvious arena for polemic and debate, and the carnivalesque atmosphere of the 1960s generally—its unbinding of Dionysiac energies fundamental to drama—was naturally one in which theatre thrived. By the mid-1970s, much of this new or expanded consciousness had begun to falter and fade, contributing to some gloomy prognoses about the future of literature, in each genre, by the end of the decade. The unpromising state of English fiction was anxiously surveyed in a forum in one of the most successful of the period's literary magazines, *Granta*, in 1980. Published in 1982, Blake Morrison and Andrew Motion's *Penguin Book of Contemporary British Poetry* was widely held to reflect lack of direction, and lack of excitement, in English writing at the time, despite the claims of the editors. In the same year, David Edgar worried in *Times Literary Supplement* about the current state of drama, and about what his generation of left-wing playwrights could make of the altered priorities of 'a privatised age' (10 Sept., p. 969). In *The Seventies: Portrait of a Decade* (1980), Christopher Booker even suggested that 'our culture . . . has reached the most dramatic dead end in the entire history of mankind' (p. 259).

By the early 1980s, in other words, it did seem that the literary imagination might simply reproduce the pattern outlined above: opening like a flower in the 1960s, fading in the next decade, then closing up again, with a snap of Mrs Thatcher's purse, thereafter. Yet different patterns developed. English writing did change character in the early 1980s, in ways discussed in the chapters which follow. But any assumption that it would simply change for the worse underestimated the complexity of relations between history and literary imagination—often readier, as the Introduction suggested, to resist than to reflect contemporary social change. If renewed materialism and social decline were often depressing, in the 1980s and later, they were also creatively provoking. In the work of novelists such as Ian McEwan and Martin Amis, for example, poets such as Peter Reading and Tony Harrison, or a new generation of dramatists including Caryl Churchill and Mark Ravenhill, literature was regularly energized by adversarial encounters with its age. In particular, it was forced to extend and sharpen satirical idioms which had re-emerged in the 1960s, darkening them with a distinctively black humour which became a characteristic of literature late in the century. Any open-and-shut model of the period's literature—or of the years from 1960 to 2000 more widely—would also underestimate the resilience of the liberal post-war trends gathering momentum in the 1960s. Along with the decade's developments generally, these trends were often reshaped or redirected later in the century, rather than altogether reversed. Change in social and cultural terms was perhaps even accelerated by its failure to materialize in the economic and political ones *New Left Review* had hoped for in 1960, and the Paris students had tried to instigate in the *événements* of 1968. Never likely to alter radically 'the people who are in control and in power', as John Lennon remarked at the time, revolutionary energies unbound in the 1960s were later deflected instead into more limited political ambitions, more moderate forms of social change. This was an easy enough transition, given the interrelation already assumed between personal and wider political issues during the decade itself.

Consequences were apparent throughout the later 1970s, 1980s, and 1990s. Even that most fundamental component of English social structure, class, eventually showed some signs of change as a result. John Lennon considered the class system to have emerged intact from the 1960s, and any later reduction in its influence—or in its interest for English writers—was certainly no more than partial. Distinctions of outlook and accent between 'Them and [uz]' in English society continued throughout the period to provide material for Tony Harrison's poetry, for example. In his survey *The Way We Live Now* (1995), Richard Hoggart still found in the 1990s 'evidence all around of the enduring power of the English sense of class-divisions' (p. 199). At the very end of the period, in his novel *How the Dead Live* (2000), Will Self envisaged these divisions not only dictating the way we live now, but even enduring beyond death itself. Yet by the end of the century there was also much evidence of weakening in the nation's hierarchies, and in the institutions on which they were based. After the Life Peerage Act of 1958, the House of Lords had ceased to be the exclusive domain of hereditary peers: in 1999, it dispensed with them almost completely. By the 1990s, the monarchy seemed to have aged, as an institution, much more thoroughly even than the monarch herself, with the outpouring of grief at the death of Diana, Princess of Wales, in 1997, suggesting affections for royal figures of a different kind.

In daily life, throughout the period, there were also many signs of class divisions growing less stringent—a slackening initiated by the levelling influences of the war, and strongly apparent by the late 1950s. Though despairing of other 'good brave causes' in *Look Back in Anger*, Jimmy Porter remains implacably determined to attack every manifestation of the class system, emboldened by its increasingly fragile, fossilized aspect at the time. The readiness of other Angry Young Men to 'beat on the doors' of established society was likewise encouraged by confidence that they might already be opening. Many factors encouraged this optimism: broader education, the egalitarianism of the Welfare State, dwindling respect for the establishment, and an affluence which brought previously exclusive privileges, such as car ownership or foreign holidays, further within the reach of the population generally. New emphasis on status symbols of this kind was extensive enough to trouble commentators at both ends of the political spectrum at the time. The novelist Simon Raven worried in *The English Gentleman* (1961) that 'material standards' tended to 'cheapen the notion of gentility' (pp. 16–17). In *The Long Revolution* (1961) Raymond Williams likewise criticized the growing influence of 'conspicuous possession of a range of objects of prestige', rather than a more authentic 'general respect', as a marker of personal worth (p. 322).

Williams nevertheless acknowledged that material factors did contribute to signs of 'the class system apparently breaking up' on the edge of the 1960s. Developments during the decade soon encouraged it to do so further (*Long Revolution*, p. 293). The younger generation, Colin MacInnes considered, was 'much more *classless* than any of the older age groups' (*England*, p. 55). Throughout the alternative culture establishing itself at the time, new distinctions of age, style, outlook, or musical taste began to cut across and diminish longer-established ones of class, accent, or background. The huge success of the Beatles, in particular, and other rock groups of working-class origin, rather belied John Lennon's conviction that class constraints remained unchanged at the end of the decade. Television, too, was generally levelling and democratizing in its influence—one rapidly expanding early in the period, and remaining enormously powerful throughout. A TV set was still a coveted 'object of prestige' in the 1950s, but television had reached 72 per cent of the population by 1960, and 98 per cent of households by 1980, making all the world's news and entertainment simultaneously, identically, available in all the nation's homes. Television 'projects a classless . . . world . . . into the remotest villages, where TV aerials stick up with the regularity of chimneypots', Anthony Sampson recorded in 1962 (p. 619). Its programming also moved steadily towards more demotic forms. Viewers themselves were increasingly involved in game shows, polls, and phone-ins, and the plummy tones favoured by the BBC's early director, Lord Reith, were gradually replaced by accents often closer to Tony Harrison's.

Conventional class divisions continued in some ways to shift and weaken under Thatcher governments in the 1980s—new, raw emphases on money, rather as Williams and Raven had feared, helping to make wealth and 'conspicuous possession' more significant markers of status than birth, accent, or education. 'She's radical all right', a character suggests of Mrs Thatcher in Salman Rushdie's *The Satanic Verses* (1988): 'what she wants . . . is literally to invent a whole goddamn new middle class in this country. Get rid of the old . . . and bring in the new. People without background, without history . . . In with the hungry guys with the wrong education . . . it's a bloody revolution' (pt. V, ch. 1). Replacement of conventional class-boundaries by deepening divisions between haves and have-nots, middle class and underclass, often seemed a revolution more 'bloody' than democratizing, as Rushdie indicates by referring to Thatcher as 'Mrs Torture' throughout *The Satanic Verses*. Her election in 1979, as Britain's first woman prime minister, had more affirmative implications for another set of factors cutting across class divisions later in the twentieth century, and radically altering its outlook generally—new awareness of gender roles, and extensive changes in the social position of women. Like the counter-culture generally, these began to develop partly in response to new economic and educational opportunities available by the 1960s. Proportions of women in higher education increased during the decade, and numbers in full-time employment also grew substantially between 1950 and 1970, creating new financial independence and greater readiness to question conventional roles in marriage, the family, and homemaking. This was reflected and consolidated in some of the progressive legislation which Labour governments did manage to introduce after 1964, despite disappointing their supporters in other ways: particularly the Abortion Act of 1967, the Divorce Reform Act of 1969, and the Equal Pay and Sexual Discrimination Acts which followed in 1975.

Though emerging nearly simultaneously, and from some of the same origins, a new sense of women's autonomy was shaped as much in reaction to the counter-culture as in further extension of its 'alternative revolution'. Its much-vaunted sexual liberation, in particular, soon seemed seriously asymmetric. Greater freedoms included still freer exploitation of the female form, regularly spreadeagled over the covers of underground magazines such as *Oz*. Supposed 'freeing or unbinding of social energies' often left women more subordinate than ever; more starkly objectified by unconstrained male desires. 'Everything is challenged, everything is new', a woman character remarks of the 1960s in scene iv of David Edgar and Susan Todd's *Teendreams* (Monstrous Regiment, 1979), 'so one does just wonder . . . why the fuck we're still doing the typing and making the tea' (Edgar, *Plays: Three*). Ian McEwan's narrator likewise recalls in *Enduring Love* (1997) that 'in England, hippiedom had been largely a boys' affair. A certain kind of quiet girl sat cross-legged at the edges, got stoned and brought the tea . . . these girls disappeared overnight at the first trump from the women's movement' (ch. 21).

Though growing audible throughout the later 1960s, this trump sounded with unmistakable clarity at the end of the decade. Angela Carter dated 'questioning of the nature of [her] reality as a woman' to the period of 'heightened awareness' in the summer of 1968 (Maitland (ed.), p. 4). 'Smouldering, bewildered consciousness . . . muttered dissatisfaction . . . suddenly shoots to the surface and EXPLODES', the underground magazine *Black Dwarf* declared when claiming 1969 'Year of the Militant Woman' (Rowbotham, p. 211). The following year, demands for equal pay and equal opportunity were formulated by a first Women's Liberation Conference, drawing support from around seventy recently established women's groups. A range of new concepts of gender were also theorized and popularized at the time by two pioneering feminist tracts, Kate Millett's *Sexual Politics* (1970) and Germaine Greer's *The Female Eunuch* (1970).

Following what Millett called 'four decades of dormancy' since the end of the suffragette period in the 1920s, a woman's movement seemed to have re-established itself powerfully and quite suddenly by the early 1970s (Millett, p. 64). It was further focused by the establishment of a feminist journal, *Spare Rib*, and of Virago Press in 1973. Three decades of activism and developing awareness, thereafter, still left much to achieve at the end of the century. Women's pay, for example, continued to lag behind men's by more than 20 per cent, on average, in the late 1990s, while in literature it was still only in the genre of fiction that women's writing was even nearly as widely accepted as work by men.[4] Nevertheless, as Alan Sinfield remarked in *Literature, Politics, and Culture in Postwar Britain* (1989), by the late 1980s 'the subordination of most women in modern western societies' had come to seem obvious, whereas thirty years previously it had scarcely been an issue at all (p. 203). Clearer perception of gender roles and growing equality for women were among the most distinctive new developments of the later twentieth century, influential throughout the life and imagination of the time.

While the early 1970s, in other words, saw a decline in some of the energies unbound during the previous decade, there were others whose influence was really only beginning. Further evidence of this appeared in the emergence of the Gay Liberation movement, likewise established in 1970 and soon focused around a journal, *Gay News*, founded in 1972. Emphases in the 1960s on sexual liberation and on 'doing your own thing' had benefited the gay community, like women, only rather obliquely, and tardily. But after the decriminalization of homosexuality, through the Sexual Offences Act of 1967, it began to enjoy freedom and public acceptance probably as great as at any time in history. This generally continued to develop in later decades, despite setbacks such as the Tory threats to Gay Liberation in 1980s 'Clause 28' legislation, forbidding affirmative references to homosexuality in education. Conservative attitudes, and the last of

[4] See p. 462, below.

an England of one kind, continued in such areas to conflict with new, emerging patterns of behaviour. But in general, broadening tolerance of individual lifestyles and sexual preferences, and of new forms of relationship, continued to appear throughout the society of the time, sharing in its general democratization of outlook.

Since many of the changes involved were as much cultural as political in their origins, literature often played a leading part in their development, perhaps especially where women's issues were concerned. Literature naturally came to reflect new perceptions of sex and gender late in the century, but it had also had an initiatory role, offering a means of exploring in imagination possibilities not yet much developed within society itself. As Kate Millett remarked in *Sexual Politics*, 'the arena of sexual revolution is within human consciousness even more pre-eminently than it is within human institutions . . . even more a habit of mind and a way of life than a political system' (p. 63). Some time before the woman's movement sounded its trump at the end of the 1960s, a form of sexual revolution was anticipated in this way in the work of several women writers, particularly Doris Lessing in *The Golden Notebook* (1962). As a construct of 'human consciousness', but also a means through which consciousness and habits of mind are constructed, literature continued to provide an important focus for the attention of the woman's movement: an 'arena' in which attitudes and prejudices could be conveniently identified and their influences discussed. Long sections of Millett's argument in *Sexual Politics* were devoted in this way to literary criticism, concentrating on the author so widely influential during the 1960s, D. H. Lawrence. In her view, if Lawrence's work was in any way religious or sacred, it was only in the service of the oppressive patriarchal cult of the phallus. Freedom to publish *Lady Chatterley's Lover* in 1960 had helped initiate the liberated mood of the decade which followed: Millett showed how far ideas had continued to develop by its end, and how effectively they could be expressed through literary criticism and cultural analysis. Feminist literary critics, and women readers generally, continued in later decades to find in male authors' constructions of reality—and of women characters in particular—useful evidence of the problems they faced, and to look for possible solutions in the work of women writers. Virago Press, and other exclusively women's imprints which soon followed, helped to establish a wider availability and influence for this work than ever.

Other factors substantially reshaping society and literature in the period can be retraced to the late 1950s and 1960s, and to the difficult phase of 'the aftermath of empire' Anthony Sampson identified at the time. Immigration from former colonies had begun slowly in the late 1940s, accelerating in the next decade under the influence of a continuing post-war labour shortage. Around a quarter of a million immigrants from the Caribbean had arrived by the end of the 1950s, with growing numbers entering Britain from Pakistan and India at the start of the 1960s: by the early 1990s, 6 per cent of the population was immigrant in origin. As well as tracing the emergence of a youth culture, *Absolute Beginners* and other novels in Colin MacInnes's *Visions of London* trilogy—*City of Spades* (1957) and *Mr Love and Justice* (1960)—record the growing influence of immigrant communities on metropolitan life, and the prejudices beginning to be directed against them. *Absolute Beginners* depicts race riots which ensued in Notting Hill in 1958: these also occurred in Nottingham at the time. They were to recur regularly in the decades that followed—again in Notting Hill in the late 1970s. Unemployment, racial prejudice, and police pressure on black communities were also factors in the countrywide inner-city riots of the early 1980s. Uneasy governments passed legislation to control immigration in 1962, 1968, 1971, 1981, and 1988, and a Race Relations Board was established in 1966 to deal with tensions and prejudices already rampant within the country. They were soon heightened further by Enoch Powell's inflammatory prediction in 1968— forcing his dismissal from the Tory Shadow Cabinet—that 'much blood' would inevitably flow on the streets of Britain as a result of racial conflict.

Yet later developments on the whole proved Powell more of a political opportunist, and more misguided, even than he seemed at the time. Despite continuing tensions, race relations had at least begun to evolve in different directions by the 1990s. Blood did continue to be shed on the streets—in further riots, and, notoriously, in the unpunished murder of Stephen Lawrence in 1993. Prejudice, injustice, and racial harassment sometimes seemed to continue undiminished. Yet there were also many streets in British cities by the

1990s—the Uxbridge Road in London, for example—and many developments in the country generally which gave evidence for the more hopeful conclusion Caryl Phillips reached in *A New World Order* (2001). Under the influence of half a century of immigrants, Phillips considered, Britain had 'changed radically': generally towards more 'open, fluid' attitudes; even those of a 'truly multicultural society'. As it had in relation to gender politics, writing played a particularly significant role in this development, Phillips remarking that the most genuinely 'multicultural and multiracial area of British life—aside from the national athletics team—has been the literature' (pp. 279–80, 295).

Along with new awareness of gender roles, this growing multiculturalism shaped a society which conceived itself very differently at the end of the period than at mid-century—in terms 'far more horizontal and diffused', Richard Hoggart suggested in 1995, in *The Way We Live Now* (p. 6). As class hierarchies changed or weakened, new divisions of gender and ethnicity contributed to a partial, half-revolution in English society: a ninety-degree rotation of some of the axes around which it defined itself; a shift of emphasis from vertical to lateral distinctions. Changes of this kind were summed up by Steven Connor in *Postmodernist Culture* (1989) as 'modulation of hierarchy into heterarchy' (p. 9). Though the move away from hierarchy was in general a liberating one, the new 'diversity of voices and interests' he considered to be involved did leave society in some ways more fragmentary than hitherto; more 'torn apart', as Marwick suggested. The progressive political energy of the post-war consensus, in particular, seemed to have dissipated into diverse micropolitics after encountering the economic barriers of the 1970s and 1980s—as though, in Connor's image, 'running its propulsive strength into the marshes and rivulets of a delta' (pp. 244, 226). Donald Davie likewise worried in his poem 'Standings' (1988) that 'the Albion of William Blake' had fragmented into a 'tessellation' of diverse social 'cantons' and 'republics', defined by outlooks varying radically 'from jurisdiction | To jurisdiction'.

Yet these new diversities of voice and interest had progressive effects on literature and culture. Long-standing literary concern with class hardly required new styles for its expression, as the formally conservative, social-realist writing of the Angry Young Men showed in the late 1950s and early 1960s. New voices and interests were naturally likelier to develop new styles, or stretch and reshape some of the old. Concerned with 'revolution . . . within human consciousness', and with altering established 'habit of mind', women writers could hardly remain content with existing literary conventions, and were among the most innovative of late twentieth-century authors as a result. Some of the same commitment to new styles and visions began to emerge in gay literature later in the period. Immigrant writers had particular reason to abandon or amend established forms. Authors whom Caryl Phillips described as 'both inside and outside Britain at the same time . . . belonging and not belonging' naturally offered new perspectives on the country's life, but also new approaches to its literary conventions (*New World Order*, p. 234). The potential of authors in each of these areas was probably still not fully apparent in the early 1980s: by the end of the century, their work had done much to refute the gloomy prognoses about the future of literature often expressed at that time, and to renovate the period's writing at the levels of form and style.

By the end of the century, too, shifts from hierarchy to heterarchy had come to affect not only ways literature was written, but the whole manner in which culture was understood. Conventional conceptions of an exclusive or 'high' culture, or a single national one, had already been challenged by the development of alternative and counter-cultures in the 1960s. In a society increasingly diverse and democratized thereafter, culture continued to be reshaped by broader accessibility and more heterogeneous influence. While television was establishing an unrestricted, mass audience for itself in the 1960s, print culture had also become accessible on a new and wider scale, better education and rising levels of literacy creating a reading public larger than at any time in history. 'It is only in our own century that the regular reading even of newspapers has reached a majority of our people', Raymond Williams pointed out in 1961, adding that 'it is probable that in the 1950s, for the first time, we had a majority book-reading public' (*Long Revolution*, pp. 156, 171). This was soon extended further by expansions in the library system, and in paperback publishing, during the 1960s.[5] Though Williams's 'Long Revolution' had hardly been completed in social or political

[5] See Ch. 4, below.

terms by the end of the century—its progress in several ways retarded or even reversed since the 1980s—its ambition to open culture to 'all people rather than to limited groups' was closer to being realized. Theatres, libraries, and bookshops were less likely than forty years earlier to seem the exclusive province of a particular caste, and television, in particular, opened up new forms of cultural engagement for the population as a whole (*Long Revolution*, p. xi).

A symptom of this change appeared in the shifting significances attached to the term 'culture' itself during the period. At mid-century, 'culture' and 'cultured' remained closely cognate. Culture still seemed to belong to and reflect the tastes of 'the cultured'— a well-educated, affluent fraction of the population. The Arts Council's determination to 'raise and spread', or to bring 'high' art to a wider public, showed a continuing version of this assumption in later years: a conviction that what was considered culture might not appeal immediately, or even seem accessible, to the majority of the public. But by the end of the period, 'culture' had become a term less often used evaluatively, or exclusively. Instead, it was regularly used thoroughly *in*clusively, to refer to the increasingly diverse tastes and outlooks of the population as a whole, and to *all* the media and signifying practices of this society. 'Culture' came to mean all the ways in which society spoke to and made sense of itself, from rock music to opera, newspaper reports to lyric poetry, fashion style to film.

The term 'literature' moved similarly towards broader, less exclusive definition. 'We know what it is, pretty well', Graham Hough remarked of literature in his *Essay on Criticism* in 1966, referring to an established canon of great works (p. 9). Even by the end of the 1970s, most critics would have been less confident: likelier to question the authority of any interpretative community defined by Hough's rather royal-sounding 'we', and to challenge any canonical conclusions it might have reached. Transitions in thinking of this kind made the period's literary criticism symptomatic of general changes in its outlook, as well as, more directly, an influence on how its literature was read and understood.[6] Increasingly diverse forms of analysis—the rapid development of feminism and postcolonialism, for example—reflected the lateral division of contemporary society into 'cantons' and 'republics', and the assumption that different but

[6] See Ch. 3, below.

equally valuable forms of imagination might be at work in each. The broadening remit of literary criticism generally—its movement towards Cultural Studies, and its openness to forms of writing previously ignored—also reproduced the priorities of an increasingly democratized age.

*

Other influences retraceable to the early 1960s began to affect English culture and self-perception towards the end of the century. In his essay 'Periodising the Sixties', Fredric Jameson related the decade's 'freeing or unbinding of energies' to 'the great movement of decolonisation' taking place around the world at its beginning. Western nations' dwindling authority abroad, he considered, encouraged 'those inner colonized of the First World—"minorities", marginals, and women—fully as much as its external subjects' to seek greater freedom and autonomy for themselves (*Ideologies*, pp. 180–1). Jameson's views help explain a new urge for independence not only among 'marginal' groups discussed above, but also in the peripheral nations of the United Kingdom. Struggle against a common enemy had strengthened Britain's cohesion during the war, but 1960s election results showed the return of political nationalism in Scotland and Wales. In Northern Ireland, the Civil Rights Association's demands for equality for the Catholic minority, typical of the 1960s, led to increasingly violent clashes with the Royal Ulster Constabulary late in the decade. After the arrival of the British Army in 1969, supposedly as a stabilizing influence, the Civil Rights initiative was generally taken over by the Provisional IRA, and accompanied by increasing violence between the religious communities. The IRA's struggle against the army soon extended into regular bombing campaigns on the mainland—adding further chilling elements to 'alarm, panic and despondency' in the 'Ice Age' which Margaret Drabble envisaged replacing the 'hopeful, safe, expansive' mood of the 1960s (*Ice Age*, p. 12). Bombings and violence continued throughout the next decades, until a political solution at last came into view late in the 1990s. By that time, measures of devolution had been accepted in Wales and in Scotland, though the electorate there had initially rejected self-government, in 1979. This left Britain still united as a kingdom at the end of the century, but with the autonomy of its constituent countries more clearly established than at any time for hundreds of years. 'Decolonization' overseas at the start of the period, in other words, was soon matched by the incipient dissolution of a longer-standing English empire nearer home. Though most of the developments discussed so far affected Britain as a whole, there were others by the end of the century which were exclusive to England itself.

'Once upon a time', Jeremy Paxman commented in *The English: A Portrait of a People* (1998), 'the English knew who they were . . . the English didn't need to concern themselves with the symbols of their own identity: when you're top dog in the world's leading empire, you don't need to' (pp. 2, 12). But in a post-imperial age, and in the 1990s especially—sometimes also troubled by the growing influence of the European Union—questions about England's identity, autonomy, and traditions began to be raised more often. For contemporary writers, these questions proved thoroughly problematic, in some areas at least. Nick Hornby's popular autobiography *Fever Pitch* (1992), for example, concluded that 'the white south of England middle-class Englishman and woman is the most rootless creature on earth', finding only 'a void' when seeking 'acceptable cultural iden-tity' (pp. 47–9). The late twentieth century turned out to be a particu-larly awkward time to raise such issues of cultural identity. Even by the start of the period, Graham Hough suggested in 1960, culture showed an 'international range . . . no longer regional, no longer national, but composite and eclectic' (*Image and Experience*, p. 57). Under the influence of increasingly globalized media, commerce, and communications, it became steadily more so in later decades. In one way, this made the need to define national culture and identity more pressing than ever, but it also made it harder to satisfy, and the issues involved more difficult to confine discretely within the nation's con-versations with itself. Instead, there were many signs, late in the century, of England encountering a problem longer recognized else-where in the United Kingdom—that a nation's sense of identity is inevitably entangled with images it has to adopt in presenting itself to the outside world. Significantly, the Department of National Heritage established in 1992 was responsible not only for the arts and for historic monuments, but also for tourism. Like the Arts Council during the previous decade, a rapidly emergent 'heritage industry' had to concentrate on what could be sold, to foreign visitors particularly. New pressures on English identity in the 1990s thus coincided awkwardly with a new need to turn English culture into foreign exchange, sometimes making artificial, or easily consumable, the very authenticities that 'heritage' supposedly sought to sustain.

This was often a target of satire at the time. Simon Armitage's poem 'The Twang' (2002), for example, highlights Ireland's greater facility in marketing itself abroad, contrasting an imaginary St George's day in New York with established St Patrick's day celebrations there. Salman Rushdie's Anglophile protagonist in *The Satanic Verses* worries about how far English culture and history might be 'altered' by the media at work in 'our degraded, imitative times, in which clowns re-enact what was first done by heroes and by kings' (pt. VII, ch. 2). 'Alteration' of this kind, and motives for it, were thoroughly explored in Julian Barnes's heritage-industry satire *England, England* (1998), which shows a theme park struggling to find convenient, convincing components of English culture and character to be used in its entertainments. Yet once these have been established, the theme park seems such an attractive alternative to the 'void' of cultural identity in England itself that it is soon able to take over the monarchy, other national institutions, and large sections of the population.

England, England satirizes the construction of a national identity principally based on the country's 'social and cultural history . . . eminently marketable, never more so than in the current climate' (p. 39). Yet the novel also retains strong historical sympathies of its own, largely for supposedly straightforward, bygone decencies of life in the English countryside. *England, England* offers in this way a symptom as well as an analysis of fears about 'the last of England', and their encouragement of forms of nostalgia widely in evidence at the end of the century. Jeremy Paxman found the subjects of his study, *The English*, to be 'a people marching backwards into the future' in the late 1990s, unable to drag their attention away from the past (p. 18). Retrospection of this kind was of course not altogether new. Stresses examined in *England, England* resemble ones explored in Nigel Dennis's survey of rootless mid-century life, *Cards of Identity* (1955)—a novel likewise examining English tendencies to 'stumble indignantly backwards into the future' (p. 100). Though intensified by pressures on national identity in the 'current climate' of the 1990s, nostalgia and historical awareness remained powerful influences on national life and imagination from the beginning of this period to its end.

Along with the advance of the heritage industry—a new museum opened somewhere in Britain every week for a time in the 1980s—another indication of this influence appeared in the expanding membership of the National Trust. This rose from 80,000 in 1960 to around a million in 1980—the year Evelyn Waugh's *Brideshead Revisited* (1945) was televised, celebrating the vanished splendours of the English country house. By the late 1990s, membership of the Trust—'The National Trust for Places of Historic Interest and Natural Beauty', to give it its full title—had risen to more than two and a half million, and ten million visits were made annually to its properties. The nostalgic cast in the national imagination these figures suggest was probably inevitable, given the recent history outlined above, and the kind of 'confusions of purpose' Sampson anticipated, for Britain as a whole, as the aftermath of empire in 1962. A country experiencing the end of empire, uncertainty in its role abroad, and radical change in social structure at home could hardly resist looking back on periods of national life apparently more successful and secure than the present, or avoid creating national myths to compensate for their loss.

Probably the clearest of these myths appeared in stories of James Bond, hugely successful throughout the period. From beginnings in a series of Ian Fleming novels running from *Casino Royale* (1953) to *On Her Majesty's Secret Service* (1963), Bond soon became a figure larger than the imagination which created him, taken up by other novelists such as Kingsley Amis, in his *James Bond Dossier* (1965), as well as in numerous film versions, beginning with *Dr No* in 1962. The success of the early films contributed to annual paperback sales in the millions for the novels by the mid-1960s: later film versions ensured that Bond remained much the most widely popular character in English narrative in the period. Patriotic, charismatic, and invincible, he exercised an inevitably wide appeal by continuing in imagination—in secret, through 'British Intelligence'—a world dominion rapidly disappearing in fact. The almost simultaneous success of Astérix adventures among French readers—starting from *Astérix le Gaulois* in 1961—further demonstrated the appeal of this kind of myth for nations anxious about their world role after mid-century. Overrun in two world wars, and also losing its last hold on empire in the early 1960s, France was naturally disposed towards Astérix's perennial, magical resistance to foreign invaders.

For English audiences, Bond's suave superiority to American allies, as well as Soviet adversaries, proved especially consoling at a time when national confidence was troubled almost as much by subordination to the United States as by the threat of the USSR. The Cold War's escalating tensions in the early 1960s nevertheless opened up a new market for spy fiction, often more sombre than Fleming's. Both Len Deighton and John Le Carré made their debuts at the time, Deighton worrying about US superiority in *The Ipcress File* (1962). Le Carré began and ended *The Spy who Came in from the Cold* (1963) with dramatic passages across the recently constructed Berlin Wall, describing the Cold War generally as 'the world . . . mankind . . . gone mad' (ch. 25). Lasting at least until the fall of the Wall, and the changes of regime in Eastern Europe in 1989, Cold War stresses helped to sustain strong sales for spy fiction in the next decades. In the 1980s and 1990s, popular appeal partly passed on to the crime novel, better equipped to reflect an uneasiness within domestic society becoming more significant at this time.

Elements of nostalgia and national myth nevertheless remained thoroughly influential in the 1980s. Salman Rushdie suggested in 1982 that the country was experiencing 'a critical phase of its post-colonial period . . . a crisis of the whole culture, of the society's entire sense of itself'. The results of this crisis included, he considered, a 'huge, undiminished appetite of white Britons for television series, films, plays and books all filled with nostalgia for the Great Pink Age' (*Imaginary Homelands*, pp. 129–30). Yet no colonial adventure in film, play, or book in 1982 matched the real one which followed Argentina's invasion of one of the few areas maps still coloured pink—the Falkland Islands. Even commentators sympathetic to Mrs Thatcher, such as Alan Sked and Chris Cook in *Post-War Britain: A Political History* (1993), acknowledge that her despatch of a military force to recover these islands—ones the government had recently been trying to give away—was 'a dangerous, even absurd adventure'

(p. 418). Yet as they affirm, Thatcher's determination 'captivated those working around her', along with the popular press, and to a great extent 'the mood of the nation'. As they conclude, the campaign eventually 'completely altered the history of British politics' (pp. 418, 394). Presiding over deepening social and economic crises in the early 1980s, Thatcher had become the most unpopular prime minister of the twentieth century. Yet she was re-elected a year after the Falklands campaign as the unchallenged leader, until 1990, of a party which then continued in power until 1997.

Though the crisis itself was 'totally unforeseen', in Sked and Cook's view, the political reversal it created had an almost inevitable aspect, given the way the campaign was interpreted to the public (p. 394). Thatcher's victory speech in July 1982 drew on nostalgia and 'huge appetites' of exactly the sort Rushdie identified, claiming that the campaign had splendidly refuted anxieties that 'we could no longer do the great things which we once did . . . that we could never again be what we were . . . that Britain was no longer the nation that had built an Empire and ruled a quarter of the world' (Rushdie, *Imaginary Homelands*, p. 131). In this version of events, the Falklands had at last restored the status, national pride, and self-confidence brought to an end at Suez a quarter of a century earlier. Obviously, this was closer to wish-fulfilment, and national myth, than to reality—Britain *was* no longer a country that could rule a quarter of the world, or even seek to—but it was all the more potent politically as a result.

Writers at the time were understandably sceptical—Ian McEwan, for example, contrasting Suez and the Falklands in his film script for *The Ploughman's Lunch* (1983). In general, too, they were more sceptical of nostalgia—or at any rate more complex in their relations to the past—than Rushdie's comments suggest. Films such as *A Passage to India* (1985) did occasionally cast a hazy visual splendour over 'the Great Pink Age'. But neither films nor television serials were altogether approving of it, nor were the recent novels they were based on, such as Ruth Prawer Jhabvala's *Heat and Dust* (1975) or Paul Scott's *The Raj Quartet* (1966–75). Reflection on past glory, in the 1980s, was more often apparent in national life and politics than in literature, whose engagement with historical memory was equally crucial, but significantly different in character. Writers at the time had good reason to consider nostalgia not all that it used to be. Towards the end of a turbulent century, those who looked back on its earlier years were likelier to do so in anger than approval—or at least in some frustration, given the lack of secure, beneficent times, 'Pink' or otherwise, on which imagination and recollection could safely come to rest.

Earlier, and especially for authors between the wars, the Edwardian age had regularly seemed to offer just such a period. Nostalgia for its relative stability contributed to emphases on memory in fiction by Virginia Woolf, James Joyce, Ford Madox Ford, and Christopher Isherwood in the 1920s and early 1930s. George Orwell's narrator in *Coming up for Air* (1939) continued to recall that '1911, 1912, 1913 . . . was a good time to be alive . . . it was always summer', and that people then were still able to enjoy 'a feeling of security . . . a feeling of continuity' (pt. 2, ch. 7). Views of this sort established the period before the First World War, in the literary imagination, as an 'Edwardian wonderland before the twentieth century went so wrong', as Malcolm Bradbury called it, and its appeal lasted some way beyond mid-century (*Modern British Novel*, p. 432). 'Never such innocence again', Philip Larkin remarked of it in 'MCMXIV' (1964), indicating even in his poem's title a lost and more leisurely means of counting the passing years. Henry Williamson took a similar view in his novel-sequence *A Chronicle of Ancient Sunlight* (1951–69), returning in early volumes to turn-of-the-century London. In some of the best of them—*A Fox under my Cloak* (1955); *The Golden Virgin* (1957); *Love and the Loveless* (1958)— Williamson went on to write from personal experience of the First World War about how this Edwardian world was destroyed. Disappearance of its values, and the implications for later years, also concerned Angus Wilson in several novels in the late 1950s and 1960s—*Late Call* (1964), for example, using a section entitled 'The Hot Summer of 1911', as a contrast for the chill materialism of contemporary society. Recollection of the vanishing values of rural life added to the wide appeal of Laurie Lee's writing, in autobiographical works such as *Cider with Rosie* (1959) and *As I Walked out one Midsummer Morning* (1969). Even after the 1960s, the 'Edwardian wonderland' and its loss continued to interest a number of authors: Anthony Burgess, in *Earthly Powers* (1980), for example, or Andrew

Waterman, reflecting in his poem 'Playing Through Old Games of Chess' (1980) on a 'long, lost summer' of 'Pax Britannica', when 'all history seemed a sort of sunlit incline upwards, | with problems ... | certainly soluble, and change meant improvement'.

Nostalgia for any period, however, is itself inevitably transitory: curtailed in the end by the limited endurance of earlier years within living memory; the gradual drift forward, through time, of what succeeding generations are able to recall. Unlike authors between the wars, or Henry Williamson, neither Angus Wilson, Philip Larkin, nor the later writers mentioned could recall the Edwardian years directly. When extolling in *Look Back in Anger* the 'high summer, the long days in the sun' of the Edwardian period, Jimmy Porter inevitably admits that his regret is not for a lost world of his own, but for 'the passing of someone else's' (I). Even by the 1950s, in other words, the Edwardian 'high summer' had become an idyllic construct, or a literary habit, rather than a remembered reality. In later decades, memory could generally reach back only as far as periods *after* the twentieth century 'went so wrong'—winters of discontent whose chill influence often still defined the climate of the present. Chief among these, obviously, was the Second World War: an inevitable, obsessive, and ubiquitous focus for cultural reflection throughout the latter half of the century.

For some writers, the commitment and common purpose of the war years did contribute to forms of nostalgia. Left-wing playwrights in the 1970s and 1980s, for example—when not regretting the carnival atmosphere of the 1960s—often looked back to the end of the war, and the years of Labour government which followed, as a period of unrivalled optimism, national unity, and socialist confidence.[7] But for most writers in later years, it was exactly this period at the end of the war, and the terrible events surrounding its conclusion, which had made nostalgia impossible, and its replacement with darker forms of historical anxiety inevitable. The whole experience of the Second World War, in Ted Hughes's apt summary, had been one of 'colossal negative revelation' (Corcoran, p. 116). This was emphasized with inescapable force in 1945 by the news of the Nazi's extermination camps—of organized mass killing on a scale new in history—and of the first use of atomic weapons,

---

[7] See pp. 321–4, below.

suppressing much of the relief that might otherwise have accompanied the end of hostilities. Perhaps inevitably, the overwhelming immensity of this 'negative revelation' also suppressed, or postponed, its imaginative exploration within English literature: the exhaustion and shock of the war contributed to reluctance to contemplate events at its conclusion immediately. As Ted Hughes suggested, English authors in the late 1940s and early 1950s shared a 'post-war mood of having had enough . . . enough of the dark gods' and 'recoiled to some essential English strengths' instead—including the kind of refuges in the past, or the countryside, discussed above (Corcoran, p. 116). Even the more ordinary experiences of the war figured fairly infrequently in writing immediately after its conclusion, and the full scale of its 'negative revelation' had barely begun to be assessed in literature even by the mid-1950s.

Much the same postponement was more generally apparent in national life. Present since 1945, the atomic threat had been quickly heightened by the Cold War which soon followed, and the development of a Soviet nuclear bomb by 1949. But the real hazards of atomic warfare seemed to become widely apparent only in the later 1950s, reflected in the rise of CND at the time, and summed up in W. H. Auden's conclusion, in *Encounter* in June 1959, that 'there has seldom been a time . . . when the present and future of the whole human endeavour on this earth have seemed questionable to so many people' (p. 72). Regular weapons tests and confrontations between the superpowers made human life seem even more questionable in the early 1960s. Forty years later, Martin Amis recalled the Cuban Missile Crisis as 'the most severe in human history': a 'long dankly gleaming twilight' which left 'the children of the nuclear age . . . weakened in their capacity to love' (*Experience*, pp. 137–8). Writing nearer the time, in *Bomb Culture* (1968), Jeff Nuttall took an almost opposite view, envisaging emphasis on love and sexuality, and the carnival atmosphere of the 1960s, generally, as a sublimation of new dreads of nuclear apocalypse: a kind of dancing in the dark. In either estimation, the late 1950s and early 1960s initiated inescapable insecurities. Uncertainties of 'the whole human endeavour', its present and its future, shadowed life and imagination throughout the rest of the century, shaping an era radically lacking confidence in the powers and endurance of its culture and civilization.

The influence of the Holocaust was eventually equally pervasive, though similarly delayed. The Nuremberg Nazi trials at the end of the war had not made the concentration camps a centre of public attention, and it was only in the early 1960s, with the capture, trial, and execution of Adolf Eichmann in 1960–2, that the Holocaust much entered general discussion and awareness. As Elaine Feinstein recorded in her novel *The Survivors* (1982), people 'had read the newspapers after the war . . . knew the facts . . . had seen the photographs', but the Eichmann trial 'brought the truth into . . . consciousness in a new way' (ch. 49). Even the term 'Holocaust' had scarcely been employed before 1960, but its influence expanded steadily thereafter: forty years later, commemoration of the concentration camps was formally established in Britain by the inauguration of a nationally organized Holocaust Remembrance Day, first observed in January 2001.

The Holocaust's entry to 'collective memory' in Britain thus exactly demarcates the period from 1960 to 2000—one whose imagination can be seen as substantially influenced, in each of the literary genres, by gradually unfolding recollection of the war; gradually developing reactions to its colossal moral and political implications. Theodor Adorno claimed in the early 1960s that writing poetry at all, after Auschwitz, might be 'barbaric': his comment defined problems which remained visible throughout the period's poetry. In its early years especially, poets could generally be distinguished in terms of quite opposite reactions to recent history. The work of 'the Movement' and its successors continued to illustrate the post-war recoil Hughes identified, turning away from 'dark gods' in favour of a milder climate of 'English strengths' and a return to the example of Thomas Hardy. Also writing in the early 1960s, A. L. Alvarez demanded of poets a contrary disposition—one Ted Hughes's own work came to exemplify—towards incorporation within their work of the darkness and violence of recent history, at least obliquely. A comparable disposition began to appear on the English stage in the late 1950s and early 1960s, in the dark laughter of the Theatre of the Absurd, and the dark gods celebrated in the Theatre of Cruelty. A later generation of political playwrights also remained concerned as much with the war's negative implications as with any affirmation that could be attributed to its conclusion.

In fiction, the war contributed to the return of a strong moral sense, apparent in the work of writers such as William Golding emerging in the 1950s. For later novelists, in the 1980s and 1990s, this often extended into renewed historical interests, regularly taking the war as their central point of reference. Literature around this time, fiction particularly, also started to explore the Holocaust and its implications directly. By the 1980s, writers seemed to have travelled far enough down the road of history to discern even the deepest shadows of the war beginning to form themselves, when they looked behind them, into manageable outlines at last. But there were few signs, even by the end of the century, of English writing travelling beyond these shadows altogether. On the contrary, disturbing recollection of recent history often coalesced, in the 1980s and 1990s, with the dispirited sense of contemporary society being increasingly 'torn apart'. This contributed to a generally dark outlook in the literature of the time, making Martin Amis's 'gleaming twilight' in many ways its distinguishing shade.

A story may have no absolute beginnings, but in the ways suggested the literary history of the period 1960–2000 might well be judged to have started with events in 1945, or at any rate with belated reactions to them. Though shaped by all the developments discussed in this chapter, the later progress of this history can be seen as particularly marked by the gradual seepage of the war's dark memory through every storey of late twentieth-century imagination. This influence also reached into and eroded many of the foundations on which European thinking, more generally, had long been based. The profound shifts of outlook which resulted, and their significance for English writing, are among issues considered in the next chapter.

2

A Postmodern Age?
Literature, Ideas, and Traditions

I. The End of the Modern

'What was Modernism?', Harry Levin enquired, in the title of a lecture published in August 1960. As a literary movement, he went on to suggest, it had given way sometime earlier to 'what has been categorized . . . as the Post-Modern Period' (*Refractions*, p. 277). 'What was Postmodernism?' was the title John Frow chose for a critical essay published towards the end of the century, in 1997. In the years between, the terms 'postmodern', 'postmodernism', and 'postmodernity' came to dominate the period's critical discussions to an extent Levin could hardly have anticipated at its opening, and which Frow scarcely condoned at its close. Rarely used before 1960, or during the decade that followed, by the 1970s they were terms beginning to be applied regularly not only to the literary area Levin had described, but in 'categorizing' the life, thought, and culture of the later twentieth century as a whole. By the middle of the 1980s, as Steven Connor commented in *Postmodernist Culture* (1989), post-modernism and postmodernity were terms that had evidently 'come to stay' (p. 6). In the early 1990s, Patricia Waugh considered them key items 'in the vocabularies not only of literary theorists but also political scientists, philosophers, geographers, media theorists and sociologists . . . even in tabloid newspapers' (*Postmodernism*, p. 1).

Yet postmodern vocabulary's widening use—often in attempts to characterize a whole age—made its meaning harder and harder to define. Even by the 1980s, as David Harvey complained in *The Condition of Postmodernity* (1990), the range of disciplines and intellectual histories involved had created 'a mine-field of conflicting notions' (p. viii). Two reliable paths through this 'minefield' are outlined in this chapter, along with various intersections between them. Section II returns to the literary developments originally identified by Harry Levin, tracing ways a postmodernist literature evolved out of modernist forms dominant earlier in the century. Section I assesses ways in which the period came to be considered postmodern in more general terms, and considers the ideas of figures principally involved—critics and thinkers such as Jürgen Habermas, Jean-François Lyotard, Jean Baudrillard, and Fredric Jameson.

These general concepts of the postmodern help to locate the outlook of the later twentieth century within a long perspective of European philosophy and history. Just how long was emphasized by Thomas Docherty in his introduction to *Postmodernism: A Reader* (1993). Rather than looking back only to modernist literature, he explained, debates about the postmodern referred increasingly to a concept of 'modernity' extending throughout 'an entire trajectory of European philosophy dating from the Enlightenment' (p. 36). This trajectory, for most twentieth-century commentators, had been initiated by the Enlightenment's decisive expansion of intellectual confidence, and the new faith in progress and modernization it introduced to the late eighteenth century. Theodor Adorno and Max Horkheimer, for example, considered Enlightenment thinking to have established an 'unshakable confidence in the possibility of world domination', based on an assumed 'concordance' between the intellect and the world it surveyed—a supposedly 'happy match between the mind of man and the nature of things' (pp. 11, 3, 4). Confidence in this 'match' contributed to a conviction that the physical world could be fully fathomed by human reason, and controlled and improved by human will.

It also extended—in Jürgen Habermas's summary of Enlightenment thinking—into an 'expectation that the arts and the sciences would promote not only the control of natural forces, but would also further understanding of the world and of the self, [and] would promote moral progress, the justice of institutions, and even the happiness of human beings'. 'Efforts to develop objective science, universal morality and law . . . for the rational organization of every-day social life' constituted for Habermas and other commentators a 'project of modernity' long sustained throughout the West, and scarcely questioned as a mainstay of its life and thought (Natoli and Hutcheon (eds.), p. 98).

Raymond Williams's description in *The Long Revolution* (1961) of 'a good society naturally unfolding itself', ever since the eighteenth century,[1] offered another account of the optimistic faith in reason, modernization, and improvement Habermas and others identified.

Optimism of this kind, however, was radically challenged throughout the twentieth century, and eventually 'shattered', in Habermas's view—though he continued to argue in favour of Enlightenment thinking's potentials. Whereas the Enlightened late eighteenth century was often defined as an 'Age of Reason', the twentieth century showed from its beginning signs of reason's un-ravelling; of radical questioning of the mind's constructions, and of their truthfulness in representing reality. Even by the end of the nine-teenth century, philosophers including Friedrich Nietzsche, Henri Bergson, and William James had expressed fundamental doubts about any 'happy match' between mind and world. Nietzsche con-sidered that thought and language operate in 'a separate world beside the other world', and that as a result 'there are *no eternal facts*, just as there are no absolute truths' (pp. 13, 16). William James like-wise concluded that 'even the truest formula may be a human device and not a literal transcript' (Schwartz, p. 14).

Scepticism of this kind extended through a number of other disci-plines early in the twentieth century. A 'separate world' of language was further explored in Ferdinand de Saussure's influential *Cours de linguistique générale* (1916), which stressed the arbitrary nature of connections between words and concepts; ultimately, between words and the world they are assumed to represent. A form of scepticism appeared even in the discipline most empowered by Enlightenment emphasis of reason: science. Albert Einstein's Theories of Relativity, in 1905 and 1916, indicated that the position of the observer crucially affects all scientific laws and observations. By 1927, some of Einstein's ideas had been developed by Werner Heisenberg into an 'Uncertainty Principle', demonstrating that only

---

[1] See p. 31, above.

probability, rather than absolute rigour or universal certainty, governs all conclusions about the physical universe. Summing up 'Changes in the Foundation of Exact Science', Heisenberg explained that the discipline had been forced to challenge its 'basis for the comprehension of the whole field of "things perceptible" '. This required scientists to 'pose again the old question of the possibility of comprehending reality by mental processes', and to qualify any conviction that science could 'lead to . . . certain truth' (Waugh (ed.), *Revolutions of the Word*, pp. 255–6).

Confidence in Enlightenment thinking, and in its match between mind and nature, diminished much further in the second half of the twentieth century, under the growing historical pressures of the times. The experience of the Second World War was strongly reflected in Theodor Adorno and Max Horkheimer's 'The Concept of Enlightenment' (1944), which influentially reassessed Enlightenment thinking in terms not only of its abstract merits but its actual results. 'The fully enlightened earth radiates disaster triumphant', Adorno and Horkheimer concluded, suggesting that the faith in progress the Enlightenment initiated had simply been misplaced, or misdirected. Instead of contributing to morality, justice, or social improvement generally, reason and rational organization had soon narrowed into a mechanical, soulless emphasis on the 'rule of computation and utility'. This emphasis had furthered the development of science, but also fostered the Industrial Revolution and the exploitative capitalist practices dominating the working world it established. Rather than genuine progress, Adorno and Horkheimer considered, the 'project of modernity' had created only an 'all-inclusive industrial technology'—some of its results only too apparent in the new apparatus of destruction at work in the Second World War (*Dialectic*, pp. 3, 6, 11). Later commentators continued to stress the war's disastrous implications for Enlightenment beliefs. Looking back in the 1980s on forces contributing to the emergence of postmodern thinking, Jean-François Lyotard explained that he followed Adorno in using 'the name "Auschwitz" to signify just how impoverished recent Western history seems from the point of view of the "modern" project of the emancipation of humanity'. This sense of impoverishment and historical failure, in Lyotard's view, created 'a sort of grief in the *Zeitgeist*'—a distress and disillusion in the spirit of the whole post-war period (Docherty (ed.), p. 48).

This disillusion, however, accumulated only gradually, after the war, and passed through a number of stages before its character as 'postmodern' thinking became clear. As Chapter 1 explained, the war's full impact on imagination and culture, and in the public sphere generally, was in some ways delayed as far as the 1960s, when the real scale of its destruction—in the Holocaust particularly— finally came to be realized and discussed. Scepticism of the project of modernity was likewise far from complete in 1945. Despite their reservations, Adorno and Horkheimer still hoped for 'a positive notion of enlightenment' which might disentangle its affirmative potentials from the destructive forces it had also unleashed (p. xvi). In 1960, Harry Levin still described his contemporaries as 'children of . . . the Enlightenment', noting contrary views only as an 'anti-intellectual undercurrent' beginning to be visible 'as it [came] to the surface' at that time (*Refractions*, p. 271).

In the immediately post-war years, 'grief in the *Zeitgeist*' was less evident in anti-intellectual or anti-Enlightenment currents of thought than in the popularity of existential philosophy. Formulated during the war in the work of Jean-Paul Sartre and Albert Camus, existentialism strongly influenced post-war French literature and thinking, and eventually a good deal of English writing as well— especially when Absurd drama moved across the Channel into English theatres in the later 1950s and early 1960s.[2] A desolate recent history broadly disposed the post-war period towards philos-ophy which emphasized the emptiness of the universe, and its lack of any foundation or authority on which coherent, meaningful experi-ence could be based. Yet despite stressing the nothingness surround-ing the self, existentialism also appealed through some residual affirmations. Life in a godless universe might lack overall meaning, or definition by any absolute, externally imposed decree, but this at least allowed individuals complete responsibility for generating a significance for themselves, and an almost unlimited freedom in deciding the nature of their own existence. Such challenging yet liberating possibilities contributed in a way to the revolutionary 1960s outlooks discussed in Chapter 1. If freedom was defined as a

[2] See pp. 346–59 and 401, below.

fundamental condition of existence by philosophers, then it was important to ensure, as Sartre recognized, that it was a social and political possibility as well.

Other thinkers popular in the 1960s extended into the decade ideas shaped through experience of the war. Herbert Marcuse had been part of the Frankfurt School in the 1930s, like Adorno and Horkheimer, and his later work developed criticisms of the project of modernity they had made in 'The Concept of Enlightenment' in 1944. Disapproval of 'computation and utility' in Enlightenment thinking, and of its results in industrial technology, reappeared in Marcuse's 1950s and 1960s criticism of 'the tyranny of repressive reason', and in his demands for alternatives to the machine-like systematization of the modern world (p. 197). Like Sartre's, Marcuse's work thus sustained critical but essentially liberational thinking from the war years into the social and political movements of the 1960s, helping to shape their development in France towards the climactic Paris *événements* of May 1968. But for many commentators, the failure of this near-revolution—and eventually of 1960s radicalism generally—replaced any optimism surviving in contemporary thought with a preference for more sceptical, postmodern modes instead. Thomas Docherty, for example, considered that the postmodern habit of mind originated in 1968, after the apparent failure of revolutionary movements and of the 'emancipatory cultural politics' they represented (p. 35). Failed revolution, in other words, seemed to question Raymond Williams's kind of 'Long Revolution', or even mark a terminus of the project of modernity itself.

David Harvey also suggested that it was 'somewhere between 1968 and 1972' that 'postmodernism emerge[d] as a full-blown though still incoherent movement out of the chrysalis of the anti-modern movement of the 1960s' (p. 38). In this assessment, by the end of the 1960s the world made by modernity ceased to appear merely flawed, as it had, deeply, at least since the war. It began instead to seem beyond repair: immune to the kind of changes that social or political criticism, or philosophy, had sought to bring about, or to hopes for 'moral progress' and 'the justice of institutions' generally. Unlike Adorno and Horkheimer, still looking for some 'positive notion' even at the end of the war, Lyotard considered that no prospect remained of a 'positive orientation' or a 'new perspective' within the project of modernity (Docherty (ed.), p. 49). The late twentieth century began in this way to characterize itself in terms of an absolute end or failure of modernity—as an age of *post-modernity*, obliged to follow in its thinking priorities quite different to those established by the Enlightenment.

Lyotard influentially outlined these new priorities in *The Postmodern Condition: A Report on Knowledge*, published in 1979. This condition, he concluded, could be defined in terms of 'the obsolescence of the metanarrative apparatus of legitimation' (p. xxiv). In a number of intellectual fields, during the two previous decades, evidence had accumulated widely of 'incredulity towards meta-narratives', or 'Grand Narratives'—towards generally shared, foundational assumptions such as Enlightenment ideas of progress, or of concord between mind and nature (p. xxiv). Resulting problems of legitimation—of logical basis and validation—radically extended incertitudes apparent earlier in the twentieth century. Thomas Kuhn's *The Structure of Scientific Revolutions* (1962), for example, expanded the kind of challenges to the foundations of exact science formulated by Heisenberg. For Kuhn, reasoned enquiry into physical nature—so valued by the Enlightenment—had never been the only factor shaping scientific progress. Science also owed its development, he considered, to 'paradigm shifts' in the rules governing its own thinking—shifts resulting not only from the accumulation of empirical data, but also from an 'arbitrary element, compounded of personal and historical accident' (p. 4). The influence of this element reduced any assurance that the discipline would 'carry scientists and those who learn from them closer and closer to the truth' or to the nature of reality (p. 170). On the contrary, Kuhn concluded that phrases like 'really there' were unreliable, and that 'the notion of a match between . . . theory and its "real" counterpart in nature' might be 'illusive in principle' (p. 206).

Questioning of legitimation in other disciplines often focused on the area of language—one obviously fundamental to relations between theory and the real—and therefore regularly returned to the linguistics of Ferdinand de Saussure. Jacques Derrida's work, in particular, developed issues raised by Saussure, and by Nietzsche, into the most thorough, influential expression of the period's scepticism and anti-foundational thinking. The linguistic domain, for Derrida, appeared as empty of secure foundations or reliable points of reference as the human sphere in general seemed to Sartre. Lacking any 'centre or origin' which could confer certitude on its signification, language is if anything still more arbitrary and problematic in its operations than Saussure had suggested. Lack of ultimate anchorage leaves words able to refer only to each other, extending 'the domain and the play of signification infinitely'. This potentially infinite incertitude contributes fundamentally to the 'universal problematic' Derrida described in 'Structure, Sign, and Play in the Discourse of the Human Sciences' (1966)—to conditions in which, inevitably, 'everything became discourse'. Without reliable foundations in which language and concepts can ground themselves, all intellectual constructs have to be recognized as no more than 'discourse', determined by internal rules and connections rather than secure relation with the real. 'Part of the totality of [the] era', in this view, was that all its thought and theory, and not only science, as Kuhn described it, required to be recognized as free-floating and detached from the world it had once sought to explain (Derrida, p. 280).

In an introduction to *The Postmodern Condition*, Fredric Jameson summed up this kind of thinking, and the general state of incertitude Lyotard described, as a 'crisis of representation': a breakdown in 'the reproduction, for subjectivity, of an objectivity that lies outside it' (Lyotard, p. xii). The Enlightenment's once-happy match of mind and nature, in other words, seemed finally to have failed: replaced, Lyotard considered, by a 'flight of reality out of the metaphysical, religious, and political certainties that the mind believed it held' (p. 77). Yet for a number of commentators, Jameson included, this 'flight' was itself only a symptom: a marker, within contemporary philosophy, of forces shaping 'the totality of the era' more generally, and still more troublingly. Crises of representation, in this view, merely extended a wider set of crises often caused *by* representation—in particular, by the growing influence of the media, and their growing powers in manipulating what is thought to be real.

Like many of the developments discussed above, concern about these powers could be retraced to the early years of the twentieth century. The literary historian Paul Fussell suggests that 'devaluation of letterpress and even of language itself dates from the Great War'— from events between 1914 and 1918 so 'shocking, bizarre, and stomach-turning' it was politically essential for them to be 'tidied up for presentation to a highly literate mass population' (pp. 316, 178). The potential for this kind of 'tidying', and for general manipulation of a mass population, obviously expanded as the century went on and the resources of media and advertising continued to develop rapidly—especially through the influence of television after the 1950s. In the next decade, Guy Debord and the Situationists criticized 'Societies of the Spectacle' developing throughout the West—ones in which 'all that once was directly lived ha[d] become mere representation', and all the world's events and their implications had come to be controlled through 'the mass dissemination of images' (Debord, pp. 12–13).

Situationist ideas and criticisms of the media were a central influence on the Paris *événements* of May 1968, and they were later developed in still more sceptical, postmodern terms by the work of Jean Baudrillard. The media image, Baudrillard suggested, naturally seems at first 'the reflection of a basic reality'. But it is possible that it actually 'masks and perverts reality', and may in the end bear 'no relation to any reality whatever', even indicating only 'the *absence* of a basic reality' (Docherty (ed.), p. 196). Images, in this analysis, become only another form of discourse, detached from the real world and readily able, through their carefully constructed glamour and simplicity, to supplant it in the attention of the public. In showing a real England gradually replaced in the public's affection by a glitzy, theme-park version of itself, the plot of Julian Barnes's *England, England* (1998), outlined in Chapter 1, exactly illustrates the kind of inversion Baudrillard discussed. Baudrillard himself considered Disneyland more 'real' than the United States, and claimed that as representations and images became more appealing and influential than their originals, they left reality a 'territory [that] no longer precedes the map, nor survives it . . . it is the map that precedes the territory' (Natoli and Hutcheon (eds.), p. 343).

Like Baudrillard, commentators such as David Harvey considered image-manipulation on this scale a result of the growing powers of a 'late' or multinational phase of capitalism, and of its voracious promotional needs. The 'rush of images' in television and advertising had become an essential marketing tool, in Harvey's estimation, offering 'escape routes to another reality' in which consumers could be seduced by more glamorous—yet apparently purchasable—versions of themselves and their world (pp. 293, 302). In constantly directing desire and spending power towards this 'other reality'—towards ever-changing fashions and ever-fleeting fulfilments—late capitalism contributed to an image-driven erosion of the real, leaving 'volatility and ephemerality' inescapable conditions of late twentieth-century life as a whole (p. 285). Fredric Jameson likewise emphasized, even in the title of his study, *Postmodernism, or, the Cultural Logic of Late Capitalism* (1991), how far the postmodern condition reflected newly powerful economic forces at work in a 'world space of multinational capital' (p. 54). In his 'logic', the fashion for change and novelty throughout contemporary culture, the fascination of theory with discourse, and the crisis of representation in the period's thinking, generally, were all mere extensions of the consumer-oriented, image-saturated, channel-surfing society late capitalism had created. In this society, all that was solid really had melted into air.

Still more had melted, too, than Jameson's description of a 'crisis of representation' immediately suggested. A 'breakdown' between the objective world and subjective consciousness implies only a failure of communication between areas remaining intact in themselves. But for most postmodern thinking, neither had. Any individual perusing Baudrillard's map came to seem as unstable and evanescent as the territory it once represented. While objective reality fled further beyond a welter of discourses and images, subjective consciousness also lost much claim to coherence or autonomy. Like so much postmodern thinking, this view of selfhood radically extended scepticisms formulated earlier in the century. Examining origins of his own ideas, and of the 'totality' of his era, Derrida referred back not only to Nietzsche but to Sigmund Freud's 'critique of consciousness, of the subject, of self-identity and of self-proximity or self-possession' (Derrida, p. 280). In introducing the concept of an unconscious, Freud's work had persuaded the early twentieth century that the mind's uncertain depths denied individuals complete self-possession. In its later years, especially under the influence of the 'hidden persuaders' discussed above, individual consciousness seemed still less securely in charge of itself—perhaps no more than an intersection of conflicting desires, unconscious influences, and external pressures. 'The unified subject', according to the critic Terry Eagleton, came to seem only 'a shibboleth': 'a hangover from an older liberal epoch of capitalism, before technology and consumerism scattered our bodies to the winds as so many bits and pieces of reified technique, appetite, mechanical operation or reflex of desire' (Waugh (ed.), *Postmodernism*, p. 158). Selfhood, in this view, seemed no more than another site of disappearing meaning: only a 'hangover', like the idea of an objective reality, from earlier, abandoned modes of thought. No wonder commentators on the postmodern often saw it offering 'a simple enough message: anything goes' (Natoli and Hutcheon (eds.), p. 503). It did seem, towards the end of the century, as though anything and everything *had* gone: not only Enlightenment reason and 'Grand Narratives', but all solid foundations, all coherent means of comprehending self, society, the world.

For a time at least, after its 'full-blown' emergence in 1968, postmodern thinking had offered some less nihilistic messages. As commentators such as Docherty emphasized, it initially retained an implicitly political aspect—a suggestion that if established authority could not be overthrown on the streets of Paris, then the 'Grand Narratives' and philosophical foundations on which it was based might be undermined conceptually instead. The liberating movement of the 1960s, in this view, frustrated politically by the end of the decade, simply translated itself from the social to the intellectual sphere, as well as the personal ones Chapter 1 described. Naturally, this was a move first strongly apparent among French thinkers—especially in the growing influence of Derrida's work by the end of the decade—though it was soon followed elsewhere. Conservative regimes reappeared in the United States and much of Europe during the 1970s, further reducing the scope and promise of overt anti-authoritarian action. A kind of covert resistance—in the form of anti-foundational, postmodern thinking—naturally broadened its appeal instead. In *The Postmodern Condition: A Report on Knowledge*, Lyotard defined intellectual conditions prevailing not in any single country, but supposedly universally, by 1979, confirming the dominance of postmodern vocabulary and concepts, by that date, outlined at the start of this chapter. His work also encouraged these concepts to spread still further in the decade that followed, offering a label and a paradigm which could conveniently accommodate uncertainties or problems in a range of disciplines and artistic practices.

Yet in the 1980s—generally a still more conservative decade than the previous one—the radical origins of these concepts seemed to recede further and further from view. This began to expose postmodern thinking to the charge most often made against it: that it had chosen simply to evade an intractable reality, inhabiting instead an aloof sphere of discourses and images supposedly unable to interact purposefully with the world. Such charges were naturally raised most often in Marxist criticism. Fredric Jameson worried, as discussed earlier, that postmodern concepts were entirely complicit with late capitalism; Terry Eagleton that they might make its practices impossible to criticize or resist. Loss of faith in the project of modernity, for Eagleton, had occasioned resignation rather than new resolution, allowing incredulity towards Grand Narratives to undermine the grounds of political thinking and action as well. In *What's Wrong with Postmodernism* (1990), Christopher Norris was likewise concerned that postmodern thinking had disabled any terms in which political convictions might be validated, creating instead 'a persuasion that "reality" is constituted through and through by the meanings, values or discourses that presently compose it, so that nothing could count as effective counter-argument, much less a critique of existing institutions on valid theoretical grounds' (pp. 3–4).

Such warnings were not entirely new. In the 1960s, almost before the postmodern debate had begun—though in writing about one of its antecedents, Nietzsche—Frank Kermode had warned that sufficiently radical scepticism might make all moral and political judgement impossible, even about 'killing six million Jews' (p. 38). The most disturbing of many paradoxes in postmodern thought was its potential to deny, in this way, the very 'grief in the *Zeitgeist*' that had helped to bring it into being in the first place. For the most part, however, a different potential developed. If anything, the spread of postmodern indeterminacy actually added to the Holocaust's influence on the later twentieth century, and to its impact on the period's imagination. As well as challenging the claims of Enlightenment reason, as Lyotard claimed, 'the name "Auschwitz"' eventually invoked a kind of ultimate, surviving certitude in itself, highlighted by the collapse of sureties all around it—a conviction that *something* must still be definable as absolutely wrong. Unfortunately for literature, as later chapters consider, writers often encountered a further paradox, finding the war's greatest horrors indescribable as well as unimpeachable, and the strongest moral convictions therefore the least communicable.

In other areas, radical scepticism allowed postmodern thinking at best an ambiguous political role, even where its potentials seemed strongest. Rejection of 'Grand Narratives' could be related affirmatively, in one way, to the democratizing social transformations—transitions from hierarchy to heterarchy—discussed in Chapter 1, and seen as a timely escape from repressive aspects of Enlightenment thinking. The 'confidence in the possibility of world domination' Adorno and Horkheimer diagnosed in the Enlightenment was primarily intellectual, based on new powers attributed to mind and reason, but it had readily taken on a political aspect, and a substantial role within European imperialism. Universal powers attributed to Western rationality were used to justify the subjugation of entire races abroad, as well as many domestic factions and interests. Postmodern denial of these powers encouraged formerly colonized nations—or groups marginalized on the grounds of ethnicity or gender at home—to construct their own narratives, and to reject roles assigned them by anyone else's.

Radical challenges to established forms and foundations of thinking could in this way be seen as more liberating than nihilistic. As Terry Eagleton explained himself, in *The Illusions of Postmodernism* (1996), postmodern scepticism was not necessarily 'some sort of theoretical mistake', but part of 'a specific historical epoch in the West, when reviled and humiliated groups [were] beginning to recover something of their history and selfhood' (p. 121). Yet as Eagleton also emphasized, any empowerment of marginalized groups was obviously limited, in turn, by lack of secure validation for *their* views. What Lyotard called 'petits recits' (little stories) were accepted more readily during the period, but perhaps only because they no longer had to be acknowledged as right. Declining faith in the 'Grand' or master narratives of Western society offered new opportunities for women's voices, and other marginalized discourses, but left their conclusions, even about centuries of injustice, no *more* than discourse—just another set of ideas floating in the wake of a vanished reality. In this way, postmodern thinking 'produced in the same breath an invigorating and a paralysing scepticism', as Eagleton explained—offering no solid defence even against 'degrading social practices', but only a 'full-blooded cultural relativism' instead (p. 27).

Moreover, prolonged postmodern discussion of the Grand Narratives of Western society—even of their inadequacy and decline—seemed to several commentators in the later 1980s and 1990s merely a continuation of imperial thinking by other means. Stephen Slemon suggested that 'for all its decentering rhetoric', the postmodern had 'paradoxically become a centralizing institution', construing as a crisis *within* Western thinking a set of influences actually extrinsic to the West in their origins (Natoli and Hutcheon (eds.), p. 435). Whereas the postmodern debate lordly claimed to have *allowed* Grand Narratives to be replaced with 'petits recits', it was primarily these 'stories' and the new pressures they brought from the margins which had made radical questioning of the universal validity of European thought inevitable. Analysis of crises within Western philosophy and linguistics, in this view, should give way to assessment of social and geopolitical forces which had brought them about—in particular, to discussion of frictions between languages and cultures during and after the colonial period. In the 1990s, ample material for such assessment began to arrive in a second post—the postcolonial. Further discussed in Chapter 3, postcolonial criticism had taken over, by the end of the century, some of the central position occupied by the postmodern debate during its last two decades.

Other problems in the debate grew more apparent in the 1990s, further encouraging critical discussion to move on, or to think of the postmodern in the past tense, as John Frow suggested in 1997. Postmodern concepts had often seemed to answer critical and media needs for definitions of the late twentieth century—an age described by Ihab Hassan, in *The Postmodern Turn* (1987), as unusually reluctant 'simply [to] live, and let others live to call us what they may' (p. 87). Like terms applied to earlier periods, such as 'Romanticism', concepts of the postmodern seemed to allow a whole cultural climate and its dominant patterns of thought to be analysed collectively. Some of this promise was fulfilled, in ways discussed above. Yet terminologies defining the thought and culture of a whole epoch are usually developed retrospectively, from an objective historical distance. Problems inevitably arose from the simultaneity of post-modern analyses, and their defining vocabularies, with the age they sought to categorize. Commentators working in the twenty-first century may continue to call the later twentieth 'postmodern', and to use the term to define a period of disillusion and readjustment following the Second World War, the end of empire, the expiry of Enlightenment, the globalization of capital, or the defeat of 1960s utopianism. Yet with hindsight they should be better able to judge the relative importance of these influences, and the extent to which each shaped developments in the age's culture and thinking generally. During the period itself, emphasis of one or other of these areas, or attempts to define a postmodern pattern in its outlook overall, naturally seemed at times premature or presumptuous—over-assured, in dealing with issues inevitably still irresolvable; problems and developments still in progress.

An irresolvable aspect in the postmodern debate was compounded by the thinking and terminology involved, often inherently indefinite or self-contradictory, despite its ambitions to define. In refuting so comprehensively the validity of 'Grand Narratives', the postmodern increasingly acquired the status of a late twentieth-century Grand Narrative itself—though one unable to offer a grand vision of much beyond itself. On the contrary, in determinedly denying the validity of thinking and analysis, even in the course of its own analysis and thinking, the postmodern debate doomed itself to a discursive doldrum: to endless circuitousness, even in trying to define the terms in which it was itself taking place. As Steven Connor pointed out, the postmodern risked becoming in this way a 'generative machine', especially in academic circles, turning out material for conferences, classes, and courses apparently endlessly, filling more and more shelves in the bookshop and the library (p. 18). Mention of the principal commentators and concepts involved, in the outline above, can give only a glimpse of the full extent of the postmodern debate. Its ever-expanding scale, and its diffusion across diverse disciplines, were often matters of concern even for some of these principal commentators themselves. At the end of his exhaustive, 400–page study of the postmodern, Fredric Jameson admits 'I occasionally get just as tired of the slogan "postmodern" as anyone else', adding that it sometimes 'raise[d] more problems than it solves' (*Postmodernism*, p. 418). Towards the end of the century, in other words, weariness with the postmodern debate—as well as wariness of some of the concepts involved—began to contribute to an urge for different or complementary modes of analysis.

This urge had always had a particular focus within the field of literary criticism. Like other contemporary commentators, Ihab Hassan worried in *The Postmodern Turn* about how far postmodern 'conundrums continue[d] unresolved'. But he suggested an alternative—a return to earlier, specifically literary modes of enquiry—in pointing out that 'the first impulse of every critic of postmodernism is still to relate it to the semanteme it contains: namely, modernism' (p. 214). Hassan's 'first impulse' was of course reflected in Harry Levin's early discussion of the legacies of modernism in 1960, and it continued to appear in the work of a number of literary critics later in the period. Brian McHale, for example, defined his subject in *Postmodernist Fiction* (1987) as 'not post modern . . . but post modern*ism*'—as a literature coming 'after the *modernist movement*' as its 'logical and historical *consequence*' (p. 5). Promising a certain clarity and directness, and a particular relevance to literary history, this line of enquiry is followed in the next section.

II. Modernist and Other Legacies

For literary critics, or literary historians, some version of Hassan's 'impulse' is in any case essential: understanding the literature of the later twentieth century requires awareness of its antecedents. Literature continually interacts with contemporary events, institutions, and thinking generally, but its forms and interests are also to an extent residual, borrowed or adapted by authors from their predecessors. For much of the later twentieth century, modernist writing offered an obvious source of such borrowings. Even in emphasizing that the movement itself was over, Levin stressed that 'the afterglow of the Moderns'—'one of the most remarkable constellations of genius in the history of the West', as he called it—continued to illumine literature in 1960 (pp. 282, 284). Much of its light still shone on at the end of the century. A full mapping of Levin's 'constellation' can be found in the Oxford English Literary History, Volume 10. *Modern Letters*. Its brighter stars and overall shape are briefly outlined below—along with later, contrary influences—before considering how far modernism's 'afterglow' might justify definition of the period as a postmodernist age.

So what *was* modernism? Looking back, like Levin, from the early 1960s, Stephen Spender described modernist authors as those 'deliberately setting out to invent a new literature' as a result of finding their age 'unprecedented, and outside all the conventions of past literature and art' (p. x). This determination to 'make it new', in Ezra Pound's famous phrase, was apparent in other contemporary art forms such as painting and music: critics usually place its literary origins in the 1890s, and consider it to have reached its height in the 1920s. Departures from convention during this period were widely apparent, at one level, in the subjects and themes of writing—in new or extended reflection of the experience of women, or of empire; of sex, or of the growing anonymity of city life, for example. Yet many authors concerned with 'unprecedented' twentieth-century experience continued to present it in styles and structures carried on more or less from the end of the nineteenth. 'Modern' or modernist writing, on the other hand, is critically defined, as its name suggests, by its determination to make literature itself a new experience: its appeal for later generations of writers principally resulted from its offer of new styles, forms, and strategies.

In James Joyce's *Ulysses* (1922) and T. S. Eliot's *The Waste Land* (1922), for example, the complex, fragmented nature of modern city life figures not only as a subject, but within the form of the texts themselves—in abrupt, fracturing alternations between different perspectives, voices, and styles. Likewise, description of sex in the work of Joyce and D. H. Lawrence caused much trouble with censorship, yet their novels were set apart less by new emphasis on this subject than by the new inwardness with which all aspects of private life and emotion were explored. Typically of modernist writers, Joyce and Lawrence rejected conventional realistic techniques, turning away from observable aspects of experience and behaviour in favour of closer attention to the inner consciousness of observers—moving, in Lawrence's own terms, away from 'objective reality' and towards 'the psychology of the free human individual' (*Literary Criticism*, p. 120).

Like many developments discussed in Section I, this modernist shift of emphasis can be retraced to the turn of the century. Its origins might even be located more exactly: between Joseph Conrad's *The Nigger of the 'Narcissus'* (1897) and the novella he wrote two years later, *Heart of Darkness* (1899). In a preface to the former, Conrad continued to define his objectives in terms of conventional realism— of using 'the power of the written word . . . before all, to make you *see*'. In *Heart of Darkness*, on the other hand, Conrad's narrator Marlow doubtfully asks his listeners 'Do you see . . . ? Do you see the story? Do you see anything?', concluding with confidence only that 'You see me, whom you know' (ch. 1). As in other Conrad novels in which Marlow appears as narrator, such as *Lord Jim* (1900), an idio-syncratic, self-questioning account of the world casts doubt on what *can* reliably be seen or known, highlighting the subjective reactions of the individual observer instead. This emphasis was also extended by Ford Madox Ford's narrator in *The Good Soldier* (1915). Henry James's concentration on what he called 'intense *perceivers*', in novels such as *The Ambassadors* (1903), similarly explored the construction of experience within an individual mind and outlook (*Art of the Novel*, p. 71).

Other early twentieth-century authors developed a whole range of stylistic devices for the representation of characters' conscious-nesses. In *The Rainbow* (1915), and in *Women in Love* (1921), D. H. Lawrence extensively represents inner thoughts through forms of Free Indirect Discourse, intermingling characters' private voices and patterns of thought with the more objective tones of the author. Another, decisive, step in reflecting mental life appears in the early volumes of Dorothy Richardson's *Pilgrimage* sequence (1915–38), in a 'stream of consciousness' style, presenting characters' thoughts with all the supposedly chaotic, associative immediacy of their actual occurrence. Alternating with Free Indirect Discourse and other forms of interior monologue, this kind of writing was further devel-oped by Joyce throughout *Ulysses*, the outstanding achievement of modernist fiction in representing inner consciousness. It also figured widely in the work of Virginia Woolf. In explaining her own prefer-ences in her essay 'Modern Fiction' (1919), Woolf summed up a new priority widely evident in contemporary writing when she demanded that authors should 'look within' and 'examine . . . the mind'.

'Modern Fiction' indicated another new priority in insisting that 'life is not a series . . . symmetrically arranged' (*Collected Essays*, p. 106). In her diary, Woolf also expressed exasperation with the 'appalling narrative business of the realist' in proceeding chronologically through a series of events, and resolved that her own fiction would move 'backwards and forwards' instead (*Writer's Diary*, p. 138). As modernist narrative focused increasingly on individual consciousness, it came to rely less on what Woolf called in *Orlando* (1928) 'time on the clock' than on 'time in the mind' (ch. 2)—on memory, allowing free movement backwards as well as forwards in time. 'I will read Proust I think', Woolf added in her diary (p. 138): reliance on memory, and the rejection of conventional 'narrative business' in favour of non-linear structures was generally encouraged in modernist fiction by the example of Marcel Proust's *A la recherche du temps perdu* ('In Search of Lost Time', 1913–27). It can also be retraced to the work of Conrad and Ford. In *Heart of Darkness* and *Lord Jim*—described by Conrad in his Author's Note as 'a free and wandering tale'—and in *The Good Soldier*, narrators tell their stories to a circle of listeners, supposedly in a single evening, or as if in this way. This allows the narrative to move from one event to another in the order of recollection rather than occurrence, of memory rather than clock or calendar. Structures of this kind were further developed by later modernists. *Ulysses* and Woolf's *Mrs Dalloway* (1925) similarly employ memory as a 'seamstress', as Woolf called it, stitching into the narrative of a single day many recollections of past experiences. These gradually accumulate into a character history as extensive as any offered by nineteenth-century fiction, though obviously very different in its construction, and in its demands on the understanding of readers.

Comparable innovations distinguished modernist poetry. *The Waste Land* is as free and wandering in its construction as any modernist narrative, switching between personae, between memory and present experience, and between several historical and cultural epochs in assembling its vision of incoherent, spiritless existence in contemporary London. Shorter modernist poems—such as those produced by the Imagist movement led by Ezra Pound—were often equally disjointed, requiring readers to reconstruct meanings which are diffused throughout the poem, or suggested by oblique associations between individual lines, rather than developed lucidly and sequentially from beginning to end. Instead of direct expression of vision or feeling, modernist poems often seemed to offer only patterns of fragmented thought, or collections of puzzling symbols, seeking for some residue of significance in a dispirited, usually urban landscape.

This fragmentary vision was generally matched by fractured conventions of poetic construction. Rejecting the regularities of established metre, much modernist poetry was written as 'free verse', loosely structured by musical or colloquial rhythms. Pound, for example, explained that he sought 'to compose in the sequence of the musical phrase, not in sequence of a metronome' (Lodge (ed.), *Literary Criticism*, p. 58). This free verse was also very sparing, sometimes almost parodic, in its adherence to other conventions such as rhyme or stanza form. Yet despite this fragmented, unconventional surface, modernist poetry still gestured at orders underlying or superintending the incoherence of the modern world. Allusions to art and culture in *The Waste Land*—or in Pound's *Cantos* (1925–70), or much of W. B. Yeats's later poetry—established an aloof vision of orderliness against which the turbid stresses of the contemporary could at least be measured. Eliot might have been referring to his own work's reliance on myth and legend when—in his essay 'Ulysses, Order and Myth' (1923)—he described Joyce's references to Homer as a means of shaping and imposing order on a purposeless, chaotic contemporary history.

As Eliot's views suggest—and Stephen Spender's, quoted earlier—modernism's formal innovations were responses, direct or indirect, to the 'unprecedented' historical pressures its authors experienced. After the First World War, history could hardly seem other than anarchic, or the 'nightmare' it appeared to Stephen Dedalus in *Ulysses*: scarcely any longer a dimension in which fictional structure or poetic vision could readily be based. Even time itself—'time on the clock' at any rate—seemed compromised. Long before the end of the nineteenth century, Karl Marx had warned that capitalist industry's wage systems inevitably commodified time and reified the individual. Under the influence of F. W. Taylor's 'scientific' management principles, and Henry Ford's industrial practices, these processes accelerated after the turn of the century, in ways disturbingly reflected in some of Lawrence's fiction, *Women in Love* particularly. Along with an apparently anarchic history, reductive, rationalizing economic forces encouraged modernism's reshaping of time and literary structure. They also contributed to its movement away from 'objective reality', towards inner spaces in which 'the free human individual' seemed to retain a more fulfilling, autonomous existence. Modernism, in other words, was wholly modern in only one sense—in rejecting convention in favour of new techniques. These new techniques themselves were generally forms of imaginative resistance to the social and historical forces of modernity, and to the 'all-inclusive industrial technology' Adorno and Horkheimer defined as their result.

Engaged in creating new artistic forms, and obviously aware of difficulties involved in shaping them out of an anarchic contemporary history, modernist authors were more than usually disposed to make art and its processes subjects of their writing. This disposition was apparent in one way in the extensive allusions to art and culture in the poetry mentioned earlier, Eliot's and Pound's particularly. It was also evident in Woolf's *To the Lighthouse* (1927) in the artist figure, Lily Briscoe, who reflects that the brush she uses for her painting is 'the one dependable thing in a world of strife, ruin, chaos' (pt. 3, ch. 1). Typically of modernist writing, her comments and activities as an artist have an immediate as well as a general relevance, providing a kind of figural analogue for the practices of the text in which she appears. Her painting's form duplicates the tripartite structure of Woolf's novel itself: a division 'there, in the centre' establishes 'unity of the whole' for both painting and fiction, and allows satisfactory, concurrent completion of the vision of each (pt. 1, ch. 9; pt. 3, ch. 13). Other modernist writers also developed self-consciousness or self-reflexiveness of this kind at a figural level, through references to visual art. Comparable instances appear in *Women in Love*, for example, and in Wyndham Lewis's *Tarr* (1918).

The title of Joyce's *A Portrait of the Artist as a Young Man* (1916) suggests a similar strategy, but the novel shows literary self-consciousness focusing instead, inevitably, not on painting but directly on the medium of literature: on words and language. Their role and nature are pondered regularly by Joyce's hero Stephen Dedalus—in considering, for example, gaps between the phrase 'a day of dappled seaborne clouds' and the reality it supposedly reflects. Language, he speculates, may be less a mirror than a prism—a colourful medium, almost an object in itself—and 'the rhythmic rise and fall of words' may hold pleasures of their own, independent of any function in representing the world (ch. 4). Gaps of this kind between word and world intrigued or troubled many other modernists. In *The Rainbow* and *Women in Love*, characters regularly question how far language can convey the depths of their passions. In *To the Lighthouse*, Lily's preference for painting reflects her conviction that 'words fluttered sideways and struck the object inches too low' (pt. 3, ch. 5). 'Language . . . dims everything', Dorothy Richardson's heroine concludes in *Pilgrimage*, 'words . . . get more and more wrong' (*The Tunnel*, ch. 4). In 'Burnt Norton' (1935), T. S. Eliot likewise reflects on the tendency of words to strain, crack or break down into imprecision and unreliability.

Gaps between word and scene identified in *A Portrait of the Artist as a Young Man* were greatly expanded—and continually explored —in Joyce's own later writing. Joyce himself emphasized of *Ulysses* that 'it is the material that conveys the image . . . that interests you'— an interest sustained throughout by the novel's extended use of parody (Budgen, p. 180). Mocking versions of the styles of contemporary journalism, literature, advertising, science, and colloquial speech ensure that the nature of language is impossible to ignore, and that means of representation are almost equal in interest to what is represented. This balance shifts still further in Joyce's 'Work in Progress' in the 1920s and 1930s, eventually published as *Finnegans Wake* in 1939. In a way, this most challenging of all modernism's experiments extends to new limits its determination to look within the mind—creating a stream of *un*consciousness; a linguistic dream-domain whose 'waters of babalong' dissolve most elements of conventional story (p. 103). Joyce's language focuses instead on its own components: on the nature and relations of words; on linguistic issues such as phonetics, etymology, and the semantics of English and other languages.

Such interests are summed up in one of the novel's many multilingual puns: 'say mangraphique, may say nay por daguerre' (p. 339).

Finnegans Wake is primarily 'graphique', writing in and for itself, sharing little in common with daguerreotype, or any other means of realistically representing the world. As a contemporary commentator, Eugene Jolas, remarked in 1929, Joyce's 'Work in Progress' suggested that 'The real metaphysical problem today is the word. The epoch when the writer photographed the life about him with the mechanics of words redolent of the daguerreotype, is happily drawing to its close. The new artist of the word has recognized the autonomy of language' (Beckett et al., p. 79). This recognition seemed to many later critics to mark a decisive transition between modernist interests and postmodernist writing—often defined in terms of its self-reflexive concern with the 'autonomy of language', the 'problem of the word', and the nature of literary representation generally. For Ihab Hassan, for example, 'the postmodern endeavour in literature acknowledges that words have severed themselves from things'. In his view, *Finnegans Wake* was therefore not so much a conclusive achievement of modernism, but also, as its title suggested, a work which begins again—as a 'prophecy of our postmodernity' and 'augur and theory of a certain kind of literature' (Hassan, pp. 113, xiii–xiv).

This was not a prophecy likely to be fulfilled immediately after the publication of *Finnegans Wake*, but one partly deferred by the Second World War and its aftermath. Some of its potential, and Joyce's influence generally, were nevertheless extended during this time by the work of two other Irish writers who followed in his wake. Samuel Beckett eventually came to seem one of the most representative, influential authors of the later twentieth century, his work exactly reflecting stresses Theodor Adorno and other critics saw imposed on the period's art by the Second World War.[3] Negotiations between word and silence—between longings for language's powers and orders, and the knowledge they could never be fully trusted— figured throughout Beckett's writing, though especially powerfully in the trilogy *Molloy, Malone Dies, The Unnamable*, first published in French in the early 1950s. Self-reflexive examination of literary imagination also featured strongly, though in a more comic vein, in one of the first of many novels about a writer writing about writing, Flann O'Brien's *At Swim-Two-Birds*. Beckett's trilogy was fully

---

[3] See p. 252, below.

translated into English only in 1959. The following year saw a successful reissue of *At Swim-Two-Birds*—partly overlooked, like *Finnegans Wake*, when it was first published in 1939. The late 1950s and early 1960s, even the year 1960 itself, might therefore be seen as a point of particular focus for postmodern 'prophecy', and of potential transition towards a 'Post-Modern period' in literature, much as Harry Levin suggested at the time.

Literary interests at this point—in the 'autonomy of language' and 'the problem of the word'—at any rate invite comparison with the postmodern thinking which appeared 'fully-blown' later in the 1960s. The 'trajectory of European philosophy' underlying its emergence might also be considered to have shaped a long-term pattern in literary history. Moves towards a postmodernist literature, in this view, could be seen as a third phase of resistance to the project of modernity, with Romanticism and modernism representing the first two. Emphases on computation and utility in the Enlightenment and the Industrial Revolution produced an almost immediate reaction, in the late eighteenth and early nineteenth century, in Romantic literature's valuing of intuition, imagination, and the natural world. Modernism supported comparable values in the early twentieth century. In exploring the inner reaches of consciousness, art, or the depths of memory, modernist authors tried to establish the kind of spaces, still resistant to the pressures of modernity, which the Romantics had found more easily in external nature. Later in the century, refuges or redeeming values sought by Romanticism and modernism seemed increasingly beyond reach, with multinational capitalism, in the view of commentators such as Fredric Jameson, more and more 'penetrating and colonizing . . . Nature and the Unconscious' (*Postmodernism*, p. 49). By the 1960s, literature might therefore have had reason, like postmodern thinking generally, to turn away from an apparently irredeemable world, confining itself within a detached, autonomous domain of its own discourse instead. Modernism's self-reflexive, language-centred modes, extended through Joyce's writing and its legacies, had certainly shown how such a course might be followed. Development later in the period of new emphases on fantasy, and new styles of 'magic realism', might seem to have added further to the technical resources required.

How far this course actually was followed, and how far literature in the period extended modernist tactics, or postmodern thinking, are issues discussed more fully in later chapters. But it is worth emphasizing at this stage that writing in the 1960s and later did not follow the pattern suggested above either comprehensively or exactly. Even when following self-conscious, self-questioning postmodernist modes, literature was rarely as inclined as postmodern theory to turn away from the world and its immediate problems, as several of the authors involved explained themselves. Salman Rushdie, for example, recorded his general agreement with postmodern scepticism, and with its rejection of 'complete, totalized explanation of the world'. But he added that

this is where the novel, the form created to discuss the fragmentation of truth, comes in . . . the acceptance that all that is solid *has* melted into air, that reality and morality are not givens but imperfect human constructs, is the point from which fiction begins . . . the challenge of literature is to start from this point, and still find a way of fulfilling our unaltered spiritual requirements. (*Imaginary Homelands*, p. 422)

Literature, Rushdie suggests, has an advantage over other representations of the world, since fictionality is an obvious, accepted part of its nature, not some kind of failure of truth or certitude. Its questioning of its own tactics and means of representation is therefore different from self-doubt expressed by postmodern theorists, and potentially still able to access the priorities Rushdie mentions—social and political as well as spiritual.

In particular, in an age Baudrillard and other postmodern commentators saw so manipulated by images and the media, there was a certain political potential in literature's scrutiny of ways language and imagination—its own included—construct and mediate the world. This potential had already been illustrated in the modernist period, in Joyce's examination, throughout *Ulysses*, of the influences of a first age of mass media. Some of these influences are reflected directly in his hero, an advertising man who spends a good deal of time in newspaper offices. But they are also highlighted by the language of the novel itself: by its extensive parodies of advertising and journalism, and its more general demonstration of ways vision and judgement of the world are shaped by the forms and styles of their expression. In the work of later authors, self-reflexive, postmodernist concern with language and form continued to highlight the still wider powers, in their age, of commercial, political, or other media interests. Authors who drew most attention to their own form and language—novelists such as John Berger, Doris Lessing, or Rushdie himself; poets such as J. H. Prynne—were in this way among the most politically committed in the period, extending into the literary medium itself a further layer of commentary on contemporary society and the forces shaping it.

Postmodernist authors also developed a number of other social and political commitments evident among their modernist predecessors. Modernist concerns about gaps between word and world were in one way thoroughly aligned with contemporary philosophy and linguistics—with scepticism of language and its operations expressed by Nietzsche and Saussure, and later developed in much postmodern thinking. Yet these concerns also had more direct, immediate connections with contemporary experience. Modernist 'crises of representation' often reflected wider political crises in the life of the time. Dorothy Richardson's heroine in *Pilgrimage*, for example, concludes that words 'get more and more wrong' as a result of her realization, during the suffragette period, of how far women are constrained by having to speak a language principally shaped by the outlook of men. Stephen Dedalus likewise indicates, in a later passage in *Portrait of the Artist*, that his linguistic interests may be less abstract and philosophical than they appeared on his 'day of dappled seaborne clouds'. He concludes of an argument with an Englishman that 'the language in which we are speaking is his before it is mine . . . His language, so familiar and so foreign, will always be for me an acquired speech. I have not made or accepted its words. My voice holds them at bay. My soul frets in the shadow of his language' (ch. 5). In the light of this passage, Joyce's own early situation—as an Irishman, like Stephen, growing up in a country still ruled from England—can be seen as a source of the parodic 'fretting' against the English language evident in his later writing, and influential on the literature which followed it.

Widely at work during the period of empire, stresses of this kind extended strongly into the decades of its dismantling in the later twentieth century—into the imagination of immigrant writers, or, more generally, of any authors whom gender or ethnicity forced to fret against established conventions. As Chapter 1 suggested, women and immigrant writers were often those most committed to reshaping established literary forms during the period, and therefore most inclined to resume or extend modernist modes of innovation, or of formal and linguistic self-enquiry. In doing so, they were certainly not turning away from a supposedly irredeemable world, but determinedly rewriting and reconfiguring its established conventions, literary and social. Despite many similarities in direction—and often, confusingly, in terminology involved—it is therefore worth trying to distinguish a specifically literary path through the postmodern 'minefield' from ones followed by the postmodern debate more widely. Postmodern thinking was usefully qualified, Section I suggested, by postcolonial ideas emerging in the 1990s. Assessments of postmodernist literature likewise benefit from postcolonial, feminist, or other forms of criticism which stress social and political influences at work throughout twentieth-century culture, rather than only the more abstract or philosophic ones often preoccupying the postmodern debate. Matters that this debate usually construed as problems—as crises of representation, or causes for intellectual resignation—postmodernist literature sometimes perceived as new occasions for committed commentary.

Questions about postmodernist literature, however, especially in the English context, often focused less on its social commitment than simply on the scale and extent of its development. Postmodernist potentials in evidence around 1960 contributed to 'a certain kind of literature', as Hassan suggested—to a continuing avant-garde, self-conscious about form and style—but did not by any means grow into dominant or exclusive influences. Nor were the legacies of modernist technique, more generally, the only factors shaping the period's writing. On the contrary, this reflected influences much more diverse than can be indicated by an account of modernism alone. Ezra Pound's praise for *Ulysses* in the *Dial* in 1922—that it added 'definitely to the international store of literary technique'—could be applied to modernist writing generally, but it did also indicate a constraint on its appeal for English authors (p. 625). As critics often pointed out, modernism was a thoroughly international movement, and its major figures, even those most influential on 'English' literature, were by no means always English in nationality or origin. Of those mentioned earlier, Henry James, Wyndham Lewis, Conrad, Pound, and Eliot all began life outside England, and the Irish writers —Joyce, Yeats, and Beckett—also kept their distance in later life. Partial or complete foreignness to England, its traditions, or even its language contributed a particular angle to modernist vision, encouraging abandonment or amendment of established conventions. But the new forms which resulted often seemed to critics, naturally enough, partly alien to domestic tradition.

Twentieth-century writing in England has often been seen in terms of conflict between this domestic tradition and innovative influences from abroad. At several stages of the century, English authors were certainly less inclined to browse in modern or international stores of literary technique than in local or longer-established ones—favouring methods consolidated in the nineteenth century, and carried over into the twentieth by Edwardian novelists such as Arnold Bennett, or poets such as Thomas Hardy. Even by the 1930s, a sense of contemporary political crisis often made modernist tactics seem less effective than the realistic description and direct social commentary the Edwardians had favoured. Preoccupied throughout with the threat of Hitler, Christopher Isherwood's *Goodbye to Berlin* (1939), for example, begins with the narrator defining himself as 'a camera with its shutter open, quite passive, recording, not thinking'. Only ten years after Eugene Jolas had concluded that realist modes of 'photographing' life were becoming obsolete, strategies of supposedly straightforward 'recording' once again seemed the best means of communicating contemporary stresses—depression and unemployment at home, as well as fascism abroad.

Modernism itself, of course, did not simply disappear during the 1930s. Other modernist writers as well as Joyce continued to publish during the decade, their styles sometimes influencing a new generation. Like most contemporary poets, W. H. Auden was thoroughly concerned with social and political pressures, but his work nevertheless extended some of modernism's characteristics: its stylistic inventiveness and complexity; its elliptical emphases of personal feeling. Among the decade's new novelists, Malcolm Lowry, Jean Rhys, and Lawrence Durrell likewise continued to practise modernist idiosyncrasies of language and form. But the mood of the 1930s and the war years postponed full appreciation of their fiction, as it did in the case of Beckett and Flann O'Brien, sometimes even as far as the 1960s. The war itself encouraged some of them—Malcolm Lowry, at any rate—to find new forms to encompass the violence and strangeness of the times. But as Chapter 1 suggested, the period which followed was perhaps inevitably one of constraint and conservatism—of wearied disdain for the wayward; of preference instead for the straightforward and unchallenging. Directness and moderation—realistic social concern in fiction, careful containment of emotion within conventional rhyme and metre in verse—seemed to critics to define a collective direction in contemporary writing, duly labelled as 'The Movement' in the 1950s. For many Movement writers—as several suggested in comments made in the late 1950s—Harry Levin's question 'What was Modernism?' would have been most welcome because it was framed in the past tense, identifying a phase of innovation and experiment which could apparently be assumed to have expired.

So for any English writers, looking over their shoulders to see what twentieth-century literature offered in terms of forms and strategies, at least two sets of possibilities were apparent by 1960. Innovative techniques and postmodernist 'prophecy' offered themselves along-side conventions modernism had never wholly displaced—ones often surviving since the nineteenth century, and recently strongly revalued by Movement writing. Twentieth-century literature could even be seen as divided almost decade by decade in terms of alle-giance to one or other set of priorities, with the revolutions dominat-ing the 1920s followed by the formally conservative writing of the 1930s and 1950s. In discussing 'the afterglow of the Moderns' in 1960, Levin duly suggested that the century's literary history thus far had been marked by an alternation of this kind: by a 'basic rhythm'; a 'cyclic oscillation' between what he called 'progresses and regres-sions' in literary history (*Refractions*, pp. 281, 282). Some of this oscillation did remain broadly apparent later in the century: in a renewed readiness for experiment in the 1960s, often drawing on the examples of modernism and its successors, followed by a return towards conservatism in the difficult years of the 1970s. Perhaps the most general conclusion that might be drawn in terms of Levin's oscillations is that they tended to dampen or flatten out towards the end of the century. Many authors in the 1980s and 1990s were ready to choose fairly eclectically from stores of literary technique, and to recombine devices they found there, rather than favouring either of the major branches too exclusively.

Rather than comprehensively fulfilling postmodern prophecies, the period's literature thus came closer in the end to justifying another of Hassan's suggestions in *The Postmodern Turn*: that 'history is a palimpsest, and culture is permeable to time past, time present, and time future. We are all . . . a little Victorian, Modern, and Postmodern, at once' (p. 88). Even this moderate conclusion was applicable only in different proportions to each of the literary genres. On the whole, the period's poetry was more conservative than its fiction. In the 1960s, modernist influences shaped the work of a number of poets, such as Basil Bunting or Geoffrey Hill, but for much of the period they remained subordinate to directions established by the Movement—even, in a way, to the kind of late Victorian manner it had borrowed from Thomas Hardy. A self-conscious, postmodernist idiom remained still harder to discern, partly for reasons inherent in the genre itself. As the poet Colin Falck pointed out, a sense of language possessing 'a kind of opacity in its own right instead of being a clean instrument for dealing with the world' is to an extent 'a necessary condition of all poetry', though it can obviously vary in degree (Hamilton (ed.), *Modern Poet*, p. 3). For much of the period, until the later 1980s and 1990s, a great deal of English poetry seemed to prefer language as a 'clean instrument', rather than one requiring much attention to its own operations. Earlier, only a small—though determined—minority of poets had entered deeply into what J. H. Prynne called 'the great aquarium of language', or used its opacities to refract much attention onto their own strategies and styles (Iain Sinclair, *Conductors*, p. 355).

Relations between the period's drama and the literary history outlined above were still more problematic, complicated by the absence of a strongly modernist phase on the English stage earlier in the century. Theatre on the Continent did develop rapidly at this time, in ways often analogous to the modernist innovations discussed above. Following the work of August Strindberg, German Expressionism attempted like much modernist writing to represent the inner movements of the individual psyche. Bertolt Brecht's 'Epic' theatre practised a modernist fracturing of conventional, linear forms of narrative, and a postmodernist element also appeared in his drama's confrontation of spectators with the artificial, constructed nature of its own presentations. Yet neither these nor other developments abroad had much contemporary impact within England. Instead, the long-delayed arrival of a number of European influences in the mid-1950s coincided, and eventually coalesced, with some long-suppressed domestic energies also released at this time. This helped to make the period's drama in many ways the most rapidly developing of all its literary genres—one in which Victorian, Modern, and Postmodern suddenly did all figure at once, and not always entirely distinguishably. Chapter 12 nevertheless discusses playwrights whose work could be defined as postmodernist, either in the general sense of extending modernist influences or in sharing the self-conscious concern with language and form, discussed above as a particular legacy in later writing.

*

A postmodern age? On the evidence of the patterns of thought and writing outlined in this chapter, the question is well worth asking. Despite the risk Fredric Jameson mentions, of raising 'more problems than it solves', the postmodern debate helps identify some of the principal stresses in twentieth-century thought, accentuated between the Second World War and the 1960s, and further troubling the period's outlook and imagination thereafter. But complex relations with modernist antecedents, and with contemporary thinking, make a question mark essential in any overall definition of late twentieth-century English literature as 'postmodern'. One part of the literary area nevertheless remained freer of such reservations. Literary theory, during the period, came to reflect postmodern thinking increasingly closely, especially in the post-structuralist modes emerging among English critics in the 1980s. Along with other developments in the period's literary theory and criticism, this is discussed in the next chapter.

3

An Age of Theory?
Critics, Readers, and Authors

High, high above the North Pole, on the first day of 1969, two professors of English Literature approached each other at a combined velocity of 1200 miles per hour.

The opening of David Lodge's *Changing Places* (1974) goes on to explain that collision is avoided, literally at any rate, by the two professors: the 'thoroughly conventional English don' Philip Swallow and the aggressively up-to-date Morris Zapp, travelling on exchange to each other's universities (ch. 1). Hurtling towards each other in the late 1960s, carrying such different intellectual baggage, they nevertheless provide a good metaphor for the high-level collisions of ideas which came to dominate academic study of English Literature over the next two decades. Later parts of Lodge's trilogy of campus novels, *Small World* (1984) and *Nice Work* (1988), further illustrate the transformations which resulted. Rapid expansion in theoretical thinking at the end of the 1960s, mostly Continental in origin, eventually impacted profoundly on established conceptions of literature, and of how it should be studied, in British universities. There were also wider influences on reading practices during the period, and often on its authors themselves. Generally, theory and criticism took on roles more prominent in the last decades of the century than at any earlier stage of literary history. In the United States, Geoffrey Hartman even claimed that critical or theoretical writing could assume a status equal to the literature it had once been thought to serve. In the *Cambridge History of Literary Criticism* (1995), Raman Selden envisaged a more modest role, but still a definitive one, suggesting that 'we may regard the period between the mid-1960s and the present day as the age of *theory*' (Selden (ed.), p. 1). No history of literature has the scope to provide a comprehensive account of criticism as well, or of theory, especially for an age of such productivity. This is in any case supplied for the period by volumes 8 and 9 of the *Cambridge History*, and by later chapters in Chris Baldick's *Criticism and Literary Theory 1890 to the Present* (1996). A literary history of the late twentieth century, on the other hand, needs at least to outline the developments which made it so particularly the 'age of *theory*' Selden envisaged. This chapter provides such an outline, before considering the wider implications of new critical theories for the literary imagination of the time.

Literary study was becoming more systematized even at the beginning of the period, some years before Zapp and Swallow took off on their respective transatlantic flights. In 1960, Graham Hough suggested in his study *Image and Experience* that 'to be entirely innocent of any concern with literary theory . . . is hardly possible now', adding that 'one of the most striking recent literary developments is the independent emergence of criticism, I will not say as an autonomous art, but as something between a profession and big business' (pp. 28, 47). Growing demand for critical texts, as well as primary ones, ensured that literature did remain a potentially profitable area for publishers in the decades that followed, if hardly ever a genuinely 'big business'. What really moved criticism towards 'big business'—at any rate, towards new sorts of systemization and professionalism—was the growth in numbers of students attending university, and the increasing popularity of English literature as an area of study. Earlier in the century, in its first two or three decades especially, much literary criticism had remained within the undemanding, rather amateur form of 'belles-lettres'. This assumed, according to Peter Widdowson, that 'great literature was universal and expressed general truths about human life, and that therefore readers required no special knowledge or language'. Critics therefore 'talked comfortable good sense about the writer's personal experience', or about 'the human interest, imaginative "genius", and poetic beauty of great literature' (Selden and Widdowson, p. 1).

As David Lodge indicates in the conventional figure of Philip Swallow, such comfortable, commonsensical assumptions still survived strongly in universities during the 1960s. In *An Essay on Criticism* (1966), Hough himself still seemed relatively innocent of literary theory, concluding that 'literary discourse is ultimately a conversation about a shared enjoyment' (p. 176). Yet in order to justify its place within an expanding university system—in particular, to compete with the influence and authority increasingly enjoyed by the sciences—literary study needed to offer more than only a shared enjoyment, accessible to anyone who had read a book with care. Instead, it had to develop its role as a genuine discipline, requiring 'special knowledge' in the form of skills, strategies, and analytic tactics which justified the expenditure of years of students' time in their acquisition, and of substantial amounts of public finance to support the staff who taught them. The first of a series of student readers edited by David Lodge, *20th Century Literary Criticism* (1972), indicated areas in which analytic tactics of this kind had developed furthest by the end of the 1960s. Lodge's anthology included sections of Formal and 'New' Criticism; of Social and Political Criticism; and of Myth Criticism and Psychoanalytical Criticism. In practice, it was the first of these areas, New Criticism, which had contributed most to the discursive idiom prevalent in English universities by the 1960s. The other major influence on this idiom—one not entirely contrary to some of the assumptions Widdowson outlined—was the work of F. R. Leavis.

Like the New Criticism, Leavis's thinking had grown more influential since the 1930s, partly through its coalescence with longer-standing critical assumptions established by Matthew Arnold in the late nineteenth century. Arnold had helped to make literature and its study into an extension of Christianity, or even a substitute for it: an alternative source of authoritative texts, and of moral and spiritual values, around which the increasingly agnostic societies of the late nineteenth and early twentieth centuries might still cohere. For Leavis, literature was likewise a bright book of life, offering vision, creative energy, and models for behaviour. Leavis particularly praised the work of D. H. Lawrence, for example, for its 'unfailingly sure sense of the difference between that which makes for life and that which makes against it; of the difference between health and that which tends away from health' (*Lawrence: Novelist*, p. 325). Judgements of this kind also contributed to Leavis's reassessment and eventual consolidation of the literary canon. Literary study had generally concentrated on a canon of the supposedly greatest writers, without always clarifying the basis on which they were selected. By judging how successfully authors might 'make for life', particularly in *The Great Tradition* (1948), Leavis seemed to offer a definite strategy for identifying the truly great.

He also suggested ways of making the best use of their strengths. Properly elucidated and disseminated by critics, values of 'life' and 'health' in great literature, Leavis considered, could oppose the cheapening effects of mass culture, the narrow rationalism of a scientific age, and the deadening commercialization of the modern industrial world. First outlined in the 1930s, such views were particularly appealing in the 1960s. They apparently coincided with those of popular thinkers such as Herbert Marcuse, and contributed directly to the contemporary revaluation of Lawrence through the reissue of Leavis's *D. H. Lawrence: Novelist* in 1964. Dominant in much 1960s critical writing, Leavisite influences also lasted long afterwards, extended by the spread of academics he had inspired throughout the English university system. Legacies of his thinking were also sustained through extensive contributions made by his collaborators and associates to Boris Ford's *Pelican Guide to English Literature*, regularly reissued after its first publication in 1961.

More nonconformist than Arnold—too much so, for the liking of the Cambridge English Faculty, where he worked—Leavis made his most enduring impact in insisting on literature's relevance to a wider world, and on its capacity to provide an oppositional, critical vision of society. Terry Eagleton remarked in the early 1980s that in this and other ways, students of English were still Leavisites 'whether they know it or not . . . that current has entered the bloodstream of English studies in England' (*Literary Theory*, p. 31)—an influence perhaps confirmed by Eagleton's sanguine choice of metaphor. Yet by the 1980s, limitations inherent in Leavis's work had become inescapably apparent. Its deliberate lack of systematization, for example, could only be partly excused as a form of resistance to an over-rationalized world. Without a firm basis or theory, values of 'life' and 'health' could be defined only by the unsubstantiated judgement of privileged intellectual initiates: the 'very small minority' upon whom, in any period, Leavis believed, 'the discerning appreciation of art and literature depends . . . upon them depend the implicit standards that order the finer living of an age' (*Mass Civilisation*, pp. 3, 5). Paradoxically, while seeming to liberate literary study from the gentlemanly exclusiveness of belles-lettres, Leavis introduced to it interpretative criteria potentially more elitist than ever.

The New Critics had established by the 1960s directions which extended still further through later critical movements: ones much less concerned with 'the living of the age'. Based around some of T. S. Eliot's critical ideas, and on I. A. Richards's exercises in 'Practical Criticism' in the 1920s—ones requiring students to analyse poems shorn of dates and their authors' names—New Criticism favoured exclusive concentration on 'the words on the page' and on 'the text itself'. During the late 1940s and 1950s, it had developed a strong theoretical base through critical work in the United States, particularly two influential essays by W. K. Wimsatt and M. C. Beardsley, 'The Intentional Fallacy' (1946) and 'The Affective Fallacy' (1949). The first of these questioned the critical habit of invoking writers as an explanation of their writing—of deriving supposed authorial intentions from a literary work, then using these to judge the text concerned. The second was a warning about subjective judgement, arguing for a literary study as far as possible independent of the personal reactions of the critic. Relieved in this way from constraints imposed either by author or critic, a literary work—usually, in the New Critics' interests, a poem—could be considered as a freestanding object; a 'Verbal Icon', in the title of one of Wimsatt's studies, or a 'Well-Wrought Urn', in one of Cleanth Brooks's. Attention could be concentrated on how its verbal medium had been wrought and shaped: on internal aspects of style, structure, ambiguity, irony, and rhetorical figure, and their various contributions to overall unity.

Concentration on technical devices seemed to move literary study away from the unsystematic, 'comfortable' talk about authors' lives or about critics' reactions predominant in earlier years, and it led to widespread adoption of New Critical methods within universities in the 1950s and 1960s. Later in the period, methods of 'close reading' or technical analysis generally remained part of the repertoire of skills students of literature were encouraged to acquire. Significantly for later developments, too, New Criticism had begun to challenge conventional conceptions of a literary work as a straightforward act of communication between author and reader, drawing attention instead to its generation of meaning exclusively through its own language, structure, and devices. A poem 'simply *is*', Wimsatt and Beardsley argued. Since 'its medium is words . . . the poem is not the critic's own and not the author's'. Instead, 'the poem belongs to the public. It is embodied in language, the peculiar possession of the public'—even if it still required the intervention of critics to elucidate its full effect (Wimsatt, pp. 4, 5).

In one way, these emphases reflected in the critical sphere, partly under T. S. Eliot's influence, the increased attention to the medium of language in modernist literature, discussed in Chapter 2. They also anticipated still wider concerns with language in much later twentieth-century writing and thought. In structuralism, critical interest in language entered a more radical phase, no longer much concerned with rhetorical, poetic, or other surface features of texts. Instead, this further 'linguistic turn' sought in the nature of language a model for the structuring, at a deeper level, of all texts, and—an interest pursued in the study of semiotics—for the functioning of sign systems throughout society generally. Developed strongly in the 1960s by Roland Barthes, A. J. Greimas, and Tzvetan Todorov, such thinking drew on the structuralist anthropology of Claude Lévi-Strauss, published in the late 1940s and 1950s, and derived in particular from Ferdinand de Saussure's analysis, early in the century, of the functioning of signs within any language.

Saussure considered all linguistic signs split into two aspects: a signifier, whether sound or written mark, and a signified, the concept that it stood for. Signifier and signified, he explained, are connected to each other only arbitrarily, through the habits and conventions of individual languages. Such arbitrary relations leave no 'positive terms'—no words immediately, reliably, and exactly representing things or concepts—but instead a language which works only differentially, generating meaning through relations between signifiers; through differences between terms contained within its system. Language, for Saussure, could not therefore simply reflect the world or express the individual's vision of it, but rather produced and shaped each itself, through its own structures and systems of relation. Based on this linguistic model, structuralist criticism sought the underlying grammar or 'code' through which elements within any sign system—or any literary text—are combined to make meaning. In doing so, it also drew on the work of the Russian formalist Vladimir Propp, whose analysis of folk tales in the 1920s had established a limited number of fundamental 'functions'—roles and activities—underlying the various surface features of these narratives. His strategy was later developed by Greimas, who reduced Propp's functions to a still more limited range of 'actants'—helper and opponent, sender and receiver, and so on—and by Todorov, who defined characters in terms of nouns, and their actions in terms of verbs. For each critic, narrative could be shown to derive from a number of underlying units, and the relations between them could be construed like the grammar of a sentence. Lévi-Strauss had treated myth in a similar way—one also familiar to literary critics from the work of Northrop Frye. In *Anatomy of Criticism* (1957), Frye traced the projection into myth of a set of Jungian elements fundamental to human consciousness, using these archetypal, mythic patterns as the basis for a taxonomy of all world literature. Though much less indebted to linguistic models, like most structuralist thinking Frye's work suggested that categories and systems underlying narrative and myth might ultimately represent the structure of human consciousness itself.

Such thinking had a number of consequences, immediate and longer term. Concerned with overall form, rather than the local devices studied by New Critics, structuralism contributed to a gradual shift in the focus of critical attention, after the 1960s, from poetry onto narrative. It also helped to provide a theoretical basis for this interest, explored in a new branch of critical study, narratology. Apart from Wayne Booth's *The Rhetoric of Fiction* (1961), concerned with point of view and narrative voice, relatively little technical analysis had been focused on the novel and its structure until Gérard Genette's *Narrative Discourse* (1972). Like much of the thinking considered above, this study developed the work of the Russian formalists: in particular, their distinction between what Genette labelled 'récit', the order of events in the text, and 'histoire', the order they might have followed had they occurred in reality. Along with other distinctions modelled on the mood and tense system of verbs, this allowed Genette to construct categories for analysing the temporality of narrative, and the range of voices, points of view, or 'focalisations' through which it is communicated to the reader. Still often used at the end of the century, these categories and methods were among structuralism's most effective longterm legacies in later critical thought.

Structuralism's immediate impact often had less to do with its actual methods than with what these implied for literary study generally. These implications were very variously perceived within the academic community. Sections of it naturally resented structuralism's threat to long-established forms of critical enquiry. If meaning developed through structures inherent in language and imagination themselves, rather than the writer's will or communicative intent, then author-oriented study—already questioned by Wimsatt and Beardsley, and further challenged by Roland Barthes's celebrated essay 'The Death of the Author' in 1968—now seemed almost completely eliminated as a valid area of enquiry. Just as disturbingly for traditionalists, structuralism was the first of several critical movements largely to ignore established cultural values, treating literature instead simply as one sign system among many— one of the range of signifying practices analysed by semioticians, likely to be equally interested in fashion, cars, or television soap operas.

To the relief of many academics, on the other hand, structuralism seemed to offer at last a reliably theoretical, objective basis for literary study, its scrutiny of underlying codes and structures finally matching the kind of methodological authority claimed by the sciences. *Small World* reflects—affirmatively, though occasionally ironically—some of this new sense of potential. David Lodge shows Zapp's and Swallow's careers rapidly developing beyond the early stages reflected in *Changing Places*, involving them increasingly in an international circuit of lecturing and conferences. Yet the world is shrunk not only by the characters' jet-setting lifestyle, but by a new confidence in the ability of critical intellect to encompass all myths and narratives—even the extravagant range which Lodge intertwines with ordinary experience through the novel's romance mode.

Yet the ambitiousness of structuralism's claims also hastened its demise, drawing attention to flaws in its logic and assumptions. Roland Barthes followed structuralist thinking in early work such as his 'Introduction to the Structural Analysis of Narrative' (1966), demonstrating how far 'narrative shares the characteristics of the sentence' (*Image–Music–Text*, p. 84). He nevertheless began to speculate that structuralism could hardly offer the ultimate or certain form of knowledge it claimed, since its own operations were in principle also open to further scrutiny and decoding. Analysis of this kind was influentially undertaken by Jacques Derrida. Categories which structuralism identified as fundamental had no real claim to scientific objectivity, Derrida showed, but were unavoidably tainted instead with the prejudices of analysts, such as Lévi-Strauss's preference for nature over culture. Derrida likewise minutely reassessed the Saussurean linguistics on which structuralist thinking was based, suggesting that the relation between signifier and signified is not so much arbitrary as non-existent. The idea that an element of the signified somehow remains present within a linguistic sign shows Saussure still covertly committed to the immediate presence of meaning which his linguistics had generally set out to deny.

Derrida also stressed that Saussure's principle of differential meaning inevitably implies deferral of meaning. Differences obviously cannot be established by a single signifier alone, but require relations with others, or with other elements within a sentence. Derrida emphasized—even enacted—the complications of this process through his celebrated play on the French term 'différance', in which both difference and deferral are implied. Différance makes the construction of meaning a potentially limitless process in a language system lacking any ultimately secure, positive term or 'transcendental signified'. Meaning, in this analysis, is interminably fugitive, receding from determinate grasp along potentially infinite chains of mutually related signifiers. Rather than representing the world, or the mind, or providing a reliable model for the structure of either, language for Derrida is only 'a world of signs . . . without truth, and without origin' (p. 292).

Such a radically sceptical view of language was in a way liberating, allowing readers new freedoms, of a kind also celebrated by Barthes, in interpreting or generating meanings from texts. Derrida himself

considered that the indeterminacies of the world of signs 'offered ...
an active interpretation'; even an 'innocence' and a 'joyous affirmation of ... play' (p. 292). New freedoms, or challenges, implied by his
views contributed to a range of new, 'post-structuralist' critical
strategies. Such freedoms were also sometimes construed as a licence
to suggest that a literary work could mean anything at all. But
Derrida's principal concern was to show more specifically—as in his
rereadings of Saussure and Lévi-Strauss—how texts implicitly contradict themselves, retain covert allegiances to ideas they explicitly
seek to refute, or depend on presuppositions they fail to acknowledge or explore. More widely employed in the 1970s and 1980s,
interpretative practices of this kind were usually labelled as 'deconstruction', developing particularly in the United States in the work of
the Yale School of critics, which included J. Hillis Miller, Geoffrey
Hartman, and Paul de Man.

New critical freedoms or forms of 'active interpretation' obviously
conflicted radically with many of the old. Extending the anti-
foundational, postmodern thinking outlined in Chapter 2, Derrida's
ideas brought to the study of literature the firmness of knowledge it
had often sought, but only, paradoxically, in the form of certain
knowledge of the impossibility of certitude. Attempting to 'pass
beyond man and humanism', as Derrida acknowledged, such thinking challenged still more fundamentally than structuralism many of
the long-standing, essentially liberal-humanist practices of English
criticism (p. 292). Deconstruction left little scope for Leavisite moral
readings of what 'makes for life', for example, since it suggested that
no text, no piece of language, reliably reflects life or the world,
morally or otherwise. It likewise undermined the New Critics'
emphases on overall textual unity, treating the contradictions and
ambiguities they analysed not as parts of a well-wrought whole, but
as one of many holes through which a determinate role for 'the
words on the page' inevitably leaks away. Any of the 'comfortable'
critical habits Widdowson saw surviving at the end of the 1960s
were likewise bound to collide with what Christopher Norris
described as deconstruction's 'affront to every normal and comfortable habit of thought' (*Deconstruction*, p. xi).

Yet such collisions were themselves subject to deferral. Structuralist thinking was well established in France by the mid-1960s, and

had already been challenged by the end of the decade by Derrida's ideas—increasingly influential after the publication in 1966 of the essay quoted above, 'Structure, Sign, and Play in the Discourse of the Human Sciences'. But as Terry Eagleton suggested in *Literary Theory: An Introduction* (1983), 'a decade or so is perhaps the customary time-lapse for ideas in transit across the Channel' (p. 123). It was not until the later 1970s that this new thinking much impacted on England, with deconstruction arriving, confusingly, almost before the impact of structuralism had been absorbed. Published in 1975, Jonathan Culler's *Structuralist Poetics* provided an influential introduction to the latter, as did Terence Hawkes's *Structuralism and Semiotics* two years later. The 'New Accents' series in which it appeared, edited by Hawkes for Routledge, helped to ensure that new theories of linguistics, narratology, deconstruction, and semiotics became widely available throughout the later 1970s and early 1980s, with Catherine Belsey's *Critical Practice* summing up a particularly influential case against conventional or 'comfortable' critical assumptions in 1980.

By that date, conflict and collision within the discipline of literary study had become inescapably apparent. On exchange in Philip Swallow's English university in *Changing Places*, Morris Zapp worried his new colleagues only mildly by discussing 'fashionable people like . . . Saussure and Lévi-Strauss' (ch. 3). Set ten years later, in 1979, *Small World* shows stronger reactions to a lecture Zapp delivers at one of the novel's many conferences. Now a confirmed 'antitheorist', Swallow concludes with horror that Zapp has been infected with 'the virus of structuralism', even though his lecture shows he has actually moved on towards deconstruction (pt. 4, ch. 1; pt. 1, ch. 1). Such reactions of hostility and partial comprehension, widespread at the time, were in one instance dramatic enough to become national news. No more tolerant of nonconformism than it had been in Leavis's days, Cambridge University refused in 1980 to reappoint Colin MacCabe, on the grounds, according to the newspapers, that he was a structuralist, though by this time he too was closer to deconstruction. Incorporating the episode into *Nice Work*, Lodge recalls that 'all hell broke loose in the Cambridge English Faculty . . . insults and libel suits were exchanged . . . for a few weeks the controversy featured in the national and even international press' (pt. 1, ch. 2).

Newspaper reports at the time made McCabe into a kind of Zapp among the Swallows, a martyr at the hands of intellectual conservatism, and the affair itself evidence of the spread throughout literary study of sensational, if incomprehensible, antagonisms.

Their extent was confirmed by Peter Widdowson in another 'New Accents' volume, *Re-Reading English*, which recorded of literary studies in 1982 that 'an increasing number of people teaching and studying in this field are aware that their subject is in the midst of some kind of crisis' (p. 1). It was a crisis which prompted a number of different reactions in universities over the next decade or so. One was to continue—as Cambridge apparently hoped to—as if nothing much had happened. Just as existential conclusions about life's meaninglessness had not stopped people getting up and going about their daily business in the 1950s and 1960s, new challenges to the subject's intellectual foundations did not prevent critics continuing to produce conventional studies of authors and their work. In many universities neither curricula nor teaching methods were much changed, at least in the early 1980s: new strategies and theories instead appeared gradually, alongside existing ones. Another response was in seeking to integrate longer-established ideas and practices *within* the new forms of linguistically centred analysis, following the example of a number of thinkers, usually French, who had initiated this process by the 1960s. This response was especially apparent where critical practices had already been substantially theorized or systematized—in particular, in two of the areas identified in Lodge's reader in 1972, psychoanalytic and 'political', usually Marxist, criticism.

Earlier in the century, most psychoanalytic criticism had straightforwardly followed Sigmund Freud's methods, either in examining the psyches of characters, much as if they were real people, or in analysing authors, treating their works as evidence of unconscious or neurotic preoccupations much in the way Freud treated his patients' dreams. After the 1970s, literary criticism instead drew increasingly on the reinterpretation of Freud in the work of Jacques Lacan, and on his reappraisal of the self and its relation to society. For Lacan, the self in earliest childhood is formless, fluid, and unable to distinguish itself from what is other or external to it. It then enters a phase in which a mirror, metaphorical or real, apparently makes available a coherent, autonomous self—though an 'Imaginary' one, in Lacan's terms, existing only as an ideal, unrealizable image. This Imaginary phase is followed by recognition of the self not as an image, but within the shifty symbolic order of language, in which it identifies with a range of subject positions implied by the 'I' used in its own utterances, and the 'he', 'she', or 'you' of other people's.

Given the vagaries of language assumed since Saussure, with no final or complete meaning residing in any signifier, this linguistically constructed subjectivity can never be complete, but in its desire for fullness only distends itself through endless differentiations and chains of signifiers. In bringing the incertitude of linguistically based thinking to analyses of the psyche, Lacan's work contributed significantly to the late twentieth-century recognition of a decentred self, discussed in Chapter 2: of individual identities lacking unity or self-presence, and constructed in ways beyond their own complete control. Lacan also helped to shift the attention of psychoanalytic criticism away from tenuous speculation about the psyches of authors or characters. It moved instead towards more text-based concerns with the operation of desire and the construction of selfhood in language, and with the involvement and identification of readers in the processes involved.

Louis Althusser was as influential in reinterpreting Marx as Lacan was in reassessing Freud. Most earlier Marxist criticism had concentrated either on the politics directly expressed by literary texts, or on tracing connections—usually quite direct ones—between the economic 'base' of productive forces identified by Marx, and the 'superstructure' of cultural, social, and intellectual processes he considered it to condition. Althusser outlined relations between base and superstructure more complex than those Marx had usually been assumed to suggest, and sometimes even inverse in terms of cause and effect. Greater emphasis on a relatively autonomous superstructure contributed to more sophisticated Marxist analysis of literature and culture generally. In particular, it concentrated attention on the role of cultural forms in generating 'ideology'—ideas and assumptions, plausible but misleading, which divert individuals from full knowledge of their economic exploitation. For Althusser, processes of self-construction envisaged by Lacan are shaped by the dissemination of ideology through the 'state apparatuses' of media, religion, law, art, and culture. These apparatuses ensure that individuals' self-recognition in the Imaginary and in language make an acquiescent position within capitalist society seem the only natural or possible one. The individual acquires in this way a 'subject' position in every sense, with subservience to the established order an inevitable condition of subjectivity and selfhood. With its glossy, seductive images of self-enhancement through the purchase of consumer products, advertising provides an obvious example of processes that concerned Althusser.

Similar ideas were developed by a number of contemporary critics —in showing, for example, how conventional realist fiction might subtly seduce readers, through 'natural' identification with plausible characters, into complicity with the status quo. Roland Barthes criticized nineteenth-century realist fiction, Balzac in particular, as 'readerly'—offering an imagined world so straightforwardly accessible to the reader that its political biases might pass unnoticed. Modernist literature came closer to Barthes's ideal of the 'writerly', since its fragmented texts demand of readers more active participation in constructing meaning—a role as 'producer of the text', rather than its passive 'consumer'—and hence more active scrutiny of political or other values involved (*S/Z*, p. 4). Preferences for social realism expressed by earlier Marxist critics such as Georg Lukács— suspicious of modernism for its fractured, subjective view of experience—were similarly challenged by other commentators at this time. Several returned to the values of the Frankfurt School, particularly to the work of Theodor Adorno, to emphasize ways that innovative, modernist, or postmodernist writing could establish critical distance from the world it represented.

Althusser's interests were extended more directly by Pierre Macherey in *A Theory of Literary Production* (1977). Analysing the role of ideology in literary works, Macherey outlined a deconstructive reading which could identify in their formal strategies—their omissions and avoidances—an implicit or unconscious critique of this ideology itself. His work extended in this way a wider movement of Marxist criticism towards politicized analysis of literary form and style. This interest in the 'politics of form' was developed further by the leading Marxist critics in England and in the United States, Terry Eagleton and Fredric Jameson. Each examined most of the stages in theoretical thinking outlined above, and in the end combined a full range of this thinking's implications within an overriding political perspective. Eagleton worked towards a politicized 'science of the text' in *Criticism and Ideology* (1976), and in *Literary Theory: An Introduction* (1983) directed a broad survey of recent ideas and practices towards a demand for a fully political criticism which could supersede them. Jameson examined structuralism and formalism in *The Prison House of Language* (1972), going on in *The Political Unconscious* (1981) to assemble some of the theories of Adorno, Althusser, Greimas, Macherey, Lévi-Strauss, Freud, and others into one of the most wide-ranging syntheses of late twentieth-century critical thought.

Both psychoanalytic and Marxist criticism thus moved towards eclectic incorporation of structuralist and poststructuralist ideas. Moves in this direction were shared, and often outpaced, by the evolution of feminist criticism and gender studies during and after the 1970s. Progress was necessarily rapid. Apart from pioneering contributions by Virginia Woolf in the 1920s, and by Simone de Beauvoir from the late 1940s, this was an area which had hardly developed before 1970. In Lodge's *Changing Places*, set just before the publication of Germaine Greer's *The Female Eunuch* and Kate Millett's *Sexual Politics*, feminism is understandably omitted from the list of methodologies—'historical, biographical, rhetorical, mythical, Freudian, Jungian, existentialist, Marxist, structuralist, Christian-allegorical, ethical, exponential, linguistic, phenomenological, archetypal'—which Morris Zapp intends to employ in an 'utterly exhaustive' analysis of the novels of Jane Austen 'from every conceivable angle' (ch. 1). Ten years later, feminism's omission from any such list would have been inconceivable, with the significant role accorded it in Lodge's *Small World* a clear acknowledgement of the change. In addressing the broad range of issues raised by sexual and gender relations, feminism had necessarily become fairly eclectic or 'exhaustive' itself, obliged to address many of the areas included in Zapp's list. Some offered methods which feminism could adopt or adapt—Marxist analyses of exploitation and subordination especially. Others demanded critical scrutiny in terms of their complicity with partriarchal values or their suppression of women's perspectives. Feminism could hardly leave unquestioned Freud's assumption that female sexuality was based on penis envy, for example, or the primacy accorded the phallus as a signifier within the symbolic order Lacan outlined.

Though thoroughly wide-ranging, feminist approaches to literature fell into three main areas. To some extent, these reproduced stages in the broader development of contemporary literary criticism. The first area, termed by Elaine Showalter 'feminist critique', could in this way be seen as loosely Leavisite in its methods (p. 129). Much of the work of Kate Millett and the critics who followed her interpreted literature as a reflection of the world, discussed values it offered, and related them to everyday life and experience. One of the early achievements of this feminist critique was in establishing literature as a useful context for analysing issues of general interest to feminism—ways that stereotypes of women are constructed and perpetuated, for example. Often highlighting negative, distorted presentations of women in male-authored texts—degradation rather than affirmation of 'life'—the results of such analysis were of course far from Leavisite. Notably in Millett's attack on D. H. Lawrence,[1] evaluations of the authors concerned were likewise very different from any proposed in Leavis's *Great Tradition*. Emphasizing the implications of reading as a woman, and not, as conventionally assumed in critical studies, as a man, another of the achievements of feminist critique was its exposure of the male-centredness of established literary values and of the canon of 'great' texts and great traditions based around them.

A second phase, labelled by Showalter as 'gynocritics', also sought to amend a male-centred canon, but less through challenging male-authored works than by promoting ones by women (p. 131). Many of these, gynocritics showed, had been unjustly excluded from attention in their own time, or left unstudied since. Fewer than 10 per cent of authors studied in university literature courses in the early 1970s were women, surveys estimated at the time. Showalter's own aptly named *A Literature of their Own* (1977), along with Sandra M. Gilbert and Susan Gubar's *The Madwoman in the Attic* (1979), sought to restore recognition of nineteenth-century women writers, a process later extended into the twentieth century by studies such as Gilbert and Gubar's *No Man's Land* (1988–94) and Bonnie Kime

[1] See p. 41, above.

Scott's *The Gender of Modernism* (1990). Studies of earlier periods likewise helped to establish a tradition of women's writing scarcely recognized or discussed previously: it was further consolidated in the 1970s and 1980s by the work of the new women's publishing houses in reissuing many of the titles involved. Within this 'newly visible world of female culture', as Showalter called it, gynocritics also sought to identify elements of women's experience overlooked or excluded in the male-oriented canon, and the themes, tropes, genres, or other devices specifically developed for their expression in literature by women (p. 131).

Much of this work was undertaken by critics in Britain or, in the case of those named above, the United States. Like feminist critique, it remained relatively conventional in its analytic strategies, concentrating on authors and the literary tradition, and on texts as expressions of their writers' interests and reflections—responsible or otherwise—of society and the world. Like literary study in the period more generally, feminist criticism and gender studies also came to be strongly affected by the influence of innovative French thinkers. Luce Irigaray, Hélène Cixous, and Julia Kristeva helped to move feminist criticism into a third phase, often referred to as 'gynesis', in which 'woman' and 'feminine', like everything else in poststructuralist theory, were considered less as sure or stable categories than as constructions generated by language and text. Arguments such as Lacan's or Althusser's—about the positioning of the subject within the order of language, and the making 'natural' of subordinate roles—could be readily extended to demonstrate how women were moulded into conventional identities and roles by language and ideology. Cixous and other critics saw an alternative in an 'écriture féminine', a fluid language or 'writing effect'—not necessarily exclusive to women authors—based around bodily impulses and rhythms, rather than the intellectual rigour and rationality conventionally claimed by masculine writing. This alternative was consistent both with Kristeva's interest in the non-rational aspects of poetic language and with a wider sense among feminist critics that too rigorous an adherence to theory—even feminist theory—might be inimical to the variable, idiosyncratic qualities they wished to celebrate within private experience.

Radical emphases on private experience also figured in the Queer

Theory which appeared within the broader area of gender studies in the 1990s. Like feminist critique and gynocritics, much of this was concerned with challenging the roles conventionally assigned gays and lesbians in literature included in the canon, suggesting its enlargement to include further texts, or identifying particular qualities within the work of writers concerned. Like feminist criticism generally, Queer Theory also moved on to consider the implications of gender and sexual categories within—and for—society's linguistic and cultural systems. In *Epistemology of the Closet* (1990), for example, Eve Kosofsky Sedgwick suggested that the 'chronic modern crisis of homo/heterosexual definition has affected our culture through its ineffaceable marking particularly of the categories secrecy/disclosure, knowledge/ignorance, private/public, masculine/ feminine, majority/minority', etc. By highlighting these 'modern crises' and their implications, she considered, feminist and gender theory had introduced to cultural analysis in general 'the recognition that categories of gender and, hence, oppressions of gender can have a structuring force for nodes of thought, for axes of cultural discrimination, whose thematic subject isn't explicitly gendered at all' (pp. 11, 34).

Recognitions of this kind—of forces structuring social categories, 'nodes of thought', and ultimately language and culture generally— extended into other new directions followed by criticism towards the end of the century. As discussed above, psychoanalytic, Marxist, feminist, and gay criticism had all developed poststructuralist phases by the later 1980s, accommodating new linguistically oriented theories rather than simply colliding with them. But for many critics, Marxists and feminists included, the last two decades of the century also suggested a need, if not to move beyond poststructuralism, at least to reconsider dilemmas some of the new thinking had created, in its more radical, deconstructive modes especially. Incipient forms of this need appeared from time to time in Lodge's *Small World*. Jetting around the 'global campus', discussing critical problems stratospherically distant from immediate experience, Lodge's academics are generally glad to find themselves 'up here, in the sun, above the clouds, [where] all is calm'. But they nevertheless remain aware, at least intermittently, of 'clashes between police and protesters . . . political murders in Turkey, meat shortages in Poland, car bombs in

Belfast, and of many other tragedies, afflictions, outrages, at various points of the globe' (pt. 1, ch. 1; pt. 2, ch. 1). During the 1980s and 1990s, both these perspectives—elevated and immediate—came to be reflected in contemporary critical developments.

Like postmodern thinking generally, literary theory at the time sometimes seemed simply to desert an intractable reality, taking refuge in a bright domain of ideas, and in a language which stressed its detachment from reliable reference to lived experience. Yet a political climate hardening throughout the 1980s, along with Thatcherite cuts in university funding beginning in 1981, forced many academics into greater awareness of the stresses of the working world—a process Lodge went on to trace in *Nice Work*. This helped to suggest that postmodern or deconstructive undermining of intellectual authority had done too little to challenge political authority: that Jacques Derrida had become, or had been made by his followers, a kind of Jacques le Fataliste, universally negating possibilities of political engagement. Like Christopher Norris, quoted in Chapter 2, Terry Eagleton complained that 'the view that the most significant aspect of any piece of language is that it does not know what it is talking about smacks of a jaded resignation to the impossibility of truth . . . it also frees you at a stroke from having to assume a position on important issues'. Eagleton went on to defend Derrida himself—a far from jaded analyst of Western metaphysics—explaining that 'deconstruction is for him an ultimately *political* practice, an attempt to dismantle the logic by which a particular system of thought, and behind that a whole system of political structures and social institutions, maintains its force' (*Literary Theory*, pp. 144–5, 148). This logical 'dismantling' had contributed strongly to Derrida's influence in France after 1968. Yet neither Derrida nor his deconstructionist followers seemed clearly to make the move Eagleton required, from intellectual systems back to explicit concern with political systems. Partly as a result, literary theory and criticism in the 1980s and 1990s tended to shift attention towards other figures: principally the French historian of thought, Michel Foucault, and another of the Russian formalists, Mikhail Bakhtin.

In different ways, each suggested that a way of analysing what language *is* talking about, or how it is talking—however shifty a medium it may be in itself—lies in the context-specific nature of its actual uses, and ways these are determined by social, historical, institutional, and ideological influences. In Bakhtin's view, interactions between these influences make language always to some extent 'dialogic': always a contested domain, in which various forces fret, collide, or coalesce. In his analysis, the novel is 'a *system* of languages that mutually and ideologically interanimate each other': one in which even individual words function as shifting counters in an interplay of the voices of author and characters, and ultimately of attitudes and assumptions which shape their outlooks (*Dialogic Imagination*, p. 47). Bakhtin's conception of language extends in this way his view of carnival, as an event or state in which social roles interact freely and dynamically, subverting conventional hierarchies.[2] Suggesting that the contestation of established social and cultural conventions—characteristic of the 1960s—might be an inherent feature of all literature, Bakhtin's views held a wide appeal for critics in the decades that followed. In particular, they offered ways of analysing literary texts in terms of the marginalized voices diffused within them, and of assessing the processes of domination and subordination through which they had been suppressed. Bakhtin's ideas also added to the late twentieth-century development of narratology, particularly its investigation of the 'hybridisation' of language in forms such as Free Indirect Discourse, strongly developed by modernist writing early in the twentieth century.

Michel Foucault likewise saw language as an area in which relations of domination and subordination are established, though with less scope for contestation than Bakhtin suggested. Just as 'academic discourse' or 'legal discourse' define for individual disciplines the terms in which knowledge and ideas can be shaped, so for Foucault communication within society as a whole is controlled in any period by general forms of discourse. Subject to unspoken rules and constraints, this discourse controls what it is possible to say, or at any rate to say with authority. Forms of language and 'discursive practice' decide which speakers are empowered and which silenced, which ideas dignified as normal or natural, and which not. Such controls, of course, are not maintained naturally or innocently, but in order to sustain the prevailing political system, strategically supporting the status quo on behalf of its beneficiaries. Thinking of this kind

---

[2] See also pp. 27–8, above.

offered possibilities Eagleton missed in deconstruction: of analysing systems of power, and their shaping of societies, through the study of textual and linguistic forms and strategies.

This offer was taken up in the 1980s and 1990s both by existing critical practices, such as feminism, and in a number of new developments at the time. One of these was postcolonialism, originating largely from the work of Edward Said in *Orientalism* (1978). Working from some of Foucault's principles, and those of the early critic of empire Franz Fanon, Said examined one of the longest-standing discursive practices in the writing of the West: its construction of a sense of the superiority of European civilization through derogatory or caricatured representations of its colonial subjects. Western culture, in this analysis, endowed colonized people with all the negative characteristics—of laziness, irrationality, immorality, or whatever—which it actually most feared in itself. As well as highlighting the role of European literature in constructing this colonized 'Other', and generally in sustaining established systems of power, postcolonial criticism offered influential modes of analysing writing in former colonies, and the frictions between languages, cultures, and identities which contributed to its development.[3]

Foucault's ideas were also a basis for cultural materialism and New Historicism. The latter's historicism was 'new' in its emphases on language and text—on the existence or recoverability of the past only through narratives and representations. It also emphasized the need to study a range of modes of writing in order to establish what two of New Historicism's founding critics, Catherine Gallagher and Stephen Greenblatt, called the 'creative matrices of particular historical cultures' (p. 16). In their view, literary works 'did not spring up from nowhere', but embody 'a whole life-world . . . social energies that circulate very broadly through a culture . . . passing from zones designated as art to zones apparently indifferent or hostile to art'. Assessment of a range of 'expressive possibilities' allows identification of these social energies, and of means used by public institutions—church, monarchy, even the theatre—to direct and contain them (pp. 12–13, 16). Greenblatt's *Renaissance Self-Fashioning* (1980), for example, examined ways individuals are shaped, or manoeuvred into shaping themselves, as subjects: again, in the

---

[3] See also pp. 70 and 82–3, above.

double sense suggested by Althusser, by being made to believe they have an autonomous subjectivity, while actually being positioned subserviently within established political structures.

Whereas New Historicism originated largely in the United States, cultural materialism was more the work of British critics—such as Catherine Belsey and Jonathan Dollimore—though it shared many of the same interests. It differed mostly in its less disillusioned assessment of the machinations of power. New Historicism sustained much of Foucault's pessimism, suggesting that subversion or rebellion were invariably contained within established state structures, possibly even contributing to their ultimate stability. Renaissance drama, for example, showed uprisings occasionally disposing of inadequate individual monarchs, but could never depict the overthrow of the monarchical system itself. Rebellion, shown in this form, ultimately strengthened existing political structures, rather than leading to genuinely radical change. Cultural materialism remained closer to Bakhtin in emphasizing the vitality of conflict, in and beyond literary texts, and the potential of acts of subversion, transgression, or intervention in the dominant discourses of earlier periods—suggesting, by extension, the possibility of challenging the established political order at the present time.

Cultural materialism and New Historicism did have in common an impulse also more widely apparent in the new movements discussed above: a determination to challenge the established category of 'literature', and the canon of 'great works' conventionally held to constitute it. The period had begun with a strong consolidation of this canon. The expansion of universities in the 1960s required redefinition of the subject matter of English literature courses, as well as firmer development of their methods. Definitions of literature consequently narrowed at this time, as Bernard Bergonzi observed, moving away from assumptions earlier in the century that 'works of history, biography, philosophy, and divinity were part of the canon' in favour of concentration on 'the obviously fictive genres, poetry, drama, and the novel' (*Exploding English*, p. 189). Even within a literature thus restricted, further contraction remained necessary. F. R. Leavis's commitment to a 'great tradition' may have been practical as much as intellectual. 'Prompted most of all by the brevity of the three-year degree course taken by his Cambridge students', Chris

Baldick commented, Leavis may have 'simply wanted to ensure that in the short time available for their studies, they should read nothing but the greatest' (p. 153).

Yet as the study of literature continued to develop and diversify in the ways discussed above, definitions of 'the greatest' came to seem less practical than indefensible, or even sinister. Since structuralism supposed the systems or grammars it outlined to be universal, it had every reason to range beyond literature, and no real reason to treat it as a special category. Derrida and deconstruction likewise shifted attention onto writing generally, finding gaps and contradictions inherent in any text, with little distinction between philosophical, literary, or other works in this respect, or in others. Though feminism initially found literature a useful field for studying the stereotypes and influences it sought to criticize, it soon asserted the need to expand or explode a canon established around male priorities and exclusions. Marxist and other left-wing critics were likewise sceptical of ways the canon—and conventional literary study generally—might ascribe universal values to texts which actually served the interests only of a class fraction. Peter Widdowson, for example, complained that criticism, 'while assuming and proclaiming its "descriptiveness", its "disinterestedness", its ideological innocence, has so constituted Literature as to reproduce and naturalise bourgeois ideology as "literary value" ' (p. 3).

Recording New Historicist concerns, in 2000, that the study of literature might 'wall off for aesthetic appreciation only a tiny portion of the expressive range of a culture', Gallagher and Greenblatt were thus extending doubts variously developing within the subject for at least two decades previously (p. 13). Catherine Belsey concluded *Critical Practice* in 1980 wondering 'whether we should continue to speak of *literature* at all' and explaining that she used the term 'reluctantly, "under erasure", as Derrida puts it' (p. 144). It remained similarly under erasure—as an essential but nevertheless unreliable term—in Eagleton's *Literary Theory* in 1983. Emphasizing that 'the present crisis in the field of literary studies is at root a crisis in the definition of the subject itself', Eagleton recommended dropping 'once and for all the illusion that the category "literature" is "objective" . . . literature, in the sense of a set of works of assured and unalterable value, distinguished by certain shared inherent properties, does not exist'. The 'so-called "literary canon", the unquestioned "great tradition" of the "national literature" ' should instead be 'recognized as a *construct*, fashioned by particular people for particular reasons at a certain time' (pp. 214, 10–11). Literary academics, for example, as Chris Baldick suggested, might have particular reason to establish 'the canon of literature upon the principle that the truly literary work is one requiring from its readers a certain labour of interpretation' (Baldick, p. 14).

For all these commentators, literature was at any rate not an extant body of texts to which criticism applied its methodologies, but rather a category of writing which it constitutes and legitimates through these practices themselves. Coinciding with new interests in discursive practices, and in analysing texts within the 'cultural matrix' which produced them, this kind of thinking naturally extended into questions about how, when, and why authors and literary works *had* come to be canonized. The most iconic, 'literary', and 'national' of all English authors, Shakespeare, provided an obvious focus for such enquiries—developed in the collection of essays edited by John Drakakis, *Alternative Shakespeares* (1985), for example, and in Jonathan Dollimore's *Political Shakespeare* (1985), as well as in Gary Taylor's study, *Reinventing Shakespeare* (1990). Each examined how far Shakespeare's reputation might have been owed not to an absolute literary value inherent in his plays, but to the ease with which later societies, especially after the mid-eighteenth century, had been able to use them to consolidate their hierarchies and political structures.

Naturally, thinking of this kind also contributed to wider changes in the study of literature, and its place in the university, later in the century. Some of these had originated well before the 'crisis in the definition of the subject' in the early 1980s. In some aspects, this was less a 'present crisis' than a continuing one, as old as the period itself, and particularly focused at its opening by the work of Raymond Williams. In *The Long Revolution* (1961), Williams declared his central interest to be in 'methods of analysis which, over a range from literature to social institutions, can articulate actual structures of feeling—the meanings and values which are lived in works and relationships—and clarify the processes of historical development through which these structures form and change'. But he also considered that 'there is no academic subject within which the questions I am interested in can be followed through' (pp. 293, ix–x). With the establishment of the influential Birmingham Centre for Contemporary Cultural Studies in 1964, such a discipline was soon in evidence. It developed further in later decades through Williams's own thinking, some of the theories discussed above, and the interests of a generation of academics who had grown up under the influence of television as well as books.

As Chapter 1 discussed, Williams's work also helped to shift the idea of 'culture' away from conventional associations with refined taste and aesthetic sophistication, and towards a definition in which 'it becomes almost identical with our whole common life' (*Culture and Society*, p. 256).[4] Definitions of this kind, and the range of cultural forms and practices considered in Cultural Studies, made it a discipline obviously much broader than literary study, and potentially likely to subsume the latter within its operations. This had occurred to a limited extent by the end of the century. In some universities, the study of literature had moved within, or alongside, new departments in the field of Cultural Studies, or established a new definition for itself as 'English Studies', while academic publishers increasingly directed their output to an area defined as 'Literature and Cultural Studies'. Elsewhere, literature departments continued intact, though most, having gradually added elements of theory to their curricula during the 1980s, went on in the next decade to devote more attention to the historical and cultural matrixes surrounding the texts they studied.

Questions such as Catherine Belsey's, about 'whether we should continue to speak of *literature* at all', or Peter Widdowson's, in *Re-Reading English*, about whether English '*should* have a future as a discrete discipline' (p. 7), thus remained incompletely resolved at the end of the century. Institutional commitment to the subject, and popular acceptance of it, suggested that literary study would retain some separateness, perhaps based around the distinction Baldick emphasized. Literary texts might be distinguished in the way he suggested: as ones particularly requiring, or particulaly repaying, 'a certain labour of interpretation', and so with some claim to greater complexity or multilayeredness than other cultural practices. Even in

---

[4] See pp. 44–5, above.

advocating wider forms of study, neither Raymond Williams nor those sharing his views renounced distinctions between literature and other forms of imaginative writing. In much the same vein as Richard Hoggart in *The Uses of Literacy* (1958), Williams complained about 'bad art' throughout *Culture and Society* (1958, e.g. p. 305), continuing to distinguish it with equal confidence from 'real art' in *The Long Revolution* (p. 336). Forty years later, while insisting on the need to read more widely, Gallagher and Greenblatt still recorded the 'deep gratification' that drew them 'in the first place to the study of literature and art' (p. 9).

Roles remained even for the much-disputed literary canon. Even at the height of the subject's sceptical self-scrutiny in the early 1980s, in *Re-Reading English* Catherine Belsey saw little need to 'reject both the institution of English and the great tradition in their entirety', providing the former was envisaged as 'a site of struggle', and the canon broadened to reflect writing's actual pluralities (Widdowson (ed.), p. 130). Eve Kosofsky Sedgwick also pointed to the canon's usefulness as an object of historical analysis. Texts establishing themselves as centres of interest in any period obviously have particular capacities to reveal the nature of these interests and how they worked, and thus 'the potential to dismantle the impacted foundations upon which a given culture rests' (p. 54). Such thinking offered a new version of the 'test of time' beloved of conventional literary judgement. It suggested a reason to continue studying works defined as 'literature and art', not on account of claims to universal value and immutable aesthetic worth, but because they offered such particular opportunities for questioning a period and its 'foundations'; for identifying forces shaping society and its imagination.

*

However literary study itself withstood the test of time in the twenty-first century, by the 1990s it was already very different, in subject and method, from the discipline students had encountered thirty years or so earlier. Published in 1966, Graham Hough's views in *An Essay on Criticism* help demarcate the scale of the change. Hough was still content to define the subject of literary study around a conventional canon, comprising 'the *Iliad, Hamlet, War and Peace*, etc.'. Of his methods, he remarked that he had 'been at pains to avoid treading on the ground of general aesthetics, linguistics, semantics, psychology or social science' (pp. 9, vi). As he suggested, literature departments at the time generally worked through a canon of great texts, usually running, as Philip Swallow recalls in *Changing Places*, from Beowulf to Virginia Woolf. In terms of method, an intelligent, fairly exclusive attention to these texts was the primary requirement, supplemented by some Leavisite evaluation of their representation of life, and by close attention to their language and stylistic devices, developed through regular exercises in 'practical criticism'.

In the 1990s, on the other hand, students were less likely to find the curriculum stretching all the way from Beowulf to Virginia Woolf, or updated to include Tom Wolfe or Christa Wolf. Overall historical coverage sometimes remained a priority, but individual courses—often chosen from a broad range, reflecting the increasing diversity of the subject—were likely to be focused around particular theories, trends, or concepts, or based on specific historical periods in which various imaginative modes and writing practices could be considered. Recent critical developments often renewed attention to certain periods, the Renaissance and Romantic ages particularly. In offering a relatively uncomplicated set of social structures, in which the emergent pressures of modernity and capitalism could be clearly traced, the former especially attracted the attention of New Historicists. Depicting nature thoroughly infused with poetic imagination, yet also supposedly inviolate, Romantic poetry proved a plentiful source of the gaps and contradictions highlighted by deconstruction.

Even by the 1960s, Hough considered that increasingly rapid change in 'the texture of living experience' had left much pre-twentieth-century English literature 'as remote as the ancient classics' (Plumb (ed.), p. 103). University courses later tended to reflect a growing preference for recent writing—especially in modernist and postmodernist modes, illumined particularly usefully by some of the new language-centred theories. In terms of method, Hough's painstaking exclusions had mostly been replaced, even by the later 1980s, by the contrary conviction offered in *Re-Reading English*—that literary theory's 'intellectual bearings are variously situated in philosophy, linguistics, psychoanalysis and marxism' (Widdowson (ed.), p. 65). Later editions of David Lodge's critical readers—following *20th Century Literary Criticism* in 1972—

confirmed this general expansion and updating of the subject's 'intellectual bearings'. Published in 1988, Lodge's *Modern Criticism and Theory* included sections on formalist, structuralist, and poststructuralist poetics, linguistics, and narratology; on deconstruction; on psychoanalysis; on politics, ideology, and cultural history; on feminism; and on hermeneutics, reception theory, and reader-response (see below). Its last section was devoted to 'cognitive literary scholarship': arguments against the current of post-structuralist thought, and in favour of sustained certitudes in interpretation, based in the case of E. D. Hirsch on qualified re-emphasis of authorial intention.

Significantly, when the contents of Lodge's reader were once again updated in 2000, exactly the same sectional divisions were retained, suggesting that by the last decade of the century the 'bearings' followed by students and critics of literature had developed into a fairly settled map. Richard Bradford used very much the same set of categories in *Introducing Literary Studies* (1996), remarking that these now constituted 'a familiar catalogue of isms and ologies' and that students would find 'a similar list in the contents page of many an introduction to literary theory' (p. xiii). Introductions or anthologies such as Rick Rylance's *Debating Texts* (1987), Raman Selden and Peter Widdowson's *Reader's Guide to Contemporary Literary Theory* (1993), Douglas Tallack's *Critical Theory: A Reader* (1995), or Julie Rivkin and Michael Ryan's *Literary Theory: An Anthology* (1998) did indeed cover much the same areas. To enter and acquire the authority of critical discourse in the 1980s and 1990s, in other words, students had to assimilate a set of well-established discursive practices, drawn from a number of disciplines and a range of theorists. As Chris Baldick reflected, literary study in the later twentieth century had to some extent replaced the conventional canon of works of literature with 'a new canon of constantly-invoked theoretical scriptures', one which had come to be 'granted an equivalent authority as canonical texts' (pp. 200, 204). In this way, the study of literature—at any rate in universities—had moved decisively towards 'the age of *theory*' Raman Selden described.

Often counter-intuitive—or as Norris suggested of deconstruction, an 'affront' to common sense—these new theoretical scriptures were not always easy to learn, or even just to read. Much critical writing and publishing was devoted to guides and anthologies, such as those mentioned above, which made them easier to understand and use. New theories also encouraged the publication of many new readings, applying innovative ideas and methods to established literary texts or fields of study. Work of this kind often showed how far criticism had departed from shared priorities or overall consensus. General acceptance of lists of 'isms and ologies' did not imply much agreement among these ideas and methods themselves. As discussed above, many post-structuralist approaches *were* potentially compatible, and much critical effort in the 1980s and 1990s was devoted to showing how they could be integrated, sometimes along with older methodologies, into enriched, diversified forms of literary study. Yet there were also approaches less susceptible to mutual integration. Lodge showed in *Small World*, often comically, how far some of them had become mutually antipathetic, or just mutually deaf. Critical judgements, studies, and positions towards the end of the century inhabited a set of separate islands, each with its own microclimate of ideas, strategies, and legitimations. These were often self-consciously provisional, and sometimes developed in the course of the analysis itself, without always much referring to the geography of the archipelago as a whole.

In one way, this made literary study, more than ever, an exciting, diverse field of enquiry. In another, as Bernard Bergonzi suggested, it made it by the 1990s simply a 'fissiparous' discipline (*Exploding English*, p. 17). Raman Selden also commented at the time on the lack of an 'emerging consensus which could constitute a new paradigm' (*Cambridge History*, p. 10). Without this 'new paradigm', those lists of isms and ologies represented about as much consensus as literary study could claim in the 1990s: an agreement about where fissures in this fissiparous subject occurred; perhaps also that the major earthquake which had caused them was over. Widdowson indicated as much in *A Reader's Guide to Contemporary Literary Theory*, in defining the end of the 1970s and the early 1980s as the 'moment of theory' (Selden and Widdowson, p. 6). As he suggested, the time around 1980 was the 'moment' when established assumptions were challenged most radically, with implications then gradually assimilated within critical practice over succeeding years. By the end of the century, this process was clear enough in overall outline to suggest several connections with the wider life and thinking of the times.

In the pattern and timing of its principal developments, literary theory offered a kind of model, or portrait in miniature, of the evolution of postmodern thought outlined in Chapter 2. Strongly influencing critical thinking in the 1960s, Leavisite commitments to 'life'—and to ways literature and criticism might contribute to its conduct—generally shared the consensual, post-war faith in social and civic improvement still widely in evidence at this time. The continuation of Leavisite and other liberal forms of critical thinking as far as the mid-1970s, or beyond, in one way confirmed Eagleton's judgement of a 'customary time-lapse' in bringing ideas across the Channel. At the time, it sometimes seemed part of a customary English reluctance to accept imported or Continental thinking at all. Just as innovations in modernist or postmodernist literature were often considered foreign to an English literary tradition, there were commentators in the 1980s and later who resisted new theories on the grounds that they were inherently alien to liberal, empirical modes of English criticism.

But in another way, new theories can be seen to have arrived tardily because it was not until the later 1970s that the situation in England entirely demanded them. The kind of political disillusion experienced in France by the end of the 1960s accumulated more gradually, across the Channel, during the following decade. It was only by the end of the 1970s that it seemed as if the post-war consensus, or Raymond Williams's 'Long Revolution'[5]—or even Enlightenment ideas of improvement more generally—might be impossible to sustain any longer. As in France a decade earlier, thinking which had recently still been much engaged with social and political life departed into a self-enclosed intellectual sphere instead —into linguistically centred scepticisms and assertions of the radical autonomy of the literary text. Looking back in *Nice Work*, Lodge describes this shift of emphasis and the 'moment of theory' occurring around 1980 as a 'revolution . . . like the sixties all over again', but 'in a new, more austerely intellectual key' (pt. 1, ch. 2). Yet the political climate of the 1980s, as discussed earlier, did not long allow critical enquiry to remain altogether austere, aloofly intellectual, or

[5] See p. 31, above.

concerned only with free-floating signifiers. Towards the end of the decade, and in the 1990s, new critical movements continued to follow the pattern of contemporary thinking more generally, returning from the more radical modes of postmodern scepticism towards qualified forms of political and historical engagement.

A survey of literary theory also suggests how widely its development shared in the democratization of late twentieth-century life discussed in Chapter 1—a connection obviously clearest in the work of feminism, postcolonialism, and Queer Theory. As Gallagher and Greenblatt concluded at the end of the century, movements of this kind had developed the interests of 'groups that in many colleges and universities had hitherto been marginalized, half hidden, or even entirely excluded from the professional study of literature' (p. 11). While these movements helped to open up the canon towards the interests of the whole population, Cultural Studies also contributed to a kind of democracy among texts and imaginative forms themselves, introducing to university curricula critically neglected genres such as detective stories, science fiction, popular romance, and television drama. Growing democratization was apparent even at the level of methodology. Many of the developments discussed above contributed to what Roland Barthes described in 1968 as 'the birth of the reader . . . at the cost of the death of the Author' (*Image–Music–Text*, p. 148). Wimsatt and Beardsley, the New Critics, structuralist, and many post-structuralist theories all added weight to Barthes's conclusion that 'a text is not a line of words releasing a single "theological" meaning (the "message" of the Author-God) but a multi-dimensional space', held together in the apprehension of the reader (p. 146). Without a single, exalted figure determining the meaning of a text, readers themselves became lords and ladies of the manner in which literature was understood and enjoyed—a kind of interpretive democracy, endowing ordinary citizens with greater freedoms and responsibilities in their reading.

Some of these were consolidated by reception theory and reader-response criticism—areas related only tangentially to other established 'isms and ologies' represented in Lodge's readers. Reception theory developed instead out of hermeneutics and the work of Roman Ingarden and Hans Robert Jauss in phenomenology—in particular, from its emphases on the nature of perception and the role of the perceiver in deriving meaning from experience. Such thinking contributed to Wolfgang Iser's conclusion that texts have less concrete existence as 'the words on the page' than through readers' constructions of them. Processes involved were discussed by Iser in *The Act of Reading* (1978), and in other studies exploring conventions and expectations which readers bring to their experience of individual works of literature. Stanley Fish further developed this kind of analysis in *Is There a Text in this Class?* (1980). If literary works exist primarily through the reading process, he suggested, then criticism should focus less on what they mean than on what they do, and how they do it—on an 'affective stylistics' tracing how they function, line by line, as an accumulating experience for their readers.

Such emphases obviously risked moving criticism back towards an extreme subjectivism—towards the reliance on individual feelings and reactions which Wimsatt and Beardsley's 'Affective Fallacy' had warned against thirty years earlier. Fish dealt with this problem by explaining that readers' reactions are in practice constrained by more or less explicit membership of 'interpretive communities'. At work most obviously in academic institutions, such groupings establish patterns of shared expectation and conventional interpretive practice which restrict the range of experiences texts can offer. Though sometimes seeming to promise ever-greater freedoms, reader-response criticism thus favoured plural, polysemic textual possibilities less enthusiastically than Roland Barthes in his celebrations of 'the birth of the reader'. It nevertheless suggested further ways of liberating the critical practices of groups Gallagher and Greenblatt saw as previously marginalized within the academy, treating their readings not as subsidiary to some objective norm, but as the work of interpretive communities as valid and worthy of development as any other. In this way, and in further rejecting the 'theology' of author-oriented interpretation, reader-response criticism did contribute to general liberalization of literary study in the period. Graham Hough still found 'a vague odour of old port and oak panelling' surrounding literary education in the 1960s (Plumb (ed.), p. 98). Stale airs of the senior common room were gradually dispelled in later years by opening critical practice towards the interests of the population as a whole, rather than those of the 'small minority' upon whom Leavis and others had thought 'the discerning appreciation of art and literature' to depend.

An obvious irony in this process was that it risked remaining invisible or inaccessible to the wider populace supposedly its beneficiary. Bernard Bergonzi suggested in *Exploding English* (1990) that at the end of the 1950s 'criticism was still part of general intellectual discourse; thirty years later it has become a form of academic professionalism' (p. 71). His recollection may not have been entirely accurate. In 1961, in his essay 'To Criticise the Critic', T. S. Eliot was already pointing to a gap opening up between academic and other forms of commentary on literature. But it was a gap which certainly seemed to widen rapidly in succeeding decades, while the role of publicly recognized author-critics of Eliot's kind apparently declined. Chris Baldick commented in the 1990s on how rarely, compared to earlier periods, a 'leading critic' was 'a leader in poetry or in fiction' (p. 14). Patrick Parrinder similarly warned, around this time, that 'the split between creator and critic has never seemed wider' (p. 346).

Like Bergonzi, Baldick also emphasized 'accelerating incompatibility' between 'the public marketplace of literary consumption in which the book-review and the literary biography have favoured places' and 'the enclosed space of the university': in general, between 'the "public" and the academic varieties of criticism and literary theory' (p. 6). As Lodge's characters in *Nice Work* consider, in other words, there seemed every possibility that where 'Derrida's critique of metaphysics . . . Lacan's psychoanalytic theory . . . Foucault's theory' were concerned—or other matters academics 'argue about and read about and write about endlessly'—'ninety-nine point nine per cent of the population couldn't give a monkey's' (pt. 4, ch. 1). By the end of the century, this possibility seriously concerned the Council for College and University English. Issues of its newsletter in 2000 (*CCUE News*) worried that apart from the Colin MacCabe affair in 1980, the subject's huge collisions of ideas had scarcely been noticed outside the 'enclosed space' of universities—small worlds apparently disseminating their understanding of literature and culture much less widely or usefully than they might.

Within the 'marketplace of literary consumption', there were areas where this did seem to be the case. Roland Barthes admitted in 1968 that despite his theories, the author was far from dead but 'still reigns in . . . interviews, magazines'. This helped to ensure that 'the image of literature to be found in ordinary culture is tyrannically centred on the author, his person, his life, his tastes, his passions' (*Image–Music–Text*, p. 143). Thirty years later, this reign had still not much changed, as any comparison of newspaper book reviews across the period could confirm. An *Observer* review of *The Great Fortune* on 24 January 1960, for example, gave an outline of Olivia Manning's plot and characters, described as 'a splendid gallery of eccentrics', praised the accuracy of her depiction of wartime Bucharest, and explained that 'one feels that the author is deeply involved yet artistically objective'. It also judged that the novel's mixture of exciting story and literary qualities might offer 'caviare to the general', adding 'who on earth doesn't like caviare if he can get it?' (p. 22). Like criticism generally, *Observer* reviews forty years later were significantly democratized in tone and assumptions: less likely to suppose that all readers were male, likely to be interested in vague impressions 'one feels', and accustomed to caviare and quotations from *Hamlet*. But they remained just as focused on issues of character and plot, or of authorial life, tastes, and passions: apparently untroubled, on the whole, by any of the problems recent critical thinking had introduced to these areas.

Yet book reviews particularly require straightforward, consumer-oriented description, and are not the likeliest area to reflect new theories and changing critical practices. Evidence of the latter's wider effects was more apparent elsewhere. Universities were after all less enclosed or exclusive spaces at the end of the century than in the 1960s, with student numbers more than quadrupling since 1965. Growing incorporation of theoretical issues within literature courses after the 1980s ensured that they reached rather more of the population than the 0.1 per cent Lodge suggested in *Nice Work*. Terry Eagleton's *Literary Theory: An Introduction* alone had sold over 100,000 copies in the United Kingdom by the end of the century, helped by Eagleton's lucid, witty exposition, and it was certainly consulted more widely still in libraries. The high proportion of former students who went on to work in education or the media ensured further dissemination of new critical thinking among a general reading public. Along with feminist and postcolonial ideas, in particular, critical terms such as 'deconstruction' often joined the postmodern vocabulary which Patricia Waugh recorded finding even in the popular press by the 1990s. It was probably in literary-critical versions, in fact, that postmodern vocabulary and thinking reached its widest audience by the end of the century. Though a huge majority of the population may have continued not to give a monkey's for Derrida, Lacan, or Foucault themselves, their ideas nevertheless—gradually, and much in the manner of any new thinking—came to exert an influence on the outlook and on the reading habits of the age.

This was extended not only by a general increase in numbers attending university, but more specifically by the high proportion of authors—novelists especially—who were among them, often as students in literature, arts, and humanities departments. Increasing numbers of authors were also involved in university work as teachers, as writers in residence, or in running creative writing courses. An obvious consequence was in the growing popularity of campus novels.[6] Several of these followed David Lodge's *Changing Places* in making contemporary literary theories and critical practices a centre of their attention—Tom Sharpe's *The Great Pursuit* (1977), for example, or Howard Jacobson's *Coming from Behind* (1983). A university teacher and critic as well as a novelist, like Lodge, Malcolm Bradbury also incorporated critical issues into much of his fiction—through parodic allusions to Russian formalism in *Rates of Exchange* (1983), for example, or to postmodern thinking in *Doctor Criminale* (1992). Ironically, given its doubts about public interest in figures such as Derrida, Lodge's campus trilogy itself reached many more readers even than Eagleton's *Literary Theory*. Nearly 350,000 copies of *Changing Places* had been sold in the United Kingdom by the end of the century, with *Small World* and *Nice Work* not much less popular. This ensured that concepts discussed in this chapter, and the broad pattern of their development, were at least loosely familiar to a broad reading public. Lodge's example also suggested that, contrary to Parrinder's worries about growing gaps between creator and critic, the two functions were sometimes closer than ever previously. While disseminating new theories in his critical anthologies, Lodge was writing imaginatively about them, almost simultaneously, in his novels.

Interest in contemporary critical theory also extended widely

[6] See also pp. 403–4, below.

beyond campus fiction. A. S. Byatt's narrator in *The Biographer's Tale* (2000) is actually in flight from the campus, overcome by 'post-structuralist semiotics . . . Foucault (or Lacan or Derrida or Bakhtin)' (p. 114). Characters in Byatt's *Possession* (1992) are similarly, though less painfully, aware of recent critical thinking. Other novelists exploring or referring to this thinking in the course of their fiction included John Fowles, Margaret Drabble, Elaine Feinstein, Michèle Roberts, Christine Brooke-Rose, and Julian Barnes, and it received further attention in some of Tom Stoppard's drama—in *Arcadia* (1993) and *Indian Ink* (1995) particularly. Several authors also examined the new theories in critical essays or other writing. Peter Ackroyd's *Notes for a New Culture* (1976), for example, discussed at length the implications of Lacan and Derrida for English writing, and of 'the emergence of LANGUAGE as the content of literature and as the form of knowledge' (p. 9).

For several other novelists, areas of recent critical thinking became partly symbiotic with their fiction, further confirming that the role of author-critic Baldick mentioned had not altogether vanished from the later twentieth century. Jeanette Winterson and Angela Carter, for example, each developed feminist thinking extensively in essays and commentary as well as throughout their novels. Salman Rushdie, in critical writing collected in *Imaginary Homelands* (1991) and *Step across This Line* (2002), or Caryl Phillips, in *A New World Order* (2002), likewise contributed strongly to the emergence of postcolonial thinking, also in many ways embodied and exemplified in their fiction. Though less explicitly, by the later 1980s and 1990s the work of many novelists showed further evidence of the influence of recent theory, or of its coalescence with the thinking and literary idioms of a postmodern age more generally. Authors such as Ackroyd, Barnes, Byatt, Graham Swift, or Lawrence Norfolk, for example, emphasized in various ways the provisional nature of language's representation of the world, and the unreliability or opacity of any construction of it in narrative, text, or history.

Though such emphases were most evident in the novel, they were also apparent in what might be called 'campus poetry'. Few poets in the period wrote directly about university life, but many were long involved in it as academics and teachers. Influences and effects of new critical ideas were sometimes apparent in their work as a result—in the writing of Christopher Middleton, for example, or Donald Davie. The clearest examples appeared in the work of poets following J. H. Prynne, whose own critical interests produced illuminating commentary on Saussure, though limited approval of theorists who followed him. Poets of the 'Cambridge School' loosely associated with Prynne were nevertheless strongly concerned with 'language as the content of literature and as the form of knowledge'. More enthusiastically than in other parts of the Cambridge academic world, their work often embraced and exemplified the more linguistically centred forms of critical thinking dominant in the last decades of the century.

Often abstract and counter-intuitive, this thinking offered authors little in the way of direct or practical advice, and the commentators quoted earlier were obviously right, in that way, to emphasize a growing gap between creator and critic late in the century. Yet in the other ways suggested, creative writing and critical theory also entered—on occasion—into interrelations whose directness and intimacy was largely new in literary history. This was part of a more general move during the period towards an 'image of literature' both broader yet more sophisticated than in many earlier ones. Shifting patterns of demand and readership within 'the marketplace of literary consumption', however, were a much stronger influence on this move than literary theory and new critical ideas themselves. These market and consumer forces are discussed in the next chapter.

4

A Golden Age? Readers, Authors, and the Book Trade

I. The More Common Reader

> No common person reads a book.
> Your telly's done for all that guff.
>
> (John Whitworth, 'The Middle-
> Sized Poem', 1989)

It hadn't, as it turned out. Yet the appeal of print culture was often doubted, naturally enough, in an age increasingly dominated by images and mass media, and eventually by other new forms of leisure technology. In influential 1960s studies such as *Understanding Media* (1964), the Canadian theorist Marshall McLuhan suggested that the cultural centrality of books and print, globally, might be nearing its end. The English critic George Steiner also wondered at the time if 'an historical era of verbal primacy' might be giving way under media and other pressures (p. 13). Concerns of this kind were sharply focused, early in the period, by the emergence of a mass tele-vision audience in England during the 1950s, especially following coverage of the Coronation, watched by 20 million people in 1953. 'Before June 2 that year' A. S. Byatt remarks in her novel *The Virgin in the Garden* (1978), many people 'had never seen a television broadcast'. Byatt also shows how quickly the 'obtrusive screen' reshaped the living room at the time, drawing attention and conver-sation irresistibly around itself (pp. 237–8). Rapid sales of television sets soon followed. By the time the commercial channel, ITV, began broadcasting two years later, the number of licences had doubled, to four and a half million, and half the population could watch at home. By the end of the 1950s, there were more than ten million licences: 90 per cent of the population were viewers by 1962, for an average of two and a half hours per day. With the advent of BBC2 in 1964, colour broadcasting in 1967, and Channel Four in 1982, daily viewing increased steadily, to an average of three and a half hours in the later 1980s. By that time, 98 per cent of households had a television, and 80 per cent a video recorder, with as many as 375 million video films borrowed annually. By the end of the 1990s, 40 per cent of homes had access to satellite, cable, and digital broadcasting as well, further expanding the small screen's influence in almost every living room, and on the attention of the later twentieth century generally.

Even by 1960, the Society of Authors saw this influence creating a 'a new and dangerous situation' for literature, and a particular threat for the stage (*Author* (Autumn), p. 99). In a survey prepared for the Society three years later, Richard Findlater identified what seemed clear signs of a decline in the reading habit. One of these was the demise of the circulating libraries. At work since the mid-eighteenth century, and particularly popular since the 1930s, these libraries had offered access to a wide range of reading material, mostly fiction, in return for a yearly subscription, or in the case of more modest libraries, for as little as twopence per volume per week. Around 200 million volumes continued to be issued annually in this way at the end of the 1950s. W. H. Smith's library still had 280 branches and 60,000 subscribers, but falling interest forced its closure in 1961: Boots soon followed, and the last of the circulating libraries closed in 1966. At the time and later, the Booksellers Association also worried that the influence of television might be changing society's whole relationship with books and reading, steadily displacing them from popular attention. 'Those who only look and listen are far better informed and knowledgeable citizens than the most voracious reader of 50 years ago', the *Bookseller* warned in the late 1970s. As a result, there might be little reason 'to assume that the child of our time will approach the book with the same reverence and awe as a child of even 40 years ago' (Dec. 1977, p. 3132). With the demand for both information and entertainment increasingly fulfilled by computers and television, the Publishers Association worried in the early 1980s that 'the future of the book itself is questioned' and that 'the oldest means of mass-communication in our society' might be growing obsolete (Oakeshott and Bradley, p. 3). During the 1990s, the need to 'approach a book' was further diminished by games packages, educational and other programmes, and eventually by Internet access available through home computers, present in a quarter of homes by the middle of the decade, and nearer half by its end.

It was often suggested that if the future of the book was in question, the publishing industry might itself be partly to blame. Richard Findlater's 1963 survey, *What are Writers Worth?*, warned of its 'anarchic conservatism' (p. 16); Michael Lane's *Books and Publishers* (1980) considered that it was 'gravely ill' (p. 128); and John Feather's *History of British Publishing* concluded in 1988 that publishing had been in 'a continual state of crisis' for the previous thirty years. Feather nevertheless added that it would be 'difficult to find a time in the last five hundred years when that would not have been true' (pp. 221, 224). Publishing did go through a particularly serious crisis in the 1970s, with consequences discussed in Section II of this chapter. But for much of the period it managed to offer readers what was in many ways an improving service. In particular, the number of new titles published in Britain each year increased steadily, often astonishingly. The *Bookseller* recorded around 18,000 of these in 1960, 24,000 in 1970, 36,000 in 1980, and 47,000 in 1990, with numbers rising even more sharply during the following decade, and more than doubling by its end.

This output left British readers in an unusually privileged position. Of around 900,000 new books published annually worldwide in the 1990s, 10 per cent came from the United Kingdom. With about a quarter of the population of the United States, Britain produced very nearly the same number of titles. By the mid-1990s, this offered readers in Britain a choice of around 600,000 books in print, with up to 100,000 new titles added annually by British publishers alone. Rising output, of course, might have indicated feverish activity rather than real health. In the difficult years of the 1970s, with average sales of individual titles falling to around 300 copies, there were warnings of 'surfeit' and 'suffocation' and of a need 'to curtail the industry's over-production' (Sutherland, p. x). Yet expansion continued unchecked in the years of recovery that followed. A *Bookseller* survey, *Book Publishing in Britain*, concluded in 1995 that it gave evidence of 'the continuing relevance of the book as a valuable and valued package' and of an industry 'remarkably resilient and capable of adaptation' (Barbanneau et al., p. v).

There were also many signs that the book trade eventually managed to adapt to conditions—and profit from technologies—once thought to threaten its very existence. The trade quickly realized, for instance, that mass media might distract from books, but could also help to sell them. During the 1960s, the *Bookseller* regularly noted radio programmes likely to create interest in particular titles. Television's still greater sales potential was confirmed by the BBC's dramatization of *The Forsyte Saga* in 1968. The first of many prestigious 'classic serials', often based on straightforwardly adaptable nineteenth- or early twentieth-century realist fiction, it helped to sell 150,000 copies of the Heinemann edition of John Galsworthy's novel-sequence, and eventually one and a half million of the multi-volume Penguin version. In the 1970s, the National Book League began to co-ordinate trade promotions with the media: thereafter, film and TV 'tie-in' sections appeared in most bookshops. By the mid-1980s, surveys suggested that as many as 22 per cent of book-buyers had been influenced by some connection between their chosen volume and television.

In less direct ways, too—contrary to early fears of its influence—television may have added to the appeal of reading.[1] The central position of a television set in every living room ensured that fictional worlds were more easily and immediately available than at any time in history, and that late twentieth-century life was daily drenched in narrative. One result—as commentators such as Jean Baudrillard warned—was an attenuation or fictionalizing of reality, swathed in ever-thickening fabrics of images. But another may have been an increasing appetite for the imaginary in all its forms, print included. New media influences also tended to highlight the particular nature of the imaginative experience reading offered. Of those questioned in surveys at the end of the century, 25 per cent felt that the counter-attraction of television and computers actually concentrated their

---

[1] Television's particular relations with the theatre are discussed on pp. 383–7, below.

attention on reading. And 50 per cent acknowledged that television offered only a form of 'chilling'—recuperative inertia—compared to the closer attention they devoted to reading. As the Irish novelist William Trevor suggested, writing in the *New Review* (Summer, 1978), reading acquired an imaginative privacy and intensity that 'may not before have been as rare, or as valuable' in periods less fraught with competition from other media, or with 'noisy, flagrant . . . jostle and buzz' in general (p. 69).

New technologies offered more straightforward benefits to the publishing industry. At the start of the period, laboriously set metal type was already being replaced by cheaper printing from rubber plates. Offset lithograph and film-setting later replaced letterpress altogether. Printruns of 40,000 had once been required by Penguin to cover set-up expenses and keep unit costs at a low level: by 1978, 1,000 copies had become a viable figure. Other production costs continued to fall later in the period. Computer typesetting, usually from floppy disks supplied by the author, reduced expenses from the mid-1980s. Savings on typesetting and printing were also made by sending work abroad. Cheaper reprints further reduced the need for long print runs, avoiding the costs of warehousing stock tied up in publishers' backlists. By the end of the century, so-called 'Just-in-Time' printing—able to produce even a handful of copies cheaply and quickly—offered still better opportunities of matching production and demand.

New technologies eventually helped book selling as well as production, particularly in dealing with problems of distribution. These were compounded by the rapidly growing numbers of titles in print, as well as the individual needs of between 3,000 and 4,000 major bookshops nationwide, along with many smaller outlets. Even by 1960, the book trade had scarcely recovered from the loss in the London Blitz of the comprehensively stocked wholesaler Simpkin Marshall, obliging bookshops to deal directly with as many as 200 individual publishers instead. A relatively low number of titles, along with cheap labour and postage, disguised problems for a time, but the industry seemed unable or even unwilling to solve them completely. In 1978, the Publishers Association was still complaining that the book trade was too complex, and produced and stocked too many different products, to be able 'to benefit as much as some other industries from sophisticated modern management techniques and methods' (*Bookseller* (Feb.), p. 1446). It did in the end. Introduced in 1967–8, International Standard Book Numbers (ISBNs) eventually allowed books to be bar-coded, improving distribution and inventorying. A narrowing range of publishers, and improved contacts with them—especially through teleordering, introduced in 1979—allowed most bookshops in the 1980s to obtain almost any title within twenty-four hours, rather than weeks or even months needed previously. Distribution was further improved during the 1990s by electronic point-of-sale tills, electronic data interchange, and computerised stock-monitoring.

Book selling was transformed in other ways in the latter decades of the century. Bookshops had struggled in the late 1950s and 1960s, when costs and wages were rising, but prices fairly static. Difficulties continued in the 1970s, average profits of only 4.5 per cent forcing many bookshops to close, or to move away from High Street locations. Problems were also caused by the shops themselves. Paul Hamlyn was eventually one of the period's most successful publishers, instrumental in expanding a mass market for books, but when addressing the Society of Young Publishers in 1960, he pointed out that most people were simply 'terrified of going into bookshops' (Norrie, p. 113). Richard Findlater confirmed in 1963 that many potential readers considered bookshops simply 'out of bounds, the precinct of another class': an impression which 'unwelcoming and unimaginative' managements did little to dispel (*What are Writers Worth?*, p. 17). There were exceptions. From the late 1940s, Tony Godwin had attempted to make his Better Books chain 'bright and unfusty . . . beguilingly attractive' and where possible a social centre with a coffee bar, poetry readings, and other literary events (Norrie, p. 206). Though financial problems forced Better Books to close in 1974, its example was followed in the next decade by the new bookselling chains Dillons and Waterstones. Each re-established well-stocked, browser-friendly shops on High Street sites—usually with long opening hours, knowledgeable staff, and regular author-events and readings.

The chains rapidly enlarged the market: by the mid-1990s, they had nearly 200 shops between them, and had increased turnover in the book trade by 63 per cent. Along with W. H. Smith, with 450

Fig. 3. Foyles bookshop in February 1960,
and a branch of Waterstones in the 1990s.

shops nationwide, they accounted for £710 million of book business annually by that time—a small lead over independent booksellers, gradually increasing later in the decade. In 1978, a government Prices Commission had warned that publishing's successful survival depended on 'widening the whole market for books and moving beyond the implicit assumption that book readers, of necessity, represent a limited clientele' (*Bookseller* (July), p. 22). This was what the chains achieved, the *Guardian* describing Waterstones as 'the bookshop that made Britain enjoy books again' (2 Mar. 2001, p. 4). New tactics gradually spread to the independent bookshops, and were extended still further by the arrival of the US giant, Borders, in 1997. Coffee bars, soft furnishings, and the generally languid atmosphere in new 'lifestyle' shops made book purchase late in the century seem almost a social event, not a socially exclusive one.

There were in any case more and more ways in which books could be easily purchased, without even leaving home. Book clubs attracted a wider membership after 1968, when they were allowed for the first time to sell new titles simultaneously with their first publication. Membership rose to around a million by 1978, and to more than two and a half million in the 1990s, encouraged by some clubs withdrawing the usual requirement of an annual minimum purchase. Book clubs accounted for between 5 and 10 per cent of all sales by this time, their high advertising costs balanced by claiming discounts of as much as 75 per cent on bulk orders from publishers. Book buying was made even easier in the late 1990s by the Internet. A rise in users from one and a half million in 1996 to as many as fifteen million by the end of the century—58 per cent of them, surveys showed, educated to A level or above—provided a good market for book selling, exploited by Amazon.com and a number of other mail-order companies. Internet shopping offered discounts, a personalized service, and electronic searches which made available a huge range of titles. It also gave purchasers the chance to post comments and assessments on the web site for the interest of other readers. Rather than only distracting from the written word, the Internet made book buying in many ways more engaging and interactive than ever before.

Congenial, in the end, for book buyers, the period was promising almost throughout for book borrowers. Declining membership of circulating libraries in the 1960s was probably caused less by competition from television than from a rapidly improving—and free—public library service. Local authority spending on libraries doubled during the decade, and annual borrowing rose from 400 million volumes to around 600 million. Comparing favourably with other European countries—such as France, with only 45 million withdrawals annually—this level was sustained for much of the rest of the century, despite retrenchment in the 1970s. Seventy-five million books were in stock in 1960, and 132 million by 1995, with 12 million being added annually. Over half the adult population borrowed books in the early 1990s, and a quarter did so every three or four weeks. Fiction accounted for more than half of these issues. Though titles borrowed belonged overwhelmingly to the thriller, romance, and crime genres, the figures did indicate—even independently of bookshop sales—that on average each member of the population read about six novels annually. By the later 1990s, however, loan figures were in quite sharp decline, by around 17 per cent since the beginning of the decade. Underfunding by successive Tory governments had damaged the library service, and the newly relaxed atmosphere of bookshops made them more attractive places in which to browse or even read at length. But reduced borrowing was generally attributed to the Internet: its effortless delivery of information to home computers could easily outdo, in scale and convenience, almost anything conventionally offered by library books. A *Bookseller* survey in 1999 noted that 670,000 pages of new information were being added to the Internet every day, with the expectation that 'within the next three years more will be published on the web than has been published in print since the invention of the printing press' (Gasson, p. 12).

Established publishers themselves, of course, were among those beginning to use the Internet extensively. In the mid-1990s, *Book Publishing in Britain* still considered that 'no one in the UK market is quite clear yet how to make serious money out of delivery down the line' (Barbanneau et al, p. 58), but there were indications of change. By the end of the century, 14 per cent of publishing worked electronically, with an expectation that this would rise to 35 per cent within three years. Many academic journals were posted on the net, to be downloaded either free of charge or through passwords released to subscribers. Academic publishers such as Oxford University Press already produced dictionaries and encyclopaedias in CD-Rom form —its capacity and search-facility ideal, like the web, for information retrieval—and were contemplating electronic delivery for minority-interest textbooks and monographs. In the field of imaginative literature, too, authors such as Frederick Forsyth and Stephen King tried placing sections of their novels on the web, to be accessed either free of charge or in return for a fee or voluntary contribution. Early in 2001, HarperCollins announced publication of the first complete novel to be available in Britain in electronic as well as printed form, with a hundred other titles planned to follow. A few years earlier, the French book chain FNAC had begun to experiment with methods of 'print-on-demand', able to produce immediately, from disk or a web-accessed data archive, a bound copy of any available volume requested by a customer. Such developments had huge implications —affirmative ones, in terms of keeping unlimited numbers of titles 'in print'—for publishing and bookshops in the future, likely in each case to become more and more 'virtual' in methods of delivery and customer contact.

This 'virtual' future also had the potential to transform imaginative literature—much more radically than other new technologies recently exploited by publishers, which had affected the format of the book in only a couple of instances. 'Audiobooks'—cassette tapes of readings or dramatizations of literature—grew increasingly popular, bought by 13 per cent of the population by the 1990s, perhaps as an antidote to the decade's lengthening traffic jams. Cheaper colour printing helped the graphic novel—pictorial in form, with added speech- or thought-bubbles, cartoon-style—to achieve some popularity by the end of the century, though never on the scale it enjoyed abroad. A computer-delivered electronic novel, on the other hand, had the potential to accompany its text with images, static or cinematic, and to offer readers a choice of variant, parallel or extended aspects of the story. Children's publishing—such as Penguin's interactive 'Fighting Fantasy' series, accompanied by computer software —had begun to develop such possibilities. But their exploitation, even at the start of the twenty-first century, still seemed some distance away in writing for adults. Novelists at the time had only just begun to recognize the literary potential even of e-mails—Helen

Fielding's popular *Bridget Jones's Diary* (1996), for example, using them to facilitate changes in setting and point of view, and as a modern, instantaneous form of epistolary romance. In the absence in Britain of the kind of hand-held print readers available in the United States, HarperCollins's plans for electronic novels still envisaged them being bought from booksellers and read on home computers—not even, for copyright reasons, printed out in bookshops, or directly sent through the Web. By the end of the century, in other words, computers and the Internet had still not much influenced imaginative literature, either in opening up new creative possibilities for authors, or even in terms simply of accessing text. A computer age sometimes seemed a less immediate influence on literature than on criticism, likely to be starved, in assessing this period, of most of the authorial letters and manuscript drafts once a mainstay of its research.

At any rate, where leisure reading rather than information delivery was concerned, convenience as a physical object still provided, throughout the 1990s, a strong component in the book's continuing appeal. As *Book Publishing in Britain* concluded in 1995, books were simply easier to read for long periods of time, and convenient objects in general: 'you can pick them up and put them down, you can skim through them, you can put them on a shelf and they look good, you can throw them about and you can read them on the beach. And they don't need batteries' (Barbanneau et al., p. 9). In the growing 'jostle and buzz' of the later twentieth century, such versatility allowed books to retain niches for themselves—in bed, on the beach, in the bath, on the bus, in the tube—still mostly beyond the reach of other media. In this and other ways, reading continued to fend off competition from other forms of entertainment. Only 58 per cent of the population had claimed it as a leisure activity in 1980, but 70 per cent did so in 2000, with surveys—though unreliable in their separation of newspapers from other forms—suggesting that reading occupied adults on average for between four and six hours per week.

There was also evidence that books were taken increasingly seriously, much as William Trevor suggested. Reading Groups discussing literary interests grew rapidly in the late 1990s, with around 50,000 members by the end of the decade. Continuing interest in the book, such figures suggested, resulted not only from better bookshops and libraries, but longer-term changes in public attitudes—even the appearance of a new kind of public, reshaped by steady expansion in education ever since the Education Act of 1944. As Raymond Williams noted, a 'majority book-reading public' had come into existence, for the first time, only at the end of the 1950s.[2] In the early 1960s, Richard Findlater anticipated a 'much vaster reading public' emerging from the extension of the tertiary education system far beyond the affluent minority it had reached before the war (*What are Writers Worth?*, p. 27). Already increasing at the time, student numbers reached 200,000 by 1970, and around a million by the 1990s. Expansion on this scale obviously greatly increased demand for books used in education itself: significantly, what became one of the country's biggest booksellers, Dillons, was initially set up as an academic bookshop by London University. The expansion fostered more widely, too, and at an early age, the habit of buying and using books, as well as patterns of study and discussion which sometimes continued into later life, as the appearance of the Reading Groups suggested.

Growth in higher education may also have contributed to general shifts in reading preferences and literary expectations. Virginia Woolf's *To the Lighthouse* (1927), for example, sold an average of 1,400 copies during each of its first five years of publication. By 1980, 30,000 copies were being bought annually—many, probably, by secondary school pupils, students, or university graduates. What had been a minority taste during the modernist period, in other words, broader education helped to make a best-seller. Library lending figures gave similar evidence. Though hardly comparing with loans of thrillers and romances, Thomas Hardy and Jane Austen novels were borrowed a quarter of a million times annually, towards the end of the century. Even the more challenging fiction of Henry James and James Joyce found substantial numbers of borrowers each year. As well as expanding the overall demand for books, broader education had accustomed a wider public, by the end of the century, to the demands sometimes made by books themselves.

More attractive bookshops, better-stocked libraries, and a more fully educated readership would surely have been enough to guarantee the book's survival, even in an age of multiplying distractions.

<hr />

[2] See p. 44, above.

Much the most important factor nevertheless remains to be discussed: the paperback revolution, which transformed publishing, reading, and culture generally in the latter half of the century. In some ways, of course, it was hardly a thoroughgoing revolution. The paperback format already existed in the nineteenth century, and was widely used abroad throughout the twentieth. But its real impact within Britain dated only from Allen Lane's foundation of Penguin Books in 1935, and even then was partly delayed until his new company's jubilee, in 1960. The *Author* in the spring of that year continued to consider paperback publishing in terms of a recent 'revolution', appealing to 'the newly-leisured masses' (pp. 52, 55). Findlater's survey recalled that paperbacks had been 'no more than a minor sideline in 1948, a promising trend in 1954'. By the early 1960s, on the other hand, Findlater defined them as 'the most dynamic factor in the publishing world', radically changing conventional relations between writers, publishers, librarians, and booksellers through their 'sheer pace and volume in the expansion of publishing *and* reading' (*What are Writers Worth?*, p. 12). Victory in the *Lady Chatterley's Lover* trial[3] late in 1960 had been excellent publicity for Penguin, and a milestone in the company's development. The huge sales of the Penguin edition of Lawrence's novel demonstrated not only changing moral and social assumptions at the start of the 1960s, but a shift in the market for reading material, and the paperback's dynamic new potential to exploit it.

This continued to develop during and after the decade. At the beginning of 1960, fewer than 6,000 paperback titles were available; ten years later, there were 37,000. By 1975, 30 per cent of all new titles were published in paperback, and by the end of the century the figure had risen to 60 per cent. Paperback publishers quadrupled in number between 1960 and 1965, increasingly forcing Penguin to compete for a share of the market it had been principally responsible for creating. Alongside longer-standing imprints such as Ace, Corgi, Panther, and Pan, established hardback publishers such as Faber, Macmillan, and Routledge had all moved into the paperback business even by the end of the 1950s. Penguin nevertheless maintained a leading place—at least as far as the early 1980s—and some of the principles on which it had been founded through the wide range of

[3] See pp. 24–6, above.

titles it published. In the mid-1960s, both Penguin and Pan were selling around 20 million books annually, but in very different ways. Penguin relied on 2,000 available titles, and Pan on only 450: several million of its annual sales were paperback reprints of Ian Fleming's James Bond novels. Penguin maintained its original commitment to diversity and quality through signing up recently established authors such as Iris Murdoch, and by initiating original work on its own, as well as reprinting cheaply—as it had from its early days—titles first released by publishers such as Heinemann, Hamish Hamilton, Faber, Chatto, and Michael Joseph. By 1956, reprints already made up less than half of Penguin's output. Ten years later, it established a hardback imprint of its own, Allen Lane, to ensure that it could compete with other publishers in securing the kind of material usually released in hard covers before going into paperback.

Commitment to new material or new editions was extended by ventures such as Penguin Classics, Penguin Modern Classics, Penguin English Library, Penguin Modern Poets, Penguin Modern Playwrights, Penguin Modern Stories, New English Dramatists, Pelican Guides and Histories. Each series established an attractive format, a lower price, and a brisker market for writing often much less saleable previously. Through Penguin's junior wing, Puffin, children's literature was a particular beneficiary. Committed to attracting readers rather than profits, the Puffin Club set up in 1967 had acquired 50,000 members by the early 1970s. Puffin's annual sales had passed three and a half million by that time, and it remained one of the largest children's publishers in the period, contributing to some general changes in children's literature. Concentrating on the contemporary rather than the classic, Puffin moved children's fiction closer to the tastes and outlooks of its readers, rather than their parents. Instead of the conventional morality of much late nineteenth- and early twentieth-century children's literature, writers such as Roald Dahl created subversive, extra-parental, excitingly provisional worlds, often placing their management in the hands of young characters themselves. Later in the period, J. K. Rowling's Harry Potter stories likewise moved beyond established conventions, using the English public school story only as a familiar basis for a fantastic world in which children, rather than being overawed by magic, were regularly wizards themselves. The huge success of Harry Potter in the

1990s added to a popularity for children's writing which often extended widely among adults. A survey of the nation's favourite authors for World Book Day in March 2000 placed Dahl, Rowling, and Terry Pratchett in the top three spots, with Dickens only thirteenth equal and Shakespeare fiftieth equal (*Book Marketing Quarterly Update*, p. 11). New attractiveness and a buoyant market for children's writing also ensured—along with the changes in education discussed above—a broadening interest in books, and the possibility of encouraging new generations and new sections of the population towards an appreciation of them.

Paperbacks contributed to this possibility in many other ways, accelerating several of the changes outlined above. Transformations in book selling in the 1980s had really begun—though more modestly—long before, often under the direct influence of Penguin. Like the commentators quoted earlier, Allen Lane judged bookshops 'forbidding places'—ones where 'you only expected lawyers, doctors and professors to be seen'—and worried that members of the broader public he sought for his cheap Penguins might not be persuaded to buy them there (Jones and Aynsley, pp. 75, 16). Part of his sales strategy in the 1930s had therefore been to use a cheap department store, Woolworths, as an outlet for Penguin's new titles. By the 1960s, Penguin had also started to make established bookshops less forbidding, setting up customized, self-service shelving units and sometimes a whole paperback shop within a shop. These tactics increased by 50 per cent the profits of the London bookshop Collett's in 1963, for example.

They also contributed to some lasting changes in the design of books. Shelving in most bookshops later in the century displayed some or even all paperbacks—and increasingly hardbacks—face-forward, ensuring that book design and cover pictures became major marketing influences. The book trade learned, as it had from television, that an age of images might distract from books, but could also help sell them. The lurid artwork of rivals such as Pan gradually forced Penguin to abandon its simple, colour-coded jackets—orange and white for fiction, green and white for crime, and so on—and eventually, in the 1980s, to adopt the sensational images and gold-embossed lettering already used by most other paperback publishers. Earlier, more sober cover designs—such as the modern art and

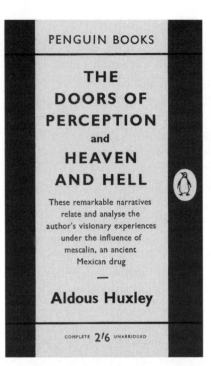

PENGUIN BOOKS

THE
DOORS OF
PERCEPTION
and
HEAVEN
AND HELL

These remarkable narratives
relate and analyse the
author's visionary experiences
under the influence of
mescalin, an ancient
Mexican drug
—

Aldous Huxley

COMPLETE 2/6 UNABRIDGED

PENGUIN PLAYS

ARNOLD WESKER
The Wesker Trilogy

Chicken Soup with Barley
Roots
I'm Talking About
Jerusalem

3/6

PENGUIN MODERN POETS 3 George Barker
Martin Bell
Charles Causley

Fig. 4. Penguin gradually replaced
plain orange-and-white covers, still
used at the end of the 1950s for
authors such as Aldous Huxley.
Distinctive new designs appeared
during the 1960s for the popular
Penguin Modern Poets series, and for
various volumes of Penguin Plays.

distinctive grey spines Germano Facetti provided for Penguin Modern Classics—had helped establish a uniform identity for some of Penguin's new ventures, encouraging readers' loyalty to a series and their readiness to experiment with new works included in it.

The broad range of titles Penguin published—even the way they were displayed—also contributed to the general democratization of culture, extending from the 1960s, discussed in Chapter 1. Penguin's most significant success at the time was not necessarily the sensational one of *Lady Chatterley's Lover*, but the less expected accumulation of a comparable sale—of 2 million copies by 1965—for Homer's *Odyssey*, first published in E. V. Rieu's translation twenty years earlier. A third of Penguin titles in print in the mid-1960s were detective novels. Displaying the *Odyssey* and *Lady Chatterley's Lover* more or less alongside them, even in different-coloured covers, created a kind of democracy among texts themselves. 'At 1s.6d. each, cheerfully coloured, brightly democratic'—Penelope Fitzgerald recalled in a novel set on the edge of the 1960s, *The Bookshop* (1978)—paperbacks elided conventional boundaries between literary genres, also reducing, quite literally, the distance between supposedly 'high' and 'low' forms of culture (p. 36).[4] As one commentator explained of titles in Rieu's Penguin Classics series, 'the very act of publishing them in Penguin editions made them considerably less forbidding to the uninitiated' (Steve Hare (ed.), p. 300). The same might have been said of most Penguin editions, and of paperbacks generally, lowering conventional cultural barriers around reading, as well as, crucially, its cost.

It was not only bookshops, in other words, which Penguin and the paperback revolution made less forbidding. Paperback publishing ensured that literature and culture, generally, came to be associated much less exclusively with a moneyed, generally male, intellectual class of lawyers, doctors, and professors. Critical positions described in Chapter 3—sceptical of canons of great texts, even of the category of literature itself—may have arisen not only from theoretical thinking but from recognizing this transformation in the market for books, gradually democratizing ways writing reached the public and was perceived by it. Some such transformation had at any rate been part of Penguin's aim since its foundation, part of Allen Lane's

---

[4] Penguin novels at the time were likelier to cost 3s. 6d.—i.e. 17.5p.

determination to establish a new reading public by 'a combination of commerce and conscience' in his publishing. 'Instruction and education in the broadest sense and on a very wide front' were priorities Lane continued to affirm in the 1960s, sometimes with reference to Lord Reith's long-sustained precept for the BBC—that 'it must educate as well as entertain' (Jones and Aynsley, pp. 16, 76; Steve Hare (ed.), p. 306). Like a number of other influential institutions, such as the Arts Council, Penguin was established around principles of social and civic improvement originating in the 1930s and 1940s and eventually realized fully in the liberal atmosphere of the 1960s. Penguin's success in the *Chatterley* trial, and its dominance of the book market at the time, made it simultaneously a source, symbol, and beneficiary of new cultural freedoms developing during the decade.

In altering the cultural status of the book, the paperback revolution also radically changed its status as an object. Following Woolworths' initiative in selling paperbacks, they could be purchased almost anywhere, eventually in supermarkets, department stores, newsagents, and filling stations. This made books a more accessible, ordinary part of daily life than ever before. Contrary to commentators still worrying about 'reverence and awe' for books in a televisual age, Ian Norrie's history of publishing offered the sensible conclusion that

> an important ingredient in the paperback revolution was the lack of taboos about how the books should be handled. Previously children had been taught not to illtreat books . . . It was not so with paperbacks. They could be stuffed into pockets, left lying open and upside down, or bent back at the page last read. Coffee cups and beer mugs could be placed upon them, and they were eminently suitable for reading on beaches and in the bath. (p. 161)

As well as helping paperbacks to colonize spaces electronic media could not reach, versatility of this kind allowed competition with them much as an equal. Bar-coded, taboo-free, and doubling as beer mat, beach gear, or bath accessory, the book became an object of mass consumption in the late twentieth century, nearly as much a part of ordinary life as television itself.

Broadened and democratized in appeal in this way, books perhaps never ran very much risk of being 'done for' by the telly, or other media, acquiring instead a far more 'common' appeal than in earlier ages. In January 1990, *British Book News* confidently concluded that 'Over the past thirty years the death of the book has been pronounced in tones sombre and portentous. First it was television, then the computer that would spell its end. But the book not only survives—it flourishes. At no time in history has this incomparable medium of communication been in greater demand' (p. 5). Expanding demand around this time continued to dispel publishing's sense of permanent crisis. Book purchase increased its share of leisure expenditure between 1985 and 1993, with strong growth in the areas of poetry, fiction, and literature generally. Consumer spending on books rose by a further 11 per cent by the end of the 1990s, increasing publishers' annual income to £2.8 billion, with a further 2.2 per cent growth forecast up to 2004. With 'the big trade houses . . . making more money than they have made at any time in the past 20 years', a *Bookseller* survey claimed in 1999 that 'this may be a golden age of consumer publishing' (Gasson, p. 15).

II. Commerce and Conscience, Ledgers and Literature

Definition of a 'a golden age' in these terms nevertheless introduces another concern about the publishing industry, often thought too ready to abandon literary or other values in favour of simply making more money. Worries of this kind had already begun to be expressed at the start of the period. In its Spring 1960 issue, the *Author* remarked that

in spite of certain high-flown descriptions of it as a Profession, a Calling, or even . . . an Occupation for Gentlemen . . . publishing in Britain is changing, is becoming Big Business, and is in fact tending to slip out of the hands of genuine bookmen ('the devils we know') into the control of those to whom books mean ledgers, not literature ('the demons who don't know us'). (p. 48)

These regrets resumed questions raised the previous year in the publisher Fredric Warburg's autobiography, which wondered whether his work was best described as 'an occupation for gentlemen' or 'a real business' (p. 11). At that time, the 'gentleman' aspect remained persuasive, not only because the great majority of those working in publishing were male, but because they shared so extensively an affluent, well-educated background. Richard Findlater's survey, *What are Writers Worth?*, recorded that 70 per cent of publishers in the early 1960s had attended public school, 25 per cent had entered the business through friends or family connections, and as many as 40 per cent had private incomes. Another publishing analyst, Christopher Gasson, helped to explain the last figure, pointing out that levels of pay 'were such that a private income was almost an essential qualification for working in publishing'. As a result, the publishing industry in the early 1960s still lacked 'democracy of opportunity' or any real chance to progress without 'family connections or personal wealth' (p. 17).

Evident for much of the earlier twentieth century, this gentlemanly cast in publishing may have added to the complicities between literary and class values feared by critics mentioned in Chapter 3,[5] potentially biasing the range of texts chosen to reach the public. Yet as the *Author* recognized at the time, new factors were already displacing these gentlemanly influences in 1960, and they were to diminish much further over the next two decades. In 1959, Warburg was still confidently advising publishers to 'look after the books . . . and the pounds will look after themselves' (p. 15)—ironically, since some of his own finance was raised privately. In a letter to the *Times Literary Supplement* of 10 June 1965, he continued to suggest that paperback publishing was a rather unworthy form of 'commodity selling', based on '*popular* appeal', rather than 'quality' (p. 481). These attitudes could not be sustained much longer. Tony Godwin warned the Society of Young Publishers in 1967 about difficulties arising for the industry because 'the upper class considered themselves . . . as the custodians of culture'. But he also suggested that 'the steady "democratization" of culture' in the 1960s was beginning to bring about change, and that 'the distinguished amateur in publishing was . . . being supplanted by the passionate professional' (Steve Hare (ed.), p. 263). This process rapidly accelerated under the financial pressures of the next decade, which quickly showed that gentlemen, bookmen, or distinguished amateurs might lack the genuine commercial urgency necessary for their own survival.

[5] See p. 110, above.

Financial pressures forced many other radical changes on publishing during the 1970s. Expansion and new ventures following the 1960s paperback revolution generally gave way—symptomatically of the movement of British life more widely at this time—to economic crises which continued to squeeze the book trade even beyond the 1970s. Trade figures clearly reflected the seriousness of the problem, showing rapidly expanding annual totals of new titles actually falling back—almost uniquely during the period—in 1974. This date, of course, coincided with the general economic crisis following the oil embargo, one which quickly affected every aspect of the book trade. The price of paper rose by 600 per cent between 1972 and 1980; printing costs by about 30 per cent annually; postal distribution to bookshops by 400 per cent between 1971 and 1975. Warehousing grew steadily more expensive, making it difficult to keep backlist items in print: the spread of remainder bookshops in the later 1970s indicated how badly publishers needed to dispose of excess stock at the time. Initially at least, there was little else they could do to counter their problems. One shrewd library analyst noticed that by the mid-1970s the average length of books had decreased, saving on paper and printing, but for the most part increased costs had to be passed on directly to the public (Wootton, pp. 23–5). Average hardback prices rose from £2.78 in 1970 to £6.64 in 1976. Printed prices began to be omitted from book covers in favour of sticky labels, easily replaced when the next rise occurred. Annual increases were far enough ahead even of inflation to lead to investigation by the Prices Commission in 1978. Rising prices naturally made books harder to sell, and publishers were further squeezed by declining demand from libraries, whose funds were reduced by as much as 75 per cent in the 1970s.

Losses were also incurred in the export trade, which had previously accounted for as much as 45 per cent of publishers' sales—especially after US anti-trust laws declared illegal, in 1976, British publishers' exclusive rights to sell in the Commonwealth. Unpredictable demand, uncontrollable price increases, high backlist costs, and money itself devaluing through inflation by as much as 20 per cent annually—all deterred publishers from new initiatives, and from taking a risk on any book that could not be sold fairly quickly. Some of the strongest and most imaginative publishers of the 1960s suffered most. Penguin was made especially vulnerable by the extent of its backlist, of more than 4,000 titles in the early 1970s. Though it shed many of the new initiatives of the previous decade—Penguin Education in 1974, for example—sales and profits continued to fall, and it declared a loss in 1979. Reducing its backlist, and emphasizing efficiency, sales, and cost-cutting—commerce rather than conscience—it did manage to return to profit by 1983, though not altogether to its leading position in paperback publishing, nor to the breadth of interests it had sustained in the 1960s.

Though the measures Penguin and other publishers adopted were often painful, they may simply have been overdue: part of an unavoidable movement towards 'real business', and beyond the gentlemanly bookmen and 'anarchic conservatism' Findlater diagnosed in 1963. Without the crises of the 1970s, many of the improvements in efficiency, marketing, and book selling considered in Section I might have occurred more slowly, or not at all. The same is true of the growing number of mergers later in the century, which showed a kind of herd instinct among publishers, huddling closer together to resist the economic chill. This instinct was not entirely new. The *Author* described the beginnings of a 'trend towards amalgamation' in Spring 1960 (p. 49), but it became much more widespread in the 1970s and 1980s. A new US market, opened up by amalgamation with Viking in 1975, helped Penguin towards recovery in the early 1980s: it went on to take over Michael Joseph and Hamish Hamilton in 1986. Along with Longman, a partner from an earlier merger, it was eventually absorbed itself within the Pearson Group. This conglomerate had moved from interests in oil, china, banking, and journalism to a concentration on publishing and entertainment which made it one of the largest media groups in the world by the 1990s.

Similar amalgamations eventually absorbed most of Britain's other major publishers, often after more than a century of independent operation. By the 1990s, Eyre & Spottiswoode (founded in 1826), Routledge (1836), and Methuen (1889) had been taken over by Thomson; and Chatto & Windus (1876), Bodley Head (1887), Jonathan Cape (1921), and Virago (1972) by Random House. By the end of the century, the greater part of Britain's publishing output was controlled by large media/publishing conglomerates. These included

Random House, Reed, and Transworld (all taken over themselves by Bertlesmann by 1998); Penguin/Pearson; News International; Hodder Headline; and Palgrave/Macmillan—one of the last of the independents until a German takeover in 1995. Such mergers followed wider patterns of corporate amalgamation throughout industry towards the end of the century, and they offered many advantages and economies in working methods. Broadly based conglomerates were better equipped to resist crises through the diversity of their interests: if one area of the market—academic publishing, for example—became temporarily depressed, it could be supported by another which might still be thriving. Costs of warehousing, distribution, marketing, design, and editing could often be reduced through centralization and other efficiencies offered by larger organizations. These also allowed wider, sometimes global, exploitation of concepts in a range of media—including paperback and hardback publishing by the same company, or even, in some of the larger ones, development into film, television, computer software, or other forms of dissemination available at the end of the century.

A more efficient, profitable industry, on the other hand, was not necessarily any more democratically oriented in its choice of texts for publication, nor more reliable in sustaining a range of literary or cultural forms. Publishing before the 1970s had after all not *only* perpetuated gentlemanly values, but often—obviously in Penguin's case—attempted to make many forms of writing more widely available, regularly supporting material considered valuable without necessarily being easily saleable. The Publishers Association insisted in 1962 that 'books should not remain unpublished simply on the grounds that they have limited demand', adding that 'among books with such limited appeal are found the most significant and valuable products of our civilization'. Collins was one of several companies continuing to believe, even in the difficult mid-1970s, that 'good fiction *must* be published . . . we owe it to the novelist and to posterity to publish novels of quality' (Sutherland, pp. 44, xiv). Such principles were harder to sustain within conglomerate publishers and media groups later in the century. In founding and developing Penguin, Allen Lane was in some ways the kind of old-fashioned individualist publisher Fredric Warburg valued, free to follow his own principles and to 'put a lot of his own personality into his firm'

(Warburg, pp. 14–15). As it turned out, Lane's principles were not only democratizing, but also outstandingly successful commercially: entirely consistent with 'commodity selling'. But they might have been harder to develop in the first place within a large corporation, less amenable to individual vision, or to concerns with conscience as well as commerce. Though publishing increasingly benefited from the security and flexibility of corporate finance, this inevitably entailed a primary commitment to corporate profit-seeking. Even by the end of the 1970s—encouraged by the appearance of weekly best-seller lists in Sunday newspapers after 1972—the key question in publishing policy seemed to have become, as John Sutherland suggested in *Fiction and the Fiction Industry* (1978), not ' "is this a good book?" but "will it sell?" ' (p. 210). In 1995, *Book Publishing in Britain* straightforwardly concluded that 'publishing is about seeing a market in a manuscript and betting on it' (Barbanneau et al., p. 3). In 2000, a publishing director in Random House likewise compared his work with 'gambling . . . placing a bet on a horse' (Leader (ed.), p. 278). This contrasted sharply with Warburg's definition of his work, forty years earlier, as a 'noble way to gain a livelihood': one involving 'friendship with the spirit' and engagement with 'the highest achievements of man's creativity' (Warburg, p. 279).

Growing emphases on market values appeared in other areas of the book trade. Waterstones may have 'made Britain enjoy books again' in the 1980s, but it was later less clear what the longer-term consequences of selling on this scale might entail. The new chains' high overheads made profitability a problem, forcing them, too, into a series of mergers. Waterstones was bought by W. H. Smith at the end of the 1980s, and Dillons was later absorbed into the same group. Financial pressures, along with their power as bulk buyers, encouraged demands for huge discounts: in the 1990s, the chains sometimes paid publishers less than 50 per cent of the cover price of books, rather than the 66 per cent usual in the previous decade. Enthusiasm for bulk selling also contributed to the demise of the Net Book Agreement (NBA), which had committed all bookshops to a cover price fixed by the publisher, effectively making discounting illegal. In place since 1900, and renewed in 1957, the NBA had been strongly defended by the Publishers Association: before the Restrictive Practices Court in the 1960s, the Prices Commission in the 1970s, and a National Heritage Select Committee in the 1990s. Publishers and many booksellers had seen it as an essential safeguard of diversity, and a necessary subsidy to smaller bookshops. Fewer would survive without it, they argued, and there would be less incentive even for large bookshops to stock a range of titles beyond immediate best-sellers. Fewer titles, in turn, would be published, damaging minority interests and ultimately the breadth of culture and imagination which print sustained. With the NBA finally succumbing in 1995, discounts came to be included in half of all book sales by the end of the century, and there were already some signs of consequences the trade had feared. The Booksellers Association recorded that as many as 10 per cent of its members had been forced to close by the end of 2000. Newspapers that year also carried stories of a Waterstones shop manager sacked 'for stocking too many good books' and for failing to follow orders 'to reduce drastically the number of books in his shop and put a high focus on best sellers'. This concentration on best sellers, the novelist Will Self warned at the time, would soon lead to 'cultural impoverishment' and 'wall to wall pulp' (*Guardian*, 1 July 2000, p. 9).

Cultural impoverishment or narrowing of this kind remained a threat for the twenty-first century, further apparent even in its first years, but there were strong commercial reasons why it was largely avoided as far as the end of the twentieth. 'Wall to wall pulp' was after all unlikely to satisfy the more educated readership discussed in Section I. Even when working within larger conglomerates, publishers were often able to maintain much of their original diversity. Virago, for example, continued its commitment to neglected women authors, with its founder, Carmen Callil, retaining a measure of editorial independence within the Random House group. New publishers such as Bloomsbury and Fourth Estate continued to appear in the 1980s and 1990s, and a number of others remained independent. Though John Sutherland had feared for the future of the 'cultural mosaic of minority readerships' supported by the book trade in the 1970s, in practice no publisher in later years could afford to ignore it (p. 102). Surveys revealed patterns of purchase increasingly influenced by diversifying tastes and lifestyles later in the century: by factors of race, class, age, and, above all, gender. In the 1990s, two-thirds of all books were being bought by women—far likelier than men to browse, and to experiment with new authors. Gender also figured significantly in choices of genre. Poetry was read much more often by women than by men. Fiction figured in the preferences of three-quarters of women, but less than half of men, with some gender stereotypes still apparent in the genres favoured by each. Romantic, historical, and contemporary novels were chosen more often by female readers; war, crime, and science fiction by males.

Titles, design, and the author's gender also had significantly differential influences on potential purchasers. Book Marketing's *Quarterly Update* concluded in Spring 2000 that books by men appealed equally to a male and female readership, but that 'women novelists have to work harder to be taken seriously by both sexes' (p. 13). Male readers could be deterred by pastel-coloured covers, or by the inclusion of certain words in a title: 75 per cent of men questioned considered Ian McEwan's *Enduring Love* (1997) to be primarily for women, and only 30 per cent considered trying it for themselves. Other evidence suggested that sales depended on appealing to niche markets which were both multiplying in number and narrowing in their focus in the 1990s. Publishers and reviewers coined more and more specific terms to define the interests involved. 'Chick lit' or 'city girl', for example, defined the idiom of writing about single women established by Helen Fielding's *Bridget Jones's Diary*; 'lad lit' the beer- and football-centred narratives initiated by Nick Hornby and John King. There was even a 'dad lit' centred on the interests of the older man. Half a dozen further categories were used regularly in book marketing by the end of the century, alongside or within the general classification of 'contemporary fiction'.

There were other commercial reasons for maintaining diversity. 'Betting' on a manuscript, after all, like betting on a horse, could never be a sure thing. 'What makes a current bestseller?', the managing director of Weidenfeld & Nicolson wondered in 1999, adding regretfully that 'just as you think you know, the kaleidoscope shifts' (Gasson, p. 53). Profitable titles remained, as ever, a minority, forcing heavy reliance on a few best-sellers to support the rest of publishers' operations. This ensured that publishers remained bookmakers in every sense: prudently inclined not to bet too exclusively on single manuscripts, but to hope that sufficient winners might emerge through backing broad fields. Logic of this kind probably contributed to the continuing dramatic increases in the number of titles published annually. Though for reasons of commerce rather than conscience, in other words, publishers late in the century remained committed to Allen Lane's principle of working on 'a very wide front', despite the crises of the 1970s.

Paths followed in reaching this position extended the patterns of development and democratization—of the disappearance of one kind of England, and the emergence of another—discussed in the Introduction and in Chapter 1. Like the Arts Council, the book trade in the 1950s still exhibited a gentlemanly concern with 'the highest achievements of man's creativity', along with a certain amount of interest in making these broadly available to the public. In the 1960s, the paperback revolution ensured much wider accessibility, part of the general cultural democratization Tony Godwin emphasized at the time. Financial pressures in the 1970s diminished democratic enthusiasms evident a decade earlier, but market forces ensured thereafter that publishing had to continue serving a wide and various public nevertheless. As a result, the book trade at the end of the century remained more diverse and imaginative than commentators such as John Sutherland had feared, and much more attuned to the taste of the general public than it had been fifty years earlier. *Book Publishing in Britain* concluded in 1995 that 'although literary critics, publishers and authors might believe that a few well promoted bestsellers are increasingly dominating publishing, the statistics show otherwise'. Despite a concentration on particular titles, sales figures revealed an 'overall trend towards greater diversity', reflecting a period in which 'both readers and authors [had] become more diverse in their tastes', and offering hopeful signs for publishing's future (Barbanneau et al., p. 7).

*

Publishing's development in the period did not, of course, ensure a uniformly golden age for all forms of literature, or for the authors producing it. Different literary genres benefited to very varied extents from developments in the book trade. If the late twentieth century could be called a golden age in publishing, it was principally for sales of fiction. Read by 50 per cent of the population, novels generally accounted for up to 10 per cent of new titles: around 2,000 annually in the 1960s, 3,000 by 1980, and as many as 9,000 by the end of the century. Not all were necessarily entirely original, many being new editions of established material, or of work from abroad. In the 1950s and 1960s, John Calder influentially imported work by Samuel Beckett and the authors of the *nouveau roman*, for example. Later, from the 1970s, Picador took over some of this role, helping to ensure that a more educated readership was also more wide-ranging in its tastes. Readers late in the century were likelier than earlier generations to be aware of writing elsewhere within the English-speaking world, or of new idioms available in translation, such as the 'magic realism' developed by Gabriel García Márquez and others at the end of the 1960s. Partly as a result, English fiction during the period remained fairly permeable to influences from abroad, and perhaps grew more generally enthusiastic for them, despite a resistance sometimes expressed by critics, or by some authors themselves.[6]

Publishing of plays was on a much more modest scale—as in most periods, given the secondary interest of the printed form to performance. Only around 100 titles appeared annually in the 1960s and 1970s, rising to 200 in 1980, 230 in 1990, and 700 by 2000. Publishers in the period nevertheless ensured that scripts of most successful new plays were quickly in print. Fourteen volumes of Penguin New English Dramatists included much of the new work, at the Royal Court and elsewhere, which transformed English theatre in the late 1950s and early 1960s. The series was supplemented by Penguin Plays, which eventually sold half a million copies of Arnold Wesker's *Trilogy*, first performed in 1960. Methuen also published playwrights emerging at this time, such as Harold Pinter and Edward Bond, and continued to keep a range of recent work in print in cheap collected editions. Contemporary drama was also strongly supported by Faber, John Calder, Samuel French, and in later years Nick Hern. In the 1990s, the Royal Court and several other theatres began to target an obvious market for drama scripts by including them in a form of extended programme, on sale during the play's run and later in the theatre bookshop.

Support for poetry was equally strong during the 1960s, a relatively buoyant time for the genre in general. Several mainstream

[6] See also pp. 83–4, above, and pp. 407–12 and 477, below.

publishers expanded their poetry lists at the time—Cape in 1963, Macmillan in 1968, and Secker and Warburg in the 1970s—while Chatto and Oxford University Press continued longer-established commitments, and Faber and Faber remained a key outlet throughout the period. As in other areas, Penguin was particularly successful in the 1960s, its Modern Poets series selling half a million volumes during the decade and in the early 1970s.[7] But the demise of the series later in the 1970s was symptomatic of the book trade's declining fortunes at the time, and of poetry's in particular. The bankruptcy of Better Books in 1974 removed an important outlet for poetry books and pamphlets, and more and more publishers decided that they could no longer afford a poetry list, despite its prestige. Michael Lane concluded that by 1980 poetry was 'universally regarded as certain to lose money' (p. 36), and John Sutherland in 1990 that it had become 'an entirely minority taste' (Coyle et al. (eds.), p. 811). By the mid-1990s, a revival was beginning to be in evidence, with the Penguin Modern Poets series relaunched in 1995 and Picador also establishing a contemporary poetry list at the time. But for most of the latter part of the period, poetry—classic or contemporary—was read by less than 4 per cent of the adult population. It was hardly surprising that it was a poet who worried that telly might have 'done for' reading altogether. In the *Writers' and Artists' Yearbook 2000*, the same author, John Whitworth, warned aspiring poets not to expect to make any money, and that any 'slim volumes' they managed to publish 'will not sell in four figures' (p. 275).

Fortunately, 1960s enthusiasm for poetry had helped to develop a range of outlets and small presses independent of the more established publishers.[8] Poetry also came to benefit more than any other area of publishing from the help of the Arts Council. In its Annual Report for 1970/1, the Chairman, Lord Goodman, suggested that where poetry was concerned 'recognition by a single perceptive mind can amply justify support to maintain an activity which can rarely find an adequate public'. He also reaffirmed the Arts Council's determination to deal with 'an economic world where it is a simple untruth that worthwhile activities must necessarily succeed' (p. 5). Such priorities suggest that Arts Council help might have arrived just

---

[7] The series is described on p. 180, below.
[8] These are outlined on pp. 261–3, below.

in time to replace some of the 'conscience' which commercial pressures forced publishers to relinquish after the crises of the 1970s. Unfortunately, literature did not figure centrally or consistently among the Arts Council's own commitments. Established only in 1965, its Literature Department never received more than 1.5 per cent of the overall budget, and 0.5 per cent or less in the 1990s. Even these limited resources were rather tentatively deployed. The New Fiction Society, for instance, was set up in 1974 to encourage promising novelists, eventually receiving £40,000 in annual subsidy, but it failed to attract a wide membership and was one of a number of measures abandoned in the early 1980s.

Other casualties around this time included subsidies for book distribution networks, bookshops, and publishers, and for augmenting literary prizes. These nevertheless continued to thrive even without Arts Council assistance. By 1995, the Book Trust and Society of Authors *Guide* listed forty-one annual awards for poetry, and fifty-four for fiction, many directed towards particular categories of writing. Novel prizes usually attracted most attention, particularly the annual shortlists for the Guardian, Whitbread, and James Tait Black awards, and, above all, the Booker McConnell Prize: Malcolm Bradbury's *Doctor Criminale* (1992) offered a comic account of the enormous media interest generated by 'the Booker' and its award ceremony. Established in 1969, and eventually offering £20,000 for 'the best full length novel by a citizen of Britain, the Republic of Ireland, the Commonwealth or South Africa', the Booker Prize was probably most valued—like much else in publishing later in the century—for its effect on sales. Though this diminished in its later years, an average 60,000 copies of the winning novel were sold in hardback, with much enhanced sales for later paperback versions, and for other novels shortlisted.[9]

In its 1980s policy document, *The Glory of the Garden* (1984), the Arts Council concluded that the impact of subsidies for literature other than poetry was 'highly marginal' (p. 29). It accordingly reaffirmed support for areas including the Poetry Society, which received £105,000 annually at this time; the National Book League, which

---

[9] A listing of fiction prizes, and of annual winners of several of the major ones, appears in Merritt Moseley (ed.), *Dictionary of Literary Biography: British Novelists since 1960* (Gale, 1999), pp. 309–18.

organized fairs, exhibitions, and book promotions (£60,000); and the Poetry Book Society, founded by T. S. Eliot in 1953 to promote understanding of poetry, and committed to reducing publisher's costs in producing it (£18,000). Low readership had forced withdrawal in 1978 of a major Arts Council investment in the *New Review*, but a number of literary magazines—*Ambit*, *Agenda*, *London Magazine*, and *London Review of Books*—all continued to receive funding at the end of the 1980s. Subsidy to several small poetry presses was increased—in particular, to Anvil and Carcanet, which had been among the first to receive public funding, of around £2,000 each annually in the mid-1970s. This had risen to around £55,000 for each by 1990. Throughout the period, many individual writers were also supported directly. The Arts Council's 1976/7 report worried that 'there is no firm evidence to suggest that a poet is encouraged to write more or better poems by being offered £2,000' (p. 30). But around fifty writers annually—not only poets—were by that date being supported in this way, though rarely at the level suggested. Instead, out of an overall annual budget of only £40,000– £50,000 in the 1970s, most received grants of less than £1,000, an amount John Sutherland described at the time as a 'pittance' (p. 135).

It did indicate how very modestly, if at all, the period fulfilled hopes Richard Findlater had expressed in his Society of Authors survey, *What are Writers Worth?*, in 1963—that 'the British writer will have better opportunities to ensure that he is paid what he is worth and treated as he deserves' (p. 28). The Society itself had regularly tried to improve authors' pay. By 1976, it had argued successfully for improving their share of paperback rights—previously split equally with publishers—and further increases followed. Agitation along with the Writers Action Group ensured that a scheme rewarding authors for library borrowings of their books, first suggested in 1951, eventually became law in 1979. Public Lending Right (PLR) payments began in 1982, though rarely offering more than a further 'pittance': £2 million was shared among 9,000 writers in 1985, and £5 million among 24,000 in 1995, with maximum grants of £6,000. Only 135 writers received more than £5,000 through PLR in that year—surveys at the end of the century suggested that the principal beneficiaries were mostly authors of popular fiction who already earned substantially from direct sales. Authors' groups continued to press governments for an increased allocation to PLR, and for the kind of preferential tax laws already operating in countries such as France and the Republic of Ireland. In terms of state subsidy, signs of real improvement appeared only in 2001, when Arts Council literature funding was increased by 75 per cent, with substantial amounts designated for distribution to poets through the Poetry Book Society and the Arvon Foundation.

Novelists, in particular, made increasing use of literary agents to secure the best advance on royalties, and to deal with the complicated matter of rights, sometimes involving film, television, US editions, translations, and eventually electronic forms. Though at a cost, usually of around 10 per cent commission, agents late in the century sometimes did succeed in securing advances far higher than anticipated royalties. As long as any excess element seemed sure to be covered by profits, publishers were willing to pay large sums—often in auctions arranged by an agent—to secure novels likely to generate a big sale, either immediately or on their backlist. The New York agent Andrew Wylie was especially successful in securing advances, for authors such as Martin Amis and Salman Rushdie, which sometimes matched those paid for thrillers: Amis was offered six-figure sums in the 1990s. Magnus Mills was said to have signed a £1 million deal in 1996 for his first novel, *The Restraint of Beasts*, and Zadie Smith rumoured to have received £250,000 for another first novel, *White Teeth* (2000). Only 6 per cent of authors in the 1990s, however, received more than £25,000 in advance: £5,000 was a more usual figure. The majority of writers had to make do with a modest advance and a basic royalty, standard throughout most of the period, of 10 per cent on hardback sales, with a lower rate, usually 7.5 per cent, for paperbacks. Even a moderately successful novel, selling 2,000 copies in hardback and going on to paperback, might in this way have earned only around £7,000–£8,000 in the 1990s. The fiction editor of Secker and Warburg estimated at the start of the decade that it might be difficult even for an award-winning novelist to make as much as £10,000 annually from writing: for poets, of course, the position was generally much less promising.

Surveys conducted throughout the period by the Society of Authors were just as pessimistic. They estimated that in the early

1960s the majority of authors made less than £500 annually, though a few still had private incomes at this time, and that earnings continued to fall in real terms throughout this decade and the next. Though there were some new opportunities for radio or television work, authors' earnings suffered seriously from a reduction in outlets for occasional journalism, and in the number of magazines prepared to pay for poetry, or for short stories—a genre whose market declined particularly sharply during the period. The Society's figures nevertheless suggested that nearly half of its authors still managed to support themselves from writing in 1966, and a third in 1971. Ten years later, after the economic crises of the 1970s, it was a sixth, and by the end of the century only one in seven.

Nor was there much compensation in terms of the better treatment Findlater had also anticipated. At the start of the period, Fredric Warburg's epigraph for *An Occupation for Gentlemen* suggested that 'it is writers who are the kings and queens of the publishing trade'. By its end, they were more likely to find themselves pawns within the financial manoeuvres of large, increasingly impersonal conglomerates. The change was disturbing enough to be reflected regularly in fiction and poetry in the 1990s. In her comic poem 'Reflections on a Royalty Statement' (1992) Wendy Cope records becoming simply a number within the bureaucratic organization of her publishers. Jonathan Coe's narrator in *What a Carve Up* (1994) discovers that the respected, long-established imprint which used to publish his work has been 'swallowed up by an American conglomerate' in which 'the only kind of . . . values anybody seems to care about are the ones that can be added up on a balance sheet' (pp. 94, 102). Jenny Diski's heroine in *Happily Ever After* (1991) is more fortunate, taken on by 'one of the last of the independent publishers on the face of the earth', still free of the 'faceless financier' and the 'American conglomerate', though only just (pp. 123–4). Compared with Warburg's generation, most authors in the 1980s and 1990s received less personal attention from publishers; less thorough editorial advice; lower standards of copy-editing and proof-reading; less control over matters of production such as cover illustration and type-size; more frequent turnover of editors. Timothy Mo indicated what was probably a more widely shared exasperation with this kind of treatment when he decided to publish his novel *Renegade, or*

Halo[2] himself—it went on to win the James Tait Black Prize for 1999—and to consider future publication only on the Internet. If the late twentieth century was a 'golden age', in other words, it was for readers, and some publishers, rather than for the most part for authors themselves.

There were signs, nevertheless, that the appeal of a writing career remained undiminished. One of these appeared in the growing popularity of creative writing as an academic subject late in the century. 'British universities will not touch creative writing', John Sutherland recorded in the 1970s (p. 150), but by the 1980s and 1990s many popular and successful courses had established themselves. Founded by Malcolm Bradbury and Angus Wilson, East Anglia's had helped to launch the careers of novelists such as Ian McEwan and Kazuo Ishiguro. Even at the height of publishing's financial crises in the 1970s, the *Bookseller* confidently concluded that the imagination remained 'unquenchable, the instinct to create as universal as that to procreate. Whatever the rewards, the hazards, the frustrations, stories will go on welling up in authors' minds' (Apr. 1978, p. 2513). Yet it would be romantic to suppose this 'welling up' unaffected, or altogether undeterred, by the quality of outlets available for it. Later in the century, there was probably more risk than in many earlier periods that imagination might sink back again without trace— unheeded by publishers craving quick successes, and reluctant to nurture authors beginning their careers. In the view of the literary agent Richard Curtis, 'more and more emphasis on buying winners instead of breeding them: acquisition without cultivation' meant that 'less and less attention [was] paid to developing writers'. 'When authors are deprived of the time to grow', he added, 'creativity will be snuffed out' (p. 58). Difficulties for new writers, even by the 1980s, were starkly highlighted when Doris Lessing, as a test, sent a typescript novel to her publishers under a pseudonym, Jane Somers. It was rejected, though widely acclaimed when eventually published as *The Diary of a Good Neighbour* (1983). New authors later in the century, in other words, would have been lucky to find the kind of support enjoyed by William Golding in the 1950s. His editor at Faber ignored a disparaging reader's report on his first novel, *Lord of the Flies* (1954), helped to reshape it by deleting the first chapter, and ensured that it remained in print long enough to accumulate gradually, despite a slow start, what was eventually a huge readership. Two million copies had been sold by the mid-1960s; seven million by the end of the century.

New imagination in the 1990s also lacked some of the specialist outlets publishing had offered in the past. For much of the period, John Calder attempted to create a new school of British literature, not only through importing influential work from abroad, but also by publishing innovative domestic writers such as the playwrights Howard Barker and Heathcote Williams. Calder remained one of the last independent publishers at the end of the century, but recorded that it had become more difficult to support the kind of avant-garde material he had helped to develop in the past. Another long-term supporter of innovative fiction, Peter Owen, lamented the loss of Arts Council subsidies in this area, warning in the *Times Literary Supplement* on 13 October 2000 that 'market conditions are so bad that it is almost impossible to launch unknown writers; this will ultimately lead to cultural stagnation' (p. 17). Faced with growing difficulties in finding a publisher, greater rewards in other media, and the greater cultural 'buzz' which they offered, potential authors later in the century may have chosen not to channel their creative instincts towards books at all. This might have led to some loss of quality in the period's literature, or at any rate a risk for its future beyond the 1990s.

Compared to complex production processes required by other media, printed text may nevertheless have continued to attract authors by its promise of a certain freedom and independence. Yet any such freedom could only be relative. Even the most congenial of publishers could never free authors completely from growing pressures within the industry, or from influences within the market for books generally. With John Betjeman the last English poet until the 1990s to reach a large audience—apart from a few popular authors such as Pam Ayers—poets could hardly remain unaware of the minority readership for their work, favouring private discourse and inward vision partly as a result. The public voice and subject matter to be found in Victorian verse—or even in the modernist writing of T. S. Eliot, W. B. Yeats, or W. H. Auden—survived only occasionally in the later twentieth century, with some loss of range and appeal in its poetry as a result.

Fiction had far fewer problems in finding readers, yet new emphasis on the detached, private nature of reading, compared to other entertainment forms in the period, probably affected subject matter in this genre, too. The privacy and singularity of reading may have been especially welcome amid the 'noisy, flagrant . . . jostle and buzz' William Trevor envisaged, but it implicitly accepted that cultural 'buzz' and immediacy had largely been ceded to other media. The popularity of cinema and television, their powers of realistic representation, and their more central roles within society, all tended to deflect the novel away from epic themes or broad social perspectives, and towards closer concentration on private, inward experience, often reflected in first-person forms of narrative. A generally more aloof, detached role for writing may even have added to the readiness, among theorists described in Chapter 3, to envisage literary texts as autonomous: as discourses distanced from direct reflection of the world. The 'autonomous text' and the pleasures critical theorists ascribed to it perhaps acknowledged, indirectly, how far the written word had ceased to be society's only or most popular means of representing life and reality to itself—even if it often remained a preferred one. Books and print survived the period successfully, but their cultural role, as Marshall McLuhan had predicted, was less central by its end.

Market forces extended other strong influences over fictional form and style. Novelists could not all be best-sellers, nor were they necessarily always urged by their publishers to try, but few could avoid an obligation to write as accessibly as possible. Though Henry James and James Joyce were still borrowed regularly from libraries at the end of the century, publishers were unlikely to encourage writers to borrow too many of their innovative methods or complex prose styles. Critics throughout the period regularly lamented the absence of 'high art' from English fiction, but did not always consider how difficult publishing conditions had made some forms of it to sustain. English fiction's most innovative or postmodernist phase coincided significantly with publishers' relative freedom from financial pressure, in the 1960s and early 1970s. Thereafter, commitments to experiment and the legacies of modernism—if they continued to appear at all—tended to be combined with more familiar, less challenging conventions, often ones well established before the modernist period. As David Lodge emphasized, by the 1990s, regardless of its other interests, contemporary writing was 'likely to be reader-friendly', and contemporary authors likely to be more firmly committed than their predecessors to direct, straightforward communication (Bradbury and Cooke, p. 214). Combination of innovation and tradition, one of the principal characteristics of the period's fiction, could be seen as motivated directly by the need to appeal to a wide audience, though one increasingly well-educated and sophisticated in its literary tastes.[10]

This need for wide appeal contributed to another characteristic set of combinations in late twentieth-century fiction: between serious and thriller genres, literary and popular forms. In reviewing *The Great Fortune* in January 1960, that *Observer* critic—quoted in Chapter 3—expressed surprise at Olivia Manning's creation of 'caviare for the general' by her combination of art and entertainment, moral seriousness and an adult adventure story. In an *Observer* interview twenty years later, Graham Greene still expressed concern about a 'division of literature into the great because hard to read, the not so great . . . because of the desire to divert, to be readable, to keep it plain' (16 Mar. 1980, p. 33). But as it turned out, Manning's novel anticipated a combination of priorities increasingly evident later in the period. 'All publishers are searching', a senior editor suggested at the end of the century, for 'a novel that is at once literary and com-mercial, a book with big ambitions that will appeal to a very wide audience' (Leader (ed.), p. 273). Reviewers later in the 1980s and 1990s—and the general public—would on the whole have been surprised had they *not* found a compelling, engaging storyline, and a certain directness of expression, even in otherwise complex novels of 'big ambitions'. In these and other areas, publishing and the book market were influences at least as decisive on the period's fiction, in particular, as the historical, intellectual, and social ones discussed in Chapters 1–3.

---

[10] This combination and those mentioned in the next paragraph are discussed on pp. 429–30, 457–9, and 513–14, below.

Part II

Poetry

5

Movement or Revival:
The Late 1950s to the 1980s

Though it is 'twenty-five years since the battle | Plucked up the sand and let it settle', the desert landscape Anthony Thwaite surveys in 'At Asqefar' (1967) is still stained and strewn with relics of war. In the literary landscape of the later twentieth century, memories of the Second World War likewise faded only very gradually, long influencing directions followed by English poetry. In the early 1960s, a time of growing recognition of the devastation wrought by the concentration camps and the atom bomb,[1] the war's implications sometimes seemed to threaten the poetic imagination's very survival. Theodor Adorno challenged at the time the ethics of continuing to write poetry at all after Auschwitz, and the question was further debated by A. L. Alvarez and Donald Davie in the first issue of the influential journal the *Review* in May 1962. Referring to his recent visits to Auschwitz, Alvarez stressed the need for a new emotional directness if English poetry was to survive and flourish: a 'new seriousness' able to 'express the complexity, the bastardy of being human and having to face all the pain and . . . remain sane'. Though sharing Alvarez's conviction that 'humanity and human relations are under an intolerable strain in our time', Davie favoured instead a 'new aestheticism', able to contain contemporary pressures 'so that human relations may as far as possible be decent' (pp. 11, 16–18).

Their debate was typical not only in the positions adopted—each

---

[1] See pp. 54–5, above.

representative of a different set of responses to the war in English poetry, described in this chapter and the next—but also in the sharpness of distinctions separating their views. Diverse in its reactions to recent history, English poetry at the time was equally variable in its response to the literary legacies of the earlier twentieth century, those of modernism particularly. As a result, it was divided more complicatedly than contemporary fiction or drama into movements and counter-movements, each attempting through poetic practice and critical discussion to establish what the true priorities of poetry should be. Anthony Thwaite suggested a means of tracing the arguments and factions involved when he remarked that 'the programmatic and polemical anthology' had offered throughout the period 'one of the most conspicuous instruments of change, or attempted change' (*Poetry Today*, p. 1). His suggestion is followed in this chapter and in Chapters 6 and 7. As well as discussing the period's principal poets, each concentrates on key anthologies which define the conflicting priorities within which these writers worked.

In his wish to avoid emotional excess, and to keep human relations as decent as possible, Donald Davie sustained into the early 1960s principles established by the most influential anthologies published in the previous decade. D. J. Enright's *Poetry of the 1950s* (1955) and Robert Conquest's *New Lines* (1956) each set out quite deliberately to function as an 'instrument of change'. Each helped establish 'the Movement': a loose grouping which included, among poets, Elizabeth Jennings, John Holloway, Thom Gunn, Philip Larkin, D. J. Enright, Kingsley Amis, and John Wain, as well as Donald Davie and Robert Conquest himself. Many of the Movement's distinguishing preferences were summed up in Conquest's introduction to the first volume of *New Lines*, which stressed 'rational structure and comprehensible language' and 'integrity and judgement enough to prevent surrender to subjective moods'. Conquest also recommended a 'reverence for the real' which could free poetry from 'mystical and logical compulsions' and leave it instead, like contemporary philosophy, 'empirical in its attitude to all that comes' (pp. xiii, xv). All these were qualities Conquest considered might rescue contemporary poetry from the supposed Romantic excesses and indulgence of the 1940s, faults often particularly ascribed to Dylan Thomas's work.

The Movement's restraint and directness also answered more general needs in a post-war age, anxious about A-Bombs and Auschwitz in the ways Davie and Alvarez discussed in 1962—a response clarified by several of the poems in the anthology, including Davie's own. In 'Remembering the 'Thirties', Davie notes that 'a neutral tone is nowadays preferred', and in 'Rejoinder to a Critic' he explains why, asking 'how can I dare to feel?', talking of 'love's radio-active fall-out' and suggesting—in recalling John Donne's question 'Who's injured by my love?'—that

> recent history answers: Half Japan!
> Not love, but hate? Well, both are versions of
> The 'feeling' that you dare me to. Be dumb!
> Appear concerned only to make it scan!
> How dare we now be anything but numb?'

Injunctions to be numb, dumb, or feelingless—though odd ones for poetry—also appeared in Philip Larkin's 'Born Yesterday', which offers 'may you be ordinary' and 'may you be dull' as wishes for a new baby. Kingsley Amis's 'Against Romanticism' similarly recommends a 'pallid' vision and 'a temperate zone' as a refuge from 'all grime of history'. Later, in 'Ars Poetica' (1977),[2] Davie stressed poetry's capacity to provide this temperate zone: a calm, historyless space which has been 'cleared to walk around in' and

> has
> Boundaries, and beyond them
> The turbulence it was cleared from.
>
> Small clearances, small poems;
> Unlikely now the enormous
> Louring, resonant spaces
> Carved out by a Virgil.

Neutral tones and cleared spaces were consolidated by Movement poetry's careful structure, and by its language—colloquial in style, but usually regular in rhyme and metre, and often assembled into tidy quatrains. Davie later indicated potential tensions between these

---

[2] Where poems do not appear in the anthologies discussed, a date of their first publication in book form is given in parenthesis. Editions quoted are listed in Works Cited, pp. 587–606, and where appropriate asterisked in Author Bibliographies, pp. 523–80. Anthologies are listed in Works Cited under the name of their editor.

aspects of style and form—between Conquest's twin requirements for 'comprehensible language' and 'rational structure'—when he pointed out that the chatty tone of Movement poetry often wasted metrical places by inserting phrases such as ' "no doubt", "I suppose", "of course", "almost", "perhaps" ' (*Poet in the Imaginary Museum*, p. 72). Yet Conquest indicated an important motive behind this apparent metrical profligacy when he referred to 'the real . . . honesty' of George Orwell as 'one of the major influences on modern poetry' (*New Lines*, p. xv). Whether or not they were committed to *real* honesty, Movement poets were determined to *sound* straightforward and down-to-earth. As Davie acknowledged, 'going much further than halfway to meet our readers' was usually a priority: like Orwell in his essays, Movement poetry sought with its audience a kind of rhetorical camaraderie, developed through styles close to ordinary speech, and through subjects close to the common experience of English daily life (*Poet in the Imaginary Museum*, p. 72). At a time when recent history had made poetic imagination seem more problematic, and more challenged, than ever, the Movement reacted through 'small poems', re-establishing a tentative, self-deprecating post-war poetic safely distanced from big issues, grandiose emotion, or 'louring' language. Relying on a language which often sounded quite *un*poetic, Movement poetry nevertheless—as if in nervous counter-reaction—remained 'concerned to make it scan'; to hold on to exact poetic forms; even to establish 'new aestheticism'. Ingenious, complex accommodations of conventional structure and colloquial speech often resulted. The expansive enjambements of Philip Larkin's 'Mr Bleaney' (1964), for example, extend poetic reflections over the last two quatrains of the poem, only to return precipitately to ordinary speech at the end:

> But if he stood and watched the frigid wind
> Tousling the clouds, lay on the fusty bed
> Telling himself that this was home, and grinned,
> And shivered, without shaking off the dread
>
> That how we live measures our own nature,
> And at his age having no more to show
> Than one hired box should make him pretty sure
> He warranted no better, I don't know.

Larkin is usually considered the typical Movement author, exemplary of the general preferences Conquest expressed. Yet his poetry was also particularized by the dispirited context and vision evident in 'Mr Bleaney', reflecting the outlook of a poet who once remarked that 'depression is to me as daffodils were to Wordsworth' (Haffenden, *Viewpoints*, p. 118). Like the photography described in 'Lines on a Young Lady's Photograph Album' (1955), Larkin's writing was usually both 'faithful and disappointing', or disappointed. In tracing the disfigurement of a sunny landscape on an advertising poster, and its eventual replacement by the grim exhortation to 'fight cancer', 'Sunny Prestatyn' (1964) is typical not only of the dilapidated world Larkin often surveyed, but of the processes of his imagination itself. 'Essential Beauty' (1964) similarly highlights disparities between huge, cheery images on advertising hoardings, in 'frames as large as rooms', and the dreary, 'rained-on streets and squares' they stand above. A kind of framing of desire and the ideal, held apart from immediate life and experience, also leads to conclusions in 'The Large Cool Store' (1964) about 'how separate and unearthly love is' and how shallow the 1960s materialism which seems the only substitute for it.

Larkin's much-admired 'The Whitsun Weddings' (1964) extends this sense of separateness, of unfulfilled desire and tauntingly unreachable communion. The long train journey the poem describes establishes a 'we' voice of collective outlook, shared with fellow travellers. Yet the scenes of 'larking' on the platforms are close to Larkin phonetically, not emotionally; remaining distanced, framed beyond train windows he leans from as a lonely 'I'. Rather as Movement work struggled to sustain a common, colloquial voice within conventional poetic structure, Larkin's poetry is both drawn towards common, collective experience and enjoyments, yet also distanced from it by the poet's role as aloof observer. 'Halfway' to readers, or to the ordinary people his poetry depicts, is as close as Larkin gets: in 'The Whitsun Weddings', this leaves him both engaged and isolated by his imagination, wondering about fulfilments which take place only 'out of sight, somewhere'. This sense of inaccessible fulfilment in 'The Whitsun Weddings', or of 'imperfect eyes | That stare beyond this world' in 'Essential Beauty', moved quite literally into a higher frame in some of Larkin's 1970s poetry. In 'High Windows' (1974), for example, it extended into the more abstract, metaphysical vision of 'sun-comprehending glass, | And beyond it, the deep blue air, that shows | Nothing, and is nowhere, and is endless'.

Other *New Lines* poets also moved on in later years, or were from the beginning further from Conquest's principles than their association with the Movement suggested at the time. Like many Movement writers, Elizabeth Jennings admired Robert Graves—one of several long-established poets who remained influential early in the period —especially for the 'reticence' and 'diffidence' of his love poetry. These were qualities extended in much of her own writing. Yet its concentration on love, relationships, and their 'subjective moods' also set her apart from Movement writers, most of whom were male and still more evasive of emotion. Jennings's religious concerns sometimes also transgressed Conquest's embargo on 'mystical compulsions'. His demand for 'rational structure' was more thoroughly fulfilled by the exact metre and rhyme of Thom Gunn's early poetry, imposing a restraint even on descriptions of the raw or raucous—the biker boys in 'On the Move' (1957), for example, or the drug pusher in 'Street Song' (1971). Yet some of this restraint was diminished by Gunn's own concern with relationships, eventually explicitly homosexual ones, and by influences arising from his move to the United States. Later poetry was often less tightly patterned in its metrics, and more interested in subjective moods, or in moving through them towards metaphysical speculations far from Conquest's preference for the empirical. 'The sniff of the real' Gunn mentions in 'Autobiography' nevertheless remains apparent in the persistent memories of English life he records in *Jack Straw's Castle* (1976).

Some of D. J. Enright's vision of England was similarly sharpened by exile. His early poetry reflected work abroad in Egypt, Thailand, Japan, or Germany, and encounters there with 'creatures . . . not like us' which highlight the particularity of English life, or of the poet's private outlook ('Taken Prisoner', 1972). Later writing continued to share the conversational candour of the Movement, though often expressed within freer verse forms, while the objective outlook of the exile was sometimes replaced—in *Paradise Illustrated* (1978) and *A Faust Book* (1979), for example—by literary perspectives allowing an equally distanced, ironic assessment of contemporary life and morals. Like Enright, Donald Davie often moved towards moral

concerns in his later poetry. 'In the Stopping Train' (1980) antici-
pates a speculative, brooding investigation of relations of self, art,
and life shaping much of the poetry which follows. Periods in the
United States, and a growing interest in the modernist writing of Ezra
Pound, also distanced him from the idiom of the Movement.

Davie's shifting allegiances helped to make him an exceptionally
insightful commentator on poetry throughout the period, unusually
wide-ranging in his sympathies, and at various times both advocate
and adversary of priorities Conquest established in *New Lines*.
Arguments in favour of rigour and exactness made *Purity of Diction
in English Verse* (1952) as much a manifesto for Movement values as
Conquest's introduction. Later, as his own interests developed,
Davie took a more distanced view of Movement priorities. These
included rejection not only of the romantic excess of the 1940s, but
of what Movement writers saw as the elitism, complexity, and foreign origins of the modernist writing which had preceded it. As Davie
discussed in *Thomas Hardy and British Poetry* (1973), Movement
poets looked on modernism as a deviation from an English tradition
last truly evident in Victorian or Edwardian writing, Hardy's particularly, and to be restored if possible by their own work.
Introducing a 1966 reissue of his early collection *The North Ship*
(1945), Larkin explained how admiration for Hardy's straightforwardness had replaced, by the 1950s, early allegiance to W. B. Yeats.
Hardy's wan wistfulness and brooding regret for the past added to
his appeal for Movement writers, often—like many other English
poets later in the period, such as C. H. Sisson—backward-looking
in theme as well as style. Nostalgic for the Edwardian era in
'MCMXIV' (1964), Larkin expresses in 'Show Saturday' (1974), 'To
the Sea' (1974), and 'Going, Going' (1974) a regret for the continuing decline of traditions and sanctities in later years, providing in
'Reference Back' (1964) an analysis of this kind of nostalgic vision
itself.

Similar nostalgia for life earlier in the century appeared in the
work of an older poet, John Betjeman, whom Larkin admired—even
worrying that he might come to seem a 'sort of cut-price Betjeman'
himself (Haffenden, *Viewpoints*, p. 119). Though not usually associated with the Movement, Betjeman's work shared many of its characteristics, particularly in containing chatty, colloquial language

within exact, conventional poetic forms. Betjeman's elegantly asserted rhymes and rhythms even reproduced some of the grander styles of the Victorians, wryly counterpointed against a disdainful vision of contemporary life. Though occasionally showing a bleaker aspect, especially in the autobiographical *Summoned by Bells* (1960), much of Betjeman's work was humorous and unchallenging. This helped to ensure for his *Collected Poems* (1958) an immediate popularity—ten impressions had appeared by 1960, and an enlarged edition followed in 1962—which he retained throughout the rest of his career, including an eccentric term as Poet Laureate from 1972 until 1984.

The huge popular appeal of poetry so retrospective in theme and form also helps account for the wider success of the Movement after mid-century, and for Edward Lucie-Smith's judgement of it—of Larkin specifically—as '*the* characteristic voice of a whole generation' (p. 121). Conventional and constrained in style, and engrossed in disappointment and unfulfilled desire, the Movement's 'small poems' were thoroughly consonant with an age exhausted by the war and by the anxieties and austerities which followed. In 'Goodbye to London' (1962), Louis MacNeice described feelings of being 'reborn into anticlimax' after 'the headshrinking war'. Such feelings were exacerbated by uncertainty and loss of status following the end of empire and the spread of the Cold War, and by the shifting values and new materialism evident within England itself at the end of the 1950s and in the 1960s. Regret about 'the last of England' —about supposed decline abroad and at home—sometimes shaped direct complaint, as in Larkin's 'Homage to a Government' (1974). More generally, it contributed to the Movement's attempts to resuscitate a 'lost' English poetic tradition, and to its celebration of longstanding features of England's way of life and sense of itself which seemed particularly threatened at the time.

So specific in its historical origins, the Movement might seem surprising in the extent and longevity of its influence over English poetry in the decades that followed. As Blake Morrison suggested, it established an idiom which long outlasted or 'transcended' the group of poets initially involved, consolidating 'certain characteristics in English writing—rationalism, realism, empiricism—which continue[d] to exert their influence' throughout the 1960s, the 1970s, and beyond (*The Movement*, p. 9). Seamus Heaney likewise concluded that 'the Movement poets, Larkin, Davie, Enright and others . . . pointed the way for much of what happened over the next twenty years' (*Government of the Tongue*, p. 41). Anthony Easthope considered that 'the poetry of the Movement . . . ha[d] expanded since the 1950s' and continued to hold 'a dominant position in English culture' even in the 1990s (Acheson and Huk (eds.), p. 26). Yet in some ways this lasting appeal is easily explained, and not only in terms of the endurance of some historical conditions the Movement originally envisaged. 'Reverence for the real', conventional structure, and comprehensible language established a thoroughly accessible poetry, dignified in the name of 'new aestheticism', and an English tradition reaching back to the august figure of Hardy. Such poetry proved agreeably easy to teach in schools, congenial and unchallenging to readers and many poets alike, and freed of demanding metaphysics or the formal complexities of modernism. Larkin remarked in the *Listener* on 25 July 1968 on a wish to 'relapse back into one's own life and write from it' (p. 111). His work offered his successors a model, and an excuse, for writing straightforwardly about theirs: for continuing an idiom described by Edward Lucie-Smith as 'post-Movement . . . naturalistic, "domestic" ' (pp. 247, 256). As Anthony Easthope suggests, there was ample evidence of the continuation of this idiom as a norm or mainstay within English poetry even at the end of the century. Supposedly representing the best of the year's writing, much of the work included in *The Forward Book of Poetry* (1999), for example, was still largely shaped around the characteristics outlined above.

The history of the period's poetry was also, of course, shaped by challenges and alternatives to this post-Movement mainstream. But these were not always much represented in anthologies published in the 1960s, 1970s, or early 1980s, only a few of which—discussed in Chapter 6—were either genuinely 'polemical' or in any way 'instruments of change'. Consolidation of Movement idioms often seemed, instead, editors' principal interest. This was naturally the case with the second volume of Conquest's *New Lines* (1963), which retained most of the authors who had appeared in the first, adding a few established poets such as Vernon Scannell, and a handful who had emerged recently, including Anthony Thwaite, Hugo Williams,

George MacBeth, and Edward Lucie-Smith. MacBeth and Lucie-Smith also figured—the latter as an editor, along with Philip Hobsbaum—in another volume published in 1963, *The Group Anthology*. The Group had met since 1955 in an early form of writers' workshop, allowing poets to read and discuss their work together, sometimes applying to it the kind of close textual analyses advocated by the New Criticism influential at that time. These methods were more innovative than most of the poetry they helped to produce. Little departure from Movement empiricism and 'reverence for the real' was suggested by Edward Lucie-Smith's foreword to *The Group Anthology*. This promised 'frank autobiographical poems' and a 'poetry of direct experience' shaped by 'reflection of the world' and firmly 'linked to the business of living' (Lucie-Smith and Hobsbaum (eds.), pp. vi, vii). Nevertheless, there were Group poets—such as Peter Redgrove, Alan Brownjohn, and Peter Porter—who did move beyond Movement idioms. Along with Martin Bell, Brownjohn and Porter were more sharply satiric than most Movement writers, and more attuned to radical moods beginning to shape the early 1960s. Brownjohn's 'William Empson at Aldermaston' (1962), for example, explored the fundamental division of attitudes beginning to appear between the CND movement and the military and government establishment it opposed. Written around the time of the Cuban Missile Crisis, Porter's 'Your Attention Please' (1962) also belonged to this phase of 1960s dissent, anticipating the kind of warning that would be broadcast minutes before a nuclear attack.

Porter later extended the style of 'Your Attention Please' into other satiric monologues, such as 'Mort aux Chats' (1972), which attacks, among other targets, racial prejudice, or the still wider critique of 'A Consumer's Report' (1970), in which 'the name of the product . . . tested is *Life*'. Migration from Australia in the 1950s equipped Porter with the objectivity of an outsider, shaping acute observation of shifting metropolitan morals and lifestyles, on the edge of the 1960s, in poems such as 'Euphoria Dies', 'Party Line', 'Made in Heaven', or 'John Marston Advises Anger', included in his early collection *Once Bitten Twice Bitten* (1961). Each anatomizes what the last-named calls 'a Condé Nast world' of 'thin richness'—one peopled by 'Classics Honours Men promoting Jazzetry | Market

Researchers married into Vogue', regular revellers at fashionable, sexy parties soon fading into sordid city dawns. Porter's aloof, satiric vision also derived from the kind of youthful tensions described in 'Eat Early Earthapples'(1963), which recalls 'reading a book | While the smut-skeined train goes homeward | Carrying the practised to the sensual city'. Throughout a career spanning the last four decades of the century, Porter remained concerned—in ways often highlighted by the exact or unusual verse forms he employed—with conflicts or coalescences between art, or the intellectual sphere generally, and sensual, smut-skeined, or still darker aspects of lived experience. While much of his work celebrated the potential of the aesthetic to order or transcend 'the business of living', in some of the best of it, such as 'An Exequy' (1978), Porter traced elegiac personal emotions for which art could provide only very limited consolation.

Departure from Movement idioms was no more in evidence in *The Young British Poets* (1971) than in *The Group Anthology*. The volume's editor, Jeremy Robson, praised his poets for their freedom from foreign influence and commitment to 'the English tradition'—even though six of them were Irish or Scottish—and for the 'craftsmanlike' qualities of work 'deeply rooted in personal experience' (Robson (ed.), p. 13). Much of this personal experience—in poetry by Brian Jones, Dom Moraes, and Douglas Hill—continued the realistic, domestic manner of the Movement. Ian Hamilton and Hugo Williams nevertheless created an atmosphere of puzzle and intensity by withholding background or contextual details a Movement poet would habitually have supplied. Described by Hamilton as ' "intelligent lyricism" in an age of versified prose-poetry' (*New Review Anthology*, p. 7), writing of this kind also featured in the work of David Harsent. It was further supported in the late 1960s and 1970s by Hamilton's editorship of the *Review* (1962–72), later relaunched as the *New Review* (1974–9).

Michael Schmidt was a similarly influential editor at this time, and later, managing Carcanet Press from 1969 and founding the journal *Poetry Nation* in 1973, renamed *PN Review* in 1977. In practice, a fairly eclectic range of poets was published by both Carcanet and *PN Review*, though the latter declared a preference for clear, formal writing and for allegiance to tradition and heritage. This preference was also apparent in Schmidt's anthology *Some Contemporary*

Poets of Britain and Ireland (1983). Poems it included by Peter Scupham, Andrew Waterman, and Jeremy Hooker continued English pastoral conventions apparently scarcely altered since Hardy, while Schmidt's preface likewise claimed Dick Davis, Clive Wilmer, and Robert Wells as 'resolutely traditional in their approach to the craft of poetry' (Schmidt (ed.), p. xiii). It also recorded Schmidt's view that contemporary poetry, more generally, 'accommodate[d] itself within the English traditions' and that a 'Victorian spirit seems to be ghosting our literary world at the far end of our century . . . the great Anglo-American modernists—who seemed so decisively to have shaken off the nineteenth century—have not been, and now perhaps never will be, assimilated into the 'mainstream' of British writing' (p. xi). Like Movement poets in the 1950s and 1960s, Schmidt continued to consider that 'English traditions' depended on a ghostly or exhumed Victorianism, and a dismissal of the modernism that had attempted to bury it. In claiming that this view was still so widely shared by poets in the early 1980s, Schmidt was in many ways reiterating the position controversially expressed the previous year by Blake Morrison and Andrew Motion in *The Penguin Book of Contemporary British Poetry* (1982). This key anthology and its challenging introduction provided a turning point in the period's poetry and its appreciation, though by no means always in ways its editors would have anticipated or welcomed.

In the light of the editors' own poetry and critical interests, there was in the first place a doubtful aspect in their claim that *The Penguin Book of Contemporary British Poetry* sought to represent 'a shift of sensibility' and a 'radical departure from the empirical mode' established by Larkin and the Movement (Morrison and Motion (eds.), pp. 11–12). Motion later published a biography of Larkin, in 1993, and he was one of a number of poets Edward Lucie-Smith considered to illustrate 'the extreme tenacity of the poetic ideals originally set up by the Movement' in later decades, even among writers of a different generation (Lucie-Smith (ed.), p. 369). In *The Pleasure Steamers* (1978) and later collections, perhaps for biographical reasons, Motion's poems show a Larkin-like distancing of strong feelings. Love is 'overtaken by echoes' in 'Over the Hills', for example, and the collection's title poem suggests an uneasy emotional suppression in its image of a stretch of water, untroubled on its surface, yet with 'somewhere beneath it I an absence of light, increasing I swelling towards me like rain'. Blake Morrison's detailed study, *The Movement*, appeared in 1980, and like much of Motion's his poetry continued Movement idioms of domestic realism, and of tidy construction in rhyme and metre, though with more frequent commentary on contemporary politics and lifestyles. Fashionable furnishings provide an image of how 'the old veneers I have been stripped away' in 'Pine' (1984) for example, while the narrative poem 'The Inquisitor' (1984) refers to contemporary issues such as the Falklands, and to Margaret Thatcher, her voice ringing 'like a grocery-till'. Much of Morrison's later work continued to reflect topical issues or news stories—in another long narrative poem, in Yorkshire dialect, *The Ballad of the Yorkshire Ripper* (1987), or in commenting on the James Bolger child-murder case in a poem written for television in 1994.

Some of the poets included in *The Penguin Book of Contemporary British Poetry,* such as Peter Scupham or Hugo Williams, departed no more radically from Movement convention than the editors. Their claims for a 'new spirit in British poetry' emerging recently in Northern Ireland soon looked equally misdirected (p. 12). Morrison and Motion's introduction described Seamus Heaney as 'the most important new poet of the last fifteen years', but in an *Open Letter* published a year later, Heaney firmly dissociated himself from their anthology, regretfully but clearly explaining 'British, no, the name's not right' (st. 33). Though acknowledging a British audience, acquired 'via Faber' and journals such as *Times Literary Supplement*, Heaney remarked 'my passport's green' and emphasized a 'deep design I To be at home I In my own place', making it impossible for him to accept being 'characterized I As British' (sts. 13, 14, 16). Though he stressed that he spoke for himself, others among the Northern Irish poets included in *The Penguin Book of Contemporary British Poetry*—Derek Mahon, Michael Longley, Tom Paulin, Paul Muldoon, and Medbh McGuckian—certainly shared his views. An outstanding new 'spirit', range, and power clearly *had* developed in the work of Northern Irish poets over the last two decades, confirmed by Morrison and Motion's wish to include so many of them in their anthology. But it emerged in ways which were at odds with any straightforward labelling as 'British', and obviously related only tangentially to the literary history of England.[3]

Appropriate evidence for a 'shift of sensibility' among English writers was provided by the women poets included in the *Penguin Book of Contemporary British Poetry*—Carol Rumens, Fleur Adcock, and Anne Stevenson—and by the regional accents of Tony Harrison.[4] Several poets also emphasized the 'primacy of the imagination' identified in Morrison and Motion's introduction as part of recent 'reformation of poetic taste' (pp. 11–12). Some of James Fenton's poems, such as 'The Kingfisher's Boxing Gloves', were shaped much more by imagination than empiricism: by reverence for the surreal rather than only the real. Fenton's 'In a Notebook' likewise showed how completely political or military violence can undermine any sense of security or familiarity with the world of ordinary experience. Poetry by Craig Raine, Christopher Reid, and David Sweetman was similarly defamiliarizing, their similes and metaphors treating domestic objects and experiences with the kind of *ostranenie* or 'making strange' recommended by Russian formalist critics.

Such tactics were not altogether new. Fenton's mentor John Fuller had sometimes favoured similarly surreal similes, including references to 'Cows . . . With ears like mouths of telephones', hounds with 'tongues like shoehorns', or 'breakers [which] fall like piano lids' in 1960s poems such as 'Band Music' (1960), 'Fairy Tale' (1960), and 'Flood Box' (1967). Yet Fuller was an allusive, erudite writer, concerned, not unlike the Movement, with the 'poetry of implication, disturbance and restraint' he mentions in 'The Wilderness' (1979). Startling similes were an occasional extravagance in work usually pensive, highly formal, and reserved. For Raine, Reid, and Sweetman, such similes were instead a central interest: much of their poetry was dominated by bizarre images—such as Raine's, in 'The Butcher' (1978), of 'a leg of pork | like a nasty bouquet' or of 'coiled coral necklaces of mince'. The improbable imagination of their work, first published in the late 1970s, contributed to a vision supposedly so alien and unfamiliar that the term 'Martian', coined by Fenton from one of Raine's titles, had already become the

---

[3] Implications of the renaissance in Northern Irish writing for poetry in England are discussed on pp. 255–6, below.

[4] These poets are discussed on pp. 223–5 and 215–16, below.

established description of it by the time the *Penguin Book of Contemporary British Poetry* was published. As Raine suggested in his later poems 'Retirement' and 'The Prophetic Book' (1996), translation of ordinary objects into Martian imagery did attempt to 'grant you the world | that is taken for granted', one which readers may have simply 'ceased to see'. Yet the world restored by the Martians' Raine-rinsed clarity of vision remained in some ways as limited as the one envisaged by Movement writers. However extraordinary the imagination of Raine, Reid, and Sweetman, it continued to focus on much the same 'temperate zone' of banal everyday experience the Movement had established, offering a reconfiguration of existing interests rather than the radical departure from convention which Morrison and Motion claimed.

They were still less convincing in suggesting that almost no such departures had occurred during the previous two decades. Any 'shift of sensibility' had taken place, they emphasized, only very recently, after 'a spell of lethargy'. This spell, they considered, had occupied 'much of the 1960s and 70s, when very little—in England at any rate—seemed to be happening, when achievements in British poetry were overshadowed by those in drama and fiction' (Morrison and Motion (eds.), p. 11). There may have been reasons to compare poetry in the whole period from 1960 to 2000 unfavourably with contemporary achievements in fiction and drama.[5] Yet as many commentators pointed out, such negative comparisons were probably *least* justified in relation to the 1960s and early 1970s, one of the few times in the twentieth century when English poetry both broadened the range of its forms and interests and also managed to expand its hold on public attention. Though *The Young British Poets* was not itself a progressive anthology, Jeremy Robson did acknowledge in its introduction 'some kind of renaissance' in the 1960s, noting that 'poetry is now remarkably popular in Britain . . . a large and growing number of people listen to it, buy it, feel it to be relevant to their lives' (p. 11). In *British Poetry 1964 to 1984*, Martin Booth suggested that it was actually in the 1980s that poetry was in a 'mess . . . a bog of indifference, apathy and artlessness', whereas during the previous two decades it had been 'alive to a huge section of the British population' (pp. 3, 4).

---

[5] See also pp. 269–70, below.

'There was something abroad in the 1960s that set a tone or mood for the burgeoning of poetry', Booth added (p. 30). Poetry had the potential to appeal more directly than fiction or sometimes even drama to the new trends, fashions, and carnival attitudes emerging during the 1960s. It offered a medium adapted since the Romantic period to the self-expression the 1960s encouraged, and to the heightened states of consciousness and emotion often pursued at the time. To a decade supposedly belonging to beautiful people—to hedonism, colourful imagination, and a desire for play—poetry seemed to promise beautiful, colourful, imaginative, and playful language. And in departing, almost by definition, from conventional forms of discourse, poetry naturally appealed to a period committed against convention and 'the establishment'. Many of the 600 or so small magazines, devoted wholly or in part to poetry, which Booth records appearing between 1966 and 1972 readily took on the aura of an underground or subversive literature. They were as likely to be sold on a street corner as through a conventional outlet, along with radical journals such as *International Times*, and the poetry they published often offered satiric statements against the Vietnam War, nuclear armaments, apartheid, or other contemporary abuses of power. Established presses also added to the contemporary popularity of poetry, Penguin particularly: two volumes in its 'Penguin Modern Poets' series were published annually for much of the 1960s and early 1970s. Regularly selling 30,000 copies or more, each contained the work of three contemporary poets, usually British, and occasionally of comparable style or interest, though most of the volumes juxtaposed writers fairly randomly. Almost regardless of authorship, the series' distinctive black covers promised a certain quality and contemporaneity, adding to a fashionable, stylish atmosphere surrounding poetry generally at the time. As well as attracting new readers, this also encouraged new authors towards the genre. John Agard summed up 1960s influences on many contemporaries when he recalled beginning to write when 'Viet Nam, the Beatles, Black Power and Peace & Love were part of our consciousness. The poems . . . grow out of that mood' (p. 5)

As Agard suggests, the Beatles—and rock and pop more generally—further extended the appeal of poetry in the 1960s. As well as growing steadily more popular, in the work of some performers rock music moved away from the trite formulas of the 1950s and towards a depth and subtlety which allowed it to be appreciated in much the same way as poetry. Reviewing Bob Dylan's 1966 English tour for *London Magazine*, Angela Carter compared him to Kierkegaard, Kafka, Dostoevsky, Pope, Swift, and Emily Brontë, also talking more soberly of a maturity and imaginativeness 'new and extraordinary in music of mass appeal' (August 1966, p. 101). As she recognized, Dylan defined the new moods of the early 1960s not only through direct statement—as in 'The Times They are a Changin' ', quoted in Chapter 1—but often through concise, understated yet provocatively imaginative images. He continued to provide this kind of lyric intensity—sometimes alongside elements of political engagement—throughout the decade, and intermittently as far as *Blood on the Tracks* (1975). Partly under his influence, and especially after their *Sergeant Pepper* album in 1967, the Beatles's lyrics likewise expanded imaginatively, sometimes into psychedelic strangeness. Towards the end of the decade, the Canadian poet and singer Leonard Cohen's sombre reflections on love, sex, loss, and death further extended affinities between poetry, rock, and pop.

While these and other performers acquired some of the status conventionally accorded poets, poetry gained, reciprocally, a new status, excitement, and breadth of appeal for itself. This association especially benefited writers who seemed to be part of the Mersey scene, almost alongside the Beatles, and soon came to be known as the Liverpool Poets—Adrian Henri, Roger McGough, and Brian Patten. Their 1967 Penguin Modern Poets collection, *The Mersey Sound*, was much the most successful volume in the series, eventually selling more than a quarter of a million copies and remaining in print at the end of the century. Poems in this volume and others reflected many aspects of the new fashions and outlooks of the times. The Liverpool Poets engaged regularly and directly with the popular politics of the 1960s, criticizing the proliferation of nuclear weapons, for example, in Adrian Henri's 'Bomb Commercials', and Roger McGough's 'Icarus Allsorts'. They stayed close to new 1960s fashions in media and music—'feeling Top of the Pops' providing one of Adrian Henri's metaphors in 'Love Is . . .'. They flirted with contemporary drug and student culture—McGough describing himself as 'stoned and lonely in the union bar' in 'The Golden Treasury

Fig. 5. Roger McGough and Brian Patten reading their poems in the late 1960s.

of Flesh' (1973), for example. As McGough's title suggests, they relished new freedoms to talk about love and sex. Funny and flippant, they cheerfully challenged conventional pieties, literary ones included—McGough describing himself in the same poem as 'in I no mood to be laid I alongside our literary heritage'—and favoured instead surreal images and a deliberately naïve, sceptical vision of the world.

Another of their departures from convention was in extending preferences for poetry on the stage rather than only on the page. New enthusiasm for readings and live events in the 1960s was highlighted by the 'First International Poetry Incarnation' held at the Royal Albert Hall in June 1965. This was an event as close to a rock concert as a poetry reading could come, attracting an audience of seven thousand, decked with flowers as they entered the auditorium. A range of poets from Britain and abroad performed work often directly concerned with contemporary politics: Adrian Mitchell's 'To whom it may concern (Tell me lies about Vietnam)' was especially well received. Other poetry reflected new 1960s interest in sex, drugs, or expanding mental horizons generally, Allen Ginsberg's chants and bells also attempting to bring an Eastern mysticism to the occasion. Robert Gittings emphasized the new excitement of live readings in a poem describing the Albert Hall event, recording that 'it began with the flowers I . . . I . . . the occasion had become religious, I With drums and bells I . . . I Names from the anthologies actually present in flesh and blood, I Their own faces'. Along with work by the performers involved, his poem was reproduced (pp. 339–40) in one of the decade's genuinely polemical anthologies: *Children of Albion: Poetry of the 'Underground' in Britain* (1969). Its editor, Michael Horovitz, acclaimed the Albert Hall readings as 'the greatest stimulus for poetry this century', emphasizing in his anthology's title how far their success had been owed to a general opposition to established values, literary or political, at the time (p. 339).

Horovitz had already helped to develop a broad audience for poetry readings, setting up tours and performances since 1959 through 'Live New Departures', an outgrowth of the avant-garde journal *New Departures*. Combining readings with music, the 'informality and excitement' of these shows had in Adrian Mitchell's estimation 'brought into the open a huge new audience for poetry, as

Fig. 6. Allen Ginsberg on stage at the Albert Hall Poetry event,
11 June 1965.

well as many new poets' by the end of the 1960s (Hampson and
Barry (eds.), p. 27). They also helped establish a reading circuit
throughout the country, eventually organized by bodies such as
the National Poetry Secretariat and the Greater London Arts
Association. Though not always maintained at 1960s levels, enthusiasm for readings, literary events, and book festivals continued to
develop in later decades, soon including authors other than poets.
The influence of television, after the 1950s, probably added to expectations that authors should be visible, like everything else, and
renounce their old role as remote figures accessible only through
what they wrote. Finding 'names from the anthologies actually present in flesh and blood' was at any rate something the public had come
to expect towards the end of the century. Interest in author-events,
readings, and book-signings was further extended by the new bookshops established in the 1980s and 1990s, and by a growing number
of literary festivals throughout the country.

   As a result, from the 1960s onwards most poets had to think of
themselves as performers as well as writers, with many consequences

Fig. 7. Readings, promotions, and book signings began to feature
more regularly in bookshops during the 1980s—this one involving
poets Craig Raine and Seamus Heaney.

for the genre, and particular incentives for certain forms of experiment within it. Readings were an obvious context for sound poetry,
for instance, just as the spread of small magazines—such as Bob
Cobbing's *And*—had encouraged concrete and visual poetry. More
generally, the success of readings changed perceptions of what a
poem should be, and of how, ideally, it should be encountered.
A correspondent to the *Listener* on 5 April 1973, for example,
defended Brian Patten's poetry by suggesting that it should be read
'with a rock group and strobe half in mind . . . with a musical score à
la [Leonard] Cohen', concluding that 'in our time . . . the Muse left
her seat to become a performing artist' (p. 449). For many writers,
the Muse never quite sat down again. In *Grandchildren of Albion:
Voices and Visions of Younger Poets in Britain* (1992), Michael
Horovitz presented work by a new generation who had continued
'giving and getting its essence in performance before print' (p. 414).
Other poets such as Brian Catling, Caroline Bergvall, or Aaron
Williamson continued into the 1980s and 1990s to treat their work

primarily as a performance medium, sometimes in combination with sculpture, graphic art, or other installations. Many writers kept a rock group or musical score more than half in mind, some of the Black British poets emerging in the 1970s particularly. Much of Benjamin Zephaniah's and Linton Kwesi Johnson's work was recorded or set to music, the latter commenting in *Dread Beat and Blood* (1975) that his poems were invariably intended to be read aloud, in the community. Though he had never published a poem on paper, the ex-Beatle Paul McCartney was regularly mentioned in discussions about who should succeed Ted Hughes as Poet Laureate in 1999, confirming how far rock had come to be equated with poetry in the popular imagination, or to function as a substitute for it. Straightforward, memorable lyrics that the later twentieth century kept at the back of its mind, or under its breath, were likelier to have been delivered by rock music than by established poets.

Radio, too, continued into the 1970s and beyond to expand an audience for whom poetry was a matter of 'performance before print'. The Third Programme (later Radio Three) broadcast several regular poetry features under George MacBeth's direction: *The Poet's Voice*, for example, and *Poetry Now*, which attracted as many as 50,000 listeners at various stages of its long run from the late 1950s. The programme's withdrawal in 1976, however, and the demise of the Penguin Modern Poets series by the end of the decade, were among many signs that the 'renaissance' initiated in the 1960s was drawing to a close. Eric Mottram entitled an essay assessing developments at this time 'The British Poetry Revival, 1960–1975', and the dates were well chosen (Hampson and Barry (eds.), p. 15): Peter Jones and Michael Schmidt likewise identified in their study *British Poetry since 1970* (1980) a movement from 'euphoria' to 'betrayed optimism' in the early 1970s (p. ix). So dependent on the expansive or 'euphoric' atmosphere of the 1960s, the poetry revival was quickly curtailed by the narrowing, chillier outlook of the mid-1970s. Like many other areas of contemporary life and art, it also suffered directly from the economic crises of the time. Less money was available from the Arts Council or local authorities to sponsor readings, while tighter finances among the population generally made attendance at poetry events or the purchase of costly slim volumes seem an unnecessary luxury. Small poetry presses as well as larger publishers suffered as a result. As Chapter 1 suggested, all genres of literature reflected in one way or another the new moods of the 1960s and the betrayed optimism which followed. At least in terms of popular appeal, poetry corresponded more simply and directly than drama or fiction to the expansiveness of the 1960s and the constraints of the next decade, flourishing and fading alongside the flower children.

Yet for several commentators the efflorescence of the 1960s and early 1970s never amounted to a real renaissance. Deliberately avoiding 'the literary heritage', writers such as the Liverpool Poets were inevitably unwelcome to those who saw themselves as its custodians, as upholders of poetic tradition. Donald Davie considered that writers 'went wrong, and failed themselves as poets . . . in running together the aesthetics of the creative and of the performing arts' (*Under Briggflatts*, p. 55). Replying to an early version of Davie's criticisms, that correspondent to the *Listener*, quoted earlier, did acknowledge that without a strobe-light or musical score Brian Patten's lines could seem 'inert' on the page. It would have been still harder to defend some of the poets Horovitz included in his *Children of Albion* anthology. Poems such as Pete Brown's three-line 'Road' —'They tore up the old road | and buried it under a new one. | I didnt mind'—lack on the page the quirkiness or irony which made them successful in performance. For critics such as Davie, it was just this demand for quirkiness and immediacy in performance which narrowed the range of poetry's possibilities and threatened its potential for profundity. Another poet sympathetic to the Movement, Anthony Thwaite, likewise worried in the *Listener* on 5 April 1973 that the *Children of Albion* anthology and other directions in contemporary poetry indicated an impending 'split in our literary culture'. On the one hand, Thwaite saw 'exuberant mind-blowers' in search of 'spontaneity, immediacy, an energy released by . . . an instant flash of communion'. On the other, there were those still conventionally concerned with 'academic rigour and complexity', or convinced that 'art has a great deal to do with shape, form, control, and that a good poem shouldn't reveal all its facets and depths and resonances at a single hearing or reading' (pp. 453–4).

Davie was further troubled by worries arising from his view of poetry readings as aesthetically undemanding occasions, ones 'obviously in keeping with the participatory democracy of the 1960s' (*Under Briggflatts*, p. 125). Other commentators looked more favourably on the effects of democratization in English society following the 1960s, considering it to have encouraged participation rather than passivity where poetry was concerned. Instead of the usual expectation that poetry came from 'a specific group of humans', with particular attributes of class, education, and temperament, Martin Booth emphasized that a premiss 'at the core of the poetry revival of the 1960s' was that 'anyone can write a poem' (p. 20). Facilitated by poetry's ease of publication, compared to other genres, this assumption was further consolidated by the writers' groups and poetry workshops proliferating during and after the 1960s, and by institutions such as the Arvon Foundation, established in 1971 by the poets John Moat and John Fairfax to provide residential courses for aspiring writers. Booth considered that the Arvon Foundation 'carrie[d] on what the 1960s started' through the belief that 'poetry exists in everyone . . . its ease of construction, with a laxity of strict techniques, has made it belong to everyman' (pp. 29–30).

For Davie, on the other hand, assumptions about 'ease' and 'laxity' of this kind 'put paid to, or at least had drastically imperilled, the practice of poetry in any sense that preserved continuity with previous centuries' (*Under Briggflatts*, p. 126). Discussing the huge entry for the annual Arvon Foundation prize, he questioned why, by the end of the 1970s,

more than 30,000 persons in the English-speaking world thought they had sufficiently mastered the principles of an ancient and intricate art . . . It began to seem that in an egalitarian century the exclusiveness of art—of *any* art—was an affront that could not be tolerated . . . the writing of poems was clearly no longer considered an art but rather a hobby. (pp. 137–8)

In his introduction to the *Oxford Book of Verse, 1945–1980* (1980) D. J. Enright likewise complained about a contemporary 'distaste for élitism and specialisation' which had led to 'abandoning the ancient poetic habit' and 'the weakening of poetry', or even its treatment as 'a self-administered form of therapy' (pp. xxi, xxii). Thom Gunn's 'Expression' (1982) gave a similarly negative view of neurotic self-indulgence and unconstrained emotion in much contemporary writing. For poets involved with the Movement, in other words, the 1960s and early 1970s had witnessed not a real renaissance in poetry, but an erosion of its traditional strengths in favour of populism, lax self-expression, cheap sensation, or what Blake Morrison called '60s Romantic notions of the poet as risk-taker, "mad genius" or bard' (Jones and Schmidt (eds.), p. 142). Morrison and Motion's improvident conclusion—that 'very little' had been happening in England in the two decades prior to the publication of *The Penguin Book of Contemporary British Poetry* in 1982—was in one way inevitable, since work which had so enlarged popular appreciation of the genre seemed irrelevant, even antithetical, to what they and authors like them conceived the 'ancient, intricate art' of English poetry ideally to be. Puzzlingly, however, their introduction was scarcely more sympathetic towards other recent initiatives with firmer claims to 'intricate art' and 'poetic habit'. These developments and reactions to them are considered in the next chapter.

6

Counter-movements and Modernist Memories: 1960 to the 1980s

Indifferent to the popular revival of the 1960s, Blake Morrison and Andrew Motion's introduction to *The Penguin Book of Contemporary British Poetry* (1982) was scarcely readier to acknowledge— and eventually dismissed—other recent directions contrary to the Movement. Some of these had been highlighted twenty years earlier —almost before they were fully apparent in English poetry—in A. L. Alvarez's 1962 debate with Donald Davie, described at the start of Chapter 5. Arguing with Davie about tactics poetry might legitimately follow after Auschwitz, Alvarez extended ideas he had introduced in *The New Poetry*, published a few weeks earlier. As he admitted himself, this anthology was polemical not for its choice of poets, many of whom—Philip Larkin, Kingsley Amis, Donald Davie, D. J. Enright, Thom Gunn, and John Wain—also figured in Robert Conquest's Movement-oriented *New Lines* volumes. Alvarez's real polemic appeared in his introduction to *The New Poetry*, highly critical of the contemporary scene, and prophetic of directions poets ought to follow in order to move 'beyond the gentility principle' (p. 21). In his view, much contemporary writing, the Movement's particularly, offered only 'a kind of unity of flatness': a ready complicity with the established hierarchies of English society, and with 'the idea that life in England goes on much as it always has' (pp. 24, 25). 'Genteel and enislanded' attitudes of this kind seemed to him strangely inappropriate in an era blighted by 'world wars . . . mass extermination . . . concentration camps . . . the hydrogen bomb' (pp. 26–7).

Alvarez was further concerned that 'recognition of a mass evil outside us ha[d] developed precisely parallel with psychoanalysis; that is, with our recognition of the ways in which the same forces are at work within us' (p. 27). New recognitions of evil, inside and out, urgently required reassessment of conventions recently dominant in English writing. Instead of withdrawal into small spaces and domestic realities, Alvarez demanded a poetry as shocked, and shocking, as the Movement's was deliberately temperate and tame. Only a 'powerful complex of emotions and sensations', or a 'nexus of fear and sensation', he considered, could begin to do justice to deep post-war disillusion and its shattered moral and ethical convictions (p. 31). Alvarez, in other words, sought to extend into poetry a transition beginning to be apparent in other genres of English writing in the early 1960s, and in national consciousness generally: from evasion or deflection of the war's implications, towards more direct responses to its overwhelming moral and historical challenges.[1]

The 'nexus' he demanded—between historic forces of disintegration and others 'at work within us'—began to appear in the work of Sylvia Plath almost at the time the first edition of *The New Poetry* was published. 'Lady Lazarus' (1965), for example, configures personal compulsions toward suicide within broader conscience of the concentration camps: within an imagined self whose face is 'fine | Jew linen', whose skin is 'Bright as a Nazi lampshade' and whose body is doomed to be burned down to 'A cake of soap, | A wedding ring, | A gold filling'. 'Daddy' (1965) likewise identifies with the experience of 'Chuffing . . . off like a Jew. | A Jew to Dachau, Auschwitz, Belsen'. The poem goes on to describe tortured relations with a father figured as 'Panzer-man'—'a man in black with a Meinkampf look' who has come from a central Europe 'scraped flat by the roller | Of wars, wars, wars'. This black vision unfolds within tripping sound-patterns and rhythms resembling nursery rhyme, as if even the most habitual accents of innocence and gentility had been enslaved by the darkening forces of modern history. Plath's biographer Anne Stevenson described her as 'the fiercest poet of our time', and the one

---

[1] See pp. 54–5, above.

best equipped to encapsulate its anxieties through 'catching the anguish of [the] age | in accents of a private rage' ('Letter to Sylvia Plath', 1990). Including Plath in a second edition of *The New Poetry* in 1966, Alvarez concluded that, 'more than anyone else's', her work had fulfilled the demands made in his introduction to the first edition four years earlier (p. 18).

This first edition had excluded her on the grounds of her origins in the United States, though she had lived intermittently in England after her marriage to Ted Hughes in 1956, and permanently from 1959 until her suicide in 1963. Without Plath, Alvarez's first edition relied principally on Ted Hughes himself to exemplify alternatives to Movement gentility. Hughes's first two collections, *Hawk in the Rain* (1957) and *Lupercal* (1960), offered fears and emotions to sensational extent, like Plath's poetry. Each collection also thoroughly challenged poetic conventions—of orderly rhythm and rhyme, and of pastoral and the use of nature especially. The opening poem of *Lupercal*, 'Mayday on Holderness', for example, is set in much the same Humberside territory Philip Larkin continued to appreciate, in wistfully Hardyesque pastoral terms in 'Here' (1964), for its 'unfenced existence' and 'solitude | Of skies and scarecrows'. 'Mayday on Holderness' also begins conventionally enough, with an image of nature personified as 'motherly summer'. But in describing decomposing leaves as a 'furnace door whirling with larvae', and the Humber as a 'loaded single vein' draining the industrial North's effluent into the 'unkillable' North Sea, the poem moves within a few lines into a very different kind of vision. Nature no longer seems benign, but rather a soiled, threatening plenitude, infested by 'length of gut . . . growing and breathing'; by 'eye-guarded eggs in the hedgerows'; by a 'nightlong frenzy of shrews'. Typically of Hughes's poetry, images of violence horribly surround birth and procreation: by the poem's end, the 'Mayday' of its title no longer suggests any welcome fecundity in 'motherly summer', but becomes a distress call in the face of feral fertilities of brute blood and gut.

Other poems in the collection develop similar fears of 'natural' yet darkly alien vitality. 'Pike' figures its subject belonging to a 'stilled legendary depth | . . . as deep as England', a 'darkness beneath night's darkness' which the poet fishes 'with the hair frozen on [his] head'. Like 'Mayday on Holderness', 'Pike' reconfigures nature poetry into the nexus Alvarez sought, tracing reciprocal implications between contemporary history and a darkly post-Freudian, primordial sense of the self. The dread depths of the fish's domain figure something of the dark reaches of the poet's own unconscious, while 'Mayday on Holderness' parallels the violence of the beast world with human conflicts extending from the First World War to the submarine missiles of the Cold War, at its height at the time. 'The North Sea lies soundless', 'Mayday on Holderness' remarks, but 'beneath it | Smoulder the wars: to heart-beats, bomb, bayonet'. Often described as an expressionist, Hughes diffused stresses of late twentieth-century history, society, and selfhood throughout his vision of nature, rather as the river in 'Mayday on Holderness' drains human detritus into the sea. These stresses were further, reciprocally, reinforced by visceral hostilities shown ruling that natural world itself. Like the moon in his 'Full Moon and Little Frieda' (1967), in relation to nature Hughes was 'an artist gazing amazed at a work | That points at him amazed'.

Historical stresses highlighted in 'Mayday on Holderness'—and in other poems in *Lupercal* such as 'A Woman Unconscious'—were usually less explicit in Hughes's later poetry. The vision they helped to shape nevertheless remained consistent throughout much of his writing. The translations published in his best-selling *Tales from Ovid* (1997) were in a way a predictable interest, since Hughes's own poetry so consistently metamorphosed nature and creatures into threatening, unexpected versions of themselves. The birds envisaged in 'Thrushes' (1960), for example, are 'coiled steel', endowed with 'bullet and automatic | Purpose', and those in 'Skylarks' (1967) 'crueller than owl or eagle', while 'The Bull Moses' (1960) is of a blackness 'beyond star | . . . | . . . nothing of our light | Found any reflection in him'. Habitually dark, physical, and bloody descriptions—such as the graphic concentration on decapitating a half-born foetus, in an account of lambing in 'February 17th'(1979)—seemed excessive to some commentators. Neil Corcoran found Hughes occasionally 'voluptuous . . . almost to a febrile degree' (p. 119), while Wendy Cope's popular comic verse included a poem, written in the manner of Gilbert and Sullivan, which imagines the ghastly job of policing Hughes's unconscious. Some of his most widely-admired poems—such as those in *Crow* (1970)—were therefore ones which contained darker obsessions within a redeeming irony. The figure of Crow flaunts cheerfully, as parts of his indestructible resilience, qualities seen in other poems as ineluctably malign. Leavening destruction and desolation with dark metaphysical laughter, this phase of Hughes's work was typical of a black comedy much more widely apparent in the period's writing, often as a legacy of the war—an aspect of much of its fiction, as well as the drama of the Absurd.[2] Looking blackly on a dark universe also allowed Crow's parables of survival to recuperate, in a kind of double negative, an almost affirmative view even of death, the torment of sexual relations, or the aloof indifference of God.

In such ways, in *Crow* and other later work Hughes attempted no less than the reconstruction of mythologies for a violent, disillusioned, irreligious, post-war age. The ambition and unusualness of this imagination contributed to his unique reputation when he died in 1998, shortly after the publication of *Birthday Letters*. Its huge sales reflected in one way a widespread, even sensational, interest in the relationship with Sylvia Plath the volume described. But its success also confirmed Hughes's status by the 1990s: as a writer who had come to share or surpass Larkin's reputation as the pre-eminent English poet of the later twentieth century. Andrew Motion claimed of Larkin that '*The Less Deceived* made his name; *The Whitsun Weddings* made him famous; *High Windows* turned him into a national monument' (Thwaite, *Poetry Today*, p. 41). Even before the end of the century, Hughes had come to seem another literary monument, though one resolutely facing the opposite way. Contrasting a Larkin nature poem with one by Hughes, Alvarez identified as early as 1962 the extent to which their work represented contrary directions in English poetry. D. J. Enright confirmed in 1980 that it had already become convenient to 'subsume the period under two poets, Philip Larkin and Ted Hughes. Their contemporaries can then be located at intervals on the line stretching between these two' (*Oxford Book of Verse*, p. xxiii). Developments still to be considered had stretched and tangled this line, even by 1980, further than this convenient synopsis suggests. Nevertheless, contrasts between Larkin and Hughes, Movement 'gentility' and Alvarez's alternatives, do help to define major directions followed by English poetry, especially

[2] See Chs. 12 and 17, esp. pp.346–59 and 452–4 respectively.

in the first half of the period—startlingly different ones, given how far each was shaped by the same set of historical circumstances, the legacies of the war in particular.

In their introduction to *The Penguin Book of Contemporary British Poetry*, Morrison and Motion acknowledged some influence on recent writing from the authors discussed above, but suggested that Hughes was 'no longer the presiding spirit of British poetry' and that Alvarez's attack on 'English decency' had 'come to seem simplistic' (p. 13). Further dismissing the Alvarez/Hughes direction in recent poetry, they reiterated the kind of scepticism Donald Davie had expressed in conversation with Alvarez twenty years earlier, quoting James Fenton's mockery of supposed emotional excesses in his 'Letter to John Fuller' (1972). Alvarez, according to Fenton,

> tells you, in the sombrest notes,
> If poets want to get their oats
> The first step is to slit their throats.
> The way to divide
> The sheep of poetry from the goats
> Is suicide.
>
> .   .   .   .   .   .
>
> For a poet, not to have cut his wrist
> Is worse than having not been kissed.

Support for Fenton's mockery of passions and extremes confirmed Morrison and Motion's membership of the Larkin/Movement camp, and further explained their conclusion that little had been happening in English poetry in the 1960s and 1970s. From their point of view, much of what might have been approved by Alvarez, or even Hughes, could be discarded—along with 1960s populism and its 'exuberant mind-blowers'—as of limited aesthetic worth.

Yet like several of Alvarez's opponents, Morrison and Motion misconstrued his introduction to *The New Poetry*. Alvarez by no means favoured extremes of passion *alone*, but also stressed their containment. Arguing with Davie in the *Review* in May 1962, he commended the contemporary US poet Robert Lowell not only for 'writing about violent neurotic breakdown', but for doing so in 'a language very disciplined, highly disciplined' (pp. 16, 19). Sylvia Plath's 'The Arrival of the Bee Box' (1965) might provide an ideal metaphor for Alvarez's poetic principles, in its description of a 'dangerous . . . box of maniacs', but nonetheless a 'clean wood box | Square as a chair . . . locked'. Alvarez at any rate emphasized what he called in *The New Poetry*, following Coleridge, the reconciliation of 'a more than usual state of emotion with more than usual order'. Such reconciliation, he suggested, required something of 'the technical skill and formal intelligence of T. S. Eliot' (p. 32). His introduction consequently complained less about passionless gentility in recent English poetry than about the extent to which modernism's technical sophistication and inventiveness had been submerged in successive waves of mediocre writing in later years, culminating in the Movement. For Movement writers and their followers, characterizing Alvarez as a wrist-slitting eccentric conveniently obscured his advocacy of forms of modernist writing whose influence they were also anxious to suppress.

This influence nevertheless reappeared strongly almost from the time Alvarez wrote, justifying his claims for a prophetic aspect in his introduction. English poetry after 1960 was characterized not only by antitheses between Larkin and Hughes, but by contrasts between the Movement idiom and surviving, or rediscovered, legacies of modernist writing. The Scottish modernist Hugh MacDiarmid's *Collected Poems*, published in 1962, introduced his work to a wider English audience early in the decade. MacDiarmid himself considered the poems of another writer often overlooked in England in earlier years, Basil Bunting, as the most important to have appeared in the English language since T. S. Eliot's *The Waste Land*. Published in 1966, Bunting's outstanding work, *Briggflatts*, resembled *The Waste Land* (1922) in a number of ways: in its complex structure of juxtaposed vignettes, with unexplained transitions in period and locale; in its uncompromising incorporation of material from other cultures; even in the division of its 700 lines into five sections. *Briggflatts* also shared some of the mood of *The Waste Land*. Though eventually more affirmative of sex and procreation, the poem begins in a late, harsh spring, comparable to Eliot's cruel April, and goes on to juxtapose starkly, throughout, images of fertility with ones of death and dissolution. Setting in the raw northern landscapes of Bunting's youth often creates only a cold pastoral, even for the poem's affirmations: its lovers lie 'Under sacks on the stone' and

> kiss under the rain,
> bruised by their marble bed.
> In Garsdale, dawn;
> at Hawes, tea from the can.
> Rain stops, sacks
> steam in the sun, they sit up.
> Copper-wire moustache,
> sea-reflecting eyes
> and Baltic plainsong speech
> declare: By such rocks
> men killed Bloodaxe.

Yet this northern landscape of becks and fells is far removed from Eliot's urban one. *Briggflatts* was indebted more directly to Ezra Pound—whom Bunting knew in Paris and Italy in the 1920s and 1930s—and to the emphases on language and sound-pattern in the work of another US poet, Louis Zukofsky. Bunting identified Scarlatti rather than *The Waste Land* as the model for his five-part construction in the poem, and refers in it to the composers Monteverdi, Byrd, and Schoenberg. The preface to his *Collected Poems* (1968) also explains that he had 'set down words as a musician pricks his score ... to trace in the air a pattern of sound'. In their extended, modulated sequence of open vowels, the lines quoted above are typical of 'patterns of sound' Bunting sustains throughout *Briggflatts*. The whole poem shapes around water, stones, stars, and memories a 'plainsong speech' comparable to the poetry of Gerard Manley Hopkins, or even the alliterative richness of Anglo-Saxon or Middle English verse. Bunting's direction of this formal invention and modernist imagination on an English landscape and tradition made *Briggflatts* for many commentators a pre-eminent achievement of English poetry in the later twentieth century. Donald Davie, for example, recorded his admiration in the title of his critical study *Under Briggflatts: A History of Poetry in Great Britain 1960–1988* (1989). *Briggflatts* also contributed to a shift of poetry's centre of gravity towards the regions at this time—one later encouraged by the Newcastle-based publisher Bloodaxe Books, founded in 1978 and named after Bunting's ancient Northern king. Regional landscapes, and often regional accents,[3] played a growing role in the poetry of the

---

[3] These are discussed on pp. 217–18, below.

period—Yorkshire, in work by Tony Harrison and Blake Morrison, for example; Cumbria, for Norman Nicholson; Cornwall, often the context for the modern ballad-forms ingeniously developed by Charles Causley.

Bunting described *Briggflatts* as 'An Autobiography'. Public rather than personal history preoccupied another writer, indebted to the modernists, who emerged in the 1960s: Geoffrey Hill. His first collections, *For the Unfallen* (1959) and *King Log* (1968), strongly developed the 'new seriousness' Alvarez demanded in relation to recent history, though in a minimal, intense poetry shorn of explicit passions. Poems in *King Log*, such as 'Ovid in the Third Reich' or 'September Song', raised as gravely as any post-war writing the difficulties of continuing to produce poetry after Auschwitz. Description of a concentration-camp victim in 'September Song' is followed by the poet's uneasy acknowledgement of his own apparently safe distance in a fertile, peaceful landscape, with only 'the smoke | Of harmless fires' in his eyes. And yet—typically of Hill's poetry—'September Song' denies the possibility of any safe or uncomplicated vision of history, unharmed or untainted by its effects. Apparently innocent, the smoke nevertheless draws the observer towards complicity with the experience of the camps, while at the same time clouding his vision.

Typically, too, this vision is further complicated by the poet refusing—like the modernists, Eliot particularly—to provide what Hill called in *King Log* 'overt narrative or dramatic structure' (p. 67), and by his drawing attention to 'the debasement of words' under historical and political pressures (Haffenden, *Viewpoints*, p. 88). Conflicting statements, speech-registers, and implied attitudes force Hill's readers to construe for themselves diverse strata of discourse, and to recognize some of the politics and pressures which shape each. From the chill register of bureaucratic planning—'Just so much Zyklon and leather, patented | terror, so many routine cries' required for organized death in the concentration camps—'September Song' moves on to a concluding line belonging to no clear or singular perspective. 'This is plenty. This is more than enough' could refer—among other conflicting possibilities—to historical circumstances which may be more than can be borne; to the poet's relative comfort and immunity from them; or even to the closure of this 'elegy' itself, its minimal consolations more than the subject might have been expected to allow. Hill found in the 'debasement' of words themselves 'a paradigm of the loss of the kingdom of innocence and original justice'. By extending the unspeakable conflicts of recent history into the splintered semantics of his own writing, he may have dealt with memories of the Holocaust as effectively as any English poet could (Haffenden, *Viewpoints*, p. 88). The regularity with which the concentration camps recurred as a subject of late twentieth-century poetry suggested that for many writers their implications remained, rather as Alvarez and Davie feared in 1962, both irresolvable yet impossible to ignore. The Holocaust, at any rate, continued to figure centrally in poetry as otherwise diverse as Peter Porter's 'Annotations of Auschwitz' (1961), Tony Harrison's 'Allotments' (1970), Lee Harwood's 'Text for two posters by Ian Brown' (1981), Ken Smith's 'Exiles' (1972), Carol Rumens's 'Outside Oswiecim' (1985), and Jon Silkin's 'Jaffa, and Other Places' (1971). It also shaped Silkin's long sequence 'The People' (1974), and several other poems by Hill himself.

Hill's attempts to free the past from the remoteness of official history, bringing to its bloodiness the 'belated witness' he felt it demanded, also extended in *King Log* to holocausts long before the twentieth century: to the battles of the Wars of the Roses, vividly relived in its 'Funeral Music' sequence (p. 68). Investigation of what 'poetry | Unearths from the speechless dead' and of 'old | Laurels wagging with the new' ('History as Poetry', 1968) continued in much of his later writing. The complex anachronisms of *Mercian Hymns* (1971), for example, suggest—like Bunting's infusion of Bloodaxe's memory into the rocks of Northumbria—that the ancient Mercian monarch Offa was not only 'King of the perennial holly-groves, the riven sandstone' but still a contemporary figure, still 'overlord of the M5' (I). Offa's battles are also shown surviving as present-day suburban house names, and several 'hymns' intermingle childhood experience of the Second World War with the immemorial life of Mercia, its legacies somehow still sustained within 'the long-unlooked-for mansions of the tribe' (IV). In such ways much of Hill's writing followed T. S. Eliot's conclusions in *Little Gidding* (1942) about the past's continuity with the present; its survival within an immediate 'now' of contemporary England. Relating history and the contemporary through amalgams of causality, memory, and metaphor, *Mercian Hymns* figures an ancient 'coiled entrenched England' as a mythic mainspring of its later life, source of a bloodline still resounding in the heartbeat of the present (XX).

Several other poets emerging in the 1960s diverged sharply from Movement idioms, extending instead, like Bunting and Hill, forms of modernist challenge to poetic convention. Charles Tomlinson disliked the 'narrowness' of Larkin (Ford (ed.), p. 479), criticizing Movement writers for lack of 'vital awareness of the continuum outside themselves' and for their indifference to 'mystery . . . in the created universe' (Corcoran, p. 84). Christopher Middleton complained that by 1964 English poetry had 'steered off into a parochial corner of the universe', far too little concerned with 'the radical remaking of techniques' (Stan Smith, pp. 16–17). Both writers shaped new techniques of their own, partly based on reassessments of relations between the poet and the 'continuum' outside the self. Peter Redgrove followed a similar course, also continuing to reshape nature poetry in ways initiated by Ted Hughes. Some of Redgrove's work—the precise description of 'The Ferns' (1966), for example— reflected straightforwardly enough the exact observation of a poet who first trained as a nature scientist. But like Hughes, Redgrove often envisaged nature as threatening or alien, rather than passive or neutral. Description of 'a cow's placenta thrown over a whitethorn' ('The Smith's Anvil', 1979) could have come from Hughes's poetry, as could the 'brute muscle' of the bird—an 'airship | Whose furnace-draught is screams'—in 'On the Screaming of the Gulls' (1966). Descriptions of this disturbing external world also raised questions about how—literally, or sometimes physically—it could be digested within the human sphere. 'The House in the Acorn' (1966), for example, describes how trees are turned into domestic architecture, and 'The Whole Music at Pod's Kitchen' (1979) and 'The Heir' (1966) how glasses of thunder-rain or beer pass into the human digestive system. Moving towards Redgrove's interest in the magical, 'Mr Waterman' (1961) even speculates about how a pond might enter the house as a lodger. In other poems Redgrove investigates, reciprocally, how apparently human qualities may be found in the natural world: in the 'great alphabets' of the forest in 'Initials of the Dead' (1979), or the landscape figured as 'a great individual', embodying 'awareness in the earth' in 'Drunk on the Moon' (1979).

Yet Redgrove describes this earthy awareness not as an extension or metaphor for human consciousness, but existing independently of it. The introduction to his *Selected Poems* (1975) talks of a need for 'rebellion . . . *against* consciousness' in order fully to recognize that 'waves and sky have meaning in themselves'. This need is emphasized in 'The Idea of Entropy at Maenporth Beach' (1972), which alludes to the US poet Wallace Stevens—a regular commentator on relations between imagination and reality—but inverts preferences he expressed in 'The Idea of Order at Key West' (1935). A modernist—also a late Romantic—Stevens highlights the human voice's capacity to 'order words of the sea' and applauds art's ability to shape 'the meaningless plungings of water and the wind'. Redgrove, on the other hand, seeks no convenient containment of nature within human constructs. On the contrary, he favours the submersion of human forms in exhilarating, muddy earthiness, leaving no human voice but rather 'the shrugged-up riches of deep darkness' somehow free to sing for themselves.

Charles Tomlinson sometimes described nature conventionally, as in 'The Snow Fences' (1966). More often, like Redgrove, he wrote about a natural sphere autonomous and distanced from the human one, and about the difficulty of maintaining connections between the two. Their separateness is emphasized in 'The Fox Gallery' (1969), for example. Swerving away from human domiciles, the fox demonstrates 'how utterly the two worlds were | disparate'. Like another of Wallace Stevens's poems, 'Notes Toward a Supreme Fiction' (1942), Tomlinson's writing regularly investigates the implications of this utter disparity for art and language. In 'Cézanne at Aix' (1960), he wonders how the painter could possibly represent a mountain whose 'silence silences' and which remains 'irreducible', 'unalterable', and 'a presence | which does not present itself'. 'Observation of Facts' (1955) likewise questions how the imagination can ever legitimately reproduce a world which is 'stripped of imagination' in itself. Words have an especially doubtful role in this process, concealing 'the observation | Behind the observer'. Language and metaphor, 'Observation of Facts' suggests, function as a 'chintz curtain' draped over the observed world. 'Bluebells' (1989) likewise reflects of the flowers that 'if they are blue | . . . | It is only our words so call and colour them'. Similar uneasiness with language, art, and their relations with reality extends through poems such as 'Winter Encounters' (1960), 'The Chances of Rhyme' (1969), or 'Glass Grain' (1960). 'Something: A Direction' (1960) even practises a kind of self-interrogating breakdown of any language in which mind and natural world might relate, discussing a 'self delimited | Regarding sun. It downs? I claim? Cannot | Beyond such speech as this, gather conviction?'. Only 'beyond speech', Tomlinson's poetry suggests, can either self or world exist fully, in copious autonomy, independent of a language which limits and distorts even when seeking only to describe. Concerned that the world contains 'more | Than the words can witness', as 'Winter Encounters' remarks, much of his work showed affinities with the language-centred postmodern poetry discussed in Chapter 7, below.

Christopher Middleton was similarly wary of words, worrying over language's role in making of the physical world 'a thing recovered into thought' (*Pursuit of the Kingfisher*, p. 96). Yet on the whole he was more affirmative than Tomlinson or Redgrove of relations between observer and observed world, stressing their significance for selfhood and identity. 'You best exist in things | outside', he claims in 'A Bunch of Grapes' (1962), explaining in his essay 'Reflections on a Viking Prow' (1979), that 'the regard resting on the object is . . . the key to self-affirmation . . . as the object reveals itself in a certain light, that self can gaze into its own depths . . . Between "I am" and "This is" there can be strange ligatures—a magico-grammatical tissue links first and third persons singular' (*Pursuit of the Kingfisher*, p. 87). Much of Middleton's poetry correspondingly strives for the 'magical substitution' described in 'Reflections on a Viking Prow': for 'structurings . . . which relate transitively to the extraneous world whose form they gaily enshrine' and which can 'put us in perceptual contact with being' (p. 84). Desire for such 'transitive' contact diversified Middleton's work into poetic forms as various as the structures or objects it sought to enshrine.

Structures, geometries, and spatial relations were also regular subjects of his poetry. 'Le Nu Provençal' (1975), for example, meticulously details a photograph's representation of objects and their positions, concluding that 'watch as you will, the mystery is . . . |

Perhaps between the things, distributing tensions. | . . . | Or in the volume of the space they occupy'. In 'Snail on the Doorstep' (1980), Middleton finds in the shape of the spiral mollusc a version of an 'infinite curve of space' repeated throughout the universe, and in 'Old Water Jar'(1986) a form whose 'long sweet wave | you can't help liking . . . | Simply for the way | It stands there'. Though the latter poem alludes once again to one of Wallace Stevens's, 'Anecdote of the Jar' (1923), Middleton's insistence on the significance of objects was generally closer to another US poet, William Carlos Williams. Much of his work seems to follow, in particular, Williams's suggestion that there are 'no ideas | but in things' ('A Sort of a Song', 1944). In 'The Green Lemon', for example, Middleton celebrates the pendulous, portentous, yet 'unremarkable . . . lemon hanging | In a lemon tree' much as Carlos Williams insisted on the significance dependent on his famous red wheelbarrow. Typically of wider political and historical interests also shaping his poetry, Middleton goes on to speculate on the exploitative economic and labour conditions in which the lemon will eventually be picked.

'The Green Lemon' appeared in Middleton's *Intimate Chronicles* in 1996, continuing a career which developed successfully, like Redgrove's and Tomlinson's, well beyond the 1960s and 1970s. During those decades, each poet might already have been counted among the 'strong individual writers' whom Morrison and Motion did acknowledge at work at this time, despite what they considered its 'lack of overall shape and direction' (p. 11). Middleton, Tomlinson, and Redgrove did not contribute an overall shape to the 1960s and 1970s, but their work did illustrate how far modernist legacies, as well as those of the Movement, remained influential at the time. It also indicated—like Basil Bunting's writing—how important the United States had become for the more innovative or modernist-influenced English poets in the period. For Tomlinson and Middleton, the attempt to conceive the natural world in its own terms might have followed from familiarity not only with the literature of the United States, but with its landscapes: often more hostile, further beyond human scale, and less amenable to conventional pastoral than the English countryside. Extensively interested in US poets, William Carlos Williams particularly, Tomlinson was a regular visitor to the States on various fellowships, describing in 'Above the Rio Grande' (1989), as clearly as in any of his poetry, a 'world of things that are merely things'. Transatlantic landscapes likewise figured regularly in poetry by Middleton, a more permanent exile from England after 1966. Some of their characteristics were also reflected in writing by other long-term exiles such as Thom Gunn, who comments in 'Flying above California' (1961) on 'a cold hard light without break | that reveals merely what is—no more | and no less'.

An exile in the United States from 1968, Donald Davie remarked in 'To Thom Gunn at Los Altos, California' (1977) that 'we are mid-Atlantic people, | You and I'. The 'mid-Atlantic' label could be appropriately applied to the exiled poets described above, and more loosely to others who remained at home but were strongly influenced by US writing. Interest in translation expanded greatly during the 1960s—a further part of the poetry revival at the time—bringing a range of European poets to the attention of English writers.[4] But for poetry, a shared language is a more important determinant of sources of influence than it is in other genres, and it was the United States which offered the styles and interests most regularly adopted by English poets who looked abroad during the period. At its beginning, several channels particularly directed attention across the Atlantic. Founded in 1958, William Cookson's journal *Agenda* regularly featured Ezra Pound's work, while Gael Turnbull's Migrant Press introduced English readers to the poetry of a generation following Pound and William Carlos Williams. This new generation was also strongly represented in Donald M. Allen's anthology *The New American Poetry 1945–1960*, published in 1960 with a postscript by Charles Olson, and strikingly different in much of its material from most poetry written in England at the time.

Yet these publications formed only a part of what Jon Silkin identified in 1973 as 'successive waves' through which writing from the United States 'impacted itself on poets in England' (*Poetry of the Committed Individual*, p. 19). A number of these 'waves' can be distinguished in the latter decades of the twentieth century, with the 'confessional' poetry developing in the USA in the 1950s, in the work of Robert Lowell and John Berryman, contributing to one of the earliest. Despite their other differences in the *Review* in 1962,

---

[4] See pp. 253–5, below.

Donald Davie and A. L. Alvarez shared admiration for Berryman and Lowell, assessing the latter as 'the best poet now writing . . . the best model in the English language' (p. 16). Work by Lowell, Berryman, and Anne Sexton—included in the second edition of *The New Poetry* in 1966 alongside Sylvia Plath's—further demonstrated the stressed connections between private and public experience which Alvarez required of English writing at the time. It also encouraged English authors towards a new kind of voice, appropriately private, modest, and reflective—even in digesting public events and historical stresses—at a time when poetry's hold on a wide readership and on the popular imagination generally was in decline. This voice continued to develop almost more strongly in later decades than it did in the 1960s.[5] In some ways, its fullest development—and the clearest example of the kind of confessional idiom Alvarez favoured—appeared in Ted Hughes's *Birthday Letters* in 1998. Though a hugely public exposure of the most famous, and troubled, relationship in late twentieth-century poetry, Hughes's collection employs throughout the reflective, inward tones of a first-person voice talking directly to Plath as 'you', as if readers eavesdropped on an intimate monologue privately addressed to her.

A second wave of US influence followed the work of the 'Beat' poets, principally Allen Ginsberg, Gregory Corso, and Lawrence Ferlinghetti, who were published together in the fifth volume of Penguin Modern Poets in 1963. This was an unusual departure from the series' concentration on British writing, reflecting a high level of interest at the time. The Beats were admired by many of the writers Michael Horovitz included in his *Children of Albion* anthology, which was dedicated to Ginsberg and took as its epigraph 'Who Be Kind To', a poem or 'prayer' he had delivered at the poetry event at the Albert Hall in 1965. Typical of Ginsberg's rhythmic, incantatory monologues, 'Who Be Kind To' is freely associative in assemblage and visionary in imagery. Showing some affinities with rock, and ideal for reading aloud, such poetry coincided conveniently with 1960s self-expression and spontaneity, and with the contemporary 'distrust of the formalized and the structured' which continued to concern Anthony Thwaite in the *Listener* in 1973.[6]

---

[5] See also pp. 229–30 and 242–3, below.
[6] See p. 187, above.

Ginsberg and the Beats particularly appealed to the Liverpool Poets, and others Thwaite referred to as 'exuberant mind-blowers'. Some of the more sober among Horovitz's 'Children of Albion' followed a third cohort of United States writers, extending the work of William Carlos Williams. Like Charles Tomlinson and Christopher Middleton, Roy Fisher mingled a sense of the nature of perception, and of the perceiver, into his precise, detailed descriptions, typically in his ironically entitled 'For Realism' (1966). His long work *City* (1961), centred on the life of Birmingham, also sought new poetic structures to represent complex relations between the observer and the scene described, and to reflect the fracturing, disparate nature of modern urban life. The resulting mixture of many different forms and registers in *City*—of prose as well as poetry—resembled William Carlos Williams's compendious account of a locale and its inhabitants in *Paterson* (1949–63).

Within the United States, the examples of Williams and Ezra Pound contributed to Charles Olson's epic *Maximus Poems* (1950–75) and to his manifesto 'Projective Verse' (1950). Olson emphasized the complexity and plurality of cognition: the existence 'at any instant' of 'any experience . . . on several more planes' than could cohere within a single strand of discursive language (Hampson and Barry (eds.), p. 216). Poetry, in his view, therefore required an exploratory, open form of composition: an 'open field', crosshatched by conflicting energies driving representation of disparate perceptions and the shaping of individual lines. Olson's work was a central influence on the 'Black Mountain' poets. One of them in particular, Ed Dorn, helped to introduce his thinking to English writers during a period in Oxford and Essex in the mid-1960s, an experience recorded in his long poem *The North Atlantic Turbine* (1967). Olson's innovations—a 'Transatlantic Dream, | Black Mountainous and vast . . . | . . . | a geography and not a view', as Neil Powell called them—had some influence on 'children of Albion' such as Andrew Crozier, Anselm Hollo, Tom Raworth, Gael Turnbull, and Lee Harwood (Jones and Schmidt, p. 150). This influence was also apparent in the fractured forms and odd lineation of early poetry by Elaine Feinstein, who was briefly part of a writing circle, at the University of Essex in the 1960s, which included Ed Dorn and Donald Davie.

'Black Mountainous' principles offered a complete escape from the formal restraints of Movement writing: a thoroughgoing alternative to its empirical conviction that significance could be readily derived from an observed world, and a stable identity assumed for the observer. Poetry by the writers mentioned envisaged instead a multifaceted experience, impacting on a consciousness conceived not as stable or unitary, but in postmodern terms, as a compound of competing discourses, fragmented perceptions and memories. Described by John Ashbery as 'open to the reader, like a meadow', Lee Harwood's writing, for example, reproduced a version of the fields of fragmented perception favoured by Olson (Harwood, p. 11). In doing so it also registered radically, at a formal level, the forces of disintegration which perplexed Alvarez and Davie in 1962, fracturing the texture and attention of poems including 'As your eyes are blue' (1966):

> a newly designed red bus drives quietly down Gower Street
> a brilliant red   'how could I tell you . . .'
> with such confusion
>   meetings disintegrating
> and a general lack of purpose only too obvious
> in the affairs of state
>   'yes, it was on a hot july day
> with taxis gunning their motors on the throughway
> a listless silence in the backrooms of paris bookshops
> why bother   one thing equal to another.

In poems such as 'The Long Black Veil' (1975) or 'As your eyes are blue', disjunctures of locale, register, and chronology create a disintegral aspect partly mimetic of modern experience, like T. S. Eliot's in *The Waste Land* (1922), though without the ulterior unity Eliot suggests through allusions to myth and earlier cultures. Instead, quoting Albert Camus in 'Text for two posters by Ian Brown' (1981), Harwood warns against 'still chasing | after an illusion of unity' at a time when 'separation is the rule. | The rest is chance'. This poem's explicit references to the Holocaust also keep in view—in a way Alvarez might have approved—disintegral historical forces underlying a sense of fracture and fragmentation in everyday contemporary experience.

Chapter 7 assesses a still further phase of United States influence, following the 'Language Poets' who succeeded Olson and open-field composition. The 'waves' considered above already indicate how regularly English writers in the 1960s and 1970s were obliged to look abroad for innovations and 'reworkings of technique' suppressed at home by the Movement and its legacies. Though Basil Bunting and Geoffrey Hill did continue writing in an established modernist idiom, any further developments of it, towards post-modernist styles, generally had to be imported or adapted from work in the United States. In one way, this might be seen as confirmation of Morrison and Motion's judgement in the *Penguin Book of Contemporary British Poetry* that little had been happening within England itself in the 1960s and 1970s. Yet in another way this conclusion ignored the extent to which US poetry *had* 'impacted' on English writing at this time. It also overlooked other new directions outlined in this chapter. In passing over these developments, the *Penguin Book of Contemporary British Poetry* nevertheless had a particular usefulness in the early eighties, and thereafter. Morrison and Motion's views highlighted the extent to which post-Movement idioms retained a dominant position at the time, yet also how far this depended on subordinating or obscuring a range of contrary initiatives also in evidence between 1960 and 1980. For some critics, Morrison and Motion's work as editors even confirmed an anxiety Donald Davie expressed in the early 1970s: that 'the smallness of England' made it 'entirely feasible for a group to secure one or two sub-editorial chairs and a few reviewing "spots", so as to impose their shared proclivities and opinions as the reigning orthodoxy' (Jones and Schmidt (eds.), p. xii). Much the same worry was reiterated by Sean O'Brien at the end of the century in his critical survey of contemporary poetry, *The Deregulated Muse* (1998).

Yet a welcome—if unintended—effect of the *Penguin Book of Contemporary Poetry* in the years that followed was in provoking a number of anthologists and critics into reasserting the real diversities of English writing. Whether or not the poetic scene was as conspiratorially manipulated as Davie feared, recognition of how narrowly it had come to be considered by the early 1980s—and how urgently different views were needed—did contribute a renewed vitality and some 'shape and direction' to the last two decades of the century. The writing involved is discussed in the next chapter. It also considers another significant new direction, probably too much in its infancy for Morrison and Motion to have recognized in 1982: poetry's growing engagement with political and social issues, in response to the stresses and divisiveness so apparent in the country's life after the late 1970s.

7

Politics and Postmodernism: The Late 1970s to 2000

'Satire to-day | Moults in silence or has flown away' Geoffrey Grigson remarked at the end of the 1970s ('To an Abusive and Ridiculous Art Historian', 1980). Its departure was especially marked in the work of older poets—including Grigson himself—who had shared the political concerns of the 'Auden generation' in the 1930s. In 1974, in an elegy addressed to Auden, Grigson recalled that 'Forty years now | Have slipped by since for some who were young | You became living's healer ... | ... | ... our fixture, our rhythm' ('To Wystan Auden'). During these forty years, Auden himself had changed many of the 'fixtures' of his poetry. Even by the end of the 1930s, he had shed some of the political commitment marking his early work, famously concluding in an elegy of his own, 'In Memory of W. B. Yeats' (1939), that 'poetry makes nothing happen'. In 'The Cave of Making' (1965)—a later elegy, for Louis MacNeice—he expressed further doubts about relations between politics and poetry following the Second World War, suggesting that 'we shan't, not since Stalin and Hitler, | Trust ourselves ever again'. Auden's early admirers seemed similarly doubtful of poetry's political potentials. Grigson remained ready to satirize Britain's entry into the Common Market (EU) in 'Entente Cordiale' (1974), or to record in 'First Public Death of the New Year Season' (1974) disgust that in 'the bloody filth of Vietnam | ... | The life of man | Must either cease or be American'. But much of his later poetry renounced the social interests of the 1930s in favour of description or celebration of nature and the countryside.

The career of C. Day Lewis, Poet Laureate from 1968 to 1972, followed a similar path, moving from 1930s commitment to later conservatism. Roy Fuller's 'Orders' (1968) likewise indicated an eventual weariness with politics, complaining that 'war . . . during my life has scarcely stopped. | And the government that I elected, like | All governments, whether elected by me | Or not, will be powerless or uncaring'. In 'The Unremarkable Year' (1973), Fuller went on to describe a resulting preference for the private over the public domain, suggesting that

> there is much to be said for a summer
> Without alarms. The plum crop is modest,
> The monarch has remained unchanged . . .
> Small differences only in one's teeth and hair and verse-forms.

Similar restraints and domestic interests excluded direct satiric or political commentary from most Movement writing in the 1950s and 1960s. Like Auden in 'The Cave of Making', Donald Davie defined disillusion with politics as part of the war's 'numbing' effect in the years that followed.[1] In 'Too Late for Satire', included in the first of Robert Conquest's *New Lines* anthologies in 1956, he suggested that contemporary poetry, his own included,

> might have been as pitiless as Pope
> But to no purpose; in a tragic age
> We share the hatred but we lack the hope
> By pinning follies to reform the age.
> To blame is lame, and satirists are late.
> No knife can stick in history or the id . . .

Satire, of course, was by no means entirely silenced in the 1950s, 1960s, and 1970s, with Auden himself occasionally continuing to criticize public affairs and 'the usual squalid mess called History' in witty late poems such as 'Moon Landing' (1972). Political stresses and changing moods in the early 1960s provoked members of the Group into regular satire, while the Movement's nostalgia sometimes extended—in Larkin's 'Homage to a Government' and 'Going, Going' (1974), for example—into explicit criticism of contemporary society. Satiric writing in the 1960s and early 1970s also appeared

[1] See p. 167, above.

regularly in the work of a post-war generation of 'Children of Albion', often directly reflecting the decade's radicalism and its politicization by the 'filth' of the war in Vietnam.[2] By the mid-1970s, too, poets were beginning to register—like other writers at the time—increasing tensions on the domestic scene following the oil embargo and the economic crises of the decade.

Filth, distress, and poverty on the streets of Britain eventually restored a strongly satiric element to the period's poetry. Satire and social commentary, however far they might have flown in previous years, came home to roost decisively in the work of many younger writers after the election of the Tory government in 1979. In 'Poet for Our Times' (1990), Carol Ann Duffy defined headlines, in the 1980s, as 'the poems of the decade'—a 'bottom line of art' sometimes used sensationally by her contemporaries to incorporate into poetry the immediate realities of urban life. Headlines, and journalism generally, were frequently employed in this way in Peter Reading's poetry, which sometimes also used press reviews of his work—real or imaginary—to emphasize his satiric intentions. Newsprint sharply highlighted these intentions in another way, in the image in *Perduta Gente* (1989) of a vagrant who has 'wound round a varicose indigo swollen | leg' a newspaper whose 'Property Pages delineate *bijou* | River-View Flatlets | £600,000 each'.

Reading had already examined, in earlier collections, a range of factors underlying social exclusion: old age, in *For the Municipality's Elderly* (1974); mental illness, in *Tom o'Bedlam's Beauties* (1981); disease, in *C* (1984). After *Ukulele Music* (1985), his poetry concentrated on gross divisions of wealth and lifestyle in a society experiencing not 'just another | crisis but a climacteric', its distresses painfully apparent throughout the violent, vandal-ruined landscapes of the inner cities ('Nothing for Anyone', 1977). Described throughout *Stet* (1986) and *Perduta Gente*, characteristics of this decaying landscape are summed up in a returned emigrant's view of England in *Evagatory* (1992) as

> an island farctate with feculence:
> chip-papers, Diet-Pepsi cans clattering,
> prams, supermarket trolleys, spent mattresses,

---

[2] See p. 183, above.

bus-rank of steel and rank uriniferous
concrete, a footbridge richly enlivened with
aerosol squirtings, daubed graffiti,

pustular simian sub-teenagers
hurling abuse and empty bottles.

In *Evagatory*, this urban decay is juxtaposed with images of NASA's planetary probe Voyager, disappearing into deep space near Sirius, as if only the drear voids between stars could match moral and social emptiness on earth.

Contemporary decay was further emphasized by ironic comparisons in *Ukulele Music*, with the volume's blackest material— accounts of a bottle smashed in a baby's face, for example—accompanied by descriptions of the trivial plinking of the ukulele. Dissonances between art and life were also highlighted by the fastidiousness—in terms such as 'farctate' or 'feculence'—of the language Reading employed, and by the ostentatious precision of his poetic forms, habitually shaping gruesome descriptions within elegant metrical patterns. Mixtures of filth with formal fastidiousness, even Latinate elegance, placed his work close to Augustan modes of satire employed by Alexander Pope and Jonathan Swift. These early eighteenth-century modes and their grotesque social vision seemed once again topical to other writers in the 1980s: among dramatists, for example, Caryl Churchill based some of her satire of the decade's sleazy politics and rampant stock market on Thomas Shadwell's *The Stockjobbers* (1692). Reading, however, was a more explicitly self-conscious satirist than the Augustans, reflecting some of the postmodern idioms of his own age. The incongruity of his forms and strategies was often deliberately highlighted: sometimes even by means of metrical analyses included in the text, or by other mockeries of his poetry's attempts to order the disintegral world it surveyed. For the cancerous decay of living bodies in *C*, for example, Reading records that '*no* metric is vindicable . . . we are beyond verse here'.

Rather than remaining 'beyond verse', the urban decline Reading surveyed seemed to provide a ubiquitous background for poetry in the 1980s and 1990s, and the social divisions created by free-market enterprise and privatization an unavoidable satiric target. Similar cityscapes of 'broken glass, corrugated tin and spraygunned ply-wood' figured in Michael Hofmman's aptly named 'Albion Market', and in his 'From Kensal Rise to Heaven' (1986). Carol Rumens wondered in 'Letter from South London' (1987) if 'the slender candle-light of democracy | ha[d] flickered out in a gloom of broken doorways | where the winos study meths-economy'. Iain Sinclair lamented in 'Serpent to zymurgy' (1985) 'the form-filling | dole-scratching, ill-tempered lumpen | mess of what we've become', and Douglas Oliver, in several poems, the consequences of what he called in 'The Infant and the Pearl' (1985) 'a country's Conservative night at its coldest'. Sean O'Brien regularly examined what he called the 'moral and economic barbarism' of life during and after the Thatcher years (Riggs (ed.), p. 879). In poems such as 'After Laforgue' (1991), he described an urban life of 'boredom and waiting, | The bus-station's just-closing teabar, | The icy, unpromising platforms of regional terminii | . . . dead docks and the vandalized showhouse', contrasting it with 'the world of Miss Selfridge and Sock Shop, | Disposable income and lycra'. Later, in 'Piers Powerbook's Prologue' (2001), he highlighted social contrasts and divisions 'between money and morals' through the fractured, disjunctive form of his poem's lines themselves.

Geoffrey Hill was rarely a commentator on contemporary life or English politics in his earlier work, but even he demanded in the 1990s, in 'To the High Court of Parliament: November 1994' (1996), where 'probity' could be found in the current government. It had left 'England—now of genius | the eidolon— | unsubstantial yet voiding | substance like quicklime', the poem suggested: a wounded country which might 'privatize to the dead | her memory'. In 'Against the Grain' (1990), Ken Smith similarly defined an England 'dying of neglect . . . | . . . a free enterprise disaster zone'. A decade earlier, in his long work *Fox Running* (1980), Smith had already broadly sur-veyed life 'way down Thatcherland', finding in 'the closed-down clinic | and the short-staffed school | such a vision of the street'. Alluding in that last line to T. S. Eliot's poetry, *Fox Running* devel-oped its vision of city life on an epic scale, as close to *The Waste Land* (1922) as anything published since. Connecting a blighted urban landscape with a disturbed central persona—sometimes accorded a redeeming vitality by figuration as the running fox—Smith's poem examined contemporary pressures not only in social and economic terms, but, like *The Waste Land*, showed their consequences for the stressed, vacant spirit of modern city life.

Satiric and political interests shaped much of the poetry of Tony Harrison. Some of it commented directly on current events—on the Gulf War, for example, in *A Cold Coming* (1991), or the Poet Laureateship, ferociously denounced, along with the monarchy, in 'Laureate's Block', published in the *Guardian* shortly after Ted Hughes's death, on 9 February 1999 (p. 15). Harrison also focused political commentary through autobiographical poems about his parents, his childhood in Leeds, and his departure from the declining North in favour of a career elsewhere—one eventually including many successes as a dramatist and verse translator at the National Theatre in London. These concerns received their fullest treatment in his long poem *v.* (1985), written in the aftermath of the miners' strike in 1984–5. Alluding ironically to Thomas Gray's 'Elegy Written in a Country Churchyard' (1751), Harrison describes in *v.* a return to Leeds to visit his parents' grave in a vandalized cemetery, and his recollection of their era's dignified expectation of 'one job all life through'. This is contrasted with a violent, divisive, contemporary society which has left 'the cunts who lieth 'ere wor unemployed' as the likeliest epitaph for many citizens, and another 'bottom line of art', graffiti, sometimes their only form of self-expression. Harrison also explores disturbing continuities between past and present, finding in the miners' strike evidence of conflicts of 'class v. class as bitter as before'. 'Personified in 1984' in bitter struggles between the miners and their employers, these conflicts reflect an 'unending violence of US and THEM'—a wider pattern of 'all the versuses of life' which Harrison traces back through the V-signs of the Second World War to still earlier histories of class exploitation. Historical depth of this kind figured in much of his work, extending patterns widely evident in the period's imagination. Like dramatists considered in Chapter 10, below, and a number of contemporary novels, Harrison's poetry in *The School of Eloquence* (1978) contrasted the end of the Second World War with later decades, attempting to account for the collapse of the post-war consensus so conspicuous after the Thatcher government came to power.

Like much of Harrison's later poetry, the sonnets of *The School of*

Eloquence and *Continuous* (1981) examined conflicts between 'US and THEM' not only historically, but in terms of region, language, and dialect—sometimes even phonetics. In 'Them and [uz]', for example, he derides the preferences for 'RP, | Received Pronunciation' which favour [ʌs] over the dialectal [uz] in the speech of officialdom, privilege, and poetry. The poem promises to fight back on behalf of the silenced working classes, and cheerfully concludes 'So right, yer buggers, then! We'll occupy | Your lousy leasehold Poetry'. This 'occupancy' is achieved throughout Harrison's work by tidily formal poetry, firmly containing ordinary speech and dialect within neatly rhyming couplets, and employing an unusual, sixteen-line form of sonnet in *The School of Eloquence*. Yet poems in this volume and others often emphasize the tensions and contradictions entailed by such firm containment, or by any art. Poetry is described in the title of a later poem as 'The Heartless Art' (1984), and one whose practice contributes to a kind of 'class v. class' struggle within the poet himself. 'The Rhubarbarians' suggests that Harrison would 'like to be the poet [his] father reads', but 'A Good Read' worries that intellectual ambitions may have made him a 'stuck-up-bugger' himself, his status as poet and intellectual alienating him from the very class on whose behalf he sought to speak. Anxieties of this kind contribute to self-divisions vividly dramatized in *v*. Complex ideas and liberal platitudes the poet delivers provoke infuriated responses in the voice of an imaginary skinhead graffitist, an alter ego who shares Harrison's name and reminds him of 'the language that yer mam spoke'. The skinhead eventually elicits the poet's admission that 'the *autre* that *je est* is fucking you'—ironically drawn from an intellectual sphere, the poetry of Arthur Rimbaud—and gradually reoccupies the poem's discourse with the local dialect and copious obscenity that mark his own.

In a period of increasing social mobility, tensions with a parental generation—with its class allegiances, or even its language—were painfully encountered by many other writers.[3] Uneasiness about moving from the working class into the life and language of a poet was comparably reflected in D. J. Enright's *The Terrible Shears: Scenes from a Twenties Childhood* (1973), and in some of Donald Davie's poems, such as 'Northern Metres' (1990). It also shaped

[3] See also pp. 36–8, above, and pp. 288–9 and 401–2, below.

Seamus Heaney's early writing—his attempt in 'Digging' (1969), for example, to retain a place among generations of agricultural labourers by equating his pen with his father's spade. The kind of local dialects and colloquial speech-forms shaping Harrison's work were also more widely significant for contemporary poetry and its politics. Employed much more regularly than in earlier periods, dialect and demotic forms contributed to fundamental changes in poetry's language and relation to its audience, also reflecting a regular shift of interest from the metropolis to the regions. In 'Yorkshire' (1974), Davie described Basil Bunting as 'master of Northern stops': various Northern dialects likewise replaced, or were mixed with, conventional poetic language in Norman Nicholson's poetry, in the work of the Newcastle poet Tom Pickard, who helped relaunch Bunting's poetic career, and in Blake Morrison's 'The Ballad of the Yorkshire Ripper' (1987), for example. Though not a dialect poet, even Charles Tomlinson recalled in 'Class' (1974) how a flat midland 'a' once cost him a job.

Another Northerner, Ted Hughes, remarked that 'Whatever other speech you grow into . . . your dialect stays alive in a sort of inner freedom, a separate little self' (Corcoran, p. 114). Like Tony Harrison, some of the writers mentioned above may have been drawn towards the genre of poetry by frictions they experienced—heightening their linguistic sensitivities—between a 'separate self' and the public forms of speech they had to grow into. For several, Harrison in particular, the use of dialect at any rate provided a certain freedom: an opportunity to encapsulate concisely, without the need of further explanation, values outwith those of the metropolitan mainstream and the status quo. As in other genres, the politics of poetry could of course be stated straightforwardly, as they often were by writers deploring the despoiled cityscapes of Thatcherland in the 1980s. Yet since poetry inevitably—almost by definition—draws attention to its own language, its politics can also be represented more subtly, through the dialects and registers it employs and the conflicts implied between attitudes, social strata, or class fractions that can be heard to speak in each. Differences of dialect, accent, and register assumed in this way a new significance during a period in which long-standing class hierarchies began to break down, or were increasingly complicated by lateral divisions of gender and ethnicity, region and metropolis, lifestyle and outlook. Poetry's emphasis on voice and language could direct attention very effectively on these divisions, even when they were not explicitly its subject. Though Harrison's skinhead suggests in *v.* that 'it's not poetry we need in this class war', it continued to offer opportunities in some ways ideal for representing the complex social politics and positionings of the later twentieth century.

This potential was especially important for black poets. Like Ted Hughes, James Berry found an inner freedom in the use of dialect, emphasizing the capacity of 'the people's language' to open up 'fertile inward areas of self expression' (*Fractured Circles*, p. 9). For the West Indian poets who began to emerge strongly in the later 1970s, Berry included, a 'people's language' was crucial not only for inward self-expression, but in establishing for the immigrant community generally a voice and identity of its own. Fred D'Aguiar emphasized the need for this when he warned in 'Dread' (1993) 'Check your history and you will see I throughout it some other body speaking for we'. Grace Nichols explained how this new voice could evolve when she recalled in 'Epilogue' (1983) 'I have crossed an ocean I I have lost my tongue I from the root of the old one I a new one has sprung'. Linton Kwesi Johnson identified similar linguistic roots, old and more recent, acknowledging the influences of 'Jamaican Creole and Jamaican English and . . . English English . . . the consequence of having been brought up in a colonial society and then coming over here to live and go to school in England' (*Dread Beat*, p. 8). Combinations of West Indian and English idioms figured distinctively in poetry which quickly developed phonetic representations of colloquial and dialectal forms. The significance of dialect was also accentuated by its regular, explicit discussion or celebration in the poems themselves. John Agard highlighted the sensual pleasure to be derived from pronouncing some of the words in 'Limbo Dancer's Mantra' (1983), showed language taking on a vital reality of its own in 'Poetry Jump-Up' (Grace Nichols (ed.), *Black Poetry*, 1988), and famously emphasized in 'Listen Mr Oxford don' (1985) that 'human breath I is a dangerous weapon', and an essential one. Agard's 'simple immigrant I from Clapham Common' finds 'mugging de Queen's English I is the story of [his] life'. For black writers generally, still more urgently than for Tony Harrison in 'Them and [uz]', only through an assault on standard English could the 'story' of the lives and communities they spoke for be fully communicated.

Black poetry also relied particularly on 'human breath' and speech since it evolved as much through performance as writing. Linton Kwesi Johnson worked in the 1970s with a performance group, the Radical Alliance of Poets and Players, and gave concerts with the punk poet John Cooper Clarke. This helped to establish for poetry a new set of contacts with rock music, superseding the harmonious celebrations of love and peace which had appealed to the 'Children of Albion' and other new poets in the 1960s. Benjamin Zephaniah looked back fondly in 'Lennon's Song' (1985) to the Beatles and the political potential of 1960s rock lyrics, but it was the harsher punk idioms of the next decade, and later the rhythms of ska, reggae, and rap, which were generally closest to black poetry. James Berry emphasized a further significance for music in black writing in his introduction to *News for Babylon: The Chatto Book of Westindian British Poetry* (1984). Black poets, he explained, sought to recover voices which had been 'lost in the cycles of time and place', but also to explore forms through which black expression *had* managed to survive and sustain itself. As well as reggae, these included 'drum, blues, jazz and gospel . . . symbols and images of a people's culture' (p. xxi). As he suggested, black poetry commented on the liberating influence of these cultural forms as regularly as it did on the particularities of black speech. They are celebrated in Johnson's 'Bass Culture' (1975), for example, and in his 'Reggae Sounds' (1975)—of 'Shock-black bubble-doun-beat bouncing | rock-wise tumble-doun sound music'. They also figured in some of Zephaniah's poetry, such as 'Beat drummers' (1985), and in John Agard's demand in 'Beat it Out' (1982) for drummers to 'beat out | a new message | from de middle | passage'.

As this reference to the middle passage suggests, black poetry often re-examined, like black fiction, the history of a doubly displaced people and the ways it continued to shape what James Berry called 'a collective psyche laden with anguish and rage' (*News for Babylon*, p. xii). Experience of the middle passage from Africa to the colonies was examined at length in David Dabydeen's 'Turner' (1994), both from a slave's point of view and through re-examining J. M. W. Turner's rather different vision of it in his famous painting *Slavers*

Throwing Overboard the Dead and the Dying (1860). Fred
D'Aguiar likewise reflects on this earlier period in 'At the Grave of an
Unknown African' (1993). Though D'Aguiar describes England as
'home | by now', the poem points out that recollection of the way
black people first reached it—through the slave trade, or escape from
the colonies—continues to provide a 'wick and petrol mix' for race
riots in the 1980s. For many black writers, the 'home' that England
offered, and the history that led to it, contributed to an anguish and
rage which made their work as powerfully politicized as any poetry
in the last decades of the century. This was a matter not only of implication, through voice or dialect, but often of entirely explicit commentary on indignities daily imposed on black life. The prejudice of
immigration officials is described in D'Aguiar's 'Home' (1993), for
example; police harassment in his 'A Gift of a Rose' (1993) and in
James Berry's 'In-a Brixtan Markit' (1985); the disappointments or
non-existence of employment in Linton Kwesi Johnson's 'Inglan is a
Bitch' (1980); and the improbability that established political parties
would deal with any of these problems in his 'Independent
Intavenshan' (1980).

As titles such as 'Fight dem' (1985) and 'Anti-society' (1985) indicate, Benjamin Zephaniah provided some of the most vehement
reactions to black experience of life in England. Yet its disappointments and disorientations, along with nostalgia for earlier life in the
West Indies, also contributed less outspokenly political themes to
Zephaniah's poetry, and to the work of the other writers mentioned.
In 'Homeward Bound' (1996), for example, Zephaniah sympathizes
with an old immigrant who is 'fed up with the weather' and 'only
wants to see his saviour | Sweet Jamaica', but instead will die in the
middle of London, in Kensal Rise, with 'all his Jamaica nights' only
'in his head'. D'Aguiar's recollections of childhood in Guyana in
Airy Hall (1989), James Berry's 'Lucy's Letters' (1979), and some of
Dabydeen's poetry likewise looked back on the sweeter climate of an
earlier life. Grace Nichols reflected the disorientations of leaving this
life in poems such as 'Beverley's Saga' or 'Wherever I Hang' (1989).
Though talking in them, like D'Aguiar, of finding England now
'home', she also describes missing 'back-home side', and concludes
only that 'divided to de ocean | Divided to de bone | Wherever I hang
me knickers—that's my home'.

Towards the end of the century, England had nevertheless been home for so long to so many black writers, some belonging to a second generation of immigrants, that black poetry had begun to be defined less exclusively around the characteristics of language and theme outlined above. Introducing black writing at the end of the 1980s, in *The New British Poetry 1968–1988* (1988), Fred D'Aguiar even suggested that 'two black poets in Britain today are likely to have less in common than two poets picked out of a hat' (Allnutt et al. (eds.), p. 4). James Berry also stressed the growing scale and diversity of black writing, pointing out that Edward Kamau Brathwaite and Derek Walcott had been the only Caribbean poets widely known in England in the 1960s. Even in the next decade, the anthology *Bluefoot Traveller* (1976) had contained only thirty-four poems and eleven poets. Berry's own collection, on the other hand, *News for Babylon* (1984) included 154 poems by forty poets. Berry acknowledged that some of them, such as E. A. Markham, had moved 'close to British mainstream writing' (p. xxiv). Publication of Linton Kwesi Johnson's selected poems as a Penguin Classic, in 2002, also indicated how far black poetry had come to be accepted by mainstream publishers, and by the reading public generally. Yet as Berry emphasized, even as black poetry's scope expanded, and its new tongue became a more familiar English poetic dialect, many of its 'distinctly different and unique qualities' continued to appear (p. xii). Black poetry developed in range and readership, as he suggested, without losing the verbal energy and political urgency distinguishing its rapid development in the 1970s and 1980s.

*

Black writing made up the first section of *The New British Poetry 1968–1988*. Its second was devoted to what its editor, Gillian Allnutt, called 'Quote Feminist Unquote Poetry'. In the view of some commentators on contemporary poetry, 'the need of those traditionally on the periphery to define their identity against "the centre"' created 'similarities of strategy or tone between certain black and women writers' (Hulse et al. (eds.), p. 18). Yet as Allnutt's tentative title suggested, women's poetry had emerged less decisively, and with less certain politics, than black writing during the 1970s and 1980s. In term of models and antecedents, it had in some ways as slender a basis to work from. Fairly few women poets had established strong reputations earlier in the century, in England at any rate, and—unlike women novelists at the time—they had scarcely been more successful in the 1960s and early 1970s. Though Michael Horovitz's *Children of Albion* (1969) was thoroughly committed to liberations taking place in other areas of 1960s life, it contained only three women poets out of the sixty or so in the anthology. No English woman had been represented in Alvarez's *The New Poetry* in 1962, and Sylvia Plath, English only by residence, scarcely restored a gender balance in the second edition in 1966. No woman poet appeared in Jon Silkin's otherwise politically aware *Stand* anthology, *Poetry of the Committed Individual*, in 1973, and Jeremy Robson considered only one promising enough to include among *The Young British Poets* in 1971. Women writers were not much better represented either in D. J. Enright's *Oxford Book of Verse 1945–1980* (1980) or Edward Lucie-Smith's *British Poetry since 1945* (1985).

Women poets' standing began to improve only towards the end of the 1970s, under the influence of the women's movements gathering momentum at the time. Recognition of their work was encouraged by Lilian Mohin's *One Foot on the Mountain: An Anthology of British Feminist Poetry 1969–79* (1979), which made widely accessible writing previously published mostly by small journals and presses. Once again, a 'polemical anthology' functioned decisively as an 'instrument of change'.[4] As one critic, Claire Buck, remarked, *One Foot on the Mountain* not only identified many new women writers, but attempted a thoroughgoing 'reformulation of the traditional territory of poetry'. In her view, this involved redirecting attention onto areas of women's lives which poetry had too rarely explored: areas such as 'day-to-day experience, and women's feelings about the experiences . . . work, friendships with women, domesticity and family relationships, abortion, childbirth, and sexual relationships—heterosexual and lesbian' (Acheson and Huk (eds.), p.91).

Concern with these areas was in evidence even before the feminist phase of writing Mohin's anthology represented, appearing in the work of the few women poets who had succeeded in establishing a reputation earlier in the period. Elizabeth Jennings was distinguished

---

[4] See p. 166, above.

from the male writers included in Robert Conquest's *New Lines* anthologies by the extent of her interest in relationships and their emotions—traced in many poems, such as 'One Flesh' (1966), 'Love Poem' (1966), and 'Absence' (1958). Hilary Corke's 'A Woman's Song' stood out from Movement writing included in Conquest's second volume in a different way: through the unusual explicitness, and scepticism, with which it described the sexual act. Similar candour later marked the work of several women poets—typically, Sujatta Bhatt's in 'The *Kama Sutra* Retold' (1988). Fleur Adcock was equally direct in descriptions of intimate stains in 'Poem Ended by Death'(1979), or of sucking 'earlobe, penis, tongue' in 'The Ex-Queen among the Astronomers' (1979). Adcock's accounts of love and relationship were various as well as explicit. They ranged from an almost sacramental view of sex in 'Folie à Deux' (1974) to a readiness in 'Against Coupling' (1971) to reject intercourse altogether in favour of 'the solitary act'—a sure way of avoiding tensions, highlighted throughout her poetry, between women's sexual expectations and those of men. In 'The Ex-Queen among the Astronomers', these are shown as part of a wider divergence of attitudes, in which the woman's point of view is generally subordinated firmly to the needs and opinions of men.

Physicality in Adcock's description of relationships extended wider awareness of the body and its significances in her poetry—of its metaphoric potentials in 'Knife Play' (1964), for example, or simply its decay, in 'Advice to a Discarded Lover' (1967). Following the loosening of taboos and the ending of censorship in the 1960s, this kind of heightened physical awareness appeared throughout the period's writing, but it was developed in particular ways by women poets in later decades. Some of these were anticipated by Sylvia Plath in poems included in *Ariel* (1965). In 'The Applicant', for example, she discusses a bodily self-alienation imposed on women by a fragmenting, anatomizing male gaze, threatening to reduce the female form merely to 'rubber breasts . . . rubber crotch'. Yet for many women poets in the years that followed, new explicitness in describing the female form also allowed new freedom to assert potentials independent of male control or even imagination. Grace Nichols, for example, affirmed the creativity of the female body in poems such as 'The Body Reclining' (1989), 'On Poems and Crotches' (1989), and

'Ode to my Bleed' (1989). Penelope Shuttle likewise described 'bleeding this fathomless blood' in 'Fosse' (1980), while her 'First Foetal Movements of my Daughter in the Womb' (1980) directed consciousness of the body specifically around the physical aspects of motherhood.

As Claire Buck suggested, childbirth and family life were interests strongly developed by women writers throughout the period. Marital and familial relations provided a regular theme for Elaine Feinstein in 1960s poems such as 'Song of Power'(1966), 'Mother Love' (1966), and 'Marriage' (1969), before her interests moved on to more inward, personal reflections in later decades. Several of Anne Stevenson's poems, such as 'The Victory' (1970), or 'The Spirit is too Blunt an Instrument' (1970)—and many of Helen Dunmore's in *The Apple Fall* (1983)—were concerned like Shuttle's work with the physical experience of maternity, and with intimate, evolving relations with children as they grow up. Emotions and relationships within the family received more detailed, extended attention in Stevenson's *Correspondences: A Family History in Letters* (1974), which used the epistolary form to contrast various subjective perspectives among successive generations of women in a family in the United States. Love, marital relations, and domestic or family life often remained a central interest of women poets emerging in the 1980s and 1990s, such as Vicki Feaver and Selima Hill.

'I have stood in the kitchen, transfixed by what I'd call love', Anne Stevenson declares in 'Himalayan Balsam' (1982). Michèle Roberts's 'Lacrimae Rerum' (1991) similarly intermingles passion and domesticity, in the voice of a woman who finds 'last night's hot sweetness | still fizzing between [her] legs'—even when 'jumping up to make tea | and rinse dishes'—and who promises that she will 'carry on | getting the roof fixed | making love | weeping into the washing-up'. Typically of new emphases on 'day-to-day experience' and domesticity in women's writing, such poetry located relationships, love, or bodily awareness firmly within a prosaic, familial domain: one whose supposedly mundane tasks and commitments it often sought to dignify and re-evaluate. For a number of poets and critics, however, this reappraisal of established gender roles provided a less than satisfactory direction for women's poetry. Affirmation of family responsibilities, or of the value of domestic commitments—even of the latent powers of women's bodies and sexualities—for some critics simply confirmed or acquiesced in positions conventionally assigned women within patriarchal society. The 'reformulation of the traditional territory of poetry' Claire Buck outlined sometimes seemed limited in other ways. Carol Rumens, for example, worried that concentration on new subjects or themes, whether affirmative of feminism or not, risked ignoring 'excellence', 'quality', or 'the art of the poem'—poetic priorities she highlighted in her introduction to *Making for the Open: the Chatto Book of Post-Feminist Poetry 1964–1984* (1985, pp. xv–xvi).

Typically of rapidly developing debates surrounding women's writing in the 1980s, these views were widely criticized in their turn. Vicki Bertram dismissed Rumens's emphases on quality and artistic integrity as 'naively optimistic about the flexibility of traditional English poetic aesthetics' and potentially irrelevant to women writers, at any rate without careful investigation of the value judgements involved (Acheson and Huk (eds.), p. 273). As critics such as Bertram pointed out, the literary tradition had been established mostly by men, based on evaluative principles potentially irrelevant to the kinds of writing women produced. This male-centred construction of tradition would explain why so few women poets were available as models for authors emerging in the 1970s and 1980s. All those 1950s, 1960s, and 1970s anthologists, mentioned earlier, were male. What women's poetry might have lacked at this time was not necessarily artistic quality, but editors and critics able to recognize particular forms of it, and to offer contexts and publishing outlets which might have allowed women's writing to develop further. This constraint was largely removed in the last two decades of the century. Contemporary women's writing was more widely disseminated, and a longer tradition more firmly established, by anthologies including *The Bloodaxe Book of Contemporary Women Poets* (1985), *The Penguin Book of Women Poets* (1986), *The Faber Book of Twentieth Century Women's Poetry* (1987), *Sixty Women Poets* (1993), and *Making for Planet Alice: New Women Poets* (1997).

Carol Rumens's emphasis on art and aesthetics nevertheless suggested a potential limitation in contemporary women's poetry, at least if its reformulations of poetic territory had gone no further than the reshaping of subject matter outlined above. Even by 1980, black poetry had established for itself particular voices and styles, largely based on shared dialects and distinctive speech-forms. Without this basis, women poets could less easily develop the political potentials for poetry discussed earlier, in terms of distinctive language, voice, and form. Even when radically new in its subject matter, much women's poetry in the 1970s remained conventional in form, and successful women poets emerging during the 1980s and 1990s— such as U. A. Fanthorpe, Lavinia Greenlaw, and Helen Dunmore— were often no more innovative. Several critics complained about this apparent conservatism, and about a failure among women writers to match radical new outlooks with experiment in poetic technique. Linda Kinnahan, for example, compared English poets adversely in this respect with 'American women experimentalists who employ language disruption to question the gendering of tradition and language' (Acheson and Huk (eds.), p. 248). Wendy Mulford likewise found English women writers in the 1990s still too 'tied to a familiar poetics' and too rarely 'formally adventurous' (Hampson and Barry (eds.), pp. 9–10).

Yet changes in subject matter could hardly occur independently of implications for form. New concentration on physicality sometimes brought to poetry a new rhythm: a pace and syntax, potentially distinctive of women's voice, evident in some of Plath's work and in several later writers. Even in lamenting an absence of 'language disruption' in English poetry, Kinnahan pointed to ways the oddly paratactic rhythms of the Scottish poet Carol Ann Duffy's writing distinguished her from less innovative male contemporaries. Wendy Mulford's own work offered some of the formal adventure and innovative poetics she thought missing elsewhere: these also shaped the writing of other poets included in *The New British Poetry*, such as Maggie O'Sullivan and Jeni Couzyn. More generally, too, the restrictive gender roles explored in much women's poetry imposed upon it, almost inevitably, some degree of formal or linguistic self-consciousness. As feminist critics such as Cora Kaplan emphasize, women writers—women generally—experience a 'special relation' to a language 'not theirs' as a consequence of being female (Acheson and Huk (eds.), p. 87). Partial exclusion by a male-owned language, as well as by a male-dominated tradition, disposed women authors generally, throughout the twentieth century, towards reformulation of established forms and styles of literature.[5] Within the linguistically oriented genre of poetry, there was particular reason for this disposition to be directed on the language of their writing itself. Introducing 'Quote Feminist Unquote Poetry', Gillian Allnutt described the language available to women poets as '"man made" but not, given a little loving attention, unmalleable' (Allnutt et al. (eds.), pp. 77–8). More often sceptical than loving, this attention appeared at some level in the work of many women poets late in the century. For several, new feminist theories of 'écriture féminine' were an interest[6]; in the writing of a few, challenges to conventional language and reformulations of its use in poetry were a distinctive feature.

Such challenges were evident from the beginning of the period in the work of Stevie Smith, who had begun writing in the late 1930s and acquired by mid-century a reputation and popularity unusual among women poets at the time. Among work she continued to publish in the 1960s, 'Pretty' (1962) opens by challenging a term conventionally associated with the feminine, asking 'Why is the word pretty so underrated?' In the rest of the poem, the word's significance is less underrated than undermined and evacuated of all conventional meaning. 'Pretty' is repeatedly applied in ludicrous ways to a natural world shown actually to mean 'nothing, and this is pretty', or to be entirely beyond humanity and its wish for prettiness. 'Pretty' is also employed repeatedly in vapid phrases, such as 'All this is pretty, it could not be prettier', which are immediately contradicted by the next—'Yes, it could always be prettier'. Wearied repetitions of words and phrases in 'Pretty'—and in poems such as 'Thoughts about the Person from Porlock' (1962) or 'Emily Writes such a Good Letter' (1966)—seem to despair of making language function convincingly. The unpunctuated gusts of verbiage that also figure in these poems indicate a kind of linguistic panic that results. Freedom from such stresses is offered only by an ultimate collapse of language, or of the need to go on working with it. 'Pretty' concludes 'Cry pretty, pretty, pretty and you'll be able | Very soon not even to cry pretty | And so to be entirely delivered from humanity | This is prettiest of all, it is very pretty'.

[5] See also p. 44, above.
[6] See p. 104, above.

The uneasy, pseudo-naïve tone and strange thought-patterns distinguishing poems such as 'Pretty' were among qualities which led critics to assess Stevie Smith as eccentric, or unique. Some of her poems might also be considered as unique, historically and socially, to England in the late 1950s and early 1960s—as parodies of the gushing superficialities of polite English conversation around this time; swansongs for the vacuous gentility whose longevity so riled A. L. Alvarez in 1962. Smith has less often been considered a precursor of late twentieth-century women's poetry. Yet in their own terms—sometimes significantly less genteel—several later writers extended her self-doubting idiom, and her inclination to question poetic language and tactics within poems themselves. Fleur Adcock's 'Poem Ended by a Death' (1979), for example, begins with warmly erotic memories of a dying ex-lover, but then remarks 'fuck that for a cheap I opener', recalls that he will simply be put 'into a box', and adds self-appraisively that 'this is my laconic style'. The Scottish poet Veronica Forrest-Thomson also continued something of Stevie Smith's idiom. 'The Garden of Proserpine' (1976), for example, amalgamates musing bleakness with nursery-rhyme naïvety, concluding ' I love you and you love me I Although we are in hell'. In 'Cordelia, or "A Poem Should not Be"' (1974), Forrest-Thomson repeats phrases, refers to other texts, and discusses her own tactics of rhyme and refrain extensively enough to make the poem's principal subject its uncertainty about its own meaning and construction.

Such interests and uncertainties were extensively explored in Denise Riley's poetry, often in combination with feminist commitments. Riley was a determined analyst of fabrics of language, even in the course of spinning them. Poems in *Mop Mop Georgette* (1993) regularly discuss with readers issues such as the 'awful I process' of composition ('Lyric'), the potential inappropriateness of the poet's voice and tone ('Cruelty without Beauty'), or the difficult, maybe misguided, attempt to transcribe self and experience. 'Representing yourself, desperate to get it right, I as if you could, is that the aim of the writing?' Riley asks in 'A Shortened Set', for example. Ironic about the 'Starry unconscious: sea body: child maintenance' demanded of women ('Lucille's Tune'), Riley's writing sometimes holds up for scrutiny—separated from her own voice by inverted commas or italics—male-oriented or other forms of public discourse, allowing these juxtaposed registers to challenge and implicitly comment on each other. Such tactics demonstrated how useful language disruption and formal adventure could be for late twentieth-century women's poetry—in identifying and challenging, at work within literary or linguistic conventions, assumptions also more widely structuring contemporary gender roles and expectations. Exploration of language as 'the place where power struggles are going on' had the potential to add significantly, as Michèle Roberts suggested, to the politics of women's poetry and its determination to 'change the world' (Horovitz (ed.), *Grandchildren of Albion*, p. 402). This potential was still being developed by women writers at the end of the century.

*

Language disruption, formal adventure, and challenges to literary convention featured much more widely in poetry late in the century, their extent emphasized by the work of several critics and anthologists towards the end of the 1980s and in the 1990s. This work often responded directly to Blake Morrison and Andrew Motion's *Penguin Book of Contemporary British Poetry* (1982), seeking to provide broader or less conservative perspectives than their controversial anthology had offered. Typically, in *The New Poetry* (1993)—its title deliberately echoing A. L. Alvarez's, thirty years earlier—Michael Hulse, David Kennedy, and David Morley emphasized that they had excluded from their anthology all the authors whom Morrison and Motion had included in theirs. Along with more established figures such as Peter Reading, *The New Poetry* concentrated instead on the work of younger poets such as Sean O'Brien, Simon Armitage, Glyn Maxwell, Michael Hofmann, Jo Shapcott, and Lavinia Greenlaw. Many of these poets were also included in the 'New Generation' defined the following year by the Poetry Society's journal, *Poetry Review*. For Hulse, Kennedy, and Morley, the work of this New Generation of 1990s poets was distinguished by 'accessibility, democracy and responsiveness', and by reaffirmation of 'the art's significance as public utterance' (p. 16).

This element of public significance was often developed through versions of the confessional mode Alvarez had favoured in 1962: many writers included in the 1990s *New Poetry* traced the stresses of the wider world through their effects within the personal sphere. These were generally recorded in a voice attuned, accessibly and reticently, to the demands of 'public utterance' in an age generally impatient with idiosyncratic or heightened forms of discourse, poetry's included.[7] In the work of the writers mentioned, the result was often a form of urbane monologue: humorous and colloquial, but sometimes also ironic or uneasy about its own procedures. Historical stresses, Alvarez considered, could be aptly represented through description of authors' tormented psyches. The New Generation of the 1990s tended instead to reflect their disruptive effects on language. 'Language is impossible | in a country like this', Jo Shapcott remarked of contemporary England in 'Motherland' (1996), demonstrating in other poems, such as 'Phrase Book' (1992), the withering effects of media and public discourse and the trite, reductive formulas they impose on modern speech. For other New Generation poets, Glyn Maxwell particularly, an impossibly warped late twentieth-century language introduced a sceptical self-awareness into the voice of poetry itself. Such scepticism naturally extended from voice to speaker. New Generation monologues regularly represented uncertain identities, able to articulate themselves only in fragmentary, fluid, postmodern terms: as 'not myself . . . just anyone', in Michael Hofmman's 'A Brief Occupation' (1986), for example. Poets such as Hofmann, Ruth Padel, Selima Hill, and others of the 'New Generation' imagined their way freely into multiple, diverse selves—like the metamorphic sea goddess in Shapcott's 'Thetis' (1996)—while remaining sharply aware of limits language imposes on the expression of any individuality or identity.

Equally dismissive of poetry favoured by Morrison and Motion, other anthologies in the 1980s and 1990s concentrated much more exclusively and austerely than *The New Poetry* on the nature and difficulties of language. In *A Various Art* (1987), Andrew Crozier and Tim Longville scorned the 'pusillanimous set of conventions' consolidated by the Movement in the 1950s, illustrating alternative possibilities in the work of poets such as Roy Fisher, Veronica Forrest-Thomson, John James, Douglas Oliver, David Chaloner, John Riley, J. H. Prynne, and Iain Sinclair, as well as their own (p. 12). *The New British Poetry 1968–1988* followed a year later, concentrating in its

[7] See also p. 205, above, and pp. 258–60, below.

four sections on areas its editors—Gillian Allnutt, Fred D'Aguiar, Ken Edwards, and Eric Mottram—considered wrongfully excluded from *The Penguin Book of Contemporary British Poetry*. The first two of these—black and women's writing—have already been discussed. In the third section, Eric Mottram stressed that the 'Poetry Revival' of the 1960s and early 1970s had contributed not only to the genre's popularity, but to the readiness of poets starting to write at the time to become 'explorers in language and form' (Allnutt et al. (eds.), p. 132). In the fourth section, Ken Edwards demonstrated how far this disposition had extended into the work of younger poets in the following decades. Mottram and Edwards included among their 'explorers' several of the writers featured in *A Various Art*, alongside others such as Tom Raworth and Lee Harwood whose interest in developing modernist legacies—often on the basis of transatlantic models—was described in Chapter 6.

Conductors of Chaos (1996) further supported the radical interests Eric Mottram defined. Iain Sinclair's introduction was sceptical of the 'public utterance' developed in the work of the New Generation, but complained more vehemently about the 'flash dudes of Blake Morrison's and Andrew Motion's *Penguin Book of Contemporary Poetry*' [*sic*]. Sinclair recommended instead poems more fully engaged with 'the complexity of the climate in which they exist', and included a range of writers similar to Mottram's, and to Crozier and Longville's, with further additions such as Denise Riley, Cris Cheek, Grace Lake, and Rod Mengham (Iain Sinclair (ed.), *Conductors*, pp. xv–xvi, xvii). His anthology also featured several recently established writers, such as Tony Lopez, Drew Milne, and Jeremy Reed, who introduced their own work alongside poetry by earlier authors who had influenced them—W. S. Graham, David Jones, and David Gascoyne, respectively. *Conductors of Chaos* emphasized in this way what Tony Lopez called 'a continuity in the Modernist tradition, even if the Movement writers managed to make it seem less visible for a time' (p. 210).

Critics writing in the 1990s also stressed the importance of this continuity, and of the explorations in language and form Mottram mentioned. Essays in Robert Hampson and Peter Barry's *New British Poetries: The Scope of the Possible* (1993) and James Acheson and Romana Huk's *Contemporary British Poetry: Essays in Theory and Criticism* (1996) concentrated on black and women's poetry, on issues of language and ideology, and on the experimental legacies of modernism. David Kennedy's *New Relations: The Refashioning of British Poetry 1980–1994* (1996) stressed how far recent writing had progressed beyond the constraints of the Movement and the modest ambitions still inhibiting poetry in the early 1980s. Each of these volumes looked in detail at the work of some of the poets included in the recent anthologies, discussing writers such as J. H. Prynne, Lee Harwood, Veronica Forrest-Thomson, and Andrew Crozier alongside more widely known figures such as Tony Harrison, Geoffrey Hill, and Jon Silkin.

Along with the anthologies mentioned, this critical work highlighted effects within English poetry of the broader literary developments outlined in Chapter 2. Despite the counter-influence of the Movement after mid-century, several English poets had continued to develop modernist writing—incipiently self-conscious about its form and medium—towards a more fully self-referential, language-centred postmodernism in evidence by century's end. Critics and anthologists in the 1990s also demonstrated how much this continuing development depended on encouragement from the United States: on transatlantic rerouting and rejuvenation of influences modernism had originally established. In addition to the models mentioned in Chapter 6, generally redirecting poetry's attention to issues of language and form, English poets late in the century were drawn towards work which had followed 'open field' composition in the United States. 'Language Poetry' was a particular interest. Produced by authors such as Charles Bernstein, Bruce Andrews, and Ron Silliman in the 1970s, this new idiom was characterized by abstract, puzzling, apparently random patterns of words, fracturing ordinary syntax, sequence, and sense. The Language Poets centred attention instead on their own linguistic processes, and sometimes their implied politics, making poems into illustrative amalgams of conflicting discourses rather than immediately coherent statements in themselves.

Stressing the common interest of poets included in *A Various Art* in post-war US poetry, Crozier described its overall influence, like Mottram, in terms of 'commitment to the discovery of meaning and form in language itself' (Crozier and Longville (eds.), p. 14). 'I am from language and will return to language', Peter Riley remarks in a poem included in *A Various Art*; 'Praise be to the continuing | independence of language', David Chaloner adds in another, 'Just Deserts'. Some of Andrew Crozier's own poems in the anthology also exemplify transitions towards this linguistic 'independence'. Like the US poet John Ashbery, Crozier repeatedly refers to light, glass, mirrors, windows, and curtains to emphasize his concern with processes of perception, rather than only what is perceived—with what 'floods the retina | then vanishes along the | optic nerve to reappear | as what we see' ('Light in the Air'). Concentrating on 'the glass | through which you witnessed' and what 'mists over it', such poetry necessarily focuses on the language in which perception is recorded, and the forms and means through which it orders experience, rather than the world its words might more conventionally have been expected to represent.

This concentration made much greater demands on readers than the work of the New Generation writers Hulse, Kennedy, and Morley included in *The New Poetry*. For the New Generation, the opacities of language partly shaded or complicated what was otherwise mostly urbane, accessible commentary on life and reality. For the poets of *A Various Art* or *Conductors of Chaos*, these priorities were virtually reversed. To ensure readers looked *at* the language on the page—rather than through it, towards a familiar, represented reality—transparency and ease of ordinary understanding had to be eliminated as far as possible. The deliberately difficult work which resulted required different reading strategies, and new forms of engagement with the poem as a literary object: even as a kind of art object, a role further suggested by the shapely, almost sculptural layout of some of this poetry. Typically of postmodernist writing, these new interpretative strategies were sometimes implied within the poems themselves. David Chaloner's reference in 'Never Let It End' to 'a panorama of images drifting sedately through the haze, intent on decorating the view from the page', suggests that readers might survey an intriguingly hazy verbal prospect, without worrying that its words and images did not immediately distil themselves into conventional sense. Drifts of words and images could also be construed as inner movements of the poet's mind: as representations of fragmentary thoughts; fringes of mind preceding firm articulated sense.

A number of poems included in *A Various Art* and *Conductors of Chaos* suggested this kind of reading: Anthony Barnett's self-questioning interior monologue, or dialogue, in 'Report to the Working Party'; Douglas Oliver's streams of impressions; some of the work of John James, Veronica Forrest-Thomson, or Grace Lake.

'Photographs of processes of thought' was a description a fellow poet, Ian Patterson, offered for the work of J. H. Prynne (Iain Sinclair (ed.), *Conductors*, p. 348). Prynne was often identified as an influence on the loose constellation of poets known as the 'Cambridge School', considered to include writers such as Veronica Forrest-Thomson, Denise Riley, Rod Mengham, Wendy Mulford, Peter Riley, John Wilkinson, and Drew Milne. But his full significance for the period's poetry began to be realized only at the end of the century, with the publication of his collected *Poems* in 1999. Prynne's strategies and their difficulties were paradigmatic of postmodernist poetry generally, and of work included in *A Various Art* and *Conductors of Chaos* in particular. These difficulties were substantial. On 23 April 1999 the *Times Literary Supplement*—not usually much daunted by difficult or cerebral writing—described Prynne's poetry, in its later phases especially, in terms of 'impenetrable enigmas . . . like the clues to a crossword no one is ever likely to crack' (p. 27). Yet like the authors mentioned above, Prynne did provide clues about his work, in critical writing as well as in poems themselves. He stressed in *Conductors of Chaos*, for example, that 'within the great aquarium of language the light refracts variously and can bounce by inclinations not previously observed' (p. 355). Though concerned as Patterson suggested with 'processes of thought', sometimes even at a neurological level, much of his poetry was more involved in processes at work within, and upon, language—like Crozier's, with ways its 'glass' could mist, refract, or obscure.

Language's indeterminacies, refractions, and unobserved 'inclinations' were also analysed in Prynne's critical essay *Stars, Tigers and the Shape of Words* (1993). In particular, Prynne reassessed the arbitrariness Ferdinand de Saussure attributed to primary relations between 'the thing and the name', and between 'the sense or meaning of a linguistic utterance . . . and the forms of its expression' (*Stars*, pp. 16, 1).[8] Prynne emphasized instead a set of '*secondary* relations'

---

[8] Saussure's views are discussed on pp. 93–4, above.

through which meaning develops more subtly and less arbitrarily than Saussure considered—ones dependent on 'historical contexts and usages . . . accumulated layers and aspects of association . . . social function . . . usage codes' (*Stars*, pp. 32, 14, 18). Much of Prynne's poetry suppressed conventional meaning—primary relations between 'thing and name'—in order to bring these secondary elements more fully into play, and to ensure readers recognized their influence. Peter Ackroyd approvingly assessed Prynne's poetry as almost entirely lacking 'extrinsic reference' and retaining at most 'only a marginal denotative potential' (p. 130). Rather than wilful or crossword opacity, this suppression of ordinary meaning could be considered an attempt to make the 'glass though which you witness' as visible as possible. As another of his admirers, Veronica Forrest-Thomson, explained, Prynne's poetry continuously sought to 'make language real again for the poet and reader' in the fullest way (*Poetic Artifice*, p. 50).

An important part of this attempt was the identification of forces—for Prynne, usually commercial or economic ones—which had most muddied the waters of language's aquarium. Rather like Geoffrey Hill, wrestling with corruptions coded into language by governments and systems of power, in his early poetry particularly Prynne sought to resist the warping and commodification of words by the relentless materialism of the modern age. Some of its pressures are indicated by references to 'mercantile notion' and 'manoeuvre | of capital' in 'Moon Poem' (1969) and 'Foot and Mouth' (1969), for example, and to 'thickening in the words | as the coins themselves wear thin' ('In the Long Run, to be Stranded', 1969). 'Sketch for a Financial Theory of the Self' (1968) also shows how readily 'bond and contract and interest' deflect into mere materialism desires once directed upon the transcendent—a corruption of language which leaves 'names . . . *necessarily false*', only 'tricks we | trust'. Corruptions of this kind could be effectively exposed by suspending conventional 'extrinsic reference' and forcing readers to question anew how language's potentials were being employed or abused in contemporary life. Though they also had wider implications, opacities in the work of Prynne and other postmodernist poets could therefore be justified by Fredric Jameson's critical conclusion about the difficulties of twentieth-century poetry generally. In an age more than ever dominated by media, advertising, and commercial interests, there were as Jameson suggested 'deeper social reasons for the stubborn insistence of modern poetry on the materiality and density of language, on words felt not as transparency but rather as things in themselves' (*Marxism and Form*, p. 24).

Poetry included in *A Various Art* or *Conductors of Chaos* could not always be entirely justified in this way. In the work of some poets, obscurities seemed gratuitous, or self-indulgent; part of a postmodernist manner adopted without genuine motive or 'social reason'. A more fundamental problem was that poetry so immersed in the shadowy depths of language's great aquarium simply deterred the interest or exhausted the patience of potential readers. Numbed by the Movement and its successors into expecting poetry to be straightforward and accessible, late twentieth-century readers had much to gain from writing which could challenge and rejuvenate their expectations. But they were also, in general, and for the same reason, poorly prepared to appreciate such work when it did appear. Poets included in *A Various Art* and *Conductors of Chaos* could not, of course, be held responsible for this element of recalcitrance in their potential audience—or not entirely, at any rate. Like any avant-garde, they might have worked less in expectation of immediate appreciation than of eventually reshaping aesthetic conventions and popular understanding around new priorities emphasized in their work. Yet neither *A Various Art* nor *Conductors of Chaos* showed much interest in such reshaping. On the contrary, each anthology envisaged any shortage of readers not as a problem to be regretted, and perhaps eventually overcome, but rather as a guarantee of integrity, even a measure of success. 'Egos puffed to a critical stage' within a 'private world' of small presses were unlikely to be deflated by their remoteness from a popular readership, even seeming to 'rather enjoy it', Iain Sinclair suggested in *Conductors of Chaos* (pp. xvii, xviii).

Though he acknowledged that poetry had become too confined in this private world, and had been 'driven too far from the sites of . . . "civic production" ', Sinclair briskly dismissed some of the 1990s authors likeliest to drive it back again (*Conductors*, p. xx). Writers of the New Generation whom he disparaged—Glyn Maxwell, for example, self-conscious in poems such as 'Tale of the Mayor's Son' (1990) about the 'modern poet thing'—combined postmodernist interests typical of Sinclair's poets with a wit and directness they often conspicuously lacked. Combining postmodernist awareness with 'civic production' and the demands of a general readership, it was the authors of the New Generation, and less often the poets in Sinclair's anthology, who offered the most promising path for poetry at the end of the century. Rather than suggesting any way forward, the emphasis in *Conductors of Chaos* on 'remote, élitist ... alienated, fractured' writing indicated the continuing hold of the past on English poetry, demonstrating in a new form the longevity of the Movement's legacies (pp. xvi, xvii). Movement influences had continued to divert innovative writing into marginal positions within the literary establishment: its example had apparently also persuaded postmodernist poets that popular appeal was so compromised that it was best to avoid it as far as possible. The next chapter considers further implications of this assumption—an improvident one, in a period when poetry's readership was generally in decline—along with other problems the genre had accumulated towards the end of the twentieth century.

8

Rosebay Revived: Language, Form, and Audience for 'This Unpopular Art'

Some nations lock up their poets. Ours have the key
to a high, clean room labelled Sensibility.

They have sat there now for a very long time,
and are clearly no threat to a democratic regime.

They are old, of course, but remarkably unspoiled;
their edges still cut, their moving parts are oiled.

Of course, they're permitted to go down to the street,
and the street may visit them, if it wipes its feet.

Here comes the guide now, telling the solemn young faces
that yes, the poets still work, but don't touch the glass cases.

(Carol Rumens, 'In the Craft Museum', 1987)

'This unpopular art' was W. H. Auden's description of poetry in 'The Cave of Making' in 1965. Rumens's 'In the Craft Museum' indicated that it later came to seem not only an unpopular art, but even a faintly obsolescent one. As they suggest, English poetry seemed to endure a troubled period late in the twentieth century, encountering many difficulties in meeting the demands of the times, and of its potential audience. Various historical pressures threatened to remove it further than ever from a popular readership, especially after the 1960s revival faded. Some of these problems arose from the continuing aura of 'high Sensibility' Rumens describes. In *British Poetry 1964–1984* (1985), Martin Booth likewise pointed to a continuing common assumption, at the beginning of the period, that poetry was about 'high-flown emotions or rhetorical ideas or . . . love', yet at a time when tolerance for high sensibility, rhetoric, or lofty emotions was generally in decline (p. 17). As the editors of *The New Poetry* warned in 1993, 'the hierarchies of values that once made stable poetics possible' had been eroded throughout the twentieth century (Hulse et al. (eds.), p. 15). Towards its end, as part of the broad democratization of life in evidence since the 1960s, the idea of hierarchy itself was increasingly questioned, not only in social but in much wider terms, artistic ones included.

Many factors were involved in this questioning. It was paralleled, first of all, and probably accelerated, by the steepening decline of Christian faith and churchgoing in the period, eventually leaving Sunday just another day for relaxation and shopping. This also left readers, by the 1980s and 1990s, unfamiliar with a rich field of biblical stories, ideas, and characters which had formed a background to English writing throughout much of its earlier history. Another consequence was in carrying any sense of the exalted or spiritual—of a higher dimension beyond the immediate one—further away from most daily lives. Without necessarily being believers themselves, poets perhaps intuited implications for their own role in this gradual failure of a Christian sense of transcendence. In any case, they reflected significantly often on religious decline, and usually with some uneasiness: like Auden in 'The Cave of Making', they mostly 'watched with mixed feelings | . . . the churches empty'. In 1955, in 'Church Going', Philip Larkin had wondered 'when churches fall completely out of use | What we shall turn them into': his question was often taken up, directly or indirectly, by poets in later decades. In 'Development' (1981), D. J. Enright noted that 'the house of God is due to be converted, | These days He has no need of so much space', and predicted—accurately—that churches would soon be used for 'bowling or housey-housey' instead. Tony Harrison mentioned in *v.* (1985) that in buildings once 'truly . . . the Lord's | . . . pews are filled with cut-price toilet rolls'. Substitution of the transcendent by materialism, marketing, and toilet rolls was also explored in Blake Morrison's 'Superstore' (1987), which found in a new shopping centre 'not a mockery of churches | but a way like them of forgetting | the darkness where no one's serving | and there's nothing to choose from at all'.

'Oh Christianity, Christianity, | . . . | . . . are you vanishing?' Stevie Smith wondered, like Larkin, in 'How do you see' (1972), anticipating a general fading of faith into mere 'beliefs we do not believe in'. Like the steady emptying of the churches, this evacuation of belief itself was reflected regularly and progressively in the period's poetry. In its earlier years, a number of older poets continued to consider religious matters, or at least, like C. Day Lewis in 'Requiem for the Living' (1962) to address a 'God, in whom we half believe, | Or not believe'. Religious concerns, often accentuated by a harsh rural landscape, figured centrally in the work of the Welsh poet and parish minister R. S. Thomas, at this time and later. They were also regularly explored by John Heath-Stubbs, and by Elizabeth Jennings, discussing in 'Letter from Assisi' (1958), 'Harvest and Consecration' (1961), and 'Annunciation' (1958) what she described in 'Lazarus' (1961) as the way 'minds moved . . . hungry for finished faith'. Much of her later poetry, such as 'Towards a Religious Poem' (1975), regretted the fading of this faith from the wider life of the times.

Many writers in later decades continued to share Jennings's 'hunger', but with less and less sure means of assuaging it. C. H. Sisson's religious longings followed naturally from his bleak preoccupations with evanescence and mortality, in poems such as 'Burrington Combe' (1980); or with a 'heart . . . armoured by intellection' in 'The Adventurer' (1968); or, in general, with solitude and the failure of love. Yet religion scarcely offered a persuasive solace, Sisson recording in 'The Usk' (1974), for example, how *'per Cristum'* only 'lies on [the] tongue'. Even this uncertain promise seemed implausible to other poets, though the attraction of 'beliefs we do not believe in' continued to figure strongly in their work. *'No God any more'* Larkin remarked in a later church poem, 'High Windows' (1974). Yet he still looked 'beyond', towards 'the deep blue air, that shows | Nothing, and is nowhere, and is endless'. 'No Saviour here', Peter Porter accepted in 'The Sadness of the Creatures' (1970). Yet he, too, continued to seek 'things of the spirit' among details of daily domesticity. In 'The Historians Call Up Pain' (1961), he also regretted—like A. L. Alvarez, complaining of the passionlessness of English life at this time—that 'we can only | Walk in temperate London, our educated city, | Wishing to cry as freely as they did who died | In the Age of Faith'. Geoffrey Hill's historical interests were often shaped by a similar attraction towards past ages of faith. A 'passion' to 'find out God in this', and for 'unearthing of the God-in-us' appears in 'Shiloh Church, 1862' (1968), for example. Hill remained more generally concerned, throughout his work, with what *Mercian Hymns* (1971) calls 'the re-entry of transcendence into this sublunary world' (XXIII). Yet he also stressed that he was 'trying to make lyrical poetry out of a . . . common situation—the sense of *not* being able to grasp true religious experience' (Haffenden, *Viewpoints*, p. 89).

Along with the general fading of the transcendent from an increasingly materialist 'sublunary world', this situation left little scope for the visionary role often accorded poets in earlier periods. An increasingly democratized, anti-hierarchical age—defined by C. Day Lewis in 'Who Goes Home' (1965) as 'restive against the uncommon'— also challenged more limited, secular concepts of poets' roles. Even their position as privileged observers of ordinary life, unusually equipped to express collective experience of it, seemed questionable. Distinctive shifts in rhetoric and outlook appeared in the period's poetry as a result. Members of an older generation still publishing in its early years—including W. H. Auden, Louis MacNeice, and Day Lewis himself—still wrote regularly and confidently on behalf of a supposedly common humanity. Poems concerned employed either a collective 'we' form, or a first-person singular expressing general experiences and perspectives through the poet's account of his own. These habits were also sustained by writers emerging early in the period: in Peter Porter's reflections, for example, quoted above, on what 'we' experience in walking through London, 'our' educated city. C. H. Sisson's habitual support for tradition and poetic convention included explicit emphasis of the individual poet's right to speak for common humanity. In 'My Life and Times' (1965), he remarks

> I would not waste this paper for
> (I hope) a merely personal bore
> But write about the singular
> Because 'I am' may read 'We are.'
>
> .   .   .   .   .

> Remember that the human race
> Grins more or less in every face.

Equations of 'I am' and 'We are', however, grew more uncertain in an age which the editors of *The New Poetry* saw lacking not only the hierarchies of values that poetry had once relied on, but many of the shared values it used to reflect.

As they emphasized, 'shared moral and religious ideals, common social or sexual *mores* or political ideologies' had been in decline throughout the century, along with any collective 'philosophy on the conduct of life' (Hulse et al. (eds.), p.15). Resulting tensions between poetry's individual voice and its wider audience were already evident even in the late 1950s and 1960s. Movement poets writing at the time often went 'further than halfway to meet . . . readers' by using common, colloquial forms of speech, though ones still carefully contained within conventional metrical patterns. They also alternated, or hesitated, between 'I' and 'we' perspectives within single poems, such as Larkin's 'The Whitsun Weddings' (1964).[1] As the kind of public festivals, traditions, and collective social expectations reflected in 'The Whitsun Weddings' faded further from English life, and the audience for poetry itself generally diminished and diversified, a confidently collective voice and vision grew still more difficult to sustain. By 1993, in 'A Shortened Set', Denise Riley was suggesting principles opposite to Sisson's, advising poets not to 'quote the "we" | of pairs nor worse, of sentient | humanity, thanks'. This was a warning apparently heeded by many of the authors represented in *The New Poetry*, published in the same year. The 'New Generation' poetry the anthology included was often deliberately self-contained and tentative, implying few assumptions about its public—even when discussing public issues—or about the poet's own powers or typicality. The urbane monologues of much New Generation poetry presumed instead to speak for—or perhaps even to—no one other than their own authors. The visions this poetry unfolded were too particular, and the views and personae concerned too provisional, to represent confidently any outlook other than the poet's own, interesting though this might nevertheless seem to anyone encountering it.

---

[1] See p. 169, above.

In this and other ways—discussed later—New Generation writing avoided some of the difficulties which came to affect poetry's relation with its public during the period. Yet these were not confined to doubts about a collective, public voice. They also extended into questions even about poetry's private one: about the introspective, lyric, 'I am'. An age 'restive against the uncommon' not only grew suspicious of any voice presuming to speak collectively on its behalf, about public life and experience in general, but also grew wary of any poets too ready to assume wider relevance for their private emotions, reflections, sensitivity, or supposedly 'high Sensibility'. As Donald Davie remarked, Movement writers in the 1950s and 1960s had rarely questioned 'by what right, if any, the lyrical sensibility can . . . subjugate to itself the physical or historical realities which it chooses to play upon'. Nor did they much challenge what he called 'the characteristic procedure of the lyrical poet . . . to station himself in a physical or mental landscape, and then have emotions about it' (*Under Brigflatts*, p. 227). But such questions and challenges were raised more and more often later in the century. Poetry's difficult relations with the mental landscapes and historical realities of the period are further considered later. Changed relations with physical landscape obviously had far-reaching consequences for a genre which had relied so substantially, especially since the Romantic period, on the imaginative potentials of nature. These potentials might have taken on still further significance at a time of declining religious faith, in ways Ken Smith suggested in 'After a journey' (1972), talking of praying 'not to a god but to stone, | to the grass, to the running hooves of the horses'. For late twentieth-century poetry, even for the period more generally, nature offered a secular transcendence potentially able to replace the religious one in which faith was increasingly failing.

Yet the consolations of nature, like those of religion, tended to fade from English poetry as the period went on. Any transcendent aspect was principally evident in its early years, or among an older generation of writers, such as George Barker or Geoffrey Grigson. In 'Crossing the Beauce by Slow Train, After the Harvest' (1980), for example, Grigson continued to describe an almost religious sense of peace communicated by physical landscape. Among Movement writers, too, admiration for late nineteenth- and early twentieth-century poets such as Thomas Hardy and Edward Thomas some-times expressed itself in a return to pastoral idioms. These appeared in Larkin poems such as 'At Grass' (1955) and 'Here' (1964), as well as in the poetry of Elizabeth Jennings, and in some of the later work of Robert Conquest. In 'Appalachian Convalescence' (1979), for example, Conquest continued to relish a sense that nature could 'confirm . . . a mind made free'. Such freedom also appealed to C. H. Sisson, describing in 'The Consequence' (1968) how 'twilight and the rose | And other such ephemera' can 'distract us to a brief repose', and in 'On the Coast' (1968) how wilder prospects could communi-cate a healing sense of insignificance to the self. Jon Silkin celebrated a comparable sense of freedom—or of redemptive insignificance—in showing 'the self . . from its being taken out' by 'purged barbaric wildness' and by 'words among branches' in 'Wildness Makes a Form' (1980). Like Peter Redgrove in his early work, in poems such as 'Flatfish' (1971) or 'Worm' (1971) Silkin pursued an immediacy of contact with the natural world through meticulous descriptions of it. Seamus Heaney's early work was similarly immediate in its repre-sentations of nature, and of his native Irish landscape, part of his wide appeal to English poets and readers at this time. Some of the material in *Death of a Naturalist* (1966), *Door into the Dark* (1969), and *Wintering Out* (1972) also moved distinctively beyond ordinary description—towards the 'vowelling embrace, | Demesnes staked out in consonants' described in 'A New Song' (1972), for example. A still closer identity between language and land developed in poems such as 'Anahorish' (1972), merging scene and syllable into a 'soft gradient | of consonant, vowel-meadow'.

Finding 'words among branches', or a 'vowelling embrace' of the natural world, seemed more problematic to many contemporary English poets. Postmodern scepticism of language and imagination —even of the identity and coherence of the observing 'I'—often com-plicated or made impossible the conventional lyrical 'subjugation' of physical landscape Donald Davie saw surviving early in the period. Veronica Forrest-Thomson's 'Pastoral' (1976) summed up one set of difficulties encountered by the period's nature poetry in transcribing 'the world that is not ours'. 'Jagged are names and not our creatures | Either in kind or movement like the flowers', the poem comments, adding that 'Silence in grass and solace in blank verdure | Summon the frightful glare of nouns and nerves'. In the work of Peter Redgrove, Charles Tomlinson, Ted Hughes, and Christopher Middleton, the sense of a natural world containing 'more | Than the words can witness', and of 'strange ligatures' connecting ' "I am" and "This is" ', allowed only a self-questioning form of nature poetry. Such scepticisms contributed to new ways of imagining the physical world, yet they also challenged poetry's capacities to represent it at all.[2]

Even among an older, more conventional generation of poets early in the period, doubts about the lyric sensibility's engagement with physical landscape tended to qualify any affirmation or transcendence to be found in it. Geoffrey Grigson's aptly named 'The Veil' (1980) worried that language might occlude the natural world in the act of describing it. In 'Villa Stellar' (1978), George Barker likewise examined both the 'glass that supervenes between all | we see and the I that sees it' and the nature of 'that observatory from which one looks out upon all things | . . . the First Person Obscura' (XLVI). Some of Elizabeth Jennings's titles—'Beyond Possession' (1955), 'World I Have Not Made' (1961), and 'Let Things Alone' (1972)— indicated a similar concern about how 'thoughts about it divide | Me from my object' ('In the Night', 1955). Questions about how the natural world 'lives | Within my mind' ('The Dog Rose', 1983) continued to appear in some of C. H. Sisson's poetry, and occasionally in the work of Anne Stevenson, Fleur Adcock, and Donald Davie himself. In 'Essex' (1974), for example, Davie provided a succinct version of postmodern, late twentieth-century anxieties about 'nouns and nerves', remarking that 'names and things named don't match', and that 'sooner or later the whole | Cloth of the language peels off | As wallpaper peels from a wall'.

Nature poetry and the conventional 'lyric sensibility' were also much troubled in the period by changes in the English landscape itself, and in ways it was popularly imagined. 'England's green and pleasant land', as William Blake defined it in 'Jerusalem' (1804), provided an adequate context for much of the idealism and pastoral imagination of the Romantics, and for poets throughout the nineteenth and early twentieth centuries. Towards the end of the twentieth century, under the growing influence of tourism, exile, and

---

[2] See pp. 192–4 and 200–4, above.

international travel, poets and the population generally were likelier to locate their ideal or pleasant landscapes outside England. For immigrant writers, those from the West Indies especially, this often invited recollection of warmer, brighter landscapes of childhood. Other poets shared directions suggested by popular travelogue—by Peter Mayle's best-selling account of a new life abroad in *A Year in Provence* (1988), for example—preferring to celebrate sunnier, holiday landscapes rather than a domestic climate of wind and rain. Like 'Crossing the Beauce', much of Grigson's later pastoral poetry was set in rural France. Elaine Feinstein, too, considered 'days lived in peace' and 'the beauties of August' accompanied most pleasingly by 'the dry wind of Provence' ('Mas-en-Cruyes', 1973). By contrast, she envisaged in 'By the Cam' (1977) an England 'puddled in | rain and mud', and remarked in 'June' (1977) that 'we've learnt on our bodies | how each Summer day is won | from soil, the old clay soil | and that long, cold kingdom'.

The weather, apparently, was one form of collective experience which did survive influentially in late twentieth-century English literature: for many other poets, a 'cold kingdom' was likewise all that England seemed to offer. After many years living and working abroad, Basil Bunting explored in *Briggflatts* (1966) an English landscape often as damp and grim as it was redeeming. In much of Ken Smith's 1960s poetry, such as 'Family Group' (1964), country life was described as equally chill, bleak, and hard-working, reflecting realities of agricultural labour in the north of England which he had known at first hand in his youth. Both Smith and Bunting nevertheless envisaged an English country world still relatively unspoiled and unpolluted in the 1960s, still able at some level to 'confirm . . . a mind made free'. As the period went on, this freedom was more and more displaced by the sense of a soiled, enclosed England, its apparently ubiquitous decay among incentives for poets to locate ideal landscapes elsewhere. In 1964, in 'Here', Philip Larkin was still able to contemplate escaping from 'industrial shadows | And traffic all night' into a 'bluish neutral distance' of 'unfenced existence'. Ten years later, in 'Going, Going', such escape seemed to him almost impossible. 'I thought it would last my time', Larkin remarks, 'the sense that, beyond the town, | There would always be fields and farms'. Instead, he fears that 'garbage . . . too thick strewn | To be swept up now' will soon leave 'England gone', and that 'all that remains I . . . will be concrete and rubber tyres'. Donald Davie duly confirmed, at the end of the 1980s, how little potential remained in the earlier twentieth-century pastoral conventions which had appealed to Movement writers such as Larkin. Edward Thomas had experienced 'that country between the North and the South Downs . . . as immemorially secret and settled and lonely', Davie recalled, whereas later in the century 'we barged along bumper to bumper between commuters' homes, to and from Gatwick airport' (*Under Briggflatts*, p. 168).

Such concerns were typical of an 'eco-depression', as Benjamin Zephaniah called it in 'City River Blues' (1996), which provided one of the dominant notes of the period's poetry. Early examples appeared throughout D. J. Enright's collection *Some Men are Brothers* (1960), and in Alan Brownjohn's much-anthologized poem 'We are going to see the rabbit' (1962)—a nearly extinct creature to be found only under 'sodium lights, I Nibbling grass I On the only patch of grass I In England'. Like Larkin, John Heath-Stubbs lamented in 'The Green Man's Last Will and Testament' (1982) that 'ditches run with pollution, I . . . hedgerows are gone' and that 'all that remains' of nature is 'rags and patches'. Pastoral poetry's 'litany of flowers', he added in 'Greensleeves' (1982), had been overwhelmed by 'coal, I Iron, methane, oil, lead'. By the 1990s, in *Evagatory* (1992) Peter Reading viewed rural landscapes nearly as disconsolately as his cityscapes, finding 'only a troubled idyll now possible, I pastoral picnic under an ozone hole'. Nature and its idylls, in other words, were banished from late twentieth-century poetry not only by the 'nouns and nerves' Forrest-Thomson referred to in 'Pastoral'. They were dismissed still more firmly by what she called 'the long summer meadows' diesel fumes'—traffic, pollution, and urban sprawl carrying into a landscape of fields and farms all the corruptions poets might once have hoped confined to the city.

'Frigid lattices I Of pylons', Charles Tomlinson likewise suggested in 'Foxes' Moon' (1974), threatened to leave 'England's interrupted pastoral' devoid of 'all the meanings we can use'. For some authors, as the Introduction mentioned, this added significantly to a sense of 'the last of England' itself.[3] Yet pastoral was more interrupted than

[3] See p. 3, above.

altogether extinguished in the later twentieth century. English poets continued to develop residual meanings for nature, even in an age of pollution and decay. If nature no longer seemed redemptive and inviolate beyond the towns, for many poets it could still function affirmatively within them. Though later despairing of the Green Man, John Heath-Stubbs emphasized this renewed potential for nature poetry as early as 1954, remarking in 'Shepherd's Bush Eclogue' that the city might itself have 'truly pastoral' aspects. Heath-Stubbs found this true urban pastoral in the 'azure and virginal | Fields of pure air that all over London lie'. Throughout the period, other poets similarly highlighted nature's survivals above, below, or in rags and patches within towns and cities, regardless of the general greyness of these areas themselves. 'The town is dead', A. L. Alvarez remarked in 'Mourning and Melancholia' (1968), yet 'foxes are out on the Heath; | They sniff the air like knives. | A hawk turns slowly over Highgate', revealing 'the hidden life of London. Wild'. Ted Hughes described intimate connections with nature, typical of his interests, covertly extending even into the heart of London: in 'Epiphany' (1998), he recalled 'escaping | Into the Underground', haunted by the 'wild confronting stare' of a fox-cub bizarrely encountered 'On the hump of Chalk Farm Bridge'. In *Fox Running* (1980), Ken Smith also located a hidden, wild vitality in 'the cold | wind of | the subway tunnels' and in 'town littorals | chicken runs long bricked over'. These 'black | fast city veins' offer an 'underground poetry' of a different sort, creating in *Fox Running* a map of secret, subterranean energies which a deadening urban life has not eradicated entirely.

Beyond the metropolis, observing a ruined mill in 'Cheshire' (1974), Donald Davie recalled W. H. Auden's conviction that 'a post-industrial landscape | . . . | . . . can bleakly solace'. He also emphasized in 'Nottinghamshire' (1974) nature's power to reoccupy and transform areas once defaced by industrialization. After the economic crises of the 1970s, and the industrial decline which followed, this resilient, restorative power was more and more regularly explored in poetry. Intrigued by the reappearance of a butterfly in 'Dark Times' (1984), Tony Harrison pondered 'turning all these tides of blackness back' since 'Yorkshire's millstacks now don't burn'. He also identified in *v.* (1985) a natural productiveness even in decay: in the 'vast, slow, coal-creating forces' released by the gradual slippage of his parent's graveyard into old mine-workings beneath it. Some of Norman Nicholson's poems, such as 'Comet Come' (1994) or 'Bee Orchid at Hodbarrow' (1992), similarly considered human agency within vaster timescales, contrasting the transience of a man-made industrial landscape with a more changeless natural one around the poet's native Millom in Cumbria. 'On the Dismantling of Millom Ironworks' (1981) took as its epigraph Wordsworth's complaint about the 'taint | Of sordid industry', going on to show how natural forces have slowly wiped this taint from the landscape, with 'scrag-end and scree ironed out, and re-soiled and greened over'.

Yet the poem concludes that perhaps only Wordsworth's ghost could look altogether approvingly on the result—on 'a peninsula bare as it used to be, and, beyond . . . a river | Flowing, untainted now, to a bleak, depopulated shore'. Showing how *un*desirable a vacant landscape can seem in human terms—devoid of activity, purpose, and employment—Nicholson's work confirmed how thoroughly economic and industrial conditions in the late twentieth century forced poetry to move beyond pastoral conventions established by Wordsworth and the Romantics. Natural and urbanized spaces, life in the country and in the town, could no longer be considered altogether alternate, or even straightforwardly contrasted in value. In an industrial or post-industrial English landscape, poets had to envisage instead more complex forms of intermingling and interaction: possibilities, for a beleaguered natural world, only of residual forms of affirmation. These were also emphasized by Helen Dunmore, acknowledging in her introduction to *The Raw Garden* (1988) that 'a profoundly human-made landscape' no longer allowed contemporary writing to 'follow Romantic poets'. Poets had to celebrate instead nature's 'resilience, adaptability, and . . . power of improvisation'—its survival 'moment by moment, fragmented and tough, cropping up like a fan of buddleia high up in the gutter of a deserted warehouse' (*Out of the Blue*, pp. 126–7).

For a significant number of Dunmore's contemporaries, an emblem of this survival was provided not by buddleia, but by rose-bay willow-herb. In Edward Thomas's conventionally pastoral 'Adlestrop' (1916), the poet's glance falls only casually on 'willows, willow-herb and grass', each a relatively insignificant part of a country landscape around the station where his train briefly halts. Later in the century, the gritty bomb sites of the Second World War offered rosebay willow-herb a new foothold, never relinquished, within English cities, and also within English poetic imagination, as a symbol both of urban dereliction and of nature's resilient capacity to profit from it. Willow-herb figured defiantly among Norman Nicholson's 'Weeds' (1981), 'every spiky belfry humming with a peal of bees'; its 'thousand towers' hiding 'old, worked-out mines: | Quarries and tunnels, earth scorched and scruffy, torn-up railways, splintered sleepers'. It provided the 'Phoenix-Flower' in Geoffrey Grigson's poem of that name (1971). It appeared as one of the 'edifiers | of ruined things' in Geoffrey Hill's 'Churchill's Funeral' (1996), and in Anne Stevenson's description in 'Willow Song' (1971) of a ruined landscape, in which other flowers are 'as nothing to the rose-bay willow'. For Donald Davie, too, in 'Nottinghamshire', it enhanced the 'bleak solace' surrounding industrial decay, its 'defiant' appearance on wasteland making 'the rosebay willow herb | . . . of all the flowers | . . . the one I remember'. Late twentieth-century nature poetry might be more generally remembered in the same way—for its transition from the idyllic 'litany of flowers' Heath-Stubbs recalled in earlier writing, towards the residual, weedy defiance rosebay willow-herb came to represent in post-war imagination.

This transition was typical of movements away from the 'high-flown emotions' Martin Booth still found in the conventional image of poetry at the beginning of the period. Other items in Booth's list of poetic emotions—other conventional accoutrements of the 'lyrical sensibility'—were similarly transformed in later imagination. Love appeared no more inviolate nor easily idealized than nature, later in the twentieth century. Favouring weeds over flowers, and finding churches replete with toilet rolls rather than the holy spirit, the period's poetry, not surprisingly, also despaired of any uncompli-cated transcendence to be found in personal relations, particularly after the 1960s. Freer sexualities celebrated at that time later came to seem complicating as much as liberating, even if they often allowed a new frankness in contemporary poetry—typically in Fred D'Aguiar's 'Whitley Bay' sonnets (1993), or Michael Hofmann's 'Fucking' (1999). Writers who had cheerfully celebrated the new moods of the

1960s—Brian Patten, in particular, among the Liverpool Poets—
later became compelling elegists for a loss of the freedoms love and
relationship had seemed to offer during the decade. This sense of loss,
and of new complexity in later years, was aptly summed up in Colin
Falck's title *Postmodern Love* (1998). Examining contemporary attitudes to affairs, seduction, and divorce, Falck's sequence updated
George Meredith's *Modern Love* (1862) for a still more tangled,
uncertain age.

Love and sex, of course, continued to be celebrated in the period,
but for many writers in its later decades, they ceased to offer the idyllic, inviolate private space they had promised earlier poetry. Instead,
the experience of relationships often seemed to echo or even amplify
the wider historical disturbance of the times. 'The century's roar is a
desert carrying | too much away', J. H. Prynne remarked in 'Airport
Poem: Ethics of Survival' (1970), adding that 'love is, always, the |
flight back | to where | we are'. Throughout the period, the 1960s
perhaps excepted, poets seemed to make love under a flightpath
which kept history's uproar, as well as their own emotions, always
disturbingly audible. In the late seventeenth century, John Donne's
amours famously made his bed seem an 'everywhere'—blithely subordinating the stresses of a public world of states and princes—but
by the end of the twentieth the roles seemed almost reversed.
'Everywhere' invariably invaded even the bedroom and the intimate
spaces of sexual encounter. Donald Davie was already emphasizing
this interfusion of public and private life in the 1950s, describing
'love's radio-active fall-out' in 'Rejoinder to a Critic' (1956).
Michael Hulse continued to stress it in the 1990s, in his aptly entitled
'Fornicating and Reading the Papers' (1991). In the middle of the
period, in 'Durham' (1978), Tony Harrison anatomized the complicity of public and private affairs particularly clearly. 'Durham'
acknowledges that 'bad weather and the public mess | drive us to
private tenderness, | . . . | love's anti-bodies in the sick, | sick body
politic'. It conjectures hopefully that 'the machinery of sudden
death, | Fascism, the hot bad breath | of Powers down small coun-
tries' necks | shouldn't interfere with sex'. Yet the poem concludes
that 'they *are* sex . . . we must include | all these in love's beatitude',
and that 'on the *status quo*'s huge edifice' lovers are 'just excres-
cences that kiss'.

Though especially disturbing for private tenderness, the 'century's roar' and the hot bad breath of its history troubled the period's poetry much more generally. 'The sword I has developed immensely', Tony Harrison remarked, contemplating the Cold War in 'Sentences' (1975), 'while the pen is still only I a point, a free ink-flow I and the witness it has to keep bearing'. Influences discussed above all contributed to the sense of poetry's partial obsolescence, defined in Carol Rumens's 'In the Craft Museum'. But the most significant factor was the dark unfolding of twentieth-century history itself, scarcely allowing the survival of any writing supposed to be 'high-flown' in language, vision, or emotion. Theodor Adorno suggested early in the period that to continue 'to write lyric poetry after Auschwitz is barbaric', and many later poets shared or extended his anxiety (Bloch et al., p. 188). Jon Silkin, for example, referred in the 1970s to George Steiner's *Language and Silence* (1967) as a focus for his own doubts about ascribing much 'civilising attribute' to literature (*Poetry of the Committed Individual*, p. 210). Seamus Heaney went on raising in the late 1980s a 'question as immense and unavoidable as whether silence rather than poetry is not the proper response in a world after Auschwitz' (*Government of the Tongue*, p. 101).

Self-evidently, of course, Heaney and Silkin did prefer poetry to silence, the latter writing directly about the Holocaust in several poems.[4] Silkin also affirmed a continuing place for poetry after the concentration camps—a role developed through political commitments in much of his own writing—when he pointed out that 'society would be even more cruel were it not for these minimal restraints and exampla that art has made' (*Poetry of the Committed Individual*, p. 22). Such views were not much different from those Adorno originally expressed. His essay, 'Commitment', actually suggested that it would be as barbaric to abandon poetry as to persevere with it, arguing that 'the abundance of real suffering . . . demands the continued existence of art while it prohibits it' (Bloch et al., p. 188). It was nevertheless significant that writers and critics later in the century focused on Adorno's apparent despair of poetry more often than his assertion of its continuing potential. Given how immensely the sword had developed since 1939, a sense of history as prohibition rather than challenge was perhaps inevitable in the period, with a

[4] See pp. 68–9 and 199, above.

resulting concern that writing might offer only a refuge or escape from sufferings it had lost the capacity to deal with directly.

This was a problem by no means confined to poetry,[5] or to literature in England, but it did have particularly troubling consequences for English poets. Some of these were indicated by the suggestion in Rumens's 'In the Craft Museum' that 'Some nations lock up their poets' whereas 'Ours . . . are clearly no threat to a democratic regime'. English writers sometimes seemed to have survived a century of abundant suffering relatively easily, encountering historical and political forces much less challengingly than authors elsewhere. Though differing widely on other issues, A. L. Alvarez and Donald Davie concurred in this suspicion in their debate in the *Review* in 1962. They concluded that the Second World War inevitably brought poets from Eastern Europe 'face to face with the brutalities and atrocities of what the human condition is in the present century', whereas English writers had by comparison experienced '*nothing*' and did not really 'know what the war was about' (pp. 24–5). Thirty years later, referring to a visit to Slovenia, Denise Riley talked similarly in 'Laibach Lyrik' (1993) of 'seeing present history | . . . hearing it at work to stammer its imperfect story' while remaining 'by accident of place of birth protected'. Seamus Heaney summed up such concerns when he remarked that in the latter part of the century English poetry had

become aware of the insular and eccentric nature of English experience in all the literal and extended meanings of those adjectives . . .
. . . our own recent history of consumerist freedom and eerie nuclear security seems less authentic to us than the tragically tested lives of those who live beyond the pale of all this fiddle. Which is why the note sounded by translated poetry from that world beyond—pitched intently and in spite of occupation, holocaust, concentration camps and the whole apparatus of totalitarianism—is so credible, desolating, and resuscitative (*Government of the Tongue*, pp. 41, 43–4)

Notes sounded by translated poetry were certainly heard more widely in this period than in most earlier ones. That first issue of the *Review* in 1962, in which Alvarez and Davie's debate appeared,[6]

[5] See pp. 55–6 and 79–80, above.
[6] See p. 165, above.

opened with a set of translations from Zbigniew Herbert. The following year, Daniel Weissbort and Ted Hughes established a new
journal of *Modern Poetry in Translation*, and Penguin initiated a
Modern European Poets series to match their promotion of contemporary writers in English. Hughes also organized a 'Poetry International 1967' festival on a scale matching the Albert Hall event two
years previously. It featured writers such as Octavio Paz, Zbigniew
Herbert, Hans Magnus Enzensberger, and Pablo Neruda, proclaiming in its programme that poetry was 'less and less the prisoner of its
own language' and that it had begun to contribute instead to 'a universal language of understanding' (Davie, *Poet in the Imaginary
Museum*, p. 156). In 1980, the editor of the *Oxford Book of Verse in
English Translation*, Charles Tomlinson, suggested that a 'trans-
lation boom' had occurred in the period since the publication of
George Steiner's *Penguin Book of Modern Verse Translation* in
1966. Interest was generally maintained in later years, with
Modern Poetry in Translation relaunched in the 1990s, and Anvil
Press, among others, continuing to publish translations from East
Europe and elsewhere. Translation figured in the output of many
of the period's leading poets, and substantially in the work of
Fleur Adcock, Donald Davie, Elaine Feinstein, Tony Harrison,
Christopher Middleton, and Carol Rumens, as well as Charles
Tomlinson's and Ted Hughes's.[7]

How far a translation boom really could contribute to a 'universal
language', or to genuinely resuscitative notes for English poetry,
were nevertheless different issues—ones sharply focused by Elaine
Feinstein in 'Debts to Marina Tsvetayeva' (1986). Feinstein recorded
her gratitude for the Russian poet's 'stern assurance of the spirit',
and for being able to turn to her reassuringly 'in thought'. But she
also acknowledged 'I can never learn from you, Marina, | since
poetry is always a question of language'. This question clearly
limited the influence of much foreign poetry in terms of style and
technique, however compelling it seemed in thought or theme. Less
intimately involved with language, English fiction and drama gained
much more than poetry from translation during the period. As previous chapters described, it was other anglophone writing—principally work from the United States—which most influenced English

---

[7] Details can be found in the Author Bibliographies, pp. 523–80, below.

poets in the latter half of the twentieth century. Even in terms only of thought or spirit, the 'tragically tested' European writing Heaney mentions was as likely to be inhibiting as resuscitative, confronting English poets, as he suggests, with the 'eccentric' or relatively insignificant nature of their own historical and political experience. Heaney pointed to Christopher Reid's *Katerina Brac* (1985), written in the voice of an imaginary East European poet, both as a symptom and an attempted resolution of this concern—a way of accessing forms of tragic experience assumed to lie elsewhere, in a 'world beyond' the insular life of England.

There was irony, or appropriateness, in Heaney's highlighting concerns of this kind, since his own poetry—moving on in collections such as *Wintering Out* (1972) and *North* (1975) from early interests in nature—so powerfully reflected another world of tragic experience, much closer to England itself. Introducing one of the last of the period's significant anthologies, *The Firebox: Poetry in Britain and Ireland after 1945* (1998), Sean O'Brien remarked that progress towards devolution in each of the peripheral nations of the United Kingdom had contributed to a 'cultural assurance' for their poets, and to a collective voice and identity, which might justly have been envied by their English neighbours (p. xxvii). Yet it was developments in Northern Ireland which had much the strongest impact on writing in English during the period. In *English Poetry since 1940*, Neil Corcoran defined the Troubles beginning in 1968 as 'the single most influential factor on the subsequent history . . . of contemporary "English" poetry' (p. 136). In *The Penguin Book of Contemporary British Poetry* (1982), Andrew Motion and Blake Morrison's low estimate of native English poetry in the 1960s and 1970s arose partly from their judgement that it had been overshadowed by a new generation of Northern Irish writers. This included Michael Longley, Paul Muldoon, Derek Mahon, Medbh McGuckian, and Tom Paulin, as well as Seamus Heaney. Much of their work embodied a tragic urgency—a compelling need for the shaping voice of poetry, in encountering intolerable events—which English writers could scarcely share directly, and which no translated writing, however credible and desolating, could communicate quite so immediately. In several cases, too, the immediacy of the Northern Irish influence was increased by the extended residence in England of poets involved, and by their thorough involvement, as critics or anthologists, with the English tradition. Seamus Heaney, for example, was appointed Oxford Professor of Poetry in 1989, and Tom Paulin was also a long-term university teacher in Nottingham and Oxford.

More regularly and explicitly than fellow Northern Irish poets, Paulin raised a question nevertheless underlying much of their writing, and also more widely relevant late in the twentieth century: the issue of how poetry *could* continue to confront and contain intolerable events. Many of Paulin's poems worry about the nature and honesty of poetry's role as part of the 'riotshield that jigs | between self and reality' ('The Sting', 1994), and as a 'form | that betters what we are' ('Amphion', 1983). Such concerns were also figured in his description in 'Klee/Clover' (1994) of the painter Paul Klee, working as a mechanic in the First World War and cutting his canvases out of the wing-fabric of crashed aeroplanes. His image aptly suggests the ingenuity and opportunism increasingly required by artists in wresting their forms out of the disorderly violence of twentieth-century history. Even if this history did not prohibit poetry, as Adorno half-affirmed, it continued later in the century to challenge conventional shapes and structures radically—a challenge extended by the general 'distrust of the formalized and the structured' critics such as Anthony Thwaite discerned in their age.[8] Many poets adopted the kind of solution Paulin demonstrated in *Walking a Line* (1994) and other late collections, avoiding contemporary 'distrust' as far as possible by practising a poetry unostentatious or colloquial in its language, minimal and unobtrusive in its use of poetic device.

Movements in this direction were more or less progressively apparent throughout the period. In the early 1960s, in *The Dyer's Hand and Other Essays* (1963), W. H. Auden still envisaged 'rhymes, meters, stanza forms, etc' as the essential 'servants' of the poet (p. 22). At the time, there were still many poets—John Fuller, Peter Porter, or John Heath-Stubbs, for example—who continued like Auden to employ complex, exact, and very various verse forms. Established structures were generally also retained, though with less variety or elegance, by Movement writers in the late 1950s and 1960s. Later, too, some of the poets most disturbed by contemporary or historical disorder continued—naturally enough, in one

---

[8] See p. 205, above.

way—to employ the most stringent of artistic forms in describing it. Geoffrey Hill's account in 'Funeral Music' (1968) of 'fastidious trumpets | Shrilling into the ruck' at the Battle of Towton was emblematic of his poetry's resolute containment—often in meditative, measured, sonnet form—of even the most grievous histories of carnage. Peter Reading was equally fastidious in the forms employed for his bleakly satiric city visions. Tony Harrison likewise remained determined to contain his ragged cityscapes and colloquial speech 'in metres . . . | with rhyme and rhythm' ('The Heartless Art', 1984), reflecting a formal exactness imparted by his classical education. Many other poets later in the period continued to employ rhyme and metre entirely conventionally, and to find in their orderliness what Carol Rumens described in 'Writing the City' (1983) as 'those slightly archaic correspondences | I look for when in trouble'.

Yet towards the end of the period, these 'correspondences' often came to seem more than slightly archaic. As social formality diminished in English life generally, and domestic servants vanished from most households, so Auden's poetic servants tended to fade from writing late in the century, increasingly superseded by free verse. This had grown gradually, ever since the modernist period, into what Donald Davie considered the predominant form of English poetry by the late 1980s. 'Many readers today neither know nor care whether what they read or hear is in metre or not', Davie added, pointing out that one of the most successful contemporary poets, Ted Hughes, used 'no discernible prosody at all'. In terms of metrics, he concluded, there was possibly no longer 'between poet and reader any form of contract whatever' (*Under Briggflatts*, p. 125). In one way, this neglect of conventional prosody was simply an appropriate or inevitable extension of late twentieth-century mistrust of form and structure. Yet in another, broken contracts with poetic convention may have unsettled conventional 'contracts' between poetry and its readers too far, or in ways more troubling for a popular audience than Davie assumed. Minimal or unobtrusive prosody risked reducing poetry to a point where it could scarcely any longer be recognized as a distinctive use of language at all. As Martin Booth noted, at the beginning of the period popular assumptions about 'what a poem was' included, along with expectations of 'high-flown emotions', a conviction that it should be 'a set of words that rhymed (or not), had

a metre . . . and was written in verses' (p. 17). Later, popular perceptions of poetry were inevitably disturbed—and some of its broader
appeal probably constrained—by its growing resemblance to what
Tony Harrison described in 'The Heartless Art' as merely 'chopped-
up prose'. Readers in the period might justifiably have shared doubts
one of Michael Horovitz's *Children of Albion* authors, Philip
O'Connor, expressed about his own 'Poem on Self'. 'Is this Poetry?',
he asked, concluding that 'if it is I do not know what is not, | And if
it is not I do not know what is'. As in areas discussed earlier, in
departing from archaic or 'high-flown' aspects of poetic form—however necessarily or appropriately—writers in the period sometimes
seemed doomed to saw down branches they might have sat on,
renouncing characteristics still widely seen as definitive of their art.

English poetry's progress, and its relations with its audience, were
further complicated by a more fundamental mistrust of the formalized, apparent in the period's attitude to language itself. In its early
years, poets were sometimes troubled not only by a decline in spirituality and religious worship, but by the nature of the language in
which vestigial faiths had come to be expressed. T. S. Eliot, in particular, was disappointed by the Church of England's adoption of the
New English Bible in 1961—straightforward and up-to-date in its
locutions, yet inevitably seeming less resonant and orotund than the
'King James' version the church had used, with little revision, since
the seventeenth century. By making the word of God once again
directly and immediately intelligible to the whole population, the
New English Bible might have pleased Martin Luther: it was at any
rate typical of the broadening and democratizing of access to culture
at work from the 1960s onwards. Yet the doubts surrounding its
introduction were also typical of fears—regularly expressed by
critics and poets throughout the period—that a variety of contemporary pressures were eroding the range, resources, and poetic
potential of the English language. 'We have . . . become alienated
from our language', Jonathan Raban suggested in *The Society of the
Poem* (1971), 'as if the language had died' or become merely 'a pro-
grammed circuit fed into one by the media' which had come to 'own
and control' it (pp. 98–9). In *Language and Silence* (1967), George
Steiner worried that 'the jingles, the oohs and ahs of modern advertisement' were among influences contributing to 'a phase of decayed

language'. Contemporary experts, he recorded, considered that 'the perfect advertisement should neither contain words of more than two syllables nor sentences with dependent clauses'—one of several factors Steiner thought were leading to 'drastic reduction in the wealth and dignity of speech' (pp. 416, 13, 45).

'Lovers of what's simple', as he called them in 'On the Tercentenary of Milton's Death' (1977), were similarly criticized by Gavin Ewart—one of the period's most successful authors of light and comic verse, along with Wendy Cope and Kit Wright. Ewart's poem opens by informing Milton that 'E. Jarvis-Thribb (17) and Keith's Mum | don't reckon you; | even students of English get lost | in your syntax'. Like critics of the *New English Bible*, Ewart went on in 'They flee from me that sometime did me seek' (1979) to contrast the supposed banalities of contemporary English with the gracefulness of earlier centuries. His poem mockingly updates Sir Thomas Wyatt's famous lines to read 'At this moment in time | the chicks that went for me | in a big way | are opting out; | as of now, it's an all-change situation' (Enright (ed.), *Oxford Book of Verse*, pp. 74, 77). Other poets saw less humour in contemporary linguistic change, worrying as much about what seemed the last of English as about the last of England. Andrew Waterman compared an apparently decaying language with late twentieth-century pollution of the countryside, describing in 'Playing through Old Games of Chess' (1976) 'the mineral ores of language processed through | to a standing slag beyond recycling'. Ten years later, Elaine Feinstein concluded in 'England' that 'the old gods are leaving. | They will no longer crack the | tarmac of the language, open generous | rivers, heal our scoured thoughts'. In this view, the defiant rosebay willow-herb might have provided an emblem not only for the period's imagination of nature, but for the survival of poetry itself, struggling to sustain vitality and colour in a decaying, linguistically polluted environment, one which old gods and graces seemed to be rapidly abandoning.

English poetry, however, sometimes seemed less likely to survive and flourish in the period than comparison with the resilient, ubiquitous willow-herb might suggest. While a supposedly 'decayed language' created difficulties for poets themselves, an age of generally simplified public discourse obviously limited the likely appeal of their work. While poets were ready to mock 'lovers of the simple', there was often evidence of reciprocal impatience with poetic language. Gavin Ewart's protagonist in 'On the Tercentenary of Milton's Death', for example, also had a regular role in the satirical magazine *Private Eye*. Numerous parodic poems by 'E. J. Thribb' mostly mocked the portentousness of amateur verse, but they also expressed an element of scepticism—reinforced by the magazine's 'Pseud's Corner' section—about any language which departed too conspicuously from the straightforwardness Steiner saw as the preferred contemporary idiom. Such scepticism obviously threatened a genre Donald Davie considered still fundamentally committed— despite simplifications in prosody by the end of the 1980s—to 'language . . . lovingly explored as a medium, not rapidly marshalled to serve merely as an expedient vehicle' (*Under Briggflatts*, p. 115). The rapid pace of life late in the century might have been expected to broaden the appeal of writing offering a profound yet succinct literary experience—the kind of quick 'swig of the sublime' Hanif Kureishi describes one of his characters ingesting from a pocket poetry book in *The Buddha of Suburbia* (ch. 8). Instead, a stressed, hasty age accustomed the public to a sound-bite culture, minimal in its demands on concentration, as well as on time. Along with other factors discussed above, this severely limited poetry's popularity, despite the years of revival in the 1960s, when Kureishi's novel was set.[9] According to an Arts Council Report, quoted in Sean O'Brien's *The Deregulated Muse* (1998), toward the end of the century 'the general public ha[d] a problem with the image of poetry . . . often perceived as out-of-touch, gloomy, irrelevant, effeminate, high-brow and elitist'. Like Carol Rumens's 'In the Craft Museum', O'Brien agreed that poetry generally had fallen into 'a vague state of public disfavour' (pp. 270–1).

Few poets could altogether overlook this disfavour. In 'The Cave of Making', W. H. Auden was by no means the first or the only poet in the latter half of the century to ponder an 'unpopular art'—one likely to appeal only to a 'handful | of clients', a 'remnant still able to listen'. In 1956, Robert Conquest's first *New Lines* anthology had included Kingsley Amis's 'Something Nasty in the Bookshop', remarking that 'Between the GARDENING and the COOKERY | Comes

---

[9] Consequences of poetry's 1960s popularity, and of its later loss, are also discussed on pp. 152–3 and 180–7, above.

the brief POETRY shelf'. In later years, poetry shelves which survived in bookshops at all were usually even briefer, and unlikely to be found anywhere near sections as popular as Gardening or Cookery. Michael Schmidt indicated a likelier location for them—in the university section—when he described 'the market for books of poems', by the 1980s, as 'now pre-eminently academic'(Hewison, p. 267). At the end of the decade, Donald Davie estimated that even the most 'successful' of contemporary poets—such as Geoffrey Hill or Charles Tomlinson—could expect no more than a very limited 'following' for their work. Only Philip Larkin and Ted Hughes, among English poets, had attained the genuinely wide recognition of what he called 'a public' (*Under Briggflatts*, p. 83). Limited interest in poetry was generally confirmed by another Arts Council Report at the end of the next decade. *Rhyme and Reason: Developing Contemporary Poetry* (2000) suggested that apart from a handful of outstanding figures, Hughes in particular, 1990s poets usually sold extremely poorly. Jo Shapcott and Fleur Adcock, for example, finished fifteenth and sixteenth in the list of best-selling poets, yet in the previous year had managed, between them, to sell substantially fewer than 1,000 copies of their books.

Fortunately, poetry's popularity in the 1960s—along with its low demand on production resources, compared to fiction and drama—had encouraged developments allowing it to survive independently of mainstream publishers or strong bookshop sales. Cheaper printing, better photocopying, and the 'alternative', do-it-yourself philosophy of the 1960s all contributed to the rapid proliferation of small magazines at the time.[10] Commenting on little magazine production in later decades, R. J. Ellis suggested that between one and two hundred continued to be regularly available in the 1990s (Hampson and Barry (eds.), p. 72). Most were open to new writers, who could in any case distribute copies of their poems or even start a magazine of their own just with access to good duplicating facilities. For some poets, involvement with their own means of production encouraged experiments with form and typography, contributing to the development of concrete poetry, for example, or of styles of 'open field' composition facilitated by the fuller space of an A4 page. Any poet who had begun to establish a reputation in the small magazines could move

---

[10] See also p. 180, above.

on to more substantial journals of the kind supported by the Arts Council. Several of these had particular fields of interest: *Agenda*, for example, in United States writing; *Poetry Nation*—later retitled *PN Review*—in formal elegance and the literary heritage; *Stand* in writing from the regions and in what it called 'poetry of the committed individual'. In practice, such interests were rarely exclusive: the pages of *Stand*, in particular, remained open to lesser-known poets as well as many of the period's established ones.

Poets could develop their work further by publishing a book with one of the many small presses which grew up alongside the new magazines in the 1960s, encouraged by cheaper typesetting, lower production costs, and sometimes Arts Council support. By the early 1970s, as many as two hundred of these were able to produce well-designed books relatively cheaply, their resources co-ordinated by an Association of Small Presses established by the concrete poet Bob Cobbing. Anvil Press was typical of several—such as Fortune, Scorpion, Marvell, or Fulcrum—which evolved into larger operations around this time. Under Peter Jay's directorship, Anvil continued to receive unsolicited manuscripts in the 1970s, and to publish authors relatively unknown at the time, such as Carol Ann Duffy, John Birtwhistle, and Dick Davis, as well as more established ones including Gavin Ewart and F. T. Prince. Around a dozen elegantly finished books were produced annually, with print runs of between 500 and 1,000 copies—equal to the output of many mainstream publishers—and with distribution organized through the Arts Council's 'Password' scheme, the Poetry Society, and Anvil's own mailing list. Other operations such as Bloodaxe in Newcastle or Carcanet in Manchester eventually moved almost beyond any definition of a 'small' press. While retaining some of the flexibility or readiness to depart from convention which had been part of their original purpose, they increasingly rivalled commercial publishers in terms of output. Carcanet had published over 400 books by the 1980s, while Bloodaxe—supported like *Stand* by the Northern Arts Council—had drawn strongly on the identity of its region, establishing a new market for poetry within it. Yet sales income could never be entirely relied on to recoup expenditure on overheads and book production. In 1987/8, for example, Anvil would have lost £42,000, or produced far fewer books, had it not received a substantial grant.

Supporting both small presses and small magazines, Arts Council help was fundamental to poetry's survival during a period of particular difficulty in the 1970s and 1980s.

The strength of this survival was confirmed, in one way, by an editor of *The New British Poetry 1968–1988* (1988), Ken Edwards, who recorded that 'the quantity of small press books . . . show[ed] no diminution' at the end of the 1980s. As a result, he considered that it was 'easier for a young poet today to get into print and to have her or his work disseminated to those interested than it ever has been' (Allnutt et al. (eds.), p. 266). On the other hand, the range of 'those interested' in poetry was unlikely to be extended by publication of this kind. Dissemination through small presses and small magazines tended instead to accept and even perpetuate poets' appeal to small audiences, encouraging an esoteric, self-interested aspect in their work itself. As Iain Sinclair acknowledged, a 'private world' of small presses helped to inflate the egos of poets included in his *Conductors of Chaos* anthology (1996),[11] contributing to the 'remote, alienated'—sometimes just uncommunicative—forms of writing they produced (pp. xvii, xviii). A poetry editor influential earlier in the period, in the 1960s and 1970s, Ian Hamilton, likewise recalled in an interview in the *London Review of Books* that he had had 'no interest in an audience . . . the audience could be very few—as few as two dozen, as long as they had got it right' (24 Jan. 2002, p. 9). Such attitudes suggested that English poetry—however puritanically 'right' in its own aesthetics—might eventually reach no more than the handful of readers Auden had pessimistically described in the early 1960s.

Not surprisingly, a new determination to resist this possibility appeared late in the century. Poets generally recognized that they might have to work harder than their predecessors to escape the 'unspoiled', glass-cased world Carol Rumens feared—one in which editors such as Hamilton and Sinclair seemed only too ready to leave them. Resisting risks of remoteness, poetry showed renewed readiness, if readers did not come to visit it, to 'go down to the street'—or even further down, into the Tube—to get hold of them. No doubt there was an irony in poetry renouncing its 1960s role as part *of* 'the Underground' in favour of a place in the late 1980s and 1990s among advertisements *on* the Underground. Initiated in 1986,

---

[11] See pp. 236–7, above.

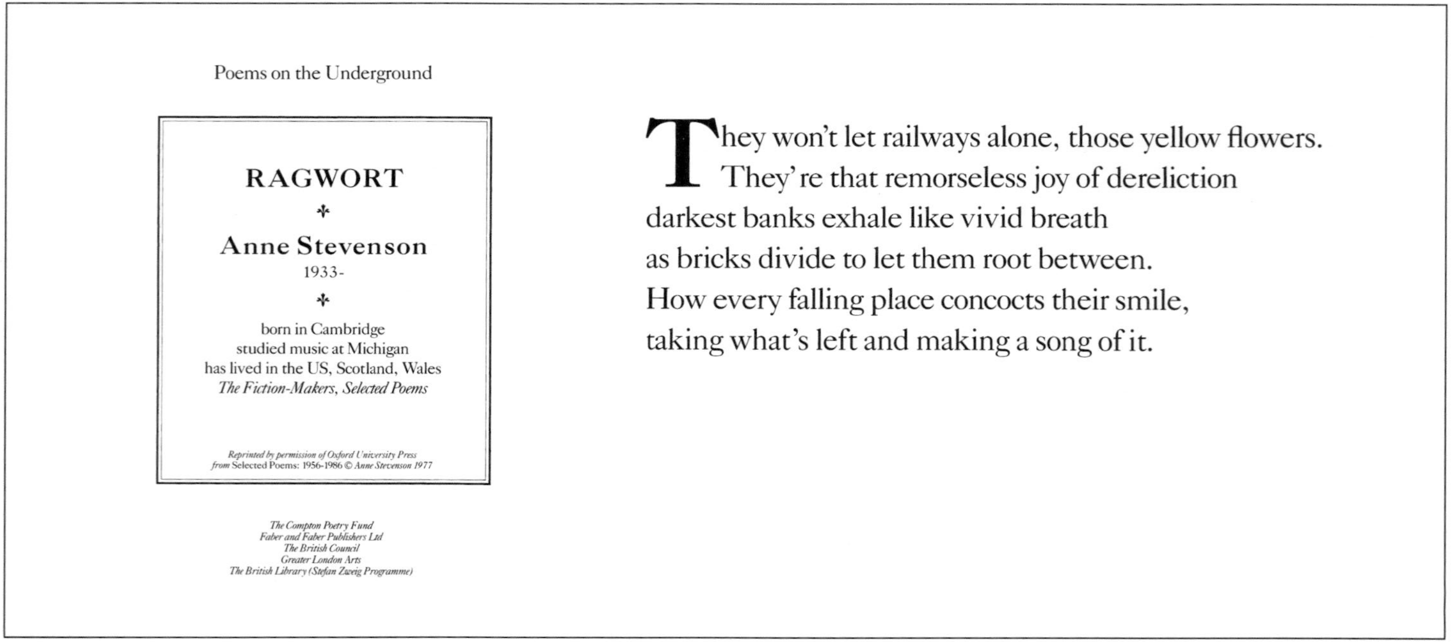

Fig. 8. Two of the series of 'Poems on the Underground' posters which began to appear in the London Tube in January 1986. 'Ragwort' shows an early, 1980s style; 'The Catch' a later design.

The Catch

Forget
the long, smouldering
afternoon. It is

of the bat; upwards,
backwards, falling
seemingly

out
of its loop
like

this moment
when the ball scoots
off the edge

beyond him
yet he reaches
and picks it

an apple
from a branch,
the first of the season.

Simon Armitage (b. 1963) Reprinted by permission of Faber from KID (1992)

Poems on the Underground
1,000 YEARS OF POETRY IN ENGLISH

9th edition
Cassell

LONDON ARTS BOARD

The British Council

CALOUSTE GULBENKIAN FOUNDATION

Books and Posters are on sale at The London Transport Museum, Covent Garden 020 7379 6344 – Poster design by Tom Davidson

London Transport's 'Poems on the Underground' series, and the anthologies which resulted, nevertheless exemplified ways poetry could survive—even thrive, in the right context—in an age of rapid reading and short attention spans. Similarly, £450,000 of National Lottery funding in 1998 helped the Poetry Society to publish poems on chip wrappers, refuse sacks, and in bus shelters, and to establish a 'Poetry Places' scheme which installed over a hundred poets in various residencies. Locations included police stations, a tin mine, law offices, theatres, the Millennium Dome, Marks and Spencers, and the Internet—already used by a number of aspiring poets as a convenient means of disseminating their work. Audiences continued to be created or consolidated in the 1990s by schemes such as the Forward Poetry Prize, accompanied each year by an anthology of new writing; the T. S. Eliot Prize; the Arvon Poetry Competition; and an annual National Poetry Day marked by readings, promotional events, and classroom discussions throughout the country. Growing numbers of literary festivals and bookshop events also extended the excitement and direct contact with audiences which the poetry revival had helped to initiate in the 1960s. Renewed interest in the 1990s was reflected in improving sales figures: these suggested that poetry's readership almost doubled during the decade, although from slender beginnings. The 1,000 most popular poetry titles sold nearly two million copies in 1998 and 1999, worth £13 million, and 2,700 poetry books were published annually by the end of the decade, more than four times as many as in the 1970s and 1980s.

For some commentators, all this suggested that poetry was once more 'experiencing a boom—an explosion of new talents, many fine small- and large-press publications, and a resultant rekindling of audience interest' (Acheson and Huk (eds.), p. viii). The signs were probably more equivocal. Contemporary writing accounted for only a fraction of overall sales of poetry, and the larger publishers were as likely to be indifferent as supportive. Though Picador began publishing contemporary poets in the 1990s, and Penguin briefly relaunched its Modern Poets series in 1995, Oxford University Press notoriously dropped its poetry list three years later. Though sales of contemporary poetry did improve in the 1990s, they were very unevenly distributed, as the Arts Council pointed out, and remained disappointing overall. Yet there were exceptional successes. By the beginning of 1999, Ted Hughes's *Birthday Letters* (1998) had sold nearly 150,000 copies in the United Kingdom, and almost as many in the United States, making it one of the best-selling volumes of poetry ever published. As Hughes's publishers, Faber, claimed in the *Guardian*, this suggested that poetry was potentially 'a much bigger business than meets the eye'—even that it might reclaim some of its old, slender prominence somewhere not too far from bookshops' gardening and cookery shelves (12 Jan. 1999, p. 3).

By the 1990s, too, some of the poetry critics mentioned in Chapter 7[12] were suggesting a less depressed view of the English language— its changing locutions and poetic potentials—than commentators such as Steiner had outlined in the 1960s. As they indicated, what had seemed to Steiner decay in contemporary language could more appropriately be considered as inevitable transition—even progress towards new flexibility, openness, and invention. The 'oohs and ahs of modern advertisement' which Steiner found so disturbing were after all often the work of poets—Gavin Ewart included—who had found a new outlet for their skills in an industry increasingly reliant on catchy verbal ingenuity. Other forms of supposedly 'decayed' locution—in newspaper headlines, or eventually in the abbreviations of e-mail or mobile-phone text messages—might also be seen to have brought new inventiveness into daily language use, rather than only new limitations or banalities. In this view, Andrew Waterman's description of language, 'processed through | to a standing slag beyond recycling', may have underestimated its inherent fluidity and capacity for regeneration—perhaps less in evidence in English poetry when he wrote, in 1976, than in later decades.

Waterman's image was at any rate surely too pessimistic for a period which eventually drew into its poetry all the new potentials of black speech, for example, and of many other dialects and demotic forms longer established in England, yet long missing from most of its literature. 'Poetry over here is, I think, still a "class" thing', Tom Raworth commented to the US poet Ed Dorn in 1961: 'there's no flow: no use of natural language. The whole thing is so artificial and contrived' (Hampson and Barry (eds.), p. 34). Class-based exclusiveness and disdain for demotic speech or 'natural language' were steadily diminished thereafter, initially and rather tentatively by

---

[12] See pp. 231–2, above.

Movement writers, and later by a whole range of poets: writers such as Peter Reading, Tony Harrison, and others discussed in Chapter 7 were merely the most conspicuous among them. As Sean O'Brien suggested in *The Deregulated Muse* in 1998, 'the balance of the relationship between the vernacular and the literary' had by the end of the century crucially altered 'since Larkin was at work'—further evidence of the democratizing influences developing throughout this period. For O'Brien, the 'New Generation' writers of the 1990s—specifically Glyn Maxwell and Simon Armitage—were 'the first rising generation in English poetry' to have found 'no difficulty in placing its speech among the other constituents of poetic language' (pp. 242, 246).[13]

Typically of the period, in other words, poetry experienced the last of an England of one kind, along with the appearance of another, and of a new literary language accompanying its emergence. Like English society more generally, poetry turned away from the 'hierarchies of values' the editors of *The New Poetry* mentioned towards a set of more lateral variations, involving conflicts and contrasts in speech and register between a whole range of voices, often newly entering the poetic discourse of the times. Poets in the 1980s and 1990s may have been less able to draw on exalted language—the 'wealth and dignity of speech' whose loss was lamented in the 1960s—or to rely on a common background of education in the classics and the Bible shared with their readers. But they more than made up for any such losses through new wealths and diversities of language—through incorporating the murmur and jostle of competing contemporary dialects, and the energizing, dialogic interplay of outlooks they represented. Sensitive to this dialogic potential, New Generation authors such as Simon Armitage often directed attention on distinctive locutions or even individual words in their poetry, highlighting the colouring and coding of each within the microprocesses of contemporary consciousness, and within idiosyncratic new idioms of dialect and language use. This alertness to 'the possibility of cliché, proverb, adspeak, slang, popular song', as O'Brien called it, was equally evident in his own work. Its widespread appearance in 1990s poetry suggested that language was perhaps explored less 'lovingly' than in the past, but nevertheless with minute attentiveness to the shifting

---

[13] See also pp. 167–8 and 230, above.

politics and values of English society at the time (*Deregulated Muse*, p. 245). Along with some of the postmodern or linguistically self-conscious writing discussed in Chapter 7, and the growing impact of black and women poets, the New Generation highlighted in this way a language not in decay but perhaps in an unusually vital phase of reinvention, fluidity, and contestation.

Shifting hierarchies and changing language use contributed, in this view, to a period not of terminal or irreversible poetic decline, but rather one demanding only redirection and reformation. Though perhaps felt unusually strongly at the time, such demands were by no means unique to the later years of the twentieth century. As the editors of *The New Poetry* suggested, 'the hierarchies of values' on which poetry had once depended were challenged—along with expectations of 'high-flown emotions', rhetoric, and conventional patterns of rhyme and metre—not only at the end of the century, but more or less throughout. If poetry in its later decades went through a difficult phase, at any rate by comparison with contemporary fiction and drama, it was because historical forces which made aesthetic change so urgent also seemed for many years to make real change peculiarly difficult for English poets to bring about. Though the Second World War was such a strong historical influence on the period, and on 'high-flown emotions' and conventional poetic forms especially, it largely failed to provoke in England the desolate but resuscitative poetry it inspired elsewhere. Instead, as Alvarez and Davie concluded in the *Review* in 1962, the immediate response to the war among most English poets was one of evasion rather than engagement. 'The agonies of the human condition in our time', they concluded, seemed only to add to incentives to 'get our heads back again as quickly as we can to this private island paradise of ours' (pp. 25, 22). The resulting conservatism and insularity of Movement writing developed, ironically, at exactly the time, in the post-war decades, when change and innovation were most required, and began to appear strongly in other genres. Progress was further delayed by the continuing influences of the Movement in later years, marginalizing domestic extensions of modernism and other radical influences, from the United States especially, which might have allowed a mainstream of English poetry to develop much more rapidly and variously than it did.

By the end of the century, the lingering languor the Movement left had at least come to be widely recognized, and at last evaded by a genuinely new generation of English poets. Debates surrounding the appointment of Andrew Motion as Poet Laureate in 1999 generally recognized the conservative nature of his appointment, and identified a number of poets who might have offered more progressive alternatives. Keith Tuma's *Anthology of Twentieth-Century British and Irish Poetry* (2001) and Sean O'Brien's *The Firebox* were the first collections to represent fully, alongside more established writers, the range of modernist and postmodernist influences which Movement and post-Movement writing had excluded from full appreciation. The success of Ted Hughes's *Birthday Letters* in 1998 also offered a sign of change. As well as reflecting sensational interest in his private life, it also suggested an eleventh-hour ascendancy of the kind of writing—readier to embody than evade the stresses of its age—which Alvarez had demanded of late twentieth-century poetry nearly forty years previously. The spectrum of English poetry D. J. Enright once described always stretched further than the limits he suggested for it, Larkin and Hughes: the latter's celebrity at the end of the century nevertheless indicated a shift of public taste towards its progressive end. Ironically, English literature was never more static than under the influence of the Movement: if the later twentieth century proved a difficult period for poetry, it was in large measure because it took so long to realize this, and move on.

Part III

Drama

9

A Public Art Form:
The Late 1950s to the 1970s

> The theatre is, or can be, the most public, the most clearly political of the
> art forms. Theatre is the place where the life of a society is shown in public
> to that society. (McGrath, *A Good Night Out*, p. 83)

Poetry went through a difficult period, Chapter 8 suggested, in the
later decades of the twentieth century. Drama, in the view of most
critics, enjoyed an unusually successful one. Martin Esslin judged the
later twentieth century 'the most vigorous period of dramatic writing
. . . since Elizabethan and Jacobean times' (Shank (ed.), p. 180). In
The Full Room: An A–Z of Contemporary Playwriting (2000)
Dominic Dromgoole talked of 'a unique and extraordinary' age, one
in which more good playwrights had been at work than at any time
in the history of the craft (p. xi). Many factors contributed to
drama's return to the forefront of English writing: one of the most
influential was its rediscovery of the role John McGrath defined in
the comment quoted above. Whereas evasiveness, rather than real
engagement, initially marked poetry's relations with recent history
and contemporary politics, drama in the period followed an opposite
course, strongly re-establishing a public voice for itself in the late
1950s and 1960s. This later developed into a phase of direct political
commentary, characteristic of the 1970s, discussed in Chapter 10,
below.

Moves in this direction in the late 1950s and 1960s appeared
exciting, even revolutionary, because they seemed to have been

missing from English theatre for so long—hardly since Elizabethan or Jacobean times, but throughout a predominantly conservative period in the first half of the twentieth century. In its earlier years, in this view, both English fiction and poetry had shared in the formal innovations of modernism, or otherwise moved on in response to the challenges of their age. Drama seemed instead to have remained static, or even regressed, ever since a period of genuine innovation at the turn of the century. In the late nineteenth century, Henrik Ibsen's plays had helped to establish on the Continent a new seriousness of moral and social debate, compellingly developed within realistic representations of ordinary domestic life. Playwrights such as Oscar Wilde, George Bernard Shaw, John Galsworthy, and Harley Granville-Barker imported debate of this kind into the English theatre, though focusing less often on ordinary life than on the concerns of the upper class or affluent middle classes. Elegant characters, refined manners, and well-furnished drawing rooms—the curtain usually rising on them just before or just after dinner—gradually became a habitual focus of mainstream English drama early in the twentieth century. It remained a dominant context between the wars—one naturally favoured by mostly middle-class audiences at the time, but strongly resistant to new influences which succeeded Ibsen's abroad. August Strindberg, Luigi Pirandello, the German Expressionists, the Russian Constructivists, Bertolt Brecht, and Erwin Piscator contributed to a wide-ranging theatrical modernism which transformed Continental drama in the 1920s and 1930s, but it had little effect in England apart from the experimental work of the Group Theatre in the 1930s.

Instead, it was another turn-of-the-century playwright, Anton Chekhov—a subtle portraitist and comic elegist of middle-class life—who most appealed to English audiences at the time. As the popularity of his work suggests, these audiences grew more and more content with a drama of character and emotion, and less interested in the wider issues introduced in the 'Plays of Ideas' of Shaw or Wilde. In his later career, Shaw himself often found it necessary to dilute the social concern of his earlier work with growing measures of comedy and entertainment. Even this kind of residual engagement with ideas was gradually replaced in the 1940s and 1950s by undemanding, usually comic surveys of middle-class manners and relations provided by Noël Coward, Terence Rattigan, and William Douglas Home. By mid-century, in other words, English playwrights seemed comfortably settled in the drawing room, and disinclined either to look beyond it, or to examine serious issues within it, even in the moderate way they had fifty years or so earlier. Recent English drama provided Harold Hobson, the most influential theatre reviewer of the period, with ample evidence for conclusions he reached at the end of the 1950s. 'It is not the principal function of the theatre to strengthen peace, to improve morality, or to establish a good social system', Hobson remarked in 1959. 'It is the duty of the theatre, not to make men better, but to render them harmlessly happy' (Lloyd Evans and Lloyd Evans (eds.), p. 90).

Very different views of recent theatre were expressed at the time by another distinguished critic, Kenneth Tynan. In 'Summing Up: 1959', Tynan mocked class bias and formal conservatism which had ensured that in London's West End

nightly, in dozens of theatres, the curtain rose on the same set. French windows were its most prominent feature . . . If we were not at Mark Trevannion's country house in Berkshire, we were probably at Hilary Egleston's flat in Knightsbridge . . .

Five years ago, anyone whose knowledge of England was restricted to its popular theatre would have come to the conclusion that its standard of living was the highest on earth . . . The poor were seldom with us . . . To become eligible for detailed dramatic treatment, it was usually necessary either to have an annual income of more than three thousand pounds net or to be murdered in the house of someone who did. (*View of the Stage*, pp. 249–50)

Tynan went on to define further a 'gentleman code' that had blighted much twentieth-century English drama, and to offer reasons why writers in the late 1940s and 1950s had been so reluctant to discard it (p. 274). Playwrights since the Second World War, he suggested, had responded clearly enough to 'the forces of contemporary reality', if only by showing a sustained wish to ignore them in favour of 'imagined worlds in which rationing and the rest of austerity's paraphernalia could be forgotten' (pp. 248, 270). English theatre in the early 1950s, in this view, continued to offer undemanding stories, gentlemanly characters, and affluent settings as a kind of comfortable *with*drawing room—a refuge from the shock and exhaustion of the post-war years comparable to Movement poetry's 'temperate zone' of emotional restraint, even numbness, at the time.[1]

Drama, however, began to move away from this zone at exactly the moment Movement poetry's commitments to it were stressed most strongly, in Robert Conquest's first *New Lines* anthology, in 1956. Tynan's comments in 'Summing Up: 1959' referred specifically to a period 'five years ago'. He went on to emphasize how thoroughly drama had been changed since then by the 'breakthrough' which had occurred 'in the spring of 1956 . . . [when] the English Stage Company's production of *Look Back in Anger* lanced a boil that had plagued our theatre for many years' (*View of the Stage*, pp. 248, 271). *Look Back in Anger* was similarly applauded by many critics at the time, and the importance of John Osborne's 'breakthrough' at the Royal Court remained unchallenged for long afterwards, discussed even by characters in later plays. David Mercer's drama critic in *After Haggerty* (RSC, 1970), for example, remarks that 'the crucial development in our theatre in nineteen fifty-six was, as has been repeated and analysed ad nauseam: Osborne's LOOK BACK IN ANGER' (I. iv).

For critics later in the century, Osborne's importance sometimes seemed to have been repeated and analysed altogether too often, at the expense of other crucial developments occurring in the mid-1950s,[2] or of the reputations of some of his predecessors. In *1956 and All That: The Making of Modern British Drama* (1999), Dan Rebellato emphasized qualities and diversities too rarely acknowledged in 1940s and early 1950s drama, and ways it anticipated changes often attributed more exclusively to 1956. Other critics also found new reason to admire the stagecraft or vision of playwrights such as Coward or Rattigan—or the work of their contemporary J. B. Priestley, his reputation restored by Stephen Daldry's revival of *An Inspector Calls* (1946) at the National Theatre in 1995. By the end of the century, denial of Osborne's significance had become almost as much of a critical commonplace as its earlier assertion, though not necessarily more helpfully. Despite genuine limitations in

---

[1] See p. 167, above.

[2] These included new influences from Bertolt Brecht's drama, discussed later in this chapter; from the Theatre of the Absurd (see Ch. 12); and from the theories of Antonin Artaud (see Ch. 13).

the importance of *Look Back in Anger*—and in its quality as a play—
it actually anticipated later interests in English drama in more and
subtler ways than critics have usually recognized.[3] Though Osborne
was obviously not solely responsible for the 'breakthrough' in
English drama, *Look Back in Anger* at the very least indicates factors, social and theatrical, which helped it to occur at the time it
did—changing attitudes to class in particular.

Osborne's hero Jimmy Porter considers that the middle and upper
classes have been 'plundering and fooling everybody for generations': his wife's affluent friends and ex-colonial family are sections
of society he has 'declared war on' and regularly vilifies in his furious
tirades (I; II. i). In one way, such feelings were typical of contemporary impatience with the hierarchies of English life—of mid-1950s
fretting against class barriers still surviving despite the new affluence
and educational opportunity of the time. In another way, Jimmy's
anger had a particular theatrical relevance, implicitly challenging the
class orientation and 'gentleman code' of much twentieth-century
English drama. This challenge was emphasized by the very ungenteel
setting of *Look Back in Anger*, startling its first audiences in May
1956—almost as much as by anything which followed—by the presence of an ironing board onstage at the beginning of the play.
Characters such as Mark Trevannion and Hilary Egleston would
presumably have had their ironing done for them: the prominent
presence of an ironing board would at any rate have been inconceivable in the kind of plays in which Tynan imagined them appearing.
In its banal, domestic setting, as well as its class-based invective,
Look Back in Anger could scarcely have departed more emphatically
from the affluent drawing room and middle-class concerns so long
dominant on the English stage.

Even Jimmy's occasional failure to find targets for his tirades—his
despair of finding 'good brave causes'—contributed a new contemporary relevance to *Look Back in Anger*. 'If the big bang does come,
and we all get killed off,' he remarks, 'it won't be in aid of the old-
fashioned, grand design. It'll just be for the Brave New-nothing-
very-much-thank-you' (III. i). His views encapsulated directionless
feelings surrounding contemporary politics, a result of the apparently indistinguishable policies of the Labour and Conservative parties

[3] These are also considered in Chs. 11, 12, and 14, below.

on the domestic scene in the 1950s. Crises in international affairs also made Jimmy's despair of 'grand design' especially topical. Significantly, the real popular success of *Look Back in Anger* came not in the spring of 1956—much as it was admired then by critics such as Tynan—but in a revival in the autumn. At the time, throughout late October and early November, the Hungarian uprising and the Suez crisis were dominating the headlines and challenging a whole spectrum of established political faiths. No one on the Right could go on confidently believing in Britain as a successful imperial power after it failed to retain control of the Suez canal. No one on the Left could remain altogether confident of communism, at any rate of the sort currently practised in East Europe, after the suppression of the Budapest rising by Soviet tanks. Grand designs and brave causes seemed easier to envisage in the earlier periods *Look Back in Anger* recalls: in one case, in the years of imperial confidence before the First World War, or, in the other, in the decade of socialist action Jimmy remembers from the 1930s. Menaced by international crises and the Big Bang, and bereft of obvious strategies for dealing with either, the mid-1950s found its anxieties compellingly expressed in the impotent urgency of Jimmy's monologues.

Catching the mood of the time in this way, *Look Back in Anger* strongly re-established contact with 'forces of contemporary reality' which Tynan complained English theatre had so long ignored. Other playwrights soon extended this direction and the others Osborne had established. Critics quickly coined the term 'kitchen-sink' to describe a new realism, indifferent to middle-class settings, which was further developed by dramatists—Arnold Wesker in particular—who had followed Osborne onto the stage of the Royal Court by the start of the 1960s. First performed in its full version at the Royal Court in 1961, Wesker's *The Kitchen* could hardly have been further from the drawing room, concentrating on working life among washers, chefs, and waitresses overwhelmed by the demands of a busy restaurant. Wesker's *Chips with Everything* (Royal Court, 1962) was similarly realistic in portraying army life and in examining the continuing pressures of class. Harold Hobson described it as 'the Left-wing drama's first real breakthrough', though Wesker was less confident about any immediate change in English society than this comment suggests. Instead, *Chips with Everything* shows an army conscript absorbed, apparently inevitably, into the very officer class he initially sought to resist (Lloyd Evans and Lloyd Evans (eds.), p. 110).

Class, working life, and the difficulties of social change also shaped the plays which had established Wesker's reputation: the trilogy *Chicken Soup with Barley* (1958), *Roots* (1959), and *I'm Talking about Jerusalem* (1960), first presented in its entirety at the Royal Court in 1960. Each play follows painful conflicts between political ideals and a recalcitrant world. In *Roots*, the heroine's torpid Norfolk family seem immune to hopes and interests she has learned from her boyfriend Ronnie Kahn. Tracing pressures on the Kahn family's own idealism, other parts of the trilogy suggest, like *Look Back in Anger*, that brave causes could most easily be envisaged in the past. *Chicken Soup with Barley* opens in the 1930s, with the Kahn family enthusiastically discussing the Republican cause in Spain and sharing in successful resistance to Oswald Mosley's fascist marches in London's East End. Wesker's second act recalls the atmosphere created by the Labour government in 1946 and the hopes for 'new cities and schools and hospitals . . . Nationalization! National health!' widespread at the time (II. i). But in a third act, set in December 1956, Ronnie struggles to come to terms with the news from Hungary, and with the shock—especially for a Jewish family— of revelations about oppression in the Soviet Union. The English population, too, seems disappointingly ready to forget about politics as soon as they have 'a few shillings in the bank and they can buy a television' (III. ii). By the end of *I'm Talking about Jerusalem*, which follows events from 1946 until the third successive Conservative victory of 1959, political idealism seems almost best forgotten, with one character concluding 'I had ideas. But not now . . . visions don't work' (III. ii).

Similar conclusions were emphasized still more strongly by the adroit structure of Wesker's *Their Very Own and Golden City* (Royal Court, 1966). Like his trilogy, this surveyed English life between the 1930s and the 1960s, but moved more freely between different periods, juxtaposing an architect's youthful determination to 'build Jerusalem in England's green and pleasant land' with his progressive exhaustion by penny-pinching and narrow-mindedness among politicians he encounters (I. vii). His failed dreams may have reflected some of Wesker's own disillusionment with the Centre 42 project around this time. Named after a Trades Union Congress resolution, passed in 1960, encouraging involvement in cultural activities, Centre 42 gained some support from the unions and from writers including Bernard Kops, Doris Lessing, Alun Owen, John McGrath, and Shelagh Delaney. A London base was eventually secured at the Roundhouse, and a series of arts festivals in 1962 took drama—as well as poetry, jazz, and exhibitions—to several areas lacking a theatre of their own. Wesker was substantially involved, though not always successfully, especially in terms of securing funding. Centre 42 did not outlast the 1960s, and its difficulties may have contributed to the disillusion and 'loss of political purpose and dramatic coherence' which critics such as Christopher Innes see in Wesker's work after the middle of the decade (p. 114). A moving later play, *Love Letters on Blue Paper* (National, 1978) was based loosely on Vic Feather of the TUC. But in others, such as *The Friends* (Roundhouse, 1970), *The Wedding Feast* (Leeds Playhouse, 1977), or *Caritas* (National, 1981), idealistic characters are often presented as more impractical or self-destructive than in Wesker's earlier writing—a disillusion reduplicated by a lack of clear directions or ideas in the drama itself.

Wesker's early plays could be compared to the work of the other outstanding playwright to have emerged at the Royal Court by 1960, John Arden, despite many differences of style. Arden was anything but a kitchen-sink realist, favouring instead colourful, stylized action, enlivened by music and song, and often set in a past owing more to the mythic atmosphere of ballad than to strict historical accuracy. As the subtitle of *Serjeant Musgrave's Dance* (Royal Court, 1959) suggested, his drama often offered 'Un-Historical Parable', its past settings generally illustrating contemporary concerns—with Britain's colonial misdemeanours in Cyprus in this play, or with recent events in the Congo in *Armstrong's Last Goodnight* (Citizens', Glasgow, 1964). These concerns, like Wesker's, often focused on the likelihood that 'visions don't work': on the impracticality of idealism, or its risks of excess. In *Serjeant Musgrave's Dance*, the central figure's determination to take news of deaths in a colonial war back to a nineteenth-century mining town initially seems admirable. But it turns out to include shooting twenty-five of its citizens in revenge for the murder of one solider abroad and the army's reprisal killing of five civilians. In Musgrave's view, this murderous arithmetic is part of a 'duty . . . drawn out straight and black for us, a clear plan', one which 'life or love' threaten to 'scribble all over' and leave 'crooked, dirty, idle, untidy, *bad*' (II. i). Yet it is obviously life and love—however untidy, shapeless, or idle—which audiences are likelier to favour in the end, especially after Musgrave aims a Gatling gun at them.

Similar tensions between life and 'clear plan' trouble many of Arden's other heroes: the Alderman in *The Workhouse Donkey* (Chichester, 1963) who painfully learns the limits of laws and ideals in regulating his dissentious community; the courtier in *Armstrong's Last Goodnight* who discovers the frailty of diplomacy in an overwhelmingly violent world; King John, in *Left-Handed Liberty* (Mermaid Theatre, 1965), who has to watch the results of all his subtle politics dissolving away as he drowns in the Wash. Comparable conflicts extend into a play Arden revised and enlarged throughout his early career, *The Island of the Mighty*. Its eventually complex, ramshackle construction helps to emphasize the hopelessness of King Arthur's attempt to maintain unity in a country irreparably fractured by factions of tribe and religion.

By the time *The Island of the Mighty* was finally produced—by the Royal Shakespeare Company in 1972—Arden had moved towards commitments to the political left much more decisive than any evident in his first plays in the late 1950s and early 1960s. His career was typical in this way of the broader movement of theatre in the later 1960s and 1970s: towards a 'left-wing breakthrough' more genuine than any evident in drama a decade earlier, still rather wary of political visions, grand designs, and plans. In achieving even the limited theatrical breakthrough they did, the playwrights discussed were fortunate in enjoying the support of a company, and a director, strongly sharing the frustrations with earlier conservatism which Tynan summed up at the end of the 1950s. New directions in English drama were sought out and supported by the English Stage Company from the moment of its establishment at the Royal Court theatre in 1956. Its inspirational first director, George Devine, considered like Tynan that drama earlier in the 1950s had remained inexcusably remote from 'forces of contemporary reality'. Since recent history had 'seen six million Jews murdered', he remarked, along with many other forms of 'drastic political and social changes', dramatists should surely have managed a response stronger than the undemanding entertainment offered by writers such as Noël Coward and Agatha Christie (Wardle, p. 169).

Believing fresh playwrights essential to this response, Devine instituted a policy of vigorous support for new writing. By the time he retired, a year before his early death in 1965, 126 new plays had been staged at the Royal Court, and many other measures introduced to help foster new talent. Sunday-night sessions offered untried plays the chance of cheap, simply staged productions. A writers' group met from 1958 to 1960 to help dramatists such as Arden, Wesker, Edward Bond, Ann Jellicoe, and Keith Johnstone to develop their work. Several new directors trained alongside more established figures such as William Gaskill, John Dexter, and Lindsay Anderson: many went on to successful careers in film and television, or in other theatres. Later directors in the Royal Court itself—Gaskill from 1965 to 1972—ensured that Devine's policies were generally maintained throughout the rest of the century. At its end, along with the Bush Theatre, the Royal Court was still the most promising venue in London for new or emerging playwrights.[4]

The English Stage Company also did what it could to encourage new audiences for its plays. After 1945, theatregoers had generally remained as affluent and middle class as they had been between the wars: continuing class complicities between audience and stage helped to extend English drama's long drawing-room doldrum at the time. Devine tried to escape this middle-class 'backwater', as Edward Bond recorded, not only by encouraging new playwrights generally, but by favouring ones from 'a social group that had largely been unheard in the theatre—working-class writers and others who shared their point of view' (Findlater (ed.), *Royal Court*, p. 121). Work from this group—Bond's included—did appeal to younger and more varied audiences, perhaps even including the 'the bus driver, the housewife, the miner and the Teddy Boy' whom Wesker dreamed of attracting to Centre 42 (Itzin, p. 109). In this way, the

---

[4] This chapter and later ones note the theatre—in London unless otherwise indicated—as well as the year of first productions, confirming how regularly the Royal Court continued to take the lead in supporting new drama.

Royal Court helped to initiate a further, gradual change in theatre's conventionally conservative image—certainly in its own. As the theatre critic Irving Wardle suggested, the Royal Court soon came 'to occupy a symbolic role quite beyond its theatrical function . . . [as] a rallying point for the whole youth protest movement that exploded in the late 1950s and which centred on the word "establishment"' (p. 191). A number of activities highlighted this anti-establishment role. The theatre had its own section on Aldermaston protest marches, for example, and Arnold Wesker—once gaoled for his CND activities—was said to have met his director, John Dexter, on one of them. Some of the Royal Court's most direct engagement with contemporary politics, in other words, occurred offstage, helping to develop channels for anger or protest its relatively moderate new plays had sometimes failed to find for themselves.

By the early 1960s, several other theatres were ready to consolidate the 'breakthroughs' made at the Royal Court. Plans for a National Theatre had originally been discussed just over a century previously, coming closer to fruition with the promise of £1 million of government money in 1949. A foundation stone was laid in London in 1951, though it turned out to be on the wrong site, and another quarter-century passed before the National Theatre (renamed the Royal National Theatre in 1988) finally opened in its new building on the South Bank of the Thames. In the meantime, a National Theatre company worked from 1963 at the Old Vic, under the overall direction of Laurence Olivier until 1972. It initially drew heavily on the expertise of the Royal Court, borrowing directors such as Gaskill and Dexter, as well as performers including Joan Plowright and Frank Finlay. Its work complemented that of another 'national' company, established in 1960 when a Royal Charter elevated the Shakespeare Memorial Theatre Company in Stratford-upon-Avon into the Royal Shakespeare Company (RSC), with Peter Hall as its first director and a new London base at the Aldwych (later, from 1982, at the Barbican). Neither of the new national companies was primarily committed to the production of new English plays. A first season including *Hamlet*, Shaw's *Saint Joan*, Chekhov's *Uncle Vanya*, and George Farquhar's *The Recruiting Officer* set a pattern for much of what followed at the National. Classics, English or translated, made up the greater part of its repertoire. The new

Fig. 9. The National Theatre building on the South Bank of the Thames, inaugurated in March 1976.

companies nevertheless offered a further, prestigious alternative to the commercial managements which continued to control much of London theatre, and each was ready to risk new plays fairly regularly. David Mercer, Henry Livings, David Rudkin, John Arden, Trevor Griffiths, and Tom Stoppard were staged in the early years of the RSC, with Charles Wood, Peter Nichols, John Osborne, James Saunders, and Peter Shaffer, as well as Stoppard and Arden, all produced by the National in the 1960s.

Opportunities for contemporary dramatists were further extended by the new independence of theatres outside the capital. For decades, many of these had operated only as receiving houses for commercial productions, despatched on tour by London managements. As many as eighty theatres throughout the country gave up this role between 1956 and 1968, usually setting up repertory companies of their own instead. These doubled in number during the same period, and around sixty were working by the end of the 1960s, sometimes in newly established theatres. Four new buildings opened in 1961 alone—at Guildford, Croydon, Nottingham, and Chichester—and twenty were established between the late 1950s and 1970, often in areas where live professional theatre had long been unavailable. Though the provincial theatres varied greatly in their commitment to new writing, several contemporary dramatists either began their careers in them, or later received significant support. These included Alan Ayckbourn, Peter Barnes, David Edgar, Willy Russell, Trevor Griffiths, Howard Brenton, David Hare, and Arnold Wesker, whose early plays were first produced in the Belgrade Theatre, Coventry before transfer to the Royal Court.

New theatres and new companies were in almost every case supported by public funds, disbursed either by local authorities or—usually in larger amounts—through the Arts Council, financed more and more generously by central government in the 1960s.[5] Much indebted to this support, the revival in English drama in the late 1950s and 1960s can be seen as another long-term consequence in English life of attitudes emerging at the end of the war—of new civic commitments underlying the foundation of the Arts Council at the time, and the agreement a few years later to establish a National

[5] The Arts Council's general role is outlined on pp. 33–4, above, and its particular influence on the theatre on pp. 388–93, below.

Theatre, after nearly a century of hesitation. By the early 1960s, post-war enthusiasm for theatre's role within national life had begun to be realized in a new kind of English drama, more varied, ambitious, and influential than its predecessors earlier in the century. The national companies could afford cast sizes, production standards, and risks with unusual, innovative staging on a scale which commercial managements could scarcely match, at any rate where contemporary plays were concerned. This offered the 'space, time, skill and technology', as Edward Bond later remarked, 'to create those images of ourselves which are essential to culture and human nature' (Shank (ed.), p. 62).

New resources, broader audiences, and new capacities to create 'essential' images naturally increased the appeal of the drama among contemporary authors. Tom Stoppard considered that 'after 1956 everybody of my age who wanted to write, wanted to write plays—after Osborne and the rest at the Court, and with Tynan on the *Observer*, and Peter Hall about to take over the RSC' (Trussler (ed.), p. 60). Worrying in the *New Review* in Summer 1978 about the fate of contemporary fiction, Ian McEwan likewise concluded that for some time previously the most promising of younger authors had 'preferred to write for the theatre' (p. 51). Looking back in 1981, David Hare remarked that a feature of the whole period since the 1950s had been the extent to which 'public forms became those in which the most gifted writers chose to work' (Peter Roberts (ed.), p. 209). Later in the century, it was often the public forms of film and television which seemed most attractive, particularly in terms of financial reward. But for thirty years or more, from the mid-1950s to the mid-1980s or beyond, theatre benefited from a new cultural centrality, and a growing hold on the attention of the age.

*

Yet it was some time before drama's potential as a public art form was fully realized. Like Stoppard, David Hare belonged to a new generation—or 'second wave', as the critic John Russell Taylor described it—whose work reached the stage only later in the 1960s. 'Osborne and the rest at the Court' continued to dominate the first half of the decade, though in ways not always sustaining expectations raised by their earlier work, particularly in Osborne's case. His

original 'breakthrough', as Stoppard suggested, had been enormously influential on contemporary writers. David Mercer, for example,
recalled being 'tremendously affected and infected by *Look Back in
Anger*, because it simply burst the doors of the bourgeois middle-
class theatre wide open' (Trussler (ed.), p. 51). But by the 1960s,
Osborne seemed ready to close these doors once again, discarding
theatre's newly acquired engagement with social issues and public
life. His later career shared in this way a direction followed by
several of the supposedly 'Angry Young Men' of the 1950s—one
partly anticipated even in *Look Back in Anger*. The extraordinary
vehemence of Jimmy Porter's tirades directs attention as much on
his uneasy personality as on any of the issues he addresses: later
plays simply focused still further on individual characters and their
stresses. The historical setting of *Luther* (English Stage Company,
1961) eliminates direct engagement with contemporary politics, and
Osborne directs most of his attention on the psychology of the original 'protestant'—the figure who has 'always [had] to resist' (I. iii)—
rather than the substance of his dissent. Individual problems and
psychologies continued to dominate *Inadmissible Evidence* (Royal
Court, 1964) and *Time Present* (Royal Court, 1968), especially in
the earlier play. This used a formal inventiveness unusual in
Osborne's work to focus attention almost exclusively within the
consciousness of the protagonist, Bill Maitland, disturbed by the
stresses of his law office and his many extramarital affairs. Later
work such as *West of Suez* (Royal Court, 1971) and *Watch it Come
Down* (National, 1975) did refer to issues such as England's supposed national decline. But wider interests in these plays and in *The
Hotel in Amsterdam* (Royal Court, 1968) were scarcely discernible
among the wordy, weary middle-class relationships portrayed—as if
Osborne was trying to reinvent the very drawing-room drama he
was usually credited with having burst apart.

Interests initially established by Osborne and the Royal Court
figured more strongly in the work of some of the new playwrights
emerging in the 1960s. The issue of class figured widely during the
decade, along with renewed rejection of the 'gentleman code'. Like
Arnold Wesker, Harold Pinter shifted theatre's attention further
from the middle classes in early plays such as *The Caretaker* (Arts
Theatre, 1960) and *The Homecoming* (RSC, 1965), partly through

meticulous reproduction of patterns of demotic and working-class speech. Edward Bond's early work also concentrated on working-class life, examined in a rural context in *The Pope's Wedding* (Royal Court, 1962) and an urban one in *Saved* (Royal Court, 1965). Like Pinter, Bond developed new forms of dialogue for these contexts. Minimal, almost monosyllabic patterns of speech—in *Saved*, for example—reproduce the emotional and imaginative effects of poverty on his characters' lives:

LEN. Down the labour Monday.
FRED *grunts*.
   Start somethin'.
Silence.
   No life, broke.
FRED. True.
Silence.

(vi)

Much of David Mercer's 1960s drama was also concerned with class distinctions, and with extending the assault on bourgeois theatre for which he praised Osborne. In *Belcher's Luck* (RSC, 1966), portrayal of a dying aristocrat and the struggles over his inheritance illustrate changing social hierarchies after the war, providing what Mercer called 'a metaphor for England and its class structure' (Trussler (ed.), p.56). David Storey offered another such metaphor in portraying working life in *The Contractor* (Royal Court, 1969), and Peter Barnes a surreal one in *The Ruling Class* (Nottingham Playhouse, 1968)—a blackly comic depiction of an aristocrat who considers himself, as a member of the upper class, naturally close to the Lord God Almighty. His spectacular insanity passes unnoticed when he takes up his traditional place in the House of Lords.

Some of David Mercer's other plays, such as *After Haggerty* and *Ride a Cock Horse* (Piccadilly, 1965), contributed less to a metaphor than to a kind of sub-genre of class-conscious writing in the 1960s. Stresses in an age of expanding social mobility were repeatedly reflected in stories—usually autobiographical—about characters who move beyond working-class origins, yet find it painfully diffi-cult to shed the outlook of their less affluent, less educated parents. Versions of this story appeared in a number of novels considered in

Chapter 15. They also shaped some of the work of Tony Harrison and other poets discussed in Chapter 7. In contemporary drama, much the same story reappeared in Dennis Potter's celebrated television plays *Stand Up, Nigel Barton* and *Vote Vote Vote for Nigel Barton* (BBC, 1965), in Alan Plater's *Close the Coalhouse Door* (Newcastle Playhouse, 1968), and in David Storey's *In Celebration* (Royal Court, 1969), which traces uneasy relations between a miner and his three sons, home in the North for their parents' fortieth wedding anniversary.

By the mid-1960s, the theatre was beginning to reflect other changes in the decade's outlook and lifestyle, and the growing influences of the counter-culture at the time. Playwrights successful in the previous decade sometimes viewed these new developments with suspicion. Like the narrator in Colin MacInnes's novel *Absolute Beginners* (1959), but less sympathetically, in Osborne's *Inadmissible Evidence* Bill Maitland surveys a generation apparently 'dreamy, young, cool... for the first time they're being allowed to roll about in it and have clothes and money and music and sex... No one before has been able to do such things with such charm, such ease, such frozen innocence... stuffed full of... marches and boycotts and rallies' (II). David Mercer's hero in *Ride a Cock Horse* also finds new freedoms with sex and drugs more confusing than liberating, while David Halliwell's *Little Malcolm and his Struggle against the Eunuchs* (Unity Theatre, 1965) suggests its author was more exasperated than attracted by protest movements and bohemian lifestyles spreading through the student community at the time. Other dramatists were readier to celebrate contemporary counter-culture and alternative lifestyles: Anne Jellicoe in *The Knack* (Arts, Cambridge, 1962), for example, or Bill Naughton in *Alfie* (Duchess, 1963). In plays such as *Kelly's Eye* (Royal Court, 1963) or *Eh?* (RSC, 1964), Henry Livings also suggested that it is those on the fringes of conventional society, and not the rich and established, who have the truest values, and enjoy the best sex.

Much the strongest attack on establishment values appeared in the work of Joe Orton. This often seemed to assume—blithely but provocatively—that new patterns of sexual behaviour were already an accepted norm, and that it was longer-established moralities and conventions which were really outrageous. Extramarital relations and casual affairs with secretaries, for example—still so troubling for Osborne's hero in *Inadmissible Evidence*—are presented in Orton's *What the Butler Saw* (Queen's, 1969) as entirely normal and altogether to be expected. *Entertaining Mr Sloane* (New Arts, 1964) and *Loot* (Jeanetta Cochrane, 1966) likewise suggest that promiscuity has become universal, restraint or abstinence improbable, and conventional heterosexual relations no more than an odd aberration or 'folk-myth'. In one way, these moral inversions were conventional enough themselves—established components of the farce mode which much of Orton's writing followed or parodied. Yet in most farce moral reversal and sexual anarchy are strictly temporary, with order carefully restored in the end. Orton's work was darker and more subversive: the open-endedness of *Loot* or *What the Butler Saw* brought the plays closer to life beyond the theatre, contributing to their capacity to comment on it. In particular, like much of R. D. Laing's work at the time, *What the Butler Saw* persuasively demonstrated that 'you can't be a rationalist in an irrational world. It isn't rational' (II). This principle is cheerfully embraced by staff in the psychiatric clinic the play depicts, convinced that 'Her Majesty's Government' and its representatives may be no more than their 'immediate superiors in madness' (I). Typically of Orton's work, representatives of established morality, authority, or law and order are portrayed as far more incompetent, corrupt, or just crazy, than the rest of the population.

Orton's plays reflected in this way an anti-establishment mood much broader and more radical than any Irving Wardle found in the Royal Court ten years or so earlier. It was a mood which increasingly—sometimes literally—reshaped theatre after the mid-1960s. Rejection of the establishment and its values extended easily into departures from dramatic convention, and often from established theatres themselves. Since mid-century, the Edinburgh Festival had offered an influential annual example of forms of 'fringe' drama thriving independently of established theatres and theatre companies. The example was increasingly followed in England in the later 1960s, sometimes as a direct result of the 'marches and boycotts and rallies' of the period. The Agit-Prop Street Players, for example, developed directly out of anti-Vietnam demonstrations in 1968. Renamed Red Ladder, after one of their favourite props, the company went on to play to tenants' groups, to striking Ford workers, and at trade union events. The Welfare State company likewise evolved from street theatre, though in a different direction. It originated in the extraordinary events organized by Albert Hunt in Bradford, including in 1967 a large-scale restaging of the Russian Revolution in the streets of the town. Later, the company developed further what Catherine Itzin recorded in *Stages of the Revolution* (1980) as interests in 'ritual, myth and magic . . . ceremonies . . . performances, processions and dances' (pp. 68–9).

Very different from Red Ladder's, these interests placed Welfare State at the opposite end of the 'spectrum' of alternative theatre Baz Kershaw defined in *The Politics of Performance* (1992)—one stretching 'from carnival to traditional-style agit prop, from the anarchic celebration of total anti-structure' towards 'energetic . . . communication of a clear, unambiguous message' (p. 82). More and more alternative companies took their place somewhere along this spectrum. Only a handful had been in operation in the mid-1960s, but by the early years of the next decade a solid reputation had already been established by companies such as Belt and Braces, North-West Spanner, The People Show, Pip Simmons, Portable Theatre, 7:84, General Will, Joint Stock, Foco Novo, and CAST, as well as Red Ladder and Welfare State. By the end of the 1970s, there were more than a hundred well-established small companies, attracting up to 12 per cent of the Arts Council's annual drama budget. While the cultural democratization of the 1960s encouraged a new, do-it-yourself populism in contemporary poetry, it also suggested that with some talent and determination any group of people might start their own drama company, or at any rate that the support of established theatres was no longer essential in order to do so.

Though the new companies were generally happy to avoid these theatres, and adept at working in ad hoc venues and temporary sites, they obviously welcomed the use of more permanent performance spaces when appropriate ones could be found. New theatres and alternative performance venues evolved to meet their needs, and in response to wider changes in drama's role and audience at the time. Edinburgh once again provided a useful model in the shape of the Traverse Theatre, founded in 1963 as a permanent venue for the fringe and alternative forms of drama which had evolved around the official festival. Virtually the first professional studio theatre in Britain, it offered a model soon followed elsewhere. The Traverse company played influential London seasons in 1966 and later, and one of its founders, Jim Haynes, used his experience in opening the Arts Lab in Drury Lane in 1968. Many other new, usually small-scale venues followed in London, including by the early 1970s the Half Moon, the King's Head, The Bush, Soho Poly, the ICA, The Open Space, and the Roundhouse. Performances in the new venues were often innovative and exciting. Efficiently publicized by the alternative London entertainments journal, *Time Out*—first published in 1968—they at last attracted audiences as young, varied and enthusiastic as those sought by the Royal Court and Centre 42 at the start of the 1960s. They also attracted new playwrights. Half the new drama staged in London in the late 1960s and early 1970s was produced in the new fringe theatres, helping to launch the careers of a number of new writers at the time.

A need to keep pace with audiences and performance trends encouraged larger London theatres to rely less exclusively on their main auditoria. The Royal Court quickly recognized that the theatrical revolution it had helped initiate required new spaces as well as new plays for its further development, opening a small studio, the Theatre Upstairs, in 1969. The national companies gradually followed this example. A studio space, the Cottesloe, was included in plans for the National Theatre, drawn up in the 1960s, and provided for the Royal Shakespeare Company by The Place in London and the Other Place in Stratford, opened in 1971 and 1974, and the Donmar Warehouse, added in London in 1977. Many of the regional repertory theatres also set up studios, or otherwise moved away from conventional auditoria. The Victoria Theatre in Stoke, for example, worked from the early 1960s in a converted cinema, set up as a theatre-in-the-round. Its director, Peter Cheeseman, considered this arrangement helped to place drama 'in a space cleared in the middle of the community'—one of several possibilities he believed might be realized 'philosophically and even politically' by 'the human structure of the environment [theatres] create' (Elsom, *Post-War Theatre*, p. 206).

As he suggested, new performance spaces reflected and encouraged a range of new relations between drama, stage, and audience in the later 1960s. The structure of the new venues helped to democratize theatregoing, avoiding old-fashioned divisions into stalls, grand circle, and gallery, and the differential ticket prices and social hierarchies these entailed. Smaller studio theatres reflected contemporary expectations in other ways, bringing to live performance some of the intimate, close-up view of actors a televisual age demanded. Yet they also encouraged a drama more innovative than either television or many larger theatres usually provided. Small-scale productions could more easily afford to risk experimental material, and the structure of studio spaces encouraged them to do so. The architecture of the bigger theatres—often built in Victorian times—had helped to sustain the vogue for drawing-room drama earlier in the century, the realistic box-sets it required fitting very conveniently onto proscenium-arch stages. Studio theatres could no longer rely on such conservative, expensive forms of staging, even had they wished to, nor, more generally, on conventional forms of dramatic illusion. Since spectators in studios or theatres-in-the-round could see each other more or less as clearly as the stage, even the most realistic set was unlikely to make them forget they were in a theatre. Instead, audiences in small venues developed a slightly more sceptical, provisional relation with the plays they saw—freer, as a result, to depart from narrowly realistic modes of performance.

Contemporary drama was led in similar directions by the new fringe and alternative companies. Often limited in resources, or even acting experience, they nevertheless needed to make a quick impact on audiences—ones who might be unused to theatre, or to watching it in bare, makeshift performance spaces. Such needs were not ideally served by conventional drama's carefully explored character psychology, extended complexities of plot, and elaborate stage furniture. Many of these conventions had survived the 'breakthrough' of the late 1950s and early 1960s more or less intact. Even when innovative in theme, or in shifting class orientation, theatre at the time had only occasionally—in Arden's plays, or the stage languages developed by Bond and Pinter—done much to develop dramatic form. The needs of new venues and companies made such development more urgent, encouraging theatre in the later 1960s—especially in its more politicized forms—to draw further on another set of resources first available to the English stage in 1956. These were offered by the drama and theories of Bertolt Brecht, introduced by the 'short but cataclysmic visit', as Kenneth Tynan called it, made to the Palace Theatre in London by his company, the Berliner Ensemble, in August 1956 (Tynan, p. 363).

Brecht's drama was not widely known in England at the time, and in London probably even less than elsewhere. There had been only a handful of professional productions in the provinces during the 1950s—most recently an uninspiring *Mother Courage and her Children* (1941), with Joan Littlewood in the lead, at the Barnstaple Arts Festival in 1955. Brecht's plays and the performance styles he developed with the Berliner Ensemble were largely a 'discovery' for English theatre in 1956, as Tynan suggested: one which he considered by the mid-1970s to have had

enormous and still reverberating repercussions on almost every aspect of theatrical style: on playwrights, obviously, but also on directors . . . on designers . . . on composers, and on such other departments of stagecraft as lighting, wardrobe, and make-up . . . our theatre has been permeated, for good or ill, by Brecht, and no influence of comparable magnitude is yet in sight. (p. 13)

'Repercussions' were felt first at the Royal Court, partly as a result of relations it had established with Brecht before his company came to London. George Devine had visited Berlin earlier in 1956: chatting with him over beer and sausages, Brecht had agreed that the Royal Court could stage *The Good Woman of Sezuan* (1943) late in the year. Though Brecht died suddenly a few months later, just before his company's visit to London, his wife Helene Weigel stayed on after the Palace Theatre season to attend Devine's rehearsals. Ideas were also offered by the Berliner Ensemble's designer, Teo Otto, and its composer Paul Dessau.

Despite their advice, the Royal Court production of *The Good Woman of Sezuan* was not outstandingly successful. The experience it offered, and the example of the Ensemble itself, nevertheless continued to exercise a strong influence on the Royal Court in the years that followed—especially on directors such as William Gaskill and John Dexter, and on Jocelyn Herbert, the designer for early plays by Arnold Wesker, John Arden, and Samuel Beckett. By the early 1960s, Brechtian influences had spread to the national companies, partly through Dexter and Gaskill's early involvement with the National Theatre. The Royal Shakespeare Company also saw a model for its own organization in the work of the Berliner Ensemble —a large, permanent, generously funded company, able to develop performers' skills collectively, and deploy them in carefully co-ordinated production styles. Throughout the period, shifting styles and fashions in contemporary English theatre were often reflected particularly clearly by the RSC's work. In several of its productions in the early 1960s, Brecht's stage devices and politically alert treatment of history were much in evidence. They were especially clear in Peter Hall and John Barton's adaptation of *Henry VI* and *Richard III* as *The Wars of the Roses* in 1963—a production reflecting convictions of Shakespeare's continuing political relevance further strengthened by the Polish critic Jan Kott.

'Repercussions' of this kind demonstrated Brecht's rapid influence on directors, designers, theatre companies, and stagecraft generally. Yet as Tynan admitted at the end of the 1950s—contrary to the later views quoted above—the Berliner Ensemble's visit had not immediately affected playwrights, nor 'inspired any plays' (p. 273). As their 1956 performances were entirely in German, it was inevitably the non-verbal aspects of the Ensemble's work—minimal sets, regular use of music and song, strong, stoical acting styles—which at first most impressed English audiences. As Tynan acknowledged, given the 'paucity of good translations' of Brecht's plays, and limited awareness of his theories, it was not always clear what his striking stage devices were intended to achieve (p. 273). Clarifications and explanations were nevertheless fairly soon available—in John Willett's *The Theatre of Bertolt* Brecht (1959), for example, or a year earlier in *Encore*, a magazine read by many of those involved or interested in new developments in English theatre in the later 1950s.

Encore published a long analysis of Brecht's staging in an article by Ernest Bornemann—an acquaintance of Brecht's in the 1920s, when he was still learning some of his tactics from the revolutionary director Erwin Piscator, author of *The Political Theatre* (1929). Bornemann's article highlighted Brecht's Marxism and described the importance for his political theatre of the famous 'alienation effect'. Brecht was determined, Bornemann explained, 'to destroy any possible impression of reality, of looking at real events rather than at a play'. A whole range of stage devices helped achieve this aim: non-naturalistic acting, non-atmospheric lighting, minimal scenery, direct address to audiences, regular songs, onstage posters, projected scene synopses and slogans. Fracturing any 'impression of reality' in this way discouraged audiences from habits Brecht thought lazy and anaesthetic—uncritical empathy with characters, or easy emotional engagement with their individual natures and psychologies. Brecht sought instead a theatre concerned with issues rather than individuals, and an audience thoughtfully distanced and detached from the immediate action it witnessed. Innovative staging and 'cool, unemotional presentation of a case', Bornemann suggested, encouraged spectators to '*contemplate* the scene and receive its full impact as a *guide to action*' in the real political world beyond the theatre (Marowitz et al. (eds.), pp. 147, 146, 148).

Well prepared by Bornemann, readers of *Encore* might have recognized that critics were sometimes overeager in identifying Brechtian effects in contemporary English drama. An actor as well as a writer, John Osborne had performed as a peasant in *The Good Woman of Sezuan*, and critics understandably looked for Brecht's influence in his second play, *The Entertainer*, produced at the Royal Court the following year with Laurence Olivier in the lead. This influence seemed to be confirmed by unconventional staging, including regular songs, and by the play's strong focus on issues such as class privilege, the Suez debacle, and the limitations of the Welfare State. Yet by using the demise of traditional music hall to represent the wider decline of England, Osborne communicated frustrated nationalism rather than any of Brecht's revolutionary socialism. Olivier's charismatic performance in any case made individual character and psychology a stronger interest than wider political themes. Even the songs seemed fairly naturalistic in the context of a family of music-hall artists. Not surprisingly, Harold Hobson suggested that John Arden's early plays showed more genuine affinities with Brecht's work, which Arden had read for himself earlier in the 1950s. Arden's plays often moved abruptly between intense, concise scenes, each offering brief illustration rather than full development of character. This did bear comparison with the episodic construction Brecht learned from the montage techniques of cinema and referred to as his 'Epic' style. Yet Arden's individual scenes scarcely allowed the 'full impact as a guide to action' which Brecht sought. Instead, as early audiences of *Serjeant Musgrave's Dance* regularly complained, Arden's ideas could hardly be grasped during the course of the play, but only—if at all—at its end. Even his distinctive use of songs may—like Osborne's—have owed less to Brecht than to a debt Arden acknowledged to the music hall, and to solidly English traditions of mumming plays and melodrama.

Affinities between Brecht's work and two playwrights popular at the start of the 1960s, Robert Bolt and John Whiting, were likewise only partial, despite larger claims at the time. In *The Devils* (RSC, 1961), Whiting shared Brecht's conciseness in constructing illustrative scenes, but these are focused less on political issues than on an imposing central character—the aptly named Grandier, destroyed by religious hysteria reminiscent of Arthur Miller's *The Crucible* (1952). New attitudes and theatrical tactics evolving at the start of the 1960s were sharply illustrated in Robert Bolt's contrasting popular successes of 1960, *The Tiger and the Horse* (Queen's) and *A Man for All Seasons* (Globe). Anti-establishment feelings—particularly focused by CND—were strongly represented in *The Tiger and the Horse*, but still contained within the drawing room of an affluent middle-class family. *A Man for All Seasons* was more adventurous theatrically, in ways Bolt claimed were owed to Brecht. Bolt's choric figure, 'the Common Man', regularly breaks the stage illusion by chatting to the audience while bringing on props, rearranging the minimal set, or ostentatiously taking on other roles in the play. Yet his interventions did little to direct audiences towards cool, critical appraisal of Sir Thomas More and his dilemma, or to diminish the ardent empathy with embattled individualism which most of the play invites. Like Whiting, Bolt concentrated on what he called 'definite vision of what an individual human person is' rather than the wider, more objective political analysis Brecht favoured (Tynan, p. 287). The same vision shaped later documentary plays, dramatizing relations between Queen Elizabeth and Mary Queen of Scots in *Vivat! Vivat Regina!* (Chichester, 1970), or among Russian revolutionaries in *State of Revolution* (National, 1977). In each, Bolt continued to use history as a context for exploring individual will, rather than the economic or social forces through which it is shaped and constrained. His introduction to *A Man for All Seasons* in any case showed a limited understanding of devices Brecht used to focus attention on these forces—particularly in suggesting that his distancing or 'alienation' effects resembled a slap in the face.

Brecht's example seemed to be followed more faithfully in Theatre Workshop productions—particularly in *Oh What a Lovely War* (1963)—but it was usually in combination with a range of other devices. Theatre Workshop had been based in Glasgow and Manchester after 1945, before moving in 1953 to Stratford in the East End of London. Some of the company's strategies were owed to lessons in politicized, entertaining forms of theatre its founders Joan Littlewood and Ewan MacColl had learned still earlier, in Salford in the 1930s. *Oh What a Lovely War* combined devices used in 'Living Newspaper' performances popular in the 1930s with ones which may have been borrowed from Piscator and Brecht—such as the projection of contemporary headlines, or of scenes of the First World War, as a background for the production's live action. *Oh What a Lovely War* also drew on modes and working methods the company had developed for itself. Ensemble performance, improvisation sessions, and research by cast members all contributed to the production's innovative style. Nostalgic First World War songs and traditional forms such as melodrama, Pierrot show, political cabaret, and music hall added to its popular success, realizing some of Littlewood's dream of replacing conventional theatres with 'fun-palaces for the people' (Shepherd and Womack, p. 358). Provocative as well as entertaining, the production highlighted the purposelessness of the war—and the incompetence of the politicians, businessmen, and generals responsible for it—in ways nevertheless familiar from Brecht's theatre, certainly to Joan Littlewood herself. In particular, the conclusion that capitalism makes war 'a political and economic necessity' (II) was one Littlewood might have drawn directly from her 1955 performance as Mother Courage—a character forced by her war-dependent business interests into perversely hoping that peace may never come.

Theatre Workshop's politicized, semi-documentary style and use of popular entertainment was highly influential, and further developed elsewhere in the later 1960s. Charles Wood's *Dingo* (Royal Court, 1967) employed similarly mixed performance styles, presenting an anti-establishment history of the Second World War as bitter as Theatre Workshop's treatment of the First. John McGrath's admiration for Joan Littlewood shaped some of his work at the Liverpool Everyman in the late 1960s, and with his 7:84 company in the next decade. Theatre Workshop also influenced Peter Cheeseman's determination to 'make theatre livelier' and to find a 'popular language' for it—one he hoped might 'bridge the cultural gap which separates the artist from the majority of the community' (Itzin, p. xii). Research into local history and working conditions contributed to a number of his documentary productions for the Victoria Theatre, Stoke. *The Knotty* (1966), for example, dramatized the history of the North Staffordshire railway through a mixture of narrative commentary, ballad, folk song, and short, illustrative scenes, alternating realism with more stylized modes. A resident playwright at the Victoria Theatre in the mid-1960s, Peter Terson, developed similarly free, inventive forms of staging in work for the National Youth Theatre, using a large, ensemble company especially successfully in *Zigger Zagger* (1967), a play about the life of football fans, and in *The Apprentices* (1968). Alan Plater acknowledged the influence of Joan Littlewood and Peter Cheeseman in his preface to another semi-documentary play, *Close the Coalhouse Door* (Newcastle Playhouse, 1968). Based on mining life in the North-East, Plater's play was typical, like Cheeseman's work, of the growing success of regional theatres in addressing their local communities.

For much of the 1960s, in other words, Brechtian tactics were taken up at most only hesitantly by playwrights, appearing most clearly in the work of small companies and community theatres, though even then in ways often difficult to distinguish from the broader legacies of Theatre Workshop. Fuller and more direct contact with Brecht's thinking developed only gradually as the decade went on. It was provided by George Tabori's compilation of Brecht's drama and theory, *Brecht on Brecht*, for example, staged at the Royal Court in 1962. More of Brecht's plays were published in English, and John Willett translated his essays and journalism as *Brecht on Theatre* in 1964, and his discussions of dramaturgy, *The Messingkauf Dialogues*, in 1965. Under the direction of Helene Weigel, the Berliner Ensemble also made an influential return visit to London in the same year. By the later 1960s, Brecht's plays and theories were more familiar to playwrights, as well as to the range of directors, designers, and other practitioners who had been impressed immediately by the unusualness of his staging. Political events and a 'second wave' of new writers—ones who had often begun their work with small alternative companies—ensured that Brecht remained an influence in the English theatre throughout the 1970s, consolidating and extending the role as a public, political art form it had redeveloped since 1956.

10

Last Year in Jerusalem: Politics and Performance after 1968

Today, it is hard to see how a vital theatre and a necessary one can be other than out of tune with society—not seeking to celebrate the accepted values, but to challenge them. (Brook, *The Empty Space* (1968), p. 150)

For about fifteen years after 1968, this challenge was extended throughout English theatre by a generation of writers including Edward Bond, David Hare, Howard Brenton, David Edgar, Howard Barker, John McGrath, and Trevor Griffiths. Most of them were strongly influenced by the emergence of the counter-culture in the late 1960s, by the new theatrical possibilities it encouraged, and above all by the 'great watershed', as Howard Brenton called it, of the near-revolution in Paris in the summer of 1968 (Trussler (ed.), p. 96). David Edgar dated 'the growth of the socialist theatre movement in Britain' to 1968, and recalled being politicized himself on a '1968-ish axis' combining 'the New Left and the counter-culture' (Itzin, pp. xiv, 139). John McGrath witnessed the May *événements* at first hand, commenting that 'the excitement of the whole complex set of attitudes to life which that para-revolutionary situation threw up, was incredible . . . the urgency and the beauty of the ideas was amazing' (Trussler (ed.), p. 106). Trevor Griffiths was similarly excited by the new ideas and their implications, reflecting their influence in Britain at the time in *The Party* (National, 1973). This showed the 1968 demonstrations unfolding dramatically on television while a political discussion group, meeting in London, analyses the rapid development of revolutionary feelings 'in London, in Paris, in Berlin, in the American cities; wherever you care to look' (I. ii).

Much of this discussion concerned the difficulty of translating radical vision in Paris into effective political action across the Channel. In Britain, revolution appeared only a remote, romantic possibility, and radical social change fairly improbable. The Labour government seemed particularly disappointing in this respect, its difficulties figuring on television, in the background of *The Party*, as a dismal contrast to events in France. For many playwrights, the failure of Harold Wilson's government to instigate real reform—confidently expected when it was elected in 1964—led to gloom almost as powerful as the optimism surrounding events in Paris. David Edgar stressed the 'failure of the 1964 Labour government' as a further key influence on his political development (Itzin, p. 139). David Hare recalled believing 'passionately in the Labour Government of 1964', only to see it soon 'sell everything down the river'(Trussler (ed.), p. 115). Barrie Keeffe likewise recorded feeling 'not disillusionment, but absolute despair' when the 'enormous social change' he had anticipated failed to materialize—a despair obviously deepened by the election of another Conservative government in 1970 (Itzin, p. 243).

Playwrights by the start of the 1970s, in other words, experienced particularly sharp divisions between ideals and party-political realities, and between a brief phase of revolutionary optimism, in the summer of 1968, and very different influences gaining ground in Britain at the start of the new decade. These were circumstances loosely comparable to ones in which a strongly left-wing theatre first developed fifty years earlier, in Germany during the 1920s. Confronted by the rise of reactionary forces at the time—following the defeat of the brief German revolution in 1918—Erwin Piscator and Bertolt Brecht created a theatre they hoped might refocus socialist energies and direct them towards more lasting revolutionary change. Many English playwrights likewise sought to restore a revolutionary vision glimpsed in 1968, confronting audiences with political problems and educating them in the possibility of alternatives. Typically of the early 1970s, Trevor Griffiths remarked that he had written *Occupations* (RSC, 1971) in response to 'the '68 revolution in France', and in the hope that portrayal of the Italian Marxist

Antonio Gramsci's leadership of the working class might contribute to 'similar struggles in Europe and Britain' at the time of writing (Griffiths, pp. 5, vii). Didactic drama resulting from such intentions could hardly have been further from Harold Hobson's conviction, quoted in the last chapter, that 'it is the duty of the theatre, not to make men better, but to render them harmlessly happy' (Lloyd Evans and Lloyd Evans (eds.), p. 90). Howard Brenton considered instead that drama should be 'a weapon of peace, to change the world', and that it should concentrate on 'only one theme . . . simply "how can we live justly"' (Wu, pp. 11, 3). Coinciding with Brecht in its didactic, politically progressive aims, this phase of drama naturally adopted many of the stage strategies and practices his work had first developed. These were already familiar to most of the playwrights concerned from their early work with fringe companies: almost all went on to use some form of Brecht's alienated style and 'epic' construction as a basis for their later plays.[1]

These plays often reflected another crucial development in 1968—one that freed authors from restrictions enforced in one way or another for centuries, and virtually unaltered since the Theatres Act of 1843. This required playscripts to be submitted to the Lord Chamberlain, empowered either to ban them altogether or to demand cuts and changes before licensing them for public performance. Freedom from this requirement contributed significantly to the development of small performance venues in the 1960s: status as a theatre club exempted some of them from the Lord Chamberlain's control, allowing much more daring expression of the decade's newly liberated mood than was usually possible elsewhere. In the established theatres, the restrictions of censorship seemed increasingly contrary to the liberalism of the 1960s, political and cultural. As Kenneth Tynan complained, the Lord Chamberlain seemed to work in 'a limbo aloof from democracy, answerable only to his own hunches' and apparently unswayed by changes in contemporary fashions and tolerances (p. 366). Play texts published in the 1960s often contained a resentful note listing alterations his office had imposed.

One of these appeared at the end of John Osborne's *A Patriot for Me* (1965), though in practice the Royal Court circumvented the

---

[1] See pp. 295–7, above.

Lord Chamberlain's dislike of the play—in particular, of its glitter-ing transvestite ball and sustained interest in homosexuality—by temporarily turning the theatre into a club, with performances ostensibly open only to members. The same tactics were used later in 1965, when Edward Bond's *Saved*—notorious for showing a baby stoned to death in its pram—proved too violent to receive a licence for ordinary performance. But on this occasion the Lord Chamberlain detected breaches of club licensing practices, and the Royal Court was prosecuted and found guilty, despite an impassioned defence from witnesses such as Laurence Olivier. Though the theatre was fined only nominally, the case provided a strong focus for resentments of an institution so at odds with its age. A campaign for reform soon followed, supported throughout the theatre profession. Parliament was persuaded to pass a new Theatres Act in 1968, removing the Lord Chamberlain altogether and leaving drama virtually as free from censorship as other forms of literature had been since the *Lady Chatterley* trial in 1960.

This had had many consequences for the theatre, some also discussed in Chapter 13, below. For left-wing playwrights working in the early 1970s, it allowed greater freedom both to comment on contemporary issues and institutions, and to shock audiences, in various ways, into recognition of the need for change. Edward Bond was among the first to exploit these freedoms, developing the violent tactics he had employed in *Saved*, in combination with Brechtian influences absorbed since the beginning of his career. Many of his early plays were directed by William Gaskill, familiar with Brecht's staging ever since the early days of the Royal Court. Bond himself worked at the time on Brecht adaptations, and arranged an evening of his songs for the theatre. Views of drama he later expressed often followed Brecht's closely. Bond explained, for example, that he sought an 'epic theatre—the theatre of change, the only theatre that can analyse and explain our condition' (Peter Roberts (ed.), p. 173). He also described this as a 'Rational Theatre'—one which 'interprets the world . . . does not merely mirror it' and is therefore able to show 'why things go wrong and how we could correct them' (Bond, *Bundle*, p. xii; *Bond on File*, p. 65).

Like Brecht, Bond often found these aims hard to realize within existing conventions of acting and staging. Drama's habitual emphasis on individual psychology had left contemporary actors merely 'private performers on a public stage', in his view—'still part of the bourgeois theatre', yet at a time when society could 'no longer be expressed politically and morally in terms of the individual' (Peter Roberts (ed.), p. 173; Bond, *Worlds*, p. 136). Like Brecht, Bond shifted attention from individuals to issues by using discontinuous, epic forms of construction—illustrating ideas rather than developing character—and by relying on plots close to parable in their strong outlines and clear implications. *Narrow Road to the Deep North* (Belgrade Theatre, Coventry, 1968), for example, used the kind of remote setting in the Far East Brecht had employed in *The Good Woman of Sezuan* (1943) to add a distanced objectivity to audiences' judgements. Bond's play also followed the fable-like plot device— discovery of an abandoned baby—which Brecht used in *The Caucasian Chalk Circle* (1948). In *The Narrow Road to the Deep North* the baby grows up to become a parable tyrant, satirizing and caricaturing British imperialism. In *The Bundle* (RSC, 1978), Bond further challenged audience expectations by returning to much the same story, but with opposite implications, the baby growing up this time to establish a juster society through resistance to the landowner class.

In another parable of power, *Lear* (Royal Court, 1971), Bond used a different distancing device, closer to Brecht's in *Galileo* (1947). In Brecht's characterization, Galileo appeared unexpectedly selfish and unheroic: *Lear* likewise forced audiences to reconsider a familiar figure, subjected to fresh critical scrutiny. The 'social moral' of Shakespeare's *King Lear*, Bond considered, was 'endure till in time the world will be made right' (*Bond on File*, p. 25). In his own play, Lear is presented less as a figure of heroic endurance than one clearly culpable, politically and personally, for ways his world has gone wrong. Bond confronts his Lear directly with responsibility for the dire character of his daughters, instigators of several cycles of civil war and revolution. This Lear also has to face the consequences of an obsession with constructing a huge wall around his kingdom. Ostensibly for defence, the wall is mostly used to keep the domestic population employed and subservient: its hugely expensive con- struction represents in the play the politics of nuclear deterrence and the Cold War. By showing revolutionary regimes reduplicating tyrannies they originally sought to destroy, *Lear* also offers a parable about Stalin, or about consequences which follow, as Bond warned in his preface, when any government chooses 'to subordinate justice to power' (*Plays: Two*, p. 11). *Lear* offers only limited hope of resistance. Lear is eventually shot while removing a single shovelful of earth from the top of his wall. His death resembles Kattrin's at the end of Brecht's *Mother Courage* (1941) but is still more minimal in its affirmation.

Unusual staging made conflicts of innocence, justice, and power disturbingly immediate in *Lear*. Long after he is murdered, the Gravedigger's Boy trails painfully after Lear as a ghost, reminding him of his responsibilities and illustrating Bond's belief that if the dead could vote, there would be no wars. The Boy's murder also exemplifies Bond's broadly based theatrical poetry, derived less from dialogue than from suggestive combinations of action, word, and image. Shot while his wife is raped, the Boy's blood instantly saturates fresh white sheets she has just strung across the stage to dry, graphically highlighting the play's concerns with innocence violated and destroyed. The violence of the scene was typical, too, of ways Bond used new freedoms in the early 1970s to move some way beyond Brecht's idioms. Other scenes in *Lear* show eyes ripped out in the name of science, eardrums punctured by knitting needles, and the lungs, stomach, and other internal organs torn from the body of one of Lear's daughters. Since Bond believed that 'violence shapes and obsesses our society, and if we do not stop being violent we have no future', such scenes in one way just represent forms of behaviour he thought it essential for audiences to confront (*Plays: Two*, p. 3). But the recurrent violence is also part of a wider dramatic strategy—comparable to Brecht's alienation, or 'A-effect', but more extreme. Bond continued to refer to an 'A-effect', but one redefined in terms of aggression rather than only distancing or alienation. This 'aggro-effect', as he called it, demanded and directed attention through shock or revulsion, as if alienation might work better, after all, as the slap in the face Robert Bolt once described. Bond considered shocking, aggressive claims on audience attention 'justified by the desperation of the situation', much as if he were shaking awake occupants of a burning house (Innes, p. 172). Discussing *King Lear*, he worried that contemporary society had 'less time than Shakespeare' (*Bond on*

Fig. 10. The death of the Gravedigger's Boy in Edward Bond's *Lear*, in a 1982 RSC revival.

File, p. 25). His own *Lear* suggested it had less time even than Brecht, still requiring the lessons his theatre offered, but in yet more challenging and immediate forms.

Bond's later plays continued to offer such lessons in various ways, though often more moderately than in *Lear*. Some continued to develop forms of parable—*The Woman* (National, 1978), for example, set at the end of the Trojan War, and *Restoration* (Royal Court, 1981), parodying late seventeenth-century drama and exposing the class-ridden society it reflected. More conventional, naturalistic strategies were followed in plays such as *The Worlds* (Newcastle Playhouse, 1979), portraying violent action against an industrialist, and *Summer* (National, 1982), examining the legacies of Nazism. An ability to develop a wide range of dramatic styles, and to combine them to serve immediate political purposes, made Bond one of the most powerful and influential playwrights in the period. Violent 'A-effects' in plays such as *Lear* also made him one of the most typical of the early 1970s. Similar effects were used by many writers emerging at the time, especially those working with small touring and alternative companies, often obliged by life on the road to seize audiences' attention as quickly and strongly as they could.

Portable Theatre was one such company, founded by David Hare and Tony Bicât in 1968. Its production of *Lay-By* in 1971 helped establish directions left-wing theatre followed during much of the 1970s. It also introduced several of the authors most involved: the script was a collaboration between Howard Brenton, Trevor Griffiths, David Hare, Stephen Poliakoff, Brian Clark, Hugh Stoddart, and Snoo Wilson. *Lay-By* featured violence, rape, pornography, and nudity throughout, eventually showing a naked, half-dead woman's body subjected to a series of abuses. Like Bond, in other words, *Lay-By* tried to use the freedoms of a stage without censorship to taunt taboos and shake audiences out of their complacency—ideally, into recognition of the 'extreme decadence . . . extreme state of crisis' which Hare diagnosed as the contemporary condition of the country as a whole (Trussler (ed.), p. 117). Similar shock tactics were used in other plays Portable produced at the time, such as Snoo Wilson's *Pig Night* and *Blow Job* (1971).

They were also widely employed by Howard Brenton, determined that a generation 'kicked awake' in 1968 was kept awake in the years that followed. 'A really great burst of nihilism', he remarked of *Lay-By*, 'is one of the most beautiful things you can see on a stage'. He added in 1972 that theatre in general is 'not a place for a rational analysis of a society—it's there to bait our obsessions, ideas and public figures' (Bull, *Political Dramatists*, pp. 41, 43). Baiting and nihilism shaped several of his early plays. *Christie in Love* (Royal Court, 1970), for example, suggested that a serial killer may be no more odious than the police and legal systems pursuing him. *Magnificence* (Royal Court, 1973) was concerned with vicious class hierarchies and the attempted murder of a Tory politician. Brenton's determination to bait audiences seemed as strong as ever at the end of the decade in *The Romans in Britain* (National, 1980)—extreme enough to provoke a prosecution for indecency against the director, Michael Bogdanov, initiated by Mary Whitehouse on behalf of her National Viewers and Listeners Association. The case was eventually withdrawn, though it seemed for a time to threaten the reappearance of censorship in a new form.

Yet as supporters of Brenton and Bogdanov stressed in the press, scenes of violence and homosexual rape in *The Romans in Britain* were never intended *only* to shock. Instead, they were supposed to add urgency to the play's analysis of a metaphoric form of rape—imperial conquest. Brenton made his analysis of empire and its legacies still more provocative by juxtaposing the Roman invasion of England with recent events in Northern Ireland. In trying to force audiences to reassess imperialism in this way, even the play's more shocking elements moved Brenton's writing rather closer to the 'rational analysis' he had rejected at the start of the 1970s, and to the Brechtian influences he began to acknowledge later in his career. Movements in this direction were in evidence even by the middle of the decade. Brenton's *Weapons of Happiness* (1976) was the first contemporary play to be staged by the National Theatre in its South Bank building, disturbing new audiences with little more than an unusually disjunctive epic construction. This was used to contrast the resilience of a former Czech communist with the lassitude of contemporary England—a country in which 'nothing will change . . . Decay, yes . . . There will never be a revolution' (I. ix). *Epsom Downs* (Joint Stock, 1977) provided what sometimes seemed a still more benign picture of English life. It was certainly a very broad one, using a public festival—rather like Ben Jonson in *Bartholomew Fair* (1614)—to bring together a huge range of diverse characters. Yet their supposedly great day out and cheerful social mixing at the Derby is shown to be no more than a picture, 'thin as paint' (I). It is regularly redrawn by characters—such as the ghost of the suffragette, killed by the King's horse—who highlight a society dominated not by engaging diversity, but by deeply engrained divisions of class and wealth.

Other members of the *Lay-By* group renounced the violent tactics of the early 1970s sooner and more decisively than Brenton. David Hare went on in 1974 to found another company, Joint Stock, this time in collaboration with Max Stafford-Clark, David Aukin, and William Gaskill. The company's ensemble methods were aptly employed in its production of *Epsom Downs*, which included carefully characterized speaking parts even for horses, and generally required performers to work closely together, doubling and trebling parts. The skills involved had been acquired through Joint Stock's production of Hare's *Fanshen* (1975), which used an equally extensive range of characters to dramatize revolutionary redistribution of land and resources in early communist China. The *Fanshen* production also radically reshaped Joint Stock's whole organization as a theatre company. As a commentator on its work remarked, 'having enacted the turning over to communism of the Chinese peasants, the company promptly applied the process to itself' (Ritchie (ed.), p. 12). Reorganized as a collective, Joint Stock shared responsibility for all aspects of its work equally among playwrights, directors, performers, and administrators. Often beginning from company research, improvisation, and workshop sessions, Joint Stock's productions and principles resembled those of Joan Littlewood and Theatre Workshop, strongly influencing a number of contemporary dramatists, Caryl Churchill in particular. William Gaskill recorded that the company's methods offered a way of realizing fully, at last, ideals he had first encountered in the work of Brecht's Berliner Ensemble almost twenty years earlier. As he suggested, Joint Stock's work after *Fanshen* illustrated particularly clearly a coalescence of politics and practices—also evident elsewhere in 1970s theatre—which Brecht's example had originally done much to encourage.

David Hare's other plays were on the whole less committed to revolutionary methods, or to revolutionary politics. A collaboration with Howard Brenton, *Pravda: A Fleet Street Comedy* (National, 1985), examined journalism's 'perpetual distortion of the truth' (II. iv) in ways more typical of his sustained concern with the lies and deceit of English public life. Like most playwrights in the 1970s, Hare was troubled by a sense of widespread national decline, with public mendacity one of its darker symptoms. In *Knuckle* (Comedy Theatre, 1974), he used a *film noir* plot to emphasize ubiquitous sleaziness behind the façades of the City of London and the supposedly cultured suburbs. Each was revealed as part of 'a jampot for swindlers and cons and racketeers', leaving 'words like honour and loyalty . . . now just a joke' (viii; ii). Declining honour and decency were similarly explored in *Plenty* (National, 1978) and in the television play *Licking Hitler* (BBC, 1978), which showed the origins in wartime propaganda of a 'steady impoverishment of the people's ideals' and of a 'thirty-year-old deep corrosive national habit of lying' (lxxiv). Later in his long, successful career Hare's interests in public lying continued, naturally enough, to concentrate on the media. *Amy's View* (National, 1997), for example, examined pressures on honesty experienced by a film and television director. In the last of a trilogy of plays examining England 'trapped in historical decline', *The Absence of War* (National, 1993), Hare presciently portrayed a Labour Party whose ideals are completely subordinated to the demands of its media image, leaving its leaders 'not allowed to say anything . . . working at speeches . . . covering up for what's really gone wrong' (II. ix).

As well as moving away from the shock or 'nihilism' marking Portable's early productions, Hare generally grew readier—unlike Edward Bond—to express social and political issues through the life of the individual. He talked in the late 1970s of trying to 'show the English their history' reflected in 'the extraordinary intensity of people's personal despair', and later plays such as *A Map of the World* (National, 1983) strongly emphasized the interrelation of private and public life (Itzin, pp. 332–3). David Edgar likewise suggested in 1984 that drama should concentrate on 'recognisable people with recognisable concerns', allowing audiences to 'recognize the characters from the inside, but be able . . . to look at how these individual journeys were defined by the collective journey of an epoch' (*Second Time as Farce*, p. 172). Edgar's own journey as a playwright had followed a path similar to those of Hare and Brenton in the previous decade, beginning with work for another small touring company, General Will. Most of its productions were designed for factories or other unconventional venues, using a strong agit-prop idiom to address issues such as the Common Market, or the building of Concorde. Later in the 1970s, Edgar moved on to work for larger theatres in a style he defined as social realism, detailed in its explorations of general principles and individual psychologies. His adaptation for the RSC, *The Jail Diary of Albie Sachs* (1978), was in this way both a broad attack on South Africa's apartheid policies and a close analysis of the effects of imprisonment on a character gaoled for resisting them. Typically, too, Edgar presented gaolers as well as prisoner in some psychological detail.

Similar breadth appeared even in plays closer to his earlier agit-prop idiom, such as *Our Own People* (Half-Moon, 1977). Directly attacking racist treatment of immigrant workers by both unions and management, Edgar nevertheless provided motives and histories for all the factions and characters involved, regardless of guilt or innocence. *Destiny* (RSC, 1976) likewise analysed adversaries of socialism as closely as its advocates. Growing 1970s support for the extreme Right is carefully retraced in the play to anxieties about immigration, the economy, the decline of traditional Conservatism—in general, to a feeling that England, after the collapse of the empire, has become 'seedy, drab, | Locked in the dreams of glories she once had' (I. iv). *Maydays* (RSC 1983) employed similar historical depth and breadth in examining the lost dreams of the Left. Though concentrating on a few epoch-defining individual journeys, Edgar used the capacious stage of the newly opened Barbican Centre to present a very wide range of characters. Most are socialists forced to adapt or abandon their convictions when faced with the injustices of Soviet communism, the Hungarian rising in 1956, the defeat of the Paris revolution in 1968, and ultimately the appearance of a powerful new Tory party under Margaret Thatcher at the end of the 1970s.

The Tory's rise to power forced other playwrights on the Left to wonder how effective their 1970s work could really have been. David Hare worried in 1978 that 'consciousness has been raised in this country for a good many years now and we seem further from radical political change than at any time in my life' (Itzin, p. 331). Failure to initiate real change suggested to a number of writers and critics that political drama had tried to raise the right sort of consciousness in the wrong sort of places, and that playwrights moving from alternative companies to established theatres might not have been following a sensible direction. Naturally, this was a move nevertheless defended by some of the playwrights involved. Trevor Griffiths stressed the need for 'strategic penetrations' of central cultural institutions in order to direct the resources they offered—the 'space, time, skill and technology' which Edward Bond admired in the National Theatre[2]—into a drama of social and political commitment (Itzin, p. 165). In discussing work for the National, Howard Brenton likewise explained that 'social action' could not be represented on the scale he sought with fewer than ten actors, claiming that 'with fifteen you can describe whole countries, whole classes, centuries' (Itzin, p. 187). Yet Brenton also acknowledged that determination to 'use the National facilities', without sharing in its 'concept', left him—along with his director David Hare and their cast and crew—merely part of 'an armoured charabanc full of people parked within the National walls' when they worked there in 1976 (Bull, *Political Dramatists*, p. 29).

When Brenton returned in 1980, it was to sound an uneasily metatheatrical note in the very first line of *The Romans in Britain*: 'Where the fuck are we?' As well as its immediate relevance within the play, the question had a certain resonance for Brenton himself, back in another charabanc, its armour soon to be severely tested by the furore surrounding the play. In this instance and others, adversarial, armoured attitudes to established theatres were perhaps less than ideal for relations with their audiences, adding too much fuel to left-wing dramatists' urge to shock—or, as Brenton once expressed it, to throw 'Petrol Bombs through the proscenium arch' (Bull, *Political Dramatists*, p. 16). Shock and confrontation could undermine audiences' complacency, without gaining their sympathy, impeding the very consciousness-raising and improved political understanding so important for the dramatists concerned. If any change in political thinking occurred, it may eventually have been most apparent in the dramatists' own. In the later 1970s and 1980s,

---

[2] See p. 286, above.

the work of Hare, Edgar, and eventually even Brenton generally grew less radical, and closer to the established 'concept' and aims of the National and the RSC.

John McGrath had his own answer to that opening question in *The Romans in Britain*, famously remarking that he would 'rather have a bad night in Bootle' than an audience in the National Theatre (Bull, *Political Dramatists*, p. 19). Following directions more or less opposite to those described above, his career had taken him by 1970, if not quite to Bootle, at any rate nearby. After an early association with the Royal Court, and the staging of relatively conventional plays such as *Events while Guarding the Bofors Gun* (1966) and *Bakke's Night of Fame* (1968) at Hampstead, McGrath decisively turned away from London theatres and from conventional dramatic forms. Late in 1969, he began work at the Liverpool Everyman with the director Alan Dossor, a fellow admirer of Joan Littlewood, and of Brecht. McGrath adapted Brecht's *The Caucasian Chalk Circle*, relocating it in Liverpool, and went on in original plays such as *Soft or a Girl* (1971) and *Fish in the Sea* (1972) to use local history, local issues, and sometimes a rock band to draw a broad popular audience back to the theatre.

Music, topical political commentary, and a cabaret style of performance also contributed to performance styles developed in productions with 7:84, the company he helped to set up in 1971. Its work over the next decade or so followed principles McGrath summarized in *A Good Night Out: Popular Theatre—Audience, Class and Form* (1981): generally, that if many natural and necessary spectators of left-wing drama might never go near a conventional theatre, then plays must be taken to them, and in styles as entertaining, accessible, and immediately relevant as possible. Sympathetic and educative in its attitude to audiences, McGrath's political drama could hardly have been further from Brenton's petrol bombs, nor moved further from metropolitan theatres. Productions such as *Lay-Off* (1975), dealing with the contemporary threat of multinational corporations, were taken by 7:84 to factories, working men's clubs, community centres, and university campuses throughout England. A separate branch of the company, set up in 1973, enjoyed even greater success in Scotland: perhaps, McGrath reflected, because of stronger socialist traditions north of the border, or because 'the public life of any "subject" nation' encourages 'Utopian speculations' in its politics (*Naked Thoughts*, p. 187). McGrath's later work in Scotland in the 1980s and 1990s at any rate sustained an unswerving commitment to post-1968 idealism, unusual in the work of fellow left-wing playwrights in England at the time.

John Arden's later career followed a similar path, intersecting with McGrath's in the early 1970s. In 1972 7:84 toured Arden's *The Ballygombeen Bequest*, along with a McGrath adaptation, *Serjeant Musgrave Dances On*. This updated Arden's late 1950s play to reflect the first of the 1970s miners' strikes and the recent 'Bloody Sunday' massacre in Northern Ireland. Later, 7:84 were to receive an odd invitation to perform *outside* the National. Comparably, in 1972, Arden engaged in a strange street performance of his own, just outside another of London's main theatres, the Aldwych. With his collaborator Margaretta D'Arcy, he picketed the RSC's rehearsal of their play *The Island of the Mighty* in protest at what they considered the company's politically neutering interpretation. Not surprisingly, Arden and D'Arcy soon departed, like McGrath, as far as possible from London theatre, and often from conventional dramatic styles. Most of their work in later years was in the west of Ireland, sometimes in modes scarcely stageable in established theatres. The six-part *Non-Stop Connolly Show*, for example, first produced at the Irish Trades Union Congress in 1975, dramatized the life of the union leader James Connolly in a range of theatrical forms whose full performance took more than twenty-four hours. Like McGrath's, Arden's career suggested that the radicalism of the early 1970s was more readily sustainable outside established theatres, and even outside England itself.

Another genuine radical, Howard Barker, was also in part an exile from metropolitan stages. The RSC produced many of his plays, but invariably in its smaller auditoria—often in the studio space in the Barbican Centre, the Pit—or on one occasion in a season of work banned from television production. Powerfully and unusually imagined, Barker's characters appealed particularly strongly to actors: in 1988, a group of them formed a new company, the Wrestling School, specifically to perform his plays. Managements of established theatres, and their audiences, sometimes found his writing less congenial. This may have been inevitable, given Barker's belief that 'to continually undermine the expected is the only way to really alter people's perceptions', and that this might best be achieved by breaking 'limits of tolerance' both in the author's own imagination and in the outlook of audiences (Trussler (ed.), p. 190; Shepherd and Womack, p. 355). In one way, Barker's tactics resembled those used by the *Lay-By* playwrights in the early 1970s to shock audiences into awareness of social and political decline in contemporary England. Yet Barker was more unremitting in emphasizing cruelty, decadence, pain, and treachery, and often more bizarre. Dislike of naturalism and a preference he expressed for 'events that are metaphorical and not commonplace' introduced strong elements of fantasy into his work, sometimes making it difficult to decipher (Itzin, p. 250).

Typically, *Downchild* (RSC, 1985) highlighted England's readiness to 'rot down like a marrow, collapsing inwards, like a corpse' by means of a darkly surreal plot, featuring hauntings, a lurid fantasy trial, odd sex scenes, and a baby casually purchased and then callously thrown over a cliff (II. iii). *Fair Slaughter* (Royal Court, 1977) was similarly surreal, depicting a British soldier who acquires the severed hand of Trotsky's train-driver while fighting in Russia in 1920 and keeps it in a bottle throughout a later career as a music-hall artist and political activist. Eventually, he flees prison in an attempt to return the hand to Russia which gets no further than the South Downs. Such narratives shared the dark, warping vision of Jacobean drama Barker occasionally adapted for the modern theatre. At times, they were still closer to the Grand Guignol manner of horror films, as if a decadent England were dreaming through problems too profound or troubling, too close to the limits of imagination and tolerance, to be represented in any other way. Projection of contemporary stresses into powerful parables and visions made Barker, with Edward Bond, the leading political poet in late twentieth-century English theatre, though with scant reward from critics or audiences in England. Like Arden and McGrath, he was sometimes more appreciated outside his own country: symptomatically, *Birth on a Hard Shoulder* (1980) was premièred in Stockholm.

Barker's debauched Restoration setting in *Victory* (Royal Court, 1983) offered especially effective metaphors for the altered outlooks and new business pragmatism—or cynicism—of the early Thatcher years. The politics of the Right were further examined in 1980s plays such as *The Loud Boy's Life* (RSC, 1980). Like Edgar's *Destiny*, this showed general 'rotting' in English life contributing to the rise of an extreme right-wing figure resembling Enoch Powell. More often, Barker's 1980s drama focused on rottenness and disillusion spreading through the politics of the Left. Described by Barker as a 'final piece on the Wilson era', *Downchild* endowed all its politicians with spectacular lubricity, complete lack of morality or ideals, and ready connivance in England's ruination by class or business factions powerful enough to override elected government (Trussler (ed.), p. 195). Politicians at a Labour Party conference in *A Passion in Six Days* (Sheffield Crucible, 1983) likewise admit they have ceased to care about the population of a 'scarred and scalded land', or about socialism, offering only more 'rotting decencies and murdered hope' in place of ideals (iii). Barker, in other words, expressed like Edgar in *Maydays* a thoroughgoing disillusion with the progress, or lack of it, made by the Left since the war. In the work of many of the dramatists discussed above, this kind of disillusion had begun to be apparent well before the 1980s began. Revolutionary idealism inspired in 1968 faded rapidly in the worsening economic climate of the next decade, leaving the weakness of the Labour Party and the profound intransigence of the political situation in England only too bleakly apparent.

Quoted earlier, Howard Brenton was already suggesting the impossibility of revolution, or even of radical change, in *Weapons of Happiness* in 1976. Barrie Keeffe's *Gimme Shelter* (Soho Poly, 1975–7) likewise stressed the hopelessness of any 'dream that . . . things, this England . . . 1976 . . . can be changed' (p. 94). David Hare delivered the same opinion around the same time, in *Teeth 'n' Smiles* (Royal Court, 1975). Encountering unchanging, unshakeable class prejudices at a Cambridge ball, Hare's rock band conclude that 'the acid dream is over' and that 'if there was going to be a revolution it would have happened by now' (iii). Later in the 1970s, and thereafter, disappointed political hopes often turned into half-sceptical nostalgia for the period in which they had so vividly been raised. In *Commitments* (Bush, 1980), Dusty Hughes looked back half-approvingly and half-critically on revolutionary allegiances and radical new attitudes surviving into the early 1970s, and on some of the theatre they inspired. David Edgar's *Mary Barnes* (Birmingham Rep., 1978) likewise examined the romantic, chaotic aspect of late 1960s

idealism, but also the scale of its imagination and of what it sometimes achieved, epitomized in the psychiatric work of R. D. Laing.
Characters in Edgar's *That Summer* (Hampstead, 1987), set during
the 1984 miners' strike, similarly acknowledge the 'silliness and
grandiosity and triviality' of the 1960s, but remain sympathetic to the
decade's 'revolutionary changes in the way we spoke and sang and
reached out to each other', and resentful of Thatcherite attempts to
write off these changes in the 'bleak, mean times' that followed (II. ii).

Willy Russell also explored legacies of the 1960s, and their
conflicts with mean times and middle-aged conformities, in *One for
the Road* (Lyric Hammersmith, 1987) and in his hit comedy *Shirley
Valentine* (Liverpool Everyman, 1986). But the real laureate of
1960s idealism and its loss was Stephen Poliakoff. Much of his best
work was written in the later 1970s, a time he described as 'grey
years when the last residue of sixties optimism was quickly fading'
(p. ix). Though set in the First World War, *Clever Soldiers*
(Hampstead, 1974) was clearly contemporary in its portrayal of
fading optimism. Characters believe in 'freedom for all', and that
'there's no limit to what can happen now', only to find that before
long 'everything's back in place. The holiday's over' (I. vii; II. vii). In
City Sugar (Bush, 1975) a disc jockey likewise recalls that 'ten years
ago, five years ago even . . . things were very different', contrasting
'the golden days of 1967 when London was alive and wriggling and
bursting at the seams' with the 'mindless' numbness he finds among
teenagers now listening to his station (II. ii; I. v). *Hitting Town* (Bush,
1975) shows this numbness extending from concrete urban landscapes into the 'grey and defeated, and miserable' young people
inhabiting them (vi). This background appears still greyer in
Strawberry Fields (National, 1977) and *Shout across the River* (RSC,
1978), darkened by 'the shadow of unemployment and recession'
which Poliakoff later described extending into 'the terrible bleakness
of the early eighties'. Though accurate, even prescient, in its portrayal of social conditions, as Poliakoff suggested *Shout across the
River* at times 'violently breaks free of any trace of social realism,
moving into a more heightened and sensual world' (p. xii). Several of
his other plays also developed this heightened vision, as though his
drama sought compensation, in its own imaginativeness, for all the
vitality that urban life had drained out of its numbed characters.

Unusual, slightly surreal elements ensured that Poliakoff's plays, not unlike Howard Barker's, undermined the expected and jolted audiences out of any easy acquiescence with the 'mean times' they addressed.

*

Some nostalgia for the 1960s was inevitable during the grey years that followed. Playwrights also had pressing reasons for looking back to the experience of the Second World War. Like other genres, drama had to do what it could to deal with the immense 'negative revelation' of the war for morality and humanity. Edward Bond showed how strongly this need was felt in the 1960s, both by paralleling an older character's war recollections with contemporary violence in *Saved*, and by later revealing the source of the play's most disturbing episode in wartime experience of his own. The scene of the baby, stoned to death in the park, derived from his memories of an equally unnatural incident, Bond explained: an occasion during the war when he found that the trees in a local park had been entirely stripped of their leaves by the blast from a bomb. *Saved* was instrumental in opening the English stage to new, uncensored forms of violence and shock. In recalling the play's imaginative origins, Bond confirmed how deeply, often covertly, the war continued to influence later decades, forcing new darkness and destructiveness into the vision of the period's literature. Like Bond in *Saved*, several other dramatists emphasized relations between the blackness of the past and bleak conditions in the present. In *Greek* (Half Moon, 1980), Steven Berkoff retraced some of the origins of an 'emotional plague' in contemporary English society to the 'pictures of Auschwitz . . . | thousands of bodies like spaghetti all entwined' which the play's characters recall (Author's Note; II. iv). 'Mountains of gold teeth and hair and the millions boiled down for soap' (I. xvi) also figured as a background to the madness Peter Barnes depicted in *The Ruling Class* (Nottingham Playhouse, 1968), and as a principal subject in *Laughter* (Royal Court, 1978). Like Barnes in the latter play, several dramatists explored the moral implications of the Holocaust directly, or sought to explain how the Nazi's atrocities could have been allowed to occur. In *Good* (RSC, 1981), for example, the Scottish playwright C. P. Taylor showed a 'good' man too bound up in private ambition and the minutiae of everyday life ever to grasp fully the growing evil of his work for the Nazis.

Playwrights on the Left also needed to examine the war's implications for contemporary British politics. In particular, they had to challenge the 'consensus' Harold Hobson considered still 'generally assumed' in 1974: that 'in May, 1940, England found a man who could, and did, save her', and that this man was an arch-Conservative, Winston Churchill (Lloyd Evans and Lloyd Evans (eds.), p. 200). Impatient as ever with 'consensus' and the establishment, Joe Orton had recently offered a different view of 'the hero of 1940' (II) in *What the Butler Saw* (Queens, 1969). This included a grotesque description of the removal of parts of Churchill's statue, shattered in an explosion, from the corpse of an innocent passer-by. Several contemporary playwrights were similarly determined to explode Churchill's myth and excise his influence from the body politic. Charles Wood began this process in his Second World War play *Dingo* (Royal Court, 1967). A former soldier himself, Wood did not share straightforwardly in the anti-establishment feelings of the 1960s, or in the anti-militarism influentially expressed for the decade by Joseph Heller's novel *Catch-22* (1960). He explained instead that he was 'anti-war but pro-army' (J. R. Taylor, p. 63). In later drama such as *H* (National, 1969), set at the time of the Indian Mutiny, or in his much-admired television play about the Falklands war, *Tumbledown* (BBC, 1987), Wood investigated sympathetically the nature of courage and the morality of military action generally.

Dingo was nevertheless firmly anti-heroic. Regular experience of 'mates cut to chunks' leaves soldiers disgusted by ideas of the 'romantic and glorious', and thoroughly fed up with being 'pissed on . . . by Mr Churchill' (II. i, ii, v). Affirmative views of the Second World War, or of military glory, were further undermined by a performance mode using farce, slapstick, travesty, and the grotesque. Howard Barker considered Wood's play 'seminal' (Trussler (ed.), p. 191). Much of his own drama followed it in style, and *All Bleeding* (RSC, 1979) portrayed Churchill in identical terms, as a defender of class hierarchies and wartime business profiteering. A still more determined attack appeared in Howard Brenton's *The Churchill Play* (Nottingham Playhouse, 1974), set futuristically among political prisoners in a British concentration camp. The inmates stage a play dramatizing Churchill's vicious treatment of the Welsh miners in 1910, along with other episodes which emphasize—much in the spirit of Angus Calder's influential history, *The People's War* (1969)—that victory in 1945 was owed not to any single leader, but to the collective efforts of the population as a whole.

Projected images and recorded speeches in *The Churchill Play* provided a wider history of post-war Britain, working back towards wartime through references to 'Macmillan. Profumo. Gaitskell. Eden. Suez . . . Attlee. Rationing. Bevin. Coal fields nationalized. Election 1945' (IV). Many of the same figures and episodes appeared in Edgar's *Maydays*, beginning from an opening scene set on May Day, 1945. Edgar had earlier used the end of the war as the starting point for *Destiny*, and for *O Fair Jerusalem* (Birmingham Rep, 1975). For playwrights, like historians, the war provided an obvious watershed, and an appropriate point to begin any account of life in the later twentieth century. Yet it was often envisaged more particularly, and more affirmatively, by left-wing writers: as a time of transition towards socialist optimism, experienced with unique intensity at its end. As well as examining the black moral implications of Nazism in *Good*, in *And a Nightingale Sang* (Newcastle Playhouse, 1977) C. P. Taylor showed the resilience of the domestic population in enduring the war, and the renewal of collective purpose and national unity at the time. Stephen Lowe took a similar view in *Touched* (Nottingham Playhouse, 1977). Though the play begins with radio commentary on the discovery of the concentration camps, it goes on to explore more cheerfully the months between the end of hostilities in Europe (VE Day) and in the Far East (VJ Day). This period is reflected in the experience of three sisters who have struggled to survive the war and appreciate the chance to celebrate at its end. Literally, in the case of pregnant Sandra, they are ready to 'give birth to the future'—one apparently full of political promise (III. ii). The landslide Labour victory of 1945 seems to suggest 'the overwhelming desire of the British people to free themselves from the sleep of Capitalism', and that 'after all that evil, good's bound to come . . . something beautiful. Clean. Jerusalem' (III. i). Still looking happily into the future, Lowe's characters reflect on VJ day that they 'never dreamt [they] could have such a day' and that 'you'd think you could see thousands of miles' (IV. iii).

Similar nostalgia for the spirit of wartime figured in the work of other contemporary playwrights. Alan Bennett was probably the most comprehensively nostalgic dramatist in the period—significantly, also one of the most popular—looking at various phases of national loss and decline in several of his plays. *Enjoy* (Vaudeville, 1980), for example, parodied the work of the heritage industry, showing the fading authenticities of Northern working-class life preserved by transferring an entire household into a living museum. Portraying a Kim Philby figure, *The Old Country* (Queen's, 1977) worried about recent betrayal and decline in Britain's world role. The Labour MP in *Getting On* (Queen's, 1971) focused more domestic anxieties about how far the war and the subsequent founding of the Welfare State had been forgotten in later years. Bennett's most comprehensive treatment of war, memory, and decline appeared in *Forty Years On* (Apollo, 1968). In the form of a school pageant, interspersed with the headmaster's recollections, *Forty Years On* plays out half-nostalgically and half-parodically 'the decline of authority, the decay of standards . . . slow collpase' in twentieth-century England generally, but with a particular focus on the Second World War (II). Like Lowe in *Touched*, Bennett recalls the confident belief that the war would see 'the end of the businessmen, the property developers' and of 'the England of Halifax who went hunting with Goering' (II).

Wartime optimism was also strongly recalled in Hugh Whitemore's *Breaking the Code* (Guildford, 1986). Whitemore's interests were generally historical, or biographical in plays such as *Stevie* (Vaudeville, 1977), a popular treatment of the life of Stevie Smith. *Breaking the Code* shows the mathematician and Bletchley Park cryptographer Alan Turing reflecting, on an 'extraordinary . . . wonderfully sunny day' of inspired war work, that he will never again experience such affirmative feelings for life—'never again a moment like that' (p. 78). Later events in *Breaking the Code* confirm the transience of his brilliantly illumining moment. The uniqueness of wartime's sense of purpose and the inevitability of its loss were also emphasized in some of the other plays mentioned above. In Lowe's *Touched*, Sandra's pregnancy turns out to be a phantom one, symbolic of hopes which may have been unrealistic in 1945, and were at any rate never entirely fulfilled thereafter. Post-war disillusion was focused especially sharply by David Hare in *Plenty* (1978). Set in another brilliantly sunny landscape, on VE day in rural France, its concluding scene shows Hare's heroine Susan enjoying undreamed-of relief from wartime work with the Resistance. Her delight is heightened by her certainty, now the war is over, that 'we will improve our world . . . there will be days and days and days like this'. Poised on the brilliantly illumined stage of the National Theatre, she stared happily out into the auditorium towards a future Hare's late 1970s audience knew only too well had never come into being.

The inverted chronology of *Plenty* had in any case already confirmed how deeply her optimism was doomed. Earlier scenes had shown her progressive disillusion in the post-war years, unable ever to recover the committed idealism she experienced with the Resistance. Hare's ironies in *Plenty* helped to make that last scene a defining moment in the period's left-wing theatre, clarifying why playwrights looked back so regularly to the war and its conclusion. In discussing *Plenty*, critics such as Peter Womack emphasized the 'unique cultural *authority*' and 'primal moment of definition' offered by the passage through shadow to purpose at the end of the war—'the last time, it seems, for good or ill, when the nation was a positive entity' (Shepherd and Womack, p. 324). In one way, looking back on the optimism of this time allowed dramatists to recover an ideal socialist vision, unsullied by the Labour Party's later limitations. It also allowed them to force on audiences bitter recognition of the distance between ideal and reality: of the scale of failures in later years; the extent to which potential had been wasted and hopes for an improved world allowed to leak away.

Hare's later plays sometimes traced further encounters between wartime idealism and tangled, disillusioning post-war life. Significantly entitled, *The Absence of War* shows a Labour leader motivated to 'fifty years' honest endeavour' by his mother's death in an air raid on South London, only to find that by the 1990s his commitment 'no longer meets the needs of the day' (II. xiii). Appropriately, *The Absence of War* opens on Remembrance Day, with a reflection that if all the soldiers who had died fighting for Britain were to form a column, it would stretch from the London cenotaph all the way to Edinburgh. A similar image appears in Howard Barker's *Birth on a Hard Shoulder*, in which a character envisages 'a line of ghosts behind [him] reaching two abreast, beyond Dunkirk, the Somme . . . decent Englishmen' (II. iv). Ghostly lines in all these plays, stretching back towards the political and cultural authority of the past, moved contemporary drama in two distinct directions. As a character remarks in another of Barker's plays, *All Bleeding* (RSC, 1979), 'social paralysis . . . [and] capitalist anaesthetics . . . make people hark back to the so-called simple issues of the war' (ix). In one way, political dramatists' harking back was a moderate version of the shock tactics they so often employed, jolting audiences out of contemporary anaesthesia by reminding them how positively their lives had been anticipated, and struggled for, during and just after the war.

Yet in another way, as Barker warns, regular retrospection risked representing in itself a form of anaesthesia, paralysis, or retreat. It showed progressive, left-wing drama engaging reverse gear after colliding with the frustrations of the later 1970s, or even returning to the more muted political idiom of the late 1950s. Playwrights once again seemed less inclined to look ahead than to look back in anger: like Arnold Wesker, 'talking about Jerusalem' in his late 1950s trilogy, their visions of the future turned increasingly into regret for the lost idealism of earlier decades. Like the angel described in Walter Benjamin's 'Theses on the Philosophy of History', in trying to move forward left-wing drama seemed unable, by the late 1970s, to drag its attention away from the past. It added in this way to Jeremy Paxman's definition of the English in the later twentieth century as 'a people marching backwards into the future', almost regardless of differences in their political persuasions.[3] Left-wing writers obviously had little reason to share in conservative laments for the last of a traditional England. Yet this disposed them to look back all the more regretfully on what seemed various lost chances—in 1945, or perhaps in 1968—for its absolute termination through truly decisive political reform.

*

In the still harsher atmosphere of the 1980s, while poets and novelists sometimes resumed modes of satire and political commentary, left-wing playwrights seemed more than ever engaged in self-doubt

[3] See p. 48, above.

and withdrawal. This often extended the questioning of their own principles and practices discussed earlier. Edgar's *Maydays* followed Hare's *Plenty* in showing post-war potentials betrayed as much by socialism's failures as the actions of its adversaries. In *A Map of the World* (1983) Hare raised still more serious doubts about sustaining socialist politics in Britain, and elsewhere in the West, at a time when people apparently believed only in 'money or sex or motor cars' (I). Howard Brenton's *Bloody Poetry* (Foco Novo, 1984) projected similar doubts into a historical context, using the lives and loves of Byron and Shelley as a focus for contemporary stresses—even for Brenton's own, as a political writer. 'There must be a revolution in England', *Bloody Poetry* concludes, while also demonstrating that the politics, lifestyle, and writing even of the most revolutionary authors seem very unlikely ever to bring one about (II. ii).

In his introduction to a later play, *Greenland* (Royal Court, 1988), Brenton confirmed that the 'reactionary, mean England' shown defeating 'Utopian dreams' in *Bloody Poetry* directly reflected the disillusioned mood of the 1980s. The first act of *Greenland* itself is set at a still more reactionary moment, on the day of the Conservatives' third successive general election victory in 1987. Characters still clinging to hopes for 'a new world . . . a new Jerusalem' find only partial fulfilment in a fantasy second act, set in a future utopia which does as much to challenge as satisfy their original idealism (I. vii). Brenton recalled that 'a generation dreaming of a beautiful utopia' had been 'kicked awake'—forced into active political awareness—by the events of 1968 (Trussler (ed.), p.97). Twenty years later, on the evidence of *Greenland*, dreams of distant utopias seemed once again the only outlet for socialist aspiration, and even those had apparently lost much of their original beauty and allure.

Left-wing drama faced still more immediate challenges by the mid-1980s. Throughout the previous decade, the alternative theatre circuit's funding was mostly sustained or increased, allowing continuing support for political drama and for new writing generally. During the early 1980s, alternative companies and venues began to be seriously affected by cuts in Arts Council and local authority spending.[4] In 1984 7:84 (England), for example, had its grant cut altogether, and ceased performing soon afterwards. The activities of

---

[4] Theatre funding in the period is further discussed in Ch. 14, below.

many other alternative and left-wing companies were curtailed, or ended, in following years. In larger theatres, worries about budgets and the growing need for business sponsorship often led to reluctance to support left-wing drama, or to risk contemporary writing of any kind. Dwindling in confidence and resources, the politically oriented theatre evolving since 1956, and flourishing after 1968, might have been expected to expire altogether after the mid-1980s. There were those who thought it had. Peter Hall—director of the National Theatre from 1973 to 1988—suggested that what he called the ' "whither Britain" school of drama' did not last beyond 1984 (Appleyard, p. 9). Dominic Dromgoole considered that 'the new direction for new writing' in the 1990s—often produced under his direction at the Bush—included 'no politics, no naturalism, no journalism, no issues. In its place, character, imagination, wit, sexuality, skin and the soul' (p. 241).

Yet the mid-1980s were in many ways a point of transition rather than termination. Several of Dromgoole's 1990s dramatists continued to imply criticism of the decade's politics—like 'New Generation' poets at the time[5]—by registering its intimate, disturbing pressures on the skin, soul, or sexuality of the individual. In the later 1980s and 1990s, several of the writers mentioned above continued to move on, or back, from the direct political polemic of the 1970s towards broader—though more muted—modes of commentary redeveloped since the mid-1950s. Examining church, judiciary, politicians, and the state, David Hare's *Racing Demon* (1990), *Murmuring Judges* (1991), and *The Absence of War* (1993) provided a theatrical 'condition of England' trilogy for the National Theatre in the 1990s. In *The Shape of the Table* (National, 1990) and *Pentecost* (RSC, 1994) David Edgar offered a kind of 'whither Europe' drama, examining what he called 'the extraordinary resilience and tenacity of various forms of social idealism' even in the rapidly changing political environments of former communist states after 1989 (*Plays: Three*, pp. x–xi). The same territory was also explored by Caryl Churchill in *Mad Forest* (Royal Court, 1990), set during and after the Romanian revolution.

Churchill's work illustrated more generally both continuities and transitions in political theatre late in the century. The style and struc-

[5] See pp. 229–30, above.

ture of her plays, and some of her comments on theatre, each indicated continuity at the level of form, evidence of the lasting legacy of Brecht. 'For writers, directors and actors working in England', she remarked, by the mid-1980s Brecht's ideas had been 'absorbed into the general pool of shared knowledge and attitudes' (Reinelt, p. 86). Non-naturalistic styles, minimal, illustrative scenes, and disjunctive construction no longer seemed as startling or 'cataclysmic' as they had when Brecht's company first visited London thirty years earlier, nor always immediately recognizable as part of his legacy at all. Instead, his modes and ideas had contributed gradually, as a central influence among several others, to the development of what David Edgar called 'a style for the presentation of public life' in English theatre in the latter decades of the century (Itzin, p. 144). Towards its end, in 1998, the *Guardian* drama critic Michael Billington continued to note the lasting effects of ' "Epic theatre", with its emphasis on montage, reason and argument', and of Brecht's 'rigorous aesthetic' and 'belief in the capacity for action and change'(10 Feb., p. 9). These were influences he considered thoroughly absorbed, as Churchill suggested, into the pool of theatrical resources at the time.

Churchill's work—*Serious Money* (Royal Court, 1987) in particular—also showed political theatre moving on, late in the century, to reflect new problems and a society divided less firmly around the old hierarchies of class. Focused by *Look Back in Anger* in 1956, class had long remained a central interest in English theatre, examined by playwrights throughout the late 1950s and 1960s. It was still a principal target of political drama in the 1970s, in David Hare's *Teeth 'n' Smiles* and Trevor Griffiths's *Comedians* (Nottingham Playhouse, 1975) particularly. In the early 1980s, Steven Berkoff's *Decadence* (New End, Hampstead, 1981) continued to portray, or caricature, a society structured 'like a pyramid' (xii). Willy Russell's *Educating Rita* (RSC, 1980) still found much comic potential in familiar class tensions of accent, culture, and outlook, highlighted by a student seeking self-improvement through study with the Open University. Playwrights later in the 1980s, on the other hand, recognized that successive Tory governments had made wealth and money into social determinants still more powerful than class, and directed more of their attention onto satiric targets already being attacked in poetry and fiction at the time. Set in the City of London, quoting the perverse contemporary slogan 'Greed is all right. Greed is healthy' (I), *Serious Money* satirized the brashly monetarist imperatives of Tory policy, highlighted by a plot involving insider dealing, corrupt takeovers, and sinister complicities between government and big business. Churchill also observed, like Salman Rushdie the following year, how far Thatcherite policies had favoured 'the hungry guys with the wrong education'.[6] One of her loutish new stockbrokers emphasizes the change, taunting a smoothly mannered upper-class predecessor with 'new faces in your old square mile, | Making money with a smile, | Just as clever, just as vile' (II).

As well as new faces at the centre of power, the 1980s saw new levels of exclusion at the fringes of society. Widening gaps between serious money and the serious lack of it further ensured that new social divisions were of more pressing concern than the old, pyramidic class system. Forms of social exclusion had already been dramatized in the later 1970s, at a time when economic decline and extensive unemployment were first threatening to create a new underclass. Some of its problems appeared in Stephen Poliakoff's plays, and in Barrie Keeffe's two trilogies, *Barbarians* and *Gimme Shelter* (Soho Poly, 1975–7). *Barbarians* portrayed a group of youths who find city life and schooling 'all fucking hopeless', and crime, the National Front, and the army—though it soon posts them to Belfast —the only available outlets for their frustrated energies (p. 16). *Gimme Shelter* showed even the most violent attacks on the establishment doomed by the unshakeable power of 'them up there, them who dash up and down compromising, keeping the status quo in balance' (p. 94). Keeffe's later plays in the 1980s and 1990s continued to examine gaps between an underclass and 'them up there'. Forms of deprivation, leaving sections of society almost beyond conventional politics, increasingly concerned other dramatists at the time. Peter Flannery's *Our Friends in the North: A History Play* (RSC, 1982) begins with a group of characters whose 'dream of being able to put things right. Get houses built. And hospitals and schools' seems still to belong to the idealistic idiom of 1970s drama, even of Arnold Wesker's late 1950s plays (I. iii). But Flannery's wide-ranging, interconnected stories show the rapid defeat of this dream by comprehensive corruption and greed, tainting the police,

[6] See p. 38, above.

judiciary, industry, and the Labour and Conservative parties throughout the entire country. With conventional channels of action corrupted and effectively closed by factions of power and wealth, Flannery's characters have good reason to feel they 'don't want to join in politics . . . It's just—them up there. And [we're] down here' (I. iii).

Jim Cartwright's *Road* (Royal Court, 1987) also attacked the hardening social divisions of the 1980s. Staging as a promenade confronted audiences unusually directly with characters who have no jobs, whose future has been 'snatched', and whose despair is intense enough—'forcing the brain out of [their] head'—to move action and dialogue into an almost surreal idiom, similar to some of Poliakoff's plays (I). City squalor and social exclusion continued to be reflected by 1990s dramatists such as Jonathan Harvey and Mark Ravenhill, though differently in the work of each. Harvey was typical of 1990s writers Dromgoole considered primarily concerned with private life and relationships. Yet urban stresses continued to be communicated strongly in *Babies* (Royal Court, 1994), for example, in the life of its central figure, a teacher, and in a group of schoolchildren as impoverished, imaginatively and emotionally, as Barrie Keeffe's characters, or, earlier, Edward Bond's in *Saved*. Ravenhill was a more direct and outspoken commentator on the society of the 1990s, satirizing rampant materialism in *Shopping and Fucking* (Royal Court, 1996), like Churchill in *Serious Money*. All the play's relationships are ultimately commercial, offering very little reassurance to the character who wants 'to find out . . . if there are any feelings left' (vii). *Shopping and Fucking* featured telephone sex, simulated homosexual intercourse, and much violence throughout. Along with Sarah Kane's *Blasted*, staged at the Royal Court the previous year, it showed 1990s drama once again using shock tactics to ensure that genuine feelings continued to be experienced at least by its audience—almost as if the theatre had turned back, full circle, to the *Lay-By* idiom first developed a quarter of a century earlier, at the start of the 1970s.[7]

Doug Lucie's plays in the 1980s and 1990s also recalled a whole cycle of political theatre evolving since the idealistic 1960s. Lucie was a more critical elegist of the decade than Stephen Poliakoff. *Progress* (Bush, 1984) traced weaknesses as well as strengths in late

[7] See also p. 378, below.

1960s liberalism—personal and political—revealed by the pressures of later decades. *Fashion* (RSC, 1987) went on to criticize, like Caryl Churchill, a 1980s society which has forgotten that 'fifteen, twenty years ago . . . politics and art were sexy': characters Lucie portrays are no longer much excited by anything apart from 'money and work' (I. ii). A materialist era was further anatomized in *Grace* (Hampstead, 1992), reflecting an England where 'nobody is honest any more' being turned over to the heritage industry, or to US tourists and capital (ii). *Gaucho* (Hampstead, 1994) used a failed Conservative candidate to highlight Thatcherism's creation of 'a culture that is unnatural, that forces people to look for ways out rather than ways in' (vi). Through the figure of a drug dealer—peddling one sort of 'way out'—Lucie nevertheless continued to examine negative influences inseparable from freedom and radicalism surviving since the 1960s.

Set in a Conservative Party advertising agency, *Fashion* showed the Tories successfully representing themselves, in the 1980s, as 'the true radical force' in a country apparently no longer interested in Labour's 'vision of a New Jerusalem' (II. i, iii). *Fashion* emphasized in this way the need for political theatre to review assumptions reaching back through the 1960s to the post-war years so often recalled by left-wing playwrights. David Edgar's *Maydays* opens with a political speech, delivered in the last week of the war, confidently demanding that 'the toiling masses rise to liberate themselves from tyranny, to fashion with their own hands their own New Jerusalem' (I. i). Four decades later, as Lucie suggested—and Edgar went on to show—such visions carried much less conviction. Politicians were unlikely to address 'whither Britain' questions in terms of a journey to a socialist or utopian 'Jerusalem', or even a mass, collective journey by a unified Britain at all. Dammed by the economic obstacles of later decades, post-war hopes for an entirely new society—revivified in the 1960s—had dispersed by the 1980s into a broad range of subsidiary interests and group-specific utopian aspirations. Vertical hierarchies of class—still so significant for Royal Court writers at the start of the period—had been replaced by new gaps between wealth and the underclass, but also by the whole set of lateral divisions of gender, ethnicity, and lifestyle outlined in Chapter 1. Caryl Churchill's work was representative of transitions in the 1980s not only in attacking monetarism and materialism in *Serious Money*, but in addressing, in other plays, gender issues which had become one of several new, modified channels for the political energies of the time.

Mark Ravenhill also emphasized changing, diversifying political commitments and postmodern failures of faith, late in the century, when a character in *Shopping and Fucking* remarks that 'a long time ago there were big stories. Stories so big you could live your whole life in them . . . the Journey to Enlightenments. The March of Socialism. But they all died or the world grew up or grew senile or forgot them, so now we're all making up our own stories. Little stories . . . But we've each got one' (xiii). Disillusioned in *Maydays* with the idea of a New Jerusalem, or a collective March of Socialism, David Edgar likewise located the 'tenacity . . . of social idealism' in a new story. The play's final hope of resisting 'a world that is demonstrably . . . dramatically wrong and mad and unjust and unfair' is centred not on an abstract, alternative Jerusalem (III. vii). Instead, it highlights the actions of women—specifically, those in the peace camp established in 1981 at Greenham Common to protest against the deployment of US nuclear missiles. *Maydays* confirmed in this way a direction often taken by political energies in the last decades of the century. 'The old left is trapped in old ideas', one of Edgar's characters suggests: 'the real revolutionaries in our society are blacks, gays and women' (II. i). Chapter 11 examines these 'revolutionaries' and the importance of their new 'stories' for English theatre at the time.

'Real Revolutionaries':
Politics and the Margins

Like much else in the period's theatre, some of the social 'revolutions' mentioned at the end of Chapter 10 were anticipated by John Osborne in *Look Back in Anger* (1956). Though more interested in issues of class, and a general lack of 'good, brave causes' in 1956, Jimmy Porter does acknowledge—grudgingly—that homosexuals 'seem to have a cause . . . plenty of them do seem to have a revolutionary fire about them, which is more than you can say for the rest of us' (I). This was a cause widely significant for the period's drama, encouraged by strong and long-standing representation of the gay community in the theatre profession. Yet any 'revolutionary fire' had to remain covert for some time after 1956, both on the stage and in society generally. The Wolfenden Report suggested partial decriminalization of homosexuality in 1957, but it was a decade before its recommendations became law, in the Sexual Offences Act of 1967. Gay issues likewise endured a ten-year limbo in the theatre. Homosexuality continued to be defined by the Lord Chamberlain as a 'forbidden subject' in 1957, though he relented significantly at the end of the following year by allowing homosexual characters to be represented on stage, although still within carefully specified limits (Shellard, p. 10).

In practice, oblique references to male homosexuality had figured in many plays earlier in the century, and gay relations had begun to appear more often and more explicitly on the stages of London theatre clubs during the 1950s, the Arts Theatre particularly (Rebellato,

pp. 208, 211). But in the larger theatres, it was only after the abolition of the Lord Chamberlain's office in 1968 that homosexuality
could be presented and explored with much freedom. Not surprisingly, in later years this exploration often included angry reflection
of problems long inflicted on homosexuals by the law. These were
examined, for example, in Alan Bennett's portrayal of a gay Tory
MP in *Getting On* (Queen's Theatre, 1971); in Julian Mitchell's
treatment of public-school homosexuality in *Another Country*
(Greenwich, 1981); in Hugh Whitemore's *Breaking the Code*
(1986), showing Alan Turing's destruction by the police and the
judiciary; and in Paul Godfrey's tracing of the relationship between
Benjamin Britten and Peter Pears in *Once in a While the Odd Thing
Happens* (National, 1990). Critics later in the century also came to
recognize how far the work of gay playwrights before the 1960s had
been shaped by enforced disguise, sublimation, and a whole discourse of hints and obliquities. Loneliness and suppressed emotions
among Terence Rattigan's heterosexual characters, for example,
began to be discussed as a projection of the difficulties of his own
experience as a homosexual.

Despite continuing caution, plays in established theatres did begin
to treat gay experience more explicitly, and eventually more positively, even during the limbo period of the early 1960s. Homosexuality was still only implied—enigmatically but inescapably—in
Rattigan's portrayal of T. E. Lawrence, *Ross* (Theatre Royal, 1960).
Rattigan was more candid in *Man and Boy* (Queen's, 1963), though
unexpectedly critical of dissembling practised by homosexuals in
order to evade public censure and the law. John Osborne viewed dissembling and disguise more affirmatively in *A Patriot for Me* (1965),
developing for the stage—helped by the Royal Court's temporary
adoption of club status—elements of dramatic excitement in the role
play forced on gay characters. Charles Dyer's *Staircase* (RSC, 1966)
was less successful in avoiding censorship, listing in its published text
many changes demanded by the Lord Chamberlain. Despite these
cuts, and the problems Dyer examined—fears of prosecution, furtive
encounters, incomprehension from families, suspicion from society
—*Staircase* offered one of the first affirmative treatments of homosexuality on the modern English stage, warmly portraying an ageing
gay couple and the long relationship they have enjoyed and endured

together. Though darker and more comic, Joe Orton's drama also displayed growing confidence in staging gay relationships—provocatively presented as more natural than heterosexual ones in *Loot* (1966) and several other mid-1960s plays.

Affirmation and re-evaluation of this kind continued to appear throughout the 1970s. Like the decade's left-wing drama, this phase of gay theatre emerged from the expansive liberal atmosphere and 'revolutionary fire' of the late 1960s, and from the new venues and performance opportunities it helped to create. Established in 1970, the Gay Liberation movement encouraged the foundation in 1975 of a fringe company, Gay Sweatshop, dedicated to creating solidarity, changing 'media misrepresentation of homosexuals', and developing 'themes to liberate rather than oppress' (Itzin, p. 235). Performing throughout the new touring circuit of small, alternative venues, the company had an early impact with plays by writers such as Drew Griffiths, Roger Baker, and Noel Greig, treating movingly and straightforwardly material often previously the subject of evasiveness or unease. Gay Sweatshop's work also encouraged several playwrights who moved on to larger theatres, taking the case for acceptance of homosexuality to wider, often more conventional audiences. Michael Wilcox's *Rents* (Traverse and Lyric, 1979 and 1982), for example, presented the gritty realities of survival as a male prostitute on the streets of Edinburgh. Martin Sherman's *Bent* (Royal Court, 1979) showed gay theatre—like much of the political drama considered in Chapter 10—seeking cultural and moral authority by returning to the experiences of the Second World War. Challengingly—sensationally, in the view of many critics—*Bent* redirected towards the gay community some of the strongest of all historical sympathies, showing homosexuals 'treated worse than a jew' in the concentration camps, yet able through the strength of their relationships to transcend the horrors inflicted upon them (I. vi).

In the later 1980s and 1990s, gay experience less often required such challenging affirmation, or even much direct commentary at all. Homosexual relations remained a central issue in Jonathan Harvey's *Babies* (Royal Court, 1994), but only as one aspect—mostly very positive—of the play's wider reflection of contemporary city life. Mark Ravenhill's *Shopping and Fucking* (Royal Court, 1996) used gay sex with similar confidence, though often portraying it disturbingly: like other relationships in the play, it highlighted a society far more shocking in its obsessive materialism than any of its sexual proclivities. Still more confident attitudes appeared in Harvey's male-centred love story *Beautiful Thing* (Bush, 1994), and in Kevin Elyot's *My Night with Reg* (Royal Court, 1994). Though Elyot reflected the AIDS crisis troubling the gay community since the mid-1980s, in other ways his play would have seemed conventionally romantic and unremarkable if the many relationships presented had not been exclusively between male characters. A relaxed, undemonstrative attitude to these relations suggested homosexuality had acquired much of the role Orton seemed so daring in proposing thirty years earlier: as a norm of social behaviour of its own, as valid as any other. Plays in the 1990s such as *My Night with Reg* reflected a society much altered since the 1950s, its new tolerance owed in part to gay theatre's positive images of homosexuality, and to its success in directing understanding on what had so long remained a 'forbidden subject'.

Though never, obviously, an actively forbidden subject, the experience of women seemed in some ways as firmly excluded as gay life from the theatre at the start of the period. Despite the promise of playwrights such as Shelagh Delaney and Ann Jellicoe at the end of the 1950s, opportunities for women dramatists remained scarce in the years that followed. Of the many new plays produced at the Royal Court between 1956 and 1975—around 250—fewer than twenty were by women. 'Plays have mostly been written by and for men for two thousand years', Charlotte Keatley pointed out at the end of the century, in an introduction to *My Mother Said I Never Should* (Contract, Manchester, 1987). Partly as a result, women playwrights often found suitable actors as scarce as supportive theatres. Like Edward Bond, worrying in the 1970s about performers' ill-preparedness for political theatre,[1] Louise Page recorded difficulty in the next decade in finding suitable male actors for her plays—ones able to play subordinate parts, rather than the substantial, controlling ones they had grown used to in conventional drama. Without easy access to performers or stages, women's movements established at the end of the 1960s generally required—like the gay

[1] See pp. 304–5, above.

community at the time—new tactics and new companies to express their interests. Two of the most influential, Women's Theatre Group and Monstrous Regiment, were founded like Gay Sweatshop in the mid-1970s. Along with other fringe groups working at this time, each helped—like Gay Sweatshop—to launch the careers of playwrights who went on to work extensively in the established theatre. The two most successful were Pam Gems, who began writing for the Women's Theatre Company in the mid-1970s, and Caryl Churchill, who worked with Monstrous Regiment around the same period. Divergent paths followed in their later careers exemplify priorities and practices developed by women dramatists during and after the 1970s.

Monstrous Regiment's declared aim was 'to shift consciousness in the area of women's relation to society' by experimenting with old forms and developing new ones to reflect 'the often very dislocated nature of women's experience' (Itzin, p. 274). Experimentation and formal development characterized much of Caryl Churchill's drama, shaped by work with Joint Stock as well as Monstrous Regiment in the later 1970s. Churchill recorded the origins of *Cloud Nine* (1979) in Joint Stock's collaborative methods—in workshop explorations of 'the parallel between colonial and sexual repression', and in company members' recognition that their sexual behaviour still reflected 'very conventional, almost Victorian expectations' (*Plays: One*, pp. 245, 246). Set in Victorian times, in colonial Africa, the first act of *Cloud Nine* uses cross-casting to explore various repressions and constraints, sexual and racial. The colonial officer's wife was played by a man, Churchill explained, 'because she wants to be what men want her to be', and a black servant 'played by a white man because he wants to be what whites want him to be' (p. 245). Setting a second act in a 'present' somehow both twenty-five and a hundred years after the first keeps the conventions of the Victorian period in view, while highlighting new opportunities to escape them through the freer behaviour—heterosexual and homosexual—of the late 1970s. Provocative historical analogies also shaped *Top Girls* (Royal Court, 1982). This showed a Thatcherite businesswoman celebrating promotion with dinner guests including Pope Joan, Patient Griselda, and other legendary women from the distant past. Each character illustrates self-betrayals forced on women if they wish to succeed—or

Fig. 11. Caryl Churchill's *Cloud Nine*, in the 1997 Old Vic revival.

just survive—in societies invariably structured, throughout history, primarily around the interests of men. Both plays, in other words, extended Monstrous Regiment's wish to challenge social conventions through departure from theatrical ones. Peculiar, often hilarious tensions between actor and role in *Cloud Nine*, in particular, forced audiences to consider gender as in part socially constructed—as a type of behaviour learned and performed, rather than altogether innate.

Churchill continued to discard or modify stage conventions in her later work. *Fen* (Joint Stock, 1983), for example, was generally realistic—even documentary—in its account of life among the rural working class, yet it contained a scene showing a suicide who returns from the other side of death to describe its loneliness and console her lover. Similar freedom and imagination often marked the work of a new generation of women dramatists emerging in the 1980s, including Louise Page, Bryony Lavery, and Sarah Daniels. Surprisingly often, their plays followed exactly Churchill's departure from realist convention in *Fen*, showing characters who return freely and easily from the dead. In *Salonika* (Royal Court, 1982), Louise Page portrayed an ageing woman searching a beach in Greece for her husband's grave, only to find him returning from beyond it to explain his death in the First World War. In *Origin of the Species* (Monstrous Regiment, 1984), Bryony Lavery showed the return to contemporary Yorkshire of a female ancestor of the human species, dead for four million years. In *Two Marias* (Theatre Centre Women's Company, 1989) Lavery illustrated the power of maternal feelings, focused on a girl killed in a road accident, but drawn back to post-mortem life and conversation with her mother. In *Nothing Compares to You* (Birmingham Rep, 1995) Lavery introduced mythic Norse creatures who helpfully remove from the mortal world characters unable to endure it any longer. A similar exit is suggested to Sarah Daniels's heroine in *Ripen Our Darkness* (Royal Court, 1981). On the brink of death by suicide, after a life 'at best monotonous, and at worst unbearably painful', she is offered a final escape from 'that war-ridden shit-heap men call earth', through entry to a feminist heaven (xiii).

Its appeal helps account for regular interest in post- or transmortem experience in women's drama. Like Howard Brenton in

Greenland,[2] women playwrights showed utopian thinking, frustrated in contemporary society, naturally seeking a new heaven or new earth entirely beyond the 'shit-heap' of daily reality. In *The Grace of Mary Traverse* (Royal Court, 1985), Timberlake Wertenbaker offered a kind of parable for this urge. Her heroine frees herself personally from the constraints of eighteenth-century society, but can do nothing to reform its wider abuses. This leaves wishes for a juster society, or an ultimate 'grace, somewhere', realizable only in a 'new world', not among the institutions of the existing one (IV. ii, i). Like 'magic realist' novelists discussed in Chapter 18, below, women dramatists found in new worlds beyond ordinary realism both an imaginative alternative to a male-dominated society, and also an opportunity to criticize its abuses from detached, inviolate perspectives.

Pam Gems exemplified the other mode principally practised by contemporary women's drama: criticism of society through conventionally realistic portrayal of its injustices. Gems provided an early, influential model in *Dusa, Fish, Stas and Vi* (Hampstead, 1976). This examined stresses experienced by a representative set of characters living together in a bedsit—a mother figure, Dusa; a disturbed teenager, Vi; Stas, who uses sex to achieve financial security; Fish, a committed socialist and feminist. Fish suffers most in the end, her suicide note summing up questions raised throughout about relations with men: 'what are we to do? We won't do as they want any more, and they hate it. What are we to do?' (II). Gems's later plays sometimes offered answers based on versions of Stas's strategy. In *Piaf* (RSC, 1978) and her Dumas-adaptation, *Camille* (RSC, 1984), she showed strong women resisting convention and escaping oppression through strategic use of their sexuality. The raucous, resilient energy created for Piaf, in particular, made her seem much more than a victim, contributing to the play's popular success in London and New York. Yet each heroine is comprehensively defeated in the end, confirming the inflexible controls of male-oriented society and the improbability of any individual ever escaping or much changing them.

Gems found in *Loving Women* (Arts, 1984) a more promising answer to Fish's question, one which also appealed to several women

---

[2] See p. 325, above.

dramatists at the time. In one way, *Loving Women* was typical of the transitions in mid-1980s drama discussed at the end of Chapter 10, above. Disillusioned by Thatcher's bleak England, Gems's heroine replaces political activism and socialist belief in 'revolution . . . fresh start' with a more specific, pragmatic focus on issues of gender (I. iii). *Loving Women* was typical in another way, in showing its heroine renouncing reconciliation with a former lover in favour of a supportive, familial relationship with the woman who supplanted her in his affections. Many other plays by women in the 1980s and 1990s suggested that relationships, families, communities, or whole societies might be improved by excluding men altogether. In *Golden Girls* (RSC, 1984), for example, Louise Page showed collaborative efforts by a female relay team almost allowing it to outdo male athletes, despite pressures focused on women by sponsors and advertisers. Nell Dunn's *Steaming* (Theatre Royal, Stratford East, 1981) similarly affirmed female community, portraying a group of women who meet by chance in a Turkish bath and gain collective trust and confidence from their campaign to keep the building open. Dunn's dialogue moves unusually easily—like some contemporary women's poetry—between descriptions of banal domesticity and sexual intimacy, sometimes in the same sentence. Free-flowing frankness in conversation affirms a solidarity among women—as diverse as Gems's characters in *Dusa, Fish, Stas and Vi*—which proves more than strong enough to annul differences of class and background.

The lesbian drama of Bryony Lavery and Sarah Daniels explored still more radical exclusions of men, often as the only means of escaping an intolerable—and intolerant—patriarchal society. Like Caryl Churchill in early plays such as *Vinegar Tom* (Monstrous Regiment, 1976), in *Byrthrite* (Royal Court, 1986) Daniels showed innocent women pilloried as witches by seventeenth-century science—early evidence of authoritarian, destructive aspects in male-centred rationality. Daniels's criticism of an 'authority, which is male oriented . . . confused, bemused and deeply threatened' extended into contemporary life in *The Devil's Gateway* (Royal Court, 1983), which used the peace camp at Greenham Common—like David Edgar in *Maydays*—as an example of 'women working together in a different way' (iv). In *Neaptide* (National, 1986) this 'working together' was further examined in the context of family relations and responsibilities for

children—eventually shared entirely by women, with males envisaged as predatory rather than even potentially supportive. In *Her
Aching Heart* (Women's Theatre Group, 1990), Bryony Lavery challenged patriarchal convention more light-heartedly, reshaping the
bodice-ripping mode of popular historical romance around relationships exclusively between women.

Affirmation of these relations—and of ones between men in gay
writing considered earlier—contributed to another direction in late
twentieth-century drama presaged in *Look Back in Anger* in 1956.
Jimmy Porter's unhappy, destructive relations with his wife—and
with the lover who replaces her—anticipate a scepticism of conventional heterosexuality much further extended in later drama. The
happily romantic or marital conclusions of classic comedy were not
much in evidence in the latter part of the twentieth century. Instead,
deepening fault-lines between the genders were often directly discussed in plays in the 1970s and 1980s, as well as demonstrated in
their action: in E. A. Whitehead's *The Foursome* and *The Sea Anchor*
(Royal Court, 1971 and 1974), for example, and in Terry Johnson's
Unsuitable for Adults (Bush, 1984). Such discussions were further
extended in 1990s plays such as Patrick Marber's *Closer* (National,
1997), which continued to present conventional relationships as
generally problematic and unfulfilling.

Marber's characters also worry that it may be 'the cop-out of the
age' to allow love and personal relations to distract so thoroughly
from wider issues and commitments (II. ix). Yet the uncertainty of
wider 'stories' and allegiances at the time—along with new freedoms
of behaviour, and new possibilities of exploring them on stage—
ensured that 'sexuality, skin and the soul' remained central concerns
of 1990s drama.[3] Like *Closer*, this highlighted fault-lines which had
continued to widen and diversify since earlier decades. 'All Sex could
have been better arranged', a character remarked in Charles Dyer's
Staircase: freedom from censorship, and freer outlooks later in the
century, allowed various 'arrangements' to be compared more
candidly than in most earlier periods of literary history, and rarely to
the advantage of uncomplicated heterosexuality (I. i). Many 1990s
plays showed eternal triangles evolving into more complicated, poly-
hedral sexualtities. Heterosexual, bisexual, and homosexual affairs

---

[3] See p. 326, above.

compete for characters' allegiances in Philip Ridley's *The Fastest Clock in the Universe* (Hampstead, 1992), for example, and in Sam Adamson's *Clocks and Whistles* (Bush, 1996). Uncomprehending or unfulfilling relations between men and women continued to seem in urgent need of rearrangement in plays such as Nick Grosso's *Peaches* (Royal Court, 1994) and Joe Penhall's *Love and Understanding* (Bush, 1997), as well as Marber's *Closer*.

When homosexual relations were directly contrasted with hetero-sexual ones—as in Philip Osment's *What I Did in the Holidays* (Cambridge Theatre Company, 1995)—it was often gay experience which seemed more innocent and desirable, as it had in Joe Orton's plays in the 1960s. Lesbian and gay dramatists retained a romantic idealism about love and sex—even a kind of evangelism—which other authors had mostly lost. Meetings of girl and girl, or boy and boy, often held out better hopes of a love story and a happy ending than any promised when boy met girl. This added to a 'real revolu-tion' or turnaround in expectations created by all the dramatists dis-cussed above. As the period went on, theatre audiences were engaged more often and more radically in a carnival plurality of sexual possi-bilities, both reflecting and advancing the reassessment of gender roles and norms of behaviour so widely evident in society at the time.

*

Radical reassessments of gender roles, in theatre late in the century, suggested that a 1950s woman playwright might have done as much as Osborne to anticipate developments in later drama. In *A Taste Of Honey* (Theatre Workshop, 1958), Shelagh Delaney displayed and affirmed what one 1990s critic described as a whole 'paradigm of alternative life-styles' (Innes, p. 449). The play's heroine, Jo, is about to become a single mother, lives in a working-class area of Manchester—further examined in Delaney's *The Lion in Love* (Royal Court, 1960)—and engages in relationships of a kind not much considered again in the theatre during the next quarter cen-tury. She is cared for by her closest companion, a gay lodger, and eventually by her mother, who has long exploited sexuality—like the heroines of Gems's 1980s plays—as a source of security and financial reward. In the end, like some of Sarah Daniels's 1980s characters, mother and daughter establish an exclusively female family unit to look after the imminent baby. Just as unconventionally, in terms of 1950s lifestyles, Jo's pregnancy results from a racially mixed relationship—the affair with a black sailor shown developing in the early scenes of the play.

This was equally unusual in terms of theatrical conventions at the time. As Michael Billington remarked, neither the new theatre establishing itself at the Royal Court in the late 1950s and early 1960s nor the drama which followed in the next decades offered 'many indications that we inhabit a pluralistic, multi-racial society' (Shank (ed.), p. 7). There were a few—plays by black dramatists such as Errol John's *Moon on a Rainbow Shawl* (Royal Court, 1958), or Barry Reckord's *Skyvers* (Royal Court, 1963). But in general, lack of openings in the established theatre forced black writers and performers to follow much the same strategy used by gays and women, developing their work with new companies they founded themselves. Several of these were set up in the late 1970s and 1980s—groups such as Temba, Tara Arts, British-Asian Theatre Company, and Black Theatre Co-operative. These new companies were varied in interest and in background, encompassing what the director of Tara Arts, Jatinder Verma, described as 'a diversity of ethnicities: Indians, Pakistanis, Bangladeshis, Caribbeans, Africans'. But most shared what Verma called a commitment to plays 'dealing with contemporary realities or with the history of Britain's relationship with its colonies', along with a general opposition to a theatrical mainstream perceived as 'white and racist' (Shank (ed.), pp. 55–6). By the 1990s, several of these companies had redirected this mainstream through all-black versions of classics—Verma directing *Tartuffe* at the National Theatre in 1990 with an Asian cast, and the Afro-Caribbean group Talawa Theatre producing *The Importance of Being Earnest*, *Blood Wedding*, and *Antony and Cleopatra*.

New companies encouraged the emergence of new writers, as they did in gay and women's theatre, and the further development of existing ones. Mustapha Matura had already had several plays produced before helping to found the Black Theatre Co-operative in 1978. His work illustrated the 'black' interests Verma defined—in the former colonies, as well as contemporary realities of life in Britain. *Play Mas* (Royal Court, 1974), *Independence* (Bush, 1979), and *Meetings* (Hampstead, 1982) were all set in Trinidad. In

Independence, a decaying grand hotel provides a particularly apt context for analysis of colonial politics and their aftermath—transitions from British 'cultural, as well as economic oppression' to rule by politicians who 'just take over wey de English leave off . . . carry on de same ting, power, power' (III; II). *As Time Goes By* (Traverse, 1971) traced transitions from Trinidad to England, while in *Welcome Home Jacko* (Riverside Studios, 1979) Matura dealt directly with contemporary realities of unemployment, boredom, and police harassment faced by black youths on the streets of London. One of few real freedoms left them is to 'talk Ja . . . genuine Rasta . . . talk Jamaican' (I). One of Matura's achievements was in transcribing Jamaican talk for the stage, either in original dialects, or in hybrid versions of English developing in immigrant communities in Britain. His work also showed—like contemporary black poetry—how deeply this talk was implicated in characters' and communities' outlook and sense of themselves. Serious issues of identity in a post-colonial age were raised—though humorously—by the character in *Play Mas* who concludes 'of course I is English, I does talk English, so I is English, we is English, all a we is English, man' (I. i).

Issues of cultural and personal identity were strongly reflected in the work of another writer dividing his attention between England and former colonies, Ayub Khan-Din. *Last Dance at Dum Dum* (Royal Court, 1999) is set in Calcutta, among an ageing Anglo-Indian community reluctant to relinquish remnants of its English identity. Set in an immigrant community in the north of England, *East is East* (Royal Court/Birmingham Rep, 1996) depicts a character similarly determined to assert a residual Pakistani identity, much to the annoyance of his children—more at ease with local life—and sometimes his English wife. Though often warm and funny, family squabbles in *East is East* provide a particularly sharp focus for conflicts between cultures, and for the stresses on emotion and identity which result. Other black dramatists emerging in the 1980s and 1990s also began to place these conflicts in a context of wider social and political pressures. These were reflected in some of Hanif Kureishi's film scripts, such as *My Beautiful Laundrette* (1985), as well as in his work for the stage. *Outskirts* (RSC, 1981), for example, offered a further view of the area David Edgar examined in *Destiny*, showing the roots of racism and National Front support in the poverty and hopelessness of a new, white underclass on the fringes of London. Winsome Pinnock similarly explored intersections of black interests with issues of socialist or gender politics in *Picture Palace* (Women's Theatre Group, 1988) and in *A Rock in Water* (Royal Court, 1989). This portrayed the black communist Claudia Jones, who helped establish the annual Notting Hill Carnival after she was deported from the United States.

Black drama, in other words, remained concerned in the 1980s and 1990s with problems of racism, injustice, and uncertain identity in immigrant life. Women dramatists worried, too, in the 1990s—April de Angelis in *The Positive Hour* (Hampstead, 1997), for example— that many social injustices remained, and that the original idealism of liberation movements might have been lost or dispersed. Yet black writers such as Kureishi and Khan-Din also reflected the experience of a second immigrant generation, for whom long-standing problems had begun to merge with other 'contemporary realities' in English society—now readier, on the whole, than earlier in the period to accept its 'pluralistic, multi-racial' nature. Improving tolerance and growing acceptance of pluralism likewise allowed women and gay dramatists to broaden their interests late in the century. As earlier chapters suggested, the 'real revolution' anticipated in the 1960s and early 1970s never occurred, but a version of it developed gradually instead: in broadly social terms rather than the radical political ones often discussed in the theatre at the time. By 'shifting consciousness' and providing fresh images of society—often well in advance of other media—black, gay, and women dramatists contributed significantly to this broader, gradual revolution. Their work added substantially, in this way, to the role for drama discussed in Chapters 9 and 10, above, and so marked throughout this period—as a major indicator, and often an agent, of social and political change.

12

Absurdism, Postmodernism, Individualism

'You're alone in the world, remember. No one can tell you what to do about it'. The remark is made by the central character in John Mortimer's popular success, *A Voyage Round my Father* (Greenwich, 1970). Earlier, Mortimer's father is described in terms of a 'great capacity for rage—but never at the Universe' (I). Much of the drama assessed in Chapters 9–11 shared a 'capacity for rage', but directed against the immediate problems of life in contemporary society. There was another drama in the period, likewise originating in the mid-1950s, which raged in different ways—metaphysically, against the lonely uncertainties of existence in an incomprehensible universe. First manifest in an English production of Samuel Beckett's *Waiting for Godot* in 1955 (Arts Theatre), this drama was influentially named and defined by Martin Esslin in his critical study *The Theatre of the Absurd*, published in 1961. Esslin discussed the work of French-language authors such as Beckett, Eugene Ionesco, Arthur Adamov, and Jean Genet; outlined their influence on writing in English; and suggested that their plays reflected 'the present situation of Western man' which Albert Camus had defined in *The Myth of Sisyphus* (1942).

Like some of the post-war poets described in Chapter 8, Camus envisaged an age tormented by 'beliefs we do not believe in'.[1] Human beings, in his view, had been 'suddenly deprived of illusions and of

---

[1] See p. 240, above.

light'—bereft of faith either in religion or in the powers of reason—but still yearned, absurdly, for consolations those vanished powers and illusions had once offered. Yet as Esslin pointed out, Camus continued—like his fellow dramatist-philosopher Jean-Paul Sartre—to write 'elegantly rationalistic . . . well-constructed and polished plays'. Dramatists of the Absurd, on the other hand, embodied the 'senseless, absurd, useless' feelings of 'Western man' within the *form* of their plays. Realistic situations and coherence of plot or character were largely abandoned in their work, in favour of direct, disturbing representations of metaphysical anxiety—typically in abstract action, black comedy, and what Esslin called 'concrete stage images' (pp. 14, 23–25). Beckett's 'power of casting a stage picture' through image and symbol was similarly praised in 1960 by Peter Brook, impressed by 'something vague made tangible' in the 'absurd and awful picture' offered by Beckett's two tramps under a tree in *Waiting for Godot* (Marowitz et al. (eds.), pp. 165–6).

Five years earlier, at a time when drawing-room realism still dominated the English stage, early audiences had found Absurdism, and *Waiting for Godot* in particular, much more puzzling than 'tangible'—Kenneth Tynan commenting that the play made it necessary to 're-examine the rules which governed all drama' (Elsom, *Post-War Theatre Criticism*, p. 70). Succeeding years had offered ample opportunity for this re-examination. As well as supporting new English drama in the late 1950s, the Royal Court had produced several of Eugene Ionesco's plays—*The Chairs* (1957), *The Lesson* (1958), and *Rhinoceros* (1960). It had also staged several of Beckett's: *Fin de Partie* in the original French production in 1957, and in translation as *Endgame*, along with *Krapp's Last Tape*, in the following year. By 1960, audiences were familiar enough with the abstract new 'rules' of Absurdist theatre to accept it in the ways Peter Brook suggested—recognizing in *Waiting for Godot* a 'stage picture' of an empty universe, with the tramps' faith in Godot one of many strategies they use as distractions from an aimless, desolate existence.

Archival tape recordings in *Krapp's Last Tape* likewise came to be understood as a stage image—highlighting perplexities of identity, time, and memory—and the pile of sand burying Beckett's heroine in *Happy Days* (Royal Court, 1962) as symbolic of detritus, mental and material, accumulated during a long life. As Absurdism grew more familiar and comprehensible to audiences, it also extended its appeal to theatre managements. Along with Brecht's work, it helped to replace expensive sets with bare stages, also allowing—unlike Brecht—economies in cast size. By the early 1960s, the initially baffling idiom of Absurdism had begun to be widely accepted on the English stage. The RSC's *Wars of the Roses* demonstrated the extent of Brecht's influence on English theatre by 1963. A year earlier, the growing importance of Absurdism was reflected in the bleak style of Peter Brook's RSC version of *King Lear*, influenced by Beckett and in particular by Jan Kott's essay 'King Lear or *Endgame*'.

Yet like Brecht's early influence, Absurdism's immediate effects were often more apparent in design and staging than directly in the work of English playwrights. Cultural factors initially limited the appeal of an idiom developed abroad and first brought across the Channel in translations by an Irishman, Beckett, of work he had written in French. As critics such as Kenneth Tynan pointed out, Beckett and Ionesco seemed to have little in common with the predominantly social concerns of the new English drama developing at the Royal Court in the later 1950s. An English Absurdism nevertheless began to be widely identified by 1960, with critics often eager to claim Harold Pinter as its principal exemplar. There were some good reasons for them to do so. Pinter himself acknowledged Beckett as a model—sometimes even a source of direct advice—and his puzzling early playlets showed clear affinities with Absurd drama. The two characters awaiting instructions in *The Dumb Waiter* (Royal Court, 1960) recalled the tramps in *Waiting for Godot*, and the action of *The Room* (Royal Court, 1960) closely resembled Ionesco's in *The New Tenant* (1956). Early full-length plays also had darkly inexplicable aspects, such as the two sinister figures who turn up in *The Birthday Party* (Arts Theatre, Cambridge, 1958) and bizarrely interrogate the central character, Stanley. Yet Pinter's drama further puzzled early audiences and reviewers by retaining strong, conventional elements of realism: if not in action, then certainly in setting, usually in recognizable, rundown parts of England, sometimes identified directly, as in *The Caretaker* (Arts Theatre, London, 1960). Pinter's dialogue also represented habits of everyday speech, usually with a working-class inflection, exceptionally accurately. Critics often explained this combination of the bizarre and the mundane as an attempt to contain the strange Continental idiom of the Absurd within forms of 'kitchen-sink' realism and social concern developing on the English stage at the time.[2]

Yet Pinter's work was shaped at least as much by longer-term influences as it was by the immediate ones of Absurdism or kitchen sink. Pinter was in many ways a postmodernist, in the literary-historical sense described in Chapter 2, recording admiration not only for Beckett but for modernist novelists such as James Joyce, Franz Kafka, Marcel Proust, and Ernest Hemingway. Much of his early drama redeveloped for the stage, unusually, tactics—and sometimes even characters—originally employed in fiction. Those two waiting figures in *The Dumb Waiter*—even the two who arrive so disturbingly in *The Birthday Party*—resemble the assassins in Hemingway's short story 'The Killers' (1928) as much as anything in Beckett's drama. Fears about individual security and domestic space in *The Room* or *The Caretaker* extend ones expressed throughout Kafka's work, in 'The Burrow' (1931) particularly. Kafka's nightmare projection of characters' stresses into the environment around them was also, more generally, a source for Pinter's habitual combination of bizarre action and realistic context. Stanley's interrogation in *The Birthday Party*, for example, is inexplicable in terms of the realistic world the play has previously portrayed, but makes every sense as a projection of his torpid, uneasy consciousness.

Covert or psychological compulsions of this kind were sometimes easily recognized in Pinter's early drama, appearing particularly clearly in the split action of *The Lover* (Arts Theatre, 1963). Its separate, Jekyll-and-Hyde sections show a suburban couple's unremarkable life in mornings and evenings, interspersed with the spicy disguises and sexual fantasies they play out during the afternoon. But psychological compulsions were usually more subtly interfused with everyday experience. *The Homecoming* (RSC, 1965), for example, follows the covert processes through which a tough London family finds a new maternal figure, Ruth, around whom to reconfigure its powerful needs. Typically of Pinter's drama, Ruth warns that her 'lips move . . . Perhaps the fact that they move is more significant . . . than the words which come through them' (II). Pinter explained that

---

[2] See p. 278, above.

his double stage action—strange yet familiar, 'realistic, but . . . not realism'—required 'a language . . . where under what is said, another thing is being said' (*Plays: Two*, p. 11; *Plays: One*, p. 14). Pinter's terse dialogues are invariably taut with subtextual negotiations of power and stress: like Ruth, many characters in his early plays communicate unmistakably, but independently of the immediate meaning of words. One of them, in *Tea Party* (BBC TV, 1965), even remarks that he has 'often wondered what "mean" means' (*Plays: Three*, p. 115). Such tactics showed further debts to modernism—to Hemingway's 'Hills Like White Elephants' (1928), or, more generally, to emphases on words' non-semantic properties in James Joyce's extended linguistic experiments.

Other modernist legacies continued to shape Pinter's later plays. In many of these, the rundown settings of his early drama were replaced by more affluent milieux, and psychological menace by less threatening attempts to deal with what Pinter called 'the immense difficulty, if not the impossibility, of verifying the past' (*Plays: One*, p. 11). Plays such as *Landscape* (RSC, 1969) and *Old Times* (RSC, 1971) examine the vagaries of memory in ways resembling much modernist fiction, Marcel Proust's particularly, as well as some of Beckett's drama. Pinter adapted *A la recherche du temps perdu* (1913–27) as *The Proust Screenplay* in 1972, following this work with further plays shaped around memory as much as psychological stress. These included *No Man's Land* (National, 1974), and *Betrayal* (National, 1978)—its scenes set in inverse order, tracing various stages of an affair back to its inception. Investigation of memory and identity continued in *A Kind of Alaska* (National, 1982) and *Moonlight* (Almeida, 1993), though sometimes with dwindling conviction. Lines in *Moonlight*, such as 'don't you remember the word games we all used to play' seem deliberately ironic about Pinter's own earlier idioms (p. 16). 'Word games' and postmodern concern with the corruption of language, especially by political interests, nevertheless remained the strongest aspect of late plays such as *One for the Road* (Lyric, Hammersmith, 1984) and *Mountain Language* (National, 1988). This late work was usually thought to reverse Pinter's 1960s refusal to involve himself in direct social or political commentary. Yet in depicting the menace of authoritarian regimes, it produced neither a strong political statement—since the regimes concerned were not firmly identified—nor an atmosphere as compelling theatrically as his plays in the late 1950s and 1960s, energized by threats and stresses arising from within individuals themselves.

Pinter's combination of Absurdism, modernism, and realism in these early plays made him one of the most original dramatists of the time, and one of the most admired in the late twentieth century generally. Reviewing a revival of *The Birthday Party*, *The Times* remarked on 19 June 1964 that 'if John Osborne fired new authors into writing, Pinter showed them how to write. He relieved them of the dead weight of naturalism, and offered a comic idiom that took its starting point from significant language' (p. 18). Along with the idiom of Absurdism generally, Pinter's writing did help English drama to abandon or amend conventional realist forms, and to escape further from the drawing room and the 'gentleman code' still prevalent in the mid-1950s. Following Beckett, Pinter also established new forms of 'significant language' for the stage, ones which grew into dominant idioms in the period's theatre. Minimal styles of dialogue—quick interchanges, punctuated by pauses and silences— suggested an emptiness underlying all speech and action, or, more particularly, sinister negotiations 'under what is said' for space and security, typically in these early exchanges in *The Caretaker*:

ASTON. You ... er. ...
DAVIES. Eh?
ASTON. Were you dreaming or something?
DAVIES. Dreaming?
ASTON. Yes.
DAVIES. I don't dream. I've never dreamed.
ASTON. No, nor have I.
DAVIES. Nor me.
    Pause
  Why you ask me that, then?
ASTON. You were making noises.
DAVIES. Who was?
ASTON. You were.
    DAVIES *gets out of bed. He wears long underpants.*
DAVIES. Now, wait a minute. Wait a minute, what do you mean? What kind of noises?
ASTON. You were making groans. You were jabbering.
DAVIES. Jabbering? Me?

Fig. 12. Michael Gambon in a 2000 revival of Harold Pinter's
The Caretaker, directed by Patrick Marber.

ASTON. Yes.
DAVIES. I don't jabber, man. Nobody ever told me that before.
> *Pause*

What would I be jabbering about?
ASTON. I don't know.
DAVIES. I mean, where's the sense in it?
> *Pause*

Nobody ever told me that before.
> *Pause*

You got hold of the wrong bloke, mate.

(I)

Pinter's styles and dialogue forms continued to appeal to playwrights throughout the period. Joe Orton's drama followed Pinter fairly directly, in the 1960s, in its shabby metropolitan settings and blackly comic idiom, and in showing conventional behaviour warped by underlying passions. But it was probably later in the period, in the 1990s especially, that Pinter's tactics and speech forms were most widely re-employed. In *Mojo* (Royal Court, 1996), for example, Jez Butterworth used terse, minimal dialogue familiar from Pinter's work to represent subtly shifting power relations among a group of 1950s club workers and minor criminals. Patrick Marber directed a revival of *The Caretaker* in 2000: his own play *Dealer's Choice* (National, 1995) offered a paradigm of the Pinteresque in the context of an extended poker game, with each player's power and prestige at stake in the subtext of every sentence. Personal and sexual relationships were presented as another Pinteresque poker game in Marber's *Closer* (National, 1997). Its characters find that lying is 'the currency of the world', that 'all the language is old', and that 'there are no new words' or any other means of fully expressing desire (II. viii; I. v). Painful, lyric precision in treating new 1990s emphases on skin, sex, soul, and the self made *Closer* one of the representative plays of the decade.[3]

Tom Stoppard's work also adapted legacies of Beckett and Absurdism into a comic idiom, much lighter than Pinter's, but likewise influential in later decades. Like Pinter, Stoppard combined Absurdist elements with other equally strong interests. If *The Dumb Waiter* was Pinter's 'Waiting for Hemingway', Stoppard created a

---

[3] Also discussed on pp. 341–2, above.

sort of 'Waiting for Hamlet' with his first success, *Rosencrantz and Guildenstern are Dead* (National, 1967). Like Beckett's tramps, his Rosencrantz and Guildenstern endure a bewildering, aimless existence, 'passing the time in a place without any visible character'(I). Yet they are troubled less by the wider meaninglessness of the universe than by their exclusion from the main action of *Hamlet*, unfolding around them without offering much sense of their role or significance. Typically of Stoppard's early work, metaphysical ideas and unusual stage images focus specifically on the nature of language, literature, and art. *Travesties* (RSC, 1974) might also have been re-entitled, as 'The Importance of Being an Artist', Stoppard using in it a revival of Oscar Wilde's *The Importance of Being Earnest* (1895) as a context for reflection on literature's representation of the world, and of political commitments in particular.

Set in Zurich in 1917, at a time when Lenin, Joyce, and the Dadaist Tristan Tzara were all living there, *Travesties* considers whether, as Stoppard put it, 'the words "revolutionary" and "artist" are capable of being synonymous, or whether they are mutually exclusive, or something in between' (Innes, p. 335). Stoppard returned to the same question in *The Real Thing* (Strand, 1982). Both plays criticized the left-wing drama described in Chapter 10, above—*Travesties* implicitly, *The Real Thing* more directly. While this drama dominated the stage, in the 1970s and early 1980s, versions of Stoppard's question naturally interested several other playwrights. In *An Audience Called Edouard* (Greenwich, 1978), for example, David Pownall showed Manet's work on his painting *Déjeuner sur l'herbe* improbably interrupted by the emergence of Karl Marx from a swim in the Seine. In *Masterclass* (Haymarket, Leicester, 1983), Pownall went on, like Stoppard, to assess the political merits of conservative and experimental art forms, contrastingly considered in the play's conversations between Stalin and the avant-garde composers Prokofiev and Shostakovich.

Travesties reproduced much of Oscar Wilde's wit and comic invention, exemplifying Stoppard's wish 'to marry the play of ideas to comedy or farce' (Trussler (ed.), p. 63). Farce predominated in some of his writing—in *Dirty Linen* (Arts, 1976), for example, and in his adaptation of Johann Nestroy, *On the Razzle* (National, 1981). More often, 'the play of ideas' described very accurately work which not only translated philosophical ideas into dramatic form, but also treated them as a game in themselves—a playing of the mind, spinning concepts and constructs sometimes remote from the reality they might be supposed to serve. Much of Stoppard's drama thus reflected the wider postmodern outlook described in Chapter 2, above, sceptical of all theories, philosophies, or forms of representation. *Jumpers* (National, 1972) showed in this way the incompetence of moral philosophy to deal with an increasingly chaotic world; *Hapgood* (Aldwych, 1988) the unreliability of perception, warped by the disposition of individual observers; *Arcadia* (National Theatre, 1993) the impossibility of biography or literary criticism ever recovering the truth of past events.

Typically of the postmodern, doubts about truth and representation focused on language and its limitations. Like ideas, language often figured in Stoppard's drama as an uncertain—even purposeless—form of play, as Rosencrantz and Guildenstern affirm:

ROS. What are you playing at?
GUIL. Words, words. They're all we have to go on.
  (*Pause.*)
ROS. Shouldn't we be doing something–constructive?
GUIL. What did you have in mind? . . . A short, blunt human
  pyramid. . . . ?

ROS. We could play at questions.
GUIL. What good would that do?

(I)

Like Pinter, or Beckett, though less darkly, Stoppard also regularly illustrated the potential of words to deceive or misrepresent, as much as to communicate. His bewildered moral philosopher in *Jumpers*, for example, both fears and demonstrates the waywardness of words:

GEORGE. . . . though my convictions are intact and my ideas coherent, I can't seem to find the words. . . .
BONES. Well, 'Are God?' is wrong for a start.
GEORGE. Or rather, the words betray the thoughts they are supposed to express. Even the most generalized truth begins to look like special pleading as soon as you trap it in language.

(I)

Typically of postmodernism, too, Stoppard's concerns with language, art, and representation were regularly self-conscious or self-reflexive, focused in plays which highlight or undermine their own theatrical tactics. *The Real Thing*, for example, soon reveals that its entirely realistic, convincing opening scene was entirely artificial, part of a play within the play. Inventiveness and ingenuity of this kind ensured that Stoppard's plays of ideas remained primarily comic and entertaining. Philosophical discussions in *Jumpers* are leavened by acrobats—who do form a 'human pyramid'—a stripper, a doomed pet tortoise, and an unfortunate hare. The perceptual perplexities of quantum physics are dramatized in *Hapgood* through the deception and disguising of a Cold War spy story. Though *The Real Thing* never moves far beyond the theme of 'infidelity among the architect class' (II. vii) it sets out to parody, nor *Night and Day* (Phoenix, 1978) beyond late 1970s platitudes about trade unions and free speech, Stoppard's capacity to amuse audiences—while flattering them with the cleverness of his material—generally made him one of the most successful and popular dramatists in the period.

Dramatists less celebrated than Stoppard or Pinter—Stanley Eveling, James Saunders, Henry Livings, Giles Cooper, and N. F. Simpson—sometimes seemed indebted more exclusively to the Absurd. In plays such as *The Balachites* (Traverse, 1963), Stanley Eveling moved from realistic contexts towards stranger or more abstract ones, or used bizarre events, like Pinter, as projections of the troubled psyches of protagonists. Eveling recorded *Waiting for Godot* as the original inspiration for his writing: it apparently had a similar effect on James Saunders. Action and dialogue in Saunders's *Next Time I'll Sing to You* (Questors Theatre, Ealing, 1962) often closely resembled Beckett's, contributing to a version of the Absurd which had some influence on Stoppard at the time. Yet Saunders suggested limits as well as strengths in the appeal of the Absurd within England, referred to in his play as a 'little haven of peace', its citizens 'well-fed, well-clad, civilized, deodorised, British, middle-class, and with impeccable consciences' (I). The description is partly ironic, but it coincided with judgements expressed at the time by one of the most perceptive of 1960s drama critics, Laurence Kitchin. In *Drama in the Sixties* (1966), Kitchin re-examined the roots of Absurd theatre in the existential philosophies of Camus and Sartre, stressing that the thinking involved had grown out of challenges to reason, morality, and politics experienced much more directly in France than in England. As well as being overrun by the Nazis, France had endured more immediate contact with what Kitchin called the 'indigestible, inconceivable facts of Auschwitz and Belsen' encountered at the end of the war (p. 38). In writing *Waiting for Godot* and most of his principal works between 1945 and 1950, Samuel Beckett was for Kitchin 'a man of the nineteen-forties, indelibly marked by the dangers of the Resistance movement' and by 'the reality of enemy occupation' experienced in wartime France, 'an ordeal we in Britain were spared' (pp. 3, 31). With the possible exception of Pinter—a Jewish playwright concerned throughout his work with menace, violence, and the invasion of private space—dramatists in England were not 'indelibly marked' in this way, and therefore not naturally or profoundly in sympathy with the 'heroic pessimism' informing the work of Beckett and Ionesco. Instead, they adopted elements of the Absurd through what Kitchin considered 'frivolous and pretentious' imitation, most often of its black or anarchic comedy (p. 31).

Comedy of this kind was strongly apparent in a play performed in the first weeks of 1960 at the Royal Court, N. F. Simpson's *One Way Pendulum*, concerned with training 'Speak-Your-Weight' machines to sing the Hallelujah Chorus. Farcical actions and demented individuals figured similarly in Giles Cooper's *Happy Family* (Hampstead, 1966), and in Henry Livings's *Big Soft Nellie* (Oxford Playhouse, 1961) and *Eh?* (RSC, 1964). To critics such as John Elsom, even the comic element in these plays showed indebtedness less to the Absurd than to a 'cheerful nonsense tradition' native to England and recently extended influentially by the Goon Shows (*Post-War Theatre*, p. 105). Featuring Spike Milligan and other radio comedians, these were first broadcast in 1953 and still popular at the beginning of the next decade. Written in collaboration with John Antrobus, Milligan's stage play *The Bed Sitting Room* (Mermaid, 1963) was equally nonsensical, though less cheerful, reflecting early 1960s dread of nuclear apocalypse. Milligan's autobiographical, blackly comic account of army life, *Adolf Hitler: My Part in his Downfall* (1971) also suggested that his nonsensical humour shared at least some of the bleak wartime origins Kitchin recognized in the

Absurd. Forms of black, surreal, or anti-establishment comedy which developed throughout the media in the 1960s—especially in the television series *Monty Python's Flying Circus* at the end of the decade—were often influenced by Milligan's desolate inanity, or faintly echoed the shock of the war in other ways. Yet England's post-war 'nonsense tradition'—even if it distantly shared some of Absurdism's origins—generally suppressed the darker reaches of philosophic enquiry and 'heroic pessimism' Kitchin admired in Beckett and Ionesco. Longer-term legacies of the Absurd in English theatre—Stoppard and Pinter apart—were on the whole apparent only loosely, as Kitchin suggested, in blacker or stranger forms of comedy, or in new emphases on the loneliness of individuals in an increasingly chaotic world.

These characteristics appeared throughout the work of one of the period's most popular dramatists, Alan Ayckbourn, most of whose plays went on to enjoy long runs in London after opening in his Library Theatre in Scarborough. Ayckbourn encountered the Absurd early in his career, acting in plays by Beckett and Pinter in the early 1960s and working in Scarborough alongside David Campton, author of *The Lunatic View* (Studio Theatre Company, 1957), a play which mixed Ionesco and the Goon Show much in the manner discussed above. Vestiges of the Absurd continued to feature in Ayckbourn's later writing, though much of his work seemed to move as far as possible from philosophic interests—or any real serious-ness—in favour of slight, farcical forms and a primary commitment to entertainment. Yet as his career went on, critics grew readier to acknowledge a particular vision—even a philosophy—underlying the hectic, funny surface of his plays. Like its characters, his drama was often considered to disguise a certain bleakness beneath a cheer-ful, attractive exterior. It was also thought to comment particularly sharply on the domestic situation of women and on the shallow commercialism of contemporary life. Plays such as *Absurd Person Singular* (1972), *Absent Friends* (1975), *Just between Ourselves* (1978), or *Woman in Mind* (1985) showed moral or emotional emptiness in family life and suburban society, and loneliness and frustration in individuals, intense enough to fracture conventional expectations of comedy.

Woman in Mind also moved beyond conventional staging,

allowing audiences to share in the subjective vision and language of an individual character much as they did in some of Pinter's work. Ayckbourn was still more innovative in other plays. *How the Other Half Loves* (1970) showed two households living out their lives and adulterous liaisons alternately on the same set, highlighting differences of class and outlook between them. In his trilogy *The Norman Conquests* (1974) Ayckbourn famously offered three successive versions of the same ghastly family weekend, one centred on the dining room, one on the drawing room, and one in the garden. Later work such as *Intimate Exchanges* (1983) used still more extravagant tactics, with actors supposedly choosing in the course of performance between different forms of plot, or in *House/Garden* (National, 2000) even dashing between neighbouring theatres to stage different parts of the same narrative. These complex, arbitrary theatrical devices extended into another dimension the stresses Ayckbourn's plays explored—adding to feelings of manipulation within families and relationships; heightening a sense of existence as an 'absurd person singular', trapped by the world's malign machinery and unmanageable forces.

By the 1980s, playwrights' attention to 'absurd persons singular' had begun to merge, almost indistinguishably, with conventional interests in individuals and their dilemmas—a more viable subject, once again, as the popularity of the issue-based political drama of the 1970s began to fade. Christopher Hampton's work was representative of this change. His biographical play *Total Eclipse* (Royal Court, 1968) traced conflicts with society resulting from the radical individualism of the poets Verlaine and Rimbaud. In *The Philanthropist* (Royal Court, 1970) he went on to consider—initially, in some Absurdist scenes, later more conventionally—a range of stresses on integrity endured by 'one little person in this enormous bloody world' (iii). Set in Hollywood during the war, at a time when Brecht and other European writers were in exile there, *Tales from Hollywood* (National, 1983) argued explicitly for the dramatic importance of 'persons singular'. Hampton's play shows Brecht encountering a more conservative dramatist, who plausibly explains that political theatre is limited by its 'profound dislike of the individual' and that audiences 'don't want instructions . . . they don't want to come into a theatre and be told what to do' (II. xvii).

Tales from Hollywood helps in this way to define the atmosphere in which left-wing drama declined or changed direction by the mid-1980s. Whereas Edward Bond had emphasized that the individual could not provide the 'metaphor for the state' required by 1970s political drama, by the early 1980s, Hampton's play suggested, audiences were quite likely to be more interested in individuals than either metaphors or the state (Bond, *Worlds*, p. 136). David Edgar also registered this change of priorities in a *Times Literary Supplement* article of 10 September 1982. By 1980, he remarked, 'the "we" decade [had] turned into the "me" decade, and the pot generation matured into the Perrier Generation'. This created a demand not for 'plays about the masses resisting the disablement of class or racial oppression' but instead for a firm focus on individual characters—sometimes, as in Brian Clark's *Whose Life is it Anyway?* (Mermaid, 1978), ones whose physical disabilities could provide a strong emotional focus for new concerns about the self (p. 969). In the figure of Smike, Edgar added to this trend himself in his popular adaptation of *Nicholas Nickleby* (RSC, 1980).

Strong individuals, of course, had hardly been altogether missing from drama earlier in the period, even in its more political phases. In the later 1970s, both Edgar and David Hare were suggesting the need for left-wing theatre to focus on the individual, and there were other politically aware playwrights who shared their views. Michael Hastings's introduction to *Three Political Plays* (1989) suggests that committed drama might usefully concentrate on 'people in legend'—newsworthy figures already strongly occupying the popular imagination (p. 13). A successful biographical dramatist in his play about T. S. Eliot's marriage, *Tom and Viv* (Royal Court, 1984), Hastings put his strategy into practice in studies of President Kennedy's assassin, *Lee Harvey Oswald* (Hampstead, 1966), and of Idi Amin's rule in Uganda, *For the West* (National, 1977). Similar concentration on strong or 'legendary' figures had also appeared in the 1960s among dramatists assumed at the time to be particularly politically aware. John Whiting believed that 'the power of the theatre' derived from 'power in the remote, isolated figure': his own plays and those of contemporaries such as Robert Bolt and David Mercer attempted to realize this dramatic potential (Elsom, *Post-War Theatre*, p. 48).[4]

---

[4] See also pp. 288 and 297–8, above.

Despite professed Marxism and a strong interest in class, Mercer concluded that 'the only possible revolution is the individual revolution', concentrating in *Ride A Cock Horse* (Piccadilly, 1965), *After Haggerty* (RSC, 1970), and *Flint* (Criterion, 1970) on 'protestant' or dissentient figures comparable to those dominating John Osborne's early drama (J. R. Taylor, p. 43).

Interest in strong, singular, individuals was obviously not new, but its reaffirmation during the early 1980s corresponded in specific ways to the 'privatization of concern', in the early Thatcher years, which Edgar described in his *Times Literary Supplement* article. As John Bull pointed out in his study *Stage Right: Crisis and Recovery in British Contemporary Mainstream Theatre* (1994), renewed focus on the individual offered mainstream and commercial theatres an ideal opportunity to recover ground they had lost to the political drama of the previous decade. At a time of growing financial difficulties, plays analysing individuals were obviously preferable, in terms of cast size, to ones seeking wide-ranging political vision and a 'metaphor for the state'. If tensions between singular individuals and a difficult world could be reflected and resolved in comic terms, then so much the better in terms of pleasing audiences. Comic idioms, Bull suggested, had been partly reshaped since the 1960s by the influence of the Absurd, but could usually be realigned, through the work of playwrights such as Ayckbourn, into humorous portrayals of conflict in conventional social contexts. This allowed a return to undemanding forms of realism, and even the middle-class drawing-room sets, popular before the theatrical revolutions of the mid-1950s. These conditions favoured a number of writers who had either stayed mostly silent in the 1970s, like Hampton, or remained otherwise untouched by the high tide of political commitment during the decade. As this tide receded in the 1980s, meeting a renewed influx of conventional interests on the way, it left English theatre quite sharply divided by opposing tactics and allegiances.

This division was highlighted satirically in Peter Nichols's semi-autobiographical play *A Piece of My Mind* (Apollo, 1987). A research student asks the author figure

Do you see your plays as advocating revolution like those of David Mercer, Edward Bond, Trevor Griffiths, David Edgar, John McGrath, John Arden, Margaretta D'Arcy . . . Willy Russell, Caryl Churchill,

Howard Barker . . . David Hare, Howard Brenton . . . or do you see them as supporting the status quo like those of Alan Bennett, John Osborne, Robert Bolt, Michael Frayn, Julian Mitchell, Tom Stoppard, Christopher Hampton . . . John Mortimer, Simon Gray, Peter Shaffer . . . Charles Wood, Peter Nichols. (I)

In *Kafka's Dick* (Royal Court, 1986), Alan Bennett had recently moved closer to the comic, literary-intellectual idiom developed by Stoppard's work, but neither he nor Charles Wood were thorough supporters of the status quo. Simon Gray offered a clearer example of the 'mainstream' drama John Bull defined. Many of his plays used middle-class social contexts to explore tensions—mostly comic—firmly focused around a single central character. These central figures were often set apart by superior wit, though occasionally by strange aloofness or reticence. In either case, they usually revealed emotional disabilities equivalent to the physical ones David Edgar identified as a growing interest of early 1980s theatre.

Reluctant to communicate with fellow teachers, the title character in *Quartermaine's Terms* (Queen's, 1981) illustrated mysterious reticence, as did the silent patriarch in *Close of Play* (National, 1979), remote from his family and its squabbles and unable to say anything to prevent its collapse around him. The disillusioned English lecturer in *Butley* (Criterion, 1971), on the other hand, is cruelly, unremittingly witty and articulate—characteristics shared with the disaffected husband in *Dog Days* (Oxford Playhouse, 1976) and the deranged publisher in *Melon* (Theatre Royal, Haymarket, 1987). As well as using supposedly rapier-like intelligence to torment less sharp-tongued characters around them, each of these wits eventually exposes a huge emptiness underlying his own carapace of glib humour. Whether garrulous or silent, all Gray's central figures, in the title of another of his plays, were 'Otherwise Engaged': less to ideals contrary to their societies than to a superior, bitter, certainty that ultimate values do not exist. Few answers were forthcoming, in Gray's drama, to the question raised in *Close of Play*: 'what is the point, the point of caring for each other and loving each other when the end is always and always the same, *sub specie* or any way you look at it?' (II). Like Ayckbourn or Hampton, Gray showed in this way a continuing trace of the Absurd's bleakness. This was nevertheless safely reconfigured, as Bull suggested, within witty, entertaining character portrayals and the familiar ambience of the middle-class drawing room.

Some of Michael Frayn's comedies also explored the difficulties of finding absolute values, or effective ways of caring for others. In *Make and Break* (Lyric, Hammersmith, 1980), religious and spiritual ideals contrast painfully with the disorderly lives of the characters who discuss them. In *Benefactors* (Vaudeville, 1984), Frayn compared two kinds of failure, placing an architect's unfulfilled visions and ruined plans alongside his inability to look after his chaotic friends. Conflicts between ideals, plans, or visions and an intractable reality or unruly individuals—natural interests for a comic writer— reappeared regularly in Frayn's novels: in *Headlong* (1999), for example, directly concerned with tensions between art and life. This kind of tension received its most celebrated theatrical treatment in Frayn's farce-within-a-farce *Noises Off* (Lyric, Hammersmith, 1982). *Make and Break* had partly prepared the way, its setting among numerous sample doors, marketed at a trade fair, creating an ideal environment for the multiple entrances and exits of farce. But *Noises Off* was unique in allowing audiences to witness a farce's action from two sides. Chaotic rehearsals and later performances are seen from the front of the set in Acts I and III, but also from behind during Act II. This shows an incompetent, argumentative cast struggling through the plot, and a desperate director trying to sustain its shape and order in the face of imminent chaos and collapse.

Though primarily an entertainment, *Noises Off* occasionally allowed the metatheatrical to move towards the metaphysical, showing characters tormented—like those in *Rosencrantz and Guildenstern are Dead*—by conflicts between their own natures or desires and demands imposed by their roles in the dramatic illusion. Frayn's plays at any rate added to the sophisticated, theatrically aware, post-Absurd comic idiom established by Stoppard's drama. Later, his work also contributed to mainstream theatres' reduction of the cast sizes often required in the 1970s to present political issues. Frayn's popular success *Copenhagen* (National, 1998) examined the menace of nuclear weapons entirely through discussions between two figures closely involved in their development during the Second World War, Niels Bohr and Werner Heisenberg. 'Metaphors for the state', or for the gravest issues of statecraft, *Copenhagen* suggested, could still be conveniently located in the outlook and moral responsibilities of strong individual characters.

Much of Peter Nichols's drama was in the form of comedy—in *A Piece of My Mind*, in the metatheatrical idiom made familiar by Stoppard and Frayn. But only a slack research student would have considered it unreservedly supportive of the status quo. On the contrary, Nichols regularly found metaphors through which he could criticize the state and its institutions—though fairly benignly, and in ways entertaining enough to ensure success in mainstream theatres. As his title suggested, in *The National Health: Or Nurse Norton's Affair* (National, 1969) he mixed romantic comedy—parodic in its excesses—with a 'state of the nation' play, using diverse characters in a hospital ward to exemplify poverty, class divisions, and racial tensions extending throughout the country as a whole. Class, privilege, and the role of the state were also examined in *The Freeway* (National, 1974). Though imposing a frustrating stasis on the action, the play's huge traffic jam aptly demonstrated the need to balance individual liberty—'democratic profusion . . . the free way'—with state intervention and control in a mass society (II. ii).

Like *The National Health*, *Privates on Parade* (RSC, 1977) and *Poppy* (RSC, 1982) combined serious issues and forms of popular entertainment in ways familiar from Joan Littlewood's *Oh What a Lovely War*. Portraying an all-male army entertainment company, *Privates on Parade* used song, dance, and repartee to enliven its assessment of empire and of the last days of British rule in Singapore. *Poppy* told a still more bitter story—of the empire's expansion in Victorian times, fostered by trade wars, opium-trafficking, and commercial exploitation—alleviated in this case by Nichols's use of a Victorian pantomime format, complete with songs, jokes, extended roles for pantomime horses, and even a pantomime elephant. Attacking Victorian values just as Margaret Thatcher was trying to reinstate them, *Poppy* was nevertheless an outstanding commercial success, in London and in New York. Its popularity suggested that by the early 1980s established theatres could fairly easily take over and redeploy tactics familiar from political drama, as well as ones derived from Absurd comedy.

Nichols reflected longer-established interests of commercial and mainstream theatre in *Passion Play* (RSC 1981), developing the theme Stoppard defined in the *Real Thing* as 'infidelity among the architect class'. Adultery had been a promising dramatic subject since the nineteenth century—even since the Restoration in the seventeenth century. Naturally involving theatrical elements of dissembling or role play, and engaging middle-class audiences compellingly with familiar forms of middle-class crisis, it continued to fascinate dramatists towards the end of the twentieth century. Adultery and its covert betrayals were often interests for Pinter, especially as his work moved away from its early working-class settings. It also figured regularly in the plays of David Mercer, Tom Stoppard, and Simon Gray, and for Alan Ayckbourn it was an almost permanent theme. In *Passion Play*, Nichols seemed to treat this perennial subject unusually ingeniously, placing separate performers on stage, close to his central characters, to express their deeper or necessarily disguised feelings. Strangely, though, ingenious staging of adultery almost became a stage convention in itself during the period. Inventive treatments of infidelity featured not only in *Passion Play*, but in Pinter's regressive structure in *Betrayal*, Stoppard's double action in *The Real Thing*, and in a whole range of Ayckbourn's innovations in stagecraft. This inventiveness may have been necessary to ensure that a long-standing theme engaged mainstream audiences as firmly as ever. Flamboyant techniques may have been designed to compensate, theatrically, for any decline in adultery's significance, morally, in a period generally growing more tolerant in its expectations of sexual roles and behaviour.

Shifting gender and sexual expectations may help to account for another striking feature in the period's mainstream drama—its concentration of interest in singular persons and individual crises almost exclusively around male protagonists. In one way, this simply reflected the continuing, centuries-old male dominance of theatre Charlotte Keatley emphasized—only beginning to change, in ways suggested in Chapter 11, in the 1980s. Yet the perennial self-interest of men writers in the period also acquired new forms, reflecting new stresses. These developed from the kind of conclusion Pam Gems expressed in *Dusa, Fish, Stas and Vi*—that women 'won't do as [men] want any more, and they hate it'.[5] Whatever their ostensible cause, personal crises in plays by male authors regularly revealed

[5] See pp. 335 and 339, above.

anxiety about women's growing autonomy, and consequent un-certainties about men's roles and sense of self. This concern in the period's drama was anticipated—yet again—by John Osborne in *Look Back in Anger*. Critics rarely recognized that Jimmy Porter's despair did not necessarily result from an absolute absence of 'good, brave causes' in 1956. It also reflected his fear that he would be 'butchered by the women' before he could find a cause of any kind—along with most contemporary men, inexplicably disposed, he claimed, to 'let these women bleed us to death' (III. i).

Women figured just as disturbingly in later Osborne plays such as *Inadmissible Evidence* (1964), and in the work of several of his con-temporaries—in David Mercer's *Ride a Cock Horse*, for example; Paul Ableman's *Green Julia* (Traverse, 1965); David Storey's *The Restoration of Arnold Middleton* (Royal Court, 1967); and Simon Gray's *Butley*. The clearest fear of being 'bled to death' appeared in E. A. Whitehead's *Old Flames* (New Vic, Bristol, 1975). Whitehead recorded in a contemporary review an 'awful fear' of what *Dusa, Fish, Stas and Vi* suggested about 'what women are thinking today' (Lloyd Evans and Lloyd Evans (eds.), p. 221). An introductory note to *Old Flames* further discussed the thinking of Germaine Greer, Kate Millett, and Doris Lessing, and the play itself showed a man's blood being drunk by a number of former partners, and his flesh eaten, too, as revenge for his many betrayals and adulteries. *Old Flames* suggested how far the crisis in heterosexual relations dis-cussed in Chapter 11—even the ingenious imagination surrounding infidelity, described above—reflected male authors' nervous aware-ness of a new independence in 'what women are thinking today'. Personal stresses endured by male characters in mainstream theatre often offered mirror images of this thinking, or half-developed nega-tives of the new pictures it offered—especially earlier in the period, when new sexual freedoms and the new women's movements were first becoming influential. In this way, too, English drama remained strongly engaged with contemporary social change, embodying shifting stresses in gender roles and sexual behaviour—so significant throughout this period—even when they were not its immediate subject.

13

Discovering the Body

Shelagh Delaney anticipated some developments in the period's drama even more directly than John Osborne, Chapter 11 suggested. So did another woman playwright in the late 1950s, Ann Jellicoe. Though she seemed to share a renewed interest in contemporary society with Osborne and other dramatists emerging at the time, Jellicoe also had much wider aims. *The Sport of My Mad Mother* (Royal Court, 1958) topically depicted Teddy Boys and 1950s teenage violence, and *The Knack* (Arts, Cambridge, 1962) freer sexual behaviour at the start of the 1960s. Yet in each play these issues were little more than a focus for choreographed, energetic staging, and for a series of games and rituals supposedly releasing characters' latent psychic energies. In a 1964 preface to *The Sport of My Mad Mother*, Jellicoe emphasized that her drama was principally 'based upon myth and . . . ritual' rather than issues, social or otherwise. 'Anti-intellect', and 'about irrational forces', her plays sought to affect audiences, she explained, 'through rhythm, noise and music and their reaction to basic stimuli' (p. 5). Whereas much of the drama emerging in the late 1950s changed the subject matter of theatre, renewing its relevance as 'a public art form', Jellicoe's work helped to renew dramatic form itself, restoring long-suppressed elements of gesture, ritual, and physicality. These elements generally expanded in influence throughout the drama of later decades, but their initial renewal was apparently at odds with many of the movements described in earlier chapters. Absurdism excepted, much of the drama considered so far remained fairly realistic, using the stage primarily to reflect experience, and to comment on the world in which it occurred. Jellicoe's work was typical of influences emerging in the 1960s which envisaged drama not so much as a mirror of experience, whether personal or political, but rather as an event or experience in itself.

This view of theatre shaped the work of one of the period's most influential directors, Peter Brook. In *The Empty Space* (1968), Brook dismissed contemporary society's 'accepted values' in theatrical as well as political terms,[1] defining established theatre as 'the Deadly Theatre' and complaining that 'all the forms of sacred art have certainly been destroyed by bourgeois values' (pp. 11, 54). Brook favoured instead a live, vital, even 'holy' drama, based on the work of the experimental Polish director Jerzy Grotowski, and on the 'Theatre of Cruelty' recommended by Antonin Artaud. Stressing the power of gesture, mime, movement, and physicality, Grotowski's ideas were collected in *Towards a Poor Theatre*, published in English with an introduction by Brook in 1968. Emphasizing the adaptability of almost any space for performance, independent of conventional paraphernalia of sets and lighting, Grotowski also encouraged fringe and alternative companies to move away from established or 'Deadly' theatres around this time, and influenced the development of site-specific productions in later years. Artaud's 'Theatre of Cruelty' manifesto was included in his study *The Theatre and its Double* (1938), first translated from French in 1958. Artaud developed in it a view of human beings as victims less of social or political circumstance than of cruelly inexorable forces in nature, or in the dark spaces of the unconscious. In the theatre, Artaud explained, 'special exorcisms' and 'distillations of dreams' could be used—in the form of powerful stage imagery, action, or ritual—to shock audiences into recognition of these forces, and of 'all aspects of an inner world' (pp. 70–1).

Brook began to develop these ideas for the English stage—following his earlier interests in the Absurd[2]—in an RSC 'Theatre of Cruelty' Season at the London Academy of Music and Drama (LAMDA) in 1964. Organized with Charles Marowitz, and with advice from Grotowski, it involved workshops in mime, improvisation, and vocal technique, leading eventually to a company-devised performance, *US* (1966), scripted by Adrian Mitchell and protesting

---

[1] See also p. 301, above. [2] See pp. 347–8, above.

against the Vietnam war. The LAMDA season also included a staging in translation of Peter Weiss's *The Persecution and Assassination of Marat as Performed by the Inmates of the Asylum of Charenton under the Direction of the Marquis of Sade* (1964). Though usually referred to just as the '*The Marat/Sade*', the full title defines the aptness of Weiss's work for the shocking, physical, and ritual staging Artaud recommended. Sensational at the time, the LAMDA season strongly affected English theatre later in the 1960s. Brook extended some of its influence through an imaginative, highly physical production of *A Midsummer Night's Dream* for the RSC in 1970, and by staging the Prometheus legend the following year, in the ruins of Persepolis, as *Orghast*, using a new language created by Ted Hughes. Other innovative productions followed in later decades, usually abroad, eventually developed mostly with his Paris-based Centre International de Créations Théâtrales. At the end of the century the *Guardian* continued to consider Brook's *Midsummer Night's Dream* 'a milestone in theatre history', and recorded that *The Empty Space* was still 'a bible for many young directors' (26 Jan. 2000, p. 12).

The same *Guardian* article quoted Brook's recollection of sharing in a struggle—along with many experimental groups in the 1960s—'to free theatre of the old complexes by which all that mattered was the text . . . the *body* . . . was ignored'. As he pointed out in *The Empty Space*, this was in part a struggle against censorship. Its abolition in 1968 had immediate effects on theatrical treatment of the body and sex: a London production of the nude musical *Hair* opened the day after the law changed. It was followed in 1970 by Kenneth Tynan's more daring evening of erotica, *Oh! Calcutta!* at the Roundhouse. Including material by Joe Orton, David Mercer, and John Lennon, *Oh! Calcutta!* was popular enough to run until 1979. For its first critics, it offered evidence of radical and lasting theatrical change. 'However daring *Hair* seemed at the time', one of them remarked, *Oh! Calcutta!* 'crashe[d] the barrier once and for all' through its 'bold and triumphant attack on the taboos which have hedged in the Western theatre for centuries' (Peter Roberts (ed.), p. 36).

Other reviewers seemed surprised to find 'poetry' in the production's 'celebration of the human body', or even just that 'the ordinary

Fig. 13. Peter Brook's 1970 RSC production of *A Midsummer Night's Dream*.

body is an object well worth attention' (Elsom, *Post-War Theatre Criticism*, 1981, pp. 194, 195). Their reactions confirmed how far the English stage—much more than most Western theatre—had previously been 'hedged in' by taboos and barriers on the physical. Coalescing with influences from the 'Theatre of Cruelty' season, contemporary slackening of taboos contributed to fundamental changes in the style and resources of English drama in the later 1960s. This affected every area of performance, eventually in established theatres as well as alternative ones. For directors, there were obvious implications in Artaud's emphasis on a 'visual language of . . . movement, attitudes and gestures', and for actors in his vision of the possibilities of 'the human body, raised to the dignity of signs' (pp. 68–9, 72). As Theodore Shank suggested, surveying English theatre late in the century, performers could no longer 'act only from the neck up', as critics had often complained, or 'focus on language and voice . . . to the exclusion of the body as an expressive instrument' (pp. 8–9).

Implications for playwrights were less positive, potentially at any rate. Greater use of the body as a sign—even as poetry—implied a diminished interest in the conventional signs of language and dramatic script. Peter Brook was sceptical of 'ciphers on paper' in *The Empty Space*, suggesting that the spoken word was not 'the same tool for dramatics it once was' (pp. 15, 54). Artaud himself had strongly emphasized the need to 'break theatre's subjugation to the text' (p. 68). Even by the end of the 1960s, it sometimes seemed that contemporary theatre had been only too successful in following this advice. The drama publisher John Calder, for example, complained in 1968 that that 'words have ceased to matter' and that audiences were 'caught up in movement and ritual' instead of 'the projection of thought through language' (Caute, *Sixty-Eight*, p. 246). Ironically, Calder had been much involved in the Edinburgh Drama Conference of 1963, which had included early discussions of 'the death of the word' and introduced the alternative potential of 'happenings'. Unscripted, supposedly spontaneous events or quasi-rituals, these were favoured by Brook as an alternative to 'the Dead Theatre', and became a regular part of the underground and alternative theatrical scene in the 1960s. Some of their manner later extended into performance art—usually highly physical, focusing attention on the body through nudity, violence, or sometimes self-inflicted injury.

New emphasis on physicality and spontaneity also featured in the work of the New York-based Living Theatre, regular visitors to Europe in the 1960s, playing an influential Roundhouse season in 1969. Several alternative companies in England shared their interests, or otherwise developed during the later 1960s and 1970s the language of 'movement, attitudes and gestures' Artaud favoured. These included Pip Simmons, Welfare State, The People Show— regular producers of happenings—and Freehold, influenced like Brook by Grotowski. Gay and Women's companies establishing themselves in the mid-1970s had their own reasons for highlighting physicality and for endowing the human body with 'the dignity of signs'. Steven Berkoff also expressed a commitment to Artaud's principles, developed in the work of his London Theatre Group, set up in 1968. Emphasis on 'gesture, mime and music' shaped most of his productions (Cohn, p. 92)—particularly forcefully in the choreographed violence of *East* (1975) and *West* (1983), described in the latter as 'East End macho-animalistic precision' (II).

Like Berkoff, many of the performers of Theatre de Complicite trained with Jacques Lecoq in Paris, developing his mime and movement techniques excitingly in their later work. Founded in 1983, Complicite helped to extend the influence of physical theatre widely in the last decades of the century. One of many company-devised productions, *Mnemonic* (1999), unusually accentuated Complicite's habitual concentration on the body as a sign: concerns with memory, desire, and identity were focused throughout around an extraordinary body—a prehistoric corpse, exhumed from ice high in the Alps. The inventiveness of productions such as *Mnemonic* was widely admired in the 1980s and 1990s by audiences and critics alike: one of the latter described Complicite's improvised work as 'far more . . . alive than that of most playwrights' (Shank (ed.), p. 221). Complicite and companies like them seemed to suggest that the life of the word might really be threatened in late twentieth-century theatre, apparently moving closer to the 'age of images' Peter Brook had envisaged (Brook, p. 54). A 1990s critical survey even defined modern British drama, in its title, in terms of 'The Death of the Playwright' (Page (ed.), 1992).

Dramatists might have been further dispirited by a wave of adaptations, often distracting attention from original plays. *Nicholas*

Nickleby and *Les Misérables* (1985) were both huge commercial successes for the RSC in the 1980s: in an irony typical of the decade, Victor Hugo's story of poverty and despair eventually earned £1 billion at theatre box offices throughout the world. Many smaller companies followed the national ones in regularly bringing novel-adaptations rather than original drama to the stage. Others began in the 1970s to use playwrights only as contributors to a collaborative process, if at all—new freedoms from censorship allowing more scope for companies to devise or improvise scripts for themselves. Mike Leigh developed these tactics with various groups of actors, initially encouraged to improvise characters and speeches which he later scripted and directed for stage or cinema. The most successful result in the theatre was *Abigail's Party* (Hampstead, 1977), its bleak satire of suburban lives and pretensions close to the comic idiom recently developed by Alan Ayckbourn.

Yet the work even of the more innovative companies mentioned did less to reject than readjust the spoken word as a 'tool for dramatics'. Steven Berkoff considered that his theatre remained primarily verbal, despite its emphasis on physicality. Even when not performing classic texts from the European repertoire, such as Friedrich Dürrenmatt's *The Visit* (1989), Complicite continued to rely heavily on the spoken word in their company-devised pieces, and to publish the texts of productions such as *Mnemonic*. Some of Mike Leigh's devised work was also published as play scripts, and later produced by other companies much like any other dramatic text. Playwrights such as Caryl Churchill often recorded the rewards of collaborative company script-work, and of the closer contacts with performers it involved.[3] The word's continuing health was in any case strongly apparent in other areas of late twentieth-century English drama. While the period's theatre was readily seduced by a new 'poetry in . . . the human body', it was also still attracted to longer-established forms of poetic or verse drama.

Christopher Fry's *Curtmantle* (RSC, 1962) and *A Yard of Sun* (Nottingham Playhouse, 1970) extended into later decades idioms developed by T. S. Eliot, W. H. Auden, and Christopher Isherwood —as well as Fry himself—during the revival of poetic drama in the 1930s, 1940s, and 1950s. Verse was used in Charles Wood's *H*

---

[3] See pp. 310 and 336, above.

(1969), and extensively by John Arden, as part of the ballad form of plays such as *Serjeant Musgrave's Dance* (1959) and *Armstrong's Last Goodnight* (1964). Berkoff affirmed his commitment to the verbal through the use of verse in plays such as *Decadence* (1981): snappy rhyming couplets likewise sharpened Caryl Churchill's satire in *Serious Money* (1987). Tony Harrison developed several fluent verse forms in work for the National Theatre—translations and adaptations including Molière's *The Misanthrope* (1973), Racine's *Phèdre* (1975), Aeschylus's *The Oresteia* (1981), and his version of Medieval cycle plays, *The Mysteries* (1985)—and in *The Trackers of Oxyrhyncus*, staged in 1988 in the ruins of Delphi. Original verse drama continued to be written late in the period by Sean O'Brien, in his political satire *Laughter When We're Dead* (Newcastle Live Theatre, 2000), and extensively by Paul Godfrey. Heightened language added to a sense of the exalted or the extraordinary in many of the relations Godfrey portrayed—between lovestruck individuals on a midsummer's night in *A Bucket of Eels* (RSC, 1994); between art and life in *Once in a While the Odd Thing Happens* (National, 1990); between astronauts' earthly and extraterrestrial experiences in *The Blue Ball* (National, 1995).

Other playwrights not only survived Artaud's influences, but incorporated into scripted theatre some of his emphases on ritual, and on natural or unconscious forces—often shown in conflict with repressive social conventions. Heathcote Williams's *AC/DC* (Royal Court, 1970) practised the kind of 'exorcism' Artaud defined, showing characters engaged in stage rituals including simulated masturbation and the evolution of an incomprehensible primal language. These rituals eventually liberate them from the 'psychic capitalism' of a media-dominated age, allowing their renewed enjoyment of late 1960s freedoms, sexual and imaginative (Heathcote Williams, p. 83). David Rudkin employed ritual in darker ways in *Afore Night Come* (Arts, 1962), depicting a group of farm workers who release in murder—perhaps sacrifice—atavistic urges repressed by a restrictive, technologized society. Conflicts of nature and technology were further examined in Rudkin's *Ashes* (Open Space, 1974). This portrayed an infertile couple treated by medical science simply as malfunctioning 'clinical objects' (I). Intimate references to sexuality sustained a strongly physical element throughout—almost a ritual one, in the shape of the 'larger-than-life anatomy-class cross-sectioned phallus' wielded by the couple's oppressive advisers (I). Divisions between an oppressive society and natural or primal forces figured equally graphically in *The Saxon Shore* (Almeida, 1986). This showed Hadrian's Wall separating Roman 'civilization'—masculine, materialist, and Christian—from the more feminine values of community and mutual support prevailing among pagan Celts on the other side.

Comparable antitheses shaped Peter Shaffer's plays. Typically, these focused on representatives of a rational, materialist society who find themselves fascinated by figures 'on the other side'—ones embodying values, either religious or imaginative, which conventional society and its 'psychic capitalism' have excluded. In *The Royal Hunt of the Sun* (National, 1964), greed, military ambition, and hollow Christianity drive Pizzaro towards the conquest of South America, but his motives are mysteriously annulled when he encounters the Incas—stilled into awed inertia by the otherworldliness of their deity-sovereign. A longing for spirituality also appears in the young soldier who hopes—in vain—that the 'world still has sacred objects', and that Pizzaro's code of honour might offer one of them (I. ix). 'Lusts for transcendence' continued to appear in *Yonadab* (National, 1985; II. xiv), adapted from Dan Jacobson's novel *The Rape of Tamar* (1970). Its central figure is reasonably convinced of the impossibility of becoming a god through sexual relations, and doubtful of the existence of any gods at all. Yet he is still tormented by 'that grain of longing we all have in us for one irrefutable and redeeming wonder' (I. viii). In *Amadeus* (National, 1980), longings and frustrations of this kind torment the composer Salieri, aware of his own mediocrity and infuriated by God's endowment of Mozart with such overwhelming musical genius. They also afflict the psychiatrist in *Equus* (National, 1973) who gradually discovers that his patient has transmuted acute stresses into a perverse religion. Faith in the god Equus, 'calling . . . out of the black cave of the Psyche' has led to his ritual blinding of a whole stable of horses (II. xxii). Professionally committed to finding a cure, the psychiatrist nevertheless begins to wonder—much in the manner of R. D. Laing—whether 'the Normal world' and its graceless materialism might offer only a poor alternative even to such destructive religious compulsions (II. xxxv).

Equus profited from a detective-story format, straightforward moral issues such as cruelty to animals; sensational interests in religion, psychiatry, and sex; and even an element of nudity. Not surprisingly, it was one of the period's most popular plays. Broad appeal sometimes encouraged evaluation of Shaffer himself as a Salieri rather than a Mozart—primarily as a commercial dramatist, like his brother Anthony, whose detective parody *Sleuth* (St Martin's, 1970) was a long-running hit in the West End. Yet Shaffer's outstanding popularity also allows his drama, more usefully, to be considered symptomatically: its characteristics highlight a number of pressures and patterns informing the period and its theatre. Sceptics still lusting for transcendence, Shaffer's protagonists naturally appealed broadly to an age which had rejected religious faith without altogether eliminating longing for 'redeeming wonder'. Residual longings of this kind shaped Absurd drama. They also appeared widely elsewhere in the period's theatre. One of Dennis Potter's stage plays, *Sufficient Carbohydrate* (Hampstead, 1983), for example, describes an 'ache in the mind' of this kind (I. i). Lengthy discussions of transcendence appeared in Christopher Hampton's adaptation of George Steiner's *The Portage to San Cristobal of A.H.* (Mermaid, 1982), and in Jane Coles's *Backstroke in a Crowded Pool* (Bush, 1993).

Even Mark Ravenhill's characters in *Shopping and Fucking* (Royal Court, 1996) experience 'a sort of glimpse' as a momentary escape from the materialism the play depicts—though as his title implied, Ravenhill saw little alternative to a spiritless world offered by sexual relations at the end of the century (ix). The possibility appealed more strongly to dramatists earlier in the period. John Whiting's hero in *The Devils*, for example, wonders if 'the body can transcend its purpose' and if 'there is a way of salvation through each other' (II). In a largely post-religious age, faith in the redemptive or even mystic powers of personal relations, sex, and the body exercised a broad appeal—one particularly focused by D. H. Lawrence's influence at the start of the period.[4] Especially in *Yonadab*, and in showing deities drawn out of the individual psyche in *Equus*—even in suggesting psychology as a substitute for religion—Shaffer's drama was indicative in this area, too, of wider preoccupations of its time.

---

[4] See p. 26, above.

Style in Shaffer's work was as symptomatic as subject matter. The staging of *Equus* was typically spectacular, using stylized movement and skeletal equine headpieces to represent spectres drawn out of 'the cave of the psyche'. Both *Equus* and *The Royal Hunt of the Sun* developed the wish Shaffer mentions in an introduction to the latter: to create ' "Total" theatre, involving not only words but rites, mimes, masks and magics'. The staging of each play showed how far mainstream English theatre acquired during the 1960s what John Elsom called 'mime, style and athleticism, with such productions as *The Royal Hunt of the Sun*, and Brook's *A Midsummer Night's Dream* (1970) with its trapezes and juggling' (*Post-War Theatre*, p. 146). 'The shock physical and psychological effects of Artaud', Elsom added, had gradually 'fed into the mainstream from . . . experimental springs' (*Theatre Outside London*, p. 109). As he suggested, influences initially most apparent among smaller, experimental companies had widely suffused English drama by the early 1970s, continuing to shape the period's staging, acting, and directing thereafter.

These influences were strengthened by concurrence with Absurdism in the 1960s, and with some other movements in contemporary theatre. The 'distillations of dreams' Artaud demanded for his Theatre of Cruelty had obvious affinities with Absurd drama's symbolic or surreal 'stage pictures'. The restricted movement or physical disablement of Beckett's characters displayed in particular the kind of expressive physicality Artaud recommended, grotesquely emphasizing metaphysical constraints on their lives. Artaudian influences might have seemed less compatible with the political theatre emerging in the early 1970s: Brechtian commitment to objective political analysis might have seemed at odds with Artaud's emphasis on the unconscious and on 'aspects of the inner world'. Yet political playwrights were often content to combine the two. David Edgar considered that left-wing drama—his own included—generally sought to integrate the 'cerebral, unearthly detachment of Brecht's theory' with 'earthy, sensual, visceral experience' (Kershaw, p. 204). Artaud's supporters took a similar view. Peter Brook's admiration for Artaud was matched by equal enthusiasm for Brecht, described in *The Empty Space* as 'the strongest, most influential and the most radical theatre man of our time . . . the key figure' (p. 80). Brook's introduction to Weiss's *Marat/Sade* likewise argued that Brecht's 'use of "distance"' could be powerfully integrated with the 'violent subjective experience' of the Theatre of Cruelty (Weiss, p. 6).

In the early 1970s, this possibility became widely apparent to left-wing playwrights, often ready to combine Brechtian tactics with directly shocking stage devices and 'A-effects'. Physical and ritual elements of the sort Artaud recommended often contributed extensively to these effects, typically in the prolonged confrontation with a naked body in Portable Theatre's *Lay-By* (1971).[5] One of the fringe companies most committed to the body as a theatrical sign, Freehold, developed directly out of Portable's production of *Lay-By*. Among playwrights involved, Snoo Wilson remained closest to Artaud in later work, his introduction to *Flaming Bodies* (ICA, 1979) describing his play's action as a 'descent into the Abyss, the unconscious', and defining the theatre in general as 'an engagement with . . . monsters within ourselves' (pp. xiii–xiv). Engagement of this kind was gradually moderated in the work of other members of the *Lay-By* generation in the later 1970s and 1980s, and in the theatre generally at the time. But it reappeared widely in the 1990s in the new drama Stephen Daldry directed at the Royal Court. Much of this was stronger in raw moral outrage at the abyss of the world's affairs than in rational analysis of ways things might be set right. Sarah Kane's *Blasted* (1995), in particular, assaulted audiences almost physically with grotesque visions of violence, cannibalism, and dismemberment, rediscovering for the 1990s the power of shock and 'nihilism' plays such as *Lay-By* had contributed to political theatre in the early 1970s.

An original source of this power, for the period's theatre generally, was identified in 1964 by *The Times* reviewer who saw Brook's *Marat/Sade* 'merging . . . political and psychological action which derives from Europe's experience of the Nazi death camps' (Elsom, *Post-War Theatre Criticism*, p. 151). His views resembled ones A. L. Alvarez expressed two years earlier in discussing contemporary poetry, worrying that psychoanalysis showed 'mass evil outside us' exactly paralleled by 'the same forces . . . at work within us'.[6] Political, psychological, and emotional horrors coalesced readily for readers of late twentieth-century literature, and for theatre

---

[5] See pp. 308–9 and 329, above.   [6] See p. 191, above.

Fig. 14. Sarah Kane's *Blasted* at the Royal Court in 1995.

audiences, aware that the darkest descents into the abyss, or the bleakest confrontations with the unthinkable, reflected only minutely the absurd cruelties of recent history. English drama needed to learn from Artaud, as well as Brecht, in order to deal as best as it could with the demands of this history. Though the two influences seemed antithetical in the abstract, in practice their combination accounted for many of the characteristics of the period's drama.

Growing interest in Artaud in the 1960s also confirms the key role played by the new energies of that decade in the continuing revival of the theatre. The liberated mood of the 1960s allowed a recovery of powers—originating in the body, sexuality, ritual, transgression of taboos—which Artaud considered fundamental to drama, and which can also be retraced to Western theatre's origins in the Dionysiac rituals of ancient Greece. Often suppressed in English drama before the mid-1950s, these powers continued to be drawn back into the theatre by the relaxation of moral, social, and sexual constraints in the next decade, and by the Dionysiac or 'carnival' atmosphere described in Chapter 1. Despite its many direct effects, the abolition of theatre censorship in 1968 was as much a symptom as a cause of dramatic freedoms developing at the time. Though the theatre never quite established itself as the 'holy' space Brook envisaged, it gained much from the decline of holiness in other areas— from the slackening not only of religious faith, but of traditional pieties, respects, and reverences throughout the life of the times. This directly encouraged the social and political drama of the 1970s: more fundamentally, it renewed access to energies within society and the body politic, even within the body itself, which allowed theatre to fulfil some of the hopes for a 'great revolution' which George Devine expressed in the 1950s (Wardle, p. 284). Though failing to bring about the political revolution 1970s dramatists sought— replaced by the broader social one earlier chapters outlined—English theatre in the later twentieth century did at least succeed in revolutionizing itself.

14

Revolution, Television, Subsidy

'Art never expresses anything but itself' (I), a playwright—clearly modelled on Tom Stoppard—suggests in Peter Nichols's *A Piece of My Mind* (1987). Theatrical art, at any rate, has always been interested in itself, plays-within-plays and other forms of metatheatre appearing regularly on English stages ever since Shakespeare's *A Midsummer Night's Dream*, or indeed much earlier. Yet in the later twentieth century—consistently with some of the postmodernist influences of the time—drama was more widely and diversely self-interested than in most earlier ages. Relations between theatre, art, and life were explored extensively by Tom Stoppard, Michael Frayn, and David Pownall, as well as by Peter Nichols himself.[1] Their interests were shared by writers including James Saunders, in *Next Time I'll Sing to You* (1962); David Storey in *Life Class* (Royal Court, 1974); Ben Elton, in comedies such as *Silly Cow* (Theatre Royal, Haymarket, 1991); Martin Crimp in *The Treatment* (Royal Court, 1993); April de Angelis in *Playhouse Creatures* (Old Vic, 1997); and Charles Wood, reflecting his work as a screenwriter in *Veterans* (Royal Court, 1972) and *Has 'Washington' Legs?* (National, 1978). A metatheatrical mode also figured in Ronald Harwood's *The Dresser* (Manchester Royal Exchange, 1980), based on the author's experiences with one of the last great actor-managers, Donald Wolfit, and his travelling company in the 1950s. One of the most popular of the period's plays, *The Dresser* was funny as well as sad, allowing its audiences a backstage insight—like Michael Frayn's in

---

[1] All are discussed in Ch. 12, above.

Noises Off (1982)—into desperate measures needed to keep *King Lear* going during the ailing star's last-ever performance.

Left-wing playwrights sometimes found a useful benchmark for later attitudes in Shakespeare, and in *King Lear* especially. Questioning of Shakespeare's political vision in Edward Bond's *Lear* (1972)[2] was extended in his portrayal of Shakespeare himself in *Bingo* (Royal Court, 1974), and by yet more Lears—Howard Barker's, in his political parable *Seven Lears* (Sheffield Crucible, 1989). Other political dramatists used plays-within-plays to high-light roles forced on individuals by governments or class structures. Metatheatre figured in this way in Alan Bennett's *Forty Years On* (1968), Howard Brenton's *The Churchill Play* (1974), David Edgar's *O Fair Jerusalem* (1975), Trevor Griffiths's *Comedians* (1975), Peter Barnes's *Red Noses* (RSC, 1985), and David Hare's *Amy's View* (1997). In *Our Country's Good* (Royal Court, 1988), Timberlake Wertenbaker also used metatheatre to examine hierar-chies in English and in colonial society, depicting a group of trans-ported convicts who explore new roles in Australia through rehearsals of George Farquhar's *The Recruiting Officer* (1706).

Another ailing Lear—and another vanishing theatrical tradition—appeared in Nigel Williams's *My Brother's Keeper?* (Greenwich, 1985). This showed a contemporary playwright arguing with his dying father, an actor of the old school, once a successful King Lear, who laments the disappearance of 'the classical gesture' from drama currently dominating the English stage (I). His hostility to his son's writing introduces a further self-reflexive, autobiographical element, as the example criticized clearly resembles Williams's own play about the Industrial Relations Bill, *Line 'Em* (National, 1980), typical of commitments shaping left-wing drama at the time. Like Harwood in *The Dresser*, in other words, in *My Brother's Keeper?* Williams examined conflicts between the generations which were as much theatrical as personal. Each play emphasized how thoroughly late twentieth-century drama had rejected manners, traditions, and the 'gentleman code' long dominant on the English stage. Directly or indirectly, this revolution in style and attitude was reflected in many of the other plays mentioned above. Their widespread use of metatheatre represented a kind of self-confidence: an expectation

[2] See p. 305, above.

that better-educated, theatrically aware audiences would share the stage's interest in its own devices, recognize references to earlier classics and traditions, and also appreciate how far contemporary drama had moved beyond them in attitude and style.

Confidence of this kind and the theatrical revolution it reflected seemed in many ways surprising developments in a period of such fierce competition from other media. Whether television's first firm influence in national life is dated to the Coronation in 1953, or to the addition of a commercial channel late in 1955, it closely coincided with the appearance of the new drama in the mid-1950s. At the time, this was not thought a happy coincidence for the theatre. Then and later, television was usually considered an adversary of the stage, often by playwrights themselves.[3] More than a hundred theatres, after all, had closed throughout the country between 1945 and 1960, and television, as well as the cinema, was assumed in later years to have contributed directly to their demise. Perhaps as a figuration of fears of the new medium, and its likely distraction of audiences, television cast a peculiarly baleful glare over several plays early in the period. In Henry Living's *Big Soft Nellie* (Oxford Playhouse, 1961) the apparently innocent question asked of the central character, 'Did you watch telly last night?' is followed by the stage direction 'for a red blinding second Stanley would like to break the room up. Then it all spins round' (I). Not surprisingly, this leads to the suggestion, confirmed by much else in the play, that he may have 'turned against television as an institution' (II). Characters in Heathcote Williams's *AC/DC* (1970) had clearly done so. Numerous television monitors focus their resentment of a 'psychic capitalism' which seeks to control imagination and all inner mental space on behalf of business and government (p. 83). Similar uneasiness appeared in Shaffer's *Equus* (1973), in the psychiatrist's conviction that 'normal' society is being warped by 'a non-stop drench of cathode-ray over our shrivelling heads' (II. xxxv).

This concern was shared by left-wing dramatists throughout the period. Arnold Wesker was already worried in 1958, in *Chicken Soup with Barley* (1958), that television created 'a world where people don't think any more' (III. ii). Peter Flannery, in *Our Friends in the North* (1982), suggested that for the population in general

[3] See p. 126, above.

television kept political issues safely 'sealed up in glass boxes . . . not real to them anymore' (II. iii). In *The Absence of War* (1993), David Hare showed television controlling politics and public life in the 1990s almost completely. Though Trevor Griffiths thought socialist playwrights should try to harness the huge new influence of television—potentially a genuine national theatre of the people—John McGrath warned in 1975 that the mass media were 'so penetrated by the ruling class ideology' as to make it impossible to do so (Itzin, p. 120). This was a pessimistic conclusion, given the social criticism often expressed in the long-running *Z-Cars* series McGrath helped create for the BBC in the early 1960s.

Playwrights were initially concerned about other problems in television. John Arden and John Osborne recorded disappointment in the early 1960s about constraints forced on their work by the technical limitations of the new medium. Dennis Potter worried at the time that even the best of what 'flickers so ephemerally on the little screen' was 'of necessity surrounded by acres of rubbish' and likely to be submerged in 'the inevitable tide of domestic chatter which . . . engulfs the TV set in the corner of the living-room' (*Nigel Barton Plays*, pp. 7, 9). Peter Nichols also regretted that all his efforts for television vanished 'after just one airing, which quite possibly no critic would write about and would never get into print' (J. R. Taylor, p. 17). The development of video recording in the 1980s eventually dispelled most of these worries about ephemerality, but in many cases playwrights' fears of television had receded long before then. In part, this resulted simply from the financial rewards the new medium offered, usually more generous than anything the theatre could afford. Even by 1980, more than 2,000 dramatic items were required annually by radio and television, helping to make the craft of play-writing more secure financially, and more attractive generally. Dramatists such as Dennis Potter and Alan Bleasdale worked almost exclusively for television, and the majority of those mentioned in earlier chapters did so at least occasionally. For some— such as Trevor Griffiths, David Rudkin, Alan Plater, or David Mercer—television gradually became a more important medium than live theatre.

By the 1960s, television had also begun to offer dramatists the new excitement of a mass audience. When ITV televised Harold Pinter's

A Night Out in its *Armchair Theatre* series in 1960, it reached more than six million viewers, leading its author to reflect that *The Caretaker*, then playing at the Duchess Theatre, would require a continuous run of thirty years to accumulate an equivalent audience (Brandt (ed.), p. 1). Television offered Pinter new tactics as well as new audiences. Scene directions in plays such as *Tea Party* (BBC, 1965) suggest that the camera allowed a concentration on the vision of individual characters less easy to sustain on the stage, yet ideal for the interests of much of Pinter's drama. Techniques of this kind, opening up some of the inner life of characters, appealed to several television dramatists who emerged in the 1960s, Dennis Potter particularly. Technical and artistic sophistication continued to develop, along with a widening audience, as the decade went on. *Armchair Theatre* had begun broadcasting in 1956: in the early 1960s, usually scheduled at a peak time on Sunday evenings, it sometimes attracted as many as ten million viewers. The BBC was often equally successful with its *Wednesday Play* series, televised from 1963 to 1970, and later with *Play for Today*. Like *Armchair Theatre*, *The Wednesday Play* mostly developed social realism and social concerns emerging more generally in drama in the late 1950s and early 1960s—especially powerfully in Jeremy Sandford's bitter examination of homelessness, *Cathy Come Home* (1966). But neither series was exclusive in style or interest, drawing widely on the work of authors successful in the theatre at the time, including Paul Ableman, Nell Dunn, David Halliwell, John Mortimer, Michael Frayn, John Osborne, and Charles Wood.

Like so much else at the time, television drama in the 1960s and early 1970s seemed to later critics to have enjoyed a 'Golden Age'—one whose promise developed only patchily in the harsher economic climate which followed (Bloom and Day, p. 181). Reports at the end of the century suggested that production of original drama had remained fairly consistent on Channel 4 and BBC2, but much less so on the main channels. BBC1 and ITV increased output of soap operas by as much as 150 per cent after 1975, while drama production on BBC1 had halved, to around 10 per cent of its total programming. Yet in other ways television's impact on playwrights—and on the population in general—remained undiminished in the 1990s. Playwrights working earlier in the period often warmly recalled the introduction to the classics, and to drama generally, offered by BBC radio around mid-century. For their successors, television was an even more familiar part of daily life, shaping imagination from childhood onwards. Hanif Kureishi, for example, recorded being impressed at an early age by *Play for Today*, and Jonathan Harvey described a love since childhood simply of television generally. For these playwrights and many others late in the century, television provided not only an early introduction to drama, but a powerful model for its pacing and construction. Pinter was an important source of minimal, tense dialogue styles developed by 1990s playwrights such as Mark Ravenhill, Jez Butterworth, and Patrick Marber,[4] but television was a more significant influence on the overall form of their work. Short scenes, quick alternations in location, and fragmentary, episodic structures became the norm in 1980s and 1990s drama, easily accepted by audiences familiar with television and film. Brecht first learned some of his strategies from the montage tactics of early cinema: even if his work had not shaped theatre so extensively from the 1960s onwards, something close to his 'epic' form of construction would eventually have developed through the direct influence of television and film.

In other ways, too, television affected the theatre more positively than had been expected in the late 1950s and early 1960s. As Pinter acknowledged, televising a single play obviously hugely increased its audience. But television also increased interest in drama more subtly, contributing throughout the period to a gradual broadening of the audience for plays, on stage as well as on screen. By offering the whole population daily experience of many kinds of performance, television made drama a more familiar part of everyday life than ever before, and the theatre, as a result, less remote and less exclusively middle class than it had often seemed earlier in the century. Styles and interests television favoured, especially in its early years, also made drama, generally, more immediate and more open to the imagination of the population as a whole. *Wednesday Plays* such as *Cathy Come Home*, or programmes such as *Coronation Street*, starting in 1960—or the *Z-Cars* series which followed in 1962—all suggested that absorbing subjects for drama could be found as easily in everyday life as in the exalted passions often supposed the mainstay of theatre. Television's new, powerful treatment of this life helped the

[4] See p. 353, above.

stage in other ways, encouraging it to develop further modes and interests of its own, and to rely on its unique communality as a live public event. Outdone by the television camera's powers of representation, the theatre had good reason to move beyond realism, towards imaginative, stylized action or the kind of surreal 'stage pictures' developed by Absurdism. Especially after the abolition of censorship in 1968, theatre also began to exploit more often freedoms not so available to the broadcast media—for improvisation or direct involvement of audiences, for example; for outspoken political commentary; or for Artaudian emphases on shock, ritual, and the body.

John Elsom concluded in 1971—contrary to worries a decade or so earlier—that the rise of television had actually 'concealed many blessings' for the stage (*Theatre Outside London*, p. 65). As he suggested, the new drama not only survived television's influence, it had often profited from it. Though the stage did initially lose audiences to television, factors discussed above ensured that they generally came back again, even by the 1970s, in a more receptive frame of mind. Later in the period, television continued to democratize culture and drama, helping to realize some of the Royal Court's late 1950s dreams of a broad popular audience. Even in 1956, at the very beginning of the Royal Court's dramatic revolution, television provided crucial assistance. Crises in Suez and Budapest added to the topical appeal of Osborne's *Look Back in Anger* during its second run in the autumn, but a still more significant factor was the extract broadcast on BBC television on 16 October. Until then, Irving Wardle recorded, attendances at the Royal Court had been 'appalling', but 'within three days applications for tickets were arriving in sackfuls' and 'a completely new audience' had appeared, of exactly the sort the theatre had hoped to find (p. 185). Stage, film, translation, and further television rights for *Look Back in Anger* earned the Royal Court more than £50,000 over the next five years, helping it through a very difficult financial period. If television had not established a new audience for Osborne in late October, the English Stage Company might not have survived beyond 1956. Many of the plays mentioned in earlier chapters might never have been produced, and the revolutionary new drama the Royal Court encouraged might have vanished almost as soon as it appeared.

Yet in the longer term the new drama owed less to a first age of television than to a first age of government subsidy for the arts.[5] By 1964, the Royal Court had received £50,000 of Arts Council funding, including £20,000 in 1962/3 alone. Rates of subsidy increased rapidly thereafter, as the Arts Council's own finances improved. By the middle of the decade, the government had apparently accepted the kind of views expressed by Kenneth Tynan—that the theatre, and the arts generally, should be 'an amenity for which the state or the municipality . . . must hold itself responsible', and not one in which 'the need or desire to show a profit' should be primary motives (Tynan, pp. 355, 361). Arts Council annual budgets doubled under the Labour government in the late 1960s, standing at £8 million by the end of the decade. They continued to rise rapidly in the 1970s, reaching £25 million in 1974. Ten years later, government subsidy to the arts had passed £100 million annually, with around a quarter spent on drama, and by the mid-1990s the figure was more than £220 million. Along with subsidies from local authorities—particularly the Greater London Council, until it was abolished in 1986—support on this scale influenced the period's drama decisively and fundamentally. Far fewer of the writers discussed in earlier chapters would have had their work staged without it. Companies and theatres producing their plays almost invariably depended on Arts Council support for their survival, or in the case of the largest and most influential—the National and the RSC—for their establishment in the first place.

By the 1970s, playwrights were also being helped directly by the Arts Council, either through bursaries, or through grants enabling theatres to commission plays and offer guarantees of royalty payments. Each scheme continued into the 1990s, along with Resident Dramatist Awards which allowed playwrights to work closely with a company and have their plays produced by it. But the main influence of Arts Council and local authority funding was in establishing and maintaining throughout the period a quite new, non-commercial sector of theatre, producing new plays and serious drama on a scale which 'the need or desire to show a profit' could never have sustained alone. Early in the period, commercial theatres had still been able to encourage several new playwrights. Harold Pinter, Joe Orton, David Hare, and Simon Gray were all staged by

---

[5] The Arts Council's general history in the period is outlined on pp. 33–4, above.

Michael Codron, one of the new producers who gradually took over the West End, controlled almost completely in the 1940s and 1950s by the HM Tennent production company under Hugh 'Binkie' Beaumont. But rising costs in the 1950s and 1960s increasingly forced on theatres dependent on the box office the 'inhibitions' John Elsom described—'timidity in choice of plays, reliance upon stars, an unwillingness to challenge popular prejudices . . . the habit of prolonging hits endlessly' (*Post-War Theatre*, p. 89).

Similar inhibitions continued to afflict commercial theatre later in the period, and they were more than ever in evidence towards its end. Peter Nichols worried in the later 1980s, in *A Piece of My Mind* (1987), about the dominance of West End theatres by 'girls got up as cats or trains' (II). The Andrew Lloyd Webber musicals he referred to—*Cats* and *Starlight Express*—were both still running a dozen years later, at the end of the century. Alongside them in central London's main theatres, in the summer of 1999, there were twenty other musicals, seven light comedies, and two thrillers—one of them, Agatha Christie's *The Mousetrap*, was in its forty-seventh year, close to its 20,000th performance. Outwith the newly completed replica of Shakespeare's theatre, the Globe, and theatres supported by the Arts Council—the National, the RSC, the Royal Court, and some smaller venues—only six items appeared in the London Official Theatre Guide's category of 'play', and of those only one was entirely new. Not surprisingly, critics in the 1990s such as Theodore Shank found reason to be 'extraordinarily grateful' for Arts Council support, given what 'the commercial theatres of the West End' indicated about the fate of drama without it (Shank (ed.), p. 184).

Yet the Arts Council never earned more than two cheers for its work, and usually less. Its funding contrasted poorly with resources available on the Continent: government support for the arts was lower in Britain than anywhere else in Europe. Per head of population, it was eight times lower than in Sweden or Holland, and fourteen times less than in Germany: three German municipalities, together, spent more than the entire Arts Council budget in the mid-1970s, expecting their theatres to derive only 15 per cent of their income from the box office. Inadequacies in Arts Council drama funding became particularly obvious in the inflationary 1970s. Grants were rapidly outstripped by the growing costs of equipment and administration, and by the new burden of Value Added Tax, imposed on theatres in 1973. Difficulties were compounded by settlements justifiably demanded by the actors' union, Equity, and the Theatre Writers Union. Founded in 1975, the latter had increased the minimum fee for a commissioned play from around £350 in the middle of the decade to £2,000 at its end: by the early 1990s, it had risen to £3,800. Faced with a £100,000 shortfall in its funding by the mid-1970s, even the Royal Court was forced to consider abandoning new writing.

As its response showed, timidity in choice of plays easily extended from the commercial sector to any theatre experiencing financial difficulties. Uncertain in their appeal to audiences or sponsors, productions of new plays generally declined in number later in the century, from about 12 per cent of work staged by London and regional theatres between 1970 and 1985, to around half that figure by the early 1990s. Eighty-seven playwrights signed an open letter—instigated by Sarah Daniels, Winsome Pinnock, Paul Godfrey, and others—pointing out the lack of opportunities for staging new work in the 1990s, and asking for increased commitments to new drama in subsidized theatres. In another open letter, to the Director of the National Theatre, Peter Nichols complained about similar difficulties experienced even by an older, established generation of writers. There was little immediate response. Hopes for improved rates of subsidy remained largely unfulfilled in the 1990s. The new National Lottery added to arts funding from the middle of the decade, but in 1996, for example, of the £250 million it contributed, only £15 million reached the theatre. The new Labour government initially did little to help: by early 2000, support for theatres through the Arts Council had fallen by 0.4 per cent in real terms since its election in 1997. Doubts were regularly expressed around this time about theatres' ability to extend late twentieth-century achievements into the new millennium, or to sustain the kind of 'perpetual revolution' in drama Peter Brook demanded in *The Empty Space* (p. 108).

Surveying the position early in 2000, the *Guardian* could point to several positive developments, such as the new or refurbished premises for Soho Theatre and the Royal Court: commitment to new writing in these theatres was shared with others including Manchester Royal Exchange, Birmingham Rep, Hampstead, the National, and the Bush. The same article claimed that the work of Joe Penhall, Nick Grosso, Sarah Kane, Mark Ravenhill, and Patrick Marber had seemed 'the most exciting in the world' in the mid-1990s. But it also worried that the energies of this 'new play renaissance' had faltered seriously after a few seasons, and might have run out altogether by 1999, when the *Evening Standard* could find no new work worthy of its annual drama award (*Guardian*, 5 Jan. 2000, p. 14). Later in 2000, an Arts Council Report likewise claimed English theatre as 'among the best in the world', but admitted that it was an 'art form in crisis', underfunded by as much as £25 million annually, and suffering from a decline in audiences and in the quality of plays (*Guardian*, 19 May, p. 7). Decisive change for the better occurred only after the end of the century, with a substantial increase in Arts Council funding from 2003, including an additional £25 million annually for the theatre. In general, the arts at the time remained nearly £50 million worse off in real terms compared to their position in 1994: where theatre was concerned, most commentators agreed that new funds were probably just sufficient, and just in time, to reverse the decline of recent years.

Yet for much of the period the theatre's financial difficulties resulted not only from an overall shortage in government funding. They were also created by some of the Arts Council's own policies and priorities, regularly criticized, by commentators such as Baz Kershaw, for being 'centrist and hierarchical . . . undemocratic' (Kershaw, p. 137). In fairness, the Arts Council could be partly defended against charges of centrism, a problem it recognized itself and introduced some measures to try and redress. Regional Arts Boards, some commitment to touring by the national companies, and the appeal to local audiences of new theatres and repertory companies developing in the 1960s[6] ensured that drama, in general, became less exclusively a metropolitan experience during the period. Northern settings and interests appeared from its early years in the work of writers such as Dennis Potter, Alan Plater, Peter Flannery, David Storey, John Godber, and Shelagh Delaney, and the life of the West Country later figured occasionally in plays by Philip Osment and Nick Darke. Yet for much of the period around 50 per cent of all arts funding continued to be spent in London. Richer resources and

[6] See p. 285, above.

the scale and diversity of its potential audience allowed metropolitan theatre to risk new plays more regularly than the regional repertory companies. As Simon Shepherd and Peter Womack suggested in *English Drama: A Cultural History* (1996), it remained all too possible in the later twentieth century to speak of ' "English drama" [as] meaning the drama of the London-centred theatrical system' (p. x).

Still less defence could be found against Baz Kershaw's other charges. Indeed, the Arts Council's own reports regularly argued that a hierarchical element was inevitable in all arts funding—an assumption obvious in its preferential treatment of prestigious national companies. In the early 1990s, for example, the National Theatre annually received more than £11 million, and the RSC nearly £9 million, while the Royal Court was awarded £840,000 and Paines Plough, a touring company committed to new writing, only £143,000. Hierarchical policies were still clearer in the overall valuation of drama relative to opera, an art form which generally retained its elite status in England during the period. While theatre as a whole received £15 million of that £250 million of Lottery funding in 1996, £78 million went to the Royal Opera House, Covent Garden alone—despite its many serious shortcomings at the time. This unstinting generosity was by no means new, reproducing in only slightly more extreme form the Arts Council's priorities at the start of the period, and indeed from its very inception. In 1957–8, the entire drama budget amounted to less than £70,000, while the Royal Opera House was allocated more than £300,000. This disproportion was an inevitable consequence, Shepherd and Womack explained, of the government initially setting up the Arts Council with the covert, undemocratic, but firm understanding that Covent Garden would be its principal beneficiary. A fuller indication of funding inequities at the end of the 1950s can be given by comparing the Royal Opera House's £300,000 with the £5,000 given to the Royal Court in 1958–9, and the meagre £1,000 allocated to the company which came closest to making theatre a genuinely popular, accessible form—Joan Littlewood's Theatre Workshop.

From the beginning of the period, in other words, despite some of the Arts Council's professed intentions, allocations of subsidy never made widening the theatregoing public a principal priority. This limited any prospect of the genuinely national theatre envisaged by the former *Observer* critic Ronald Bryden in 1976—one which could be 'a majority art, a theatre for the nation, not just for its university graduates . . . a genuine popular theatre . . . a stage of conversation, journalism, popular debate and millennial visions; a theatre of hope for the whole nation' (Peter Roberts (ed.), pp. 135, 137). Instead, when the 'National Theatre of Great Britain and Northern Ireland'—to give it its full official title—began working in its new building that year, it related only rather partially to the country it was supposed to serve. Its interest in drama from the peripheral nations of the United Kingdom remained extremely patchy, and there were limitations in its appeal even to the English public on its own doorstep, around Waterloo on the South Bank. Though the late twentieth century witnessed what Martin Esslin called 'the most vigorous period of dramatic writing . . . since Elizabethan and Jacobean times', the witnesses—in the National and many other established theatres—probably remained a good deal narrower in social background than would have been the case on the South Bank in Shakespeare's day (Shank (ed.), p. 180).

And yet, though English theatre may have lost much since the 1590s, it had nevertheless gained a great deal since the 1950s. By the end of the century, audiences were at any rate much more numerous, and more varied, than fifty years earlier. In the early 1990s, the Arts Council estimated that one adult in four was a theatregoer, that there were around eleven million theatre attendances annually, and that audiences had generally developed in expectation and discrimination as well as just in numbers. Influences from other media, from broader patterns of education, and from within theatre itself, all helped drama during the period to shed much of its exclusive image, and to share and extend the wider cultural democratization of the age. Playwrights, and plays themselves, were particular beneficiaries of a more relaxed cultural climate. In 2000, Dominic Dromgoole's study of contemporary play-writing concluded that

We live in an age of greater enfranchisement than any previous. It's not universal, it's not perfect, but it's considerably more inclusive than anything that's gone before. Many of today's boldest and brightest talents would not even have developed an appetite for drama in previous ages, let alone the confidence to create. This breadth of authorship has led inevitably and happily to an enormous broadening of content. Ideas, rhythms, worlds and concerns have reached the stage that would not have been mentioned in the drawing room just fifty years ago. Or even the toilet. Democracy flowers into represented life faster on the stage than in any other medium. (p. vi)

As he suggested, fading hierarchies, new cultural divisions, and a range of newly enfranchised voices made the theatre a natural centre for late twentieth-century society's conversations with itself—even if that society was still not represented quite as fully as the Royal Court and other theatres had sometimes hoped in the late 1950s.

Part IV

Narrative

15

To the Crossroads: Style and Society in the 1960s and 1970s

'A veil, a thick curtain, had fallen between "now" and "before the war"', Anthony Powell records in *The Soldier's Art* (1966, ch. 2). Many authors in the period tried to lift this veil from the past, tracing the features and stresses of recent history in the form and vision of their fiction. Longer-term moral and historical implications of the war are described in Chapters 16 and 17. In the years just after 1945, there was a more immediate need to lift the curtain separating 'now' and 'before'—to reconnect individual life with a broader history, and to re-establish a sense of continuity in each. This need shaped three long novel-sequences appearing at the time, each looking back across the changeful life of the twentieth century and seeking some pattern in its public and private affairs. C. P. Snow's *The Light and the Dark* (1947) extended an earlier novel, *George Passant* (1940) towards an eleven-volume sequence, *Strangers and Brothers*, completed in 1970. The twelve novels of Anthony Powell's *A Dance to the Music of Time* began to appear shortly afterwards, in 1951: *The Soldier's Art* was the eighth, and the sequence ended with *Hearing Secret Harmonies* in 1975. Henry Williamson also began publishing the fifteen volumes of *A Chronicle of Ancient Sunlight* in 1951. Completed in 1969, his sequence offered the longest historical perspective, following an individual life from the early childhood years, in London's rapidly sprawling suburbs at the turn of the century, described in the first volumes.[1]

[1] See also p. 52, above.

Snow and Powell were more broadly social in their interests, and concentrated on later periods, particularly around the Second World War. Each explored the huge transformations in English society and class assumptions occurring at the time, extended through the foundation of the Welfare State in the late 1940s. Both *Strangers and Brothers* and *A Dance to the Music of Time* illustrate in this way concerns which continued to develop throughout the 1950s, remaining a dominant influence on English fiction at the start of the period. Powell used chance meetings, dinner parties, and other social occasions to draw his many characters into dance-like patterns and relations—tactics which seemed ideally adapted to broad portrayal of English society. Yet in Powell's fiction, and in Snow's, a broad view is made relatively straightforward, in any case, by the limited scale on which 'society' is conceived. Snow's narrator talks in *The Sleep of Reason* (1968) about 'ten thousand jobs which really counted' in 'the compact English professional world, where, if you didn't know someone, you at least knew someone else who did' (chs. 7, 27). In *The Military Philosophers* (1968), Powell's narrator Nicholas Jenkins likewise records the view that only 'four or five hundred families' dominate substantial sections of English life (ch. 3). Each author envisaged the public affairs, arts, government, and industry of England being run, for much of the century, more or less by an old-boy network—a coterie based on private education, wealth, and pedigree. Each was also centrally concerned with growing, possibly terminal pressures on this self-contained society—with the last of an England structured and administered in this way.

Snow and Powell nevertheless viewed the decline or disappearance of this England with different degrees of enthusiasm. In *A Dance to the Music of Time,* Nicholas Jenkins's restrained outlook often makes him disdainful of tortuous relationships and unstable marriages, unravelling and reforming in the affluent milieu he inhabits, but he remains largely sympathetic to its values. He is therefore both repelled and fascinated by the sequence's principal outsider: Widmerpool, son of a liquid manure manufacturer, and a character as awkward and obtrusive as his name. By the time of *The Military Philosophers*, set in the Second World War, Widmerpool has grown into 'an archetypal figure, one of those fabulous monsters' in Jenkins's 'private mythology' (ch. 5). The war forces on Widmerpool himself the realization that he greatly enjoys power. Remorseless will continues to propel him up the social ladder in later years. But he occupies heights of industrial, governmental, or academic power with none of the grace or gentlemanly good manners such positions were once thought to require. His inexorable progress is exemplary in this way of what *The Acceptance World* (1955) calls 'the general disintegration of society in its traditional form . . . the significant crumbling of social foundations' (ch. 4). Especially as they accelerated after the war, these disintegral processes provided the principal interest of *A Dance to the Music of Time*. They were also examined by Simon Raven, in two further novel-sequences, *Alms for Oblivion* (1964–75) and *The First Born of Egypt* (1984–). Each reflected what Raven described, in the England of 1961, as 'the decay of manners and morals which ha[d] perverted public taste and brought disrepute on an imperial class' (*English Gentleman*, p. 17). Each sequence portrayed much the same widely interconnected upper- and upper-middle-class social world as Powell's, though one more than ever ruled by the selfishness and opportunism which made Widmerpool seem so monstrous to Jenkins.

It was mostly Jenkins's 'private mythology', of course, or ultimately Powell's, which made Widmerpool's progress seem so monstrous. From other points of view, he is simply a figure—though sometimes a genuinely unpleasant one—who demonstrates the shifting and lowering of class barriers during and after the war. Much of *A Dance to the Music of Time* examines with regret the disappearance of a 'gentleman code' which other commentators—Kenneth Tynan, for example—were happy to see expunged from the theatre, and from English life more generally, towards the end of the 1950s.[2] C. P. Snow was closer to this point of view in *Strangers and Brothers*. Based largely on the author himself, Snow's narrator and central figure Lewis Eliot is naturally presented more sympathetically than Widmerpool, but he is nevertheless a kind of Widmerpool seen from the inside. Like Widmerpool, he is deeply and continuously interested in power, and in gaining access to the public positions through which it is exercised. The sequence shows these positions opening up agreeably, especially in the post-war years, to anyone with education, expertise, and determination, rather than only the right

[2] See p. 275, above.

connections. Along with the patient, liberal intelligence of the perfect committee man, these are all attributes which Eliot learns to exercise very effectively. They take him from schooldays in the provinces through a successful academic career and eventually—in the phrase Snow's title *The Corridors of Power* (1964) added to the English language—to positions within the upper reaches of government. His progress illustrates how far consensual post-war politics, the Welfare State, and broadening patterns of education and affluence helped to open up new 'corridors' after the war.

The title of John Braine's *Room at the Top* (1957)—and a plot following another determined ascent of the social ladder—further confirmed this new sense of opportunity and class mobility. By the later 1950s, it had contributed to a phase of socially concerned writing—realistic, even documentary in style, and often directly encouraged by Snow's work as a fiction reviewer at the time. It was also influenced by Colin MacInnes and William Cooper. MacInnes's *Visions of London* trilogy—*City of Spades* (1957), *Absolute Beginners* (1959), *Mr Love and Justice* (1960)—moved down the social scale as enthusiastically as Braine's and Snow's figures moved up, following the lives of teenagers, immigrants, and drifters on the fringes of metropolitan society. Cooper's setting and his narrator's sceptical, disaffected tone in *Scenes from Provincial Life* (1950) offered another useful model for fiction in the later 1950s. Younger writers emerging at the time regularly concentrated on provincial, usually Northern settings. They also showed characters torn between new affluence or values and the continuing constraints of working-class life. Alan Sillitoe depicted Nottingham factory work in this way in *Saturday Night and Sunday Morning* (1958), and Keith Waterhouse a drab existence, demanding regular escape into fantasy, in *Billy Liar* (1959). Stan Barstow explored the morals of a close Northern community in *A Kind of Loving* (1960), and David Storey the tough, often violent demands of professional rugby league in *This Sporting Life* (1960).

Often popularized by grittily realistic film adaptations, the work of these authors opened up a much wider range of social strata than had usually figured in fiction in earlier decades. Part of the general democratization beginning to reshape culture at the time, this development was consolidated by the later work of these authors and by new ones emerging in the 1960s. Alan Sillitoe continued to show working-class figures constrained by class and social pressures in later novels, such as his trilogy *The Death of William Posters* (1965), *A Tree on Fire* (1967), and *The Flame of Life* (1974). In *Billy Liar on the Moon* (1975) Waterhouse followed his fantasizing hero into a life in urban environments as bleak as outer space. Later novels such as *Maggie Muggins* (1981) examined a similarly deprived metropolitan setting, dominated by alcoholism and unemployment. Like David Storey in *This Sporting Life*, in *The Blinder* (1966) Barry Hines depicted a working-class hero empowered by success in professional sport. In *A Kestrel for a Knave* (1968)—retitled *Kes* after Ken Loach's successful film in 1974—Hines went on to show care for a pet hawk temporarily transforming a Northern schoolboy's miserable existence. In most of the novels mentioned, perspectives on working-class life and outlooks were firmly male-centred, but several women writers soon offered a different view—Maureen Duffy, in her autobiographical *That's How it Was* (1962); Gillian Freeman, in much of her early fiction; Australian-born Christina Stead, describing life in her adopted country in *Cotter's England* (1967).

Other authors extended 1950s and 1960s interests in class and society into new areas in their later careers. New, soulless materialism on the edge of the 1960s appalled but also attracted David Storey's central figure in *This Sporting Life*. In *Radcliffe* (1963), Storey moved on to a wider assessment of conflicts between material and spiritual values, often presented symbolically—sometimes luridly and fantastically—as an ailment affecting 'the whole of Western society' (ch. 36). *Pasmore* (1972) showed interests in class and social mobility extending into deeper questioning of identity, role, and self. Such questions were often shaped for English writing in the late 1950s and 1960s—in the work of Colin Wilson particularly—by the spread of existentialist ideas from France.[3] In *Pasmore*, the hero's dreams of 'the pit and the blackness' which 'existed all around him' suggest the nothingness philosophers such as Jean-Paul Sartre and Albert Camus saw surrounding the self (ch. 13). More immediately, of course, they arise from guilty recollection of his father's work in the mines. Like some of the dramatists considered in Chapter 9, Storey included, and poets such as Tony Harrison, many novelists reflected social change

---

[3] Also influential in contemporary theatre: see Ch. 12, above.

and historical pressures in tensions within family life, between generations. 'A father is more than a person, he's in fact a society, the thing
you grow up into', Raymond Williams suggested in *Border Country*
(1960), another novel examining class mobility at the beginning of
the period (pt. 1, ch. 9). Like Williams himself, the central figure in
Border Country moves from a working-class childhood on the borders of Wales, and from the formative influence of his father, towards
a very different life in the academic world, away 'from what used to
be real' (pt. 2, ch. 1). Lost fathers and difficulties with parents continued to reflect changing lifestyles and class affiliations throughout the
period—in Christina Stead's account of leaving a torrid family for
work in the Labour movement, in *Cotter's England*, for example.
Similar tactics figured in some of Margaret Drabble's later fiction,
such as *The Radiant Way* (1987), and in Hilary Mantel's *An
Experiment with Love* (1995). Family conflict was also used by these
authors, and others in the period, to highlight differences between
provincial life and the metropolis—gaps steadily widening, socially
and economically, towards the end of the century.

Like the fiction considered above, John Wain's first novel, *Hurry
on Down* (1953) and Kingsley Amis's, *Lucky Jim* (1954), each followed journeys up or down the social scale. Amis's hero moved up,
only to be irritated by pretensions he encounters when employed in a
provincial university. Wain's moved down, choosing a number of
unpromising jobs rather than the professional life. Yet each is conveniently rescued in the end by well-paid employment, and a match
with a desirable, affluent woman. Neither turns out to have been
interested in changing society, but only his own place in it—like
William Cooper's central figure, as the titles of later novels, *Scenes
from Married Life* (1961) and *Scenes from Metropolitan Life* (1982)
suggest. Though Wain and Amis were often grouped with the provincial writers mentioned above, and with dramatists such as John
Osborne, as 'Angry Young Men', associations with the restrained
idiom of the Movement, in contemporary poetry, were more appropriate. Both Wain and Amis were included as poets in Robert
Conquest's *New Lines* in 1956, and most of their work—in the novel
as well as poetry—belonged to the 'temperate zone' his anthology
helped to define.[4] Rather than the 'angry' or even revolutionary

---

[4] See p. 167, above.

novels they were sometimes supposed at the time, *Lucky Jim* and *Hurry on Down* were mild comedies, gently satiric of the changing 1950s society Wain's novel sometimes explicitly discussed.

Lucky Jim was nevertheless influential, especially in suggesting the usefulness of campus fiction for social observation. This potential was further emphasized in the early 1950s by a volume of C. P. Snow's *Strangers and Brothers* sequence, *The Masters* (1951), set in a Cambridge college. As the upper classes shifted away from the centre of attention in English life, interest also faded away from the country-house novel developed in the 1920s, 1930s, and 1940s by writers such as Aldous Huxley and Evelyn Waugh. In later decades, universities provided a convenient, alternative setting for significant social interaction: one in which characters from a range of backgrounds could be confined together, set to relate to one another, and plausibly allowed to expound theories and ideas. Rather as Howard Jacobson suggested in his campus novel *Coming from Behind* (1983), after the 1950s the country-house novel moved to Bradbury Lodge, with the publication of Malcolm Bradbury's *Eating People is Wrong* in 1959 and David Lodge's *The British Museum is Falling Down* in 1965. In later Lodge novels, campus settings continued to provide a natural context for the discussion of ideas—recent movements in literary theory in *Changing Places* (1975)—and a convenient one for examining social and economic conditions, in *Nice Work* (1988).[5] Though sharing most of Lodge's intellectual interests, Bradbury's fiction was generally closer to *Nice Work* in its broad concern with contemporary life and society. Bradbury examined new politics and attitudes in the 1960s in *The History Man* (1975), for example, and life in Eastern Europe both before the late 1980s collapse of communist regimes, in *Rates of Exchange* (1983), and after, in *Doctor Criminale* (1993). Like Lodge, Bradbury often explored in these novels encounters between liberal English attitudes and a world which seemed increasingly to threaten them. Confinement to the relatively safe space of academic work, and a surviving liberal optimism, nevertheless allowed such conflicts to be envisaged largely in comic terms.

Social change contributed in more direct ways to campus fiction's popularity: through the growing familiarity with university contexts,

---

[5] See Ch. 3, above.

among readers and authors, following the expansion in education after the war. From the 1960s onwards, increasing numbers of potential readers passed through higher education. On the evidence of *Contemporary Fiction*—a comprehensive guide to the work of authors achieving critical or popular success—by the 1990s around 66 per cent of novelists, too, had had first-hand experience of university life. It proved useful in many other novels in the period, including Thomas Hinde's *High* (1968), David Caute's *The Occupation* (1971), Pamela Hansford Johnson's *The Good Listener* (1975), A. N. Wilson's *The Healing Art* (1982), Anita Brookner's *Providence* (1982), and A. S. Byatt's *Possession* (1990) and *The Biographer's Tale* (2000). Unlike Bradbury's and Lodge's work, none of these was primarily a comic novel, though—typically of his writing—an ironic humour strongly marked A. N. Wilson's examination of religion, love, and death in *The Healing Art*. A wider reading of late twentieth-century fiction might nevertheless suggest that universities were among the last amusing places in a troubled contemporary world, useful sooner or later to almost all comic novelists. Tom Sharpe's complex, mechanical, farce plots were applied to university contexts in *Porterhouse Blue* (1974) and in *The Great Pursuit* (1977). J. I. M. Stewart offered a generally comic account of life in an Oxford college in another novel-sequence, *A Staircase in Surrey* (1974–8). Howard Jacobson managed to make even literary history funny in *Coming from Behind*, leavening his appraisal of critical influences from D. H. Lawrence, F. R. Leavis, post-structuralism, and contemporary football with a Jewish humour unusual in English fiction.

Kingsley Amis's best comic writing appeared long after the 1950s, in novels such as *Jake's Thing* (1978) and *The Old Devils* (1986). *Jake's Thing* is impatient with feminism and tetchy about other aspects of contemporary English life, but most of the 'anger' in each novel is directed more firmly—sometimes movingly—at personal rather than social stresses. Each is principally concerned with the problems of age. Each deals with a lifetime of unresolved personal emotions, and with the difficulties of finding the spirit—sometimes just beer and spirits—painfully confined within a failing physical frame. In attempting broader social satire instead, in his 1960s fiction, Amis often only highlighted problems novelists successful in the 1950s experienced in adjusting to the next decade. Amis's hero in

Jake's Thing might have been speaking for his author, and several of his contemporaries, when he recalls that 'I was doing fine when things really were repressive, if they ever were, it's only since they've become, oh, permissive that I've had trouble' (ch. 25). Relative repressiveness in the 1950s allowed the resentments of characters such as Amis's Lucky Jim to seem like significant rebellions. More liberal attitudes in the 1960s—and a shift of attention from class to issues of lifestyle and sexual behaviour—left a number of 1950s authors lacking a clear subject, or a clear vision of contemporary interests. Confusions on the edge of the new decade were unpleasantly evident in Amis's *Take a Girl Like You* (1960), for example. Tangled encounters between the heroine's 'old Bible-class ideas' and the 'free-and-easy way of going on' exemplified by her would-be seducer were scarcely resolved by an ending in rape and the conclusion that this is only 'rather a pity' (chs. 4, 27). C. P. Snow showed similar uneasiness and confusion in the penultimate novel of his *Strangers and Brothers* sequence, *The Sleep of Reason* (1968). From its first volume in the 1940s, *Strangers and Brothers* had located a flawed form of Lawrentian, utopian idealism in the figure of George Passant. But *The Sleep of Reason* took a still darker view of these ideals, and a negative one of 1960s student dissent and liberal sexuality in general. Snow presented each as the result merely of failed rationality and restraint, also identified as a cause of horrors such as the concentration camps, or, more recently, the Moors murders.

Developments in the 1960s made much of the fiction discussed above seem conservative stylistically, as well as often in moral terms, as Rubin Rabinovitz confirmed in his study *The Reaction against Experiment in the English Novel 1950–1960* (1967). Many novelists emerging in the 1950s turned away from modernism as firmly as Movement poets did at the time. Interests in class and society—even the serial method of publication—resumed much of the manner of Victorian fiction in novel-sequences by Snow and Powell. Concern with social change likewise encouraged other writers in the late 1950s and early 1960s to return, if not directly to the manner of Victorian fiction, at any rate to the example of early twentieth-century authors modernism had rejected. John Wain, C. P. Snow, and Kingsley Amis all expressed preferences for Arnold Bennett's style. Snow and William Cooper also favoured the social concern

and realistic manner of H. G. Wells. Cooper summed up a wider suspicion of modernism among his contemporaries in remarking that
'the Experimental Novel' had to be 'brushed out of the way before
we could get a proper hearing'(Rabinovitz, p. 6). Snow's reviewing
influentially extended the conclusion he recorded in *Times Literary
Supplement* on 15 August 1958—that 'Joyce's way is at best a cul-
de-sac' (p. iii).

During the 1960s, on the other hand, novelists once again grew
disposed to view modernism as a tour de force rather than a cul-de-
sac: as in poetry and drama, the decade's progressive, innovative
outlook gradually extended from lifestyle to literary style. This new
disposition was exemplified by the career of John Fowles. In portraying a lower-class figure who kidnaps a privileged girl, Fowles seemed
close to the class interests of late 1950s fiction in his first novel, *The
Collector* (1962). Yet its action is bizarre and obsessive enough to
make it more fantastic than realistic—a kind of parable, as Fowles
himself explained, about growing materialism and possessiveness in
contemporary society. Fowles followed similar directions in *The
Magus* (1965). Throughout, the novel provides a parable about relations between fantasy and reality, imagination and lived experience,
sustained through a series of 'godgames': illusions, masks, and performances orchestrated by a Prospero-figure. Fowles's most celebrated investigation of such interests appeared in *The French
Lieutenant's Woman*, published in 1969. Set a hundred years earlier,
the novel offers extended criticism of realist conventions, through
frequent parody and pastiche of Victorian fiction, and a strong
attack on Victorian conventionality more generally. Taking his
epigraph from Marx—'every emancipation is a restoration of the
human world and of human relationships to man himself'—Fowles
contrasts life in Victorian England with a whole range of new freedoms the 1960s had supposedly established.

These also shape the plot. *The French Lieutenant's Woman* shows
its central figure undergoing an existential process of liberation,
gradually freeing him from the 'iron certainties . . . rigid conventions
. . . repressed emotion' of the Victorians (ch. 48). He eventually
reaches a position of anguished but free self-determination, confronted at the end of the novel only by the formless openness of 'the
unplumb'd, salt, estranging sea' (ch. 61). Typically of Fowles's

fiction, too, much of this progress is owed to the liberating sexual influence of a mysterious heroine. The novel regularly contrasts her behaviour—sometimes with the help of extended footnotes—with constraining, hypocritical sexual conventions at work elsewhere in Victorian society. Criticism of fictional conventions is often equally explicit, as well as working through parody. Fowles's authorial voice famously intrudes at the start of chapter 13 to explain that the story he has so far told has been 'all imagination. These characters I create never existed outside my own mind'. In 'the age of Alain Robbe-Grillet and Roland Barthes', he adds, authors themselves should be existentially liberated, no longer functioning as 'the gods of the Victorian image, omniscient and decreeing; but in the new theological image, with freedom our first principle, not authority' (ch. 13). Several author figures turn up later in the novel to demonstrate this conclusion. New principles of freedom are further forced on readers through the obligation to choose between different endings to the story.

The French Lieutenant's Woman, in other words, reflected a range of new 1960s freedoms—political and conceptual, sexual and textual. Fowles also indicated a particular source of textual innovation in referring to 'the age of Alain Robbe-Grillet' and to 'the theoreticians of the *nouveau roman*' (ch. 55). Early in *Look Back in Anger*, Jimmy Porter puts down his Sunday newspaper and complains that he has 'just read three whole columns on the English Novel. Half of it's in French' (I). At the time of John Osborne's play—1956—and for a decade or so thereafter, English fiction did mostly look to France, at any rate for new, innovative influences. A student of French literature while at university, Fowles was particularly aware of these: not only of the existentialism of Sartre and Camus, but of the *nouveau roman* or 'new novel' developed in the 1950s by Robbe-Grillet, along with Michel Butor and Nathalie Sarraute. Like postmodern writers described in Chapter 2, the authors of the *nouveau roman* were sceptical of the novel's conventional creation of tidy forms and coherent meanings for life. Instead, they replaced attention to character with minute description of the object world, and conventional plot with puzzling, fractured forms and unresolvable actions, highlighting what Robbe-Grillet called 'the movement of the writing' itself (p. 64). New emphases of this kind reappeared in the work of several English authors, in the 1960s and later. One of them, naturally enough, was Robbe-Grillet's English translator Christine Brooke-Rose. She modelled *Out* (1964) partly on Robbe-Grillet's *La Jalousie* (1957), continuing its exhaustive, scientific description of objects. Similar tactics were followed in *Such* (1966) and *Between* (1968). Multilingual puns and eccentric typography in *Thru* (1975) question 'the movement of the writing', and language in general, in ways further developed in Brooke-Rose's later fiction through interests in post-structuralist literary theory and the work of Jacques Derrida.

Like Brooke-Rose, Brigid Brophy began her writing career conventionally enough in the 1950s, but went on to experiment throughout *In Transit* (1969) with a range of devices similar to those in *Thru*. Like Fowles, Rayner Heppenstall was a former student of French, changing the habits of a long-established career in the 1960s to develop some of the strategies of the *nouveau roman*. Its meticulous observation and puzzling plot reappear in *The Connecting Door* (1962), for example, in a story inexplicably located in two different periods of time at once. Some of the manner of the *nouveau roman* also figured in the early novels of Muriel Spark—a Scottish author, but one widely influential on English fiction in the 1960s and later. The heroine of Spark's first novel, *The Comforters* (1957), begins by writing a critical study of modern fiction, and later decides to write a novel about 'characters in a novel', but remains concerned throughout that she may herself be more creation than creator. A persistent faint sound of typing adds to her worries that 'a writer on another plane of existence' may be writing about *her*, and organizing her life into 'a convenient slick plot' (chs. 9, 3, 5). Self-reflexive, metafictional questions of this kind—about 'the movement of the writing', and about relations of plot, power, and authorial control—remained in evidence in much of Spark's 1960s fiction, and a particular concern of *The Driver's Seat* (1970) at the end of the decade. Some of Nicholas Mosley's 1960s fiction, such as *Accident* (1965), was similarly self-reflexive, questioning the ethics of narrative and its powers. His later novels continued to experiment unusually widely with forms and ideas.

Metafictional investigations of the nature of narrative and imagination were further extended at the end of the 1960s in the work of

David Caute, an admirer of Brooke-Rose, and of Jean-Paul Sartre. Some of Sartre's interest in literature's relation to politics reappeared in Caute's extraordinary trilogy, *The Confrontation*. Its first part, *The Demonstration* (1969), takes the form of a play, one of whose characters, an academic, ostensibly writes the second, *The Illusion* (1971). An extended critical essay, *The Illusion* speculates about whether 'a literature which invites its audience to question the prevailing social structure and social consciousness must constantly question and expose itself' (p. 22). The same character reappears in the trilogy's third part, *The Occupation* (1971), a novel which does question, throughout, the strategies and responsibilities of fiction, its own included. Its setting amid student activists, in a university in the United States, further emphasizes the interconnectedness of challenges to all conventions, social and political as well as literary, by the end of the 1960s. It also showed Caute following influences not only from French but from contemporary US fiction—regularly credited, throughout the later twentieth century, with more vitality and inventiveness than its English counterpart. Its innovative influences appeared in several other English novels at the time, often the work of writers, like Caute, or like David Lodge, who had visited the United States on 1960s academic scholarships. Thomas Hinde, for example, produced in *High* (1968) a metafiction similar to Caute's in *The Occupation*. In *The Undiscovered Country* (1968), Julian Mitchell alternated sections of realism and fantasy with discussion of his own methods and interests. Andrew Sinclair's *Gog* (1967) extended the idiom of Jack Kerouac into a kind of English road-novel. Alan Burns's *Babel* (1968) used the 'cut-up' techniques of William Burroughs to emphasize 'some sort of social and political fragmentation, some sort of dissolution' related to contemporary events including the war in Vietnam (p. 20).

The metafictional, self-questioning mode of all this 1960s writing showed the contemporary novel, as Robbe-Grillet suggested, 'more and more moving towards an age of fiction' in which 'invention and imagination may finally become the subject of the book'. Robbe-Grillet also defined this contemporary movement as postmodernist, following 'after Joyce' and the work of other modernist authors (pp. 46, 63). In focusing attention on the nature of literature and art, innovative influences from France and the United States often did

extend modernist ones—established earlier in the century, and modified or reinforced in other cultures before reappearing in the English
novel in the 1960s. Modernist strategies were in any case, of course,
as often Irish as English in origin. These, too, were reinforced for the
1960s by Irish intermediaries particularly significant at the start of
the decade, Flann O'Brien and Samuel Beckett.[6] Another of these
intermediaries, though only half-Irish, was Lawrence Durrell: widely
admired at the time, his tetralogy *The Alexandria Quartet* (1957–60)
first appeared in a single volume in 1962. Shifts in perspective
between its four parts, and repeatedly within them, created what the
novel itself describes as 'a multi-dimensional effect . . . a sort of prism-
sightedness': a 'palimpsest where different sorts of truth are thrown
down one upon the other' (*Justine*, pt. 1; *Balthazar*, ch. 10). Durrell
continued to develop interests in the nature of reality, art, illusion,
and 'different sorts of truth' in his *Avignon Quintet* (1974–85).

Conflicting sorts of 'truth', or constructions of it, also appeared
throughout Beckett's trilogy *Molloy*, *Malone Dies*, and *The
Unnamable*, originally published in French (1950–2), and first collected in a single volume, translated into English by the author, in
1959. Like his drama, Beckett's fiction was widely influential on
English writing, at that time and later. Effects on the metafictional
modes of the 1960s were also owed to Flann O'Brien's *At Swim-
Two-Birds*, reissued in 1960. These were particularly apparent in
B. S. Johnson's fiction. Johnson professed himself 'besotted by Irish
writers like Sam Beckett, James Joyce and Flann O'Brien', and he
began his first novel, *Travelling People* (1963) with a section parodying *At Swim-Two-Birds* (Gordon, p. 155). This includes the claim,
paraphrasing one made by O'Brien, that 'it was not only permissible
to expose the mechanism of a novel' but that through doing so fiction
could 'come nearer to reality and truth' (B. S. Johnson, p. 12). These
ideas were explored through diverse narrative forms and conflicting
versions of events in *Travelling People*. Johnson also highlighted
them in *Albert Angelo* (1964), appearing in his own persona—like
Fowles in *The French Lieutenant's Woman*—to announce that the
story he has told so far has been nothing but lies. *Albert Angelo* also
featured a set of holes cut through several pages to allow readers to
see into the future of the narrative.

---

[6] See pp. 79–80, above, and pp. 452–3, below.

Johnson challenged conventional linear narrative still more radically in one of the most celebrated of 1960s experiments, his novel-in-a-box, *The Unfortunates* (1969). Made up of numerous loose-leaf sections, intended to be shuffled and read in any order, the novel's extraordinary form was in a way imitative of the random operations of memory, one of Johnson's principal interests in *The Unfortunates*. It could also be seen as a radical, postmodernist extension of modernist departures from chronological sequence. In the modernist fiction of Virginia Woolf or Marcel Proust, for example, the conventional construction of the novel was fractured comparably—though not so literally—by reliance on character's memories as an ordering principle. Johnson continued to extend modernist tactics—of interior monologue, in particular—in *House Mother Normal* (1971), and in *Christy Malry's Own Double Entry* (1973) developed further the self-conscious, experimental modes of the previous decade. These also shaped the work of several younger writers emerging at the time. In *Bibliosexuality* (1973), Clive Sinclair was much concerned with 'the intercourse between writer and reader', and with the reliability of narrative in general (ch. 1). Similar concerns, along with traces of the *nouveau roman*, or even of the Theatre of the Absurd, also appeared in the work of Gabriel Josipovici. Novels such as *The Present* (1975) explored the unreliability of characters' perceptions and challenged readers, too, with puzzling, barely comprehensible fictional worlds.

Innovative, self-conscious modes were employed especially effectively by John Berger in *G.*, a Booker Prize winner in 1972. Along with Fowles's equation of sexual, textual, and other forms of freedom, *G.* developed Caute's interest in challenging established political structures through reshaping conventional literary ones. Insisting that 'the writer's desire to finish is fatal to the truth. The End unifies. Unity must be established in another way', *G.* offers readers little refuge, within the conventional consolation of completed literary form, from the historical challenges of a wider world (ch. 3). Instead, rather like Bertolt Brecht's drama, Berger's novel uses gaps and fractures in its fictional illusion—even in the layout of the text itself—as apertures through which historical forces can be framed and focused, and political understanding directed. Throughout *G.*, readers are required to draw their own political conclusions out of a fragmentary, inconclusive, self-questioning narrative, mixing stories of a sexually subversive Don Giovanni figure with historical accounts of revolutionary activity in nineteenth- and early twentieth-century Europe. Unity and other ideals, *G.* suggests, must be pursued politically, and not only aesthetically: by overthrowing conventional constraints, social as well as textual, and by using art not to transcend the world's disorders, but to direct progressive political vision upon them.

By the early 1970s, in other words, several influences—mostly originating abroad—had contributed an experimental, innovative, element to the English novel, reflecting the liberated mood and ideals of the time, and often encouraged by them. This was a marked contrast to the main direction at the start of the previous decade, when a formally conservative social realism had vigorously avoided modernist strategies and foreign idioms. David Lodge provided an influential model for these contrasting developments, and the contrary possibilities they had established, in his study *The Novelist at the Crossroads and Other Essays*, published in 1971. Its title essay defined 'the realistic novel' as 'the main road, the central tradition, of the English novel, coming down through the Victorians and Edwardians' at least as far as the 1950s. But Lodge also emphasized 'formidable discouragements to continuing serenely along the road of fictional realism' later in the twentieth century, and the extent to which modernist and postmodernist developments offered alternative directions (pp. 18, 22). Lodge's assessment of these directions as only minor roads, though unflattering, nevertheless fairly reflected the status of postmodernist and metafictional writing by the end of the 1960s: of the authors discussed above, only John Fowles and Muriel Spark had firmly established themselves in a mainstream of popular or critical attention. His discussion also offered a key insight into some of the most successful mainstream writers in the period— William Golding, Iris Murdoch, and Anthony Burgess in particular—in recognizing a recent reluctance to opt wholeheartedly either for tradition or innovation. Instead, Lodge pointed out, contemporary novelists often found it necessary to 'hesitate at the crossroads', and then 'to *build their hesitation into the novel itself*'(p. 22). Most of the authors concerned, however, had arrived at Lodge's 1970s crossroads by a different route from those discussed so far. This was shaped less by shifting social interests or literary fashions in the late 1950s and 1960s than by deeper moral and historical challenges extending from the Second World War. These challenges are considered next, before assessing the significance of Lodge's 'hesitation' for the period's fiction generally.

16

A Darker Route: Morality and History in the 1960s and 1970s

The period's opening was marked by a new readiness among writers to respond to the challenges of the Second World War.[1] The war had obviously remained a huge influence on English life and society in the years immediately following, as several 1960s novels confirmed: Elizabeth Jane Howard's *After Julius* (1965), for example, traces the continuing, inescapable consequences, for more than twenty years afterwards, of a death during the evacuation of Dunkirk in 1940. Yet extended treatment of the war in English fiction seemed long delayed —surprisingly, given the narrative opportunities it offered. Along with its many moral and imaginative challenges, the war's violent action obviously offered contexts in which lives, emotions, and relationships could be pressured, intensified, and if necessary terminated more rapidly and compellingly than in the normal run of affairs. These proved useful to novelists throughout the later decades of the twentieth century, but neither challenges nor opportunities were much taken up at the end of the 1940s, or for much of the 1950s. In the exhausted years after 1945, writers and readers may simply have preferred to turn their attention elsewhere, with Evelyn Waugh's *Sword of Honour* trilogy (1952–61), one of few substantial treatments of war experience to appear at the time.

Renewed interest in the next decade was quickly indicated by Olivia Manning's *The Great Fortune*, published early in 1960. In

---

[1] See pp. 54–5, above.

this novel and later ones in her *Balkan Trilogy* (1960–5), Manning traced the effects of war on Guy and Harriet Pringle, working in a colourful, doomed Bucharest until the Nazi threat forces them to flee to Athens. Manning later continued their story in *The Levant Trilogy* (1977–80), set around the desert war in Egypt. In *The Balkan Trilogy*, she developed for the 1960s the straightforward narrative excitements and potentials mentioned above, showing her characters encountering a wartime world in which 'the only thing certain is that nothing is certain' (*The Great Fortune*, ch. 6). *The Balkan Trilogy* was also among the first novels to raise deeper questions about how Nazism had been allowed to develop, and the war itself to occur. These concerns are aptly focused around Guy Pringle. His physical short-sightedness is matched by improvident generosity and idealism—a naïve extension of some of the utopian politics of the 1930s. This makes him uncomprehending of 'fascist savagery . . . a new thing in the civilized world', in ways typical of British attitudes generally at the time (*The Spoilt City*, ch. 5).

Several other 1960s novels attempted to grasp how fascism could ever have overtaken supposedly civilized societies. Gerda Charles was one of a number of Jewish-English novelists to consider the issue. In *A Logical Girl* (1966), her narrator finds deceit and cruelty, comparable to the Nazis', lurking in wartime behind the respectable façades of an English seaside town: she concludes that 'Hitlers exist . . . all around us and must be taken into account' (ch. 29). In trying to understand fascism from the German point of view, two early 1960s novels made good use of characters sharing Guy Pringle's kind of naïvety. Gabriel Fielding's central figure in *The Birthday King* (1962) is too short-sighted to recognize the real nature of pacts he makes, on behalf of his rich, ambitious family, with the new powers prevailing in Hitler's Germany. Like Gerda Charles, Fielding locates the supposedly unimaginable horrors of recent German history within a painfully intelligible microcosm of family frictions and betrayals. *The Birthday King* ends by showing the United States diluting the news impact of Nazi crimes in order to retain Germany as an ally against communism—confirming the view that the Holocaust is a horror from which 'no one can dissociate themselves . . . Not Germany nor Europe nor America' (ch. 12).

This was a conclusion especially resonant in 1962, at a time when the concentration camps were once again made world news by the trial and execution of Adolf Eichmann. It was further reinforced by Fielding's flat, non-censorious narrative tone, requiring readers to apply their own moral judgement to the action described. Richard Hughes's *The Fox in the Attic* (1961) made similar demands on judgement. The ingenuousness of the central figure, Augustine, aptly represents English liberalism, leaving him poorly equipped to judge for himself the political situation he finds on a visit to Germany in 1923. Like *The Birthday King*, *The Fox in the Attic* locates the origins of the Second World War in the period during and after the First. Germany's traumas at this time, Hughes suggests, were suppressed into a 'deeper levels of nightmare', only to erupt again with redoubled violence later in its history (bk. 2, ch. 2). Much of *The Fox in the Attic* extends this Freudian rereading of history. Augustine even envisages the emergence of a new generation, 'a new kind of human being, *because of Freud!*'—one whose aggressiveness, so widely evident in the twentieth century, arises from the need for an antagonistic 'other' in order to substantiate a sense of the self (bk. 1, ch. 19).

This reinterpretation of recent history was characteristic of the early 1960s. Like some contemporary drama, Hughes's novel could be compared with A. L. Alvarez's discussion in *The New Poetry*, published the following year, of parallels between 'mass evil' revealed by the war and darker inner forces identified by psychology.[2] A self-confessedly slow writer, Hughes might have developed this historical vision more clearly had he finished *The Human Predicament*, a projected trilogy of which *The Fox in the Attic* was the first part. Only the second, *The Wooden Shepherdess* (1973), centred on Hitler's 'night of the long knives', was fully completed before his death. Yet the scale and nature of historical analysis even in *The Fox in the Attic* confirms how deeply recent history continued to press upon the imagination of writers in the 1960s. Emmanuel Litvinoff was among several other authors who began at this time to consider German experience of the war, showing in *The Lost Europeans* (1960) Jewish characters returning to a Berlin haunted by Nazism. Like Gabriel Fielding, Piers Paul Read traced in *The Junkers* (1968) the complicities of the German aristocracy with the politics of

[2] See pp. 191 and 378–9, above.

the Holocaust. Gillian Freeman later followed a similar theme in examining an aristocratic supporter of Hitler in *Nazi Lady* (1978), extending her earlier fiction's interest in the class system in England.

Related legacies of the war in the period's fiction were also high-lighted by *The Fox in the Attic*—immediately, by the startling open-ing image of blighted innocence, in Hughes's description of a child, dead and hanging upside down. Hughes further anticipated later interests in showing how the century's wars, and the propaganda surrounding them, had resuscitated 'the almost-forgotten terms of *right* and *wrong*' (bk. 1, ch. 27). In a contemporary study of the novel, *Tradition and Dream* (1964), Walter Allen suggested that even when the war was not an immediate subject of fiction, it never-theless remained 'the ineluctable shadow under which characters and events have their being' (p. 262). This shadow was clearly visible in the period's repeated concerns with right and wrong, light and dark: with moral and spiritual conflict, and with innocence destroyed or inverted, like that child at the start of *The Fox in the Attic*. Julian Mitchell concluded in *The Undiscovered Country* (1968) that after Hiroshima 'the doctrine of original sin seemed tem-porarily irrefutable' (pt. 1, ch. 1), and C. P. Snow, in *The Sleep of Reason* (1968), that the concentration camps worked in later imag-ination as 'a primal, an original, an Adamic fact' (ch. 28). Along with Walter Allen, each suggested a reason for the absence of much serious fiction dealing directly with the war until 1960. Its historical challenges and narrative opportunities may have been suppressed not only by post-war fatigue, but by post-war moral shock. Authors who might have developed wartime experience in their fiction found themselves confronted by the gates of Eden instead.

It was at any rate the primal or 'Adamic' moral implications of recent history, rather than its actual events, which shaped the writing of several highly successful novelists who first emerged in the mid-1950s, including William Golding, Iris Murdoch, Muriel Spark, and Anthony Burgess. Golding was particularly explicit about the importance of the war in his writing. Recognition of 'deliberate, specific human evil at work' in the Nazi regime, he explained, replaced his 'progressive view of humanity' with the conviction that 'Man is a fallen being . . . gripped by original sin': a creature who 'produces evil as a bee produces honey' (Haffenden, *Novelists in*

Interview, pp. 112–13; Golding, *Hot Gates*, pp. 87–8). These conclusions were demonstrated in his first novels, *Lord of the Flies*
(1954) and *The Inheritors* (1955), each set in distant, Edenic sur-
roundings, among children or childlike adults bitterly experiencing
what *Lord of the Flies* calls 'the end of innocence, the darkness of
man's heart' (ch. 12). The war figured more explicitly in *Pincher
Martin* (1956) and *Free Fall* (1959). After *The Spire* (1964), a symbolic account of a medieval cleric's obsessive architectural ambitions, and *The Pyramid* (1967), Golding did not publish a full-length
novel for more than a decade, returning to the war in the opening
pages of *Darkness Visible* (1979). Not usually considered his best
novel, *Darkness Visible* nevertheless illustrates Golding's moral
vision unusually clearly, along with some of its implications for his
fictional technique.

The novel begins in ways emblematic of the concerns discussed
above. It shows a child, Matty, miraculously emerging from the fiery
centre of war in the London blitz—one side of his face still light,
the other burned almost black—and entering apparently universal
struggles between powers of good and evil, half-spiritual and half-
earthly. *Darkness Visible* was unusual, in Golding's fiction, in showing redemptive as well as evil influences exercised in the earthly
sphere by higher powers. Yet in doing so it stretches readers' imagination and credulity between narrative modes nearly as antithetical as
Golding's moral ones. The first part of the novel belongs to 'the
world of spirit' (ch. 13): allegorical episodes feature regularly in it,
including a half-comic crucifixion and a passage through the under-
world, and Matty is envisaged alternately as 'a human shape or
merely a bit of flickering brightness' (ch. 1). The second part continues to consider evil in terms of 'the darkness between the stars' and
the entropic running-down of the universe (ch. 11). But it is also
firmly located in the tawdry streets and supermarkets of contemporary England—'the Liberal club closed for repairs, graffiti on every
available surface'—and in the actions of conventionally realistic
characters (ch. 12). These divergences between allegory and realism,
vision and daily life, never fully allow the unity claimed for the novel
in the title of its third part, 'One is One'. Instead, they emphasize a
problem Golding acknowledged when describing his 'method of
presenting the truth . . . in fable form': the difficulty of 'keeping a

relationship between the fable and the moralized world' (*Hot Gates*, pp. 86, 97).

Tensions between fable and world in *Darkness Visible* suggested that Golding's writing was more effective when it remained further from realistic reflection of contemporary life, confining itself more exclusively to 'fable form'. Contexts remote historically, as in *The Inheritors* or *The Spire*, or geographically, in *Lord of the Flies* and *Pincher Martin*, allow moral issues to be presented starkly, purged of distracting details of the quotidian. Distant settings also benefit from the immediacy of Golding's description of natural forces: their hostility or indifference often painfully expose limitations in characters' physical and moral resources, as in much of Joseph Conrad's fiction. Golding successfully returned to this idiom in his late trilogy 'To the Ends of the Earth': *Rites of Passage* (1980), *Close Quarters* (1987), and *Fire Down Below* (1989). These novels were once again confined to what *Rites of Passage* calls 'a separate world, a universe in little': to the experience, during an eighteenth-century journey to Australia, of 'men at sea who live too close . . . to all that is monstrous under the sun and moon' (pp. 191, 278). Golding's narrative was also largely confined to a highly particular perspective: to the journals of a protagonist scarcely able to recognize the real nature of monstrous events he witnesses. His limitations require of readers unusual responsibilities of judgement, as in the other novels centred on inadequate innocents discussed above. Responsibilities of this kind were generated throughout Golding's writing. Particular perspectives—or radical shifts between them, such as occur at the end of *Pincher Martin* or *The Inheritors*—stress for readers how far moral judgement must be a matter of perception, not presupposition. Innocent narrators and protagonists further demonstrate—aptly, given recent historical experience—how far any 'progressive view of humanity' risks overlooking 'deliberate human evil'. The depth and diversity of Golding's engagement with such issues made him one of the pre-eminent English novelists in the latter half of the twentieth century, a recipient of the Nobel Prize in 1983.

'We have not recovered from two wars and the experience of Hitler', Iris Murdoch remarked in 1961, adding that modern literature nevertheless offered surprisingly few 'convincing pictures of evil' (Bradbury (ed.), *Novel Today*, pp. 23, 30). As part of her long-sustained moral concerns, this was a lack Murdoch regularly redressed in her own fiction. *A Fairly Honourable Defeat* (1970), for example, offers a complex picture of evil in the figure of Julius. A wartime inmate of Belsen, Julius extends the malign shadow of the concentration camps into his later conduct and his conviction of the rottenness of human nature. In tracing this shadow, *A Fairly Honourable Defeat* sometimes seemed close to the spiritual interests of *Darkness Visible*, or to Golding's use of fable and allegory. Julius is described as a 'magician', or 'really . . . a *god*', while another character has visions of 'principalities and powers . . . demons', and the novel itself occasionally discusses original sin (pt. 2, ch. 19; pt. 1, chs. 13, 17). Yet like most of Murdoch's fiction, *A Fairly Honourable Defeat* generally remained more realistic than Golding's writing, reflecting a contemporary social context and describing in detail the 'disastrous compound of human failure, muddle and sheer chance' which rules characters' complicated lives (pt. 2, ch. 23).

Realism of this kind, faithfully representing observed life, was for Murdoch not only an aesthetic preference but a moral and philosophic requirement. Work as a university lecturer in philosophy, and as an academic author—of studies such as *Metaphysics as a Guide to Morals* (1992)—further shaped moral concerns established for her by the war. Her first novel, *Under the Net* (1954), clearly reflected some of these philosophic interests—in Sartrean existentialism particularly, though she was subsequently attracted to another French philosopher, Simone Weil. In various ways, each thinker indicated the risks of imposing a set—or 'net'—of pre-established ideas on experience, constraining life in general and misconstruing the nature of other individuals. Murdoch emphasized Weil's view that 'morality was a matter of attention, not of will' and indicated in *A Fairly Honourable Defeat* the dangers of 'some general view which makes you blind to obvious immediate things in human life' (Bradbury (ed.), *Novel Today*, p. 30; *Defeat*, pt. 1, ch. 18).

These are dangers which Murdoch's characters regularly have to recognize and avoid. Characters in her aptly named novel *A Severed Head* (1961), for example, discover that attempts to cut themselves off from 'the dark gods' of their physical and sexual natures are inevitably doomed to fail, and that they cannot live through concept, reason, and intellect alone (ch. 9). Especially at this early stage of her career, Murdoch's fiction often encountered much the same dangers itself. Demonstration of the powers of 'dark gods' in *A Severed Head* requires an operatic or dance-like swapping of sexual partners which sometimes seems 'a little improbable' even to the novel's narrator (ch. 16). Murdoch herself described it as 'giving in to the myth' (Bradbury (ed.), *Novel Today*, p. 115). Philosophical concepts and moral patterns, in other words, sometimes tugged Murdoch's work towards abstraction, myth, or contrivance, and away from the full attention to lived experience it generally sought to commend. Her awareness of this danger appeared in a number of characters in whom a manipulative nature, moral irresponsibility, and artistic talent are all closely combined.

In *A Fairly Honourable Defeat*, for example, the evil Julius claims 'I am an artist' (pt. 2, ch. 21). In *The Sea, the Sea*, a Prospero-like theatre director learns that 'the trickery and magic of art' has damagingly prevented him from 'looking at the reality', either in his own life or those of his friends (pp. 29, 499). Similar semi-mage characters turned up in many of Murdoch's novels, including some of her best, from *The Flight from the Enchanter* (1956) to *The Message to the Planet* (1989). Tensions between art, life, power, and freedom, and the various moralities involved, provided her writing with imaginative involutes teased out in more than two dozen novels. Her engaging, often eccentric characters, the sexy gyrations of their relationships, and the seriousness of the issues involved ensured popularity as well as critical esteem for her work. This popularity reached a new height shortly after her death, following her husband John Bayley's memoir, *Iris* (1998), and its adaptation as a film. Appropriately, it was life, rather than only art, which finally secured Murdoch's fame.

'Dachau and Auschwitz', Anthony Burgess considered—quoting Jean-Paul Sartre—ensured that 'we have been taught to take Evil seriously' (*Novel Now*, p. 184). A Catholic childhood also contributed to Burgess's interest in what he described as literature's potential to 'make clearer the whole business of moral choice' (Plimpton (ed.), p. 348). This potential was variously developed throughout an exceptionally prolific writing career. Burgess produced early novels of colonial life in *The Malayan Trilogy* (1956–9) and several entertainments centred on an irascible poet—*Inside Mr*

Enderby (1963), *Enderby Outside* (1968), *The Clockwork Testament* (1974), and *Enderby's Dark Lady* (1984). He also wrote novels reflecting the life and times of Shakespeare—*Nothing Like the Sun* (1964), *A Dead Man in Deptford* (1993)—as well as occasional thrillers and science fiction. Some of his most successful novels, such as *A Clockwork Orange* (1962) and *Earthly Powers* (1980), were those most directly concerned with moral choice. *A Clockwork Orange* set this concern within a disturbing vision of the future: portrayal of a society overtaken by teenage 'ultra-violence' and technologized, Orwellian forms of social control made it one of the most controversial novels published in the 1960s. Stanley Kubrick's stylish, shocking film version in 1971 increased its notoriety, without always fully developing its strengths. In particular, Burgess's invention for his narrator of a teenage slang, based around Russian roots and vocabulary, created for the novel a peculiar vividness in descriptions such as the following:

Pete and Georgie had good sharp nozhes, but I for my own part had a fine starry horrorshow cut-throat britva which, at that time, I could flash and shine artistic. So there we were dratsing away in the dark, the old Luna with men on it just coming up, the stars stabbing away as it might be knives anxious to join in the dratsing. (pt. 1, ch. 2)

Partly an oblique satire on the Americanization of British culture during the Cold War, this language did risk creating a sinister verbal stylishness, like the film's visual elegance, for the acts of 'ultra-violence' depicted. But it also sought to establish for readers a necessary distance from these acts, less easily sustained in the cinema. This was essential for Burgess's measured examination of an issue which also interested Golding and Murdoch: the need for evil to exist, in order to allow genuine free will and moral choice.

Similar issues were considered at greater length, and in historical depth, in *Earthly Powers*. Like Henry Williamson's *A Chronicle of Ancient Sunlight* (1951–69), *Earthly Powers* returned to the relative innocence of the twentieth century's opening years before examining the increasing turmoil of its later history. Burgess's narrator Kenneth Toomey is an author—often thought to be based on Somerset Maugham—whose homosexuality forces him into an eventful, itinerant existence. It eventually takes him close to Hitler, Mussolini, and many of 'the rest of the terrible people this terrible century's thrown up': he meets 'nearly everybody who counted in the Nazi Party', and visits the concentration camps shortly after they are liberated in 1945 (chs. 80, 49). He also enjoys lifelong acquaintance with another public figure, Campanati, an Italian cardinal who eventually becomes Pope. His range of encounters and the disparate moralities involved dispose Toomey to view twentieth-century history in terms of a Manichaean struggle between balanced, universal forces of good and evil. As its title suggests, *Earthly Powers* also considers whether such forces originate within or beyond the human sphere. For Toomey, the evidence of the Holocaust fundamentally contradicts belief in the goodness of humanity—in particular, Campanati's conviction that human beings are merely the innocent victims of diabolical figures such as Hitler, or of 'a kind of moral virus that had landed in Eden in a spaceship' (ch. 71). Toomey develops for himself a more existential vision of the individual's personal responsibilities within a desolate, purposeless universe. This is shown to be equally limiting. *Earthly Powers* points instead towards religious commitments which neither ignore nor diminish moral responsibility, but demand its continuing engagement with the huge challenges of twentieth-century history.

Similar views were expressed around this time in the novels of another Catholic writer, Graham Greene. As one of the century's most successful English authors, Greene did contribute strongly to moral and spiritual elements in the period's fiction. But in the course of a long career, his work also reflected a wider range of commitments.[3] It was shaped initially by the left-wing allegiances of the 1930s, entering a phase of religious reflection—and generally tragic vision—only around the time of the Second World War. After *A Burnt-Out Case* (1961), Catholicism remained a concern, but less centrally, becoming only one of several factors contributing to what Greene called in a 1945 essay on François Mauriac 'the sense of the importance of the human act' (*Collected Essays*, p. 91). Novels such as *The Comedians* (1966) sharply distinguished between characters who share this sense and those who do not. But in Greene's later fiction 'the human act' generally took place in a world summed up in the epigraph chosen for *The Honorary Consul* (1973), from Thomas

---

[3] These are also considered in Ch. 20, below.

Hardy: one in which 'all things merge in one another—good into evil, generosity into justice, religion into politics'.

Later fiction also moved beyond the tragic phase of the war years, showing central figures surviving, or achieving a precarious enlightenment, in an atmosphere sometimes tending towards romance or even comedy. Tensions between Greene's conflicting allegiances, religious and political, expressed themselves in the deadly antagonism between Priest and Lieutenant in *The Power and the Glory* (1940). Forty years later, they were translated into largely comic terms in the arguments between a priest and a communist ex-mayor which occupy much of *Monsignor Quixote* (1982). Elements of romance or comedy also figured in *Travels with My Aunt* (1969), appearing more darkly in *The Captain and the Enemy* (1988), which emphasized mortal love as the only antidote to the Devil. Perhaps because Greene increasingly found the heart of the matter in the human factor, and in the human act, few Catholic novelists later in the century appeared to follow his example directly. Piers Paul Read was an exception. In portraying a reluctant Labour candidate in *A Married Man* (1979), for example, Read outlined a tawdry, strike-bound 1970s England as sharply as Greene had some of the landscapes of the 1930s, while also examining a number of issues of morality, faith, and redemption. Like Greene's *The End of the Affair* (1951), too, *A Married Man* suggested divine powers directly, miraculously at work within the human sphere.

For another Catholic writer, Muriel Spark—also part-Jewish—evil and moral choice remained central concerns. Spark indicated some of their origins in her autobiographical novel, *The Mandelbaum Gate* (1965), set in Jerusalem at the time of the Eichmann trial, described as revealing 'an empty hole in the earth, that led to a bottomless pit' (ch. 7). Other early works such as *Memento Mori* (1959), *The Ballad of Peckam Rye* (1960), and *The Girls of Slender Means* (1963) had already dealt with death, Satanism in the suburbs, and moral conflict at the end of the Second World War, respectively. Spark envisaged another kind of evil in her most influential novel at the time, later successfully filmed, *The Prime of Miss Jean Brodie* (1961). This used her Scottish background for the story of a 1930s schoolteacher, one whose godlike moulding of her pupils into a 'Brodie set . . . Miss Brodie's fascisti' is compared to the tactics of contemporary dictators whom she admires (ch. 2). Spark's departures from conventional narrative chronology highlight how disastrously the Brodie set's later lives are shaped by her influence, but it is also shown to have an almost artistic aspect. Brodie has a penchant for 'making patterns with facts', and for shaping or narrowing the world to match her vision of it, which particularly appeals to the novel's most imaginative character, despite strong moral reservations (ch. 3). Vision, manipulation, and pattern creation make Brodie a kind of author figure, or author analogue: the novel's wariness of her extreme form of authority—a kind of fascism—indirectly reflects an uneasiness about authorship itself. This extends into her later fiction concerns Spark first expressed in *The Comforters* (1957), about novelists' organization of life into 'a convenient slick plot' (ch. 5). Spark, in other words, focused moral issues widely concerning English authors in the late 1950s and early 1960s by means of metafictional tactics—questionings of the nature of writing and authorship—initially close to the idiom of the *nouveau roman*. In this way, her work offers a particularly clear example of the 'hesitation' between previously distinct directions in the novel, traditional or innovative, which David Lodge discussed at the beginning of the 1970s.[4]

Though Spark provides an especially clear, early example of this 'hesitation at the crossroads', it was by no means the only one. 'Hesitations' of this kind were a feature of English fiction in the 1960s and later, regularly shaping the work of the authors discussed above. Strong moral interests, traditional to the English novel, did not preclude unconventional forms for their investigation—indeed, often seemed to require them. Like Spark, Iris Murdoch was concerned not only with issues of power and morality, but with their implications for art—also, self-consciously, for the ethics of narrative practice itself. Godlike or mage-like figures, comparable to Jean Brodie, often focused this interest in her writing, as they sometimes did in John Fowles's. Murdoch also worked occasionally in a more directly metafictional mode, in novels such as *The Black Prince* (1973). Anthony Burgess's narrator Kenneth Toomey likewise established a metafictional element in *Earthly Powers*, drawing attention from the first page to his 'cunning' and 'contrivance' in

[4] See p. 412, above.

presenting his story, and often pausing throughout to discuss literary technique. Linguistic inventiveness in *A Clockwork Orange* was partly owed to admiration for modernist innovation, and for the work of James Joyce in particular: Burgess produced two critical studies of Joyce, along with an abbreviated edition of *Finnegans Wake* and a musical version of *Ulysses*.

Burgess further clarified his position at Lodge's crossroads in remarking that 'we must welcome experiment in the novel . . . but it would be a pity to throw overboard all that the novel has learned throughout the slow centuries of its development' (*Novel Now*, p. 192). Dual allegiances of this kind were also apparent in much of William Golding's fiction. Though generally moving towards fable and allegory, Golding showed in several novels, *Darkness Visible* particularly, a reluctance to abandon realist conventions entirely. Like Murdoch in *The Black Prince*, Golding also moved into a meta-fictional mode in *The Paper Men* (1984). Naturally enough, further evidence of the crossroads Lodge identified appeared in his own fiction, and in some of the other campus novels discussed in Chapter 15. In one way, extensive parody and pastiche of modernism in *The British Museum is Falling Down* (1965) reflected what Lodge described in an afterword as 'critical admiration for the great modernist writers'. Yet strong elements of parody in Lodge's reworkings of modernist writing also highlighted a contrary set of allegiances—ones underlying a 'creative practice' as a novelist which he felt he owed principally to 'the neo-realist, anti-modernist writing of the 1950s' (p. 170).

Comparable syntheses of styles and traditions appeared in the 1960s in the work of two of the period's most widely admired writers, Doris Lessing and Angus Wilson. Like many 'neo-realist' authors at the time, Angus Wilson professed himself in 1958 'against experiments in technique' and on the whole in favour of 'traditional, nineteenth century forms' (*London Magazine* (Apr.), p. 44). These preferences shaped the broad, Dickensian social concerns of *Anglo-Saxon Attitudes* (1956), and they continued to appear in *Late Call* (1964) whose setting in a new town offers a 'microcosm', a character suggests, which 'reflects very accurately the country at large', highlighting the limitations of 'the nice neat England we've built' (chs. 2, 4). Like Henry Williamson and Anthony Burgess, Wilson also returned in each of these novels to the tranquil Edwardian years, contrasting them with the uncertainties and materialism of the present. The Edwardian period was also the starting point for Wilson's combination of family saga and wider history in *No Laughing Matter* (1967). His novel went on to show public affairs intertwined throughout the rest of the century with the experiences of a family of six children, and eventually their descendants, 1960s habitués of pot and the pill.

While maintaining this broad historical perspective—and a moral concern with what Wilson called 'the evil I have actually known in my own time'—*No Laughing Matter* nevertheless continued a movement away from 'traditional, nineteenth century forms' (*Diversity and Depth*, p. 281). This new direction was first apparent in Wilson's 1960s writing in *The Old Men at the Zoo* (1961), more apocalyptic fantasy than conventional social commentary. *No Laughing Matter* was equally unconventional formally. Long sections took the form of parody, or sometimes even dramatic dialogue, and Wilson also extensively employed styles of interior monologue and stream of consciousness. By using these styles in a novel still broadly social and historical in its interests, Wilson showed growing admiration for Virginia Woolf's modernism coexisting with his continuing respect for the nineteenth-century realist technique of George Eliot. Wilson confirmed his interest in this kind of combination when he remarked—echoing Anthony Burgess—that 'we may make use of all that experiment has taught us, may indeed experiment ourselves, without losing contact with our good old English tradition' (*Diversity and Depth*, p. 196).

Doris Lessing's writing underwent a similar change of direction in the 1960s, one of several in her long, distinguished career. In the late 1950s, she still found 'the highest form of prose writing' in 'the novel of the nineteenth century . . . the realist novel, the realist story' (Maschler (ed.), p. 14). Early novels in her *Children of Violence* sequence (1952–69)—such as *Martha Quest* (1952), a semi-autobiographical account of growing up in an African colony—belonged in the context of 1950s realism. Yet in looking ahead to the year 2000 in the sequence's final volume, *The Four-Gated City* (1969), Lessing moved towards fantasy and apocalypse, like Wilson in *The Old Men at the Zoo*. In the meantime she had also departed from conventionally realistic modes—and thoroughly challenged their validity—in one of the key novels of the 1960s, *The Golden Notebook* (1962). This contained fragments of a conventional novel, along with sections from notebooks kept by its central character, Anna Wulf, a 'blocked' author who records in them her activities as 'free woman', socialist, private being, and writer. None of these areas, nor the ideas attached to them, provide much coherence for her life. Some time before postmodern theorists began discussing the collapse of Grand Narratives,[5] *The Golden Notebook* reported the breakdown of attempts to formulate 'a world-mind, a world ethic'. Lessing concentrated on the problems of psychoanalysis and Marxism in this respect, but also reflected a general sense of breakdown in the uncertain period in Britain in which the novel is set, shortly after the Suez crisis (p. 15). Crucially for the emerging women's consciousness of the 1960s, too, *The Golden Notebook* reported throughout on the breakdown of conventional gender roles and relations.[6]

These wider feelings of breakdown compound Anna's narrative difficulties, highlighted throughout by self-reflexive, postmodernist scrutiny of ways conventional literary strategies and languages distort experience, or fail to represent it altogether. Words and their limitations are sometimes considered in the light of earlier 'novels about the breakdown of language, like Finnegans Wake' (*Golden Notebook*, p. 299). Notebooks include disgruntled commentary on the shortcomings of their own language and methods; fragments of unfinished short stories and reviews; even samples of the newspaper cuttings Anna uses to paper the walls of her home. Newspaper descriptions of 'war, murder, chaos, misery' accentuate what Lessing describes as 'fear of chaos, of formlessness—of breakdown' (pp. 251, 6). They confirm Anna's view that a novel 'claimed by the disintegration and the collapse'—such as *The Golden Notebook* itself—may be the only possible response to a 'world . . . so chaotic art is irrelevant' (pp. 124, 60). Some of Lessing's later novels were equally innovative. Disintegration and collapse, through personal breakdown, continued to figure in *Briefing for a Descent into Hell* (1971). Categorized on its title page as 'inner-space fiction', it developed through a range

---

[5] See p. 63, above.
[6] See pp. 38–42, above, and p. 463, below.

of inner voices a possibility suggested in *The Golden Notebook*—for a novel about 'a man whose "sense of reality" has gone', leaving 'a deeper sense of reality than "normal" people' (p. 520). The tranquillity of this 'deeper sense' and its distanced vision of human history anticipated Lessing's further move into fantasy in the *Canopus in Argos: Archives* series (1979–83). This projected some of the moral concerns so apparent in fiction after mid-century into outer-space fiction, describing distant cosmic manoeuvrings and their influence on human fate.

Some of Lessing's later work nevertheless returned to more realistic forms, and to more immediate social or political interests. *The Summer before the Dark* (1973), for example, portrayed a heroine whose personal breakdown and fears of ageing are heightened by the wider weariness of a world wracked by strikes, pollution, and political crises. In title and theme, *The Summer before the Dark* identified astutely, even presciently, the atmosphere of mid-1970s crisis in which the energy and imagination of the previous decade faded or expired. This changed mood threatened what had begun to seem a particularly promising phase of fiction. Lodge's metaphor of hesitation at a crossroads of innovative and traditional techniques barely did justice to some of the work discussed above, which showed more confident, thoroughgoing combinations of these influences than his image suggested. Later critics were readier to stress the extent, and fruitfulness, of these stylistic syntheses in the period's writing. In *Post-War British Fiction* (1995), Andrzej Gąsiorek even suggested that they had made 'distinctions between "realist" and "experimental" or between "traditional" and "innovative"', useful earlier in the century, 'so irrelevant to the post-war period that they should be dropped altogether' (p. v).

Since Gąsiorek's own study continued to employ these terms throughout—suggesting that distinctions could still usefully be defined by them—this was not a wholly convincing conclusion. Yet it was one which did emphasize the growing difficulty of assigning the period's novelists exclusively to any one category. By the early 1970s, as Gąsiorek remarked, authors were generally much readier than earlier in the century to 'cross-breed narrative modes' and to engage in productive 'interanimation of forms, styles and techniques' (p. 19). Malcolm Bradbury also remarked on how far 'Victorian and "modern" fiction started to intersect' around this time, with John Fowles's *The French Lieutenant's Woman* (1969) an unusually clear example of this combination (*Modern British Novel*, p. 362). By the early 1970s, previously divergent strands in English fiction—modernist or postmodernist on the one hand; realist, moral, or conventional on the other—showed every sign of 'interanimation' or coalescence. This promised a challenging, progressive English fiction, sustaining established strengths and interests within renewed imagination about form and technique.

Even in the 1960s, however, renewed modernist or postmodernist interests had tended to provide only a subsidiary direction in English fiction.[7] After the oil crisis of the early 1970s, it seemed possible that this minor road might be poorly maintained, or that there would be less energy available to travel along it. Rather than 'cross-breeding' or 'interanimating' anything, it seemed likelier that novelists might simply follow the line of least resistance and return again to the main road of realist convention. Like some of the poets and dramatists discussed in earlier chapters, novelists did begin to see the experimental styles of the 1960s—in life or literature—as a leisurely, carefree summer before energy crises and miners' strikes plunged the country quite literally into the dark. The epigraph from Marx vanished from later editions of *The French Lieutenant's Woman*: 1960s politics and the emancipated imagination they supported seemed less viable in the next decades, in financial terms particularly. The crisis in the book trade which followed the economic downturn in the early 1970s made publishers reluctant to risk novels-in-boxes or other unfamiliar forms of writing. 'The oil crisis indicated the fragility of our little world', the critic Bryan Appleyard recorded, adding that in this context 'rarefied' modernist experiment was 'the last thing that was required . . . randomly ordered novels reeked of the indulgent megalomania of growth' (p. 97).

Conventionally ordered fiction and conservative interests often seemed, instead, to be making a comeback in the mid-1970s, or never to have gone away. An older generation of writers continued to favour the 'gentleman code', setting novels in the social echelons explored in *A Dance to the Music of Time*, despite Anthony Powell's recognition of their fading significance for English life. Pamela

---

[7] See p. 412, above.

Hansford Johnson's hero in *The Good Listener* (1975) suggests that deference to the aristocracy is 'an attitude of another day and age', but the novel questions class boundaries gently enough to seem virtually an endorsement of continuing divisions in English society, and of upper-class influences within it (p. 173). Similarly affluent contexts figured in Elizabeth Taylor's *The Wedding Group* (1974), though they provided a basis for sharper examination of contemporary social change. They also appeared in the work of a novelist who did make a comeback in the 1970s, following a period of neglect after her publisher rejected *An Unsuitable Attachment* in 1963— Barbara Pym. Like Taylor's characters, and Johnson's, the central figures in Pym's *The Sweet Dove Died* (1978) choose only the most genteel involvement in the working world, in the art and antique trade. Precious, elegant objects they handle or exchange define emotions and relationships supposedly equally subtle and refined. Interests of this kind led critics to compare Pym with Jane Austen, though her vision was sometimes bleaker. Frustrations and failures of communication figured regularly in her later fiction. Pym also entered a more contemporary mode in *Quartet in Autumn* (1977), portraying characters who do work for a living, and face poverty and mortality more immediately than in some of her earlier novels.

Comparison with Jane Austen nevertheless confirmed how thoroughly interests such as Pym's could be sustained in nineteenth-century forms, untouched by modernism or its 1960s legacies. As Bernard Bergonzi suggested at the end of the 1970s, the 'novel of character' continued to offer ways of 'seeing the nineteenth century as still a going concern' (*Situation of the Novel*, p. 60). Later in the century, many other authors—Stanley Middleton or Nina Bawden, for example—went on writing entertainingly and perceptively about life among the middle classes, without moving fiction any further from established, conventional forms. Middleton summed up this mode in 1978, admitting that he viewed experiment with suspicion and citing the innovative composer Arnold Schoenberg in support of his conclusion that 'there's plenty of good music still to be written in C major' (*New Review* (Summer), p. 54). Fascinating recent forays into minor keys or atonalities did seem to risk being drowned out, in the later 1970s, by the kind of conventional preferences he indicated.

Along with the depressed state of contemporary publishing, this risk contributed to a number of troubled assessments of English fiction at the time. In *Notes for a New Culture* (1976), Peter Ackroyd suggested that 'England ha[d] insulated itself from the development of modernism', sustaining instead 'a false context of realism'. This 'false aesthetic' underlying English writing, he considered, 'could not be in greater contrast to the French "nouveau roman" ' (pp. 147, 103). Similar concerns were expressed two years later in a symposium on contemporary fiction in the *New Review* (Summer 1978), and they continued to appear in 1979 and 1980 in early numbers of another literary journal, *Granta*. In its third issue, the editor Bill Buford worried that English fiction had become 'immune to the philosophical and intellectual' (p. 9), concentrating instead on a 'postwar, premodern variety of the middle class monologue, with C. P. Snow on one side and perhaps Margaret Drabble and Melvyn Bragg on the other (Kingsley Amis will always be nearby . . .)'. Worries of this kind were not new. The conservatism and limited ambition of Snow and Amis, and of fiction generally in the 1950s, led to expectations of the death of the English novel which had proved hard to shake off, even as fiction developed in the ways described above. In 1973, *The Pelican Guide to English Literature* continued to see English fiction 'turning aside from the mainstream of European literature' after the Second World War, and 'retreating into parochialism or defeatism' (Ford (ed.), p. 490). Further assessments of the English novel as 'a backwater, parochial and archaic' were surveyed in both editions of Bernard Bergonzi's *The Situation of the Novel*, in 1970 and 1979 (2nd edn., p. 67).

Perhaps an underlying conservatism in English writing in the early part of the period was indicated by the confinement of experiment to a minor road, or by the tendency to incorporate it within more established forms. Yet the achievements discussed in this chapter and in Chapter 15 suggest that by the early 1970s the English novel had become less 'insulated' from philosophy, modernism, the *nouveau roman*, and the Continent generally than the commentators quoted above considered. It was certainly less 'insulated', and more ambitious, than it had been during the 1950s. Faltering energies during the cash-strapped 1970s probably made the reappearance of pessimistic assessments inevitable by the end of the decade. But more promising developments soon occurred in the next, and further reasons for optimism continued to appear in the progress of the novel after the 1980s. Fiction in the last two decades of the century generally extended the 'interanimation' of techniques discussed above, developing a new vision and inventiveness already strongly marked in women's writing by the mid-1970s. The parochialism often seen in English fiction was also avoided through renewed importation of forms and strategies from abroad. In a way, John Fowles offered an apt figuration of the state of the contemporary English novel in the memorable opening scene of *The French Lieutenant's Woman*, showing his heroine standing on the coast of England, looking across the Channel for an absent object of desire. In the 1960s and the early 1970s, as often earlier in the century, English novelists had regularly drawn their inspiration from outside the country: from France, from across the Irish Sea, sometimes from across the Atlantic, or from a vital Spark in Scottish writing. In the later 1970s, and much of the next two decades, the English novel was further revitalized by the imagination of other sorts of outsider, as well as by a new generation of writers growing up within the country itself. These developments are considered in the next three chapters.

17

Longer Shadows and Darkness Risible: The 1970s to 2000

The Second World War's 'ineluctable shadow' remained strongly evident in the moral vision of late twentieth-century English fiction, but it also shaped its imagination in other ways. Throughout the period, the war functioned as an ineluctable marker—a kind of gnomon—casting a shadow sharply across memory, history, and the dimension of time itself. Earlier in the century, modernist writers such as D. H. Lawrence, in *Lady Chatterley's Lover* (1928), and Virginia Woolf, in her essays, saw the First World War as a 'cataclysm' cutting across the previously 'smooth road' of history (*Lady Chatterley*, ch. 1; *Collected Essays*, p. 167). The cataclysm of the second war obviously re-emphasized this sense of disjuncture, as Anthony Powell suggested in his image of the 'veil' or 'thick curtain' it had dropped across contemporary life, cutting off the past.[1] Any surviving sense of historical continuity was further threatened by developments at the war's end. For much of the rest of the century, the age of Cold War and atomic armament beginning in 1945 sustained a more or less imminent possibility of an end to all history and all human time. Many novels in the period attempted to imagine future nuclear conflict, or its consequences—Maggie Gee's *The Burning Book* (1983), for example, or Russell Hoban's *Riddley Walker* (1980), set far in the future, amid the ruins of England, and of its language, after atomic holocaust.

---

[1] See p. 397, above.

For less apocalyptic reasons, too, the later twentieth century was not a period which much favoured smooth temporality or long, steady historical perspectives in its fiction. Jumpcut or montage forms of assembly in the visual media, the channel-surfing conveniences of television, the increased pace of travel, communication, and life generally, all suggested different priorities. Like the modernists, several novelists in the period directly expressed scepticism of extended historical narrative—described as an 'impossible thing' in Graham Swift's *Waterland* (1983, ch. 10)—and of linear temporality, or at any rate of conventional means of its measurement. A suspicion of 'clumsy cogs and springs' disturbs Angela Carter's heroine in *Nights at the Circus* (1984), for example (pt. 1, ch. 2). Similar resentments of 'a horrible clockwork universe . . . straitjacket of thought' (pt. 2, ch. 8) were expressed at length in Brian Aldiss's *Frankenstein Unbound* (1973). They also appeared in Ian McEwan's *The Child in Time* (1987): in a distant echo of Laurence Sterne's *Tristram Shandy* (1759–67), McEwan's narrator discovers that he owes his very existence to a clock's refusal to function properly. Views of this kind were summed up by the Italian postmodernist Italo Calvino's conclusion, in *If on a Winter's Night a Traveller* (1979), that 'the continuity of time' existed only in the fiction of earlier periods. For the late twentieth century, Calvino considered, 'the dimension of time has been shattered, we cannot love or think except in fragments of time each of which goes off along its own trajectory and immediately disappears' (ch. 1).

This fragmented temporality obviously had fundamental effects on the form of fiction, generally shaped by narrative treatment of the dimension of time. In one way, it might have been expected to contribute to an outstanding age for the short story, a genre favouring the fragmentary, the inconsequential, or the momentary revelation, and one which critics such as Charles E. May naturally considered to 'thrive best in a fragmented society' (p. 13). Short-story authors such as V. S. Pritchett also emphasized this potential. Writing in the 1950s, Pritchett concluded that a 'collapse of standards, conventions and values' had bewildered novelists earlier in the century, but that it had 'been the making of the story writer who can catch any piece of life as it flies' (Shaw, p.18). The short story might have been expected to benefit further simply from its conciseness. In the hectic life of the later twentieth century, short stories offered—like poems—a quick imaginative experience to readers potentially impatient with the demands of longer literary forms. Yet the short story turned out to be a genre whose fortunes generally declined during the latter half of the century, and still more markedly than poetry's. Scarcer resources of time, concentration, or energy perhaps seemed to readers more profitably invested in the more substantial form of the novel. There were even critics in the period ready to suggest that 'the English . . . have never excelled in the form' of the short story, at least in comparison with authors in the United States (May, p. 13).

V. S. Pritchett's comments, at any rate, turned out to be much less relevant to the second half of the century than the first, when the reputations of writers such as Rudyard Kipling, Somerset Maugham, H. E. Bates, and Katherine Mansfield were based largely or exclusively on their short stories. Sylvia Townsend Warner and Pritchett himself were almost the only such authors surviving into the later twentieth century, and much of their best work had been done before the 1960s. Pritchett was even ready, in the *London Magazine* in September 1966, to describe the short story as now among literary 'lost causes', though possibly still an 'inextinguishable' one. Commercial factors contributed to this decline. Though radio continued to provide an occasional outlet for short stories, Pritchett recorded in his *London Magazine* article that 'the periodicals on which the writer can rely have almost all vanished', adding that 'the public is painfully small' (p. 6). Publishers and agents naturally pressed their authors to move on quickly from short stories—often still favoured by writers such as Ian McEwan or Adam Mars-Jones at the beginning of their careers—towards the more established, lucrative form of the novel. Authors such as Rose Tremain, A. L. Barker, and Angus Wilson continued to intersperse successful story collections between publication of their novels: John Fowles, in *The Ebony Tower* (1974), and Angela Carter in *The Bloody Chamber* (1979) did so particularly influentially. Yet even these collections did little to alter the novel's principal claim on popular and critical attention.

Aesthetic factors strengthened this claim. Any collapse of standards or conventions of the kind Pritchett mentioned had not necessarily 'bewildered' novelists earlier in the twentieth century. Instead, it had often challenged them—in the modernist period especially—to amend novelistic form, either to reflect contemporary fragmentation directly, or to contain it within subtler structures and more complex fictional styles. Later in the century, postmodern writers grew still more familiar with a generally discontinuous, fractured experience, and still readier to accept it as the basis of their fictional forms and aesthetics. Potential strengths of the short story form continued in this way to be usurped by the novel instead. Fragmentation was spectacularly evident in some of the innovative fiction of the 1960s—in the work of authors such as John Fowles, John Berger, Clive Sinclair, or B. S. Johnson particularly.[2] But it also affected the construction of novels more subtly and pervasively. Like contemporary plays, novels in the period were generally more episodic and discontinuous than in earlier years. They were also, on the whole, shorter. Declining economic confidence among publishers, and dwindling stamina or leisure time among readers, encouraged some novelists almost to usurp the short story's usual dimensions. When Ian McEwan moved on from short-story writing, it was to produce a first 'novel', *The Cement Garden* (1978), not much in excess of one hundred pages, and likelier to have been described in previous ages as a novella. On the evidence of some of McEwan's early writing, the form and tactics of the novel and the short story, towards the end of the twentieth century, grew increasingly interfused.

'Long novels written today are perhaps a contradiction', Italo Calvino suggested (ch. 1). The shattering of time and continuity he described was particularly evident in the fate, throughout the twentieth century, of the more extended fictional forms popular in previous periods. Little place was eventually left, in particular, for the huge novels of personal education and development— *Bildungsromane*, such as Charles Dickens's *David Copperfield* (1850)—popular in the nineteenth century. By the 1960s, as Doris Lessing remarked, the *Bildungsroman* form had been 'out of fashion for some time': its demise was symptomatic of wider changes in the novel's relations with history (*Four-Gated City*, p. 671). The *Bildungsroman* reflected Victorian confidence in progress and development through time, and it survived strongly in the relatively calm Edwardian years at the start of the twentieth century, sharing in the 'feeling of continuity' George Orwell ascribed to that age.[3] It even

---

[2] See pp. 406–7 and 410–12, above.   [3] See p. 52, above.

outlasted the First World War, in Marcel Proust's novel-sequence, *A la recherche du temps perdu* (*Remembrance of Things Past*, 1913–27). Moving more deeply into art, memory, and the writer's own vision, Proust sustained a sense of continuity and coherence which the war had severely challenged in contemporary life itself. Widely admired in the 1920s, Proust's work continued to influence several English writers later in the century—including, naturally, two of those still undertaking long novel-sequences after the Second World War, Anthony Powell and C. P. Snow. Though generally more conservative in their tactics, each relied regularly, like Proust, on characters' memories to re-establish continuities on a long timescale between present and past. Proust was cited directly, too, throughout *A Dance to the Music of Time*, and quoted at length in *The Military Philosophers* (1968), which showed Powell's narrator visiting the seaside resort of Cabourg—the original of Proust's 'Balbec'—just after the war.

As Chapter 15 suggested, Snow and Powell were among the writers still most determined, shortly after the war, to draw back the curtain it had dropped across contemporary life and history. But for many novelists later in the century, it was exactly in this period, just after the war and in the 1950s, that historical connections and continuities seemed finally to have fractured. A. S. Byatt, for example, also admired Proust, and some of her fiction still sought extended patterns and coherences linking individual life with a wider society and its evolving history. In *The Virgin in the Garden* (1978) and its sequel, *Still Life* (1986), Byatt followed her heroine's development through late childhood, tense family relations, education, and some of the broader social and artistic experience of the 1950s. Extended realistic and psychological detail also kept these novels close to the manner of the *Bildungsroman*. Yet contrasts in *The Virgin in the Garden* with the reign of the previous Queen Elizabeth, in the sixteenth century, highlighted the shapelessness of the new Elizabethan age in the 1950s, and the frustrating uncertainty of characters' struggles for personal development or fulfilment within it. Uncertainty and inconclusiveness likewise marked the development of Doris Lessing's central figure in her *Children of Violence* sequence (1952–69), despite her wish to redevelop some of the manner of the *Bildungsroman* in it.

John Fowles's *Daniel Martin* (1977) might have seemed closer to the manner of the *Bildungsroman* in its title and its extended, semi-autobiographical portrayal of an individual. Yet Fowles's shifting narrative perspectives and episodic story—starting in wartime, moving on to 'the national misery of that first decade after the war' (p. 169)—ultimately undermined pattern and coherence within individual life more than they affirmed them. Several authors later in the century did continue to work towards a coherent vision through long sagas of personal or family life. Tim Pears's *In a Land of Plenty* (1997) was more optimistic than the novels mentioned in showing a family—and the country generally—gradually emerging from the Second World War and the austerity and 'national misery' of the years which followed. But it generally grew more difficult, in a century of wars and violence, to ignore the kind of question a character raises in Salman Rushdie's *The Satanic Verses* (1988): 'what does a famine, a gas chamber, a grenade care how you lived your life?' More and more evidence supported his answer—that 'in this century history stopped paying attention to the old psychological orientation of reality . . . these days, character isn't destiny any more. Economics is destiny. Ideology is destiny. Bombs are destiny . . . your pathetic individual self doesn't have a thing to do with it' (pt. VII, ch. 2).

Such views help account for the scarcity of conventional tragedy—traditionally dependent on ideas of character as destiny—in late twentieth-century drama. They also help to explain the contemporary success of biography, produced in the period on a new scale of extended scholarly detail, and by an outstanding generation of authors. Some of the best of them concentrated on literary figures: Michael Holroyd in his five-volume *Bernard Shaw* (1988–92), for example; Peter Ackroyd in *Dickens* (1990) and other studies; Hermione Lee in *Virginia Woolf* (1996); and Claire Tomalin and Richard Holmes in a range of literary lives in the 1980s and 1990s. As Holroyd first demonstrated in his pioneering *Lytton Strachey* (1967–8), the success of this work was owed in one way to the relaxed outlook of the later twentieth century, allowing and inviting newly comprehensive, revealing reassessments of respected figures from the past. Lytton Strachey himself had been admired after the First World War for his candid, irreverent reconsideration of the Victorians. By the late 1960s, biographers were able to bring substantially greater candour to their re-evaluations of past lives: in Holroyd's unconstrained description of Strachey's homosexual relationships, for example. 'Even the bedrooms and beds are explored for data', Holroyd recalled one of his first readers remarking: new freedoms to examine these areas, and new levels of scholarship in acquiring and interpreting data generally, helped biography to be fuller, more honest, and often more interesting than in earlier periods (p. xxii).

But the success of biography late in the century, and its exceptional popularity with readers, probably also derived from subtler sources and displacements. In particular, biographies may have offered a substitute source of satisfactions once found in the *Bildungsoman* and similar fictional forms. In ways often missing from the contemporary novel, biography generally still offered a satisfying sense of the significance of the self, continuing to present character as destiny, and usually finding psychological, or just logical, explanations for the nature and development of individual lives. A paradigm for the appeal this offered appeared in Richard Holmes's influential combination of biography and travelogue in *Footsteps: Adventures of a Romantic Biographer* (1985). Holmes recorded several journeys he made towards self-discovery, and towards understanding of his own era, through 'identification or self-projection': through forms of 'imaginary relationship' developed in actually following the footsteps of literary figures, such as Shelley and Robert Louis Stevenson, and in intellectually exploring their lives, travels, and experiences. The popularity of this 'encroachment of the present upon the past', and of biography more generally, suggested a displaced, half-nostalgic attraction towards 'the old psychological orientation of reality' (pp. 66–7). Readers in the later twentieth century were particularly disposed to share the journeys Holmes described, seeking in the lives of earlier ages a substance and coherence which literary fiction seemed less and less able to provide for the present, and which contemporary postmodern thinking mostly challenged or refused. Biographers' frequent concentration on writers also satisfied interests displaced from the period's literary criticism, generally convinced of 'the death of the author', rather than the relevance of anything a life might reveal.[4]

*

[4] See Ch. 3, above.

'Both World Wars have fused and become a foundation on which all our assumptions are based', William Golding remarked in 1975 (*Moving Target*, p. 99). Fragmented literary narratives were only one marker of the lasting effects of a violent history on the century's imagination, even towards its end. Authors were inevitably drawn to reflect or explore in other ways, too, the wars' foundational influences on life in later years. Throughout the 1980s and 1990s, these influences continued to appear as strongly and broadly as they had in the writing of the 1960s and 1970s, also shaping fiction into some of the same patterns. Like novels by Henry Williamson, Anthony Burgess, and Angus Wilson, fiction late in the twentieth century continued to look back across its troubled history as far as the First World War. The Scottish novelist William Boyd followed this pattern in *The New Confessions* (1987), for example. It also appeared in Paul Bailey's *Old Soldiers* (1980). Bailey had been concerned with isolation, old age, and disturbed personalities since his first novel, *At the Jerusalem* (1967). In *Old Soldiers*, this interest extended into a long history of loss, including memories of the trenches—a kind of lasting shell shock—which continue to cast their darkness over the hot summer of 1976. In *A Month in the Country* (1980), J. L. Carr explored equally long memories, and an equally painful sense of loss, personal and historical, stretching back to the aftermath of the First World War, or even further, towards currents more deeply submerged in England's past. 'We can ask and ask but we can't have again what once seemed ours for ever . . . you can only wait for the pain to pass', Carr's narrator remarks, summing up feelings for the last of an England lost in the Edwardian years, or even earlier (p. 111). Sebastian Faulks likewise traced intense emotional consequences of the First World War as far as the late 1970s in *Birdsong* (1993), examining them further in a sequel, *Charlotte Gray* (1998), through the memories of a heroine closely involved herself in covert operations in occupied France in the 1940s.

There were other authors to whom the First World War seemed the main key to understanding the century's history,[5] but for most novelists in its later years, it was the Second which naturally seemed of more immediate concern, and a more direct influence on recent life. In her aptly named novel *Change* (1987), for example, Maureen

[5] See pp. 466–8, below.

Duffy used several overlapping stories to examine the Second World War's levelling effect on class hierarchies—tactics and interests shared with 1950s novelists such as C. P. Snow and Anthony Powell, but differing in her concentration on the life of the working class. Duffy shared and developed another direction in late twentieth-century fiction, much less in evidence before the 1980s, by showing her characters appalled by 'pictures of hell, of Doomsday, of the damned' taken in the concentration camps and at Hiroshima (ch. 5). Like writers discussed in Chapter 16, novelists later in the century continued to reflect the war's impact in terms of moral shock. But they were often readier than their predecessors to look directly at the horrors and depravities involved—at Nazi atrocities, and at the concentration camps in particular. Like Richard Hughes and Gabriel Fielding in the 1960s, David Hughes assessed German experience of the war in *The Pork Butcher* (1984), but portrayed a guiltier representative of it, showing a former solider returning to the village whose inhabitants he helped massacre in wartime France. Bernice Rubens's account of several generations of Jewish family life in *Brothers* (1984) centred its third part in Nazi Germany, and on the experiences of Buchenwald and Auschwitz. Elaine Feinstein likewise traced a Jewish family's life through the period of the Second World War in *The Survivors* (1982), and returned to the Hitler years in *The Border* (1982), *Mother's Girl* (1988), and *Loving Brecht* (1992).

D. M. Thomas offered a comprehensive account of the psyche of one of the Nazi's victims in *The White Hotel* (1981). Thomas presented in extended—sometimes sensational—sexual detail Freud's analysis of a patient, Lisa, whose violent fantasies originate less in past trauma than in strange precognition of her murder at Babi Yar. The narrator in Ian McEwan's novel *Black Dogs* (1992) warns that imagination is 'denied . . . its proper sympathies, its rightful grasp of the suffering' by Nazi crimes: by their 'extravagant numerical scale, the easy-to-say numbers—tens and hundreds of thousands, millions' (pt. 3). Thomas's novel attempts to restore some grasp of this suffering through the intensely intimate sympathy it establishes for a single individual and her 'psychological orientation'. *The White Hotel* shows Lisa eventually murdered alongside a quarter of a million other individuals, 'every single one of [whom] had dreamed dreams, seen visions and had amazing experiences . . . as rich and complex' as her own (ch. 5). Like Richard Hughes in *The Fox in the Attic* (1961), *The White Hotel* also attempts to reinterpret history in Freudian terms, envisaging the twentieth century's wars and violence as manifestations of 'a *universal* struggle between the life instinct and the death instinct' (ch. 3). How far *The White Hotel* offered a 'rightful grasp' of history nevertheless became a hotly debated question, with Thomas sometimes accused of pornography, on account of the explicitness of Lisa's sexual fantasies, or plagiarism, on the grounds of his extensive borrowings from Freud.

The Second World War, all these novels suggested, continued to cast a shadow over fiction in the 1980s and 1990s as dark as any that had appeared earlier in the period. Authors in the 1960s had envisaged horrors at the war's end as a kind of 'original sin', or 'a primal, an original, an Adamic fact':[6] McEwan's narrator in *Black Dogs* continued to find the Holocaust 'our universal reference point of human depravity' in the 1990s (pt. 1). The war remained in this way, for novelists throughout the period, a moral centre of gravity as well as a historical one. Continually tugging authors' attention back into the past, it provided the 'unavoidable focus' D. J. Taylor described in *After the War: The Novel and England since 1945*: a source of what he saw as 'the whole tendency of the post-war novel' towards the retrospective (p. 5). This tendency added further to the urge to depart from a 'shattered' linear temporality, discussed earlier, and had extensive consequences for the form and construction of narrative throughout the later twentieth century. From Elizabeth Jane Howard's *After Julius* (1965), mostly set in 1961, to Zadie Smith's *White Teeth* (2000), which concludes on the last day of 1999, fiction in the period habitually located primal events or moral reference points in wartime. As in *White Teeth*, this could involve starting stories with key events during the war, and going on to trace their unfolding significance in later decades. As in Howard's *After Julius*, it also often involved more recursive, retrospective forms of construction, moving back from a fictional present—repeatedly, if necessary—to examine the foundational wartime events which had helped to bring it into being.

The clearest example of this retrospective tendency, late in the century, appeared in Martin Amis's aptly named *Time's Arrow* (1991).

---

[6] See p. 417, above.

Amis's novel showed a Nazi war criminal supposedly experiencing in reality what so many novelists sought to achieve in their fiction. He lives time backwards, as if in a film of his life shown in reverse, starting from his death and old age, returning to wartime work in Auschwitz, and eventually beyond, to his birth in Adolf Eichmann's home town. Contemporary critics sometimes saw Amis's strategy as facile, or, like D. M. Thomas's, sensational. It was at any rate highly representative: of history's gravity, reshaping fictional narrative and shattering the dimension of time, and of the need for extraordinary imaginative tactics in representing the extravagant evil of the Holocaust. It was also more widely symptomatic. Showing victims of mass murder miraculously restored to life, and massively destructive acts transformed into creative ones, *Time's Arrow* was a late twentieth-century wish-fulfilment: an escape from the past's evils, veils, and shadows into a redemptive, Edenic temporality freed of the war's 'primal facts'.

Ian McEwan's *Black Dogs* engaged in less redemptive forms of retrospection. Its narrator looks back across a range of recent European history, recalling a trip to Berlin, after the fall of the wall, and an earlier one, to the remains of a Polish concentration camp. But his narrative concentrates on the recollections of his wife's parents, Bernard and June. Their memories centre on a honeymoon in France, just after the war, which permanently changed their lives. Bernard is overwhelmed by realization of the war's appalling legacy, one of 'boundless grief . . . a weight borne in silence by hundreds of thousands, millions' (pt. 4). It inspires him towards the 'thirty years' devoted advocacy of numerous causes for social and political reform' described in the narrator's 'Preface'. Bernard is in this way a figure representative of long-sustained post-war political commitments, ones whose origins around 1945 were often examined in 1970s drama: his original inspiration in rural France particularly resembles the heroine's epiphany at the end of David Hare's *Plenty* (1978).[7] June's defining experience, on the other hand, is spiritual rather than political. An encounter with two huge dogs, recently used by the Nazis to terrorise the local population, convinces her of the existence of 'a malign principle . . . in human affairs'. Yet she sees this principle as part of a Manichaean equilibrium, intuiting 'a

---

[7] See p. 323, above.

luminous countervailing spirit, benign and all-powerful', to whose service she dedicates a life of meditation and spirituality ('Preface'). Secular and spiritual, 'rationalist and mystic', Bernard and June's experiences reflect a historical vision still close to William Golding's in *Darkness Visible* (1979), or Anthony Burgess's in *Earthly Powers* (1980). McEwan continued to show in the 1990s—like these authors—forces of light and dark, and of earthly and spiritual commitment, issuing from the war and extending throughout the life and imagination of later decades.

Yet *Black Dogs* also showed how complicated historical vision of this kind had become for a younger generation of writers, late in the century. McEwan's narrator has to piece together June's story from her hazy recollection, almost on her deathbed, and several other key memories—of Bernard's defining encounter with 'boundless grief', for example—turn out to have no verifiable basis in fact. Holocaust fiction such as *Time's Arrow* or *The White Hotel* indicated one set of difficulties in dealing with the war. Complex narrative strategies in each suggested that the war's most significant events, morally, might also be the hardest to communicate in literature—nearly unspeakable, or almost beyond the 'old psychological orientation' of the novel. William Golding emphasized this difficulty in remarking that 'Belsen, Hiroshima and Dachau cannot be imagined . . . Those experiences are like black holes in space. Nothing can get out to let us know what it was like inside. It was like what it was like and on the other hand it was like nothing whatsoever. We stand before a gap in history . . . a limit to literature' (*Moving Target*, p.102). But for a later generation of novelists, these experiences had also begun to enter a black hole in time, along with experience of the war more generally. By the end of the century, as *Black Dogs* confirmed, a 'thick curtain' had fallen not only across the years before the war, but between the present and the war itself—penetrable only through the uncertain recollections of an older generation, or through potentially unreliable forms of historical documentation. Many novelists thus found themselves drawn towards 'primal facts' or moral reference points they could scarcely deal with either through conventional narrative tactics, or with complete historical conviction. The war tended as a result not only to fracture conventional narrative continuities. It also encouraged authors to multiply and diversify narrative forms, within single novels, directly communicating to readers the difficulties of arbitrating between competing or contradictory versions of the past. This tendency added generally, in the period's fiction, to self-reflexive, postmodern questions about the nature of narrative and the 'limit to literature'. It appeared particularly clearly in several novels by Graham Swift, Penelope Lively, and Lawrence Norfolk. In each, the validity of historical narratives and war recollections figured as central issues.

As in *Black Dogs*, these issues were examined in Swift's *Shuttle-cock* (1981) through conflicting accounts of wartime experience and complex relations between the generations. 'Born in August 1945 ... a product of those times', Swift's narrator Prentis offers another version of late twentieth-century stories about lost fathers (ch. 27).[8] He discovers that the archive where he works holds evidence suggesting that his father might have falsified and glamorized his wartime career when writing an autobiography—also entitled *Shuttlecock*, and reproduced in Swift's text. But its veracity can never be determined, since the war is now literally unspeakable for Prentis senior, following a breakdown which has left him unable to talk. Prentis himself finds the resulting incertitude oddly consoling—preferable to trying to emulate his supposedly illustrious father. Relief from Oedipal stress makes him in turn a more equable parent, allowing the novel an affirmative concluding vision. Showing Prentis's children running off across a sunny beach, 'no longer running towards the sea, but running, being impelled, towards the future', this ending suggests that a *third* generation may at last be able to free itself from lengthening, paling shadows of war (ch. 35).

Several other novels were similarly hopeful, late in the century, showing the war's painful immediacies subdued by the passage of the years, by fading memory, or by the interventions of art itself. Penelope Gilliat's *A Woman of Singular Occupation* (1988) and Louis de Bernière's *Captain Corelli's Mandolin* (1994) each described a romance formed then fractured during the war. Each showed relationships sustained in memory, and by the transmutation of passions into musical composition—oddly, in each case, for the mandolin. Both novels concluded with now-aged lovers on the brink of full reunion, decades later, suggesting that narratives of war

---

[8] See pp. 401–2, above.

might eventually move towards a romance mode—of restitution and reconciliation, of personal and artistic harmony. Some of this mode also appeared, along with a simply elegiac one, in Graham Swift's *Last Orders* (1996). Like several of the novels considered above, *Last Orders* traced its central figure's life from its end back to defining experiences during the Second World War. These are recalled, along with many other reflections on past and present, within the inner consciousnesses of friends fulfilling his last wish by taking his ashes to be scattered in the sea.

In *Waterland* (1983), Swift offered a more baleful account of the war's legacy, and his fullest view of its effect on historical narrative. Set in the vividly described landscape of the Fens, the novel follows a history teacher's thoughts about a chain of events, beginning in 1943, still deeply troubling his present life. He also recalls how 'a vision of the world in ruins' in 1946—like Bernard's in *Black Dogs*—first encouraged his interest in history, which seemed to offer a means of dealing with the way 'things go wrong . . . with trouble, with perplexity, with regret' (chs. 31, 10). But his narrative shows history as ultimately only one of many stories he encounters: 'made-up stories, true stories; soothing stories . . . meanings, myths, manias' (chs. 1, 6). Each is used, he realizes, simply 'to convince ourselves that reality is not an empty vessel' (ch. 6). History, supposedly the 'Grand Narrative, the filler of vacuums' is not necessarily any more reliable than the others (ch. 8). Similar scepticism figured in much of Penelope Lively's fiction. Her heroine in *Moon Tiger* (1987), for example, is a historian trying 'to align [her] own life with the history of the world', like Swift's central figure, and to deal with perplexity and regret through narratives of the past (ch. 1). Late in life, she is engaged on an account of the twentieth century, based on personal experiences as journalist, writer, and mother—above all, on memories of her lover, killed during the desert war, in 1942. Throughout, diverse perspectives, diaries, and memories complement her recollections, but they often complicate or contradict them, too. *Moon Tiger*, like the other novels mentioned, once again showed the past—its grief and its power—slipping beyond easy narrative control.

In *Treasures of Time* (1979) and *Cleopatra's Sister* (1993), Lively used the work of palaeontologists, or of archaeologists—like

J. L. Carr in *A Month in the Country*—to demonstrate further the difficulties of delving into history. In tracing its continuing power over the present, both her novels nevertheless showed history as what the latter called 'a chimera, a construct of the human intellect', made up of 'myths and fables, distortions and elaborations of something that may or may not have happened' (*Cleopatra's Sister*, pt. 1, ch. 2). Lawrence Norfolk's fiction took a view of the past similarly complex and multilayered. *In the Shape of a Boar* (2000) opens with an account of a semi-mythic boar hunt in ancient Greece. In later sections, this account becomes a metaphor for the pursuit of a Nazi by partisans the novel's central figure encounters in Greece. It may even be a version of the long poem he writes in response to this experience. Years after the war, when a former lover makes a film based around this poem, many question are raised about whether it ever truly represented events, or can ever be verified. These mutually interrogating layers of history, myth, metaphor, poetry, fiction, and film continued the complex historical interests of Norfolk's first novel, *Lemprière's Dictionary* (1991). Like much of the fiction described above, they also showed the events of the war fading towards the impalpable, late in the century—towards dark spaces beyond official documentation, history, or even individual memory and imagination. Appropriately, *In the Shape of a Boar* ends obscurely, in a cave: literally, a black hole, from which no reliable information can be retrieved.

Questions about the reliability of historical narrative—or any narrative—extended much more widely towards the end of the century. As Chapter 2 described, the shock of the war was among several factors contributing to self-questioning, postmodern uncertainties about all theories, narratives, and representations of life. This scepticism was evident in most intellectual disciplines during the period, and eventually extended into the thinking of historians as much as literary critics and authors. New examinations of gaps between text and event featured extensively in the discussions of historians and historiographers, following Hayden White's influential arguments in studies such as *Metahistory* (1973). Literary critics often considered new incertitudes in historical narratives and in fictional ones as mutually reinforcing. Linda Hutcheon, in particular, suggested that the sceptical, self-questioning idiom of postmodernist literature could be seen as primarily a form of 'historiographic metafiction' (*Poetics of Postmodernism*, p. 5). Writing of this kind was by no means confined to novels in which the history of the Second World War was directly an issue. Walter Allen found the war's 'ineluctable shadow' falling across novels in later years regardless of their subject: its consequences in terms of historical and narrative incertitude were eventually just as widely influential. For much of the period, uncertainties created by recent history confirmed and coalesced with postmodern thought: post-war and postmodern influences coincided in a self-doubting, self-questioning idiom particularly evident in novels of historical interest, even when these were set outside the twentieth century altogether.

Evidence of this appeared widely in the 1980s and 1990s. It was especially clear in the work of an author who emerged alongside Swift, Amis, and McEwan: Julian Barnes. In his first novel, *Metroland* (1980), Barnes portrayed a character living in Paris in 1968 who somehow manages to overlook the *événements* of student revolution at the time. History occupied a similarly oblique, wayward role in Barnes's later fiction. In *Flaubert's Parrot* (1984), the narrator's realistic account of his fascination for Flaubert alternates with many other textual forms, including critical essays, conversations with the reader, a kind of dictionary, a bestiary, and even an exam paper. Collectively, these demonstrate the inevitable disappearance of historical events beneath the conflicting perspectives and narratives which attempt to represent them. Points of view ranging from a woodworm to an astronaut make a similar case in *A History of the World in 10½ Chapters* (1989). Barnes continued to examine conflicts between divergent views of events in *Talking it Over* (1991) and *Love, etc* (2000). Though more conventional novels, dealing with marriage and divorce, each highlighted what *Love, etc* describes as the gap between 'the story of our life' and 'form, control, discrimination, selection, omission, arrangement, emphasis ... that dirty, three-letter word, art' (ch. 2).

Other contemporary authors followed the example John Fowles offered in *The French Lieutenant's Woman* (1969), juxtaposing past and present styles of narrative in order to highlight particularities and limitations—gaps between art and life—in each. Like Fowles, in *Possession* (1990) A. S. Byatt contrasted the literary manners of

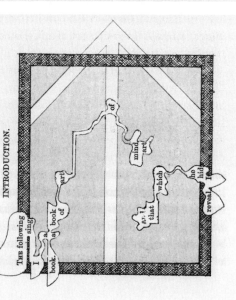

Fig. 15. Two pages from another reconfiguration of nineteenth-century fiction: Tom Phillips's *A Humument*. *A Treated Victorian Novel* (1973). Phillips began in 1966 to replace sections of W. H. Mallock's *A Human Document* (1892) with text and designs of his own, eventually reworking the whole novel.

the nineteenth century with the modern sensibilities of a pair of academic researchers, now equipped with the theories not only of Alain Robbe-Grillet and Roland Barthes but also their post-structuralist successors. Pastiche forms of letters, journals, and poems reproduce in the novel the evidence through which they redis-cover a long-lost literary love affair and even reduplicate some of its characteristics within their own relations. Peter Ackroyd's *Hawksmoor* (1985) alternated present-day narratives and styles with those employed in a more distant past, in the journals of an early eighteenth-century Satanist—a professed enemy of Christian-ity, and of the rational, scientific outlook of the early Enlightenment. Human sacrifice figures in his attempts to instil older, darker powers into the fabric of the London churches he constructs as an assistant to Sir Christopher Wren. Other sections of the novel show the reasoning powers of a present-day policeman bedevilled by recent murders committed on the sites of these churches. Often disdainful of conventional realism, and of logical, temporal orders of cause and effect, *Hawksmoor* is an unresolved detective story, reproducing some of the manner of the *nouveau roman* Ackroyd admired[9] and emphasizing postmodern scepticism of Enlightenment values, even as these first appeared in the early eighteenth century. An interest in dark powers, transcending the normal order of time and reason, extended into another story of archaeology and detection, *First Light* (1989). In *Chatterton* (1987) and later fiction such as *English Music* (1992), Ackroyd continued to show the past determining the present, yet receding beyond its certain cognition.

Uncertainty of this kind figured less darkly in the work of other novelists late in the century. Difficulties in accurately representing the past simply offered them a licence to imagine it more freely. Robert Nye reworked the lives of literary, historical, or legendary figures in this way in a number of novels, including *Faust* (1980) and *The Memoirs of Lord Byron* (1989). *The Late Mr Shakespeare* (1998) was typical of his work in freely mixing documentation and invention, particularly sanctioned in this case by the genuine short-age of information about its subject. 'Town history . . . facts and figures . . . ruled by the head' mingle throughout with 'country history . . . wild and mystical and passionate . . . ruled by the heart'

---

[9] See pp. 407 and 432, above.

(ch. 18). Rose Tremain's *Restoration* (1989) was likewise both historically faithful and freely fanciful. Carefully detailed in depicting a late seventeenth-century 'Age of Possibility', *Restoration* also showed what its narrator calls 'a visionary side'—typically, in his account of grasping a living human heart as it beats on, 'utterly without feeling' in its owner's body (chs. 1, 3). Andrew Miller's central figure in *Ingenious Pain* (1997) appears equally—and equally miraculously—immune to suffering, though otherwise a plausible-enough inhabitant of the late eighteenth century. Julia Blackburn's *The Leper's Companions* (1999) was also half-magical as well as realistic in its narrator's imaginings of fifteenth-century pilgrimage. Similar combinations of magic and realism characterized the historical imagination of some of the 1980s and 1990s novelists discussed in Chapter 18, Jeanette Winterson particularly. Though less fanciful, Adam Thorpe's *Ulverton* (1992) was as diverse in style and point of view as any of the novels mentioned, presenting three centuries in the life of an English village in forms ranging from stream of consciousness to film and radio scripts.

*

Hawksmoor was typical of attitudes not only to history, but to the depressed aspects of life in the 1980s and 1990s. Along with much contemporary poetry and drama, novels regularly envisaged bleakly what Malcolm Bradbury described in *Rates of Exchange* (1983) as an 'age of Sado-Monetarism'. Throughout the country, Bradbury suggested—and throughout contemporary fiction—this 'time of recession and unemployment, decay and deindustrialization' produced the kind of urban landscape in which 'vandalism marks the spaces, graffiti the walls, where the council pulls down old substandard housing, to replace it with new substandard housing . . . rain falls over factories which stand empty with broken windows . . . rubbish and abandoned cars litter the hard shoulder of the motorway' (pt. 1, ch. 2). Urban decline and the depressed mood of the 1980s focused, or refocused, darker forms of imagination—and darker forms of humour—which had developed through various intermediaries ever since the war. Later fiction sometimes extended the blackly comic vision of Samuel Beckett's Absurd plays, or the bleak wit of his grotesque, debilitated narrators in the trilogy, *Molloy, Malone Dies,*

The Unnamable (1959).[10] Muriel Spark was also a strong influence on English fiction after the early 1960s, and on its use of black humour especially. Spark's dark examinations of power and evil were usually characterized by aloof, ironic wit. As well as relieving some of the grimness of the contemporary life she described, this also provided a firm satiric perspective through which its shortcomings could be highlighted.

This aloof vision may have owed something to her conversion to Catholicism in the 1950s. Catholic writers, at any rate, often seemed readiest to recognize depression and deficiency in late twentieth-century life, and yet to treat them with humour. Clear moral standards and faith in another world, safely above and beyond the immediate one, perhaps encouraged confidence and aloof irony even in examining the darker vicissitudes of earthly life. Satire and irony of this kind appeared throughout Evelyn Waugh's fiction, including his *Sword of Honour* trilogy (1952–61), firmly moral, yet blackly comic in tone. Anthony Burgess also showed himself a darkly funny author in his *Enderby* novels. Catholic novelists emerging in later decades continued to use black humour resembling Spark's. *The Bottle Factory Outing* (1974) was typical of Beryl Bainbridge's manner in her early fiction. As dryly and dispassionately as Spark, Bainbridge describes a heroine who escapes a depressing life by cheerfully attending funerals, until she is accidentally killed herself. Stuffed into an empty wine-barrel by her workmates, she is dispatched to oblivion with only a plastic tulip to accompany her grotesque, bulging corpse.

Similarly dispassionate vision characterized much of the work of Alice Thomas Ellis. The narrative perspective of *The 27th Kingdom* (1982), for example, is unusually distant from any of the novel's human characters, often even sharing the point of view of an aptly named cat, Focus. Complete emotional detachment enables him 'to take a removed and measured view of affairs—human, feline and, indeed, divine' (ch. 3). Ellis's tone was generally just as measured, and her interests equally wide-ranging. Her satiric vision of a tawdry, complex world of human relationships was often relieved by transitions into dimensions above or outside it—involving sainthood and miracles in *The 27th Kingdom*; ghosts, spirits, and a domain

---

[10] See pp. 79–80 and 346–8, above.

beyond death in *The Inn at the Edge of the World* (1990). Supernatural, macabre, or grotesque elements of this kind, strongly apparent in Ellis's fiction, and in Bainbridge's, also figured much more
widely in late twentieth-century writing—in several of Emma
Tennant's novels, for example, and in Susan Hill's portrayal of murderous conflict between children in *I'm the King of the Castle* (1970).

These elements showed the renewed influence in the period's
fiction of Gothic modes of imagination, complementing its black
humour. Some of their origins were indicated in another of Bainbridge's darkly comic novels, *A Quiet Life* (1976), which considered
'the effects of war on the younger generation' in terms of 'fear . . .
dreams . . . symptoms of one sort or another' (ch. 3). Chapter 1 considered the war's effects in generally darkening the vision of writers
in the period[11]—an influence working in one way straightforwardly,
at a conscious level. But the war also had subtler, longer-term effects
on imagination, as William Golding emphasized: whatever 'goes on
at the conscious level', he remarked, 'beneath, in some deep cavern
of the soul, we are stunned' (*Moving Target*, p. 99). The twentieth
century did not necessarily witness the emergence of 'a new kind of
human being, *because of Freud*', as Richard Hughes suggested in *The
Fox in the Attic* (1961), and other early 1960s authors often considered (bk. 1, ch. 19). But recent history did unleash into immediate
experience and imagination, with new force, the levels of nightmare
Freud's work had made familiar. Hiroshima and the Holocaust
brought death and horror—'pictures of hell'—into immediate
history on a scale hitherto scarcely imaginable. A likely effect was the
exhuming of Gothic fears and dreams from whatever cavern of the
soul contained them, eroding rational restraints which might have
continued to suppress them within the unconscious. A strongly neo-
Gothic element reappeared in English fiction directly after the war, in
the malign fantasy of Mervyn Peake's *Gormenghast* trilogy (1946–
59)—the work of an author who had visited Belsen in the wake of the
liberating armies. Sustained in intervening years by authors mentioned above, Gothic and grotesque elements were easily readopted
in describing the depressed life of the 1980s, and readily combined
with the black humour also steadily developed since the war.

*

[11] See pp. 53–5, above. Gothic imagination is further discussed on p. 476, below.

Naturally enough, this combination often appeared in the work of two authors, discussed earlier, particularly concerned with the war's continuing influence, in *Black Dogs* and *Time's Arrow*—Ian McEwan and Martin Amis, among the most successful of new novelists emerging in the late 1970s. McEwan's early short-story collections *First Love, Last Rites* (1975) and *In Between the Sheets* (1978) were unusual enough in their imagination to establish his reputation almost immediately. Stories in each offered sensational elegies for the demise of the 1960s, showing sexual freedoms pressured towards cruelty and perversity in the harsher climate of the next decade, or declining of their own accord into grotesque or obsessive forms of relationship. McEwan's prose retained a cool grace even in depicting perverse emotions and dismal 1970s cityscapes, establishing for his work, in another way, some of the aloof, ironic perspective distinguishing Catholic writers discussed above. Early stories also established an interest in childhood innocence rather like Golding's in *Lord of the Flies* (1954), though McEwan was particularly concerned with characters unable to *escape* childhood—with sexual or emotional natures trapped in permanent pre-adolescence. This interest continued to shape many of his novels. The narrator's sexual awakening in *The Cement Garden* (1978) is inevitably confused by its coincidence with the gruesome burial of his mother in the cellar of the family home. *The Comfort of Strangers* (1981) follows the origins, in childhood, of a perverse 'sexual imagination . . . which distorted all relations, all truth' (ch. 10). A senior politician in *The Child in Time* (1987) madly regresses into pre-adolescent boyhood, and obsessive, childish forms of attachment continue to appear in *Enduring Love* (1997).

Most of McEwan's novels also followed the short stories in using highly particular first-person narrators. This was a tactic shared in one way or another by many late twentieth-century authors: idiosyncratic, indivdualized vision provided for their work a convenient, even essential means of representing a fragmenting, non-consensual society. McEwan's fiction was nevertheless particularly disturbing in extending into characters' individual narratives the oddity and perversity of the worlds they witness. This engaged readers unusually immediately with the depressed experience of the 1980s, and with responsibilities for judging it. In *The Cement Garden*, for example, the narrator's numbed reactions extend the particular weirdness of his family situation, but they also express a general emotional negligence in contemporary life, emphasized by the wasteland of rotting tower blocks in which the novel is set. In *The Child in Time*, the narrator initially seems partly redeemed, through parenthood, from the sexual uneasiness so evident elsewhere in McEwan's writing. But for much of the novel's duration, the disappearance of his daughter induces in his narrative, too, a nervously heightened response to 1980s conditions of poverty and social breakdown. These are further accentuated by McEwan's projection of contemporary stresses into a slightly futuristic Britain, governed with more demented authoritarianism than was in evidence in the late 1980s.

Martin Amis used similar tactics, setting *London Fields* (1989) in a millennial future threatened by global catastrophe, and employing sharply characterized narrators, in this novel and others, to focus readers' judgement of a tawdry, declining society. The narrator of *Money* (1984), for example, John Self, is both a celebrant and eventually a victim of the glitzy new affluence of business and media communities on both sides of the Atlantic in the 1980s. In describing his grotesque addictions to alcohol, junk food, pornography, and—above all—cash, Self is nevertheless chatty, funny, and street-wise. His narrative both seeks and repels readers' sympathies, rather in the manner of the 'lad lit' which followed in the 1990s:

Two forty, and I was out on Broadway, heading north. Now, how bad do you assume I'm feeling? . . . Well, you're wrong. I'm touched by your sympathy (and want much, much more of it: I want sympathy, even though I find it so very hard to behave sympathetically). But you're wrong, brother. Sister, you slipped. I didn't feel too great this morning, true. A ninety-minute visit to Pepper's Burger World, on the other hand, soon sorted that lot out. I had four Wallies, three Blastfurters, and an American Way, plus a nine-pack of beer. (p. 29)

Amis challenged reader's sympathies more strangely in *Other People: A Mystery Story* (1981), highlighting poverty and social deprivation by focusing on a character apparently recovering from complete amnesia. Lacking established moral or even perceptual capacities, her perspective reflects with painful immediacy 'the lost, the ruined, the broken, the effaced . . . [in] clinks and clinics and soup-queues . . .

hostels and borstals and homes full of mad women' (chs. 7, 11). In her vision, as in Peter Ackroyd's *Hawksmoor*, London sometimes seems a suburb of hell: only Iain Sinclair's *Downriver* (1991), among contemporary novels, offered a stranger or grimmer perspective on the capital. But *Other People* is made still more disturbing by the sinister, perhaps even murderous nature of the novel's narrative voice— apparently as depraved as the central character is utterly innocent, and gleefully familiar with all the miseries and perversities she encounters.

Another shady figure narrates *London Fields*. Murderous designs on characters he describes raise self-reflexive questions about the morality—or lack of it—in the narrative, extending ones Amis directs at the dispirited society portrayed. Strangely, D. J. Taylor concluded that *London Fields* showed it to be 'practically impossible to function as a satirist at the present time', complaining in particular about Amis's central figure, a would-be darts champion who shares many of John Self's ambitions and addictions. For Taylor, this 'worst character' lacks life or moral substance, illustrating instead only 'endless manipulation by his creator' (pp. 189, 192). But the immediate creator of this 'bad guy . . . the worst guy' is of course the narrator and not Martin Amis (*London Fields*, ch. 1). Rather like Muriel Spark and Iris Murdoch in the 1960s, one of Amis's achievements for contemporary fiction was in showing how effectively artistic, 'creator' or narrator figures, quite possibly bad guys themselves, could be used to focus the moral and satiric attention of the novel. In the work of the Catholic writers considered earlier, for example, much twentieth-century satiric narrative relied on ironic superiority to the deficient world portrayed. But Amis challenged readers' judgement further, with an extra layer of cynicism, flaunting a provocative moral deficiency within the process of narrative itself. The dexterity of such tactics, and his sharp contemporaneity of vision, made Amis a natural contender for the Booker Prize. He was sometimes thought to have been passed over on account of negative attitudes to women—in the case of *London Fields* especially—which the judges ascribed to the author himself, rather than to his carefully characterized narrators.

In other ways, too, Martin Amis was a novelist characteristic of his age. Social and economic problems in the 1980s and 1990s might have encouraged a return to conventionally realistic fiction, as they had in the 1930s, and there were authors towards the end of the century who did explore an age of 'sado-monetarism' and its stresses in this way. Contemporary social problems were conventionally highlighted in Geoff Nicholson's *Bleeding London* (1997), for example, in Ben Richards's *Don't Step on the Lines* (1997), in Stephen Blanchard's *Wilson's Island* (1997), and by Christopher Hart, concentrating on a rural context rather than an urban one in *The Harvest* (1999). Yet like writers considered earlier—such as Graham Swift or Peter Ackroyd—Amis confirmed that historical and social interests could be combined very effectively with self-questioning narratives and innovative postmodernist forms. This was a combination Amis had set out to develop almost from the beginning of his career. He remarked in the *New Review* in Summer 1978 that he intended his novels to be 'as tricksy, as alienated and as writerly as those of, say, Robbe-Grillet while also providing the staid satisfactions of pace, plot and humour with which we associate, say, Jane Austen' (p. 18). This ambition remained steadily in evidence in his work. *Other People*, for example, recalled Robbe-Grillet's *nouveau roman* in its indecipherable identities and time schemes, while still retaining some of the satiric wit and social vision characterizing Jane Austen's fiction, though obviously directed on a very different milieu. It was an ambition Amis loosely restated at the end of the period. In his autobiographical *Experience* (2000) he defined Vladimir Nabokov and Saul Bellow as his 'twin peaks' in twentieth-century writing—the former cerebral, inventive, and tricksy, the latter broadly realistic and socially concerned (p. 119).

Along with the example of many other writers discussed in this chapter, these dual preferences indicated the continuing relevance, in the 1980s and 1990s, of the 'crossroads' of tradition and innovation David Lodge identified in the early 1970s. Lodge himself continued to consider 'The Novelist Today: Still at the Crossroads?' a question worth asking in 1991, though acknowledging that the metaphor of the crossroads had been partly superseded by 'the astonishing variety of styles on offer today, as if in an aesthetic supermarket' (Bradbury and Cooke (eds.), p. 209). The novel initially arrived at Lodge's 1970s crossroads through evolutions of literary history discussed in earlier chapters: gradual coalescences between once-divergent modes, modernist, postmodernist, and traditional. In the years that followed, further factors encouraged fiction to remain at this crossroads, or to develop still greater stylistic pluralism. Along with the particular stresses and historical memories of the times, these factors included an 'aesthetic supermarket' better stocked in response to broader education, a more democratic culture, and new tastes developing as a result among writers and readers. Higher education familiarized growing numbers of authors with a range of literary styles. Readers, too, generally grew more sophisticated and wider in their interests: readier to be stimulated by narrative invention, as well as entertained by conventional realism, pace, and plot.[12] Towards the end of the century, crossroads or cross-breedings of forms and styles simply became part of market demand, and of literary production, continuing to shape much of the fiction of the 1990s.

Novels at the time also remained cross-bred with the kind of Gothic or grotesque modes, discussed earlier, exhumed from a troubled history in the devitalized 1980s. Fiction could hardly have been less vital, in a way, or more grotesque, than Will Self's *How the Dead Live* (2000). The novel's gruesome vision is particularly focused by its deceased narrator's physical self-descriptions, but also by her wider recollections of a century of war and destruction, and of a daughter trapped by drug addiction in a form of living death. The quick and the dead, post-mortem society and the living one, each inhabit a familiar London landscape in Self's satire, and are often disturbingly hard to distinguish. Self's English adaptation of 'wiseacre Jewish-American humour' also confirms that the authors most inclined to view life as desperate, late in the century, were often those, like Samuel Beckett, least disposed to view it as serious (ch. 4). Jonathan Coe provided another example in *What a Carve Up* (1994), using memories of a black comedy film as the basis for his satiric attack on a huge range of targets, including the tabloid press, factory farming, arms manufacture, the aristocracy, and the shortcomings of the National Health Service. By regularly discussing narrative tactics, Coe's narrator also sustained a satirical, postmodernist scrutiny of the representative capacities of the novel itself. Similarly black humour appeared in Jenny Diski's ironically entitled *Happily Ever After* (1991), along with a still stranger writer, a geriatric seductress

[12] See pp. 136 and 160–1, above.

who may be the source of much of the novel's own narrative. It sadly extends anxieties about childhood and innocence in the period's fiction, describing a social worker who concludes that painless death, following a single day of genuine happiness, may be the best that contemporary society can offer some of its children. Along with Muriel Spark, Beryl Bainbridge, and Alice Thomas Ellis, Diski also showed how particularly and extensively the period's black humour, grotesque vision, and postmodernist narrative modes were developed by women writers. These developments and others in this area are considered in the next chapter.

18

'Double Lives': Women's Writing and Gender Difference

'Women writers seem best placed now to use the novel seriously to open out relatively unexplored areas of individual and social experience', Ian McEwan commented in the *New Review* in Summer 1978 (p. 51). His remark reflected a growing recognition, by the late 1970s, that new and challenging areas had been opened up for the imagination—and in contemporary experience generally—by radically changing assumptions about gender. As Chapter 1 described, literature contributed significantly to these changes, not only by reflecting new outlooks and ideas, but often by initiating them—identifying and exploring, in imagination, potentials not yet much developed in society itself. The novel proved especially useful for this exploration. In the early 1960s, writers such as Doris Lessing and Margaret Drabble were already establishing a firmer focus around women characters' experiences and perspectives, diminishing or displacing conventional fictional concentration on men. Several novelists at the time also identified and criticized injustices and constraints in women's roles well in advance of the feminist movements emerging towards the end of the decade.

In later years, fiction continued to be the genre women writers used most widely and successfully. In a critical study in the late 1980s, Rosalind Miles suggested that the novel had been 'the preferred form for women writers almost since women began to write', and that they had 'yet to make any substantial impact in large numbers on any other literary form' (p. 2). Surveys of authors achieving popular and critical success in the 1990s continued to confirm her judgement, in terms of numbers at any rate. Despite significant contributions to the genres of drama and poetry, described in earlier chapters, women still made up only 16 per cent of English writers included in *Contemporary Dramatists*, and 18 per cent in *Contemporary Poets*, but 33 per cent of those appearing in *Contemporary Novelists*.[1] Women novelists, of course, were not always principally concerned with the late twentieth century's new emphases on questions of gender. Their work, on the contrary, contributed to the period's fiction in all its phases, and is discussed throughout Chapters 15–20. Yet the novel's importance for many women writers—and the nature of their work in the genre—also developed in ways related quite specifically to the exploration of gender issues, and of the new areas of 'individual and social experience' McEwan mentions. This exploration encouraged innovations in form and style, considered later. In terms of subject matter, it contributed to four fairly distinct phases of interest, developing more or less successively throughout the period.

The first of these reflected more relaxed attitudes towards sex and relationships in the 1960s, and greater freedom to describe them in the novel, following the *Chatterley* trial at the start of the decade. For male writers successful in the previous decade, C. P. Snow and Kingsley Amis in particular, these new attitudes and freedoms sometimes seemed more disturbing than enabling,[2] and it was often women novelists who made the best use of them. Earlier literature offered them still less than men in terms of tactics for describing sexual experience, but it began to feature regularly in their writing in the 1960s nevertheless. Sex and relationships were treated with new explicitness in the Irish author Edna O'Brien's *Country Girls* trilogy (1960–4), for example; in Iris Murdoch's *A Severed Head* (1961), Brigid Brophy's *Flesh* (1962), and Margaret Drabble's *The Waterfall* (1969). These novels began a long process through which the period's fiction gradually extended its treatment of relationships to include their most intimate sexual aspects. The range of sexual experience envisaged also expanded in the 1960s and later. Lesbian relationships figured centrally in Maureen Duffy's *The Microcosm*

---

[1] Details of these volumes appear in Suggestions for Further Reading, pp. 581–6, below.

[2] See pp. 404–5, above.

(1966), for example, and in some of Michèle Roberts's fiction, and in Jeanette Winterson's, in *Oranges are Not the Only Fruit* (1985) particularly. Yet for women at the beginning of the period, new freedoms offered by the 1960s sometimes simply emphasized, or exacerbated, the unsatisfactory nature of gender and sexual roles at the time. Novels such as Hilary Mantel's *An Experiment in Love* (1995) later recorded the difficulties of a generation of women forced to develop 'double lives' in the 1960s, mixing supposed sexual liberation with continuing social expectations of female propriety (ch. 6). In novels during the decade, difficulties experienced by Drabble's heroine in *The Waterfall*, and unsatisfactory relationships endured by Doris Lessing's, in *The Golden Notebook* (1962), likewise suggested that new sexual freedoms sometimes just allowed women to be still more fully and freely exploited by men.

Conclusions of this kind encouraged the emergence of a strong women's movement by the end of the decade.[3] They also contributed to a second, more explicitly feminist phase of fiction which began to appear around the same time. Prejudices and injustices troubling feminists in the early 1970s were quickly reflected in Fay Weldon's *Down among the Women* (1971), for example, which followed three generations of women from the end of the war until the more promising days of women's liberation. Weldon shows each generation enduring a 'terrible world . . . where men seduce, make pregnant, betray, desert'—one in which, by the end of her life, a woman may have 'cooked a hundred thousand meals, swept a million floors, washed a billion dishes' (chs. 3, 6). Injustices of this kind figured equally explicitly in much of Weldon's later writing, and in the work of a number of other novelists, such as Michèle Roberts, or Zoë Fairbairns. In *Stand We at Last* (1984) Fairbairns looked at women's roles in still greater historical depth than *Down among the Women*, moving through five generations from the mid-nineteenth century to the 'liberated' early 1970s.

The difficulties of these roles also figured centrally in several of Margaret Drabble's early novels—along with some rewards previously not much explored in twentieth-century fiction. Like Lynne Reid Banks in *The L-Shaped Room* (1960), in *The Millstone* (1965) Drabble showed a determined single mother achieving a measure of

[3] See pp. 38–40, above.

independence for herself, against considerable odds, partly through growing love for her accidentally conceived baby daughter. Children also played an important role within a complex set of relations in *The Waterfall*. Experiences of childbirth, motherhood, and relations with children explored in these novels continued to concern feminists and women writers generally. Similar interests appeared in contemporary women's poetry, and eventually in drama, in plays such as Charlotte Keatley's *My Mother Said I Never Should* (1987). In fiction, they were reflected in Michèle Roberts's *A Piece of the Night* (1978), for example; in Buchi Emecheta's *Second-Class Citizen* (1974), Fay Weldon's *Puffball* (1980), and Eva Figes's exploration of troubled mentalities and identities in *Days* (1974). Equivalent concern with parenthood and childbirth had been largely missing from fiction by men since D. H. Lawrence's *The Rainbow* (1915), reappearing only in Ian McEwan's *The Child in Time* in 1987.

Despite her interests, Drabble was reluctant to be defined exclusively as a feminist. Description of herself as 'a social historian documenting social change' (Brown (ed.), p. 272) accurately characterized 'condition of England' novels such as *The Ice Age* (1974) and *The Radiant Way* (1987), as well as her accounts of middle-class and professional life in *A Natural Curiosity* (1989) and *The Gates of Ivory* (1991). The place of women's experience within this wider range of interests continued to reflect views Drabble expressed in the 1970s— that 'none of my books is about feminism, because my belief in the necessity for justice for women (which they don't get at the moment) is so basic that I never think of using it as a subject. It is part of a whole' (Vinson (ed.), p. 373). Her comments summed up the priorities of a third phase of women's writing, the broadest in the period. As some of feminism's original aims began to be achieved, its demands for justice came to be expressed less explicitly and exclusively in the novel. Instead, they were examined more frequently as 'parts of a whole'— alongside a range of other issues; by implication rather than direct statement; or simply through increased concentration on the point of view of female characters.

These general trends in the later 1970s, 1980s, and 1990s can be illustrated by examples taken from each decade. Penelope Fitzgerald's fiction often focused on strong heroines, exemplifying various forms of independence—in trade, in *The Bookshop* (1978), for example, or in raising a family on a leaky houseboat, in *Offshore* (1979). Though Anita Brookner's heroines were generally more passive, like Fitzgerald's they usually chose independence rather than alliance or compromise with men. Typically, *Hotel du Lac* (1984) portrayed several women tempted by convenient relationships, focusing on a central figure sensible enough to reject two unsuitable offers of marriage in quick succession, despite the dispirited, isolated life which Brookner describes with painful intimacy throughout. Rose Tremain's heroine in *Sacred Country* (1992) experiences still stranger isolations, and practises a still fiercer independence. She grows up on broad levels of unkempt farmland beneath an indifferent Suffolk sky, flees violent, crazy parents, vehemently rejects conventional roles and behaviour, and eventually seeks to escape even biological identity as a woman. Tremain was one of several novelists in the period who followed Virginia Woolf's example in *Orlando* (1928). Like Woolf's novel, *Sacred Country* highlights gender identities by means of a character who tries to move between them, or to remain in 'a country in between'—a 'country that no one sees' which nevertheless offers especially clear perspectives on conventional assumptions and behaviour (ch. 8).

Sacred Country was also a novel of intense historical vision, tracing the impact within individual lives of events such as the death of King George VI, the Cuban Missile Crisis, and England's 1966 victory in the World Cup. Tremain explored throughout the effect of radio and television in making these events suddenly, bewilderingly immediate as well as remote, poured into domestic living rooms pell-mell, along with popular culture ranging from country music to Muffin the Mule. *Sacred Country* shared in this way in a fourth phase of women novelists' interests, particularly evident late in the period—in relations between public and private life, and in the conflict of women's private values and vision with those of the broader history they have to endure. The conflicts and tensions involved were broadly examined in Beryl Bainbridge's historical novel *Master Georgie* (1998), for example. Bainbridge's disjointed, diverse narratives highlight many gaps between the will of women characters and men whom they have to look after nevertheless, subordinating their own interests to the wider demands of various struggles culminating in the Crimean War.

Equally diverse narratives figured in Marina Warner's *The Lost*

Father (1988), extended by various fragments of notebooks, news-papers, and memories. These are pieced together by an archivist attempting to reconstruct her grandfather's life in a peasant commu-nity in Southern Italy—and as an emigrant to the United States—and to find the truth about his early death. Events in this community are richly and lyrically described throughout, but fade nevertheless beyond reliable documentation. *The Lost Father* shared many of the characteristic uncertainties of late twentieth-century historical fiction, discussed in Chapter 17, with Warner's puzzled archivist obviously comparable to Graham Swift's in *Shuttlecock* (1981). Yet Warner's historical vision was also particular to women's writing, in the roles it ascribed to men and to the public life that generally absorbs them. These male roles are shown in *The Lost Father* to be partly tangential, or disruptive, in a community whose survival and evolution is essentially matrilineal. Warner's narrative establishes in this way an almost affirmative implication for her novel's title—qualifying its more obviously elegiac aspects, and providing a still further variant on the late twentieth-century theme of fractured rela-tions with parents.

Comparable views shaped the work of other women novelists con-cerned with the wars and violence of recent history. Like Marina Warner's, their historical vision often diverged slightly from the writ-ing discussed in Chapters 16 and 17. Many of the male authors con-sidered in these chapters took a generally tragic view of historical events, as *faits accomplis* whose dark effects on subsequent life might be recognized and regretted, but ultimately just had to be endured. Women writers were more often prepared to consider cause as well as consequence: to examine circumstances in which conflict had been allowed to occur, and ways these related to civilian society and private life at the time. Some of this disposition was evident in *The Balkan Trilogy* (1960–5), in Olivia Manning's intertwining of private and public life as the Second World War reaches Romania. More often, interests of this kind centred on the First World War, per-haps because greater distance in time facilitated objective historical analysis. Isabel Colegate's fiction regularly returned to the period of the First World War, also examining the fate of the English aristoc-racy throughout the century. In *The Shooting Party* (1980), she concentrated on a glittering assembly of the ruling classes in 1913.

Though some of its members exemplify a vanishing 'Age of Humanism', many lack democratic vision and balanced emotion in ways darkly portending 'a bigger shooting party . . . in Flanders' (pp. 181, 175). Susan Hill offered a comparable picture in *Strange Meeting* (1975), taking her title from Wilfred Owen and showing the disasters of war arising from the suppression of emotion and imagination in contemporary life, and to some extent redeemable by their return.

Similar views were developed in the most substantial of the period's re-examinations of the First World War, Pat Barker's *Regeneration* trilogy: *Regeneration* (1991), *The Eye in the Door* (1993), *The Ghost Road* (1995). Along with Siegfried Sassoon, Wilfred Owen appears as a character in its first volume, a historically accurate account of the treatment of war-damaged patients by W. H. R. Rivers, a pioneer analyst working in Craiglockart Hospital in Edinburgh. Rivers is committed to a Freudian talking cure rather than crasser methods, including electric shock to deal with shell shock, used by other therapists. Yet he acquiesces in the return to the trenches, and to probable death, of patients he has taken infinite pains to help. The contradictions of this position introduce the trilogy's wider analysis of double standards—divisions between private or humane values and public or military commitments—which allow the war to continue and are further consolidated as it progresses. Pressures involved sometimes even impose double identities on the patients Rivers treats. Sassoon has 'always coped with the war by being two people', and another patient, Billy Prior, is likewise described in *The Eye in the Door* as equipped with 'a warrior double, a creature formed out of Flanders clay'. Their analyses lead Rivers to the ironic, Laingian conclusion that 'contrary to what was usually supposed, duality was the stable state; the attempt at integration, dangerous' (chs. 18, 19).

In the trilogy's second and third parts, Prior's encounters with wartime society and with growing dissociations within his own personality offer more evidence for Rivers's conclusion. Problems it indicates are further highlighted—though in a way also redressed—by the trilogy's concentration on the inner thoughts of its principal characters, transcribed in a range of Free Indirect and other inward styles.[4] At one level, the horrors of war are made peculiarly

---

[4] See p. 74, above.

immediate by their communication through the minds and thoughts they have most disturbed: through combatants' terrible and weirdly warped recollections. This adds to the effectiveness of *Regeneration* simply as anti-war fiction. But Barker's concentration on individual consciousness is also subtly affirmative, engaging readers fully with just those dimensions of private thought and emotion the novel shows wartime events threatening to diminish or suppress. As well as highlighting pressures exerted by public life, the form and style of *Regeneration* emphasize the continuing vitality of the private sphere: its redemptive capacities to resist and survive.

Similar emphases appeared in Barker's earlier novels. *Blow Your House Down* (1984), for example, shows a group of prostitutes menaced by a Yorkshire-Ripper figure: Barker strongly communicates their solidarity and resilience through Free Indirect Discourse and other transcriptions of the private thoughts of each. Barker's fiction, in other words, not only shared new interests shaping women's writing in the period, whether in history or in contemporary life. It also ensured, like much of this writing, that fictional forms were adapted and developed specifically to represent these new interests, particularly through techniques presenting inner thought and accentuating private rather than public experience. Adaptation and stylistic development of this kind was widely in evidence from the beginning of the period. In their exploration of the new perspectives and experiences considered above, women writers regularly departed from conventional forms, often sharing renewed 1960s interests in modernist or other innovative modes developed by novelists earlier in the century. Many found Virginia Woolf's recommendation to 'look within' and 'examine the mind' especially appropriate to renewed emphases on the values of private experience. Several modernist authors— Dorothy Richardson and May Sinclair as well as Woolf—had initially developed registers for inner thought, along with a wider reshaping of fiction around women's points of view, partly in response to a first phase of feminist awareness, during or just after the Suffragette period. Techniques developed at that time naturally renewed their appeal during a second such phase later in the century.

There were also more direct connections. Modernist techniques were extended into the 1930s and beyond by the work of Rosamond Lehmann and Elizabeth Bowen, and by the use of interior monologue and stream of consciousness styles in much of Jean Rhys's fiction. The influence of some of this work was strongly renewed in the mid-1960s. Finding little encouragement for her writing in the 1940s and 1950s, Rhys had ceased publishing novels and virtually vanished from public view until *Wide Sargasso Sea* appeared in 1965. This reconsidered the early life in the West Indies of the first Mrs Rochester, the mad first wife allotted only a minor role in Charlotte Brontë's *Jane Eyre* (1847). *Wide Sargasso Sea* adopts her point of view throughout its opening section, showing her sensitive nature destroyed by stressful experiences and the harshness of her new husband. Rhys thought the novel's success had come too late in her career, but it did re-establish interest in her work generally. Along with reissues of her 1930s novels, this helped to renew the appeal of modernist techniques at the beginning of the period. Lehmann and Bowen also continued publishing into the 1960s. Their influence, too, was extended into the next decade, and beyond, by Virago Press reissues of earlier work.

Direct indebtedness to modernism was clear, and often explicit, in the work of several women writers emerging at the time—in the resonances of the name, Anna Wulf, Doris Lessing gave her central figure in *The Golden Notebook*, for example, as well as in the innovative form of her novel generally. It was also apparent in much of the writing of Eva Figes, who followed her unusual first novel, *Equinox* (1966), with an early, influential feminist statement, *Patriarchal Attitudes* (1971). Figes continued to affirm in the *New Review* in Summer 1978 her determination to 'shake off the shackles' of 'the social realist tradition of the nineteenth century'—inadequate, she considered, for reflection of the more disturbed historical experience of the twentieth (p. 39). Modernist influences on this unshackling were clearest in *Waking* (1981), close to Woolf's *The Waves* (1931) in its meditative style, and in its structure, recording seven separate moments of waking consciousness. Similarly diverse, fragmented sections of thoughts and reflections appeared in Maureen Duffy's *The Microcosm* (1966). Modernist legacies remained equally clear in the work of women writers emerging later in the period. Anita Brookner dedicated *Hotel du Lac* to Rosamond Lehmann: its novelist heroine even looks like Virginia Woolf, and finds at a moment of stress that she has 'taken the name of Virginia

Woolf in vain' (ch. 6). Admiration for Woolf and modernism was also evident in Brookner's style, shaping various interior monologue and Free Indirect forms used in *Hotel du Lac* and much of the rest of her fiction.

Even when debts to modernism were less obvious, or less specific, women's writing showed a general disposition towards subjective forms and inner registers. These might have been expected to appeal equally to men writers, later in the century, especially as they had been developed in the first place as much by James Joyce as by women modernists such as Woolf. Men's writing in the period, of course, did regularly record the subjective experience of its characters—directly, in Graham Swift's *Last Orders* (1996), for example. Yet it relied only rarely on supposedly immediate transcriptions of inner thought, mostly preferring report or description, or styles closer to written or spoken monologue. These were used by Julian Barnes, in *Love, etc* (2000), for example, and by Martin Amis, in *Money* (1984) and elsewhere. Similar effects were achieved by idiosyncratic first-person narratives frequently used by Ian McEwan and Graham Swift, and by Barnes and Amis in other novels.[5] Though a generalization, there would be some truth in the conclusion that women novelists in the period engaged readily with individual consciousness, whereas the inner life figured less often, and less directly, in fiction by men. Forms of interior monologue, stream of consciousness, or Free Indirect Discourse were at any rate developed very widely in the period by women writers. As well as shaping the fiction mentioned above, they also appeared extensively in the work of novelists as otherwise diverse as Elaine Feinstein, Elizabeth Jane Howard, Maggie Ross, and Zadie Smith. Perhaps this was because the 'room of one's own'—that private space, allowing free reflection of women's experience, which Woolf had sought in the 1920s— seemed more readily available within inner consciousness than anywhere else in a male-dominated society.

Yet women novelists in the period also showed how rarely this inner space could be supposed reliably private, or entirely free. For many of their characters, the inner life did provide an alternative to a male-dominated society, but at the same time a heightening, through contrast, of awareness of its demands. Engagement with inner

[5] See Ch. 17, above.

thoughts, emotions, or desires often simply confirmed how far these diverged from established social conventions. Woolf talked in *A Room of One's Own* (1928) of a 'splitting off of consciousness' which women experience as a result of feeling in some ways part of established society, yet also 'outside of it, alien and critical' (p. 96). Fiction later in the century often showed tensions between private and public expectations—between desire for independence, and pressure to go on accepting conventional roles—creating a split *in* consciousness, or in personality generally. In *Providence* (1982), for example, after adjusting details of her dress and appearance, Brookner's rather reserved central figure watches with surprise the emergence of an 'other self'—apparently 'a cynical, capable . . . woman who knew how to please' (ch. 13). Penelope Mortimer's narrator in *Long Distance* (1974) likewise finds that glamorous dress and accoutrements encourage the appearance of 'she, the other' (ch.17). This is one of several alternative roles endured in a kind of purgatory, fantastically extending pressures on women Mortimer had earlier examined in novels such as *The Pumpkin Eater* (1962). Sensitive inner feelings in Figes's *Waking* similarly conflict with the demands of an 'other body'—a social self, defined and assessed by 'eyes in the street'(ch. 5).

Typically, Doris Lessing's heroine in *The Summer before the Dark* (1973) concludes that '*her* self, *her* mind, *her* awareness' exist for others only as a 'façade' of dress and hairstyle. This realization releases in her 'a rage . . . she had been suppressing for a lifetime', driving her close to breakdown (pp. 44, 207). Social pressures and their demands for a second self were sometimes shown leading in this way towards a kind of schizophrenia, or a complete self-enclosure in private thoughts and fantasies. States of mind involved were communicated compellingly by the epistolary form of Jane Gardam's *The Queen of the Tambourine* (1991). Readers discover only gradually that its central figure has been 'having a bit of trouble with what is and what isn't', compensating for past traumas and the current blandness of suburban life through fantasy roles created in her copious letters (p. 214). Emma Tennant's *The Bad Sister* (1978) also featured thoroughgoing escape into fantasy, magic and demonic obsession. In this novel and in *Two Women of London: The Strange Case of Ms Jekyll and Mrs Hyde* (1989) Tennant provided a

comprehensive analysis of gaps between private and public personae, ones often a subject of characters' conversations. Various
figures in each novel discuss what *The Bad Sister* refers to as the
'double female self' and 'the inherent "splitness" of women' (pp.
101, 137).

The form and structure of women's fiction often extended this
'splitness'. In several novels, it was highlighted and explored through
alternating first- and third-person narratives. Women's writing in
the period was distinguished not only by its concentration on subjective experience, but by ways this was often startlingly intercut with
external perspectives. Sometimes this occurred only locally. Anita
Brookner replaced inner thoughts with an aloof, objective third-
person voice at several points throughout *Providence*. In *The
Summer before the Dark*, Lessing occasionally alternated between
accounts of inner thoughts and a tactic her heroine learns for herself
in the course of the novel—of directing 'a sight on herself from across
the room, as . . . men were seeing her' (p. 42). Similar transitions also
shaped the overall structure of several novels. In *Sacred Country*,
Rose Tremain accentuates a sense of dislocation—of unfathomable
gaps between public and private life; of strange worlds-in-between—
by dividing the novel into sections of third-person authorial description, alongside others presenting female characters' thoughts and
emotions in the first person. Fay Weldon likewise alternated between
sections of first- and third-person narrative in *Down among the
Women* and in *Praxis* (1978). Similar tactics were employed in
Drabble's *The Waterfall*, and also directly discussed. Much of the
novel is in the first person, though in several sections its narrator
attempts to describe intimate details of her affair in the third. An
author herself, she concludes that her writing in these sections
'won't, of course do: as an account, I mean, of what took place . . .
lies, lies, it's all lies . . . I've misrepresented . . . I had him, but I can't
describe the conditions of that possession . . . description is treachery' (pp. 46, 84). Self-conscious commentary of this kind highlighted
difficulties authors often experienced, in the 1960s, in beginning
to make use of new freedoms to present sex. It also placed *The
Waterfall* close to the metafictional modes appearing in the
decade, and in particular to Lessing's interests in *The Golden
Notebook*. Sceptical throughout of conventional narrative's powers

of representation—of women's experience particularly—Lessing's novel was also, like Drabble's, deeply divided in its narrator's vision of herself. This is split four ways in her notebooks, before she envisages the 'golden' possibility of reintegration in the fifth.

Like Drabble in the comments quoted earlier, Lessing nevertheless warned in her preface that *The Golden Notebook* should not be considered solely 'a tract about the sex war' (p. 10). As Chapter 16 described, *The Golden Notebook* was characteristic of its times in several other ways as well. Neither Lessing's fracturings of narrative and identity, nor the others mentioned above, are necessarily best assessed exclusively in gender terms. Many women novelists, after all, remained content with conventional constructions of character and perspective—Drabble herself, for example, in 'documenting social change' in much of the rest of her career. And men novelists in the period were also ready to use forms of split perspective: Julian Mitchell, in *The Undiscovered Country* (1968), or John Fowles, moving freely between first- and third-person accounts of his central figure in *Daniel Martin* (1977). Male characters, too, were sometimes shown experiencing the kind of doubling or self-splitting discussed above: in Christopher Priest's *The Affirmation* (1981), for example, or Lessing's *Briefing for a Descent into Hell* (1971), as well as throughout Barker's *Regeneration* trilogy.

'Splitness', in other words, need not be considered only in the terms characters discuss in *The Bad Sister*, as an *inherent* condition of women's experience, or of women's writing. Instead, late twentieth-century fiction showed various splittings as possible consequences, for either gender, of tensions between private consciousness and public life—ones likely to be accentuated, as Barker showed, in periods of particular social or historical stress. Yet as *The Bad Sister* emphasized, there were many social stresses in this period which made women more *likely* to encounter forms of self-division, and women novelists more disposed to reproduce the 'divided consciousness' and 'double-voiced discourse' identified and discussed by feminist critics such as Elaine Showalter (Showalter (ed.), pp. 141, 266). Some of these stresses were highlighted by Emma Tennant in *The Bad Sister*, in showing the influences of advertising, and of the growing commercialization of women's image in terms of clothes and cosmetics. These influences also extended into the 'cynical' other selves emerging in Anita Brookner's *Providence* and Penelope Mortimer's *Long Distance*. Along with the perennial male gaze, shown defining women in terms of physical appearance and attractiveness in *The Summer before the Dark*, such influences ensured that divisions in identity, tensions between inner self and outer façade, were inflected particularly forcefully on women in the period.

Disturbing in life, such divisions were nevertheless productive in art. If women writers, as Ian McEwan suggested, were among those best placed in the period to analyse individual and social experience, it was partly because tensions they encountered between the two—between private and public worlds—sharpened and particularized their visions of each. It was also because this dual vision, along with new perspectives on women's experience generally, made new development of fictional forms and style particularly necessary, as in the modernist period. It was a need memorably emphasized towards the end of *The Golden Notebook*, when Anna Wulf finds her fragile selfhood menaced by her lover's endlessly selfish repetition of 'the word *I* . . . . I, I, I, I, I . . . as if the word I was being shot at [her] like bullets', 'I, I, I, I, like a machine-gun ejaculating regularly' (pp. 538, 605). Fractured, fragile, or fluid forms of the self seem altogether preferable, in Lessing's novel, to such mechanical, assertive male egotism. More generally, the diversity in style and perspective in *The Golden Notebook* and other novels discussed above allowed women writers to avoid the reductive, narrowing certitudes of male ego or male gaze. James Joyce had warned against narrow or literally monocular vision in the 'Cyclops' chapter of *Ulysses* (1922), demonstrating alternatives in the novel's huge diversity of styles, and in sustained parodies highlighting the nature and limitations of each. Diverse, fluid vision, scepticism of convention, and inventiveness in style and form necessarily remained strong priorities for women writers late in the century. This was evident in the work of novelists discussed in earlier chapters—such as Muriel Spark, Christine Brooke-Rose, or A. S. Byatt—as well as those mentioned in this one, and others emerging in the 1990s, such as Lucy Ellmann. This disposition towards a postmodernist idiom—towards experiment and innovation generally—made women writers among the most progressive in the period, as McEwan suggested. Their work developed and cross-bred fictional forms in ways which further dispelled fears of stagnation expressed in the later 1970s, further extending into later decades David Lodge's 'crossroads' of traditional and innovative fictional techniques.

Fluid perspectives in women's writing also extended regularly, and naturally, into fantasy. The constraints of a male-oriented society obviously offered good reasons for departing, in imagination, into dimensions beyond it. This motive was emphasized by novels such as *The Bad Sister* and *The Queen of the Tambourine*. In each, realistic vision of contemporary society gives way to dreams and illusions through which its problems, fantastically enlarged, can be conveniently exposed and satirized. Similar tactics figured in some of Doris Lessing's later fiction, in the *Canopus in Argos: Archives* series (1979–83) in particular, concentrated on the voice and vision of women. They also appeared throughout the work of Angela Carter—author of an influential, controversial feminist essay, *The Sadeian Woman* (1979), and one of the writers to move most decisively in this period beyond conventional realism and the constraints of male-dominated culture generally. *The Infernal Desire Machines of Doctor Hoffman* (1972) offered early evidence of Carter's radical freedom of imagination, often expressed in picaresque, freewheeling forms of construction. The novel's narrator is another unlikeable exponent of reductive male vision, seeking to exercise a bleak 'impulse of restraint' in a city 'buffeted by phantoms', and to resist desires which have 'modified the nature of reality' and allowed fantasy and imagination to 'run wild' (chs. 8, 1).

Wildly 'modified' realities continued to figure freely in most of Carter's later fiction. Like *Wise Children* (1991), *Nights at the Circus* (1984) was set in a recognizable, realistic theatrical world at the end of the nineteenth century, yet its principal character is a celebrated trapeze artist, Fevvers, apparently born with wings. Miraculous gifts as an *aerialiste* make her a 'Winged Victory' emblematic of the narrative's own rapid, magical flights between London, St Petersburg, and Siberia. She is also representative of hopes for a new century 'waiting in the wings', a 'New Age in which no women will be bound down to the ground' (pt. 1, ch. 1). Hopes for a new age, and continuing constraints in the old, were examined still more fantastically in *The Passion of New Eve* (1977), set in a futuristic, Kafkaesque version of the United States. Carter's central character is initially male, but soon transformed into 'Eve' by female guerrillas—led by 'Mother . . . the

Great Parricide . . . the Castratrix of the Phallocentric Universe'—
only to be captured in turn by a one-eyed poet and patriarch: another
Cyclops, literally as well as metaphorically narrow in vision (ch. 6).
Eventually, s/he is married to an ancient Hollywood diva who turns
out to be a man in disguise. As in Rose Tremain's *Sacred County*, but
as if in fast-forward mode, sex changes and role swapping explore
distinctions between biological and culturally constructed gender,
showing Eve still learning supposedly female attributes long after she
has physically become a woman.

Details of bizarre mansions, darkly transgressive passions, and of
outrages performed on the anatomy all strongly extend the kind of
Gothic, grotesque, blackly comic imagination—characteristic of this
period—retraced in Chapter 17 to the Second World War. Carter's
work suggested a further source of this imagination, one confirmed
by other women writers, such as Fay Weldon—in *The Life and Loves
of a She-Devil* (1983) for example—as well as by male novelists such
as Ian McEwan. In the 1960s and later, new freedoms to describe the
body and all its functions, decent or indecent, obviously allowed and
encouraged new forms of grotesque imagination. More fundamentally, loosening of conventional sexual identities and roles required
psychic readjustments—or created unconscious tensions—sometimes issuing in black humour and dark, nightmarish imagination in
the period's writing. Apparently engaging with deep or unconscious
stresses in this way, Carter's disturbing imagination gained widespread admiration for her work—often claimed as particularly representative of its age by the many critics and academics it attracted.
They also found much to discuss in her reworking of the Brothers
Grimm's fairy tales, in terms of feminist and Freudian theory, in *The
Bloody Chamber* (1979). Like Ian McEwan's, Carter's imagination
was distinctive enough to ensure success, rare in the period, in the
short-story form. Her challenging, feminist renewals of fairy stories
also exemplified a tactic regularly employed by women writers:
reworking of established narratives, or well-known novels, to highlight their patriarchal assumptions and suggest alternatives. Jean
Rhys followed this strategy in *Wide Sargasso Sea*. Sue Roe provided
another example, alluding to Charles Dickens's *Great Expectations*
(1849) in *Estella: Her Expectations* (1982), but updating the story
by concentrating on women's desire.

Strategies Carter favoured reappeared in the work of Jeanette Winterson. *Boating for Beginners* (1985) offered a feminist version of the biblical story of the Flood, and a number of reshaped fairy tales featured in *Sexing the Cherry* (1989). In this novel and another with a historical setting, *The Passion* (1987), Winterson also illustrated 'magic realist' influences beginning to appear in English fiction around this time, especially in its historical modes. Carter used the term in discussing an absence of 'difference between fact and fiction . . . a sort of magic realism' in *Nights at the Circus* (pt. 3, ch. 8): the origins of writing it described were indicated by her South American ambience in *The Infernal Desire Machines of Doctor Hoffman*. In novels such as Gabriel García Márquez's influential *One Hundred Years of Solitude* (1967), several South American writers had begun to incorporate fantastic or improbable events seamlessly, without logical explanation or fluctuation of tone, within otherwise plausibly realistic narratives. 'Modified realities' such as Fevvers's wings, in *Nights at the Circus*, or the webbed feet of Winterson's heroine in *The Passion*, seem normal and unexceptional in magic realist writing. Salman Rushdie was one of the first authors to use this kind of writing extensively in anglophone fiction, in *Midnight's Children* (1981), emphasizing in his essays the political potential offered by its free reimagining of the status quo, and its refusal of any single, immutable construction of the world.

Magic realism's convincing contact with ordinary experience, alongside fantasies commenting on it, obviously assorted easily with some of the particularities of women's writing discussed earlier, and with its wish to challenge the gender politics of established society. In one way, *Sexing the Cherry* empowered women's imagination comically and directly, through its central figure: a giantess, heavier than an elephant, who is readier to eat men than be bound by their social conventions. But Winterson's writing also freed readers from conventional constraints more subtly, mocking established expectations and the usual boundaries of space and time, and using fantastic narratives to suggest alternatives to social norms, in the seventeenth century and in the twentieth. Alternating regularly between narrators, between different gender positions they encounter through cross-dressing, and between feminist assessments of various historical periods, *Sexing the Cherry* illustrated particularly fully the inventiveness, fluid perspective, and rejection of convention gener-ally apparent in women's writing in the 1980s and 1990s. Fantasy, magic realism, and formal innovation also figured strongly in a number of other areas at this time, further contributing to the vital-ity of English fiction late in the century. These are considered next.

19

'The Century of Strangers': Travellers and Migrants

Late twentieth-century history, Chapter 17 suggested, no longer allowed the faith in personal development through time that was once the mainstay of the *Bildungsroman*, even threatening more limited forms of 'psychological orientation' employed by novelists in earlier periods.[1] Towards the end of the century, geography and dimensions of space often seemed as fractured and disorienting as recent history and experience of the temporal. Multinational corporations, communications, and economic forces contributed to a postmodern condition inevitably entailing, in the view of critics such as Fredric Jameson, 'our insertion as individual subjects' into 'new and enormous global realities', a 'world space of multinational capital'.[2] Overwhelming in scale, and 'inaccessible to any individual . . . consciousness', this world-space was in Jameson's view potentially beyond any 'cognitive mapping' which existing forms of fiction could provide (*Postmodernism*, pp. 413, 411, 54). As he suggested, the world's old boundaries and sureties often seemed to be vanishing, late in the century, without leaving societies or individuals means of dealing with their absence, or with the new frictions between cultures and outlooks which resulted. This chapter considers later the consequences of historical forces, in the aftermath of empire, which inserted large sections of the world's population—quite literally, as immigrants—into new realities, countries, and cultures.

[1] See pp. 434–40, above.
[2] See p. 66, above.

But it begins with more innocent forms of dislocation, based on desire rather than historical or economic necessity, and therefore still able to offer some of the 'psychological orientation' Salman Rushdie mentioned. One new 'global reality' towards the end of the twentieth century was after all the new and exciting accessibility of the globe itself, at least to citizens of Western countries. Cheaper fares and package holidays ensured that foreign travel ceased to be a privilege of the few and became a widely shared experience in the life of the times, and a significant part of its broader democratization. Three and half million British people holidayed abroad even in 1961—twice as many as in 1950—and numbers continued to expand hugely in later decades. One direct result was in new patterns of book buying, and increased volumes of sales. Significantly, paperbacks' usefulness for reading on the beach was often emphasized in the affirmative accounts of publishing quoted in Chapter 4. 'Holiday reading' became a catchphrase for publishers late in the century, and the book trade's best marketing opportunity after Christmas.

There were also more complex consequences. New 'global realities' created by multinational industries depended heavily on global dreams—on corralling individuals' desires through advertisers' glitzy lifestyle images. Few of these images offered more alluring, enhanced visions of self and circumstance than the publicity generated by the travel and holiday industries. Regardless of actual complexities, foreign countries were presented through safe, simple images of sunshine, leisure, and languor, and tourists pictured as uniformly, seductively, bronzed and relaxed. New mass travel not only sold more books. It also came to offer more and more members of the population attractive ways of 'reading' their individual selves, projected into contexts brighter and more fulfilling—sometimes more adventurous, rather than only more relaxing—than anything offered by daily life at home. 'Travel' had always offered a metaphor for a reader's progress through a text, and 'holiday' for fiction's imaginative departure from the routines of ordinary life. In this period, dreams and imagination involved in the marketing of 'going abroad', and in the experience itself, ensured that the terms 'holiday', 'reading', 'travel', and 'literature' moved into new and much closer relations with each other. Novelists naturally exploited more regularly these ways of 'reading' or exploring the individual, and of expanding the imagination of narrative. It was still relatively unusual for foreign travel—rather than longer-term work, exile, or colonial posting abroad—to be used to develop or illumine character in English fiction earlier in the century. Towards its end, there were novelists who sometimes seemed to use little else: David Lodge in *Small World* (1984), for example, or Malcolm Bradbury in *Doctor Criminale* (1992).

Travel literature itself naturally grew more popular, recounting adventures now closer to the reach, actual or imaginative, of a majority of the population. English audiences were generally enthusiastic, late in the century, for writers such as Jonathan Raban, Colin Thubron, Bruce Chatwin, and, from the United States, Paul Theroux—best known for his accounts of long train journeys, such as *The Great Railway Bazaar* (1975). Each was a novelist as well as a travel writer, often reproducing some of the idiom of travelogue within fiction. The connections were particularly clear in the work of Bruce Chatwin, whose *In Patagonia* (1977) helped initiate a vogue for travel writing—matching the growing popularity of biography at the time—in the late 1970s. Chatwin described a nineteenth-century account of Patgonia by W. H. Hudson as 'a book so quiet and sane it makes Thoreau seem a ranter'(ch. 6): his own writing was likewise marked by a cool, equable reserve, even in describing what he considered a lifelong 'search for the miraculous' (*What am I Doing Here*, p. 282). Largely excising personal or emotional reflections, Chatwin's narrative offered readers unusually immediate, unfettered engagement with the extraordinary experiences his travel writing described. The same distanced, dispassionate clarity characterized much of his fiction. This was also shaped by a strong sense of place and topography: in the description of characters isolated by life in the Welsh mountains in *On the Black Hill* (1982), for example. Often, too, the anxieties or allures of *dis*placement were a central concern: in the account of the early nineteenth-century slave trade in *The Viceroy of Ouidah* (1980), based on Chatwin's own wanderings in West Africa, or in *Utz* (1988), reflecting his perennial compulsion to travel. Like the author, the central figure in *Utz* finds contentment only through regularly leaving and returning to his usual home—in Utz's case, in Prague, defined as 'a city that suited his melancholic temperament' (p. 82). Throughout the novel, the city is described in terms similarly reflecting the distanced vision of the outsider—almost of a travel guide. Distinctions between novel, travel writing, and other forms were further blurred in Chatwin's mixture of auto-biography, fiction, anthropology, and mysticism in *The Songlines* (1987), his bestselling account of travels in the Australian outback.

Other contemporary authors brought the novel close to travel writing. Travelogue elements figured darkly in Hilary Mantel's novel of life in Saudi Arabia, *Eight Months on Gazzeh Street* (1988), and more cheerfully in Esther Freud's account of Morocco in *Hideous Kinky* (1993). Jenny Diski's *Happily Ever After* (1991) shared some characteristics of the 'books . . . set in far-off, exotic places' which appeal to her characters (ch. 15). Lisa St Aubin de Terán's affection for railways appeared, like Paul Theroux's, in an autobiographical travel book, *Off the Rails: Memoirs of a Train Addict* (1989). It also shaped a novel, *The Slow Train to Milan* (1983), which celebrated 'the luxury of moving on' through landscapes and cities—such as 'Bologna, the basin of flames, secret and proud and neglected' (chs. 1, 13)—often described in travelogue terms resembling Chatwin's in *Utz*. De Terán's narrator shares appreciation of 'travelling . . . for the sake of not staying still' with a group of South American émigrés, one of whom gives her 'a little book by García Márquez' (chs. 3, 10). It seems to influence a narrative as unconstrained imaginatively as it is geographically: traces of South American magic realism were still more evident in de Terán's account of family life in a remote valley in the Andes, *Keepers of the House* (1982).

Elements of magic realism appeared in the work of another writer, Louis de Bernières, much concerned with travel and distant locations. Like de Terán, de Bernières lived for a time in South America, the setting for early novels such as *The War of Don Emmanuel's Nether Parts* (1990). Influences he acknowledged from South American writers extended into *Captain Corelli's Mandolin* (1994), a highly romantic account—negligent in its historical details—of the Italians' wartime occupation of the Greek island of Cephalonia. De Bernières begins *Captain Corelli's Mandolin* with a near-miracle, later describes several others, and sustains throughout some of the imaginative profligacy characteristic of magic realist writing. A measure of his popular success appeared in greatly increased numbers of English tourists visiting Cephalonia in the later 1990s—further evidence of new interconnections between travel, holiday, and fiction in the imagination of this period.

In a way, these connections were apparent from its beginning, before any of García Márquez's imaginative strengths lent themselves to English fiction. They figured in the romance atmosphere of Lawrence Durrell's *The Alexandria Quartet* (1957–60), for example. They also appeared in John Fowles's *The Magus* (1966), set on another Greek island, distant and exotic enough, in Fowles's description, to make credible the half-magical events and holidays from reality which shape the central figure's search for identity. 'The past is a foreign country', L. P. Hartley famously remarked at the start of *The Go-Between* (1953), 'they do things differently there'. For several of the historical novelists discussed in earlier chapters, the past did offer a separate domain, one in which things could plausibly be done differently and the imagination allowed freer play. For authors mentioned above, foreign countries obviously offered more straightforward access to the same range of possibilities. Exotic locations—or even ordinary foreign ones—offered a holiday freedom to depart from conventional realism in favour of more imaginative or 'magic' forms. They also offered characters opportunities for 'psychological orientation', wider imagination, or self-discovery, of a kind more often developed gradually, in the fiction of earlier periods, through the evolving life in time.

Foreign locations also reflected—usually more sombrely—shifts in international relations and in Britain's world role. In the early 1960s, the Iron Curtain made East European states seem the most alien and hostile of foreign countries. Contemporary genre fiction regularly explored the stresses involved.[3] These also appeared, when the Cold War was at its height, in Frank Tuohy's account in *The Ice Saints* (1964) of English naïvety encountering an austere, threatening regime in Poland. Similar conflicts of values, surrounding relative innocents in foreign societies, later shaped Piers Paul Read's *A Season in the West* (1988), as well as some of Malcolm Bradbury's novels, such as *Rates of Exchange* (1983). Towards the end of the period, in a bleakly comic account of the Hungarian uprising, *Under the Frog* (1992), Tibor Fischer even brought into English fiction some of the style of East European authors—in particular, a black

---

[3] See p. 510, below.

humour familiar from translations of the Czech novelist Milan Kundera.

English fiction, however, was naturally most affected throughout the period by the country's major international experience in the twentieth century, next to the two world wars: the final flourishing and eventual loss of the British empire. Its disappearance in one way entailed a loss of opportunity for English novelists, depriving them of foreign contexts regularly useful, earlier in the century, for authors including Rudyard Kipling, Joseph Conrad, E. M. Forster, Somerset Maugham, Joyce Cary, and Graham Greene. Colonial settings were often used by these writers much in the manner described above, though usually with more sombre implications: difficult experiences of unfamiliar cultures and values, or of the loneliness of extended exile, offered deeper challenges to characters' sense of self, values, and identity. Stresses of this kind continued to figure during the period in Graham Greene's later writing,[4] and in a number of novels set in former colonies. Like Greene, P. H. Newby often linked political and personal disturbance in his fiction. In *Something to Answer For* (1968), typically, Newby showed public events surrounding the Suez crisis contributing to the difficulties of a central figure already struggling to separate dream and reality, truth and hallucination, in his private life. Confusing experiences in chaotic former colonies were also explored in William Boyd's *A Good Man in Africa* (1981) and in Giles Foden's adventurous, morally challenging account of Idi Amin's regime in Uganda, *The Last King of Scotland* (1998). Work abroad for the British Council exposed Francis King to a range of cultural stresses and encounters with foreign societies: these were regularly reflected throughout a long writing career, continuing to shape late novels such as *Visiting Cards* (1990) and *The Ant Colony* (1991).

Fiction in the period reflected some general feelings of loss and regret occasioned by the end of empire. Julian Mitchell's account of life in London and in Africa in *The White Father* (1964), for example, emphasized connections between dwindling dominion in external affairs and diminished confidence at home. Returning from years of 'serving a vanished ideal', in the kind of African colony liberated at the beginning of the 1960s, Mitchell's central figure finds

---

[4] See pp. 507–9, below.

much changed in what has become only 'poor little old Great Britain' (ch. 7). Vanishing ideals and changing assumptions were highlighted by the structure of Paul Scott's *Staying On* (1977). The novel begins with the death of another former colonial official, then moves freely between the thoughts—often funny and nostalgic—of various characters who reflect on his life, on imperial and post-imperial times in India, and on the moment of transition between the two:

the evening of August fourteen, Nineteen forty-seven, down there on the parade ground... the flagpole lit with the Union Jack flying from it... God Save the King, and . . . that terrible, lovely moment when the Jack was hauled down inch by inch in utter, utter silence . . . on the stroke of midnight the Indian flag began to go up . . . and then the band began to play the new Indian national anthem and all the crowds out there in the dark began to sing. (ch. 10)

Scott's major work, *The Raj Quartet* (1966–74)—successfully televised in the 1970s—employed similar tactics on a larger scale. Letters, reports, and memories offer diverse accounts—often contradictory ones—of India's progress towards independence through a period of violence and change including the 'Quit India' riots of 1942. Centred on a rape and its consequences, *The Raj Quartet* was often compared to E. M. Forster's *A Passage to India* (1924). Scott's view of the English community was nevertheless sympathetic as well as sceptical, finding imperial administrators neither uniformly complacent nor corrupt, but often genuinely committed to vanishing ideals.

The Anglo-Irish novelist J. G. Farrell described the decline of empire as the most interesting historical development of his lifetime. He assessed it with reductive wit and irony in a series of novels, sometimes referred to as his 'Empire Trilogy', centred on key moments of crisis which revealed the failings of imperial rule particularly starkly. *Troubles* (1970) examined the Irish risings just after the First World War; *The Singapore Grip* (1978) the loss of British possessions to the Japanese during the Second; *The Siege of Krishnapur* (1973) the circumstances surrounding the Indian Mutiny in the 1850s. Historically detailed, and vividly descriptive of military action and adventure, *The Siege of Krishnapur* emphasized fatal flaws in imperial vision even when it was at its most powerful, in the mid-nineteenth century.

For Farrell, any idealism in the spread of empire generally vanished virtually as soon as it appeared: like Conrad in *Heart of Darkness* (1899), he showed ideals and principles invariably subordinate to the materialist motives of colonization. Numerous ironic episodes in *The Siege of Krishnapur* demonstrate 'the material world . . . constantly encroaching on the shrinking spiritual sandbank' (ch. 10). The novel describes, for example, Indian mutineers horribly maimed by house-hold materials, such as silver cutlery, used as shot during the siege, and depicts characters confidently discussing the benefits of a profitable opium trade for the empire, and hence for civilization generally. Confrontations with 'the dark foundation of . . . civilized life' in the siege highlight the 'sham' of Victorian culture in general, and of the 'hollow wonders' of science and industry recently celebrated in the Great Exhibition (chs. 32, 31). Farrell won the Booker Prize for *The Siege of Krishnapur*: the dark foundations of civilization, and the sham of imperial idealism, were examined equally scathingly in another winning novel, Barry Unsworth's epic account of the slave trade, *Sacred Hunger* (1992). Like Farrell, Unsworth described a supposedly 'expanding age', yet one whose apparent 'enterprise and vision' disguised 'death and degradation and profits on a scale hitherto undreamed of' (chs. 17, 18). *Sacred Hunger* also hinted that mid-eighteenth-century obsessions with private enterprise, free markets, and 'wealth creation' remained close to a modern age—to some of the Thatcherite thinking of the late 1980s in particular (ch. 20).

*

Anthony Burgess was directly concerned with the subject of empire in his early writing, in *The Malayan Trilogy* (1956–9). But he indicated the empire's principal importance for the period's fiction when he remarked in *The Novel Now* (1971) that 'British colonialism . . . exported the English language, and a new kind of British novel has been the eventual flower of this transplanting' (p. 165). The end of empire was accompanied by the emergence of a whole new group of authors, ones whose work greatly expanded the range and vision of the novel in English throughout the period, though especially after 1980. Authors in the colonies had sometimes adopted English as the language of their work much earlier in the century—the Indian novelist R. K. Narayan, for example, was first published in the 1930s—and they did so in increasing numbers in the later years of empire, and after its demise. Effects of 'transplanting' the English language in this way are fully considered in the Oxford English Literary History Volume 13. *The Internationalization of English Literature*. But one of its principal results, through immigration from former colonies later in the century, was as Burgess suggested the emergence of a new kind of fiction within Britain: in practice, most of the writers concerned were domiciled in England. For many of them, the 'great subject' of the novel naturally remained the one defined by V. S. Naipaul in *The Enigma of Arrival* (1987): the 'great movement of peoples . . . in the second half of the twentieth century', and the 'cultural mixing' which was its result (ch. 2). Fictional treatments of this 'great subject' generally concentrated on one of two areas, sometimes both: arrival and new experience in England, or recollection of colonies or former colonies authors had left.

The latter interest was established early in the period in the work of Wilson Harris, an immigrant from Guyana in 1959. Much of his fiction in the decades that followed matched in its complex imagination—and the peculiar brilliance of its language—the dazzling but impenetrable landscapes he had left behind. References to 'one dead seeing eye and one living closed eye' were repeated, with variations, throughout the first volume of his *Guyana Quartet* (1960–3), *Palace of the Peacock* (ch. 1). They emphasized the difficulties of separating 'the brilliancy and the gloom of the forest' from mental and imaginative reactions it provokes, or of containing either landscape or thought within a single coherent vision (ch. 2). Allusions to Conrad's *Heart of Darkness*, in the novel's dreamlike journey upriver, are among many cultural or mythic patterns Harris invokes: their conflicts and inadequacies suggest how far imagination and experience transcend conventional expression. Looking through 'the spiritual eye of the soul' towards 'the palace of the universe', *Palace of the Peacock* develops instead a visionary aspect largely unique to Harris's writing (ch. 11). Yet its dreamlike qualities anticipated, to an extent, magic realist techniques evolving in the work of other novelists of South American origin. These techniques were also used later by immigrant writers such as Ben Okri. In *The Famished Road* (1991), Okri mixed social and political analysis with the supernatural imagination of Nigerian folk tale, developed earlier in the fiction of Amos Tutuola. Okri's story of a 'spirit-child' offers on one level a colourful description of a Nigerian childhood, and of the country's progress towards independence, corrupted by domestic politicians as much as by Western powers. This realistic account of a 'world in which black people always suffered' is also interfused with 'the songs and fragrances of another world, a world beyond death'— one nevertheless simply and straightforwardly described in Okri's prose (bk. 8, ch. 1; bk. 7, ch. 11).

Abdulrazak Gurnah's account of an East African childhood in *Paradise* (1994) also moved at times towards magic realism, though of a darker sort. Set in an early phase of colonialism, it showed a population beginning to fall under the shadow of 'amazing' Europeans, imagined by one character as 'famed breakers of nations', able to 'eat metal . . . and the whole of the earth' (pt. 3, ch. 5). Their rapacity is extended by locals whose 'intrigues and hatreds and vengeful acquisitiveness had forced even simple virtues into tokens of exchange and barter' (pt. 6, ch. 4). Like *Heart of Darkness*, *The Siege of Krishnapur*, and *Sacred Hunger*, Gurnah's novel emphasized the complete interfusion of empire with soulless materialism and the remorseless pursuit of wealth. Ironically entitled, *Paradise* showed the absolute reversal—in another journey, like Conrad's, into the interior—of the kind of fulfilment achieved through travel in the novels discussed above. Travel literature and the fiction of empire did share elements of wonder, or of fascination with strange places, but in other ways they were radically contrasting, almost opposite modes in contemporary writing. Encounters with economic and historical forces in *Paradise* illustrate the overwhelming constraints on individuality experienced by a colonized population. Self-discovery in the novel is not a matter of fulfilling desire, but of painfully recognizing the impossibility of its fulfilment, or of any real freedom for the individual.

Gurnah's fiction was close in this way to the work of a number of black writers, concerned not only with recent life in former colonies, but with ways the gigantic cruelties of imperialism had shaped them in the first place—in particular, through the slave trade. Endurance of the 'middle passage' from Africa across the Atlantic was powerfully examined in Caryl Phillips's *Higher Ground* (1989) and Fred D'Aguiar's *Feeding the Ghosts* (1998), and life on colonial plantations in Phillips's *Cambridge* (1991) and D'Aguiar's *The Longest Memory* (1994). Each author also confronted a problem Ben Okri stressed at the end of *The Famished Road*. Like immigrant poetry, contemporary fiction emphasized that the history of black people had been 'manipulated . . . rigged out of existence' by the colonizers, and that new versions of it had to be created out of slaves' own voices and visions (bk. 8, ch. 1). These were incorporated into D'Aguiar's *The Longest Memory* through a range of dramatic monologues, offering sharply conflicting accounts of events as they are perceived by slaves and by their overseers.

Caryl Phillips offered similarly diverse perspectives on plantation life in the three sections of *Cambridge*. In the first of these, the narrator reproduces the genteel tones of the early nineteenth-century English fiction she admires: sent to deal with her father's West Indian possessions, she seems a relatively reliable figure until her 'thinly disguised disgust' for the black population is revealed in the second section. This is narrated by an educated slave—the Cambridge of the title—who has survived the middle passage and returned to establish a new life in England, only to be betrayed into servitude once again. The third section offers a further, more distanced view of all the participants. Divergences between the three—repeated in the tripartite structure of Phillips's *Higher Ground*—force readers to experience the difficulties of recounting the colonial past, and to engage directly with suppressions and falsifications imposed on lives and histories by imperial power. Similar tensions between historical narrative, memory, and actual experience were explored in David Dabydeen's portrayal of another educated slave in *A Harlot's Progress* (1999). Though his dreadful earlier life is already fading beyond his reliable recollection, he feels it must in any case be distanced from the conveniently sentimental accounts of it which the abolitionists are trying to construct.

Life in former colonies, recent or historical, continued to interest many other novelists late in the century. Vikram Seth, for example, set his story of romance and relationships, *A Suitable Boy* (1993), in the turbulent phase of India's history between independence and the early 1950s. In *Reef* (1994), Romesh Gunesekera looked back to a tranquil 1960s life, on the brink of violent change, in his native Sri Lanka. But immigrant fiction, especially early in the period, naturally focused not only on the former colonies, but on how an old life there came to be exchanged for a new one in England. 'Everybody is coming to London', Buchi Emecheta recorded in a novel set in the early 1960s, *Second-Class Citizen* (1974), 'the West Indians, the Pakistanis and even the Indians' (ch. 3). Each group reflected the experience in fiction. Emecheta's account of its difficulties was disturbingly focused by a narrator already sharply disadvantaged, as a woman, in Nigerian society, and then doubly so when bringing up her adored children in London, struggling against racial prejudice as well as her husband's fecklessness. Accounts of arriving from the West Indies were already established before the period began, in novels reflecting a first substantial phase of immigration from that area in the 1950s. George Lamming's title, *The Emigrants* (1954) accurately reflected a story concerned as much with departure from the Caribbean as with the strangeness of a new life in England. Sam Selvon's *The Lonely Londoners* (1956) focused more firmly on experience in England, and O. R. Dathorne's *Dumplings in the Soup* (1963) was similarly set in a tenement, crowded with immigrant students and lodgers. Selvon's *Moses Ascending* (1975) and *Moses Migrating* (1983) looked ironically at changing patterns of immigrant experience in later years, showing growing integration accompanied by continuing difficulties with racial prejudice and cultural adjustment.

Though reflecting a lesser scale of difficulties, several white authors in the period were also concerned with problems of adjustment or readjustment to English life. These appeared in some of Doris Lessing's early fiction, and in her autobiographical account of the transition from Africa to a difficult life in London, *In Pursuit of the English* (1960). Christopher Hope usually examined the politics and history of his native South Africa—in *Kruger's Alp* (1984), for example—but he also portrayed the turbulent London life of political exiles in *The Hottentot Room* (1986). In *The Hiding Place* (2000), Trezza Azzopardi traced pressures on a quite different immigrant community, the Maltese first establishing themselves in Cardiff in the 1950s, and on a second generation growing up there in the decades that followed. *The Hiding Place* was typical in this way of a new generation of immigrant narratives late in the century. Novels in the 1980s and 1990s were often concerned not with immediate problems of arrival, but with the experience of immigrants' children, and with their response to compromises and accommodations their parents had made when first establishing new lives in England. Immigrant experience often provided in this way new versions of the period's recurrent stories of lost fathers or difficult relations between generations.[5] One of these appeared in Meera Syal's account of growing up in an isolated immigrant family in *Anita and Me* (1996), for example; others, reflecting more widely on recent social change, in novels by Hanif Kureishi and Zadie Smith.

Kureishi's half-Indian narrator, Karim, defines himself early in *The Buddha of Suburbia* (1990), as 'an Englishman born and bred, almost'—though 'a funny kind of Englishman, a new breed as it were, having emerged from two old histories . . . [an] odd mixture of continents and blood, of here and there, of belonging and not' (ch. 1). In recounting a friend's attempt to escape an arranged marriage, as well as some of his own difficulties, he goes on to explore a second generation's different pace of adjustment between continents, between 'old histories', between India and England. Despite family tensions which result, and the continuing 'swamp of prejudice' Karim encounters, his narrative remains predominantly comic, even optimistic (ch. 17). In England since the 1950s, his father eventually develops expansively in the atmosphere of 'mysticism, alcohol, sexual promise, clever people and drugs' which the 1960s establishes, while Karim himself escapes from the suburbs into a life of metropolitan success (ch. 1). Progress through several areas of society, and his status as 'a funny kind of Englishman', help to make him an acute satiric observer. 'Part of England and yet . . . outside it', he directs on contemporary life a vision both objective and intimate, reflecting especially accurately the 'cults and experiments in living' fostered in the later 1960s, and ways these succumb to the 'new nihilism' of punk in the next decade (chs. 15, 5, 10).

A still wider set of trends and transitions appeared in Zadie Smith's *White Teeth* (2000), a kind of millennial compendium of recurrent themes and narratives shaping English fiction late in the century. As well as problems and conflicts in a rundown contemporary Britain, the novel examines a whole range of influences from the past. One of the families portrayed retraces its ancestry to the first

---

[5] Discussed on pp. 401–2, above.

rebel in the Indian Mutiny, the other to colonial times in the West Indies. Both encounter shadows still cast over their lives by the Second World War, and tensions with parents drive children in each to take refuge in a still further cultural context—with a Jewish family which half-adopts them. Smith was also an acute, streetwise observer of recent racial friction, recording, for example—like Kureishi in *The Black Album* (1995)—the disturbances which followed the Iranian *fatwa* death sentence on Salman Rushdie, for the blasphemy which figured in *The Satanic Verses* (1988).[6] Yet like *The Buddha of Suburbia*, *White Teeth* retains throughout a strong sense of humour. Its popular success was also owed to a consoling optimism, suggesting that different races and cultures in England have 'finally slipped into each other's lives with reasonable comfort', albeit very late in 'the century of strangers . . . the century of the great immigrant experiment' (ch. 12).

Effects of this 'experiment' on contemporary narrative—on its powers of satiric observation, in particular—were further exemplified in the work of Kazuo Ishiguro, though he was an unusual immigrant, arriving from Nagasaki as a child. His first novels, *A Pale View of Hills* (1982) and *An Artist of the Floating World* (1986), looked back on Japanese settings and concerns, even resembling some Japanese art in their subtle, meticulous observation. In *The Remains of the Day* (1989), Ishiguro turned instead to English society, examining a broad period of decline through the recollections of a country-house butler, Stevens, whose employer turns out to have been an aristocratic ally of the Nazis in the 1930s. Long-sustained loyalty to him, and to ideals of domestic service, generally exclude emotion from Stevens's personal life—and from his carefully formal narrative—and leave him with an outdated set of assumptions about English society. On a long journey across England in the summer of 1956, these attitudes nevertheless make him a revealing observer of a country on the verge of further radical change. In looking satirically at Stevens, and, through him, at the wider life of his times, Ishiguro demonstrated a detached clarity of vision derived, rather like Kureishi's, from being 'part of England, yet outside it'. Immigrant writers in the period were sometimes best placed to recreate the distanced observation developed early in the century by exiles

---

[6] See p. 572, below.

such as Henry James. In the novels mentioned, and in *When We Were Orphans* (1999), Ishiguro explored history's pressures on individual life mostly very obliquely. His narrators' complex webs of irony, evasion, and implication often resembled James's tactics in novels such as *What Maisie Knew* (1897) and *The Ambassadors* (1903).

V. S. Naipaul's later writing relied on more straightforward observation, though his long career—rewarded by the Nobel Prize in 2001—exemplified many approaches to the 'great subject' and 'great experiment' discussed above. His much-admired *A House for Mr Biswas* (1961) was typical of his early fiction, looking back on life in his native Trinidad. The novel uses its broad range of characters and their conflicts for comic effect, but they also offer extended insight into a complex, multiracial society, both hopeful and fearful for its future. Much of Naipaul's later writing was similarly wide-ranging, though often darker in tone. In the ironically entitled *In a Free State* (1971), for example, Naipaul juxtaposes narratives set in the United States, in England, and in Africa. Each examines failed or partial integrations in a new society, and the stresses which accompany immigrants' realization that 'it's their country. But it's your life. In the end you don't know what you feel about anything' (pt. 4, ch. 8). Naipaul's fullest treatments of immigration and integration in England appeared in *The Enigma of Arrival* (1987), a title which would have been appropriate for many of the novels discussed above. Its autobiographical aspects were also broadly typical—of his own work, and more widely. Often taking the form of travelogues or essays, much of Naipaul's work shared in a movement in late twentieth-century writing towards 'the higher autobiography' which Martin Amis identified, and in a way developed himself, in *Experience* (2000, p. 176). This movement was naturally extended both by immigrant novels, and by the fiction of travel discussed earlier: tensions between 'their country' and 'your life'—provocative, disturbing, or illuminating—provide an immediate, pressing, autobiographical subject for any displaced person. Elements of autobiography figured strongly in many novels about the difficulties of original arrival, such as Buchi Emecheta's *Second-Class Citizen*, and continued to shape the work of a later, more settled generation, including Hanif Kureishi and Zadie Smith.

The Enigma of Arrival explored both of these phases of immigrant experience within a single life, showing original uncertainties followed by more thorough acceptance of England. Naipaul looks back on youthful departure from Trinidad around mid-century, and on a first, disillusioning experience of London at that time, offering at most only the last of the England he had anticipated. The city's 'grandeur belonged to the past', he concludes, no longer resembling 'the England, the heart of empire, which (like a provincial, from a far corner of the empire) I had created in my fantasy' (ch. 2). This disappointment underlies a later attempt at 'coming to rest in middle life': at finding the heart of England not in its capital but in the depths of its countryside, and not in fantasy but through exceptionally meticulous recording of the real. Determination to be 'in tune with the landscape . . . for the first time in England' almost excludes incident from *The Enigma of Arrival*. Naipaul's narrative favours instead an intense, torpid concentration on rural life, and on its implications for his outlook and understanding of England. The countryside remains 'full of reminders of its Edwardian past', further reflecting the disappearance of 'grandeur' from England generally (ch. 1): in one way, Naipaul was concerned with the enigma of the whole nation's arrival, diminished and untidy, in the life of the later twentieth century. But he was concerned above all with a personal transition, and a change in his capacity to represent this life: with 'the writer's journey, the writer defined by his writing discoveries, his ways of seeing, rather than by his personal adventures'. *The Enigma of Arrival* registers the completion of this journey in Naipaul's 'delight in language' (ch. 5). The novel demonstrates and celebrates throughout the achievement of a style lucid and transparent enough to convince the immigrant author, and his readers, that he really has arrived: that he has at last found a way of seeing clearly, through his grasp of writing and the nation's language, right to England's enigmatic heart.

Naipaul's 'legendary, unforgiving prose', as Caryl Phillips called it, was unusually elegant and distinctive (*New World Order*, p. 187). His writer's journey was nevertheless one which had to be undertaken in one way or another by most immigrant authors. Not all of them shared the confidence Naipaul expresses in *The Enigma of Arrival*, remarking that 'migration, within the British Empire, from India to Trinidad had given me the English language as my own' (ch. 1). Buchi Emecheta's narrator in *Second-Class Citizen*, for example, worries that 'English was not her mother tongue . . . she could not write those big, long, twisting words'. Yet fairly few immigrant novelists—not even Emecheta herself, in this novel—much followed one solution she considers, 'to do her own phrases in her own way' (ch. 13). Sam Selvon incorporated a muted form of dialect into the narrative voice of *Moses Ascending,* but solutions of this kind were more often adopted in immigrant poetry, by West Indian writers such as Benjamin Zephaniah or Linton Kwesi Johnson. The work of each illustrated what Johnson defined as combinations of 'Jamaican Creole and Jamaican English and . . . English English':[7] novelists often seemed to share instead Naipaul's ambition to show the English that he could 'beat them at their own language' (Phillips, *New World Order,* p. 206). If any variation from standard English did appear in their work, it was often, as in *The Enigma of Arrival,* in a distinctively measured, meticulous use of words—suggesting particular care in dealing with a culture, and a language, sometimes foreign as well as familiar. Evident in the work of some of the earliest immigrant writers, this disposition continued to appear among authors emerging in the 1990s. Amit Chaudhuri, for example, admired Naipaul and reproduced some of his scrupulous grace in comparing Indian and English experience in *Afternoon Raag* (1993), as if anything less might allow that 'strange place, Oxford' to elude description altogether (ch. 22).

Yet there were sophisticated stylists, among novelists considered above, who undertook 'writer's journeys' very different from Naipaul's—Wilson Harris, and Caryl Phillips, for example. Limitations in Naipaul's realism, as a terminus for the immigrant writer's journey, were also indicated by two of the period's most widely admired novelists, Timothy Mo and Salman Rushdie. Like Harris and Phillips, each was thoroughly inventive formally, in vision and perspective, as well as thoroughly diverse—like Naipaul—in considering the 'great immigrant experiment' in countries old and new. Mo initially examined conflicts between diverse customs fairly conventionally in *Sour Sweet* (1982). Fierce allegiances to traditional Chinese values create many tensions—painful, funny, and revealing—in his heroine's relations with the English

---

[7] See p. 218, above.

community, and with her own family, struggling to make a success of a takeaway restaurant in London. In *An Insular Possession* (1986), Mo moved on to a more complex form, and an extended view of colonial history—of his birthplace, Hong Kong, and the opium wars which financed the colony's foundation in the nineteenth century. Like J. G. Farrell and Barry Unsworth, he emphasized in *An Insular Possession* the global corruption and materialism the empire encouraged, using newspaper reports, contemporary journals and letters, and a range of other documentary perspectives to broaden and add historical immediacy to this analysis.

Renegade, or Halo² (1999) also relied on letters, and on a range of vividly represented dialects and perspectives. These contributed to an equally broad analysis of exploitation at the end of the twentieth century, and of ways multinational economic forces continued— even extended—injustice and expropriation supposedly superseded by the end of empire. Set in the Philippines, Hong Kong, Malaysia, Thailand, the Arabian peninsula, Cuba, London, and aboard a Ukrainian freighter, *Renegade, or Halo²* showed these forces developing new forms of domination and reducing entire nations—the Filipinos, in particular—to a massively exploited international working class, almost a slave class. The epic scale on which these forces are envisaged was only rarely—too rarely—matched in contemporary English fiction. It made Mo's novel one of the most ambitious of the 1990s, confirming an ability to provide the 'cognitive mapping' Fredric Jameson thought essential—but scarcely realizable—for fiction confronting the 'global realities' of capitalism late in the century.

Salman Rushdie's fiction worked on a similarly epic scale, historical and global. One of the many successes of *Midnight's Children* (1981) is its focusing of this broad vision through Rushdie's use of magic realism, still known at the time mostly through the work of South American writers. Elements of fantasy help him to deal with a problem perplexing many authors discussed in earlier chapters: how to contain diverse, chaotic historical experience within the novel's conventional 'psychological orientation' and concentration on the life and vision of the individual. Ingeniously, Rushdie ensures that his narrator, Saleem Sinai, finds himself magically 'handcuffed to history' by the exact coincidence of his birth with Paul Scott's 'terrible, lovely moment'—or, as he calls it, 'the precise instant of India's arrival at independence' in 1947. Along with other midnight's children, whom he contacts through magical gifts of telepathy, this leaves Saleem's destiny 'indissolubly chained' to that of his country as a whole (bk. 1, ch. 1).

The experience of these 'midnight's children' provides a framework for broad, satiric examination of India's development later in the twentieth century. Digressions natural in a supposedly oral narrative also facilitate attention to earlier years. Lost fathers offer Rushdie more potential than perplexity: accounts of Saleem's bizarrely complex genealogy open up much discussion of the imperial past. An urge 'to encapsulate the whole of reality' in India is further extended by the range of narrative forms Saleem employs, and by his repeated discussion of the difficulties they present (bk. 1, ch. 5). Emphasis of the artificial, unreliable quality of his personal story prevents it distracting too far from the broader political and historical experience it seeks to focus. Fantastic imagination, conflicting perspectives, and self-conscious, self-questioning commentary also exemplify a postmodern aspect in Rushdie's writing. Scepticism of narrative, history, or ultimately any account of reality was typical of English fiction in the 1980s,[8] but perhaps especially relevant to Indian experience. In discussing magic realism, in an essay on Gabriel García Márquez, Rushdie suggested that it might be particularly suited to the expression of 'a genuinely "Third World" consciousness'—to political contexts in which 'truth has been controlled to the point at which it has ceased to be possible to find out what it is' (*Imaginary Homelands*, p. 301).

Rushdie went on to direct equally sharp satire over near-contemporary Pakistan in *Shame* (1983), and to extend some of the manner of *Midnight's Children* into a family history extending throughout the late nineteenth and twentieth centuries, and between India and Spain, in *The Moor's Last Sigh* (1995). But his most significant achievement for English readers may have been in *The Satanic Verses* (1988): not in representing remote periods of history, or 'Third World consciousness', but in directing magic realist imagination on racial tensions and cultural schisms within contemporary England. From its first page, *The Satanic Verses* shows that 'the world of

[8] See pp. 445–9, above.

dreams was leaking into that of the waking hours, that the seals dividing the two were breaking' (pt. V, ch. 2). The novel opens with its two central figures, clutched together in Yin and Yang position, miraculously surviving a fall from a hijacked Air India flight. 'Two fundamentally different *types* of self', they go on to follow contrary paths through English life. Previously a successful film actor, adept at changing roles, Gibreel Farishta nevertheless comes to fear 'above all things the altered states . . . which his dreams leak into' (pt. VII, ch. 2). He takes refuge instead in a single-minded obsession: that he must redeem London, like his angelic namesake, through apocalyptic fire. Saladin Chamcha, on the other hand, already has a solidly constructed persona as a typical Englishman, complete with bowler hat, but it is shattered by his nightmare experiences of racial prejudice. Transformed actually and physically into a caricature of the immigrant, complete with horns and hooves, he learns that this bestial metamorphosis can at least be used against his oppressors, as an image of sinister power. Newly sceptical of English life, and reconciled with his Indian roots, Chamcha concludes that a solid, inflexible version of the self may be inappropriate in a diverse, multicultural world, and worth replacing with a more 'hybrid' or 'conglomerate nature', open to imagination and change (pt. VII, ch. 1).

His conclusion helps to make him 'a creature of *selected* discontinuities . . . *willing* re-invention' (pt. VII, ch. 2). This kind of creature, and creativity, are strongly supported by the nature of the narrative itself: by its many discontinuities between fantasy and reality, and by the unsettling way these are framed. In *Midnight's Children*, disparate narratives, visions, and fantasies are partly held together by the controlling figure of Saleem, even though his body, symbolically, begins to crack and fissure under the strain. *The Satanic Verses* lacks a reassuring narrator figure of this kind, allowing instead literally diabolical uncertainties to surround the novel's religious visions and the origins of its story generally. Though disturbing, this indeterminacy is ultimately creative, challenging readers with the same fluid, hybrid interrelation of reality, vision, and fantasy which eventually broadens Saladin Chamcha's mind and transforms his character. The novel's notoriety heightened this challenge. Bernard Bergonzi concluded in 1979 that it was 'inconceivable in England' that literature could ever be 'taken with the kind of seriousness that means that writers are, on occasion, persecuted, imprisoned, or even shot' (*Situation of the Novel*, p. 47). One effect of the *fatwa* pronounced on Rushdie ten years later[9] was to emphasize for English readers the continuing seriousness of imaginative fiction's interrelation with religion, politics, and life in general. Ironically, this was also a conclusion offered by the novel itself: that dream, vision, imagination, fantasy, faith, and fiction all continually intermingle with daily experience, determining character, outlook, and ways life is lived even in the apparently solid centre of London.

Appropriately, it is in the form of a dream that *The Satanic Verses* first emphasizes the importance of plural, hybrid forms of imagination, and the limits of narrowing, singular visions of the real. In one way, the kind of lucid realism developed by V. S. Naipaul offered immigrant writers the clearest of 'ways of seeing' their adoptive English culture, and the most direct imaginative engagement with it. Yet clarity or transparency of this kind corresponds to Saladin Chamcha's dream of 'a bizarre stranger, a man with a glass skin'—a 'brittle membrane' which seems to imprison him, and soon breaks painfully into fragments. When Chamcha emerges from this dream, he finds his own speech 'unaccountably metamorphosed into the Bombay lilt he had so diligently (and so long ago!) unmade' (pt. I, ch.3). The experience prefigures the unravelling of his adopted, carefully perfected English identity. In the 'Bombay lilt' which he has ultimately failed to discard, it also suggests the continuing, inherent potential of originary as well as adoptive cultures. In an illuminating essay on *The Satanic Verses* and *The Enigma of Arrival*, Abdulrazak Gurnah suggested that in Naipaul's novel

the migrant arrives at understanding through unwavering 'looking' . . . the migrant's 'labour' inevitably leads to self-insertion into 'England'. Rushdie's text, on the other hand, contends the possibility of walking back and forth through the mirror, and argues the virtues of the transformation of the self as well as the irresistibility of change in the societies the migrant experiences. (Lee (ed.), p. 17)

Naipaul was often criticized for too thoroughgoing a 'self-insertion' into England, or into the cultures of the West generally—one which

<hr>

[9] See p. 572, below.

seemed to prompt his many scathing comments on the kind of former colony he had grown up in himself. Comments in Rushdie's essays, on the other hand, extend the warnings of Saladin Chamcha's dream, highlighting the dangers of unreserved self-insertion, and of the kind of 'unwavering looking'—in conventionally realistic fiction, particularly—which might facilitate it. Indian and other immigrant authors in Britain, Rushdie stresses in the essays of *Imaginary Homelands* (1991), 'are at one and the same time insiders and outsiders'. As a result, they need to work with 'stereoscopic vision . . . in place of "whole sight"' (p. 19).

Vision of this kind contributed to the distanced, satiric perspectives—'part of England and yet . . . outside it'—in fiction by writers such as Hanif Kureishi or Kazuo Ishiguro. But further effects on immigrant writing were indicated by Rushdie's conclusion in *Imaginary Homelands* that 'mass migrations' had created

radically new types of human being . . . people in whose deepest selves strange fusions occur, unprecedented unions between what they were and where they find themselves. The migrant suspects reality: having experienced several ways of being, he understands their illusory nature . . .

Migrants must, of necessity, make a new imaginative relationship with the world . . . plural, hybrid, metropolitan. (pp. 124–5)

Wilson Harris also suggested at the beginning of the period—in complicated metaphors of eyes open and closed, seeing or unseeing—that the 'stereoscopic vision' of the migrant offered more than only new satiric perspectives on society. No author aware of two different cultures can remain unquestioningly content with either of them. Contacts with other languages, literatures, and ways of seeing require writers to identify the nature and limitations of their own, encouraging the pursuit of alternative possibilities, hybrid forms, and, in general, innovation and change.

Migrants' 'new imaginative relationship with the world', in other words, strongly motivated reshaping of the form and style of English fiction during the period. It encouraged the suspicion of conventional realism evident in writers such as Harris and Rushdie, the multiplication of styles and perspectives in the work of Phillips and Mo, and the self-conscious questioning of established strategies more widely apparent in immigrant fiction. Writing of this kind offered further evidence for a conclusion discussed in Chapter 2—that developments often labelled 'postmodern' actually owed their origins principally to postcolonial 'cultural mixing' and the many stresses which resulted. But it also confirmed a conclusion reached in Chapter 18: that pressures which are debilitating socially or politically may nevertheless be enabling artistically and imaginatively. What history refuses, culture provides. New 'global realities' and 'cultural mixing' may have been bewildering, late in the century, but they were also imaginatively challenging, potentially extending the novel's capacities, rather than altogether overwhelming them as Fredric Jameson feared. Like women writers, immigrant novelists were 'insiders and outsiders' at the same time, as Rushdie suggested: part of English society, yet also partly 'outside of it, alien and critical', their work was often strengthened by the doubling and diversifying of vision this entailed. Relatively little of this potential was apparent at the end of the 1970s: its realization in the next decades helped to dispel the pessimism about the novel expressed around that time. Other 'strange fusions' and 'unprecedented unions' contributed further to the strength of the novel late in the century: these are considered in the next chapter.

20

Genres, Carnivals, Conclusions

David Lodge talked in 1991 of an 'aesthetic supermarket' of diverse fictional styles.[1] Malcolm Bradbury also figured the novel's diversity in the 1990s in terms of retailing, describing a 'great shopping mall world of pluri-culture' in which 'genres leak freely into one another', and in which 'various layers and categories of culture, from the avant garde to the populist, constantly interpenetrate' (Brown (ed.), p. viii). As Bradbury and Lodge suggest, new combinations of styles appeared more and more often late in the century, evidence of an increasingly multicultural, or 'pluri-cultural', crossroads in English writing at the time. Boundaries between 'the literary novel' and so-called 'genre fiction'—popular romances, thrillers and detective stories, spy novels, and science fiction—also grew more permeable, partly in response to the pressures of marketing and retailing. Throughout the century, the market had continued to expand for writing assigned to these 'populist' genres. But they had usually been firmly separated from 'serious' novels, not only by literary critics, but simply by the shelving arrangements in most bookshops and libraries. This gradually changed towards the end of the century, further evidence of the period's general shift towards a more broadly democratic culture. Movements in literary theory encouraged less exclusive perceptions of literature among critics, students, and eventually readers generally. Distinctions also came to be less clearly marked in bookshops. Following the paperback revolution during the 1960s, previously distinct categories—classics and thrillers—came to rub shoulders, or spines, more regularly.[2] Overwhelming

---

[1] See p. 458, above.   [2] See p. 141, above.

numbers of novel-titles published each year ensured that they continued to do so. Some bookshops retained separate sections for each of the categories of genre fiction, and a few placed them all together in a 'popular' area distinct from the 'literary' one. But by the end of the century, many just lumped everything together—covers sombre or sensational, grave or gaudy—simply as 'fiction'.

Novelists shared and encouraged these shifting perceptions. Graham Greene strongly influenced genre writing in the period, and his evolving attitudes towards it were symptomatic of its changing status at the time. In the 1930s, Greene had coined the term 'entertainment', as a kind of subtitle, to distinguish spy and crime novels from his other fiction, and it reappeared on the title page of a novel he published in 1958, *Our Man in Havana*. Twenty years later, he no longer found it necessary to describe *The Human Factor* (1978) in this way, though it was just as much of a spy story, if in a more sombre vein. Later in the century, novel and entertainment continued to coalesce, with literary authors drawing more and more regularly on the excitement and broad appeal of genre fiction. Cohabiting in bookshops, literary and genre novels became increasingly intimate partners in writers' imaginations as well. The implications of this relationship for each partner—and for the period's attitudes and imagination generally—are assessed below, examining in turn the genres of romance, thriller, science fiction, and fantasy.

By the end of the century, changing assumptions about sex had profoundly altered fictional treatments of love and relationships, whether in 'serious' literature or in popular romance. Yet new attitudes and openness developed only gradually. Authors early in the period still worked within long-established patterns of interest in relationships, a perennial subject of the novel, and took time, perhaps inevitably, to incorporate the sexual freedoms of the 1960s, and the new opportunities to describe them following the *Chatterley* trial. Difficulties of adjustment to these new freedoms often appeared in fiction at the time,[3] and there were commentators who considered they remained a problem, or a risk, for novelists throughout the period. D. J. Taylor suggested in the 1990s that 'the freedom to write about sex in whatever way you choose is generally agreed to have been an aesthetic disaster' (p. 233). Evidence for his views

[3] See pp. 404–5 and 462–3, above.

continued to appear, late in the century, in the annual 'Bad Sex in Fiction Prize', offered by the *Literary Review* for the most embarrassing or hilarious description of a sexual episode in the novel. As Lawrence himself had sometimes demonstrated earlier in the century—in novels including *Lady Chatterley's Lover* (1928)—the most private, physical, and emotional experiences might naturally be the ones most to resist expression in the largely public, cerebral medium of language. New attitudes to sex and relationships challenged established fictional structure as much as style. In the nineteenth century, and earlier in the twentieth, writers had often used sexual or—more usually—marital union to provide a sense of completion and closure for their fiction. Novels such as Kingsley Amis's *Take a Girl Like You* (1960) and Stan Barstow's *A Kind of Loving* (1960) indicated the growing awkwardness or obsolescence of this kind of conclusion—also evident in the period's drama—even by the beginning of the 1960s. By the 1990s, more than one marriage in four in England ended in divorce: growing scepticism of matrimony, and more relaxed attitudes to sex, steadily diminished the usefulness of either as a climax or grand finale for the novel.

Gradually, nevertheless, sexual relations simply became part of the novel's continuing music—part of fictional forms in any case more open, fragmentary, or inconclusive in the period. More explicit accounts of sexual relations began to figure in women's writing during the 1960s, in the work of authors including Margaret Drabble and Doris Lessing.[4] Later, women authors such as Angela Carter and Fay Weldon helped to develop an intimate awareness of the body—sometimes of a grotesque physicality—largely excluded from earlier English fiction. Men writers followed, though more gingerly. John Fowles explained the absence of sexual details in the first edition of *The Magus* in 1966 as a failure of nerve: their inclusion in the revised version of 1977 indicated his own greater confidence, and novelists' growing freedoms in the period generally. These were also developed extensively by John Berger in *G.* (1972), and by many other authors in the 1970s and later—by Ian McEwan, in particular, in fiction from the middle of the decade. Towards the end of the century, too, several male novelists began to employ more of the physical consciousness or grotesque fascination with the body often

---

[4] See pp. 462–3, above.

apparent earlier in women's writing—McEwan and Martin Amis, in several novels, or Rupert Thomson in *The Book of Revelation* (1999), for example.

Sexual directness also extended into descriptions of love between women, in novels by Jeanette Winterson and others mentioned in Chapter 18, and, eventually, into accounts of relations between men. Habitual reticence remained evident in the 1960s and 1970s: in Angus Wilson's fiction, in Christopher Isherwood's *A Single Man* (1964)—even in describing the relaxed attitudes of California, where he had long been an exile—and in E. M. Forster's long-suppressed *Maurice* (1971), eventually published the year after his death. Greater directness appeared in the later fiction of Paul Bailey, and more widely after Alan Hollinghurst's influential, highly explicit writing in *The Swimming Pool Library* (1988). This was a historic novel in other ways, obviously in looking back on prejudice against homosexuals extending throughout earlier decades. It was also historically specific in celebrating a relatively carefree phase of gay life, before the AIDS epidemic: Hollinghurst's account of gay experience was darker in *The Folding Star* (1994). Literary history was reshaped, in a way, by the intense gaze of gay appraisal reproduced in his fiction, charging minute details of physical observation and appearance with renewed emotional force. This kind of revivified realism, bodily and erotic, continued to figure strongly in later gay fiction, such as Paul Golding's *The Abomination* (2000). Writing of this kind developed the novel in ways scarcely imaginable a hundred or even fifty years previously: by the end of the century, English fiction portrayed confidently, and in physical detail, relationships gay, extramarital, or heterosexual—sometimes promiscuously intermingled in a single novel, such as Hanif Kureishi's *The Buddha of Suburbia* (1990). Though the tact and tactics required were learned gradually, and sometimes awkwardly, one of the period's decisive achievements was in expanding and normalizing literary imagination by showing sex as an intimate, integral aspect of characters' unfolding emotions and relations.

Popular romantic fiction was a less certain beneficiary of these new freedoms, and sometimes a clearer indicator of the difficulties they created. Anita Brookner's heroine in *Hotel du Lac* (1984), Edith, is an author of popular romances, warned by her agent that 'the romantic market is beginning to change. It's sex for the young woman executive now, the *Cosmopolitan* reader' (ch. 2). As he suggested, sex began to figure more regularly in romantic novels during the period. Even the traditional romance publishers, Mills and Boon, allowed it to be described much more explicitly by some of their authors in the 1990s, such as Sharon Kendrick. Yet as Catherine Belsey emphasized in her critical study *Desire* (1994), unlike other authors at the time romantic writers generally continued to work towards the socially acceptable, sustained form of relationship institutionalized in marriage. This entailed the difficulty—for authors and characters—of bringing 'physical sensation, the overwhelming intensity of erotic desire . . . into harmony with rational and moral commitment, a shared life of sympathy and support'. Heroines of popular romance often experienced as a result intense conflicts between what Belsey describes as forces 'the Enlightenment so relentlessly put asunder—the body and its pleasures on the one hand, the mind and its values on the other' (p. 23). Viewed in this way, popular romance showed more clearly than other forms of fiction why the body acquired a new fascination, even a grotesque will of its own, in the contemporary novel.[5] Growing sexual liberation, along with postmodern scepticism of Enlightenment thinking, inevitably required many readjustments between physicality, morality, and rationality throughout the imagination of the age. Often more conservative in its social and moral attitudes, popular fiction reflected especially clearly new stresses as well as new freedoms involved.

Popular romance also shared, and sometimes clarified, other broad developments in the period's writing. Several of these appeared, for example, in the work of one of the most successful and prolific of romance novelists, Catherine Cookson—author of more than ninety novels, with a total sale of more than 100 million copies. Aimed almost exclusively at a female readership, like much romantic fiction, her work reversed male authors' priorities even more emphatically than many of the women writers considered in Chapter 18. Though men are carefully characterized in Cookson's fiction, their principal role is as objects of desire, and they generally remain firmly subordinate to a heroine whose thoughts and emotions occupy the centre

[5] See also p. 476, above.

of attention throughout. Like much late twentieth-century English fiction, Cookson's writing also extensively explored the English class system and the freedom, or lack of it, of characters to change strata within it. This interest had grown slightly old-fashioned by the 1990s, but it remained appropriate to the historical setting of novels such as *A Ruthless Need* (1995), which examined the Second World War and its effects on class hierarchies in ways comparable to several novels discussed in earlier chapters. Martin Amis remarked that 'even the best kind of popular novel just comes straight at you; you have no conversation with a popular novel', but in the areas mentioned novels such as *A Ruthless Need* sustained much the same dialogue with readers as literary fiction (*Experience*, p. 224). 'Conversation' faltered only in ways indicated in *Hotel du Lac*—in Edith's confession that 'the facts of life are too terrible to go into my kind of fiction. And my readers certainly do not want them there'(ch. 2). As in most popular romance, the plot of Cookson's novels generally did come at you in predictable ways, teasing readers throughout with variously deferred expectations of the heroine's ideal marriage. Wish-fulfilment of this kind was obviously a necessary and successful part of romantic novels' popular appeal: their sales continued to account for a 35 per cent share of the paperback market in the 1990s. But it did depart decisively from 'the facts of life' as they appeared in other forms of fiction in this period—wary of happy endings of any kind, and likely to view marriage as part of characters' problems, not a solution to them.

Wish-fulfilment and romance played important roles in Graham Greene's writing, though ones not always readily recognized. In an *Observer* interview on 16 March 1980, Greene drew attention instead to his role as 'a straight writer', and to his preference for 'straight sentences, no involutions, no ambiguities', presenting 'the outside world economically and exactly' (p. 33). These preferences had been evident in Greene's writing ever since the 1930s: his economy of style and realistic presentation of 'the facts of life'—however grim or disillusioning—extensively influenced the thriller genres, as well as English fiction more generally, later in the century. Yet he was an idiosyncratic realist. The seedy settings of his novels, deepening the dispiritedness of characters inhabiting them, were distinctive enough for critics to coin the term 'Greeneland' to describe them.

Hopeless, graceless domains, their manifold shortcomings implicitly emphasized the need for a transcendent dimension beyond them. Around mid-century, during and after the war, Catholic religion fulfilled this requirement in Greene's work, making him the leading religious novelist of his time.[6] But in the late 1950s a different reaction to the world's shortcomings appeared in *Our Man in Havana*, when Greene's hero, Wormold, points out that 'a romantic is usually afraid . . . in case reality doesn't come up to expectations' (pt. 5, ch. 6). Greene had followed romance modes in some of his earliest novels, in the late 1920 and 1930s: a romantic element reappeared in fiction after the 1950s, regularly showing secular rather than divine love compensating for the disappointments of the world. As well as replacing religious faith, individual relationships in Greene's later spy stories often displaced loyalty to intelligence agencies, and ultimately to the nation itself. In *Our Man in Havana*, Wormold's girlfriend suggests he should be 'loyal to love and not to countries' (pt. 5, ch. 4), and the central figure in *The Human Factor*, Castle, is likewise reminded by his wife that 'We have our own country. You and I . . .' (pt. 5, ch. 1).

Divided between private and professional allegiances, Wormold and Castle are double agents of a kind, and typical of complicated, contradictory characters, haunted by betrayal, who appear throughout Greene's fiction. Divided loyalties experienced in childhood, Greene explained—as a pupil in the school where his father was headmaster—helped to initiate an interest in such figures. He stressed their lasting importance for his work in his autobiography, *A Sort of Life* (1971), remarking

if I were to choose an epigraph for all the novels I have written, it would be from [Robert Browning's] *Bishop Blougram's Apology*:

> 'Our interest's on the dangerous edge of things.
> The honest thief, the tender murderer,
> The superstitious atheist . . .'
>
> (ch. 5)

Ambiguous figures of this kind—culpable yet idealistic—helped Greene to sustain a sense of courage and significance for the individual, even in the dispirited domains his novels envisaged, and in the

---

[6] See pp. 423–4, above.

disillusioned age in which he wrote. Looking back on heroic figures celebrated in the Edwardian period, Greene's narrator in *The End of the Affair* (1951) remarks that 'it seemed curiously dated now, this heroism . . . Two wars stood between us and them' (bk. 5, ch. 6). Much of the enduring popularity of Greene's work was owed to its half-romantic realism, still showing forms of heroism, compromised but credible, extending into the later twentieth century, and love and personal loyalty still surviving even in a world dominated by impersonal state and military powers. A real double agent, whom Greene knew from his own wartime intelligence work, strangely confirmed close interrelations between his fiction, in its thriller modes especially, and the life and imagination of the times. Kim Philby quoted one of Greene's spy novels, *The Confidential Agent* (1939)—supposedly 'an entertainment'—in defence of his defection to Moscow in 1963. Greene, in turn, was often said to have based *The Human Factor* on Philby's experience.

Foreign settings often sharpened the 'dangerous edge of things' in Greene's fiction. Though he returned to the scenes of his Berkhamstead childhood in *The Human Factor*, most of his later novels used distant contexts familiar to him from work as a journalist and travel writer, or from world-wandering attempts to resist lifelong boredom, or from his friendship with political leaders such as Fidel Castro. *Our Man in Havana* strangely anticipated the Cuban Missile Crisis; Papa Doc's Haiti provided the background for *The Comedians* (1966); and terrorism in Argentina for *The Honorary Consul* (1973). Settings in areas of political tension added to the potential described in travel-related writing in Chapter 19. Strange, exciting, or even actively hostile foreign contexts naturally heightened pressures on characters, and within them, highlighting the particularity of their outlook and values by contrast with those around them. In various ways, this potential was further developed by several of the period's spy and thriller writers. In Ian Fleming's James Bond novels, and in the films that followed,[7] foreign locations mostly provided only an added element of glamour, at a time when travel abroad was increasingly catching the imagination of the general public. Hammond Innes, on the other hand, set much of his fiction not just abroad, but on remote edges of civilization: lonely conflicts with

[7] See pp. 49–50, above.

topography and the elements starkly focus his characters' under-standing of their personal strengths and limitations.

At the start of the period, at the height of the Cold War, East Europe offered especially revealing contrasts, not only with the out-look of individual characters, but with English life in general. These contrasts were often explored by Len Deighton—regularly con-cerned, like Greene, with moral or emotional dilemmas in a world of cynical, unstable political interests. Typically of fiction at the begin-ning of the 1960s, some of his early novels also examined shifting influences of class, education, and background. The narrator of *The Ipcress File* (1962), for example, sometimes finds himself almost equally threatened 'by the Communists on one side and the Establishment on the other', as well as by growing US military superiority worldwide (ch. 13). East Europe was also a regular con-text in John le Carré's novels. Le Carré explained that the melo-dramatic qualities of Fleming's James Bond fiction, along with the contrary example of Greene, encouraged him to write spy fiction in which realism and depth of characterization tempered the excite-ment of the thriller. The results appeared in novels such as *The Spy who Came in from the Cold* (1963) and *Smiley's People* (1980): dark, complex explorations of the moral confusion, covert brutality, and chess-like strategic manoeuvres of the Cold War. More grimly than Greene, each novel showed the disappearance of decency, love, and integrity from a world ruled more and more ruthlessly by state agencies, indifferent to anything except their own grasp of power.

In a later autobiography, *Ways of Escape* (1980), Greene recorded an 'ambition to create something legendary out of a contemporary thriller' (ch. 3). In his own work, and in the fiction of authors such as Deighton and Le Carré who followed him, spies became, if not legendary figures, ones at any rate peculiarly representative of their age. Ever since the modernist period, authors had emphasized isola-tion, alienation, and uncertainty as pervasive conditions of life in the twentieth century. These conditions were experienced still more sharply after the war's huge challenges to morals and values, and in the uncertain age of Cold War and nuclear weaponry which followed. A figure in Julian Mitchell's *The Undiscovered Country* (1968) summed up wider feelings, early in the period, when he remarked that 'all these modern spy stories about people being double-counter-bluffed—they're exact images of my mental state . . . Life is so chaotic' (pt. 1, ch. 6). Spy fiction's lonely agents offered a natural focus for anxieties about global systems of power, distant or indifferent to personal fate, and about the increasing uncertainty of values and loyalties in contemporary life. In these ways, 'modern spy stories' represented some of the principal stresses of their age more directly than much supposedly serious fiction. Not surprisingly, spy novels were produced occasionally by several 'serious' authors, as well as Graham Greene—Kingsley Amis, for example, in *The Anti-Death League* (1966) and *Russian Hide and Seek* (1980). Amis also published a James Bond novel, *Colonel Sun* (1968), under a pseudonym, and Anthony Burgess parodied Ian Fleming's extravagances of violence and sex in *Tremor of Intent* (1969).

As the international tensions of the Cold War eased, later in the period, and stresses within domestic society increased, detective and crime fiction more often provided figures representative of its age. Criminals, obviously, and detectives, frequently, are as much isolates and outsiders as spies. Each can conveniently highlight established society's values, either by contrast, in the criminal's case, or through resilient allegiance, in the detective's. Nicholas Freeling considered that 'the behaviour of a criminal (a man by definition set at odds with his society)' can also raise 'wide moral, metaphysical, and philosophic problems', and that in addressing these, the 'natural function and legitimate ambition' of the crime novelist should be art (Brown (ed.), p. 355). Modestly, this was not an ambition Freeling judged to have been fully realized in his own work. Many critics and readers considered it was achieved in the writing of other crime novelists. Julian Symons used complex crime plots as a basis for wide-ranging analysis of contemporary life, or, occasionally, nineteenth-century society. P. D. James's later fiction extended and deepened interests in character and psychology already evident in novels such as *Death of an Expert Witness* (1977). Ruth Rendell's prolific fiction often mixed conventional elements of crime writing with exploration of strange or obsessive states of mind. These interests were extended by several authors emerging late in the century—not necessarily dedicated writers about crime, but ones for whom its psychopathology offered ways of examining darker forms of individual behaviour, or, more widely, a society increasingly damaged, divided, and unruly in the 1980s and 1990s.

Depths both psychological and literal were deftly juxtaposed in Tobias Hill's *Underground* (1999), for example, incorporating into an account of intended murder on the London Tube recollections of dark experiences stretching back to the concentration camps. Iain Pears's historical imagination stretched back further, to a vividly described seventeenth-century Oxford in his complex detective story *An Instance of the Finger Post* (1997). Patrick McGrath's *Asylum* (1996) described love and its imaginings as much as murder, extending the excitement of the thriller format across a whole set of boundaries between reality and illusion, madness and sanity, normal and abnormal sexual behaviour, ordinary and obsessive emotion. McGrath had summed up the macabre aspect of his own writing in his earlier title *The Grotesque* (1989). It also indicated the particular importance for the thriller genres of darker phases of imagination more widely characteristic of the late twentieth century. Toby Litt's blackly comic *Corpsing* (2000), for example, extended grotesque fascination with the body to new extremes in its long, meticulously detailed descriptions of the impact of an assassin's bullets. Jim Crace anatomized his characters in similarly extended physical detail in *Being Dead* (1999). His novel worked on the fringes of the crime genre, and on the boundaries of mortal experience, mingling elegiac recollections of a murdered couple's earlier lives with minute, strangely graceful descriptions of their decaying corpses. The unusualness of this imagination was in a way typical of Crace's writing— especially diverse, among authors emerging in the 1980s and 1990s, in its range of modes and interests.

Longer-established novelists were also ready either to work straightforwardly within the detective genre—in the case of Julian Barnes, who published streetwise mystery stories under the pseudonym 'Dan Kavanagh'—or to use it as a vehicle for the moral or metaphysical problems Freeling mentioned. Several writers adapted crime fiction to explore gender issues, refocusing often male-centred thriller genres around the point of view of women characters: Zoë Fairbairns, for example, in *Here Today* (1984), and Elaine Feinstein in *Dark Inheritance* (2000). English novelists who developed the metaphysical concerns of the *nouveau roman* were also led towards the detective format. Alain Robbe-Grillet considered the unravelling of mysteries in crime fiction exemplary of literature's more general commitment to pattern, coherence, and explanation of 'the world around us'. 'We thought we had come to terms with [this world] by giving it a meaning', Robbe-Grillet remarked, 'and the whole art of the novel, in particular, seemed dedicated to this task'. He added, however, that this task had involved 'only an illusory simplification ... we no longer consider the world as a possession, our private property, designed to suit our needs, and domesticable' (pp. 56–7). Accordingly, Robbe-Grillet began his career with a parody detective story, *Les Gommes* (1953), its impossible chronology and conflicting perspectives rebutting the genre's usual promise of logical conclusion and rational solution.

Writers who first extended the interests of the *nouveau roman* into English fiction[8] often did so through similar travesties of the detective story. These were used by Rayner Heppenstall in *The Connecting Door* (1962), for example, and by Muriel Spark in *The Driver's Seat* (1970). Her heroine's bizarre determination to be murdered ensures the novel itself resembles the 'whydunnit in q-sharp major' she claims to have been reading (ch. 7). For writers later in the period, such as Peter Ackroyd in *Hawksmoor* (1985), the detective story continued to provide a means of investigating the postmodern outlook Robbe-Grillet's remarks suggest—one of waning faith in Enlightened reason's capacity to explain 'the world around us'. It was also used in this way by Martin Amis. Elements of Robbe-Grillet's 'tricksy' writing combined with the hard-boiled manner of US crime fiction in *Night Train* (1997), and with English settings in *Other People* (1981) and *London Fields* (1989)—each a kind of murder mystery. These combinations contributed to the representative role of Amis's novels in the 1980s and 1990s. His visions of sleaziness and corruption, typical of detective writing, were disturbingly focused by postmodern scepticism of any means of enlightening contemporary society, or of making much sense of 'the world around us', in the later twentieth century, at all.

Amis was equally representative in his attraction to conventional pace and plot, as well as literary 'tricksiness'. In making the combinations between tradition and innovation discussed in Chapters 16

[8] See also pp. 407–8, above.

and 17, several other writers were similarly drawn towards the conventions of thriller genres. Ian McEwan's *Enduring Love* (1997), for example, examined character and emotion in disturbing depth, but his story also involved a shooting, violent death, and a number of whirlwind journeys across the country. In one way, such tactics exemplified the continuing influence of Graham Greene: not only in adding new moral and psychological depth to the thriller genres, but in finding—like his mentors Robert Louis Stevenson and Joseph Conrad—fresh elements of pace, action, and adventure for literary fiction. In another way, they simply reflected the breakneck economics ruling the 'shopping mall' or 'aesthetic supermarket' of late twentieth-century publishing and bookselling. Pressures of retailing encouraged 're-taleing', or reorienting of the novel's priorities: of all the conventions authors might choose to shape their literary vision, those of the thriller genres were obviously the most likely to sell books. Cinema, too, offered Greene and many later novelists—like dramatists, towards the end of the century—influential models of pacy narrative construction.[9]

In another of Ian McEwan's novels, *The Child in Time* (1987), a quantum physicist suggests how far literary authors might have moved towards another genre, science fiction. Her claim that no one had 're-invented the world and our place in it as radically and bizarrely as the physicists of this century' could even have been strengthened by reference to other branches of science and technology (p. 44). Huge advances by the end of the century in fields such as genetics, geology, cosmology, and space travel had further 'reinvented' humanity's conception of itself and its place in the universe. The imaginative impact of planetary missions and manned moon landings was often reinforced by contemporary science fiction, in the novel and the cinema. The popularity of a pioneer novelist in the genre, Arthur C. Clarke, was greatly increased by Stanley Kubrick's film *2001: A Space Odyssey* (1968), for example. Yet as McEwan's physicist complains, writers and students of literature sometimes seemed to have given barely a moment's thought to this 'scientific revolution . . . intellectual revolution . . fabulous story', or to its imaginative potentials (*Child in Time*, p. 44). Instead, the period's literature largely justified fears expressed at its beginning in C. P.

---

[9] On film, see also p. 386, above, and on publishing, p. 161, above.

Snow's controversial lecture, *The Two Cultures and the Scientific Revolution* (1959). This concluded that the arts and sciences had increasingly 'split into two polar groups', ones which 'had almost ceased to communicate at all'. As a result, Snow feared, 'very little of twentieth-century science has been assimilated into twentieth-century art' (pp. 3, 2, 16).

There were exceptions in the poetry of the period, in the work of J. H. Prynne and Lavinia Greenlaw, for example, and in drama, in plays such as Paul Godfrey's *The Blue Ball* (1995) or Michael Frayn's *Copenhagen* (1998)—perhaps even in the lunatic disillusion with moon landings in Tom Stoppard's *Jumpers* (1972). Novels, too, did occasionally appear in which scientific disciplines at least formed an important background: astronomy, in Colin Thubron's *Distance* (1996) and Peter Ackroyd's *First Light* (1989); genetics, in Simon Mawer's *Mendel's Dwarf* (1997), for example. Descriptions in Doris Lessing's *Briefing for a Descent into Hell* (1971) reflected images which NASA missions returned from space in the later 1960s, showing 'the Earth, hung in its weight, coloured and tinted here and there, for the most part with the bluish tint of water' (p. 94). Some of this newly distanced vision of human affairs also extended into Lessing's later writing in her *Canopus in Argos: Archives* series (1979–83). Yet *Canopus in Argos* was more visionary than directly scientific. McEwan's quantum-inspired departures from conventional chronology in *The Child in Time*, or Jeanette Winterson's descriptions of matter as 'mostly empty space. Empty space and points of light' in *Sexing the Cherry* (1989) were likewise more imaginative than strictly convincing scientifically (p. 8). In an age of postmodern scepticism about the capacity of theories to assign meaning to 'the world around us', it was perhaps inevitable that even writers genuinely excited by science were tempted to view it in almost mystical terms, and not very strictly in its own. Rather than carefully reflecting reasoned, scientific analysis of a known world, authors in the period often seized on what seemed new possibilities—supposedly sanctioned by science—of ignoring or transcending the ordinary limits of knowledge and reason.

These possibilities, of course, encouraged the rapid development of science fiction itself during the period. Some of it interacted strongly with the literary novel. Christopher Priest, for example, trod much the same path as Doris Lessing, though in a contrary direction, beginning as a writer of science fiction novels such as *Inverted World* (1974) before moving on towards a kind of 'inner-space fiction'. Fantastic events and the whole imaginative world described in novels such as *The Affirmation* (1981) may be no more than projections of the disturbed psyches of the characters—sometimes vaguely aware that what they 'had imagined . . . had come to be' (ch. 2). Brian Aldiss remarked that he had 'never experienced that great divide some people detect between science fiction and the ordinary contemporary novel' (Brown (ed.), p. 22). Much of his own writing was 'ordinary' and realistic enough in its interests, and much of it explicitly literary—in describing a time traveller's encounter with Byron and the Shelleys in *Frankenstein Unbound* (1973), for example. Even in its fantastic modes, Aldiss's work often shared in the wider movements of contemporary fiction: in the obsessively observed *nouveau roman* form of *Report on Probability A* (1968), for example, and in the linguistic experimentation, regular transitions into poetry, and late 1960s drug-laden atmosphere of *Barefoot in the Head* (1969).

Like Aldiss, J. G. Ballard thought science fiction's capacity 'to respond imaginatively to the transforming nature of science and technology' made it the truly 'authentic literature of the 20th century' (Brown (ed.), p. 68). His own fiction, at any rate, reflected some of the stresses of its age as authentically as any 'ordinary contemporary novel'. This was evident in one way in the autobiographical, realist *Empire of the Sun* (1984). Like novels described in Chapters 16 and 17, *Empire of the Sun* looked back at some of the definitive disasters of the twentieth century, towards the end of the Second World War, communicating them with particular immediacy through the perspective of a partly comprehending child. He survives the fall of Shanghai to the Japanese, only to be interned in a kind of concentration camp, eventually witnessing the dawn of an age of nuclear warfare in a distant flash of light which reaches him from Nagasaki. Desolate refractions of that distant light shaped some of Ballard's apocalyptic 1960s fantasies: his 1970s novels also extended concerns recorded in *Empire of the Sun*. In particular, they developed a troubled fascination with the powers of the machine, and with its increasingly deadly interaction with human beings.

New forms of intercourse between animate and inanimate were a central interest of *Crash* (1973)—another late twentieth-century investigation of the grotesque body, though of mangled car bodies along with human ones. Ballard's narrator is allured as well as appalled by 'a new sexuality born from a perverse technology . . . the perverse eroticism of the car-crash' (ch. 1). Throughout *Crash*, he shows machines forcing themselves, often literally, upon the humanity they were once supposed to serve, and on a landscape increasingly dominated by airports and motorways, while human beings are reduced to subordinate, mechanized roles. Similar concerns were examined in a more redemptive mode in *The Unlimited Dream Company* (1979), concentrating on 'inner space' and on visionary, utopian alternatives to a materialist, technologized society. The dreary, apathetic Thameside town the novel portrays is initially dominated by machines, but its 'shrines' of 'dishwashers and television sets' are in the end 'ornamented with sunflowers, gourds and nectarines' (ch. 1). As in Angela Carter's *The Infernal Desire Machines of Doctor Hoffman* (1972), 'impossible dreams' and fantastical forms of the natural world rush in to reanimate the town, under the supernatural influence of Ballard's narrator, Blake (ch. 29).

Like *Crash*, *The Unlimited Dream Company* suggested that fantasy could communicate contemporary stresses at least as compellingly as the realism employed in *Empire of the Sun*. Each novel disturbingly expanded responses to 'the transforming nature of science and technology', shaped more often in the period by anxiety or horror, rather than the imaginative excitement suggested in *The Child in Time*. Science fiction writers, and authors such as Aldiss and Ballard, owed much of their new freedom of imagination to this 'transforming nature'. It was nevertheless often used not to celebrate science or technology, but to criticize the responsibilities of each for the 'machine landscape', described in *Crash*, steadily gaining ground in the later twentieth century (ch. 5). At its end, Ballard's aptly named *Super-Cannes* (2000) showed this landscape still further dehumanized by 'the sanctity of the workstation and the pieties of the spreadsheet', and by 'the crime wave . . . called consumer capitalism' (chs. 1, 38). Like much of his later fiction, *Super-Cannes* offered a millennial warning that 'the whole world will soon be a business-park colony', and that 'everything is for sale now—even the human soul has a barcode' (chs. 37, 38).

Allusion to Blake in Ballard's fiction, and to Byron and Shelley, in Aldiss's, suggested that the period's 'unlimited dreams' could be seen as renewed, late Romantic celebrations of vision and imagination, and of antidotes they offered to a machine landscape and the barcoding of the soul. Dreams and fantasies could also be seen to extend contemporary, postmodern suspicions of reason, and of Enlightenment thinking generally: as discussed earlier, scepticism of this kind was often even clearer in genre fiction than elsewhere in the period's literature. In *Postmodernist Fiction* (1987), Brian McHale emphasized particularly 'close affinities' between postmodernism and science fiction and fantasy (p. 74). Postmodern distrust of language and representation, as well as reason, in one way simply encouraged authors and readers to abandon realism and everyday reality altogether. If the immediate world could no longer be rendered reliably in realistic writing, there were obviously added incentives to imagine alternative, fantastic worlds instead. Like science fiction, fantasy at any rate developed a particularly strong appeal for the later twentieth century. J. R. R. Tolkein's *Lord of the Rings* trilogy (1954–5) was one of the most popular novels, for adults and children alike, from the 1960s onwards, its influence reinforced by publication of *The Silmarillion* in 1977. Legendary, fantastic worlds appeared throughout Michael Moorcock's prolific writing; epic struggles and journeys in Richard Adams's *Watership Down* (1972); and a humorous, almost parodic version of Tolkein's interests in magic and sorcery in Terry Pratchett's popular 'Discworld' novels. Like Tolkein and Adams, Pratchett appealed to adults and children almost equally. His fiction regularly appeared in adult best-seller lists late in the century, alongside J. K Rowling's highly successful Harry Potter novels and stories by Roald Dahl. Their broad popularity not only indicated the growing appeal of fantasy during the period, but the erosion of another generic boundary in bookshops, which had previously tended to keep adult and children's fiction more firmly apart.

*

Earlier chapters discussed another way fantasy entered the period's literature—in forms of magic realism, originating in South America and following various routes to England—via India, in Salman Rushdie's case. As Malcolm Bradbury suggested, boundaries between cultures in the period grew as permeable as those separating genre fiction from other modes of literature. Many new influences from abroad, arriving in the work of immigrant writers, eventually added to those from the Continent, Ireland, Scotland, or the United States significant early in the period. Towards its end, the range of forms and influences shaping English fiction suggested a certain obsolescence in the metaphor of 'the novelist at the crossroads' David Lodge had coined in the early 1970s. Lodge implied as much himself when surveying the 'aesthetic supermarket' of contemporary fiction in 1991 (Bradbury and Cooke (eds.), p. 207). The volume of actual traffic in England, after all, had long since overwhelmed simple crossroads, requiring the construction of spaghetti junctions instead. Their complexity, and faintly foreign flavour, made them better metaphors for an era of more involved literary route-planning. Long-established main roads—of tradition and innovation, conservatism and modernism, realism and fantasy—remained discernible, but increasingly overlaid by new tracks and interchanges, leaving no single direction clearly dominant at the end of the century.

What this new diversity *did* clearly indicate was an imaginative potential either less visible earlier in the period, or at any rate underestimated by critics convinced at the time of the imminent death of the novel. Many of these commentators[10] had assumed that its well-being was fundamentally linked to liberal views of the individual, and of society, which seemed to be growing untenable, especially towards the end of the 1970s. Robert Hewison suggested that 'by 1975, the liberal world view, both inside and outside the novel, was at breaking point' (p. 256). Bernard Bergonzi likewise remarked in *The Situation of the Novel* in 1979 that 'the liberal and individualistic virtues so marvellously preserved and crystallised in the traditional novel are indeed in retreat' (p. 51). Yet English life in later years continued in many ways to become *more* liberal, continuing the gradual democratization and loosening of hierarchies evident since the 1960s. This 'disintegration of society in its traditional form', feared by Anthony Powell—even seen by others as marking 'the last of England'—in the end probably damaged only 'the

---

[10] See pp. 3–4 and 431–3, above.

traditional novel'. It did erode class demarcations which had continued to be useful in many 1950s, 1960s, and 1970s novels, providing
clear differentiations between characters, firm frameworks for their
interaction, and new perspectives based on what Ian McEwan
described in an essay as 'the internal exile of social mobility' (Leader
(ed.), p. 37). But commentators who nailed the novel's overall well-
being to the sinking vessel of 'society in its traditional form' underestimated its ability, as D. H. Lawrence might have said, to cut loose
and swim away with the nail. Threats to the 'individualistic virtues'
continued—as they had throughout the century—to provide the
novel with provocative subjects, rather than a death threat, in ways
discussed in this chapter and earlier ones. Any 'breaking point' in
1970s society, as Hewison recognized, had the effect of throwing
literature open to a greater range of voices and viewpoints—most
obviously where women and immigrant writers were concerned—
and to productive dialogue and combination between them.

Developments of this kind, of course, affected all areas of writing
in the period, drama and poetry as well as fiction, though contributing to a different pace of change in each. It was only in the later 1980s
and 1990s that English poetry finally seemed fairly free of the class-
marked constraints of the Movement and its legacies, and readier to
develop and profit from a fuller range of voices and styles. Dominic
Dromgoole's claim that 'democracy flowers into represented life
faster on the stage than in any other medium'[11] helps explain the particularly rapid progress of English drama, empowered throughout
the period by the expanding range of voices, dialects, and social
strata represented on the stage. Yet 'flowering' of this kind was probably just as crucial to the development of the novel—most diverse
and capacious of literary forms, and one whose constitution, not
necessarily privileging any single voice or vision, suggests an inherent
democracy. This possibility was explored by several commentators
on the period through the narrative theories of Mikhail Bakhtin.
Diverse cultural strata, voices, languages, and ways they 'interanimate each other' were emphasized by Bakhtin as fundamental to
the 'dialogic' constitution of the novel (*Dialogic Imagination*, p. 47).
This constitution he considered retraceable, by analogy at least,
to the carnivals of the middle ages: to their parodic, subversive

---

[11] See pp. 393–4, above.

performances and grotesquely physical energies, mocking as well as celebrating official culture.[12] Though energies of this kind are present more or less within any society, and within any novel, they may have been especially influential later in the twentieth century, as a legacy of the carnivalized decade of the 1960s, and within the 'pluri-culture' of English life in later years. Loosening hierarchies, new diversities and democracies of vision—as the century drew to its close—increasingly created the kind of interfusion of cultural and imaginative possibilities Bakhtin outlined, providing a context perhaps particularly congenial for fiction. At any rate, despite the great advances of drama, the novel more than sustained its dominant position within the literary field. In terms of public and critical attention, it outstripped poetry and the theatre even more completely, by the end of the century, than it had in 1960.

The potential of developments discussed above had nevertheless probably not been fully realized by 2000. In the 1970s, in *The Situation of the Novel*, Bergonzi recorded adverse comparisons regularly made between contemporary writing in England and in the United States. Any need for English literature to envy its transatlantic counterpart, diminishing by the end of the century, seemed likely to be further reduced as England moved closer to a multi-ethnic and relatively classless society longer envisaged across the Atlantic. Through the growing role of English as an international language, too, England had every chance of continuing to draw a widening range of styles and cultural perspectives into its literature, as it had so productively in the last two decades of the century. Salman Rushdie talked at its end of the emergence of 'a new novel . . . a post-colonial novel, a de-centred, transnational, inter-lingual, cross-cultural novel', and it seemed likely that literature in English generally, and not only fiction, might continue to evolve in this direction (*Step across This Line*, p. 57).

How far writing of this kind might be defined as 'English', in the sense of belonging to a single nation—even just to a land mass north of the Channel, south of the Tweed, and east of Offa's Dyke—is another question. 'Traditions slide over borders', Malcolm Bradbury suggested in 1996, and 'national cultures reach seamlessly one into another' (Brown (ed.), p. vii). Broadening forms of Bradbury's 'world

[12] See pp. 27–8 and 106–7, above.

pluri-culture' may leave future histories of 'English' literature less confident even than the present one about nationhood, or even just geographical area, as a basis for literary analysis. Though perplexing for critics—perhaps marking the last of a specifically English literary history—this openness and indeterminacy nevertheless appeared likely to remain productive for literary imagination itself, broadening still further the democratization of voice and vision so evident in the period just considered. The last of England? Perhaps some of the most interesting years, for writing around these parts, were still to come.

So at any rate it seemed in 2000, which proved in many ways as decisive an end point as 1960 had a beginning—not only in the millennial numbering of the years, but in terms of political and historical developments. Events within a few months of the year's end threatened a new age of suspicion and closure, one in which imagination might be more than ever necessary to override borders, cultural or political, once again hardening around the world.

Author Bibliographies

Studies relevant to the period as a whole, or to broad areas of it, are listed in Suggestions for Further Reading. The entries below note the principal works of authors successful in the period, and exemplary of its main developments. They also provide a biographical outline of each, and a brief bibliography of secondary reading. An asterisk indicates editions of primary texts quoted in earlier chapters: these are also listed in Works Cited. Dates for plays indicate first production rather than first publication.

ACKROYD, PETER (1949–)

Born in London, he grew up there, attending a Catholic school in Ealing. He went on to study at Cambridge University and as a postgraduate in the USA, at Yale. While there, he completed *Notes for a New Culture: An Essay on Modernism* (Vision, 1976), a study scathing of English conservatism and insularity, and enthusiastic instead for modernist legacies and for Continental approaches to literature. These preferences developed throughout his later fiction, and were immediately apparent in his 1970s poetry: later collected in *The Diversions of Purley and Other Poems* (Hamish Hamilton, 1987), it showed influences from J. H. Prynne and the US poet John Ashbery. On his return to London in 1973 Ackroyd worked as literary editor of the *Spectator*, then as its joint managing editor and film critic; in 1986, he became chief book reviewer of *The Times*. *The Great Fire of London* (1982), his first novel, described a contemporary film of Charles Dickens's *Little Dorrit* (1855–7), introducing his interests in the past and present life of London, in relations between the two, and in their reflection in art and writing. These interests were extended in *London: The Biography* (Chatto and Windus, 2000) and in later novels including *Hawksmoor* (1985), *The House of Doctor Dee* (1993), *Dan Leno and the Limehouse Golem* (1994), and *The Plato Papers* (1999). Other novels such as *The Last Testament of Oscar Wilde* (1983), *Chatterton* (1987), *First Light* (1989), and *English Music* (1992) were equally inventive in interweaving fictional and historical narrative, and in exploring new possibilities for imaginative vision—sinister or spiritual—lying somewhere between the two.

Ackroyd was also highly innovative in his approach to biography, challenging its conventional distinction from fiction and including invented conversations between author and characters in *Dickens* (1990), for example. *Ezra Pound and his World* (Thames and Hudson, 1980), *T. S. Eliot* (1984), *William Blake* (1995), and *The Life of Thomas More* (1998) further reshaped biography's conventions, adding to its growing popularity during this period. Ackroyd also published a study of transvestism, *Dressing Up* (Thames and Hudson, 1979), and *The Collection: Journalism, Reviews, Essays, Short Stories, Lectures* (Chatto and Windus, 2001). His novels were published until the 1990s by Hamish Hamilton, with Penguin and other paperback editions following, then by Sinclair-Stevenson, who also issued most of the biographies. Critical commentary includes sections in Alison Lee, *Realism and Power: Postmodern British Fiction* (1990) and in Steven Connor, *The English Novel in History: 1950–1995* (1996). Full-length studies include Susana Onega, *Metafiction and Myth in the Novels of Peter Ackroyd* (1999) and Jeremy Gibson and Julian Wolfreys, *Peter Ackroyd: The Ludic and Labyrinthine Text* (2000).

ADCOCK, FLEUR (1934–)

Born in Papakura, New Zealand, her mother a Northern Irish emigrant and her father a British-born psychology professor. She spent much of her childhood in England around the time of the Second World War, returning to New Zealand and studying classics at the University of Wellington, then lecturing briefly at the University of Otago before becoming a librarian. She moved permanently to England after her second marriage ended in 1963, continuing to work as a librarian before becoming a full-time writer and Arts Fellow in 1979. Her first volume of poems, *The Eye of the Hurricane*, was published in Wellington in 1964: the second, *Tigers* (1967), in Britain—like all her later collections, by Oxford University Press. Both New Zealand and British anthologists have claimed her ever since. Her *Selected Poems* (1983) drew on six previous collections, including *High Tide in the Garden* (1971) and *The Inner Harbour* (1979). Later volumes include *The Incident Book*, exploring autobiographical episodes, *Time-Zones* (1991), and *Looking Back* (1997). Much of this work developed her wish for an open, flexible poetry, directly recording immediate experience, relations between people, and between poet and language itself. Her objectivity and candour also reflected the vision of a partial outsider to English life.

Adcock translated work from medieval Latin, and from Romanian, several of her own poems originating in visits to East Europe in the 1980s. She also edited *The Oxford Book of Contemporary New Zealand Poetry* (OUP, 1982), *The Faber Book of Twentieth Century Women's Poetry* (1987), and, with Jacqueline Simms, *The Oxford Book of Creatures* (1995). A collected *Poems 1960–2000* was published by Bloodaxe in 2000. An interview with her appears in Robert Crawford, Henry Hart, David Kinloch, and Richard Price (eds.), *Talking Verse* (1995). Critical analyses include Julian Stannard's *Fleur Adcock in Context: From Movement to Martians* (1997) and sections in Gary Day and Brian Docherty (eds.), *British Poetry from the 1950s to the 1990s: Politics and Art* (1997), and in Sean O'Brien's *The Deregulated Muse* (1998).

Amis, Martin (1949–)

Born in Oxford, he spent his early years in Swansea, where his father Kingsley Amis remained a little-known university lecturer until the publication of *Lucky Jim* in 1953. Attendance at more than a dozen schools in Britain, Spain, and the USA followed, and a period acting in the film of *A High Wind in Jamaica*, before he reached Oxford University to study English, graduating in 1971. He worked in the early 1970s as an editorial assistant at the *Times Literary Supplement*, and later as its fiction and poetry editor, moving on in 1977 to the *New Statesman* and to full-time writing after 1980. Three novels appeared in the 1970s, satirizing the contemporary decline of 1960s idealism into hedonism and egotism: *The Rachel Papers* (1973), *Dead Babies* (1975), and *Success* (1978). *Other People: A Mystery Story* (1981) adopted a more complex, puzzling, narrative form. *Money: A Suicide Note* (1984) developed a racy, cynical, demotic narrative voice owed partly to US novelists Amis admired. Similar modes shaped *London Fields* (1989) and his pastiche of US detective fiction, *Night Train* (1997). Along with *Money* and *London Fields*, *The Information* (1995) completed a loose grouping of novels sometimes referred to as his 'London trilogy'.

With a famous father—though one sympathetic neither to his son's politics nor his writing—Amis was doomed to lifelong media attention, particularly directed on the end of his first marriage, his publishers' lucrative advances, his sacking of his agent, even on his excruciating dental problems. One of the period's best-known authors, he was also one of its most representative, exploring its materialism, cynicism, and apocalyptic dreads—also reflected in *Time's Arrow* (1991) and the short stories of *Einstein's Monsters* (1987)—through fictions whose moral challenges were sharply focused by his inventive narrative voice and tactics.

Experience (Jonathan Cape, 2000) gives a moving account of relations with his father and other family members. He also wrote essays, criticism, and journalism extensively, some of it collected in *The Moronic Inferno and Other Visits to America* (1986), *Visiting Mrs Nabokov and other Excursions* (1993), and *The War against Cliché: Essays and Reviews 1971–2000* (2001). Most of his work was published by Jonathan Cape, with *Penguin editions following. Critical considerations include James Diedrick's *Understanding Martin Amis* (1995) and sections in John Haffenden, *Novelists in Interview* (1985); Adam Mars-Jones, *Venus Envy* (1990); Rod Mengham (ed.), *An Introduction to Contemporary Fiction: International Writing in English since 1970* (1999); Stephen Baker, *The Fiction of Postmodernity* (2000); and Richard J. Lane, Rod Mengham, and Philip Tew (eds.), *Contemporary British Fiction* (2003).

ARDEN, JOHN (1930–)

Born in Barnsley, son of a factory manager, he attended school in Yorkshire. After National Service in the Intelligence Corps he studied architecture at Cambridge University and at Edinburgh College of Art, where his first play, *All Fall Down*, was produced by the drama society in 1955. He became a full-time author after working briefly in architecture, marrying the dramatist and performer Margaretta D'Arcy in 1957: many later plays were written in collaboration with her. Arden was one of the most innovative of writers emerging at the Royal Court in the late 1950s, plays such as *Live Like Pigs* (1958) and *Serjeant Musgrave's Dance* (1959) abandoning conventional realism in favour of broad, ballad-like styles, influenced by music hall and epic theatre. Equally innovative in form, later work with D'Arcy—such as *The Island of the Mighty* (1972), *The Ballygombeen Bequest* (1972), and *The Non-Stop Connolly Show* (1975) —was much more directly politicized. Firm convictions and unusual theatrical techniques sometimes led to conflict with directors and theatre managements. In the later 1970s, Arden recorded disillusion with the English theatrical establishment, and dramatists' lack of artistic control within it, and subsequent work was mostly produced in D'Arcy's native Ireland.

He also published several novels, including *Silence among the Weapons* (Methuen, 1982), and wrote scripts for television, such as *Soldier, Soldier* (1960), and regularly for the radio—notably in the series *Whose is the Kingdom* (1988), tracing the rise of Christianity and its political implications. His collected *Plays: One* was first published in 1977 by Eyre Methuen: the same publisher issued texts of many individual plays, and a new, fuller edition of *Plays: One*, along with *Plays: Two*, in 1994. Arden's own views of drama appear in *To Present the Pretence: Essays on the Theatre and its Public* (Eyre Methuen, 1977) and in another collaboration with D'Arcy, *Awkward Corners: Essays, Papers, Fragments* (Methuen, 1988). Critical studies include Albert Hunt's *Arden: A Study of his Plays* (1974); Frances Gray's *John Arden* (1982); Jonathan Wike (ed.), *John Arden and Margaretta D'Arcy: A Casebook* (1995); and Javed Malick, *Towards a Theatre of the Oppressed: The Dramaturgy of John Arden* (1995).

ARMITAGE, SIMON (1963–)

Born in Huddersfield, he studied geography at Portsmouth Polytechnic and worked with young offenders for a time before qualifying in social work at Manchester University: he was later employed as a probation officer in Oldham. Poetry collections include his popular debut *Zoom!* (Bloodaxe, 1989), *A Book of Matches* (Faber and Faber, 1993), *CloudCuckooLand* (Faber and Faber, 1997), and **The Universal Home Doctor* (Faber and Faber, 2002). *Selected Poems* and his first novel, *The Little Green Man*, were both published by Faber in 2001. He also worked extensively for radio and television, wrote four stage plays, and edited with Robert Crawford *The Penguin Book of Poetry from Britain and Ireland since 1945* (1998). *Moon Country* (Faber and Faber, 1996) was written with his friend Glyn Maxwell, describing a trip to Iceland, following W. H. Auden and Louis MacNeice's 1930s journey there. Like Maxwell, Armitage observed contemporary life acutely and wittily, exploring the diversifying dialects and idioms entwining popular culture, public life, and private languages in the 1980s and 1990s. He was also one of a new generation of male writers who began to reflect intimately on marriage, children, and family life. An interview with him appears in Robert Crawford, Henry Hart, David Kinloch, and Richard Price (eds.), *Talking Verse* (1995), and there are sections on his work in Sean O'Brien's *The Deregulated Muse* (1998) and David Kennedy's *New Relations: The Refashioning of British Poetry, 1980–1994* (1996).

AYCKBOURN, ALAN (1939–)

Born in London, his father the lead violin of the London Symphony Orchestra and his mother a journalist and author of stories for women's magazines; they divorced when he was 4, and she later married a bank manager. Ayckbourn developed an enthusiasm for theatre while at school in Hertfordshire, and went on to join Donald Wolfit's touring company in the mid-1950s, as an actor and assistant stage manager. He moved to Stephen Joseph's studio theatre in Scarborough in 1957, returning there—eventually, from 1970, as artistic director—in 1964, after working for two years with Peter Cheeseman in another theatre-in-the round, in Stoke-on-Trent. He also worked as a drama producer for BBC Radio in Leeds between 1964 and 1970. Early plays written under the pseudonym 'Roland Allen' were produced at Scarborough or Stoke: his farce *Relatively Speaking* (1967) set the pattern of numerous later commercial successes, opening in Scarborough and transferring to London's West End. Though his view of middle-class life and manners was generally comic or farcical, loneliness and bleakness were increasingly evident in plays such as *Woman in Mind* (1985) and *Henceforward* (1987). His staging also grew more complex, using simultaneous action or multiple, alternate endings in plays such as *Sisterly Feelings* (1979) and *Intimate Exchanges* (1982), and requiring the flooding of the stage of the National Theatre—famously and nearly disastrously—for his state-of-the-nation play *Way Upstream* in 1982. As well as his own work, he successfully directed productions of Arthur Miller and Anton Chekhov, among others, and provided lyrics for several musicals. He was knighted in 1997, remarrying in the same year.

His many plays had several publishers, including Faber and Faber, Longman, and Samuel French. Collections include *Three Plays* (Chatto & Windus, 1977), and *Plays: One* (Faber, 1995) and *Plays: Two* (Faber, 1998), which contains some of his drama for children. Paul Allen's biography, *Alan Ayckbourn: Grinning at the Edge* was published by Methuen in 2001, and critical studies include Michael Billington, *Alan Ayckbourn* (2nd edn., 1990); Bernard F. Dukore (ed.), *Alan Ayckbourn: A Casebook* (1991); and Albert E. Kalson, *Laughter in the Dark: The Plays of Alan Ayckbourn* (1993). Ayckbourn gives his own views in Ian Watson, *Conversations with Ayckbourn* (new edn., Faber, 1988).

BALLARD, J[AMES] G[RAHAM] (1930–)

Born in Shanghai, where his father managed a textile firm, he grew up and was interred there by the Japanese, with his parents, for three years during the Second World War. An influence throughout his writing, disturbing early experiences were reflected directly in his autobiographical novels *Empire of the Sun* (1984) and *The Kindness of Women* (1991), the former filmed in 1988 by Steven Spielberg, with a screenplay by Tom Stoppard. Ballard returned to England in 1946, studied medicine at Cambridge

University, then English at London University, and worked in advertising, for brief periods in each case, before marrying in 1954; his wife died suddenly, ten years later. Enrolment in the RAF in 1955 took him for a time to Canada, where he encountered North American science fiction: in 1956, he began publishing experimental short stories in *New Worlds* magazine, later edited by Michael Moorcock. Work in scientific journalism followed until the publication of his first novel in 1962. In *The Drowned World* (1962), *The Burning World* (reissued as *The Drought*, 1965), and *The Crystal World* (1966), Ballard followed the 1950s English science-fiction writer John Wyndham in depicting global disasters. In the 1970s, fantasies such as *The Atrocity Exhibition* (1970), **Crash* (Cape, 1973)—controversially filmed by David Cronenberg in 1996—*High-Rise* (1975), and **The Unlimited Dream Company* (1979; Panther, 1985) moved on to explore disturbing interfaces between humans and machines, the reifying threats of technology, and alternate possibilities offered by 'inner space'. Political satire, or allegory, figured in 1980s fiction such as *The Day of Creation* (1987) and *Running Wild* (1988). It developed further in later dystopias such as *Cocaine Nights* (1996) and **Super-Cannes* (Flamingo, 2000), in which Ballard used thriller formats to examine moral anaesthesia afflicting sophisticated, hyper-affluent societies. Significantly, his early fiction was first published in the United States: more than any of his English contemporaries, Ballard shared the anxieties of US novelists such as Thomas Pynchon about corporate capitalism, media powers, wrecked landscapes, reduced humanity, and galloping paranoia in a highly technologized machine age. Flat, mechanical prose, dispassionate narrators, and passive protagonists in his novels emphasized this age's new psychopathologies, sometimes even seeming to extend them.

Complete Short Stories (Flamingo, 2001) collected Ballard's extensive shorter fiction, and *A User's Guide to the Millennium* (HarperCollins, 1996) his essays and reviews. His novels had many different publishers, including Cape, Gollancz, and HarperCollins, with paperback versions following from Panther, Paladin, and Flamingo. Critical commentary includes Roger Luckhurst, *The Angle between Two Walls: The Fiction of J. G. Ballard* (1997) and Michel Delville, *J. G. Ballard* (1998).

BARKER, HOWARD (1946–)

Born in London, his mother a cashier and his father a printing-factory worker, he attended Battersea Grammar School and studied history at Sussex University. Various casual jobs led to increasing involvement in fringe theatre, and the production of a first play at the Royal Court in

1970; his second, *No One Was Saved*, was written in reaction to Edward Bond. Barker's work nevertheless resembled Bond's. It directed a dark, highly politicized vision over contemporary and historical life, presented in disturbing yet poetic language and action, sometimes more surreal even than Bond's. Unusual staging and painful emphases on struggle, lust, and treachery made this 'Theatre of Catastrophe', as Barker called it, less than congenial to established theatres, though it appealed strongly to theatre professionals. Members of the Leicester Haymarket and Sheffield Crucible companies combined in 1988 to form The Wrestling School, dedicated to production of his work, sometimes directed by Barker himself, often by Kenny Ireland.

Barker was an occasional librettist, and produced several collections of poetry. Individual plays were published by *John Calder, who also produced three volumes of *Collected Plays* (1990–6). Barker's views of drama appear in *Arguments for a Theatre* (3rd edn., Manchester University Press, 1997), and critical studies include David Ian Rabey's *Howard Barker: An Expository Study of his Poetry and Drama* (1989) and Charles Lamb's *Howard Barker's Theatre of Seduction* (1998).

BARKER, PAT (1943–)

Born Patricia Drake, near Middlesbrough. She never learned the true identity of her father, and spent her early life with her grandmother and her grandfather, who still bore the scars of a German bayonet attack in the First World War. After attending school locally, she studied international history at the London School of Economics, teaching history and politics until her two children were born in the early 1970s. She met her future husband, David Barker, in 1969: a zoologist, he was a source of her interest in the psychologist and anthropologist W. H. R. Rivers. He also encouraged her early interest in writing, further shaped by a course taught by Angela Carter in 1979. Her first novel, *Union Street*, an assemblage of interlinked narratives, followed in 1982, and *Blow Your House Down*, likewise examining the lives of Northern working-class women, in 1984. Her aptly named *The Century's Daughter* (1986) looked back across eighty years of history to the First World War, the subject of her celebrated *Regeneration* trilogy: *Regeneration* (1991), *The Eye in the Door* (1993), and *The Ghost Road*, winner of the Booker Prize in 1995.

Virago published her early novels, and *Viking/Penguin the *Regeneration* trilogy, which was filmed in 1997. Critical commentary includes Sharon Monteith, *Pat Barker* (2002) and sections in Ian A. Bell (ed.), *Peripheral Visions: Images of Nationhood in Contemporary British*

Fiction (1995); George Stade and Carol Howard (eds.), *British Writers* (suppl. IV, 1997); Alistair Davies and Alan Sinfield (eds.), *British Culture of the Postwar: An Introduction to Literature and Society, 1945–1999* (2000); and Richard J. Lane, Rod Mengham, and Philip Tew (eds.), *Contemporary British Fiction* (2003).

BOND, [THOMAS] EDWARD (1934–)

Born in London, where his parents had moved to escape the depression in East Anglia, he was evacuated back to his grandparents' house in East Anglia during the war, and to Cornwall. He attended school in London, leaving aged 15 for work in factories and offices, and was first attracted to the theatre by a Donald Wolfit production of *Macbeth* in 1948—though he had previously watched performances in the music hall, where his sister worked as a magician's assistant. He began writing during his National Service in the early 1950s: after submitting material to the English Stage Company, he was invited to join the writer's group at the Royal Court. His first play, *The Pope's Wedding*, set in East Anglia, was staged there in 1962; the violence of the second, *Saved*, generated still more controversy in 1965, eventually leading to the abolition of stage censorship two years later. After *Lear* (1971), the black comedy *The Sea* (1973), and the portrait of the poet John Clare in *The Fool* (1975), Bond moved on to stage plays such as *The Woman* (1978) at the National Theatre, which seemed to offer the resources his broad, complex, often-historical parables required. Later, he was more sceptical of the ethos of the National, though he continued to work with the RSC on *The War Plays* (1985), a trilogy warning of the risks of militarism and nuclear conflict. In most of this drama—the 'Rational Theatre', as he called it—Bond mingled extreme violence and shock with Brechtian techniques of staging, construction, and political emphasis. His work was in this way an important early influence on the development of political theatre in the 1970s, though among contemporary dramatists only Howard Barker matched the imaginative, darkly poetic forms of his staging.

Bond directed some of his own plays, and also wrote poetry, an opera libretto, the scenario for a ballet, *Orpheus* (1979), television plays, and a number of screenplays, including those for Nicholas Roeg's *Walkabout* (1971) and, collaboratively, Michelangelo Antonioni's *Blow-Up* (1967). Individual plays were published by *Eyre Methuen, who also produced a collected *Plays: One* and *Plays: Two* in 1977 and 1978; four further volumes followed by the end of the century. Ian Stuart edited two volumes of *Selections from the Notebooks of Edward Bond*, covering the periods

1959–80 and 1980–95 (Methuen, 2000 and 2001). Critical studies include Tony Coult, *The Plays of Edward Bond* (rev. edn., 1979); Malcolm Hay and Philip Roberts, *Bond: A Study of his Plays* (1980); David L. Hirst, *Edward Bond* (1985); and Jenny S. Spencer, *Dramatic Strategies in the Plays of Edward Bond* (1992). Some of Bond's own views, along with reviews of his plays, are collected in *Bond on File, compiled by Philip Roberts (Methuen, 1985).

BRENTON, HOWARD (1942–)

Born in Portsmouth, his mother a shop worker and his father a policeman who later became a Methodist minister and a director of amateur drama. Brenton wrote a first play, based on a comic-book character, at the age of 9, and went on to study English, rather reluctantly, at Cambridge University. After graduating he worked as a stage manager for various repertory companies, and in 1968 joined Brighton Combination, adapting Rabelais's *Gargantua* for the company. The Royal Court produced his first full-length play, *Revenge*, in 1969. At the same time he was beginning his collaborations with David Hare—later to include *Brassneck* (1973) and *Pravda* (1985)—working with him and other playwrights on Portable Theatre productions such as *Lay-By* (1971). This work was typical of shock tactics used by small, early 1970s touring companies to maximize political impact; another Portable production, *Fruit* (1970), demonstrated the manufacture of a petrol bomb, then supposedly thrown into the auditorium. Like many left-wing playwrights in the later 1970s, Brenton moved towards more reasoned political analysis, and from productions with touring companies or at the Royal Court—which staged other early plays such as *Magnificence* (1973)—to work with the main national companies. The RSC staged *The Churchill Play* in 1974; *Weapons of Happiness* (1976) and *The Romans in Britain* (1980), privately prosecuted for obscenity by Mary Whitehouse, appeared at the National Theatre. His drama remained typical of political theatre in the 1980s, in the disillusion with revolutionary possibilities shown in plays such as *Bloody Poetry* (1984) and *Greenland* (1988).

His work included numerous plays for television, adaptations of Brecht, such as *The Life of Galileo* (1980) for the National Theatre, and *Iranian Nights*, written with Tariq Ali in 1989 in support of Salman Rushdie. A novel, *Diving for Pearls*, appeared in 1989, and a volume of diaries, journalism, and essays, *Hot Irons*, in 1995, each published by Nick Hern. Individual plays were published by *Methuen, who also produced a collected *Plays: One (1986) and *Plays: Two* (1988). Critical studies include Richard Boon, *Brenton the Playwright* (1991); Ann Wilson (ed.), *Howard Brenton: A Casebook* (1992); and sections in John Bull's *New British Political Dramatists* (1984); Christopher Innes's *Modern British Drama 1890–1990* (1992); and Janelle Reinelt's *After Brecht: British Epic Theater* (1994).

BUNTING, BASIL (1900–1985)

Born at Scotswood, Newcastle-on-Tyne, his father a doctor and his mother the daughter of a local mine manager, he was educated at Quaker schools, and gaoled as a conscientious objector at the end of the First World War. Brief study at the London School of Economics was followed by work as a music critic, and by an itinerant life—in Paris, where he worked with Ford Madox Ford as an assistant editor on the *Transatlantic Review*, and in the USA, where he met William Carlos Williams and Louis Zukofsky. He also spent time in the Canary Islands, and in Italy, encountering W. B. Yeats and Ezra Pound in Rapallo. He married a literature student from the USA, Marian Gray Culver, in 1930; his first volume of poetry, *Redimiculum Matellarum*, was published privately in Milan in the same year. Pound strongly featured his work in his *Active Anthology* (Faber and Faber, 1933)—T. S. Eliot later rejected him as a Faber poet because he was too Poundian.

Bunting joined the RAF during the Second World War, and after a period at sea served in Persia (now Iran) as an interpreter. By 1945, he was British vice-consul in Isfahan, continuing to work in Persia in Intelligence and as a correspondent for *The Times*. In 1948 he married for a second time, to a 14-year-old Armenian, Sima Alladallian, with whom he had a son and a daughter. They returned to Northumberland in the early 1950s, and Bunting worked for twelve years as a sub-editor on the *Newcastle Chronicle*. A long period of poetic silence was broken in 1965 by *Loquitur*, and a year later by *Briggflatts*, each published by Fulcrum Press. Usually considered his masterpiece, *Briggflatts* revivified the influence of modernism for a generation of English poets late in the century, also highlighting the poetic potentials of the landscape and working life of the north of England.

Collected Poems was published by Fulcrum in 1968, with a new edition from *Oxford University Press in 1977. Richard Caddel edited *Uncollected Poems* in 1991, and the *Complete Poems* in 1994 (both OUP). Keith Alldritt's *The Poet as Spy: The Life and Wild Times of Basil Bunting* (1998) describes Bunting's eventful life, and critical studies include Victoria Ford's *The Poetry of Basil Bunting* (1991), Peter Makin's

Bunting: The Shaping of his Verse (1992), and *The Star You Steer By: Basil Bunting and British Modernism*, ed. James McGonigal and Richard Price (2000). Bunting's own views appear in Peter Makin (ed.), *Basil Bunting on Poetry* (Johns Hopkins University Press, 1999). Donald Davie's *Under Briggflatts: A History of Poetry in Great Britain 1960–1988* (1989) defines the central importance of his work for English poetry towards the end of the twentieth century.

BURGESS, ANTHONY [John Anthony Burgess Wilson] (1917–1993)

Born in Manchester into a staunchly Catholic, part-Irish family. His father was an amateur pianist and his mother a music-hall singer and dancer: she died when he was 2, a victim of the 'flu epidemic following the First World War. His ambition to study music at Manchester University was thwarted by a lack of entrance qualifications, and he became a student of English language and literature instead. After graduation in 1940, he worked in the Royal Army Medical Corps, and later the Education Corps in Gibraltar. He married Llewela Isherwood Jones in 1942; she was attacked in the street by US army deserters a year later, an episode reflected in the violence of *A *Clockwork Orange* (1962; Penguin, 1976). Burgess taught in schools and colleges after the war, then from 1954 as an education officer and teacher-trainer in Malaya and Borneo, a basis for his first published novels, the *Malayan Trilogy: Time for a Tiger* (1956), *The Enemy in the Blanket* (1958), and *Beds in the East* (1959).

Ill health, Burgess explained, drove him back to England at the end of the 1950s: suspecting a brain tumour, doctors gave him a year to live, and he began writing rapidly to secure future royalties for his wife. Five novels resulted, including the comic *Inside Mr Enderby* (1963): some were published under the pseudonym 'Joseph Kell' to deflect criticism of over-production. Reprieved by the doctors, Burgess outlived his wife—she died of alcoholic cirrhosis in 1968—and continued writing almost as prolifically. Over thirty novels resulted. Though their styles and interests ranged widely, *Earthly Powers (Hutchinson, 1980) was typical of concerns with good, evil, and moral responsibility which long outlasted their author's early renunciation of Catholic religion. Burgess married an Italian contessa, Liliana Macellari, in 1968: considering himself an outsider ever since his Catholic childhood, he lived his later years abroad, in Italy, Malta, and eventually Monaco.

He continued playing music throughout his life: his many compositions included *Blooms of Dublin*, a musical *Ulysses*, to mark James Joyce's centenary in 1982. He also wrote libretti, stage adaptations, children's literature, translations, verse, short stories, journalism, and two volumes of autobiography: *Little Wilson and Big God* and *You've Had your Time* (Heinemann, 1987 and 1991). As well as studies and editions of authors such as Joyce, his many critical works include *The Novel Now* (2nd edn., Faber and Faber, 1971) and *Ninety-Nine Novels: The Best in English since 1939* (Allison and Busby, 1984)—each a useful guide to the period's fiction. His novels were published mostly by Heinemann and Hutchinson, with Penguin and other paperback versions following. Critical commentary includes John J. Stinson's *Anthony Burgess Revisited* (1991) and sections in most general works on the period's English fiction. Other studies are listed in Paul Boytinck, *Anthony Burgess: An Annotated Bibliography and Reference Guide* (1985). Roger Lewis's speculative biography, *Anthony Burgess* (2002), cast doubt on several long-accepted versions of his life—such as his suspected brain tumour—challenging their bases in Burgess's own account of events.

Byatt, A[ntonia] S[usan] (1936–)

Born in Sheffield, the older sister of the novelist Margaret Drabble. Their mother was an English teacher, and their father a barrister, later a judge; both sisters attended a Quaker boarding school in York and went on to study English at Cambridge University. After a year of postgraduate work in the USA, Byatt began a PhD in Oxford University, continuing until her marriage in 1959. Teaching jobs in London followed and eventually, from 1972 to 1983, a lectureship in English at University College. Her first two novels, *Shadow of a Sun* (1964) and *The Game* (1967), were loosely autobiographical: the former examining conflicts of emotional, literary, and family life; the latter tracing intense relations with an ambitious sister. After more than a decade away from fiction—during which she remarried, and endured her son's death in a car accident—she included further *Bildungsroman* elements in *The Virgin in the Garden* (1978), the first part of a long-evolving tetralogy. Later volumes—*Still Life* (1986), *Babel Tower* (1996), and *A Whistling Woman* (2002)—continued to trace the experiences of members of a Northern family, much involved in art and intellectual life between the early 1950s and 1980, and in the new experiences of the 1960s in particular. Byatt achieved her greatest celebrity with *Possession: A Romance*, a Booker Prize winner in 1990. This used playful, parodic, postmodern modes to explore her recurrent interests in criticism and creativity, in Victorian and modern modes of writing, and in the often-conflictual engagement of women in intellectual life.

These interests reappeared in the novellas of *Angels and Insects* (1992)—one was filmed in 1995—and in *The Biographer's Tale* (2000).

Byatt published four volumes of short stories and worked extensively as a commentator and reviewer. She also produced critical studies of Wordsworth and Coleridge, and of Iris Murdoch, an influence on her own fiction. Other critical work included editions of George Eliot; introductions to fiction by Elizabeth Bowen, Willa Cather, and Grace Paley; and editorship of the *Oxford Book of English Short Stories* (1998). Selections of her essays appeared as *Passions of the Mind* (1991) and *On Histories and Stories* (2000): both were published by *Chatto and Windus, who also issued all her fiction, with Vintage paperback editions following. Critical commentary includes Kathleen Coyne Kelly, *A. S. Byatt* (1996); Celia M. Wallhead, *The Old, the New and the Metaphor: A Critical Study of the Novels of A. S. Byatt* (1999); and Christien Franken, *A. S. Byatt: Art, Authorship, Creativity* (2001).

CARTER, ANGELA (1940–1992)

Born Angela Stalker in Eastbourne, she was evacuated during the war to her resourceful maternal grandmother's home in Yorkshire. She went to school in South London, leaving to work as a journalist—like her Scottish father—on a local newspaper. She married Paul Carter in 1960, moving with him to Bristol: bored as a housewife, in the exuberant 1960s, she enrolled in the university there, studying medieval literature, psychology, and anthropology. Her first novel, the Gothic detective story *Shadow Dance* (1966), appeared a year after her graduation. *The Magic Toyshop* followed in 1967, setting the mood of dark, often violent fantasy and Freudian stress developed in much of her later fiction. *Several Perceptions* (1968) won the Somerset Maugham Award, funding a trip to Japan: she remained for three years, working in broadcasting and completing *The Infernal Desire Machines of Dr Hoffman* (1972; Penguin, 1982). She settled back in London in the mid-1970s, teaching creative writing in various universities and publishing much journalism and criticism—including the controversial feminist study *The Sadeian Woman* (Virago, 1979)—as well as her most admired novels, *The Passion of New Eve* (1977; Virago, 1985), *Nights at the Circus* (1984; Vintage, 1994), and *Wise Children* (1991). Her celebrated feminist reworking of Grimm fairy tales, *The Bloody Chamber* (1979), was filmed as *The Company of Wolves* in 1984. She remarried in 1991, to her partner of ten years, Mark Pearce. She was diagnosed with lung cancer in the same year, and died shortly afterwards. For a time in the 1990s, she was the English author most studied in British universities: her unconstrained narrative and imagination explored the period's shifting stresses on gender, sexuality, and physicality unusually compellingly, expanding the scope of English fiction and interesting many contemporary writers, as well as academics.

Carter also wrote poetry, children's stories, and radio plays, and edited and translated fairy tales. Journalism and other writing appears in *Nothing Sacred* (Virago, 1982), *Expletives Deleted* (Chatto and Windus, 1992), and *Shaking a Leg*, ed. Jenny Uglow (Chatto and Windus, 1997). Her early novels were issued by Heinemann, later ones by publishers including Chatto and Windus, Gollancz, Vintage, Virago, and Penguin. Extensive critical commentary includes Lorna Sage (ed.), *The Flesh and the Mirror: Essays on the Art of Angela Carter* (1994); Sarah Gamble, *Angela Carter: Writing from the Front Line* (1997); Aidan Day, *Angela Carter: The Rational Glass* (1998); Linden Peach, *Angela Carter* (1998); and Alison Easton (ed.), *Angela Carter* (2000).

CHATWIN, BRUCE (1940–1989)

Born in Sheffield. His father, later a lawyer, was regularly absent on service with the Royal Navy during the war years and a rootless childhood resulted, much of it spent with aunts in Stratford-upon-Avon, where he regularly attended Shakespeare productions. After a public school education, he was employed in 1958 by the auctioneers Sotheby's, initially as a porter and eventually, helped by a good eye for art, as director of impressionist painting: his novel *Utz* (1988) later explored the outlook and obsessions of art collectors. Marriage in 1965 followed, and a period at Edinburgh University studying archaeology, a long-standing interest. He began travelling more extensively in the late 1960s, and writing for *The Sunday Times* from 1972. A journalistic idea of following the footsteps of Butch Cassidy and the Sundance Kid led to **In Patagonia* (1977; Vintage, 1998); it contributed to a vogue for travel writing which expanded throughout the 1980s and later. It also established Chatwin's distinctively restrained style, reflecting his admiration for the short stories of Ernest Hemingway's *In Our Time* (1925). The minimal, dispassionate description and careful research of *In Patagonia* reappeared in his novels: in *The Viceroy of Ouidah* (1980), filmed by Werner Herzog as *Cobra Verde* (1988), and *On the Black Hill* (1982), as well as in *Utz*. Though a strong influence on contemporary travel writing, Chatwin disliked the term and the distinctions it implied: fictional and factual modes intermingled in his account of the Aborigine's mystic mapping of the Australian desert in *The Songlines* (1987).

Uncollected shorter writings appeared posthumously as *What am I Doing Here* (1989) and *Anatomy of Restlessness*, ed. Jan Borm and Matthew Graves (1996). The titles sum up a life devoted to travel—professionally, for Sotheby's, but even more widely in following the writer's own interests, which led him to Afghanistan, Russia, and China, as well as South America, West Africa, and Australia. David King and Francis Wyndham edited another posthumous volume, *Bruce Chatwin: Photographs and Notebooks* (1993): like all his writing, this was first published by *Jonathan Cape, with Picador and Vintage paperbacks following. Cape also published Susannah Clapp's *With Chatwin: Portrait of a Writer* (1997), and, in association with Harvill, Nicholas Shakespeare's biography, *Bruce Chatwin* (1997). Critical commentary includes Nicholas Murray, *Bruce Chatwin* (1993) and Patrick Meanor, *Bruce Chatwin* (1997). Chatwin's friend Salman Rushdie describes travelling with him in two essays in *Imaginary Homelands* (1991). Controversy surrounded his early death, assumed to have resulted from AIDS.

CHURCHILL, CARYL (1938–)

Born in London, her mother an actress and model, her father a political cartoonist. She moved to Canada with her family at the age of 10 and attended school in Montreal, returning in 1957 to study English at Oxford University, where her first play, *Downstairs*, received a student production the following year. She married in 1961 and had three children during the 1960s, continuing to write mostly for radio at the time. This work often used song and documentary material, and helped to develop unusual forms of dialogue—sometimes of simultaneous or overlapping speeches—which later figured in her stage plays. *Owners* was one of the first to receive a major production, at the Royal Court in 1972. But it was work later in the 1970s, with Joint Stock on *Light Shining in Buckinghamshire* (1976) and *Cloud Nine* (1979), and with Monstrous Regiment on *Vinegar Tom* (1976), which did most to develop her distinctive idiom. Churchill worried that the male-centredness of theatre made it overdependent on conflict and climax: the collaborative approach of Joint Stock and Monstrous Regiment introduced her to working methods allowing a more open-ended drama, fluid and provisional in its approach to character and gender role, in *Cloud Nine* especially. Her work typified in this way, and encouraged, the development of new forms to match the new gender politics of the 1970s and 1980s. *Top Girls* (1982) and *Serious Money* (1987) illustrated continuing commitments to socialism and to feminism, further extended in innovative plays in the 1990s such as *Mad Forest* (1990) and

The Skriker (1994). Ironically, in the case of the stock-market satire *Serious Money*, her work was often highly successful commercially, regularly produced in New York as well as London.

Individual plays had several different publishers. Methuen produced two collected volumes, **Plays: One* (1985) and **Plays: Two* (1990); like much of her later work, *Plays: Three* (1998) was published by Nick Hern. Critical studies include Geraldine Cousin, *Churchill the Playwright* (1989); Amelia Howe Kritzer, *The Plays of Caryl Churchill: Theatre of Empowerment* (1991); and sections in Christopher Innes's *Modern British Drama 1890–1990* (1992) and in Janelle Reinelt's *After Brecht: British Epic Theater* (1994).

D'AGUIAR, FRED (1960–)

Born in London, though his parents were from Guyana and he spent most of his childhood there, an experience reflected in early poetry collections, *Mama Dot* and *Airy Hall* (Chatto and Windus, 1985 and 1989). He returned to England in 1972, training as a psychiatric nurse before studying African and Caribbean literature at the University of Kent, later taking on a number of writing fellowships and moving to a professorship in the United States in 1994. Later poetry includes **British Subjects* (Bloodaxe, 1993), largely concerned with life in England, and the long narrative work *Bloodlines* (Chatto and Windus, 1992). His first novel, *The Longest Memory* (Chatto and Windus) won a Whitbread Prize in 1994: it was followed by *Dear Future* and *Feeding the Ghosts* (Chatto and Windus, 1996 and 1997). Two of his plays were produced in London: *High Life* (1987) and *A Jamaican Airman Foresees his Death* (1991). Much of this work was informed by provocative wit and highly articulate anger, directed on the outrages of imperialism—slavery in particular—and the continuing injustices of the post-colonial world. Like Caryl Phillips, d'Aguiar was typical in this way of black British writers emerging in the 1980s, helping to consolidate some of the new directions they established through his editorship of a section of *The New British Poetry 1968–1988* (Paladin, 1988). An essay on D'Aguiar and Phillips appears in Marc Delrez and Bénédicte Ledent (eds.), *The Contact and the Culmination* (1997).

DAVIE, DONALD (1922–1995)

Born in Barnsley, of Baptist parents, his mother a schoolteacher who was devoted to poetry, his father a shopkeeper. He attended school locally, and went on to study English at Cambridge, encountering the work of F. R.

Leavis—a lasting influence, though Davie's university life was interrupted by wartime service in the navy, including postings to Murmansk and Archangel. He married in 1945, completed a PhD in 1951, and lectured at Trinity College Dublin, and in Cambridge from 1958 until 1964, when he helped found the University of Essex, teaching there for four years. Thereafter he took up various professorships and visiting lectureships in the USA, becoming a permanent resident there until retirement to Devon in 1988.

His first volume of poetry, *A Winter Talent and Other Poems*, appeared in 1957: *The Shires* (Routledge and Kegan Paul, 1974) and *In the Stopping Train and Other Poems* (Carcanet, 1977) were among the best-received of many later collections. Davie was also an influential critic. His early studies *Purity of Diction in English Verse* (Chatto and Windus, 1952) and *Articulate Energy: An Inquiry into the Syntax of English Poetry* (Routledge and Kegan Paul, 1955) could be considered as manifestos for the Movement. He was usually assumed to be one of its leading members, but broadening interests later appeared in several studies of Ezra Pound, and in the increasingly eclectic sympathies of **The Poet in the Imaginary Museum: Essays of Two Decades* (Carcanet, 1977) and **Under Briggflatts: A History of Poetry in Great Britain 1960–1988* (Carcanet, 1989), as well as in his own poetry. Interests in Polish, Hungarian, and Russian writing—Boris Pasternak's in particular—resulted in numerous translations, adaptations, and edited volumes. Growing religious commitment appeared in his editorship of *The New Oxford Book of Christian Verse* (1981), and in his late collection *To Scorch or Freeze: Poems about the Sacred* (Carcanet, 1988).

Carcanet published *Selected Poems* in 1985, and the last of several editions of **Collected Poems*, edited by Neil Powell, in 2002. An autobiography, *These the Companions: Recollections*, was published in 1982 (Cambridge University Press), and Davie comments on his own technique in C. B. McCully (ed.), *The Poet's Voice and Craft* (Carcanet, 1994). Critical studies include a Donald Davie issue of the journal *Agenda* (Summer 1976) and George Dekker (ed.), *Donald Davie and the Responsibilities of Literature* (1983). Most general studies of the period's poetry comment on Davie, one of the most respected of poets to emerge from the Movement idiom. Its direct diction, formal constraint, and temperate vision were for Davie not only poetic preferences, but qualities he considered might contribute positively to the conduct and civic virtues of late twentieth-century life generally.

DRABBLE, MARGARET (1939–)

Born in Sheffield, the younger sister of the novelist A. S. Byatt. Their mother was an English teacher, and their father a barrister, later a judge; both sisters attended a Quaker boarding school in York and went on to study English at Cambridge University. Margaret Drabble married an actor, Clive Swift, the week she graduated, in 1960, and went on to act with him in the Royal Shakespeare Company in a number of walk-on and understudy roles. Her three children and her first three novels—*A Summer Bird-Cage* (1963), *The Garrick Year* (1964), and *The Millstone* (1965)—were all produced in the next five years. Following the success of *Jerusalem the Golden*, which won the James Tait Black Prize for 1967, she became a full-time writer, gradually moving on—through *The Needle's Eye* (1972) and *The Realms of Gold* (1975)—from early interests in determined, independent young women and their sexual or familial relations. *The Ice Age* (1977), *The Middle Ground* (1980), and the trilogy *The Radiant Way* (1987), *A Natural Curiosity* (1989), and *The Gates of Ivory* (1991) were broader 'condition of England' novels, exploring divisions of class and wealth, or between North and South. They nevertheless retained the traditional realist forms—sometimes strongly marked by an ironic narrative voice—employed in most of her fiction.

Drabble remarried in 1982, to the biographer Michael Holroyd, though they continued to live in separate houses. She acquired a reputation of her own as a critic and biographer with studies such as *Arnold Bennett* (Weidenfeld and Nicolson, 1974), *Angus Wilson* (Secker and Warburg, 1995), and her editorship of the *Oxford Companion to English Literature* (5th and 6th edns., Oxford University Press, 1985 and 2000). She also wrote short stories and screenplays, and very extensively as a journalist and commentator. Most of her novels were published by Weidenfeld and Nicolson, with *Penguin editions following. Critical studies include Lynn Veach Sadler, *Margaret Drabble* (1986) and Valerie Grosvenor Myer, *Margaret Drabble: A Reader's Guide* (1991). Others are listed in George Soule, *Four British Women Novelists: Anita Brookner, Margaret Drabble, Iris Murdoch, Barbara Pym—An Annotated and Critical Secondary Bibliography* (1998).

EDGAR, DAVID (1948–)

Born into a theatrical family in Birmingham: he first went to the theatre aged 4, wrote a biography of Shakespeare when he was 10, and acted and directed extensively at school and at Manchester University. After graduating with a BA in drama in 1969, he worked as a political journalist and occasionally an actor in Bradford—a base at the time for much fringe theatre, centred around directors such as Albert Hunt and Chris Parr. Companies involved included Welfare State, and eventually Edgar's own touring group, The General Will. His first professionally produced play, *Two Kinds of Angel*, was staged there in 1970, commissioned by Parr. Edgar became a full-time dramatist in 1972, briefly collaborating with Portable Theatre on *England's Ireland*, and taking up writing residencies at Leeds Polytechnic and at Birmingham Repertory Theatre. He also began lecturing on drama at Birmingham University, an involvement which led to a professorship in playwriting studies in the 1990s.

Edgar described early work for General Will, such as *The National Interest* (1971) and *State of Emergency* (1972), as straightforward agitprop. Though he continued working occasionally with radical groups such as 7:84 and Monstrous Regiment, in later writing such as *O Fair Jerusalem* (1975) for Birmingham Rep, and *Destiny* (RSC, 1976), he moved like several of his contemporaries towards the psychological and political complexity often demanded by established theatres. *Maydays* (1983) was typical of another, later development in left-wing drama— towards disillusionment and self-questioning in the 1980s. Edgar sometimes turned at this time to adaptations, including the commercially successful *Life and Adventures of Nicholas Nickleby* (1980), or to community projects such as *Entertaining Strangers* (1985), returning to earlier idioms in *The Shape of the Table* (1990) and *Pentecost* (1995), each examining recent history in East Europe.

He also wrote extensively for radio and television. Essays in **The Second Time as Farce: Reflections on the Drama of Mean Times* (Lawrence and Wishart, 1988) comment insightfully on theatre in the 1980s. Individual plays later in his career were published by Nick Hern; earlier, by Methuen, who also produced three collected editions, **Plays One* (1987), *Plays Two* (1990), and **Plays Three* (1991). Critical commentary includes Elizabeth Swain, *David Edgar, Playwright and Politician* (1986); Susan Painter, *Edgar: The Playwright* (1996); and a section in Christopher Innes's *Modern British Drama 1890–1990* (1992).

FEINSTEIN, ELAINE (1930–)

Born in Bootle, near Liverpool, into a family of Russian-Jewish origins. She attended school in Leicester, and was a student of English at the University of Cambridge, where she met Donald Davie. She went on to study law, and to work in publishing and as a journalist, marrying in 1956.

The first of many volumes of poetry, *In a Green Eye* (Goliard), appeared in 1966, and her first novel, *The Circle* (Hutchinson) in 1970. In this early phase, her work often explored issues of women's identity and independence, within or beyond the family, and her poetic style shared some affinities with modernist and later developments in the United States, Charles Olson's especially. Later poetry's intense emotion yet quiet communication showed more of the influence of Marina Tsvetayeva, also the subject of a biography, *A Captive Lion* (Hutchinson, 1987), and one of several writers whose work Feinstein translated. Like many of the period's Anglo-Jewish writers, she retraced in later fiction such as *The Survivors* (1982), *Mother's Girl* (1988), and *Loving Brecht* (1992) (all Hutchinson) the terrible impact of twentieth-century history on Jewish life and experience.

A wide-ranging career included work for television and radio, short stories, and further biographical studies, including *Lawrence's Women: The Intimate Life of D. H. Lawrence* (HarperCollins, 1993) and *Ted Hughes: The Life of a Poet* (Weidenfeld & Nicolson, 2001). Carcanet published her *Selected Poems* in 1994. Critical studies include essays in Peter Jones and Michael Schmidt (eds.), *British Poetry since 1970* (1980) and in Jay L. Halio (ed.), *Dictionary of Literary Biography*, 14. *British Novelists since 1960* (1983).

FOWLES, JOHN (1926–)

Born in Leigh-on-Sea, a town he described as depressingly respectable; brief wartime evacuation to rural Devon began affections for landscape and nature often reflected in his novels and non-fiction writing. Schooling near London was followed by training in the Royal Marines from 1945 to 1946, and a degree in French at Oxford University: his fiction showed influences from several French authors, particularly the existentialists popular after the war. After graduation, he taught briefly at the University of Poitiers, and at schools in England for much of the 1950s—though also, for eighteen months, on the Aegean island of Spetsai, the 'Phraxos' of *The Magus* (1966; rev. edn. 1977) and the place he met Elizabeth Whitton, whom he married in 1954. His first published novel was *The Collector* (1963), filmed in 1965; still greater popular success with *The Magus*, begun earlier, allowed him to write full time. It also helped him to acquire a permanent home in Lyme Regis, where he later became curator of the local museum and an author of local histories: Lyme figures as a background for much of *The French Lieutenant's Woman* (1969). Filmed in 1981, with a screenplay by Harold Pinter, the novel is typical of Fowles's interests in freedom, authenticity, relationships and their illusions, and in the imagination as a subject as well as the source of fiction. Later writing included the short stories of *The Ebony Tower* (1974), the semi-autobiographical *Daniel Martin* (1977), and *A Maggot* (1985). He considered his career as a novelist to have been ended by a stroke in 1988.

Fowles also wrote plays, introduced or translated several French texts, and published two volumes of poetry. *The Aristos: A Self-Portrait in Ideas* appeared in 1965, and *Wormholes: Essays and Occasional Writings* in 1998. Like most of his fiction, both were published by Jonathan Cape; paperback editions of his novels were issued by *Triad/Panther and Vintage. Critical commentary includes Bruce Woodcock, *Male Mythologies: John Fowles and Masculinity* (1984); Simon Loveday, *The Romances of John Fowles* (1985); Thomas C. Foster, *Understanding John Fowles* (1994); and James Acheson, *John Fowles* (1998). Other studies are listed in James R. Aubrey, *John Fowles: A Reference Companion* (1991).

GEMS, PAM (1925–)

Born Iris Pamela Price, in the south of England; her father died when she was 4, and she was brought up in difficult circumstances by her mother and grandmothers. She left school aged 15, worked in the Women's Royal Naval Service from 1944 to 1946, and went on to study psychology at Manchester University after the war, graduating in 1949 and marrying Keith Gems in the same year. Though she worked briefly as a BBC researcher in the early 1950s, marriage and family demands occupied much of the next twenty years: she had four children, one of whom, Jonathan Gems, also became a playwright and screenwriter. Her long-standing interests in drama developed more fully only in the early 1970s, when she began writing for Ed Berman's Almost Free Theatre, including a piece for its all-women season in 1973. Her first play for a mainstream theatre, *Queen Christina* (1977), was also the first by a contemporary woman playwright to be staged by the RSC. It was followed by other biographical treatments of women famous from history or the stage, including *Piaf* (1978), her adaptation of *Camille* (1984), and *The Blue Angel* (1991), examining the life of Marlene Dietrich. Many of her other plays—particularly *Dusa, Fish, Stas and Vi* (1976) and *Loving Women* (1984)—further demonstrated her conviction of society's need for new norms of behaviour and gender relations. These were also explored in 1990s drama including *Deborah's Daughter* (1995) and *Stanley* (1996), based on the life of the artist Stanley Spencer. She also wrote two novels, adaptations of Ibsen and Chekhov, and drama for television.

Later plays were published by Nick Hern; earlier ones by various

Author Bibliographies 545

publishers—Samuel French for *Dusa, Fish, Stas and Vi*. *Three Plays* (Penguin, 1985) contains *Piaf, Camille*, and *Loving Women*. Critical commentary includes sections in James Acheson (ed.), *British and Irish Drama since 1960* (1993); in William W. Demastes (ed.), *British Playwrights, 1956–1995* (1996); and in Elaine Aston and Janelle Reinelt (eds.), *The Cambridge Companion to Modern British Women Playwrights* (2000).

GOLDING, WILLIAM (1911–1993)

Born in Cornwall, he grew up in Wiltshire, living there for much of his later life. He attended a local grammar school, where his father was a teacher, and studied English at Oxford University, switching from natural sciences. He went into social work after graduation, also writing, producing, and acting in plays with several small theatres and publishing a book of poems in 1934. A teaching job in Salisbury was interrupted by five years of wartime service in the navy, eventually as a lieutenant in charge of a rocket ship. In spare hours during the war, he taught himself ancient Greek, adding to a childhood interest in ancient Egypt, reflected in the novellas of *The Scorpion God* (1971). He returned to teaching after the war, continuing until 1961; his first novel, *Lord of the Flies* (1954), was a success with critics and gradually accumulated a huge readership, guaranteeing lifelong financial security and allowing him to write full time. Later novels such as *The Inheritors* (1955) and *Free Fall* (1959) further explored his view—drawn from experience of the war—of *homo sapiens* as a fallen, inherently vicious species. Concerns with good and evil, and with relations between will, ambition, morality, and religion, extended into *Pincher Martin* (1956), *The Spire* (1964), *Darkness Visible* (1979), and the sea trilogy 'To the Ends of the Earth': *Rites of Passage*, which won the Booker Prize for 1980, *Close Quarters* (1987), and *Fire Down Below* (1989). Throughout his fiction, these concerns were sharply highlighted by shifting, unreliable narrative perspectives. Sustained, ingenious, moral vision made him one of the most admired English authors of a morally uncertain age. He was awarded the Nobel Prize in 1983 and knighted in 1988. A draft novel, *The Double Tongue*, appeared posthumously in 1995.

Golding also published a play, a journal of Egyptian travels, and two volumes of essays, *The Hot Gates and *A Moving Target* (Faber and Faber, 1965 and 1982). His novels were also published by *Faber, in hardback and paperback editions. Critical considerations include Mark Kinkead-Weekes and Ian Gregor, *William Golding: A Critical Study* (1984); Philip Redpath, *William Golding: A Structural Reading of his Fiction* (1986); Stephen J. Boyd, *The Novels of William Golding* (1990);

and Kevin McCarron, *The Coincidence of Opposites: William Golding's Later Fiction* (1995).

GREENE, [HENRY] GRAHAM (1904–1991)

Born in Berkhamsted, and educated there, in a school where his father was headmaster. Divisions of loyalty which resulted, Greene considered, later reappeared in the conflicting allegiances portrayed in his fiction. More immediately, they contributed to a troubled adolescence—he was one of the first schoolboys in England to be psychoanalysed, in 1920. He went on to study history at Oxford University, and then to work as a sub-editor on *The Times* from 1926 to 1930, and as film critic and literary editor for the *Spectator* from 1937 to 1941, experiences which added to the distinctive pace and conciseness of his novels. Most were filmed, particularly success-fully in the case of *The Third Man* (1950). Early historical interests were replaced in the 1930s by contemporary settings—usually English, and reflective of the left-wing politics of the time. Daring journeys described in his 1930s travel writing, along with work for MI6 in Sierra Leone during the Second World War, encouraged him to set much of his later fiction in distant locations, ones often riven by political or military conflict. He con-tinued travelling extensively in the 1950s, and lived abroad after the mid-1960s, mostly in Antibes.

Greene converted to Catholicism in 1926, in order to marry Vivien Dayrell-Browning: while political commitment to the Left remained unswerving throughout his career, interests in religious and in secular forms of transcendence alternated in his later writing. Religious concerns predominated around the time of the war, in *Brighton Rock* (1938), *The Power and the Glory* (1940), *The Heart of the Matter* (1948), and *The End of the Affair* (1951), but from the late 1950s his fiction was more often concerned with redemption through secular love, sometimes explored in comic or romance form. Though most admired for his tragic, religious phase, Greene remained strongly influential on novelists in later decades—not only in the thriller genres but also more widely—through his mixture of psychological intensity with exciting story; and of compelling, disillusioned realism with strong moral or political commitment.

As well as his two dozen novels, Greene produced children's fiction and two volumes of autobiography, *A Sort of Life* (1971; Penguin, 1977) and *Ways of Escape* (Bodley Head, 1980). His *Collected Essays* appeared in 1969 (Penguin, 1970), *Collected Plays* in 1985, and *Collected Short Stories* in 1986. His film criticism was collected as *Mornings in the Dark*, ed. David Parkinson (Carcanet, 1993), and his letters to the press, selected and introduced by Christopher Hawtree, as *Yours, etc* (Reinhardt, 1989). Initially, much of his writing was published by Heinemann; later, by Bodley Head, with *Penguin paperback editions following, and a set of Vintage reissues at the end of the century. Jonathan Cape began publishing Norman Sherry's three-volume biography in 1989. Extensive critical commentary includes Brian Thomas, *An Underground Fate: The Idiom of Romance in the Later Novels of Graham Greene* (1988); Maria Couto, *Graham Greene: On the Frontier—Politics and Religion in the Novels* (1988); Jeffrey Meyers (ed.), *Graham Greene: A Revaluation—New Essays* (1989); Cedric Watts, *A Preface to Greene* (1997); and Robert Hoskins, *Graham Greene: An Approach to the Novels* (1999).

HARE, DAVID (1947–)

Born in Sussex and educated at public school. He studied English at Cambridge University, graduating in 1968: in the same year he wrote and directed his first play, *Inside Out*, an adaptation of Kafka's diaries, and founded Portable Theatre with Tony Bicât. The company often relied on shock tactics to communicate political urgency: it involved a number of left-wing playwrights, including Howard Brenton, with whom Hare co-authored *Brassneck* (1973) and *Pravda* (1985). He co-founded another company, Joint Stock, in 1973, directing it from 1975 to 1980. Collaborative methods concretized this company's commitment to collectivist politics, particularly exemplified in its production of Hare's adaptation *Fanshen* (1975). Early plays with other companies—such as *Slag* (1970), *Knuckle* (1974), and *Teeth 'n' Smiles* (1975)—concentrated on amorality and mendacity in public life—broad political issues firmly focused around the experience of individuals, often strong women characters. This was particularly effective in *Plenty* (1978), less so in later condition-of-England plays such as the National Theatre trilogy *Racing Demon* (1990), *Murmuring Judges* (1991), and *The Absence of War* (1993). Hare explored England's post-war history as widely as any dramatist in the period, but the commitment which initiated this interest was gradually diffused by the breadth of landscapes in which it was explored, and by the growing moderation of the views offered of them.

Hare became an Associate Director at the National Theatre in 1984 and was knighted in 1998. He remarried in 1992, to the fashion designer Nicole Farhi. Many of his stage plays were televised: he also wrote and sometimes directed original scripts for television and film, and worked extensively as a director in the theatre—of plays by Trevor Griffiths, Howard Brenton, Christopher Hampton, and William Shakespeare, as well as his own. Most of his individual plays and scripts were published by *Faber and Faber, who also produced several collected editions: *The History Plays* (1984), *The Asian Plays* (1986), *The Early Plays* (1992), *Plays: One* (1996), and *Plays: Two* (1997). An account of the research for his National Theatre trilogy was published as *Asking Around*, ed. Lyn Haill (Faber/RNT, 1993). *Acting Up: A Diary* (Faber, 1999) reflected the trip to Israel and the Palestinian territories described in the theatrical monologue *Via Dolorosa*, which he performed in 1998. Critical studies include Hersh Zeifman (ed.), *David Hare: A Casebook* (1994); Carol Homden, *The Plays of David Hare* (1995); Finlay Donesky, *David Hare: Moral and Historical Perspectives* (1996); and Scott Fraser, *A Politic Theatre: The Drama of David Hare* (1996).

HARRISON, TONY (1937–)

Born in Leeds, the only son of a housewife and a bakery worker: their deaths in the 1970s strongly influenced his poetry. He won a scholarship to Leeds Grammar School and went on to Leeds University, studying classics and linguistics and publishing poetry in university magazines. He first married in 1960 and taught in the University of Zaria in northern Nigeria from 1962 to 1966, moving on to the Charles University in Prague and later visiting Cuba, Brazil, Senegal, and Gambia on a UNESCO fellowship. He won the Geoffrey Faber Memorial Prize with his first full-length collection, *The Loiners* (London Magazine Editions, 1970). He was soon equally successful in the theatre, as a translator and adapter, notably of *The Misanthrope* (1973), *The Oresteia* (1981), and *The Mysteries* (1985), each performed at the National Theatre, where he was resident dramatist from 1977 to 1979. He went on to produce several plays designed for specific sites, such as *The Trackers of Oxyrhyncus* (1988)—based on fragments of a satyr play—and *The Labourers of Heracles* (1995), performed in Delphi, and *Poetry or Bust* (1993), staged in a former wool-mill in Yorkshire.

Later poetry collections such as *Continuous: Fifty Sonnets from the School of Eloquence* (Rex Collings, 1981) sustained strongly dramatic, vernacular qualities, usually within conventional or classical forms of containment—part of Harrison's commitment to high art, but also to wide communication, and to poetry as public speech. His work encouraged English poetry's increasingly demotic voice late in the period, also reporting influentially—often in candidly autobiographical poems—on continuing frictions between classes, and between North and South. These interests coalesced most successfully in his long, highly political poem *v.* (Bloodaxe, 1985), shocking religious leaders and Tory politicians with its strong language when a version was broadcast by Channel Four television in 1987. Often writing for television or radio, or publishing his poems in newspapers, he continued to comment outspokenly in the 1990s on issues such as the fiftieth anniversary of the bombing of Hiroshima, the Gulf War, and the conflict in Bosnia, concerns reflected in *Laureate's Block and Other Occasional Poems* (Penguin, 2000).

Penguin published an edition of *Selected Poems* in 1984, and another in *1987, Bloodaxe following in 1995 with *Permanently Bard: Selected Poetry*, ed. Carol Rutter. Faber and Faber published four volumes of work for the stage (1999–2002). Critical assessments include Neil Astley (ed.), *Tony Harrison* (1991); Luke Spencer, *The Poetry of Tony Harrison* (1994); Sandie Byrne (ed.), *Tony Harrison: Loiner* (1997); and Sandie Byrne, *H, v. & O: The Poetry of Tony Harrison* (1998).

HILL, GEOFFREY (1932–)

Born in Bromsgrove, Worcestershire, the son of a policeman. After studying English at Oxford, he lectured at the University of Leeds from 1954 to 1980, then in Cambridge until 1988, when he remarried and moved to a professorship of literature and religion in the United States. His first full collection, *For the Unfallen: Poems 1952–1958*, was published by André Deutsch in 1959, winning the Eric Gregory Award. His reputation was consolidated by volumes including *King Log* (André Deutsch, 1968), the prose poems of *Mercian Hymns* (André Deutsch, 1971), *Tenebrae* (André Deutsch, 1978), *The Mystery of the Charity of Charles Péguy* (Agenda, 1983), and *Canaan* (Penguin, 1996). Minimal, enigmatic poetry in all these collections—humorous only occasionally—reflected fallen worlds, historical or contemporary, in which myth, religion, the English landscape, and language itself offer at most equivocal consolations.

Hill adapted Ibsen's *Brand* for the National Theatre in 1978 and published two volumes of literary commentary: *The Lords of Limit: Essays on Literature and Ideas* (Deutsch, 1984) and *The Enemy's Country: Words, Contexture, and Other Circumstances of Language* (Clarendon Press, 1991). A volume of *Collected Poems* was published by Penguin in 1985, and by Deutsch a year later. An insightful interview appears in John Haffenden, *Viewpoints: Poets in Conversation* (Faber and Faber, 1981). Critical studies include Peter Robinson (ed.), *Geoffrey Hill: Essays on His Work* (1985); Vincent Sherry, *The Uncommon Tongue: The Poetry and Criticism of Geoffrey Hill* (1987); E. M. Knottenbelt, *Passionate Intelligence: The Poetry of Geoffrey Hill* (1990); and W. S. Milne, *An Introduction to Geoffrey Hill* (1998).

HUGHES, TED (1930–98)

He was born in Mytholmroyd, a remote mill town in West Yorkshire where his parents ran a stationery and tobacco shop; his father was one of seventeen men, from a regiment of hundreds, to have survived the Gallipoli landings in the First World War. Hughes attended grammar school in Yorkshire and also completed his National Service there. He won a scholarship to Cambridge University, switching from English to study archaeology and anthropology, and reading W. B. Yeats and Old English literature in his spare time. He went on to various jobs as a gardener, nightwatchman, teacher, and zoo keeper. In 1956 he married the US writer Sylvia Plath: they spent two years in the United States, partly supported by a Guggenheim Fellowship, before returning to Cambridge, and had two children before separation and Plath's suicide in 1963. One of his lovers, Assia Wevill, committed suicide, with their child, in 1969. Hughes remarried in 1970 and eventually settled in Devon, as a farmer as well as a writer.

His second collection, *Lupercal* (1960), won the Hawthornden prize. Influential later volumes, published like all his work by Faber and Faber, included *Wodwo* (1967), *Crow* (1970), the long prose poem *Gaudete* (1977), *Moortown* (1979), and—part of his extensive work as a translator—*Tales From Ovid* (1997). He edited Plath's *Collected Poems* (Faber, 1981) and published the bestselling *Birthday Letters* (1998), a series of poems about his relationship with her, shortly before his death. Some of his work as Poet Laureate—he was appointed in 1984—appears in *Rain-Charm for the Duchy and Other Laureate Poems* (1992). He was also a regular adapter or translator of drama, and a prolific writer for children, of plays as well as poems, editing the popular anthology *The Rattle Bag* with Seamus Heaney in 1982. *Shakespeare and the Goddess of Complete Being* (1992) offers a comprehensive account of Shakespeare's imagination; other critical writing and essays are collected in *A Dancer to God: Tributes to T. S. Eliot* (1992), and *Winter Pollen: Occasional Prose* (1994). His *Collected Animal Poems* were published in four volumes in 1995, and *New Selected Poems 1957–1994* in the same year; a later selection by Simon Armitage appeared in 2000.

Mingling personal stress, mythopoeic imagination, a sense of the violence of twentieth-century history, and a disturbingly immediate vision of the natural world, Hughes was one of the most powerful poets in the period, and for many years the most successful adversary of constraints imposed on it by the Movement. His work attracted much attention from critics: their work is documented, along with the author's own output, in

Keith Sagar and Stephen Tabor, *Ted Hughes: A Bibliography, 1946–1995* (1998). Book-length studies include Nicholas Bishop, *Re-Making Poetry: Ted Hughes and a New Critical Psychology* (1991); Keith Sagar (ed.), *The Challenge of Ted Hughes* (1994); Paul Bentley, *The Poetry of Ted Hughes: Language, Illusion and Beyond* (1998); and Keith Sagar, *The Laughter of Foxes* (2000). Janet Malcolm's *The Silent Woman: Sylvia Plath and Ted Hughes* (1994) is one of several studies examining the period's most famously troubled literary relationship. Elaine Feinstein's biography, *Ted Hughes: The Life of a Poet* was published by Weidenfeld and Nicolson in 2001.

Ishiguro, Kazuo (1954–)

Born in Nagasaki, he moved to Britain, aged 5, when his father, an oceanographer, began work for the North Sea oilfields. He grew up in Guildford, continuing to speak and study Japanese at home, and learning English only, he explained, as a form of mimicry. School in Woking and failed ambitions as a rock musician were followed by travel in North America, and jobs including grouse-beating on the Queen Mother's Balmoral estate. He also spent time as a social worker before studying English and philosophy at the University of Kent, returning briefly to social work, with the homeless in London, until he was accepted for the creative writing course at the University of East Anglia. Tutored by Malcolm Bradbury and Angela Carter, he began publishing short stories; *A Pale View of Hills* followed in 1982, and *An Artist of the Floating World* in 1986, each centred largely on Japanese life. *The Remains of the Day* (1989)—a Booker Prize winner in 1989, filmed in 1993—moved on to an English context, and *The Unconsoled* (1995) to a more anonymous, Kafkaesque one. *When We Were Orphans* (2000) extended his use of obliquely self-revealing narrators, their memories highlighting both personal regret and its connections with wider historical forces they have endured.

Ishiguro became a British citizen in 1982, returning to Japan for the first time in 1989. Faber and Faber published his novels in hardback and paperback editions. Critical studies include Barry Lewis, *Kazuo Ishiguro* (2000); Cynthia F. Wong, *Kazuo Ishiguro* (2000); and sections in Steven Connor, *The English Novel in History 1950–1995* (1996) and in Richard J. Lane, Rod Mengham, and Philip Tew (eds.), *Contemporary British Fiction* (2003).

LARKIN, PHILIP (1922–1985)

Born in Coventry, the son of the city treasurer, he attended school there. He studied at Oxford University during the war, part of a generation including Kingsley Amis and John Wain: a medical examination exempted him from military service. He went on to work in university libraries in Leicester and in Belfast, becoming Head Librarian at the University of Hull in 1955 and remaining in this job for the rest of his life. His second collection, *The Less Deceived*, was published by Marvell Press in the same year and marked a change in his literary career. He had published more fiction than poetry in the late 1940s—the novels *Jill* and *A Girl in Winter* appearing in 1946 and 1947—while the poems of *The North Ship* (1945) reflected the influence of W. B. Yeats and W. H. Auden. Larkin recorded the importance, instead, of Thomas Hardy for his later writing, which was generally conversational in its language, everyday in its interests, and tidily conventional in its forms. A wry, usually dispirited tone expressed a disillusioned, weary mood in England, lasting long after the war, and made him a pivotal figure in the Movement emerging in the 1950s. Often considered the most successful poet in the early part of the period, he refused the Laureateship in 1984. A measure of his appeal was its slender basis. After *The Less Deceived*, only two further collections were published, both by Faber: *The Whitsun Weddings* in 1964, and *High Windows* a decade later. His reputation suffered after his death as a result of revelations about his private affairs, and of resentment, among critics and writers, of the conservatism and constraint Movement styles had continued to impose on English poetry later in the century. Yet along with its negative qualities his work had progressive aspects, especially in moving the period's poetry towards the use of everyday vernacular language.

He edited a controversial *Oxford Book of Twentieth-Century English Verse* (1973), favouring Hardy over the modernists, and produced a good deal of journalism, including jazz reviews for the *Daily Telegraph* from 1961 to 1971. Much of this appears in *Required Writing: Miscellaneous Pieces 1955–1982* (Faber, 1983); in *Further Requirements: Interviews, Broadcasts, Statements and Book Reviews*, ed. Anthony Thwaite (Faber, 2001); and in *Larkin's Jazz: Essays and Reviews 1940–84*, ed. Richard Palmer and John White (Continuum, 2001). Anthony Thwaite edited *Collected Poems (Marvell Press and Faber and Faber, 1988) and also *Selected Letters of Philip Larkin: 1940–1985* (Faber, 1992). Andrew Motion's *Philip Larkin: A Writer's Life* (1993) provides a full biography, and Blake Morrison's *The Movement* (1980) an account of his place among his contemporaries. Extensive commentary on Larkin includes

A. T. Tolley, *My Proper Ground: A Study of the Work of Philip Larkin and its Development* (1991); James Booth, *Philip Larkin: Writer* (1992); Stephen Regan (ed.), *Philip Larkin* (1997); and James Booth (ed.), *New Larkins for Old: Critical Essays* (2000).

LAVERY, BRYONY (1947–)

Born in Wakefield, she studied English at the University of London: her first play, *Of All Living*, was produced in 1967 while she was still a student there. Her work was typical of dramatists emerging in the later 1970s who used the stage to challenge and change gender expectations. She was involved early in her career with the pioneering women's company Monstrous Regiment, collaborating on their 1977 cabaret, *Floorshow*, with Caryl Churchill and Michelene Wandor, and continuing to work in the 1980s with Monstrous Regiment and with the Women's Theatre Group, who staged *Her Aching Heart* in 1990. Lavery considered her best work came towards the end of the century, after the death of her parents had forced a new seriousness on her writing. This phase included *Goliath* (1997), concerned with housing-estate riots in 1991; *Frozen* (1998), examining maternity and paedophilia; and *A Wedding Story* (2000), exploring marriage and the nature of love. She also wrote extensively for television, radio, and children's theatre, and worked as an artistic director for several alternative companies, including Gay Sweatshop.

Individual plays were published by Faber and Faber, and a collected *Plays: One* by Methuen in 1998. An interview is included in Lizbeth Goodman and Jane de Gay's *Feminist Stages: Interviews with Women in Contemporary British Theatre* (Harwood, 1996), along with an article by Lavery; another appears in Susan Todd (ed.), *Women and Theatre: Calling the Shots* (Faber and Faber, 1984).

LESSING, DORIS (1919–)

Born Doris Tayler in Kermanshah, Iran, where her father was working for the Imperial Bank of Persia. The family moved in 1924 to a maize farm in Rhodesia (now Zimbabwe). She was educated at a convent school in the capital, Salisbury, but left at 14, working as a nursemaid, writing and reading widely while on the farm, before returning to various jobs in the city. Marriage in 1939 produced two children who were left with their father after divorce in 1943. Drawn increasingly towards radical politics, Lessing met and married Gottfried Lessing, a German exile and Communist party activist—later, German ambassador to Uganda. Her autobiographical *In Pursuit of the English* (1960) describes how, after the break-up of that marriage, she moved to London with their son and the manuscript of her first published novel—several earlier ones had been destroyed—*The Grass is Singing* (1950). Its popular and critical success was consolidated by the *Children of Violence* quintet—its opening novel, *Martha Quest* (1952) continuing to reflect early experience in Rhodesia; the closing one, *The Four Gated City* (1969; Panther, 1972), moving towards an apocalyptic vision of Britain. Lessing's most influential novel—her formally inventive exploration of writer's block and break-down, *The Golden Notebook* (1962; Granada, 1976)—had meanwhile begun to shape and reflect the new women's consciousness of the early 1960s.

  Briefing for a Descent into Hell (1971; Granada 1982) and *The Summer before the Dark* (1973; Penguin, 1975) continued to explore psychological breakdown and 'inner space': the *Canopus in Argos* quintet (1979–83) developed outer-space settings and forms of science fiction in which, among other interests, the potentials of women could be more freely imagined. Later fiction such as *The Good Terrorist* (1985), *Love, Again* (1996), and novels written under the pseudonym 'Jane Somers' mostly returned to the realism of her early work. Political commitment and a rootless, unsettled life contributed to her alertness to late twentieth-century stresses, making her one of the most admired of the period's novelists, and one of the most wide-ranging. In particular, her fiction's themes and its formal innovations anticipated and strongly influenced narratives reflecting the new women's consciousness emerging in the 1960s.

  In a prolific career Lessing also published plays, many collections of short stories, and two volumes of autobiography: *Under my Skin*, covering the period up to 1949, and *Walking in the Shade, 1949–1962* (HarperCollins, 1994 and 1997). Her early writing was published by Michael Joseph and MacGibbon and Kee; later work by Jonathan Cape and HarperCollins, with paperback editions issued by Penguin, Granada, and Flamingo. Carole Klein's *Doris Lessing: A Biography* was published in 2000. Extensive critical study includes Lorna Sage, *Doris Lessing* (1983); Margaret Moan Rowe, *Doris Lessing* (1994); and Gayle Green, *Doris Lessing: The Poetics of Change* (1994).

LODGE, DAVID (1935–)

Born in London, his mother a Catholic of part-Irish background and his father a dance-band musician. As Lodge acknowledged, much of his fiction was autobiographical. *Out of the Shelter* (1970) reflected wartime childhood and evacuation; *The Picturegoers* (1960) a south London adolescence; *Ginger, You're Barmy* (1962) his National Service; and *The British Museum is Falling Down* (1965) the anxieties of an impoverished Catholic research student. After studying at the University of London, he was appointed in 1960 as a lecturer at the University of Birmingham, where he met Malcolm Bradbury, who collaborated with him on theatre revues and encouraged him to write comic fiction. From the mid-1960s, he enjoyed an increasingly successful academic career, travelling in 1964 and 1969 on fellowships to the United States—later, much more widely—and publishing critical studies including *The Language of Fiction* (1966), *The Novelist at the Crossroads* (1971), *The Modes of Modern Writing* (1977), and *Working with Structuralism* (1981). Some of this experience reappeared in the popular campus trilogy *Changing Places* (1975), *Small World* (1984), and *Nice Work* (1988). Like Bradbury's fiction, the trilogy reflected the more accessible role of universities in British life, and the excitement of new forms of literary understanding at work within them, showing a corresponding readiness to move beyond conventional realist styles. After his retirement in 1987, novels such as *Paradise News* (1991) and *Therapy* (1995) continued in a comic vein, but with a return to some of the Catholic themes of his early fiction.

Lodge also wrote for television, edited classic texts and anthologies of literary theory, and produced further works popularizing literary study and criticism such as *After Bakhtin* (1990) and *The Art of Fiction* (1992). Most of his critical writing was published by *Routledge and Kegan Paul, early novels by MacGibbon and Kee, and later ones by Secker and Warburg, with *Penguin editions following. Critical assessments include Robert Morace, *The Dialogic Novels of Malcolm Bradbury and David Lodge* (1989); Bruce K. Martin, *David Lodge* (1999); and sections in John Haffenden, *Novelists in Interview* (1985); Thomas Woodman, *Faithful Fictions: The Catholic Novel in British Literature* (1991); and James Acheson (ed.), *The British and Irish Novel since 1960* (1991).

McEWAN, IAN (1948–)

Born into a military family stationed at Aldershot, his father an NCO who had joined the army to escape the 1930s depression in Scotland. The family moved to Singapore and then Libya in McEwan's early childhood, and he later spent holidays from boarding school at army posts in Germany. He went on to study English at Sussex University, and was the first and briefly the only student to take the new creative writing course at the University of East Anglia. Idle periods, various jobs, and a bus trip to

Afghanistan followed, before the publication of his short-story collections *First Love, Last Rites* (1975) and *In Between the Sheets* (1978). Each was cool, elegant, and explicit in describing sensational, sometimes perverse sexuality. His first novels, *The Cement Garden* (1978) and **The Comfort of Strangers* (1981; Picador, 1983)—filmed with a screenplay by Harold Pinter—continued in the same vein. After his marriage in 1982 and the birth of his children, novels such as **The Child in Time* (Jonathan Cape, 1987), *The Innocent* (1990), **Black Dogs* (1992; Vintage, 1998), **Enduring Love* (Jonathan Cape, 1997), and *Atonement* (2001) showed new breadth and historical depth, along with extended concerns for family life and, often, contemporary politics. His novels were regularly short-listed for the Booker Prize, which he won with *Amsterdam* in 1998. He remarried the previous year.

McEwan also wrote children's fiction, an oratorio, and screenplays—including *The Ploughman's Lunch* (1983), and treatments of Timothy Mo's *Sour Sweet*, and of his own novel *The Innocent* (1990). His novels were published by Jonathan Cape, with Picador and Vintage paperback editions following. His account of early life and the origins of his feminist sympathies appears in 'Mother Tongue: A Memoir' in Zachary Leader (ed.), *On Modern British Fiction* (Oxford University Press, 2002). Critical commentary includes Kiernan Ryan, *Ian McEwan* (1994); Jack Slay, Jnr., *Ian McEwan* (Twayne, 1996); and sections in Adam Mars-Jones, *Venus Envy* (1990) and Rod Mengham (ed.), *An Introduction to Contemporary Fiction: International Writing in English since 1970* (1999).

McGOUGH, ROGER (1937–)

Born in Liverpool; his father was a docker, and his family of Irish origins. After studying French and Geography in the University of Hull, he taught in schools in Liverpool, lectured in the College of Art, and enjoyed brief stardom with the pop group The Scaffold. Intended primarily for performance, his poems were also popular when they appeared in print—along with work by the Liverpool poets Adrian Henri and Brian Patten—in the bestselling Penguin Modern Poets volume **The Mersey Sound* in 1967, and in *The Liverpool Scene*, ed. Edward Lucie-Smith (Carroll, 1967). He later collaborated with the same writers on a *New Volume* (Penguin, 1983). His many collections included *Watchwords* (Cape, 1969), *Gig* (Cape, 1973), *Waving at Trains* (Cape, 1982), *Defying Gravity* (Penguin, 1993), and *The Way Things Are* (Penguin, 1999). He wrote a number of plays—including an adaptation of *The Wind in the Willows*, seen on Broadway in 1995—and prolific poetry for children, also editing *The Kingfisher Book of Comic Verse* (1986). *Selected Poems 1967–1987* was published by Cape in 1989, and **Blazing Fruit: Selected Poems 1967–1987* by Penguin a year later. With the other Liverpool poets, he contributed to a new image for poetry in the 1960s and 1970s as a performance form, drawing on the excitement of pop and rock and relying on irreverent wit and verbal ingenuity to create immediate appeal.

McGrath, John (1935–2002)

Born in Birkenhead, into a family with strong Irish connections, he attended school in Wales. After National Service—reflected in *Events While Guarding the Bofors Gun* (1966)—he studied English at Oxford University, where he met Elizabeth MacLennan, his lifelong artistic partner: they married in 1962. A first play, *A Man has Two Fathers*, was produced in 1958 while he was still a student. After university, he worked briefly for the Royal Court and more extensively in television, initiating in the early 1960s—with Troy Kennedy Martin—the *Z-Cars* series, introducing social concerns into popular, exciting stories of police work. Like many of his contemporaries, McGrath was politicized more deeply by the *événements* of May 1968, which he witnessed for himself in Paris. A period at the Liverpool Everyman followed, working on productions—such as *Soft or a Girl* (1971)—which combined popular entertainment with a strong social and political message. This combination was further developed with 7:84, the touring company he founded with Elizabeth MacLennan in 1971, its name reflecting ownership, revealed in contemporary statistics, of 84 per cent of the nation's wealth by only 7 per cent of the population. The company performed in unconventional venues throughout the country, McGrath working prolifically for both its English and Scottish branches throughout the 1970s and beyond. He wrote more than sixty plays during his career, and directed even more widely. The greatest successes of 7:84 came in Scotland, particularly with *The Cheviot, the Stag and the Black, Black Oil* (1973). But McGrath was also highly influential in English theatre, as practitioner and theorist, extending the legacies of Joan Littlewood—more distantly, of Brecht—into flexible, committed modes of performance for the later twentieth century. Like John Arden, he remained a revolutionary in vision as well as form, demonstrating even in the disillusioned 1980s both the need for social change and its perennial possibility. He worked almost as extensively in film, as a producer, director, and author of several screenplays.

Individual plays were published by Methuen and by Pluto Press. His views of theatre appear in **A Good Night Out: Popular Theatre—*

Audience, Class and Form (Eyre Methuen, 1981), *The Bone Won't Break: On Theatre and Hope in Hard Times* (Methuen, 1990), and **Naked Thoughts That Roam About: Reflections on Theatre 1958–2001*, ed. Nadine Holdsworth (Nick Hern, 2002). Catherine Itzin discusses his drama in *Stages in the Revolution: Political Theatre in Britain since 1968* (1980), and Janelle Reinelt in *After Brecht: British Epic Theater* (1994). Accounts of his work with 7:84 appear in Elizabeth MacLennan's *The Moon Belongs to Everyone* (1990) and Maria diCenzo's *The Politics of Alternative Theatre in Britain 1968–1990* (1996).

MAXWELL, GLYN (1962–)

Born in Welwyn Garden City, of Welsh parents, he studied English at Oxford University, later winning a scholarship to Boston University, where he joined a creative writing programme. His successful debut collection, **Tale of the Mayor's Son* (Bloodaxe, 1990) was followed by volumes such as *Out of the Rain* (Bloodaxe, 1992) and *The Breakage* (Faber and Faber, 1998). He also published several verse plays and two novels, *Blue Burneau* (Chatto and Windus, 1994), and the verse narrative *Time's Fool* (Picador, 2001).

The *Boys at Twilight: Poems 1990–1995* was published by Bloodaxe in 2000, and *Gnyss the Magnificent* (Chatto and Windus, 1993) collects three of his plays in one volume. An interview appears in Robert Crawford, Henry Hart, David Kinloch, and Richard Price (eds.), *Talking Verse* (1995), and critical commentary in Sean O'Brien's *The Deregulated Muse* (1998) and David Kennedy's *New Relations: The Refashioning of British Poetry, 1980–1994* (1996). Like his friend Simon Armitage, with whom he published *Moon Country* (Faber and Faber, 1996), Maxwell was one of the most accomplished of the 'New Generation' of poets emerging in the 1990s: conversational in tone, yet complex and witty in the range of forms, personae, and perspectives employed in surveying contemporary life.

MIDDLETON, [JOHN] CHRISTOPHER (1926–)

Born in Truro, Cornwall, he went to school in Essex and studied German and French at Oxford University. He served in the RAF from 1944 to 1948 and lectured at the Universities of Zurich and London before emigrating to the United States in 1966, remaining until his retirement professor of Germanic Languages and Literature at the University of Texas. Though he had published earlier, Middleton considered his first significant collection *Torse 3: Poems 1949–1961* (Longman, 1962). Subsequent volumes include *Our Flowers and Nice Bones* (Fulcrum, 1969), *The Lonely Suppers of W. V. Balloon* (1975)—published like all his later work by Carcanet—*Carminalenia* (1980), and **Intimate Chronicles* (1996). A volume of **Selected Writings* was published by Paladin in 1989, and his literary essays are collected in *Bolshevism in Art and Other Expository Writings* (1978), **The Pursuit of the Kingfisher* (Carcanet, 1983), and *Jackdaw Jiving: Selected Essays on Poetry and Translation* (1998). He worked extensively as a translator or editor of German writing—of material ranging from Nietzsche's and Kafka's letters and von Hofmannsthal's verse drama to Goethe's poetry and stories by Gert Hofmann, father of the English poet Michael Hofmann. His intellectual interests ensured that Middleton remained unusually open, among English poets in the period, to innovative influences both from European modernism, and from modernist and postmodernist developments in the United States. Each contributed to his poetry's attempt to confront and contain the darker stresses of twentieth-century history. His work is analysed in Neil Corcoran's *English Poetry since 1940* (1993) and in Ian Gregson, *Contemporary Poetry and Postmodernism: Dialogue and Estrangement* (1996).

Mo, Timothy (1950–)

Born in Kowloon, Hong Kong, the son of a Cantonese lawyer and an English mother: when she remarried in 1960, he moved with her to London, attending school there and going on to study history at Oxford University. After graduating he worked for diverse publications including *Times Education Supplement*, the *New Statesman*, and *Boxing News*: boxing and scuba diving remained interests in later life, and journalism a focus for *An Insular Possession* (1986), surveying the early colonial years of Hong Kong. Dark domestic comedy shaped earlier novels: *The Monkey King* (1978), set in Hong Kong, and *Sour Sweet* (1982)—filmed in 1987 with a screenplay by Ian McEwan—in a Chinese restaurant in London. A bleaker vision appeared in *The Redundancy of Courage* (1991), tracing military struggles against Indonesian annexation in East Timor. *Brownout on Breadfruit Boulevard* (1995) and *Renegade, or Halo²* (1999) each examined characters displaced by economic or political forces, moving into a multi-voiced, multi-perspectival, multi-locational mode satirizing the renewed, late twentieth-century imperialism of multinational capital. An acute analyst of empire and its aftermath, international in vision and interests, Mo returned to living abroad himself, mostly in Hong Kong, in the late 1990s.

Early novels were issued by André Deutsch and by Chatto and Windus. Disillusioned by conglomerate publishers, Mo established his own imprint, Paddleless Press, to produce *Brownout on Breadfruit Boulevard* and *Renegade, or Halo²*, and to reissue earlier fiction. Critical commentary includes Elaine Yee Lin Ho, *Timothy Mo* (2000), and a section in Steven Connor, *The English Novel in History: 1950–1995* (1996).

MURDOCH, [JEAN] IRIS (1919–1999)

Born in Dublin, of Anglo-Irish parents. Her father was a civil servant, and her mother an amateur singer: they moved to London with her while she was still a baby. She attended public school in Bristol, studied classics and philosophy at Oxford University—joining the Labour Club and acting in *The Winter's Tale*—and was employed as a wartime civil servant for two years after graduation. Work for the United Nations Relief and Rehabilitation Administration followed from 1944 to 1946: periods in London, Belgium, and Austria—reflected in *The Flight from the Enchanter* (1956)—sharply exposed her to suffering the war had caused. She met Jean-Paul Sartre at this time—later writing the first English study of his work, *Sartre: Romantic Rationalist* (1953)—and also the author Raymond Queneau, dedicatee of her first published novel, *Under the Net* (1954). She went on to study as a philosophy postgraduate in Cambridge in 1947, meeting Ludwig Wittgenstein. The following year, she was appointed to a philosophy fellowship in Oxford, marrying John Bayley, eventually professor of literature there, in 1956, and teaching until she became a full-time writer in 1963. Her 1950s novels largely renounced contemporary interests in class and society, favouring profounder engagements with morality and ideas. These interests were sustained throughout the prolific fiction that followed. Much of it offered a kind of moralized existentialism, seeking authenticity and goodness in personal experience, relationships, and connections between art and life—issues presented in characteristic amalgams of realist style and extravagant, romantic plot. She won the Booker Prize for *The Sea, the Sea* (Chatto and Windus) in 1979, and was made a Dame of the British Empire in 1987; Alzheimer's disease, described in John Bayley's *Iris: A Memoir* (1998)—filmed in 2001—increasingly overtook her in the next decade.

Her fiction was published by Chatto and Windus. Novels including *A Fairly Honourable Defeat* (1970) were reissued by Penguin (1984); others such as *A Severed Head* by Triad/Panther (1984). A set of Vintage reissues followed in the late 1990s. Several philosophical works followed her study of Sartre: *Metaphysics as a Guide to Morals* (Chatto and

Windus, 1992) summed up her interests even in its title, and *Existentialists and Mystics: Writings on Philosophy and Literature* (Chatto and Windus, 1997) collected her many articles. Peter Conradi published a biography, *Iris Murdoch: A Life* in 2001, along with a reissue of his critical assessment, *The Saint and the Artist: A Study of the Fiction of Iris Murdoch.* Other critical commentary includes A. S. Byatt, *Degrees of Freedom: The Early Novels of Iris Murdoch* (rev. edn., 1994), and Barbara Stevens Heusel, *Patterned Aimlessness: Iris Murdoch's Novels of the 1970s and 1980s* (1995). Many other studies are listed in John Fletcher and Cheryl Bove, *Iris Murdoch: A Descriptive Primary and Annotated Secondary Bibliography* (1994).

NAIPAUL, V[IDIADHAR] S[URAJPRASAD] (1932–)

Born in Chaguanas, Trinidad, into a family of Indian Brahmin origin: his father was a journalist and writer, and his brother Shiva also became a novelist. He attended school in Port of Spain, winning a scholarship to study English at Oxford University: after graduation in 1954 he became a freelance writer, working for BBC radio's *Caribbean Voices* series, and as a fiction reviewer for the *New Statesman*. Satire of Trinidadian life shaped his early fiction—*The Mystic Masseur* (1957), *The Suffrage of Elvira* (1958), *Miguel Street* (1959), *The Mimic Men* (1967), and the outstanding *A House for Mr Biswas* (1961). Encouraged by a grant from the Trinidadian government in 1961, he began to travel widely, initially in the Caribbean, later in India, Uganda, Pakistan, the USA, and elsewhere. Later novels such as **In a Free State* (André Deutsch, 1971), set in the USA, Africa, and England, and *A Bend in the River* (1979), examining African dictatorship, were likewise wide-ranging, often exploring the isolation of immigrants or exiles. Much of his work at this time was non-fiction or travel writing, titles such as *An Area of Darkness* (1964), or *India: A Wounded Civilization* (1977) typifying dismissive judgements for which he was often criticized. A more generous attitude, to India at any rate, appeared in *India: A Million Mutinies Now* (1990). As he explained, fiction, travel writing, and autobiography were integrally connected throughout his work: in all its modes, this explored the global rootlessness of post-imperial experience, often with a self-concerned interest—typically in **The Enigma of Arrival* (Penguin, 1987)—in its implications for artistic intellect. Exacting examination of such issues, and the precise prose in which it was sustained, were rewarded with the Nobel Prize in 2001; he was knighted in 1989.

In addition to studies of India, his travel writing includes two unsympathetic accounts of Islamic society, *Among the Believers* (1981), and *Beyond Belief* (1998). Views of the Caribbean appear in *The Middle Passage: Impressions of Five Societies* (1962) and *The Loss of El Dorado* (1969). Essays were collected in three volumes: *The Overcrowded Barracoon* (1972), *The Return of Eva Peron* (1980), and *The Writer and the World* (2002). Gillon Aitken edited his revealing *Letters between a Father and Son* (Little, Brown, 1999). Most of his writing was published by André Deutsch, with Penguin and other paperback editions following, and a full set of Picador reissues at the end of the century. Critical studies include Peter Hughes, *V. S. Naipaul* (1988); Rob Nixon, *London Calling: V. S. Naipaul, Postcolonial Mandarin* (1992); Bruce King, *V. S. Naipaul* (1993); Judith Levy, *V. S. Naipaul: Displacement and Autobiography* (1995); and Fawzia Mustafa, *V. S. Naipaul* (1995).

NICHOLS, PETER (1927–)

Born in Bristol, the son of a salesman, and educated there. He returned to Bristol Old Vic theatre school after serving in the RAF from 1945 to 1948—an experience later reflected in his musical play *Privates on Parade* (1977). He worked as an actor and teacher throughout the 1950s, writing television drama extensively at the end of the decade. Success in the theatre followed in 1967 with *A Day in the Death of Joe Egg* (1967), a partly autobiographical play about strategies parents invent to deal with their severely handicapped child. Later plays such as *The National Health* (1969), **The Freeway* (1974, Faber and Faber, 1975), *Poppy* (1982), and **A Piece of my Mind* (Methuen, 1987) continued to examine serious issues in broadly accessible, entertaining forms. Another strand of his work, exploring the more private difficulties of marriage and family life, appeared in *Forget-Me-Not Lane* (1971), *Chez Nous* (1974), and *Passion Play* (1981). In moving from television to the stage, Nichols followed a direction contrary to many of his contemporaries, though he later recorded frustration that the theatre never completely fulfilled the promise of greater artistic freedom that had first attracted him to it. Radical potentials in his drama, political and imaginative, remained constrained by the demands of commercial production.

Nichols wrote several screenplays and published an autobiography, *Feeling You're Behind* (Weidenfeld and Nicolson, 1984) and a volume of *Diaries 1969–1977* (Nick Hern, 2000). Individual plays were published by Faber and Faber and by Methuen, who also produced collected editions: *Plays: One* (1987; rev. 1991) and *Plays: Two* (1991). Critical commentary includes sections in James Acheson (ed.), *British and Irish Drama since 1960* (1993) and in William W. Demastes (ed.), *British Playwrights, 1956–1995* (1996) and Andrew Parkin's *File on Nichols* (1993).

O'Brien, Sean (1952–)

Born in London but grew up in Hull and studied at the Universities of Cambridge, Hull, Birmingham, and Leeds, where he qualified as a teacher. He taught in schools during the 1980s, moving on to work as a creative writing fellow in Dundee, Leeds, Durham, and Newcastle, as a broadcaster and literary journalist, and as writer-in-residence at Live Theatre, Newcastle, where his political verse drama *Laughter When We're Dead* was produced in 2000. Poetry collections include *The Frighteners* (Bloodaxe, 1987), **HMS Glasshouse* (Oxford University Press, 1991), **Downriver* (Picador, 2001), and *Cousin Coat: Selected Poems 1976– 2001* (Picador, 2002). He edited **The Firebox: Poetry in Britain and Ireland after 1945* for Picador in 1998, publishing in the same year a wide-ranging study of contemporary British and Irish poetry, **The Deregulated Muse* (Bloodaxe). A judicious critic of contemporary poets, O'Brien was more explicitly politicized than most of them in his own writing, acutely analysing England's recent history and its current phase of social and industrial decline. An interview with him appears in Robert Crawford, Henry Hart, David Kinloch, and Richard Price (eds.), *Talking Verse* (1995).

Orton, Joe (1933–1967)

Born in Leicester, his mother a factory machinist and his father a council gardener. He was hindered by ill health at school, and by his own reluctance with courses of vocational training which followed. But two years after his stage debut—as a messenger in an amateur *Richard III* in 1949— he won a scholarship to the Royal Academy of Music and Drama, where he met his lifelong partner Kenneth Halliwell, seven years his senior and a mentor for his writing career. Along with several unpublished novels, such as *The Last Days of Sodom* (1955), their collaborations included the insertion of obscene pictures and marginalia into public library books, for which they were gaoled for six months in 1962. From prison, Orton sent the BBC a reworking of another collaboration with Halliwell: the verse satire *The Boy Hairdresser*, re-entitled *The Ruffian on the Stair*. It was broadcast on BBC radio in 1964. His stage play *Entertaining Mr Sloane* transferred to the West End in the same year. Though supported by Terence Rattigan, it provoked fierce moral controversy in the newspapers, joined disapprovingly by Orton himself under the pseudonym 'Edna Welthorpe (Mrs.)'. The success of *Loot* (1966) and work on a screenplay for the Beatles added to the rapid growth of Orton's fame, and of Halliwell's jealousy. He killed his lover with a hammer in August 1967 before committing suicide himself. Orton's black farce *What the Butler Saw* was first produced two years later, then more successfully under Lindsay Anderson's direction at the Royal Court in 1975.

Many artistic and social influences intersected in Orton's career. His plays showed some debts to Absurdism and Harold Pinter; to an English farce tradition reaching from Ben Travers to N. F. Simpson; to the gay wit of Ronald Firbank and Oscar Wilde—even to Restoration comedy and the Jacobean city drama of Ben Jonson. Above all, Orton's life and writing shared in the rapid mid-1960s unravelling of hierarchies, moralities, sexual conventions, and respect for institutions, hastening the demise of theatre censorship a few years later, and adding new excitement and topicality to the contemporary stage.

Methuen published individual plays, and in 1976 * *The Complete Plays*, ed. John Lahr. The same editor assembled *The Orton Diaries: Including the Correspondence of Edna Welthorpe and Others* (Methuen, 1986). Lahr also published a biography—the anagrammatically entitled *Prick Up Your Ears* (Allen Lane, 1978), soon filmed with a screenplay by Alan Bennett. Nick Hern issued a novel in 1998, and in 1999 *The Boy Hairdresser*, along with another of Orton's collaborations with Halliwell. Critical assessments include Maurice Charney, *Joe Orton* (1984); Simon Shepherd, *Because We're Queers: The Life and Crimes of Kenneth Halliwell and Joe Orton* (1989); and sections in most of the general studies listed in Suggestions for Further Reading, pp. 584–5, below.

OSBORNE, JOHN (1929–1994)

Born in London, the son of a barmaid and a commercial artist, he attended a minor public school in Devon. He was a journalist on trade papers from 1947 to 1948 before touring with various companies as an actor and stage manager, often working in small venues such as Ilfracombe and Kidderminster. He began acting with the English Stage Company at the Royal Court in the spring of 1956, continuing to perform there, and occasionally on film and television, in the late 1950s. The ESC produced his first major play, *Look Back in Anger*, in May 1956. Catching the restless mood of the bland mid-1950s, and restoring the stage's potential for social criticism, *Look Back in Anger* quickly established the reputation of the Royal Court, as well as Osborne's own. This was consolidated by *The Entertainer* in

1957, with Laurence Olivier in the lead, and by plays such as *Luther* (1961) and *Inadmissible Evidence* (1964), also with strong central roles, played by Albert Finney and Nicol Williamson respectively. Later work continued to narrow its focus around the private feelings and disaffections of individuals, and Osborne repudiated wider criticisms of the establishment he had made outside the theatre, in the late 1950s, as well as within it. The excitement of his drama declined partly as a result: after the poor reception of *Watch it Come Down* in 1976, he wrote little for the stage until *Déjàvu* (1992), a return to the idiom of *Look Back in Anger*, but now in firmly illiberal mode.

He wrote several adaptations for the stage, and extensively for television and film, including screenplays for his own drama, and for *Tom Jones* (1963). Two volumes of autobiography—*A Better Class of Person* and *Almost a Gentleman* (Faber and Faber, 1981 and 1991)—reflect, often bitterly, on a changeful life, including five marriages: the novelist Penelope Gilliatt was his wife from 1963 to 1968. *Faber and Faber published individual plays, three volumes of collected plays (1996–8), and a volume of essays, *Damn You, England* (1994). John Russell Taylor's *Anger and After: A Guide to the New British Drama* (2nd edn., 1969) records Osborne's initial impact. Later criticism includes Arnold P. Hinchliffe, *John Osborne* (1984); Patricia D. Denison, *John Osborne: A Casebook* (1997); and Luc M. Gilleman, *John Osborne: Vituperative Artist—A Reading of his Life and Work* (2002).

PAGE, LOUISE (1955–)

Born in London, she grew up and attended school in Sheffield, showing an early interest in writing. She studied theatre and drama at Birmingham University, where she worked with David Edgar, and as a postgraduate at the University of Wales in Cardiff in 1977: her first plays, *Want-Ad* and *Glasshouse* were produced that year. She returned to Sheffield as a university creative writing fellow from 1979 to 1981, later working as writer-in-residence at the Royal Court. *Salonika* was produced there in 1982, reversing romantic expectations usually attached to youth and age; later plays such as *Real Estate* (1984) and *Golden Girls* (1984) likewise challenged audiences with new views of gender roles and conventions, and with a more disillusioned view of feminism's progress in *Diplomatic Wives* (1989). She also wrote drama for children, and for radio and television. Methuen published individual plays, and a collected *Plays: One* in 1990. Critical commentary includes sections in William W. Demastes (ed.), *British Playwrights, 1956–1995* (1996) and in Trevor R. Griffiths and Margaret Llewellyn-Jones (eds.), *British and Irish Women Dramatists since 1958* (1993). An interview appeared in Lizbeth Goodman and Jane de Gay's *Feminist Stages: Interviews with Women in Contemporary British Theatre* (1996).

Phillips, Caryl (1958–)

Born on the Caribbean island of St Kitts, migrating with his family to Leeds a few months later. He attended school there and in Birmingham— at a time when racial prejudice was particularly fuelled by Enoch Powell's speeches—and went on to study English at Oxford University, working extensively in student drama and founding the *Observer* Oxford Festival in 1978. *Strange Fruit*, his first play, was produced by the Sheffield Crucible in 1980. It was followed in London by *Where There is Darkness* (1982), likewise dealing with immigrant experience, and *The Shelter* (1983). He also wrote several radio, television, and film scripts at this time. A brief return to St. Kitts, on the brink of independence in 1983, contributed to his first novels: *The Final Passage* (1985), examining 1950s life in the Caribbean and in London, and *A State of Independence* (1986). Complex narratives in later novels such as *Higher Ground* (1989), *Cambridge* (1991), *Crossing the River* (1993), and *The Nature of Blood* (1997) examined slavery, African diaspora, and their legacies in terms of temporal as well as geographic dislocation; historical as well as social and cultural disorientation. All this material influentially fulfilled his ambition—inspired by reading Richard Wright's *Native Son* (1940) and Ralph Ellison's *Invisible Man* (1952) during a student holiday in the USA—to resist the exclusion of black experience from literature in England.

The exclusions of English life were further examined in his collection of essays by various immigrant writers, *Extravagant Strangers: A Literature of Belonging* (Faber and Faber, 1997). His own essays in *The European Tribe* (Faber, 1987) record a continental respite from Thatcher's Britain in the mid-1980s, and in **A New World Order* (Secker and Warburg, 2001) the mid-Atlantic identity and influences he experienced when visiting the Caribbean and West Africa, taking up writing fellowships and eventually a professorship in the USA, and dividing his time between London and New York in the later 1990s. He also edited *The Right Set: The Faber Book of Tennis* (Faber, 1999) and wrote the screenplay for V. S. Naipaul's *The Mystic Masseur* (2002). Publishers including Faber, Bloomsbury, and Viking issued his novels in hardback, with *Picador paperbacks usually following. Critical studies include Bénédicte Ledent, *Caryl Phillips* (2002) and sections in Marc Delrez and Bénédicte Ledent (eds.), *The Contact and* *the Culmination* (1997) and Richard J. Lane, Rod Mengham, and Philip Tew (eds.), *Contemporary British Fiction* (2003).

PINTER, HAROLD (1930–)

Born in east London, the son of a tailor. He was evacuated several times, but witnessed much of the Blitz in London, returning permanently in 1944 and winning a scholarship to Hackney Downs Grammar School. He acted Macbeth and Romeo in school productions, also reading James Joyce at this time, and beginning a lifelong affection for cricket. Kafka, Hemingway, and Beckett were among other early literary interests eventually influential on his plays. As a conscientious objector he avoided National Service—though risking imprisonment—and studied at the Royal Academy of Dramatic Art, briefly and reluctantly, before moving on in 1949 to repertory acting with various companies: Anew McMaster's in Ireland; Donald Wolfit's, for a time. Pinter directed his first short play, *The Room*, for Bristol University in 1957. *The Birthday Party* followed a year later, slated by critics on its transfer from Cambridge to London. His reputation nevertheless grew steadily: by 1960, with *The Birthday Party* and *A Night Out* televised, *The Room* and *The Dumb Waiter* at Hampstead and *The Caretaker* also a London success, Pinter was launched on the most successful career of any English dramatist in the period—one which developed several further phases. Mysterious action, sinister language, and covert power-struggles established a 'Pinteresque' idiom in the plays mentioned, and in *The Homecoming* (1964). This gave way to more lyrical reflection on memory and identity in *Landscape* (1967), *Silence* (1968), *Old Times* (1970), and *Betrayal* (1978). Exasperated by Thatcherism and world politics, Pinter emerged in the 1980s as a regular commentator on public affairs, sometimes alongside his second wife, the biographer Lady Antonia Fraser. This phase of political commitment was loosely reflected in short plays such as *One for the Road* (1984), *Mountain Language* (1988), and *Ashes to Ashes* (1996). **Moonlight* (Faber and Faber, 1993) returned, perhaps ironically, closer to earlier idioms.

Pinter continued as an occasional actor on film, stage, and television, and a regular director in the theatre—of most of the plays of Simon Gray, for example—and as an associate director of the National Theatre from 1973 to 1983. He was one of the most successful of screenwriters in the period—of over twenty filmscripts, including *The Servant* (1963), *Accident* (1967), *The Go-Between* (1971), *The French Lieutenant's Woman* (1981), *The Comfort of Strangers* (1990), and *The Remains of the Day* (1991). Faber and Faber issued three volumes of *Collected*

Screenplays in 2000; along with Methuen, they also published most of his individual plays. Four volumes of collected *Plays* were published by *Methuen in the late 1970s and early 1980s, and another four—much expanded—by Faber in the 1990s; *Collected Poems and Prose* was issued by Methuen in 1986. Faber published Michael Billington's *The Life and Work of Harold Pinter* in 1996, and the author's own views in *Various Voices: Poetry, Prose, Politics 1948–1998* (1998). Challenging and original, Pinter's work encouraged very extensive critical analysis. Useful studies, representative of developing views of his writing, include Austin E. Quigley, *The Pinter Problem* (1975); Alan Bold (ed.), *Harold Pinter: You Never Heard Such Silence* (1984); Elizabeth Sakellaridou, *Pinter's Female Portraits* (1988); Martin Esslin, *Pinter the Playwright* (5th edn., 1992); Peter Raby (ed.), *The Cambridge Companion to Harold Pinter* (2001); and Steven H. Gale (ed.), *The Films of Harold Pinter* (2001). The author's award-winning website at http://www.haroldpinter.org offers a useful introduction.

PORTER, PETER (1929–)

Born in Brisbane, he experienced an isolated childhood there, his mother dying when he was 9. He worked as a journalist before emigrating to London in 1951, in pursuit of early ambitions as a poet. He was employed as a bookseller and for ten years in advertising before becoming a full-time writer, broadcaster, and literary journalist in 1968, later holding various writing fellowships in Britain and Australia. He married Janice Henry in 1961 and they had two daughters before her early death in 1974: elegies for her appear in *The Cost of Seriousness* (1978), published like all his later poetry by Oxford University Press. His first collection, *Once Bitten, Twice Bitten* (Scorpion Press, 1961) contained poems written since the mid-1950s, some influenced by membership of the Group. His many later collections include *The Last of England* (1970), *Living in a Calm Country* (1975), *Fast Forward* (1984), *The Automatic Oracle* (1987), *Possible Worlds* (1989), and *Millennial Fables* (1994). These collections were less directly satiric than his early work, offering instead complex, witty analyses of relations between life and art, and of the strengths and limits of aesthetic forms in dealing with the distress, personal or historical, of modern life. Such interests helped to make Porter one of the most formally various English poets since W. H. Auden. He was also a prolific editor: of numerous Aurum Press editions of classic authors such as John Donne, Thomas Hardy, and William Blake; and of collections including *The Faber Book of Modern Verse* (4th edn., 1982) and *The Oxford Book of Modern*

Australian Verse (1996). His *Collected Poems* first appeared in 1983, with a new edition, *Collected Poems 1961–1999*, in 1999, both published by OUP. Critical studies include Bruce Bennett's *Spirit in Exile: Peter Porter and his Poetry* (1991) and Peter Steele's *Peter Porter* (1992).

PRYNNE, J[EREMY] H[ALVARD] (1936–)

Born in Kent, his mother the head of a private school, his father an engineer. He attended school in London and studied English at Cambridge University. After National Service and a year in Harvard he became a fellow in English and a librarian in Gonville and Caius College, Cambridge, remaining there until the end of the century, lecturing regularly on the language of poetry and on the work of the Black Mountain poets. His first volume, *Force of Circumstance and Other Poems*, was published by Routledge in 1962: thereafter, he mostly relied on small or private presses, perhaps in order to resist appropriation by commercial forces often critiqued in his poems. Later collections include *Kitchen Poems* (Cape Goliard, 1968), *The White Stones* (Grosseteste Press, 1969), *Down Where Changed* (Ferry Press, 1979), and *Her Weasels Wild Returning* (Equipage, 1994). Cryptically intellectual and arcane, his poems played on extreme horizons of understanding—often, though alluringly, beyond them. His work influenced poets sometimes described as the 'Cambridge School', reaching a wider audience only with the publication of his collected *Poems* (Bloodaxe, 1999). Critical studies of his importance for the period's poetry, in its postmodernist phases particularly, include sections in Veronica Forrest-Thomson, *Poetic Artifice: A Theory of Twentieth-Century Poetry* (1978); in James Acheson and Romana Huk (eds.), *Contemporary British Poetry: Essays in Theory and Criticism* (1996); and in Anthony Easthope and John O. Thompson (eds.), *Contemporary Poetry Meets Modern Theory* (1991). Fuller studies are offered by N. H. Reeve and Richard Kerridge's *Nearly Too Much: The Poetry of J. H. Prynne* (1995), and Birgitta Johansson, *The Engineering of Being: An Ontological Approach to J. H. Prynne* (1997). Prynne offers a useful insight into his interests in *Stars, Tigers and the Shape of Words: The William Matthews Lectures 1992* (Birkbeck College, 1993).

READING, PETER (1946–)

Born and attended school in Liverpool, and studied fine art and painting at Liverpool College of Art. He was briefly a schoolteacher in Liverpool, then returned to the College of Art as a lecturer in art history from 1968 to 1970.

Thereafter he worked as a labourer and weighbridge operator in the animal feed industry in Shropshire until sacked in 1992, amidst much publicity, for refusing to wear his uniform correctly. His poetry was also a centre of controversy in 1984, when 'Cub', published in *Times Literary Supplement*, drew accusations of anti-Semitism. He followed his first full collection, *For the Municipality's Elderly* (Secker and Warburg, 1974), with many others, including *Tom o'Bedlam's Beauties* (1981), *C* (1984), *Perduta Gente* (1989)—all published by Secker and Warburg—*Evagatory* (Chatto and Windus, 1992), and *Work in Regress* (Bloodaxe, 1997). Describing terminal cancer in one hundred prose sections, each of one hundred words, *C* was typical of the extreme, self-conscious formalism which shaped Reading's dire vision of contemporary life—one which mingled bleak disdain with a kind of fascinated relish, continuing to attract controversy throughout his career. *Essential Reading* (Secker and Warburg, 1986) offered an early selection: Bloodaxe published *Collected Poems 1970–1984* in 1995, and a second volume, *Collected Poems 1985–1996*, in the following year. Critical studies include Isabel Martin's *Reading Peter Reading* (2000) and sections in Gary Day and Brian Docherty (eds.), *British Poetry from the 1950s to the 1990s: Politics and Art* (1997), in Sean O'Brien's *The Deregulated Muse* (1998), and in David Kennedy's *New Relations: the Refashioning of British Poetry, 1980–1994* (1996).

REDGROVE, PETER (1932–2003)

Born in Kingston, Surrey, his father an advertising copywriter, he attended school in Somerset, and studied natural sciences at Cambridge University, where he began an acquaintance with Ted Hughes. After a traumatic period of National Service, when he was thought to be incipiently schizophrenic, he was employed in advertising and as a scientific researcher, journalist, and editor during the 1950s. He went on to work as an author-in-residence at Leeds University from 1962 to 1965, and at Falmouth School of Art in Cornwall from 1966 to 1983, also taking up several other writing fellowships. His second marriage was to the poet and novelist Penelope Shuttle, with whom he wrote a novel and two studies examining menstruation and the taboos surrounding it. Associated with the Group in the late 1950s, he published his first volume of poems, *The Collector*, with Routledge and Kegan Paul in 1960. Numerous later collections include *Dr Faust's Sea-Spiral Spirit* (Routledge, 1972), *The Weddings at Nether Powers* (Routledge and Kegan Paul, 1979), *The Apple-Broadcast* (Routledge, 1981), *In the Hall of the Saurians* (Secker and Warburg, 1987), and *My Father's Trapdoors* (Cape, 1994).

He was almost as prolific as a dramatist, for radio and television as well as the stage, and published several novels. His study *The Black Goddess and the Unseen Real: Our Unconscious Senses and their Uncommon Sense* (Grove Press, 1987) suggested in its title the interests of poetry which traced powerful animacies in the natural world and their resonances with the human psyche. Like Ted Hughes's, his work reconfigured, for the later twentieth century, nature poetry and the benign relations between mind and world on which it had conventionally depended. *Sons of My Skin: Redgrove's Selected Poems 1954–1974* was published by Routledge and Kegan Paul in 1975, a collected *Poems 1954–1987* by Penguin in 1989, and a new *Selected Poems* by Cape in 1999. Critical studies include Neil Roberts, *The Lover, the Dreamer and the World: The Poetry of Peter Redgrove* (1994); Jeremy Robinson, *Peter Redgrove: A Flood of Poems* (1994); and a section in Gary Day and Brian Docherty (eds.), *British Poetry from the 1950s to the 1990s: Politics and Art* (1997).

RUMENS, CAROL (1944–)

Born Carol Lumley, in South London, she was educated at convent schools in London and Surrey. She studied philosophy briefly at the University of London, married in 1965, and worked in publicity, advertising, literary editing, and journalism, also taking up several writing fellowships. These included a period in Queen's University, Belfast: Northern Irish life and poetic influences figure in some of her later writing. Her first collection of poetry was *Strange Girl in Bright Colours* (Quartet, 1973); later ones included *Unplayed Music* (Secker and Warburg, 1981), *Direct Dialling* (Chatto and Windus, 1985), *From Berlin to Heaven* (Chatto and Windus, 1989), and *The Miracle Diet: Poems* (Bloodaxe, 1998). She also edited *Making for the Open: The Chatto Book of Post-Feminist Poetry 1964–1984* (1985). Her early work often commented directly on contemporary English society, and on women's places within it; poetry in the later 1980s and 1990s increasingly reflected wider stresses in recent European history, in the East especially. These interests extended into several translations from Russian, and a novel set in Moscow, *Plato Park* (Chatto and Windus, 1987). *Selected Poems* was published by Chatto and Windus in 1987, and an updated volume, *Thinking of Skins: New & Selected Poems* by Bloodaxe in 1993. Commentary on her work appears in James Acheson and Romana Huk (eds.), *Contemporary British Poetry: Essays in Theory and Criticism* (1996); in Gary Day and Brian Docherty (eds.), *British Poetry from the 1950s to the 1990s: Politics and Art* (1997); and in Sean O'Brien, *The Deregulated Muse* (1998).

Rushdie, [Ahmed] Salman (1947–)

The only son of a Cambridge-educated businessman, he was born two months before Indian independence into an affluent Muslim family in Bombay. He was educated there and, from the age of 13, at Rugby School in England, where he was abused for being Indian and poor at sports. He went on to study history at Cambridge University, specializing in Arab and Islamic areas; during a visit to his family—who had joined the Muslim exodus to Pakistan—he witnessed the Indo-Pakistan war in 1965. Work with a fringe theatre group after graduation immersed him in late 1960s counter-culture: rock music later featured in *The Ground beneath her Feet* (1999), and in his acquaintance with the rock band U2. Following brief employment in television in Pakistan, he worked in England throughout the 1970s as an advertising copywriter; a science fiction novel, *Grimus*, appeared with limited success in 1975. Reflecting Indian history both before and after independence, **Midnight's Children* (1981; Picador, 1982) showed influences from magic realism, Günter Grass, 'Bollywood', and other fantastic cinema styles, winning the Booker Prize for 1981 and the 'Booker of Bookers' in 1993, as the best novel in the first quarter-century of the award.

Rushdie shifted his political and historical vision from India to Pakistan in *Shame* (1983). **The Satanic Verses* (1988; The Consortium, 1992) proved still more controversial. Though directly attacking Margaret Thatcher's Britain, it provoked outrage for the blasphemy against Islam voiced by one of its characters. India was the first of many countries to ban the novel, which was burned on the streets of Bolton and Bradford. Riots and fatalities ensued throughout the world, and the Japanese translator was murdered. Sentenced to death himself in 1989, along with his publishers, by the *fatwa* of the Iranian leader Ayatolla Khomenei, Rushdie was forced into hiding under police protection. The pressures ended his second marriage, and he returned to public life only tentatively, in the mid-1990s, remarrying in 1997. His move to New York was reflected in *Fury* (2001). *The Moor's Last Sigh* (1995) had continued the intermingling of familial and national history developed in *Midnight's Children*. Like his hero in that novel, Rushdie himself seemed 'handcuffed to history', encapsulating some of the period's post-imperial and religious stresses in his life as well as his fiction.

He also wrote a children's novel, *Haroun and the Sea of Stories* (1990); a volume of short stories, *East, West* (1994); and a travelogue, *The Jaguar Smile: A Nicaraguan Journey* (Picador, 1987). Influential post-colonial reflections appeared in **Imaginary Homelands* (Penguin/Granta Books,

1991); and in another essay collection, *Step across This Line* (Jonathan Cape, 2002). His fiction was mostly published by Jonathan Cape—though *The Satanic Verses* by Viking/Penguin—with Picador and other paperback editions following. Differing accounts of the *fatwa* and its implications appear in Malise Ruthven's *A Satanic Affair: Salman Rushdie and the Wrath of Islam* (1991) and in M. M. Ahsan and A. R. Kidwai's *Sacrilege versus Civility: Muslim Perspectives on the Satanic Verses Affair* (2nd edn., 1993). Critical studies include James Harrison, *Salman Rushdie* (1992); Catherine Cundy, *Salman Rushdie* (1996); and D. C. R. A. Goonetilleke, *Salman Rushdie* (1998).

SHAFFER, PETER (1926–)

Born in Liverpool, a few minutes after his twin Anthony—also a successful dramatist with *Sleuth* (1970)—with whom he wrote two detective novels in the early 1950s. He moved to London with his family in 1936 and attended school there, studying music extensively. Poor eyesight kept him out of the army: he was conscripted instead as a 'Bevin Boy', working in the Kent coalmines from 1944 to 1947 before studying history at Cambridge University. Following a period in New York, he worked in publishing and as a literature and music critic throughout the 1950s. Directed by John Gielgud, the family drama *Five-Finger Exercise* (1958) was an immediate success. *The Royal Hunt of the Sun* (1964) established more firmly Shaffer's recurrent interest in encounters—reduplicating relations between audience and stage—of an ordinary, material world with visionary, transcendent possibilities lying beyond it. This interest extended into later plays such as *Equus* (1973), *Amadeus* (1979), *Yonadab* (1985), and *Lettice and Lovage* (1987). The physicality of *The Royal Hunt of the Sun* and *Equus* showed debts to Antonin Artaud, adding to spectacular stage effects. Along with straightforward presentation of moral conflicts, these helped to ensure the commercial success of his plays. His farce *Black Comedy* (1965) also exemplified a facility with plot construction perhaps developed through early writing in the detective mode: its fascination with darkness and light may even have reflected his early days in the mines.

Shaffer also wrote radio drama, two 1950s television plays, and filmscripts including treatments of *Equus*, *Amadeus*, and, with Peter Brook, of William Golding's *Lord of the Flies* (1963). Individual plays had a range of publishers, including Deutsch, Samuel French, *Penguin, and *Longman (*Royal Hunt*). Critical commentary includes Gene A. Plunka, *Peter Shaffer: Roles, Rites, and Rituals in the Theater* (1988); Dennis A.

Klein, *Peter Shaffer* (1993); and M. K. MacMurraugh-Kavanagh, *Peter Shaffer: Theatre and Drama* (1998). Other studies are listed in Eberle Thomas, *Peter Shaffer: An Annotated Bibliography* (1991).

STEVENSON, ANNE (1933–)

Born in Cambridge, where her father, later an academic philosopher, was studying with Ludwig Wittgenstein. Both her parents were from the United States: she grew up there, studying music at the University of Michigan before returning to England in 1954. She continued recrossing the Atlantic, teaching at various schools in England, Scotland, and the USA before settling permanently in Britain in the 1970s. She married four times, worked as a writer-in-residence in several universities, and helped found the Poetry Bookshop in Hay-on-Wye in 1979. Her first collections, *Living in America* (1965) and *Reversals* (1969), appeared only in the USA: later ones, all published by Oxford University Press, include *Correspondences: A Family History in Letters* (1974), *Minute by Glass Minute* (1982), *The Fiction-Makers* (1985), *The Other House* (1990), and *Four and a Half Dancing Men* (1993). Her poetry reflected the experience of an itinerant life, tracing uncertainties of selfhood and emotion occasioned by diverse relationships and physical landscapes. Oxford University Press published *Selected Poems 1956–1986* in 1987, and ** The Collected Poems of Anne Stevenson: 1955–1995* in 1996: the latter volume was reissued by Bloodaxe in 2000. Her controversial biography of Sylvia Plath, *Bitter Fame* (Viking) appeared in 1989. Critical assessments include sections in Neil Corcoran's *English Poetry since 1940* (1993); in Jan Montefiore's *Feminism and Poetry: Language, Experience, Identity in Women's Writing* (1994); and in Jay Parini (ed.), *British Writers* (suppl. VI, 2001). Stevenson discusses her own work and technique in C. B. McCully (ed.), *The Poet's Voice and Craft* (1994).

STOPPARD, TOM (1937–)

Born Tomas Straussler in Zlin, Czechoslovakia, where his father, a doctor, worked for the Bata shoe company. The family moved to Singapore in 1939. His father remained there after the Japanese invasion in 1942 and did not survive the war. The rest of the family moved on to India; after the war, his mother remarried, to a major in the British army, and they returned to England in 1946. This changeful childhood may have contributed to Stoppard's concern with the relativity of truth and the fickleness of language—also to specific interests in East European politics, in plays such as *Every Good Boy Deserves Favour* (1977) and *Professional Foul* (1977), and in colonialism in *Indian Ink* (1995).

After attending secondary school in Yorkshire, he worked in Bristol as a journalist—often as a drama critic, an occupation satirized in *The Real Inspector Hound* (1968). His first play, *A Walk on the Water*, was televised in 1963 and reached the stage as *Enter a Free Man* in 1968. Several plays were broadcast in the meantime, and some staged; much wider recognition followed Ronald Bryden's rave review of *Rosencrantz and Guildenstern are Dead* at the Edinburgh Fringe in 1966, and its London transfer. Subsequent successes such as *Jumpers* (1972), *Travesties* (1974), and *Arcadia* (1993) continued to mix vestiges of absurdism with Wildean verbal wit and the play of ideas. Though still relying on tricksy theatrical inventiveness, *Night and Day* (1978) and *The Real Thing* (1982) depicted emotional relationships in greater depth, also reflecting right-wing political convictions unusual in theatre at the time. Translations and adaptations occupied much of his later career; he also continued to write extensively for radio, television, and film, including screenplays of *The Human Factor* (1980) and *Empire of the Sun* (1988). He was knighted in 1997.

Individual plays and five volumes of collected *Plays* (1995–99) were published by *Faber and Faber; they also issued *Stoppard: The Plays for Radio 1964–1983* (1990) and *The Television Plays, 1965–1984* (1993). Stoppard's wit, ideas, and unusual dramatic forms occasioned much critical commentary, including Anthony Jenkins's *The Theatre of Tom Stoppard* (1987); Paul Delaney, *Tom Stoppard: The Moral Vision of the Major Plays* (1990); John Fleming, *Stoppard's Theatre: Finding Order amid Chaos* (2001); and Katherine E. Kelly (ed.), *The Cambridge Companion to Tom Stoppard* (2001).

STOREY, DAVID (1933–)

Born in Wakefield, the son of a miner, he attended school there, moving on to Wakefield College of Art in 1951 and the Slade School in London two years later. In the same period, he played professional rugby league for Leeds, an experience reflected in his first novel, *This Sporting Life* (1960), and in his play *The Changing Room* (1971). Drama such as *The Contractor* (1969) and *Life Class* (1974) drew on later jobs as a labourer and as an art teacher; in *Home* (1970) and *Early Days* (1980), he went on to examine disturbed or ageing individuals. Conflicting personal experience of art, sport, and working life focused the period's shifting social stresses particularly sharply in his writing. Tensions between North and South, working class and new middle class, figured strongly in drama such as *In Celebration* (1969). They also shaped novels such as *Flight into Camden* (1961), and developed further in later ones including *Pasmore* (1972), *Saville* (1976), and *A Prodigal Child* (1982). Like his fiction, his plays often reflected a failure of cohesion in family life or modern experience generally, and were sometimes seen as lacking clear coherence themselves: as plotless 'slices of life'. Yet Storey also suggested forms of unity surviving within working life, or even within the vision of stressed individuals.

His plays were published by Jonathan Cape, with collected editions, *Plays: One*, *Plays: Two*, and *Plays: Three* produced by Methuen in 1992, 1994, and 1998. His novels were published by Longman until the 1980s, then Cape, with *Penguin or Vintage paperback editions following. Cape also published *Storey's Lives: Poems 1951–91* (1992). Critical assessments include William Hutchings, *The Plays of David Storey: A Thematic Study* (1988); William Hutchings (ed.), *David Storey: A Casebook* (1992); Herbert Liebman, *The Dramatic Art of David Storey* (1996); and a section in Dominic Head, *The Cambridge Introduction to Modern British Fiction, 1950–2000* (2002).

Tomlinson, [Alfred] Charles (1927–)

Born in Stoke-on-Trent, he attended school locally and studied English at Cambridge University, where he began a friendship with Donald Davie, and at the University of London. After working briefly as a schoolteacher, and as secretary to the critic and biographer Percy Lubbock, he began lecturing at the University of Bristol in 1957, continuing there until the end of the century, though also taking up many writing fellowships in North America. An interest in US writers appeared throughout his poetry—also in his editorship of William Carlos Williams's *Selected Poems* (Penguin, 1976), and of collections of critical essays on Williams and on Marianne Moore. Personal acquaintance with US poets, and debts to them, are described in *Some Americans: A Personal Record* (University of California Press, 1981), reproduced as a section in *American Essays: Making it New* (Carcanet, 2001), along with discussions of Ezra Pound, William Carlos Williams, Wallace Stevens, Charles Olson, and others. Debts to US poetry are also traced in Barry Magid and Hugh Witemeyer (eds.), *William Carlos Williams and Charles Tomlinson: A Transatlantic Connection* (1999).

An artist as well as a poet, he included much physical description in his writing, though usually in ways challenging relations between perceiver and perceived, object and consciousness. 'Phenomenological poetry' was his description of his own work: along with writing by Ted Hughes, Peter Redgrove, and Christopher Middleton, it reconfigured relations between poetic imagination and nature during the period. His first substantial collection, *Seeing Is Believing*, was published in the USA in 1958, and then in 1960—like all his later poetry—by Oxford University Press. Later collections included *American Scenes and Other Poems* (1966), *The Way In and Other Poems* (1974), *The Return* (1987), **Annunciations* (1989), and *Jubilation* (1995). **Selected Poems 1951–1974* appeared in 1978, followed by *Collected Poems 1951–1981* in 1985 (rev. edn., 1987) and *Selected Poems 1955–1997* in 1997. Literary criticism includes the lectures reproduced in *Poetry and Metamorphosis* (Cambridge University Press, 1983). Some of his extensive work as a translator was collected in *Translations* (1983): he also edited the *Oxford Book of Verse in English Translation* (1980). Critical analyses include Brian John, *The World as Event: The Poetry of Charles Tomlinson* (1989); Richard Swigg, *Charles Tomlinson and the Objective Tradition* (1994); and Michael Kirkham, *Passionate Intellect: The Poetry of Charles Tomlinson* (1999).

TREMAIN, ROSE (1943–)

Born Rose Thomson in London, her father a writer. Her parents divorced when she was 10: she was educated at boarding school and spent a year in Paris at the Sorbonne. Interest in Angus Wilson drew her to study English at the University of East Anglia: she returned to lecture on the creative writing course from 1980 to 1995. After graduating in 1967 she worked as a schoolteacher and editor, marrying in 1971; after a further marriage, she lived in Norfolk and London with the biographer Richard Holmes. She published a history of the suffrage movement, *The Fight for Freedom for Women* in 1973, and a biography of Stalin in 1975. *Sadler's Birthday* (1976) began her career as a novelist of diverse interests—in old age, which featured in early novels, and often in history, throughout her career. Twentieth-century history figures extensively in the background of *The Cupboard* (1981) and *Sacred Country* (1992), and the seventeenth in *Restoration* (1989)—filmed in 1996—and in *Music and Silence* (1999). Likewise varied in style, her fiction often employed highly characterized narrators, male or female, sometimes moving in a single novel between first- and third-person accounts of events—divergent perspectives which helped fulfil her aim of combining the extraordinary with the quotidian. Her three volumes of short stories were followed by a collected edition in 1996: she also wrote extensively for radio and television. Her fiction was published by Hamish Hamilton, Sinclair-Stevenson, and Chatto and

Windus, with *Sceptre paperback editions following. Critical assessments include sections in Jay L. Halio (ed.), *Dictionary of Literary Biography, 14: British Novelists since 1960* (1983) and in Neil Schlager and Carol Howard (eds.), *Contemporary Novelists* (2001).

WESKER, ARNOLD (1932–)

Born in east London, of Jewish immigrant parents. After wartime evacuation, he attended school in Hackney, leaving aged 16 to work in carpentry. Following National Service in the RAF, he was employed as a farm labourer and kitchen porter in Norfolk, where he met Dusty Bicker, whom he married in 1958. Work as a pastry cook earned enough to allow enrolment in the London School of Film Technique in 1955. While there, he was encouraged by an *Observer* competition and by John Osborne's *Look Back in Anger* to write *Chicken Soup with Barley* and *The Kitchen*. Produced in Coventry in 1958 and 1961, each transferred to the Royal Court. Adding *Roots* (1959) and *I'm Talking about Jerusalem* (1960) to *Chicken Soup with Barley*, Wesker completed a trilogy which established his own reputation and consolidated the Royal Court's role as a theatre of new, realistic writing, firmly involved with contemporary issues. After *Chips with Everything* (1962), however, and perhaps as a result of experience with Centre 42, his plays accentuated the disillusion with political action sometimes evident in the trilogy. The failure of ideals provided a strong theme for *Their Very Own and Golden City* (1966). But in concentrating still further on private emotions rather than public issues, in plays such as *The Four Seasons* (1965) and *The Old Ones* (1972), Wesker's writing lost some of its earlier appeal. Like *The Friends* (1970), several later plays premiered abroad: *The Merchant* (1976)—later renamed *Shylock*—in Stockholm. Both the RSC and the National turned down *The Journalists* (1977). Like Osborne's work, Wesker's drama did not easily outlast the phase of rapid social change which had shaped it in the late 1950s and early 1960s, though some of his strengths reappeared in a series of monologues for women performers written in the 1980s and 1990s.

Wesker directed several productions of his plays, and wrote extensively for children, for radio and television, and as an essayist; views of his drama and work for Centre 42 appear in *Fears of Fragmentation* (Cape, 1970). Individual plays were published by *Cape: Penguin followed their best-selling *The Wesker Trilogy*, published in 1964, by issuing or reissuing five further volumes of collected plays in 1990, and an edition of *One Woman Plays* in 1989. *As Much as I Dare: An Autobiography (1932–1959)* was published by Century in 1994. John Russell Taylor's

Anger and After: A Guide to the New British Drama (2nd edn., 1969) discusses Wesker's initial impact. Later critical studies include Glenda Leeming's *Wesker the Playwright* (1983); Robert Wilcher, *Understanding Arnold Wesker* (1991); and Reade W. Dornan (ed.), *Arnold Wesker: A Casebook* (1998).

WILSON, ANGUS (1913–91)

Born in Bexhill, Sussex, he was educated at public school in London, and at Oxford University. He worked for Intelligence during the war, mostly on code-breaking, then as Deputy Superintendent of the Reading Room at the British Library until 1955, concentrating on writing thereafter. From 1966 to 1978 he was a professor at the University of East Anglia, establishing the MA in Creative Writing there, with Malcolm Bradbury, in 1970. Satire of middle-class life and values shaped early short-story collections, *The Wrong Set* (1949) and *Such Darling Dodos* (1950), and 1950s novels including *Hemlock and After* (1952) and *Anglo-Saxon Attitudes* (1956). Broad, Dickensian scrutiny of contemporary society extended into *Late Call* (1964). Other novels in the 1960s were more typical of the decade's innovative mood, *The Old Men at the Zoo* (1961) moving towards fantasy, and *No Laughing Matter* (1967) developing modernist legacies of style and structure. Later fiction was more conventional, looking back appraisively on 1960s lifestyles in *As if by Magic* (1973), and exploring relations between life and art in *Setting the World on Fire* (1980). Wilson was one of the first English novelists to present homosexual relations extensively, although—like his treatment of family life, the liberal outlook, and the contemporary world generally—these remained subject to his unremitting critical wit.

Knighted in 1980, Wilson also wrote a play—*The Mulberry Bush* (1956), produced in the early days of the Royal Court—and extensive non-fiction, including studies of Charles Dickens, Rudyard Kipling, and Émile Zola. A collection of his critical essays, **Diversity and Depth in Fiction* (Secker and Warburg, 1983) was edited by Kerry McSweeney; his travel writing was published as *Reflections in a Writer's Eye* in 1986. Most of his work, fiction and non-fiction, was published by Secker and Warburg, with Penguin and *Granada editions following. Margaret Drabble's *Angus Wilson: A Biography* appeared in 1995. Critical studies include Peter Faulkner, *Angus Wilson: Mimic and Moralist* (1980); Averil Gardner, *Angus Wilson* (1985); and Jay L. Halio (ed.), *Critical Essays on Angus Wilson* (1985).

WINTERSON, JEANETTE (1959–)

Born in Manchester, she was adopted and brought up in Accrington, Lancashire, by parents who were Pentecostal Evangelists and wanted her to be a missionary. Most books were banned from their house, though Malory's *Morte d'Arthur* remained, and a Saturday job in the local public library allowed her to read freely. She had to leave home at 16, after falling in love with another girl, and worked for two years in ice-cream vans, a funeral parlour, and a mental hospital before gaining a place to study English at Oxford University. Further temporary jobs followed, briefly at the Roundhouse Theatre, before she impressed an editor at Pandora Press with her storytelling abilities while applying for a job. Published by Pandora in 1985, *Oranges are Not the Only Fruit* reflected some of her own early experience. *Boating for Beginners* (1985) offered a more whimsical retelling of the Genesis story of Noah. *The Passion* (1987) and *Sexing the Cherry* (1989) developed her characteristically lyrical expression and smooth transitions between realism, history, fable, and fantasy. *Written on the Body* (1992), with its unnamed and ungendered narrator, *Art and Lies* (1994), and *The.PowerBook* (2000) further assessed relations between love, sex, and artistic creation. High-profile affairs and confident claims about her own talents made her later career controversial. Throughout, her unusually free imagination explored the period's reassessed gender roles particularly radically and compellingly.

Winterson published a book of short stories, *The World and Other Places* (1998), regular journalism for the *Guardian*, and commentary collected in *Art and Lies: Essays on Ecstasy and Effrontery* (1995). She also wrote plays for radio and television, and a successful adaptation of *Oranges are Not the Only Fruit* for BBC2 in 1990, and worked as a series editor for Vintage reissues of Virginia Woolf's fiction in the late 1990s. Early novels were published by Pandora, and later ones mostly by Jonathan Cape, with Penguin and *Vintage paperback editions following. Critical studies include Christopher Pressler, *So Far So Linear: Responses to the Work of Jeanette Winterson* (2000) and sections in Laura Doan (ed.), *The Lesbian Postmodern* (1994); Andrea L. Harris, *Other Sexes: Rewriting Difference from Woolf to Winterson* (2000); and Richard J. Lane, Rod Mengham, and Philip Tew (eds.), *Contemporary British Fiction* (2003).

Suggestions for Further Reading

The Author Bibliographies (pp. 523–80) list critical works about individual writers. The British Council/Book Trust Website (http://www.
contemporarywriters.com) also offers profiles of many contemporary
authors, several of whom have their own web pages, usually found easily
by any web search. Listed below are works which offer more general views
of the period. Where possible, these are recent studies, though the list also
includes a number of works particularly influential at the time of their
publication, or useful in illustrating the development of criticism and
thinking about the period's literature.

Histories and Surveys

Political and Social History

Gamble, Andrew, *Britain in Decline: Economic Policy, Political Strategy
and the British State*, 4th edn. (1994)

Gilbert, Martin, *A History of the Twentieth Century, 3. 1952–1999*
(1999)

Hoggart, Richard, *The Way We Live Now* (1995)

Marwick, Arthur, *British Society since 1945*, The Penguin Social History
of Britain, 3rd edn. (1996)

Morgan, Kenneth O., *The People's Peace: British History since 1945*
(1999)

Sked, Alan, and Cook, Chris, *Post-War Britain: A Political History*, 4th
edn. (1993)

Cultural and Literary History

Appleyard, Bryan, *The Pleasures of Peace: Art and Imagination in Post-
War Britain* (1989)

Bloom, Clive, and Day, Gary (eds.), *Literature and Culture in Modern
Britain, 3. 1956–1999* (2000)

Davies, Alistair, and Sinfield, Alan (eds.), *British Culture of the Postwar:
An Introduction to Literature and Society* (2000)

Ford, Boris (ed.), *The Cambridge Cultural History, 9. Modern Britain*
1992)

Ford, Boris (ed.), *The New Pelican Guide to English Literature*, 8. *The Present* (1983)

Hewison, Robert, *Too Much: Art and Society in the Sixties 1960–1975* (1986)

Sinfield, Alan, *Literature, Politics and Culture in Postwar Britain* (1989)

Spittles, Brian, *Britain since 1960: An Introduction* (1995)

Waugh, Patricia, *The Harvest of the Sixties: English Literature and its Background 1960–1990* (1995)

Williams, Linda R. (ed.), *The Twentieth Century* (Bloomsbury Guides to English Literature, 1994)

Postmodernism and Postcolonialism

Adam, Ian, and Tiffin, Helen (eds.), *Past the Last Post: Theorizing Post-Colonialism and Post-Modernism* (1991)

Baker, Stephen, *The Fiction of Postmodernity* (2000)

Connor, Steven, *Postmodernist Culture: An Introduction to Theories of the Contemporary* (1989)

Hutcheon, Linda, *A Poetics of Postmodernism: History, Theory, Fiction* (1988)

Jameson, Fredric, *Postmodernism, or, the Cultural Logic of Late Capitalism* (1991)

McHale, Brian, *Postmodernist Fiction* (1987)

Smyth, Edmund (ed.), *Postmodernism and Contemporary Fiction* (1991)

Many anthologies and readers offer surveys of postmodern or postcolonial thinking. Among the best of these are:

Ashcroft, Bill, Griffiths, Gareth, and Tiffin, Helen (eds.), *The Post-Colonial Studies Reader* (1995)

Docherty, Thomas (ed.), *Postmodernism: A Reader* (1993)

Natoli, Joseph, and Hutcheon, Linda (eds.), *A Postmodern Reader* (1993)

Nicol, Bran (ed.), *Postmodernism and the Contemporary Novel* (2002)

Waugh, Patricia (ed.), *Postmodernism: A Reader* (1992)

Williams, Patrick, and Chrisman, Laura (eds.), *Colonial Discourse and Postcolonial Theory: A Reader* (1993)

Literary Criticism and Theory

Baldick, Chris, *Criticism and Literary Theory 1890 to the Present* (1996)

Eagleton, Terry, *Literary Theory: An Introduction*, 2nd edn. (1996)

Knellwolf, Christa, Norris, Christopher, and Osborn, Jessica (eds.), *The Cambridge History of Literary Criticism*, 9. *Twentieth-Century Historical, Philosophical and Psychological Perspectives* (2001)

Selden, Raman (ed.), *The Cambridge History of Literary Criticism*, 8. *From Formalism to Postructuralism* (1995)

—— and Widdowson, Peter, *A Reader's Guide to Contemporary Literary Theory*, 3rd edn. (1993)

Several essay anthologies and readers offer surveys of the main positions in critical thinking towards the end of the century:

Leitch, Vincent B. (gen. ed.), *The Norton Anthology of Theory and Criticism* (2001)

Lodge, David (ed.), *Modern Criticism and Theory: A Reader*, 2nd edn., rev. and expanded by Nigel Wood (2000)

Rice, Philip, and Waugh, Patricia (eds.), *Modern Literary Theory: A Reader*, 3rd edn., (1996)

Rivkin, Julie, and Ryan, Michael (eds.), *Literary Theory: An Anthology* (1998)

Publishing and the Book Trade

Richard Findlater's pamphlet, *What are Writers Worth?* (Society of Authors, 1963) summarizes the position at the start of the period. Developments over the next twenty years or so are described in Michael Lane's *Books and Publishers: Commerce against Culture in Postwar Britain* (1980), Ian Norrie's *Mumby's Publishing and Bookselling in the Twentieth Century*, 6th edn. (1982), and John Sutherland's *Fiction and the Fiction Industry* (1978). The state of the trade at the end of the century is indicated by Christopher Gasson's *Book Publishing in Britain* (1999) and Dan Franklin's article, 'Commissioning and Editing Modern Fiction' in Zachary Leader (ed.), *On Modern British Fiction* (2002).

Poetry

Acheson, James, and Huk, Romana (eds.), *Contemporary British Poetry: Essays in Theory and Criticism* (1996)

Booth, Martin, *British Poetry 1964 to 1984: Driving through the Barricades* (1985)

Corcoran, Neil, *English Poetry since 1940* (1993)

Davie, Donald, *The Poet in the Imaginary Museum: Essays of Two Decades*, ed. Barry Alpert (1977)

—— *Under Briggflatts: A History of Poetry in Great Britain 1960–1988* (1989)

Day, Gary, and Docherty, Brian (eds.), *British Poetry from the 1950s to the 1990s: Politics and Art* (1997)

Hampson, Robert, and Barry, Peter (eds.), *New British Poetries: The Scope of the Possible* (1993)

Jones, Peter, and Schmidt, Michael (eds.), *British Poetry since 1970: A Critical Survey* (1980)

Kennedy, David, *New Relations: The Refashioning of British Poetry 1980–1994* (1996)

O'Brien, Sean, *The Deregulated Muse: Essays on Contemporary British and Irish Poetry* (1998)

Riggs, Thomas (ed.), *Contemporary Poets*, 7th edn. (2001)

Robinson, Alan, *Instabilities in Contemporary British Poetry* (1988)

Schmidt, Michael, and Lindop, Grevel (eds.), *British Poetry since 1960: A Critical Survey* (1972)

Thwaite, Anthony, *Poetry Today: A Critical Guide to British Poetry 1960–1995* (1996)

Two anthologies published around the end of the century offer particularly wide-ranging surveys of its last decades, including introductory notes on individual poets:

O'Brien, Sean (ed.), *The Firebox: Poetry in Britain and Ireland after 1945* (1998)

Tuma, Keith (ed.), *Anthology of Twentieth-Century British and Irish Poetry* (2001)

Drama

Billington, Michael, *One Night Stands: A Critic's View of Modern British Theatre* (1993)

Boireau, Nicole (ed.), *Drama on Drama: Dimensions of Theatricality on the Contemporary British Stage* (1997)

Bull, John, *New British Political Dramatists* (1984)

——*Stage Right: Crisis and Recovery in British Contemporary Mainstream Theatre* (1994)

Callow, Simon, *The National: The Theatre and its Work 1963–97* (1997)

Cohn, Ruby, *Retreats from Realism in Recent English Drama* (1991)

Craig, Sandy (ed.), *Dreams and Deconstructions: Alternative Theatre in Britain* (1980)

Demastes, William W. (ed.), *British Playwrights, 1956–1995: A Research and Production Sourcebook* (1996)

Dromgoole, Dominic, *The Full Room: An A–Z of Contemporary Playwriting* (2000)

Edgar, David, *The Second Time as Farce: Reflections on the Drama of Mean Times* (1988)

Elsom, John, *Post-War British Theatre*, rev. edn. (1979)

—— (ed.), *Post-War British Theatre Criticism* (1981)

Esslin, Martin, *The Theatre of the Absurd* (1961; new edn. 2001)

Findlater, Richard (ed.), *At the Royal Court: 25 Years of the English Stage Company* (1981)

Goodman, Lizbeth, *Contemporary Feminist Theatres: To Each her Own* (1993)

Innes, Christopher, *Modern British Drama 1890–1990* (1992)

Itzin, Catherine, *Stages in the Revolution: Political Theatre in Britain since 1968* (1980)

Kershaw, Baz, *The Politics of Performance: Radical Theatre as Cultural Intervention* (1992)

Lloyd Evans, Gareth, and Lloyd Evans, Barbara (eds.), *Plays in Review 1956–1980: British Drama and the Critics* (1985)

Page, Adrian (ed.), *The Death of the Playwright?: Modern British Drama and Literary Theory* (1992)

Reinelt, Janelle, *After Brecht: British Epic Theatre* (1996)

Riggs, Thomas (ed.), *Contemporary Dramatists*, 6th edn. (1999)

Shank, Theodore (ed.), *Contemporary British Theatre* (1996)

Shellard, Dominic, *British Theatre since the War* (1999)

Taylor, John Russell, *Anger and After* (1969)

—— *The Second Wave: British Drama of the Sixties* (1971)

Trussler, Simon (ed.), *New Theatre Voices of the Seventies: Sixteen Interviews from Theatre Quarterly 1970–1980* (1981)

Wandor, Michelene, *Drama Today: A Critical Guide to British Drama 1970–1990* (1993)

Fiction

Bradbury, Malcolm, *The Modern British Novel* (1993)

—— *No, Not Bloomsbury* (1987)

Bergonzi, Bernard, *The Situation of the Novel*, 2nd edn. (1979)

Bloom, Clive, *Bestsellers* (2002)

Callil, Carmen, and Tóibín, Colm, *The Modern Library: The Two Hundred Best Novels in English since 1950* (1999)

Connor, Steven, *The English Novel in History: 1950–1995* (1996)

Gąsiorek, Andrzej, *Post-War British Fiction: Realism and After* (1995)

Head, Dominic, *The Cambridge Introduction to Modern British Fiction, 1950–2000* (2002)

Lane, Richard J., Mengham, Rod, and Tew, Philip (eds.), *Contemporary British Fiction* (2003)

Leader, Zachary (ed.), *On Modern British Fiction* (2002)

Lee, Alison, *Realism and Power: Postmodern British Fiction* (1990)

Lee, A. Robert (ed.), *Other Britain, Other British: Contemporary Multicultural Fiction* (1995)

Lodge, David, *The Novelist at the Crossroads and Other Essays on Fiction and Criticism* (1971)

Massie, Alan, *The Novel Today: A Critical Guide to the British Novel 1970–89* (1990)

Schlager, Neil, and Howard, Carol (eds.), *Contemporary Novelists*, 7th edn. (2001)

Stevenson, Randall, *A Reader's Guide to the Twentieth-Century Novel in Britain* (1993)

—— *The British Novel since the Thirties* (1986)

Taylor, D. J., *After the War: The Novel and England since 1945* (1993)

Works Cited

ABRAMS, M. H., and GREENBLATT, STEPHEN (gen. eds.). *The Norton Anthology of English Literature*, vol. 1, 7th edn. (W. W. Norton and Co., 2000).

ACHESON, JAMES, and HUK, ROMANA (eds.). *Contemporary British Poetry: Essays in Theory and Criticism* (State University of New York Press, 1996).

ACKROYD, PETER. *Notes for a New Culture: An Essay on Modernism* (Vision, 1976).

ADCOCK, FLEUR. *Poems 1960–2000* (Bloodaxe, 2000).

ADORNO, THEODOR, and HORKHEIMER, MAX. *Dialectic of Enlightenment*, trans. John Cumming (1944; Verso, 1992).

AGARD, JOHN. *Mangoes & Bullets: Selected and New Poems 1972–84* (Pluto Press, 1985).

ALDISS, BRIAN. *Frankenstein Unbound* (1973; Triad/Granada, 1982).

ALLEN, WALTER. *Tradition and Dream: The English and American Novel from the Twenties to Our Time* (1964; Hogarth Press, 1986).

ALLNUTT, GILLIAN, D'AGUIAR, FRED, EDWARDS, KEN and MOTTRAM, ERIC (eds.). *The New British Poetry 1968–1988* (Paladin, 1988).

ALVAREZ, A. L., FULLER, ROY, and THWAITE, ANTHONY. *Penguin Modern Poets 18* (Penguin, 1970).

——(ed.). *The New Poetry: An Anthology* (1966; rev. edn. Penguin, 1978).

AMIS, KINGSLEY. *Jake's Thing* (Hutchinson, 1978).

—— *Take a Girl Like You* (1960; Penguin, 1984).

AMIS, MARTIN. *Experience* (Jonathan Cape, 2000).

—— *London Fields* (1989; Penguin, 1990).

—— *Money: A Suicide Note* (1984; Penguin, 1986).

—— *Other People: A Mystery Story* (1981; Penguin, 1982).

APPLEYARD, BRYAN. *The Culture Club: Crisis in the Arts* (London: Faber and Faber, 1984).

ARDEN, JOHN. *Plays: One* (Eyre Methuen, 1977).

ARMITAGE, SIMON. *The Universal Home Doctor* (Faber and Faber, 2002).

ARTAUD, ANTONIN. *The Theatre and its Double*, trans. Victor Corti (John Calder, 1970).

ARTS COUNCIL OF GREAT BRITAIN. *Annual Report and Accounts* (1970/1–1985/6).
—— *The Glory of the Garden: The Development of the Arts in England—A Strategy for a Decade* (Arts Council, 1984).
AUDEN, W. H. *Collected Poems*, ed. Edward Mendelson (Faber and Faber, 1976).
—— *The Dyer's Hand and Other Essays* (Faber and Faber, 1963).
BAINBRIDGE, BERYL. *A Quiet Life* (1976; Fontana, 1983).
BAKHTIN, MIKHAIL. *The Dialogic Imagination: Four Essays*, ed. Michael Holquist, trans. Caryl Emerson and Michael Holquist (University of Texas Press, 1981).
—— *Rabelais and his World*, trans. Helene Iswolsky (1968; Indiana University Press, 1984).
BALDICK, CHRIS. *Criticism and Literary Theory 1890 to the Present* (Longman, 1996).
BALLARD, J. G. *Crash* (Jonathan Cape, 1973).
—— *Super-Cannes* (Flamingo, 2000).
—— *The Unlimited Dream Company* (1979; Panther, 1985).
BARBANNEAU, JEAN-LUC, CROOM, DAVID, FISHWICK, FRANCIS, WALKER, ALAN GORDON, KINGTON, CHRIS, McKAY, ROBERT, PEARCE, L. A., and RICHARDSON, PAUL. *Book Publishing in Britain* (Bookseller Publications, 1995).
BARKER, GEORGE. *Collected Poems*, ed. Robert Fraser (Faber and Faber, 1987).
BARKER, HOWARD. *A Passion in Six Days* and *Downchild* (John Calder, 1985).
—— *The Love of a Good Man* and *All Bleeding* (John Calder, 1980).
—— *Two Plays for the Right: The Loud Boy's Life* and *Birth on a Hard Shoulder* (John Calder, 1982).
BARKER, PAT. *The Eye in the Door* (1993; Penguin, 1995).
BARNES, JULIAN. *England, England* (Jonathan Cape, 1998).
—— *Love, etc* (Jonathan Cape, 2000).
BARNES, PETER. *The Ruling Class* (1969; Heinemann, 1980).
BARTHES, ROLAND. *Image–Music–Text*, essays selected and translated by Stephen Heath (1977; Flamingo, 1984).
—— *S/Z*, trans. Richard Miller (Hill and Wang, 1974).
BECKETT, SAMUEL, BRION, MARCEL, BUDGEN, FRANK, et al. *Our Exagmination Round his Factification for Incamination of Work in Progress* (1929; Faber and Faber, 1972).
BELSEY, CATHERINE. *Critical Practice* (Methuen, 1980).
—— *Desire: Love Stories in Western Culture* (Blackwell, 1994).

BENJAMIN, WALTER. *Illuminations*, ed. Hannah Arendt, trans. Harry Zohn (1968; Fontana, 1992).

BENNETT, ALAN. *Forty Years On* (Faber and Faber, 1969).

BERGER, JOHN. *G.* (1972; Chatto and Windus/Hogarth Press, 1985).

BERGONZI, BERNARD. *Exploding English: Criticism, Theory, Culture* (Clarendon Press, 1990).

—— *The Situation of the Novel*, 2nd edn. (Macmillan, 1979).

BERKOFF, STEVEN. *Decadence and Other Plays* (Faber and Faber, 1989).

BERRY, JAMES. *Chain of Days* (Oxford University Press, 1985).

—— *Fractured Circles* (New Beacon, 1979).

—— (ed.). *News for Babylon: The Chatto Book of Westindian British Poetry* (Chatto and Windus, 1984).

BHATT, SUJATTA. *Brunizem* (Caracanet, 1986).

BLOCH, ERNST, LUKÁCS, GEORG, BRECHT, BERTOLT, BENJAMIN, WALTER, and ADORNO, THEODOR. *Aesthetics and Politics* (NLB, 1977).

BLOOM, CLIVE, and DAY, GARY. *Literature and Culture in Modern Britain*, 3. *1956–1999* (Longman, 2000).

BOND, EDWARD. *Bond on File*, compiled by Philip Roberts (Methuen, 1985).

—— *Plays: One* (Eyre Methuen, 1977).

—— *Plays: Two* (Eyre Methuen, 1978).

—— *The Bundle, or, New Narrow Road to the Deep North* (Eyre Methuen, 1978).

—— *The Worlds*, with *The Activists Papers* (Eyre Methuen, 1980).

BOOKER, CHRISTOPHER. *The Seventies: Portrait of a Decade* (Allen Lane, 1980).

BOOTH, MARTIN. *British Poetry 1964 to 1984: Driving through the Barricades* (Routledge and Kegan Paul, 1985).

BRADBURY, MALCOLM. *Rates of Exchange* (1983; Arena, 1984).

—— *The Modern British Novel* (Secker and Warburg, 1993).

—— (ed.). *The Novel Today: Contemporary Writers on Modern Fiction* (Fontana, 1977).

—— and COOKE, JUDY (eds.). *New Writing* (Minerva/British Council, 1992).

BRADFORD, RICHARD (ed.). *Introducing Literary Studies* (Harvester Wheatsheaf, 1996).

BRANDT, GEORGE W. (ed.). *British Television Drama* (Cambridge University Press, 1981).

BRENTON, HOWARD. *Bloody Poetry* (Methuen, 1985).

—— *Greenland* (Methuen, 1988).

—— *Plays: One* (Methuen, 1986).

BRENTON, HOWARD. *The Romans in Britain* (Eyre Methuen, 1980).

—— and HARE, DAVID. *Pravda: A Fleet Street Comedy* (Methuen, 1985).

BROOK, PETER. *The Empty Space* (1968; Penguin, 1977).

BROOKNER, ANITA. *Hotel du Lac* (Jonathan Cape, 1984).

—— *Providence* (1982; Triad/Panther, 1984).

BROWN, SUSAN WINDISCH (ed.). *Contemporary Novelists*, 6th edn. (St James's Press, 1996).

BROWNJOHN, ALAN. *The Railings* (Digby Press, 1962).

BUDGEN, FRANK. *James Joyce and the Making of Ulysses* (Grayson and Grayson, 1937).

BULL, JOHN. *New British Political Dramatists* (Macmillan, 1984).

—— *Stage Right: Crisis and Recovery in British Contemporary Mainstream Theatre* (Macmillan, 1994).

BUNTING, BASIL. *Collected Poems*, 2nd edn. (1977; Oxford University Press, 1987).

BURGESS, ANTHONY. *A Clockwork Orange* (1962; Penguin, 1976).

—— *Earthly Powers* (Hutchinson, 1980).

—— *The Novel Now: A Student's Guide to Contemporary Fiction*, 2nd edn. (Faber and Faber, 1971).

BURNS, ALAN. *Babel* (Calder and Boyars, 1969).

BYATT, A. S. *The Biographer's Tale* (Chatto and Windus, 2000).

—— *The Virgin in the Garden* (Chatto and Windus, 1978).

CALVINO, ITALO. *If on a Winter's Night a Traveller*, trans. William Weaver (1979; Picador, 1982).

CARR, J. L. *A Month in the Country* (Harvester, 1980).

CARTER, ANGELA. *Nights at the Circus* (1984; Vintage, 1994).

—— *The Infernal Desire Machines of Doctor Hoffman* (1972; Penguin, 1982).

—— *The Passion of New Eve* (1977; Virago, 1985).

CARTWRIGHT, JIM. *Road* (Methuen, 1986).

CAUTE, DAVID. *Sixty-Eight: The Year of the Barricades* (Hamish Hamilton, 1988).

—— *The Illusion: An Essay on Politics, Theatre and the Novel* (André Deutsch, 1971).

CHARLES, GERDA. *A Logical Girl* (Eyre and Spottiswoode, 1966).

CHATWIN, BRUCE. *In Patagonia* (1977; Vintage, 1998).

—— *Utz* (Jonathan Cape, 1988).

—— *What am I Doing Here* (Jonathan Cape, 1989).

CHAUDHURI, AMIT. *Three Novels: A Strange and Sublime Address, Afternoon Raag, Freedom Song* (1991, 1993, 1998; Picador, 2001).

CHURCHILL, CARYL. *Plays: One* (Methuen, 1985).

—— *Plays: Two* (Methuen, 1990).

COE, JONATHAN. *What a Carve Up* (Penguin, 1995).

COHN, RUBY. *Retreats from Realism in Recent English Drama* (Cambridge University Press, 1991).

COLEGATE, ISABEL. *The Shooting Party* (Hamish Hamilton, 1980).

COLLS, ROBERT. *Identity of England* (Oxford University Press, 2002).

CONNOR, STEVEN. *Postmodernist Culture: An Introduction to Theories of the Contemporary* (Blackwell, 1989).

CONQUEST, ROBERT. *Forays* (Chatto and Windus/Hogarth Press, 1979).

—— (ed.). *New Lines: An Anthology*, 1 (1956; Macmillan, 1962).

CONRAD, JOSEPH. *Heart of Darkness* (1899, Penguin, 1995).

—— *Lord Jim* (1900; Penguin, 1968).

—— *The Nigger of the 'Narcissus' and Other Stories* (1897, etc; Penguin, 1968).

COPE, WENDY. *Serious Concerns* (Faber and Faber, 1992).

CORCORAN, NEIL. *English Poetry since 1940* (Longman, 1993).

COYLE, MARTIN, GARSIDE, PETER, KELSALL, MALCOLM, and PECK, JOHN (eds.). *Encyclopaedia of Literary Criticism* (Routledge, 1990).

CROZIER, ANDREW, AND LONGVILLE, TIM (eds.). *A Various Art* (1987; Paladin, 1990).

CURTIS, RICHARD. *This Business of Publishing: An Insider's View of Current Trends and Tactics* (Allworth Press, 1998).

D'AGUIAR, FRED. *British Subjects* (Bloodaxe, 1993).

DANIELS, SARAH. *Plays: One* (Methuen, 1991).

DAVIE, DONALD. *Collected Poems*, ed. Neil Powell (Carcanet, 2002).

—— *The Poet in the Imaginary Museum: Essays of Two Decades*, ed. Barry Alpert (Carcanet, 1977).

—— *Under Briggflatts: A History of Poetry in Great Britain 1960–1988* (Carcanet, 1989).

DAY LEWIS, C. *The Complete Poems of C. Day Lewis* (Sinclair-Stevenson, 1992).

DEBORD, GUY. *The Society of the Spectacle* (1967), trans. Donald Nicholson-Smith (Zone, 1995).

DEIGHTON, LEN. *The Ipcress File* (1962; HarperCollins, 1995).

DENNIS, NIGEL. *Cards of Identity* (1955; Penguin, 1983).

DERRIDA, JACQUES. *Writing and Difference*, trans. Alan Bass (Routledge and Kegan Paul, 1978).

DE TERÁN, LISA ST AUBIN. *The Slow Train to Milan* (Jonathan Cape, 1983).

DISKI, JENNY. *Happily Ever After* (Hamish Hamilton, 1991).

DOCHERTY, THOMAS (ed.). *Postmodernism: A Reader* (Harvester Wheatsheaf, 1993).

DRABBLE, MARGARET. *The Ice Age* (1977; Penguin, 1983).

—— *The Radiant Way* (1987; Penguin, 1988).

—— *The Waterfall* (1969; Penguin, 1971).

DROMGOOLE, DOMINIC. *The Full Room: An A–Z of Contemporary Playwriting* (Methuen, 2000).

DUFFY, CAROL ANN. *The Other Country* (Anvil Press, 1990).

DUFFY, MAUREEN. *Change* (Methuen, 1987).

DUNMORE, HELEN. *Out of the Blue: Poems 1975–2001* (Bloodaxe, 2001).

DURRELL, LAWRENCE. *The Alexandria Quartet: Justine, Balthazar, Mountolive, Clea* (1957–60; Faber and Faber, 1983).

DYER, CHARLES. *Staircase* (Penguin, 1966).

DYLAN, BOB. *Writings and Drawings* (Panther, 1978).

EAGLETON, TERRY. *Literary Theory: An Introduction* (Blackwell, 1983).

—— *The Illusions of Postmodernism* (Blackwell, 1996).

EDGAR, DAVID. *Plays: One* (Methuen, 1987).

—— *Plays: Three* (Methuen, 1991).

—— *The Second Time as Farce*: *Reflections on the Drama of Mean Times* (Lawrence and Wishart, 1988).

ELLIS, ALICE THOMAS. *The 27th Kingdom* (Duckworth, 1982).

ELSOM, JOHN. *Post-War British Theatre* (Routledge and Kegan Paul, 1976).

—— *Theatre Outside London* (Macmillan, 1971).

—— (ed.). *Post-War British Theatre Criticism* (Routledge and Kegan Paul, 1981).

EMECHETA, BUCHI. *Second-Class Citizen* (1974; Heinemann, 1994).

ENRIGHT, D. J. *Collected Poems* (Oxford University Press, 1981).

—— (ed.). *The Oxford Book of Verse, 1945–1980* (1980; Oxford University Press, 1995).

ESSLIN, MARTIN. *The Theatre of the Absurd* (1961; Penguin, 1968).

FARRELL, J. G. *The Siege of Krishnapur* (1973; Penguin, 1984).

FEATHER, JOHN. *A History of British Publishing* (Routledge, 1988).

FEINSTEIN, ELAINE. *Selected Poems* (Carcanet, 1994).

—— *The Survivors* (Hutchinson, 1982).

FENTON, JAMES. *The Memory of War: Poems 1968–1982* (The Salamander Press, 1982).

FIELDING, GABRIEL. *The Birthday King* (Hutchinson, 1962).

FIGES, EVA. *Waking* (Hamish Hamilton, 1981).

FINDLATER, RICHARD. *What are Writers Worth?: A Survey of Authorship*

Prepared by Richard Findlater for the Society of Authors (Society of Authors, 1963).

—— (ed.). *At the Royal Court: 25 Years of the English Stage Company* (Amber Lane Press, 1981).

FITZGERALD, PENELOPE. *The Bookshop* (Duckworth, 1978).

FLANNERY, PETER. *Our Friends in the North* (Methuen/RSC, 1982).

FORD, BORIS (ed.). *The Pelican Guide to English Literature*, 7. *The Modern Age*, rev. edn. (Penguin, 1973).

FORREST-THOMSON, VERONICA. *Collected Poems and Translations* (Agneau 2, 1990).

—— *Poetic Artifice: A Theory of Twentieth-Century Poetry* (Manchester University Press, 1978).

FOWLES, JOHN. *Daniel Martin* (1977; Triad/Panther, 1979).

—— *The French Lieutenant's Woman* (1969; Triad/Panther, 1977).

FROW, JOHN. *Time and Commodity Culture: Essays in Cultural Theory and Postmodernity* (Clarendon Press, 1997).

FULLER, JOHN. *Collected Poems* (Chatto and Windus, 1996).

FULLER, ROY. *New and Collected Poems 1934–1984* (Secker and Warburg, 1985).

FUSSELL, PAUL. *The Great War and Modern Memory* (Oxford University Press, 1975).

GALLAGHER, CATHERINE, and GREENBLATT, STEPHEN. *Practising New Historicism* (University of Chicago Press, 2000).

GARDAM, JANE. *The Queen of the Tambourine* (Sinclair-Stevenson, 1991).

GĄSIOREK, ANDRZEJ. *Post-War British Fiction: Realism and After* (Edward Arnold, 1995).

GASSON, CHRISTOPHER. *Book Publishing in Britain* (Bookseller Publications, 1999).

GEMS, PAM. *Dusa, Fish, Stas and Vi* (Samuel French, 1977).

—— *Three Plays: Piaf, Camille, Loving Women* (Penguin, 1985).

GILBERT, MARTIN. *A History of the Twentieth Century*, 3. *1952–1999* (HarperCollins, 1999).

GOLDING, WILLIAM. *A Moving Target* (Faber and Faber, 1982).

—— *Darkness Visible* (1979; Faber and Faber, 1983).

—— *Lord of the Flies* (1954; Faber and Faber, 1967).

—— *Rites of Passage* (1980; Faber and Faber, 1983).

—— *The Hot Gates and Other Occasional Pieces* (Faber and Faber, 1965).

GORDON, GILES. *Beyond the Words: Eleven Writers in Search of a New Fiction* (Hutchinson, 1975).

GREENE, GRAHAM. *A Sort of Life* (1971; Penguin, 1977).

—— *Collected Essays* (1969; Penguin, 1970).

—— *Our Man in Havana* (1958; Penguin, 1974).

—— *The End of the Affair* (1951; Penguin, 1976).

—— *The Honorary Consul* (1973; Penguin, 1975).

—— *The Human Factor* (1978; Penguin, 1980).

—— *Ways of Escape* (Bodley Head, 1980).

GRIFFITHS, TREVOR. *Plays One* (Faber and Faber, 1996).

GRIGSON, GEOFFREY. *Angles and Circles* (Victor Gollancz, 1974).

—— *Discoveries of Bones and Stones and Other Poems* (Macmillan, 1971).

—— *History of Him* (Secker and Warburg, 1980).

GUNN, THOM. *Jack Straw's Castle* (Faber and Faber, 1976).

—— *My Sad Captains and Other Poems* (Faber and Faber, 1961).

—— *The Passages of Joy* (Faber and Faber, 1982).

—— *The Sense of Movement* (Faber and Faber, 1957).

GURNAH, ABDULRAZAK. *Paradise* (1994; Penguin, 1995).

HAFFENDEN, JOHN. *Novelists in Interview* (Methuen, 1985).

—— *Viewpoints: Poets in Conversation* (Faber and Faber, 1981).

HAMILTON, IAN (ed.). *The Modern Poet: Essays from 'The Review'* (Macdonald, 1968).

—— (ed.). *The New Review Anthology* (Paladin, 1985).

HAMPSON, ROBERT, and BARRY, PETER (eds.). *New British Poetries: The Scope of the Possible* (Manchester University Press, 1993).

HAMPTON, CHRISTOPHER. *Tales from Hollywood* (Faber and Faber, 1983).

—— *The Philanthropist: A Bourgeois Comedy* (Faber and Faber, 1980).

HARE, DAVID. *A Map of the World* (Faber and Faber, 1983).

—— *Plays Two* (Faber and Faber, 1997).

—— *The Absence of War* (Faber and Faber, 1993).

—— *Teeth 'n' Smiles* (Faber and Faber, 1976).

—— *The History Plays: Knuckle, Licking Hitler, Plenty* (Faber and Faber, 1984).

HARE, STEVE (ed.). *Allen Lane and the Penguin Editors, 1935–1970* (Penguin, 1995).

HARRIS, WILSON. *The Guyana Quartet* (1960–3; Faber and Faber, 1985).

HARRISON, TONY. *Selected Poems* (1984; Penguin, 1987).

HARTLEY, L. P. *The Go-Between* (1953; Penguin, 1983).

HARVEY, DAVID. *The Condition of Postmodernity: An Enquiry into the Origins of Cultural Change* (Blackwell, 1990).

HARWOOD, LEE. *Crossing the Frozen River: Selected Poems* (Paladin, 1999).

HASSAN, IHAB. *The Postmodern Turn: Essays in Postmodern Theory and Culture* (Ohio State University Press, 1987).

HASTINGS, MICHAEL. *Three Political Plays: The Emperor, For the West (Uganda), Lee Harvey Oswald* (Penguin, 1990).

HEANEY, SEAMUS. *An Open Letter* (Field Day, 1983).

—— *Selected Poems 1965–1975* (Faber and Faber, 1980).

—— *The Government of the Tongue: The 1986 T. S. Eliot Memorial Lectures and Other Critical Writings* (Faber and Faber, 1988).

HEATH-STUBBS, JOHN. *A Charm against the Toothache* (Methuen, 1954).

—— *Collected Poems 1943–1987* (Carcanet, 1988) .

HENRI, ADRIAN, McGOUGH, ROGER, and PATTEN, BRIAN. *The Mersey Sound*, rev. edn. (Penguin, 1983).

HEWISON, ROBERT. *Too Much: Art and Society in the Sixties 1960–1975* (Methuen, 1986).

HILL, GEOFFREY. *Canaan* (Penguin, 1996).

—— *King Log* (André Deutsch, 1968).

—— *Mercian Hymns* (André Deutsch, 1971).

HOFMANN, MICHAEL. *Acrimony* (Faber and Faber, 1986).

HOGGART, RICHARD. *The Way We Live Now* (1995; Pimlico, 1996).

HOLMES, RICHARD. *Footsteps: Adventures of a Romantic Biographer* (1985; Flamingo, 1995).

HOLROYD, MICHAEL. *Lytton Strachey*, new edn. (Chatto and Windus, 1994).

HORNBY, NICK. *Fever Pitch* (Victor Gollancz, 1992).

HOROVITZ, MICHAEL (ed.). *Children of Albion: Poetry of the 'Underground' in Britain* (Penguin, 1969).

—— (ed.). *Grandchildren of Albion: An Illustrated Anthology of Voices and Visions of Younger Poets in Britain* (New Departures, 1992).

HOUGH, GRAHAM. *An Essay on Criticism* (Gerald Duckworth, 1966).

—— *Image and Experience: Studies in Literary Revolution* (Gerald Duckworth, 1960).

HUGHES, RICHARD. *The Fox in the Attic* (1961; Triad/Panther, 1979).

HUGHES, TED. *Birthday Letters* (Faber and Faber, 1998).

—— *Lupercal* (Faber and Faber, 1960).

—— *Moortown* (Faber and Faber, 1979).

—— *Wodwo* (Faber and Faber, 1967).

HULSE, MICHAEL, KENNEDY, DAVID, and MORLEY, DAVID (eds.). *The New Poetry* (Bloodaxe, 1993).

HUTCHEON, LINDA. *A Poetics of Postmodernism: History, Theory, Fiction* (Routledge, 1988).

INNES, CHRISTOPHER. *Modern British Drama 1890–1990* (Cambridge University Press, 1992).

ISHERWOOD, CHRISTOPHER. *Goodbye to Berlin* (1939; Triad, 1983).

ITZIN, CATHERINE. *Stages in the Revolution: Political Theatre in Britain since 1968* (Eyre Methuen, 1980).

JAMES, HENRY. *The Art of the Novel: Critical Prefaces*, ed. R. P. Blackmur (Charles Scribner's Sons, 1934).

JAMESON, FREDRIC. *Marxism and Form: Twentieth-Century Dialectical Theories of Literature* (Princeton University Press, 1971).

—— *Postmodernism, or, the Cultural Logic of Late Capitalism* (Verso, 1991).

—— *The Ideologies of Theory: Essays 1971–86, 2. The Syntax of History* (Routledge, 1988).

JELLICOE, ANN. *The Sport of my Mad Mother* (Faber and Faber, 1964).

JENNINGS, ELIZABETH. *Collected Poems 1953–1985* (Carcanet, 1986).

JOHNSON, B. S. *Travelling People* (Constable, 1963).

JOHNSON, LINTON KWESI. *Dread Beat and Blood*, introd. Andrew Salkey (Bogle- L'Ouverture Publications, 1975).

—— *Inglan is a Bitch* (Race Today, 1980).

JOHNSON, PAMELA HANSFORD. *The Good Listener* (Macmillan, 1975).

JONES, LINDA LLOYD, and AYNSLEY, JEREMY. *Fifty Penguin Years* (Penguin, 1985).

JONES, PETER, and SCHMIDT, MICHAEL (eds.) *British Poetry since 1970: A Critical Survey* (Carcanet, 1980).

JOYCE, JAMES. *A Portrait of the Artist as a Young Man* (1916; Penguin, 1973).

—— *Finnegans Wake* (1939; Faber and Faber, 1971).

KEATLEY, CHARLOTTE. *My Mother Said I Never Should* (1988; Methuen, 1997).

KEEFFE, BARRIE. *Barbarians: Killing Time, Abide with Me, In the City* (Eyre Methuen, 1977).

—— *Gimme Shelter: Gem, Gotcha, Getaway* (Eyre Methuen, 1978).

KERMODE, FRANK. *The Sense of an Ending: Studies in the Theory of Fiction* (Oxford University Press, 1967).

KERSHAW, BAZ. *The Politics of Performance: Radical Theatre as Cultural Intervention* (Routledge, 1992).

KITCHIN, LAURENCE. *Drama in the Sixties: Form and Interpretation* (Faber and Faber, 1966).

KUHN, THOMAS. *The Structure of Scientific Revolutions* (1962; 2nd enlarged edn., University of Chicago Press, 1970).

KUREISHI, HANIF. *The Buddha of Suburbia* (Faber and Faber, 1990).

LANE, MICHAEL. *Books and Publishers: Commerce against Culture in Postwar Britain* (Lexington Books, 1980).

LARKIN, PHILIP. *Collected Poems*, ed. and introd. Anthony Thwaite (Marvell Press and Faber and Faber, 1988).

LAWRENCE, D. H. *Lady Chatterley's Lover* (1928; Penguin, 1982).

——*Selected Literary Criticism*, ed. Anthony Beal (Heinemann, 1956).

LEADER, ZACHARY (ed.). *On Modern British Fiction* (Oxford University Press, 2002).

LEAVIS, F. R. *D. H. Lawrence: Novelist* (1955; Penguin, 1964).

——*Mass Civilisation and Minority Culture* (The Minority Press, 1930).

LEAVIS, Q. D. *Collected Essays, 1. The Englishness of the English Novel*, ed. G. Singh (Cambridge University Press, 1987).

LE CARRÉ, JOHN. *The Spy who Came in from the Cold* (1963; Coronet, 1994).

LEE, A. ROBERT (ed.). *Other Britain, Other British: Contemporary Multicultural Fiction* (Pluto Press, 1995).

LESSING, DORIS. *Briefing for a Descent into Hell* (1971; Granada, 1982).

——*The Four-Gated City* (1969; Panther, 1972).

——*The Golden Notebook* (1962; Granada, 1976).

——*The Summer before the Dark* (1973; Penguin, 1975).

LEVIN, HARRY. *Refractions: Essays in Comparative Literature* (Oxford University Press, 1966).

LIVELY, PENELOPE. *Cleopatra's Sister* (Penguin, 1993).

——*Moon Tiger* (1987; Penguin, 1988).

LLOYD EVANS, GARETH, and LLOYD EVANS, BARBARA (eds.). *Plays in Review 1956–1980: British Drama and the Critics* (Batsford, 1985).

LODGE, DAVID. *A David Lodge Trilogy: Changing Places, Small World, Nice Work* (1975–88; Penguin, 1993).

——*The Novelist at the Crossroads and Other Essays on Fiction and Criticism* (Routledge and Kegan Paul, 1971).

——*The British Museum is Falling Down* (1965; Penguin, 1985).

——(ed.). *20th Century Literary Criticism: A Reader* (Longman, 1972).

LOWE, STEPHEN. *Touched* (Woodhouse Books, 1979).

LUCIE, DOUG. *Plays: One* (Methuen, 1998).

LUCIE-SMITH, EDWARD (ed.). *British Poetry since 1945*, rev. edn. (Penguin, 1985).

——and HOBSBAUM, PHILIP (eds.). *A Group Anthology* (Oxford University Press, 1963).

LYOTARD, JEAN-FRANÇOIS. *The Postmodern Condition: A Report on*

Knowledge (1979), trans. Geoff Bennington and Brian Massumi (Manchester University Press, 1986).

McEwan, Ian. *Black Dogs* (1992; Vintage, 1998).

—— *Enduring Love* (Jonathan Cape, 1997).

—— *The Child in Time* (Jonathan Cape, 1987).

—— *The Comfort of Strangers* (1981; Picador, 1983).

McGough, Roger. *Blazing Fruit: Selected Poems 1967–1987* (Penguin, 1990).

McGrath, John. *A Good Night Out: Popular Theatre—Audience, Class and Form* (Eyre Methuen, 1981).

—— *Naked Thoughts That Roam About: Reflections on Theatre 1958–2001*, ed. Nadine Holdsworth (Nick Hern, 2002).

McHale, Brian. *Postmodernist Fiction* (Methuen, 1987).

MacInnes, Colin. *England, Half English* (MacGibbon and Kee, 1961).

—— *Visions of London: City of Spades, Absolute Beginners, Mr Love and Justice* (MacGibbon and Kee, 1969).

MacNeice, Louis. *The Collected Poems of Louis MacNeice*, ed. E. R. Dodds (Faber and Faber, 1966).

Maitland, Sara (ed.). *Very Heaven: Looking Back at the 1960s* (Virago Press, 1968).

Manning, Olivia. *The Balkan Trilogy: The Great Fortune, The Spoilt City, Friends and Heroes* (1960–5; Penguin, 1984).

Mantel, Hilary. *An Experiment in Love* (1995; Penguin, 1996).

Marber, Patrick. *Closer* (Methuen, 1997).

Marcuse, Herbert. *Eros and Civilisation: A Philosophical Enquiry into Freud* (1955; Beacon Books, 1966).

Marowitz, Charles, Milne, Tom, and Hale, Owen (eds.). *New Theatre Voices of the Fifties and Sixties: Selections from 'Encore' Magazine 1956–63* (Eyre Methuen, 1965).

Marwick, Arthur. *British Society since 1945* (The Penguin Social History of Britain), 3rd edn. (Penguin, 1996).

Maschler, Tom (ed.). *Declaration* (MacGibbon and Kee, 1957).

Matura, Mustapha. *Six Plays* (Methuen, 1992).

Maxwell, Glyn. *Tale of the Mayor's Son* (Bloodaxe, 1990).

May, Charles E. *The Short Story: The Reality of Artifice* (1995; Routledge, 2002).

Mercer, David. *After Haggerty* (Methuen, 1970).

—— *Ride a Cock Horse* (Calder and Boyars, 1966).

Middleton, Christopher. *Intimate Chronicles* (Carcanet, 1996).

—— *Selected Writings* (Paladin, 1989).

—— *The Pursuit of the Kingfisher: Essays* (Carcanet, 1983).

MILES, ROSALIND. *The Female Form: Women Writers and the Conquest of the Novel* (Routledge and Kegan Paul, 1987).

MILLETT, KATE. *Sexual Politics* (1970; Virago Press, 1977).

MITCHELL, JULIAN. *The Undiscovered Country* (1968; Panther, 1970).

—— *The White Father* (Constable, 1964).

MORGAN, KENNETH O. *The People's Peace: British History 1945–1989* (Oxford University Press, 1990).

MORRISON, BLAKE. *Dark Glasses* (Chatto and Windus, 1984).

—— *The Ballad of the Yorkshire Ripper and Other Poems* (Chatto and Windus, 1987).

—— *The Movement: English Poetry and Fiction of the 1950s* (Oxford University Press, 1980).

—— and MOTION, ANDREW (eds.). *The Penguin Book of Contemporary British Poetry* (Penguin, 1982).

MORTIMER, JOHN. *A Voyage Round my Father, The Dock Brief, What Shall we Tell Caroline?* (Penguin, 1982).

MORTIMER, PENELOPE. *Long Distance* (Hutchinson, 1974).

MOTION, ANDREW. *The Pleasure Steamers* (Carcanet, 1978).

MURDOCH, IRIS. *A Fairly Honourable Defeat* (1970; Penguin, 1984).

—— *A Severed Head* (1961; Triad/Panther, 1984).

—— *The Sea, the Sea* (Chatto and Windus, 1978).

NAIPAUL, V. S. *In a Free State* (André Deutsch, 1971).

—— *The Enigma of Arrival* (Penguin, 1987).

NATOLI, JOSEPH, and HUTCHEON, LINDA (eds.). *A Postmodern Reader* (State University of New York Press, 1993).

NEVILLE, RICHARD. *Play Power* (Jonathan Cape, 1970).

NICHOLS, GRACE. *I is a Long-Memoried Woman* (Karnac House, 1983).

—— *Lazy Thoughts of a Lazy Woman and Other Poems* (Virago, 1989).

—— (ed.). *Black Poetry* (Blackie, 1988).

NICHOLS, PETER. *A Piece of My Mind* (Methuen, 1987).

—— *The Freeway* (Faber and Faber, 1975).

NICHOLSON, NORMAN. *Collected Poems*, ed. and introd. Neil Curry (Faber and Faber, 1994).

NIETZSCHE, FRIEDRICH. *Human, All Too Human: A Book for Free Spirits* (1878), trans. R. J. Hollingdale (Cambridge University Press, 1986).

NORRIE, IAN. *Mumby's Publishing and Bookselling in the Twentieth Century*, 6th edn. (Bell and Hyman, 1982).

NORRIS, CHRISTOPHER. *What's Wrong with Postmodernism: Critical Theory and the Ends of Philosophy* (Harvester Wheatsheaf, 1990).

—— *Deconstruction: Theory and Practice* (Methuen, 1982).

NYE, ROBERT. *The Late Mr Shakespeare* (Chatto and Windus, 1998).

OAKESHOTT, PRISCILLA, and BRADLEY, CLIVE. *The Future of the Book, Part I: The Impact of New Technologies—A Report Prepared for the Publishers Association* (Unesco, 1982).

O'BRIEN, SEAN. *Downriver* (Picador, 2001).

—— *HMS Glasshouse* (Oxford University Press, 1991).

—— *The Deregulated Muse: Essays on Contemporary British and Irish Poetry* (Bloodaxe, 1998).

—— (ed.). *The Firebox: Poetry in Britain and Ireland after 1945* (Picador, 1998).

OKRI, BEN. *The Famished Road* (1991; Vintage 1992).

OLIVER, DOUGLAS. *Three Variations on the Theme of Harm: Selected Poetry and Prose* (Paladin, 1990).

ORTON, JOE. *The Complete Plays* (Eyre Methuen, 1976).

ORWELL, GEORGE. *Coming up for Air* (1939; Penguin, 1962).

OSBORNE, JOHN. *Inadmissible Evidence* (1965; Faber and Faber, 1974).

—— *Look Back in Anger* (1957; Faber and Faber, 1978).

—— *Luther* (1961; Faber and Faber, 1979).

PAGE, ADRIAN (ed.). *The Death of the Playwright?: Modern British Drama and Literary Theory* (Macmillan, 1992).

PARRINDER, PATRICK. *Authors and Authority: English and American Criticism 1750–1990* (Macmillan, 1991).

PAULIN, TOM. *The Liberty Tree* (Faber, 1983).

—— *Walking a Line* (Faber, 1994).

PAXMAN, JEREMY. *The English: A Portrait of a People* (Michael Joseph, 1998).

PHILLIPS, CARYL. *A New World Order: Selected Essays* (Secker and Warburg, 2001).

—— *Cambridge* (1991; Picador, 1992).

PINTER, HAROLD. *Moonlight* (Faber and Faber, 1983).

—— *Plays: One* (Eyre Methuen, 1976).

—— *Plays: Two* (Eyre Methuen, 1977).

—— *Plays: Three* (Eyre Methuen, 1978).

PLATH, SYLVIA. *Ariel* (1965; Faber and Faber, 1976).

PLIMPTON, GEORGE (ed.). *Writers at Work: The* Paris Review *Interviews*, 4th ser. (Secker and Warburg, 1977).

PLUMB, J. H. (ed.). *Crisis in the Humanities* (Penguin, 1964).

POLIAKOFF, STEPHEN. *Plays: One* (Methuen, 1989).

PORTER, PETER. *Collected Poems* (Oxford University Press, 1983).

POTTER, DENNIS. *Sufficient Carbohydrate* (Faber and Faber, 1983).

—— *The Nigel Barton Plays: Two Television Plays* (Penguin, 1967).

POWELL, ANTHONY. *The Acceptance World* (1955; Flamingo, 1982).

——*The Military Philosophers* (Heinemann, 1968).

——*The Soldier's Art* (Heinemann, 1966).

PRIEST, CHRISTOPHER. *The Affirmation* (1981; Arena, 1983).

PRYNNE, J. H. *Poems* (Bloodaxe, 1999).

——*Stars, Tigers and the Shape of Words: The William Matthews Lectures 1992* (Birkbeck College, 1993).

RABAN, JONATHAN. *The Society of the Poem* (Harrap, 1971).

RABINOVITZ, RUBIN. *The Reaction against Experiment in the English Novel 1950–1960* (Columbia University Press, 1967).

RAINE, CRAIG. *Collected Poems 1978–1999* (Picador, 2000).

RAVEN, SIMON. *The English Gentleman: An Essay in Attitudes* (Anthony Blond, 1961).

RAVENHILL, MARK. *Shopping and Fucking* (Methuen, 1996).

READING, PETER. *Collected Poems, 2. 1985–1996* (Bloodaxe, 1996).

——*Essential Reading*, selected and introd. Alan Jenkins (Secker and Warburg, 1986).

REBELLATO, DAN. *1956 and All That: The Making of Modern British Drama* (Routledge, 1999).

REDGROVE, PETER. *Sons of my Skin: Redgrove's Selected Poems 1954–1974*, chosen and introd. Marie Peel (Routledge and Kegan Paul, 1975).

——*The Weddings at Nether Powers and Other New Poems* (Routledge and Kegan Paul, 1979).

REINELT, JANELLE. *After Brecht: British Epic Theatre* (University of Michigan Press, 1996).

RICHARDSON, DOROTHY. *Pilgrimage, 2. The Tunnel, Interim* (1919; Virago, 1979).

RIGGS, THOMAS (ed.). *Contemporary Poets*, 7th edn. (St James Press, 2001).

RILEY, DENISE. *Mop Mop Georgette: New and Selected Poems 1986–1993* (Reality Street, 1993).

RITCHIE, ROB (ed.). *The Joint Stock Book: The Making of a Theatre Collective* (Methuen, 1987).

ROBBE-GRILLET, ALAIN. *Snapshots and Towards a New Novel*, trans. Barbara Wright (Calder and Boyars, 1965).

ROBERTS, MICHÈLE. *Psyche and the Hurricane: Poems 1986–1990* (Methuen, 1990).

ROBERTS, PETER (ed.). *The Best of Plays and Players 1969–1983* (Methuen, 1989).

ROBSON, JEREMY (ed.). *The Young British Poets* (Chatto and Windus, 1971).

ROLPH, C. H. (ed.). *The Trial of Lady Chatterley: Regina v. Penguin Books Limited* (Penguin, 1961).

ROSZAK, THEODORE. *The Making of a Counter Culture: Reflections on the Technocratic Society and its Youthful Opposition* (1968; Faber and Faber, 1971).

ROWBOTHAM, SHEILA. *Promise of a Dream: Remembering the Sixties* (Penguin, 2001).

RUDKIN, DAVID. *Ashes* (Pluto Press, 1978).

RUMENS, CAROL. *Selected Poems* (Chatto and Windus, 1987).

——(ed.). *Making for the Open: The Chatto Book of Post-Feminist Poetry 1964–1984* (Chatto and Windus/The Hogarth Press, 1985).

RUSHDIE, SALMAN. *Imaginary Homelands: Essays and Criticism 1981–1991* (Penguin/Granta Books, 1991).

——*Midnight's Children* (1981; Picador, 1982).

——*Step across This Line: Collected Non-fiction 1992–2002* (Jonathan Cape, 2002).

——*The Satanic Verses* (1988; The Consortium, 1992).

SAMPSON, ANTHONY. *Anatomy of Britain* (Hodder and Stoughton, 1962).

SAUNDERS, JAMES. *Next Time I'll Sing to You* (André Deutsch, 1963).

SCHMIDT, MICHAEL (ed.). *Some Contemporary Poets of Britain and Ireland: An Anthology* (Carcanet, 1983).

SCHWARTZ, STANFORD. *The Matrix of Modernism* (Princeton University Press, 1985).

SCOTT, PAUL. *Staying On* (1977; Panther, 1984).

SEDGWICK, EVE KOSOFSKY. *Epistemology of the Closet* (1990; Harvester Wheatsheaf, 1991).

SELDEN, RAMAN (ed.). *The Cambridge History of Literary Criticism*, 8. *From Formalism to Postructuralism* (Cambridge University Press, 1995).

——and WIDDOWSON, PETER. *A Reader's Guide to Contemporary Literary Theory*, 3rd edn. (Harvester Wheatsheaf, 1993).

SELF, WILL. *How the Dead Live* (2000; Penguin, 2001).

SHAFFER, PETER. *Three Plays: Five Finger Exercise, Shrivings, Equus* (Penguin, 1976).

——*Lettice and Lovage* and *Yonadab* (Penguin, 1989).

——*The Royal Hunt of the Sun* (Longman, 1966).

SHANK, THEODORE (ed.). *Contemporary British Theatre* (1994; Macmillan, 1996).

SHAPCOTT, JO. *Her Book: Poems, 1988–1998* (Faber and Faber, 2000).

SHAW, VALERIE. *The Short Story: A Critical Introduction* (Longman, 1983).

SHELLARD, DOMINIC. *British Theatre since the War* (Yale University Press, 1999).

SHEPHERD, SIMON, and WOMACK, PETER. *English Drama: A Cultural History* (Blackwell, 1996).

SHERMAN, MARTIN. *Bent* (Amber Lane Press, 1979).

SHOWALTER, ELAINE (ed.). *The New Feminist Criticism: Essays on Women, Literature, and Theory* (Virago, 1986).

SHUTTLE, PENELOPE. *The Orchard Upstairs* (Oxford University Press, 1980).

SILKIN, JON. *Selected Poems* (1980; Sinclair-Stevenson, 1993).

——(ed.). *Poetry of the Committed Individual: A Stand Anthology of Poetry* (Gollancz, 1973).

SINCLAIR, CLIVE. *Bibliosexuality* (Allison and Busby, 1973).

SINCLAIR, IAIN. *Flesh Eggs and Scalp Metal: Selected Poems 1970–1987* (Paladin, 1989).

——(ed.). *Conductors of Chaos* (Picador, 1996).

SINFIELD, ALAN. *Literature, Politics and Culture in Postwar Britain* (Basil Blackwell, 1989).

SISSON, C. H. *Collected Poems 1943–1983* (Carcanet, 1984).

SKED, ALAN, and COOK, CHRIS. *Post-War Britain: A Political History*, 4th edn. (Penguin, 1993).

SMITH, KEN. *The Heart, the Border* (Bloodaxe, 1990).

—— *The Poet Reclining: Selected Poems 1962–1980* (Bloodaxe, 1982).

SMITH, STAN. *Inviolable Voice: History and Twentieth-Century Poetry* (Gill and Macmillan, 1982).

SMITH, STEVIE. *The Collected Poems of Stevie Smith* (Allen Lane, 1975).

SMITH, ZADIE. *White Teeth* (Penguin, 2000).

SNOW, C. P. *The Sleep of Reason* (Macmillan, 1968).

—— *The Two Cultures and the Scientific Revolution: The Rede Lecture 1959* (Cambridge University Press, 1959).

SPARK, MURIEL. *The Comforters* (1957; Penguin, 1982).

—— *The Driver's Seat* (1970; Penguin, 1974).

—— *The Mandelbaum Gate* (1965; Penguin, 1967).

—— *The Prime of Miss Jean Brodie* (1961; Penguin, 1982).

SPENDER, STEPHEN. *The Struggle of the Modern* (Hamish Hamilton, 1963).

STEINER, GEORGE. *Language and Silence: Essays 1958–1966* (Faber and Faber, 1967).

STEVENS, WALLACE. *The Collected Poems of Wallace Stevens* (Faber and Faber, 1955).

STEVENSON, ANNE. *The Collected Poems 1955–1995* (Oxford University Press, 1996).

STOPPARD, TOM. *Plays Five* (Faber and Faber, 1999).

—— *Jumpers* (Faber and Faber, 1972).

—— *Rosencrantz and Guildenstern are Dead* (1967; Faber and Faber, 1978).

STOREY, DAVID. *Pasmore* (1972; Penguin, 1976).

—— *Radcliffe* (1963; Penguin, 1984).

SUTHERLAND, JOHN. *Fiction and the Fiction Industry* (Athlone, 1978).

SWIFT, GRAHAM. *Shuttlecock* (1981; Penguin, 1982).

—— *Waterland* (1983; Picador, 1984).

TAYLOR, D. J. *After the War: The Novel and England since 1945* (1993; Flamingo, 1994).

TAYLOR, JOHN RUSSELL. *The Second Wave: British Drama of the Sixties* (Eyre Methuen, 1971).

TENNANT, EMMA. *The Bad Sister* (1978; Picador, 1979).

Theatre Workshop and CHILTON, CHARLES. *Oh What a Lovely War* (1965; Methuen, 1998).

THOMAS, D. M. *The White Hotel* (1981; Penguin, 1984).

THWAITE, ANTHONY. *Poetry Today: A Critical Guide to British Poetry 1960–1975* (Longman, 1996).

—— *The Stones of Emptiness: Poems 1963–1966* (Oxford University Press, 1967).

TOMALIN, CLAIRE. *Several Strangers: Writing from Three Decades* (Viking, 1999).

TOMLINSON, CHARLES. *Annunciations* (Oxford University Press, 1989).

—— *Selected Poems 1951–1974* (Oxford University Press, 1978).

TREMAIN, ROSE. *Restoration* (1989; Sceptre, 1990).

—— *Sacred Country* (1992; Sceptre, 1993).

TRUSSLER, SIMON (ed.). *New Theatre Voices of the Seventies: Sixteen Interviews from Theatre Quarterly 1970–1980* (Eyre Methuen, 1981).

TYNAN, KENNETH. *A View of the English Stage: 1944–1965* (1975; Methuen, 1984).

UNSWORTH, BARRY. *Sacred Hunger* (Penguin, 1992).

VANSITTART, PETER. *In Memory of England: A Novelist's View of History* (John Murray, 1998).

VINSON, JAMES (ed.). *Contemporary Novelists*, 2nd edn. (St Martin's Press, 1976).

WARBURG, FREDRIC. *An Occupation for Gentlemen* (Hutchinson, 1959).

WARDLE, IRVING. *The Theatres of George Devine* (Jonathan Cape, 1978).

WATERMAN, ANDREW. *Over the Wall* (Carcanet, 1980).

WAUGH, PATRICIA. *The Harvest of the Sixties: English Literature and its Background 1960 to 1990* (Oxford University Press, 1995).

——(ed.). *Postmodernism: A Reader* (Edward Arnold, 1992).

——(ed.). *Revolutions of the Word: Intellectual Contexts for the Study of Modern Literature* (Arnold, 1997).

WEISS, PETER. *The Persecution and Assassination of Marat as Performed by the Inmates of the Asylum of Charenton under the Direction of the Marquis of Sade*, English version by Geoffrey Skelton, verse adaptation by Adrian Mitchell (John Calder, 1965).

WELDON, FAY. *Down among the Women* (1971; Penguin, 1984).

WENNER, JANN. *Lennon Remembers: The Rolling Stone Interviews* (Penguin, 1972).

WERTENBAKER, TIMBERLAKE. *The Grace of Mary Traverse* (Faber and Faber, 1985).

WESKER, ARNOLD. *Their Very Own and Golden City* (Jonathan Cape, 1966).

——*The Wesker Trilogy* (1960; Penguin, 1977).

WHITEHEAD, E. A. *Old Flames* (Faber and Faber, 1976).

WHITEMORE, HUGH. *Breaking the Code* (Amber Lane Press, 1987).

WHITING, JOHN. *The Devils: A Play Based on a Book by Aldous Huxley* (Heinemann, 1961).

WHITWORTH, JOHN. *Tennis and Sex and Death* (Peterloo Poets, 1989).

WIDDOWSON, PETER (ed.). *Re-Reading English* (Methuen, 1982).

WILLIAMS, HEATHCOTE. *AC/DC* (1971; John Calder, 1982).

WILLIAMS, NIGEL. *My Brother's Keeper?* (Faber and Faber, 1985).

WILLIAMS, RAYMOND. *Border Country* (Chatto and Windus, 1960).

——*Culture and Society: 1780–1950* (Chatto and Windus, 1958).

——*The Long Revolution* (Chatto and Windus, 1961).

WILLIAMS, WILLIAM CARLOS. *The Collected Later Poems of William Carlos Williams* (MacGibbon and Kee, 1965).

WILSON, ANGUS. *Diversity and Depth in Fiction: Selected Critical Writings of Angus Wilson*, ed. Kerry McSweeney (Secker and Warburg, 1983).

——*Late Call* (1964; Granada, 1982).

WILSON, SNOO. *The Number of the Beast* and *Flaming Bodies* (John Calder, 1983).

WIMSATT, W. K. *The Verbal Icon: Studies in the Meaning of Poetry* (1954; Methuen, 1970), with two preliminary essays written in collaboration with Monroe C. Beardsley.

WINTERSON, JEANETTE. *Sexing the Cherry* (1989; Vintage, 1990).

WOOD, CHARLES. *Has 'Washington' Legs?* and *Dingo* (Eyre Methuen, 1978).

WOOLF, VIRGINIA. *A Room of One's Own* (1928; Penguin, 1975).

—— *A Writer's Diary: Being Extracts from the Diary of Virginia Woolf*, ed. Leonard Woolf (1953; Triad, 1985).

—— *Collected Essays*, 2 (Hogarth, 1966).

—— *Orlando* (1928; Penguin, 1975).

—— *To the Lighthouse* (1927; Penguin, 1973).

WOOTTON, CHRISTOPHER B. *The British Library Research and Development Reports: Trends in Size, Growth and Cost of Literature since 1955* (British Library, 1977).

Writers' and Artists' Yearbook 2000 (A. and C. Black, 2000).

WU, DUNCAN. *Six Contemporary Dramatists: Bennett, Potter, Gray, Brenton, Hare, Ayckbourn* (St Martin's Press, 1995).

ZEPHANIAH, BENJAMIN. *Propa Propaganda* (Bloodaxe, 1996).

—— *The Dread Affair: Collected Poems* (Arrow, 1985).

Index

Reference is made to persons, topics, and primary texts. Separate works of an author are listed only in cases where there is substantial discussion of more than one work. Critics and commentators are listed only when their work is discussed or quoted extensively. Numbers in bold refer to the relevant pages of the Author Bibliographies.

624 *Index*